A WORLD HISTORY OF
RAILWAY CULTURES, 1830–1930

A WORLD HISTORY OF RAILWAY CULTURES, 1830–1930

Edited by
Matthew Esposito

Volume I
The United Kingdom

LONDON AND NEW YORK

First published 2020
by Routledge
2 Park Square, Milton Park, Abingdon, Oxon OX14 4RN

and by Routledge
52 Vanderbilt Avenue, New York, NY 10017

Routledge is an imprint of the Taylor & Francis Group, an informa business

© 2020 selection and editorial matter, Matthew Esposito; individual owners retain copyright in their own material.

The right of Matthew Esposito to be identified as the author of the editorial material, and of the authors for their individual chapters, has been asserted in accordance with sections 77 and 78 of the Copyright, Designs and Patents Act 1988.

All rights reserved. No part of this book may be reprinted or reproduced or utilised in any form or by any electronic, mechanical, or other means, now known or hereafter invented, including photocopying and recording, or in any information storage or retrieval system, without permission in writing from the publishers.

Trademark notice: Product or corporate names may be trademarks or registered trademarks, and are used only for identification and explanation without intent to infringe.

British Library Cataloguing-in-Publication Data
A catalogue record for this book is available from the British Library

Library of Congress Cataloging-in-Publication Data
A catalog record for this book has been requested

ISBN: 978-0-8153-7722-1 (set)
eISBN: 978-1-351-21184-0 (set)
ISBN: 978-0-8153-7751-1 (Volume I)
eISBN: 978-1-351-21180-2 (Volume I)

Typeset in Times New Roman
by Apex CoVantage, LLC

Publisher's Note
References within each chapter are as they appear in the original complete work

TO MY PARENTS MICKEY AND DONALIN,
WHO INTRODUCED ME TO THREE OF THE
MOST ENDURING POSSESSIONS IN LIFE –
LOVE, THE IMAGINATION, AND BOOKS.

CONTENTS

Acknowledgements   xvi

Railways and their metonyms: technology and terminology that transformed world cultures, 1830–1930   1

VOLUME I   The United Kingdom   47

England as epicenter of railway cultures and the *Pax Britannica*   49

PART 1
The *Rocket*, Rainhill Trials, and early promotion of railways   89

1 Early illustrations of the *Rocket* and Liverpool and Manchester trains   91

2 The Rainhill Trials and Inauguration of the Liverpool & Manchester Railway, 'Account of the Competition of Locomotive Steam-Carriages on the Liverpool and Manchester Railway', in *Mechanics' Magazine* 12: 322 (October 10, 1829), 114–116; 12: 323 (October 17, 1829), 135–141; 12: 324 (October 24, 1829), 146–147; 12: 325 (October 31, 1829), 161; 14: 372 (September 25, 1830), 64–69   94

3 Charles Maclaren, *Railways Compared with Canals & Common Roads, and Their Uses and Advantages Explained* (Edinburgh: Constable, 1825), pp. 48–54   108

4 Nineteenth-century engravings, lithographs, and prints   112

PART 2
Engineering enemies — 117

5 Joseph Sandars, *A Letter on the Subject of the Projected Rail Road between Liverpool and Manchester*. Second ed. (London: W. Wales, 1824), pp. 3–32 — 119

6 'Second Prospectus of the Liverpool and Manchester Railway Company', *Liverpool Mercury* XV, December 30, 1825, 203 — 135

7 George Eliot, *Middlemarch*. New edition. (Edinburgh and London: W. Blackwood, 1874), pp. 407–414 — 141

8 *The Creevy Papers: A Selection from the Correspondence & Diaries of the Late Thomas Creevy*. Ed. Sir Herbert Maxwell. (New York: E. P. Dutton, 1904), pp. 429–431, 545–546 — 149

9 William Wordsworth, 'On the Projected Kendel and Windermere Railway', 147, 'Letters on the Kendal and Windermere Railway, 301–311', from Vol. 8 of *The Poetical Works of William Wordsworth*. Ed. William Angus Knight. (Edinburgh: W. Paterson, 1888–1889), pp. 147, 301–311 — 151

PART 3
Cultures of railway construction — 159

10 John Francis, *A History of the English Railway: Its Social Relations and Revelations*. 2 vols. (London: Longman, Brown, Green, & Longmans, 1851). Vol. 2, Chapter 3 pp. 67–91 — 161

11 Benjamin Disraeli, *Sybil or The Two Nations* (London: Longmans, Green, and Co., 1913), pp. 433–441 — 170

12 Stephen W. Fullom, 'The Brawl Viaduct', 'English and Irish', and 'The Reward of Merit', in *The Great Highway: A Story of the World's Struggles*. Third ed. (London: G. Routledge & Co., 1854), pp. 119–146 — 176

13 Patrick MacGill, *Children of the Dead End: The Autobiography of a Navvy* (London: H. Jenkins, 1914), pp. 129–145, 209–212, 225–229, 254–262 — 192

14 Patrick MacGill, 'A Platelayer's Story' and 'The Navvies' Sunday' and from *Gleanings from a Navvy's Scrapbook*. Second ed. (Derry, North Ireland: Derry Journal, 1911), pp. 52–53, 55 — 211

PART 4
Novel impressions: early Victorian railway cultures — **215**

15 Frances Ann Kemble, *Records of a Girlhood*. Second ed. (New York: H. Holt, 1884), pp. 278–284 — 217

16 'Railroad Travelling', *Herapath's Railway Journal* (The Railway Magazine) 1 (Mar.–Dec. 1836), 110–112 — 222

17 Charles Greville, *Memoirs (Second Part): A Journal of the Reign of Queen Victoria from 1837 to 1852*. 3 vols. Ed. Henry Reeve. (New York: D. Appleton and Co., 1885), I, p. 11 — 224

18 William Makepeace Thackeray, 'Two Days in Wicklow', in *The Paris Sketch Book of Mr. M.A. Titmarsh, The Irish Sketch Book, & Notes of a Journey from Cornhill to Grand Cairo* (New York: Caxton, 1840), pp. 491–493 — 225

19 William Makepeace Thackeray, 'Physiology of the London Idler', *Punch* 3 (1842), p. 102, 'Railway Parsimony', *Punch* 13 (1847), 150, 'Natural Phenomenon', *Punch* 14 (1848), 87, and 'Railway Charges', *Punch* 14 (1848), 218 — 228

20 Albert Richard Smith, *The Struggles and Adventures of Christopher Tadpole at Home and Abroad* (London: Willoughby, 1847), pp. 481–483 — 233

21 Charles Dickens, 'Paul's Second Deprivation', in *Dombey and Son*. 2 Vols. (New York: Harper & Bros, 1852), I: 70–72 — 236

22 Charles Dickens, 'Mugby Junction', in *Stories from the Christmas Numbers of "Household Words" and "All Year Round."* (New York: Macmillan and Co., 1896), pp. 464–465, 500–512 — 239

23 Charles Dickens, *Our Mutual Friend* (New York: Macmillan, 1907), p. 720 — 250

24 Charles Dickens, 'A Flight', in *Reprinted Pieces* (New York: University Society, 1908), pp. 151–161 — 251

PART 5
Timetables, calendars, and stations: Mid-Victorian railway cultures — **259**

25 Henry Booth, 'Considerations, Moral, Commercial, Economical', *An Account of the Liverpool and Manchester Railway* (Liverpool: Wales and Baines, 1830), pp. 85–94 — 261

26 'Easter Travelling', *Illustrated London News*, April 29, 1905, 626 — 266

27 William Powell Frith, 'The Railway Station', (Paddington Station) (1862) — 269

28 George Catlin, *Adventures of the Ojibbeway and Ioway Indians in England, France, and Belgium.* Third ed. (London: n.p., 1852), pp. 15, 17, 20–26, 34–35, 123–127, 129, 145–146 — 270

29 John Overton Choules, *Young Americans Abroad* (Boston: Gould and Lincoln, 1853), pp. 48–52, 92–95 — 278

30 Miss (Julia) Pardoe, 'On the Rail', *Reginald Lyle* (New York: Burgess & Day, 1854), pp. 103–106 — 282

31 Elizabeth Gaskell, 'Mischances', *North and South* (London: Oxford University Press, 1908), pp. 312–317 — 285

32 George Augustus Sala, 'The Art of Sucking Eggs', in *Temple Bar* 1 (1861), 558–564 — 289

33 Miss. Muloch (Dinah Maria Mulock Craik), *A Life for a Life: A Novel* (New York: Carleton, 1864), pp. 196–197 — 296

34 Frances Eleanor Trollope, *Veronica*, 'The Railway Waiting Room', in *All the Year Round*, New Series V.2 (September 25, 1869), p. 386 — 297

35 G. K. Chesterton, 'The Prehistoric Railway Station', in *Tremendous Trifles* (New York: Dodd, Mead, 1909), pp. 260–267 — 298

CONTENTS

PART 6
Subterranean railways and the underground: high Victorian railway cultures — **301**

36 'The Metropolitan Subterranean Railway', *The Times* (London), November 30, 1861, p. 5 — 303

37 Mortimer Collins, *The Vivian Romance* (New York: Harper, 1870), pp. 31–32 — 308

38 M. E. Braddon, 'On the Track', from *Henry Dunbar: The Story of an Outcast*, Three Vols. (London: J. Maxwell, 1866), III, pp. 187–201 — 309

39 M. E. Braddon, *The Lovels of Arden* (Leipzig: B. Tauchnitz, 1871), pp. 92–97 — 314

40 Gustave Doré, The Workmen's Train, Ludgate Hill, and Over the City by Railway. Illustrations originally printed in Doré and Blanchard Jerrold, *London: A Pilgrimage*. (London: Grant, 1872) — 318

41 Lady Margaret Majendie, 'A Railway Journey', *Blackwood's Magazine* 121 (April 1877), pp. 497–503 — 319

42 Cover Illustration of H. L. Williams's adaptation of Dion Boucicault's play *After Dark* (1880s), depicting railway rescue scene in the London Underground/Subterranean Railway — 328

43 Dion Boucicault, scene II from *After Dark: A Drama of London Life in 1868, in Four Acts*. (New York: DeWitt, n.d.) pp. 36–37 — 329

PART 7
Netherworlds and nostalgia: late Victorian and Edwardian railway cultures — **331**

44 George Gissing, '10 Saturnalia!', in *The Nether World* (London: Smith, Elder, & Co., 1890), pp. 105–113 — 333

45 James John Hissey, *Through Ten English Counties* (London: Richard Bentley & Son, 1894), pp. 392–393 — 339

46 Thomas Hardy, *Jude the Obscure* (New York: Harper and Brothers, 1896), pp. 341–343 — 340

47 Arthur Quiller-Couch, 'The Cuckoo Valley Railway' and 'Punch's Understudy', in *The Delectable Duchy: Stories, Studies, and Sketches* (New York: C. Scribners' Sons, 1898), pp. 61–69, 107–115 — 342

48 George John Whyte-Melville, *The Brookes of Bridlemere* (London: Ward, Lock, 1899), pp. 156–161, 200–205 — 349

49 H. G. Wells, *When the Sleeper Wakes* (New York: Harper & Bros., 1899), pp. 201–211 — 355

50 Henry James, 'London', *English Hours* (Boston: Houghton, Mifflin and Co., 1905), pp. 36–39 — 361

51 Henry James, 'Isle of Wight', *Portraits of Places* (Boston: Houghton, Mifflin and Co., 1911), pp. 292–294 — 363

52 E. Nesbit, 'Saviours of the Train', *The Railway Children* (London and New York: Macmillan, 1906), pp. 127–137 — 365

53 E. M. Forster, *Howards End* (New York: G. P. Putnam Sons, 1911), pp. 12–19 — 370

PART 8
The railway accident, public health, and military deployment — 375

54 'Wolverhampton', *The Spectator*, February 24, 1838, pp. 176–177 — 377

55 'In the Temple Gardens', *Temple Bar* 2 (July, 1861), pp. 286–287 — 378

56 'Armagh', *The Spectator*, June 15, 1889, 813 — 380

57 'The Influence of Railway Travelling on Public Health', *The Lancet*, 1862, pp. 15–17 — 381

58 John Charles Hall, 'Railway Accidents', in *Medical Evidence in Railway Accidents* (London: Longmans & Co. 1868), pp. 27–42 — 388

CONTENTS

59 'Navvies for the Crimea' and 'The Balaclava Railway Corps', *Illustrated London News*, 13 January 1855, 28–29, 304 — 398

60 'The Invasion of the Free State', *The Spectator*, March 17, 1900, 229 — 403

61 *Boer War: Diary of Eyre Lloyd, 2nd Coldstream Guards, Assistant Staff Officer, Colonel Benson's Column, killed at Brakenlaagte, 30th October 1901* (London: Army and Navy Cooperative Society, 1905), pp. 3–6, 17–19, 27–28, 43, 45, 56–58, 63, 66–67, 71–78, 105–118, 124, 131, 137–141, 153, 169–171, 187, 242, 249–250, 260, 288–289 — 406

PART 9
The Great War and interwar railway cultures — 417

62 'Railways and the War', in *The Times History of the War* 6 (1915), pp. 161, 167, 169–174 — 419

63 Edwin A. Pratt, 'Employment of Women and Girls', in *British Railways and the Great War: Organisation, Efforts, Difficulties and Achievements*, 2 vols. (London: Selwyn and Blount, 1921), pp. 475–482 — 426

64 Thomas Hardy, 'Midnight on the Great Western', in *The Poetical Works of Thomas Hardy*, 2 vols. (London: Macmillan, 1919), I, p. 483 — 434

65 Lord Monkswell, 'Making Up Lost Time', *The Railway Magazine* 50 (Jan.–June 1922), pp. 157–160 — 435

66 'Railway Art and Literature in 1922', *The Railway Magazine* 51 (July–Dec. 1922), pp. 59–66 — 441

67 'Flying Scotsman's First Run', *Times* (London), 2 May 1928, p. 13 — 452

68 Frank Parker Stockbridge, 'Cargoes through the Clouds', *Harper's* 140, 1919–1920, pp. 189–191 — 454

PART 10
Railway cultures of Scotland and Ireland   **459**

69 Anon. (David Croal), *Early Recollections of a Journalist, 1832–1859* (Edinburgh: Andrew Eliot, 1898), pp. 8–10   461

70 Charles Richard Weld, *Two Months in the Highlands, Orcadia, and Skye* (London: Longmans, Green, Longman, and Roberts, 1860), pp. 4–6   462

71 W. Edmondstoune Aytoun, *Norman Sinclair* 3 vols. (Edinburgh: William Blackwood and Sons, 1861), I, pp. 250–251, 271–274, II, pp. 102–114   464

72 C. F. Gordon Cumming, *In the Hebrides* (London: Chatto & Windus, 1883), pp. 201–204, 420–422   473

73 C. F. Gordon Cumming, *Memories* (Edinburgh: W. Blackwood, 1904), pp. 440–441   477

74 'The Dublin and Kingstown Railway', *Dublin Penny Journal* 3, 113, 30 August 1834, pp. 65–68   479

75 J. Jay Smith, *A Summer's Jaunt across the Water* (Philadelphia: J. W. Moore, 1846), pp. 46–47   487

76 Frederick Richard Chichester, *Masters and Workmen: A Tale Illustrative of the Social and Moral Condition of the People*, 3 vols. (London: Newby, 1851), I, pp. 7–17   488

77 Andrew Dickinson, *My First Visit to Europe* (New York: G. P. Putnam, 1851), pp. 48–50   491

78 Sir Francis Bond Head, *A Fortnight in Ireland*, 2nd ed. (London: John Murray, 1852), pp. 70, 108–114   493

79 George Foxcroft Haskins, *Travels in England, France, Italy and Ireland* (Boston: P. Donahoe, 1856), pp. 265–266, 269   497

80 Michael Cavanagh (ed.), *Memoirs of General Thomas Francis Meagher Comprising the Leading Events of His Career* (Worcester, Mass.: The Messenger Press, 1892), pp. 245–253   499

CONTENTS

81 C. O. Burge, *The Adventures of a Civil Engineer: Fifty Years on Five Continents* (London: Alston Rivers, 1909), pp. 8–13, 47–53 ... 506

82 J. M. Synge, *In Wicklow, West Kerry and Connemara* (Dublin: Maunsel, 1911), pp. 65–67, 157–165 ... 511

83 J. M. Synge, *The Aran Islands*, 4 vols. (Dublin: Maunsel, 1912). I, pp. 115–120 ... 515

84 Joseph Tatlow, *Fifty Years of Railway Life in England, Scotland and Ireland* (London: The Railway Gazette, 1920), pp. 110–111 ... 518

85 Padraic Colum, 'Into Munster: On the Train', *The Road Round Ireland* (New York: Macmillan, 1926), pp. 416–419 ... 520

ACKNOWLEDGEMENTS

I must express my gratitude to those who assisted me with this *scholarly production*, foremost among them scholars, librarians, and editors. The Drake University Center for the Humanities and Arts and Sciences College provided research and travel grants to help me pursue my investigations into railway cultures. I especially thank A&S Deans Joe Lenz and Gesine Gerhard, History Department Chairs Glenn McKnight and Karen Leroux, and Humanities Center Directors Craig Owens and Jennifer Harvey for administrative assistance, moral support, and funding. For five uninterrupted years, Kristine Mogul of Drake University's Cowles Library led a staff of librarians and students to obtain hundreds of books and other research materials for this specific project on railway cultures. Lorraine Hopper, Karl Schaefer, Marcia Keyser, Bruce Gilbert, Bart Schmidt, and Mark Stumme all expressed interest in the titles and subject areas of my requests and helped me track down information related to the authors, historical figures, and railroad companies that are included in this collection. These fellow faculty members share my bibliophilism and dragged a reluctant Philistine into the magnificent realm of electronic resources. The future is now and scholarly access to materials in transportation libraries and national archives all over the world has never been better. I also want to thank the librarians of the Bancroft Library at the University of California, Berkeley, Tulane University, Texas Christian University, the Nettie Lee Benson Library at the University of Texas, Austin, the British Library, the National Library in Melbourne, Australia, and the Biblioteca Nacional's Hemeroteca and several other archives and libraries in Mexico City for assistance with newspapers and railway-related materials. I also wish to thank the Routledge editors, Kimberley Smith, Rachel Douglas, and Simon Alexander, whose professionalism, sound advice, and patience have made this project worthwhile.

I have not met many of the scholars whose works on the railways of different geographical regions served as essential touchstones for this world history collection, but to say that I have been inspired by their writings is a gross understatement, considering the prominence of their names in the endnotes and headnotes. Scholars of the U.S. Constitution refer to the famous fifty-five, not as the signers of the Constitution, but as the fifty-five words of the Declaration of Independence that have become its lofty preamble. The famous fifty-five of these volumes

ACKNOWLEDGEMENTS

are the prominent wordsmiths of the cultural history of railways and technology whose conceptual approaches, innovative historical arguments, and prosaic interests continue to inform historians and their students worldwide. The fifty-five are listed here with the understanding that they cannot be held responsible for any errors in this work: Ian J. Kerr, Michael Freeman, John Coatsworth, Wolfgang Schivelbusch, Steven Ericson, Robert Carlson, William Beezley, Miguel Tinker Salas, Ramón Ruiz, Marian Aguiar, Karen Morin, Eugen Weber, Paul Youngman, John Hurd, Jack Simmons, James McPherson, Ian Carter, Tony Rosenthal, Myron Brightfield, Dan Free, A. Kim Clark, Leo Marx, Richard White, Daniel Headrick, Michael Adas, William Cronon, William E. French, Laura Bear, Philip Pacey, Michael Robbins, Ritika Prasad, Trish Ferguson, Anne Green, R. W. Kostal, Lynne Kirby, Michael Matthews, Amy Richter, Abigail Green, Paul Noguchi, Jeffrey Richards, John M. MacKenzie, James Brophy, Sean McMeekin, David Haward Bain, Alan Knight, Anna Despotopolou, Manu Goswami, John Gunn, Robert A. Lee, Adam Smith, David Burke, Alfred Crosby, Jonathan Kellet, Charlotte Mathieson, and Christian Wolmar.

RAILWAYS AND THEIR METONYMS

Technology and terminology that transformed world cultures, 1830–1930

In 1894, John Pendleton published a unique work on the "origin, development, incident, and romance" of *Our Railways*. A regular contributor to *The Times*, Pendleton set forth to capture "the wondrous variety of event and circumstance . . . inseparable from railway travel."[1] Two volumes later, he amassed over 1,000 pages chronicling the countless ways that English railways transformed the British Isles. The work blended history, anecdotes, storytelling, and the contemporary observations of an insightful Victorian who both preserved truths and perpetuated myths about the first two generations of steam locomotive travel. *Our Railways* remains captivating as a compilation of the kaleidoscopic sources and voices that informed it. Only Wolfgang Schivelbusch's scholarly work *The Railway Journey* and Michael Freeman's superbly illustrated *Railways and the Victorian Imagination*, encapsulate so thoughtfully and comprehensively the railway experience.[2] Historians Ian J. Kerr and John Hurd II, along with a handful of multidisciplinary scholars of India that include Ian Derbyshire, Manu Goswami, Laura Bear, Marian Aguiar, Harriet Bury, and Ritika Prasad continue to advance our understanding of the cultural impact of railways on the subcontinent.[3] We look to them and dozens of other railway scholars and historians cited in the references of this collection for new directions in research.

A World History of Railway Cultures attempts to elaborate "the wondrous variety of event and circumstance" that railways inaugurated on a global scale from 1830 to 1930. Toward the end of that period, E. M. Forster reflected on how railway stations served as gateways to the infinite. In his masterpiece *Howards End* (1910), Forster writes: "They are our gates to the glorious and the unknown. Through them we pass out into adventure and sunshine, to them, alas! we return."[4] The author describes King's Cross station as a portal to unlimited destinations, but since passengers returned home after their journeys, it also fulfilled its role as a "terminus." Forster designates Paddington as the threshold to Cornwall and the west. Liverpool opened to the fenlands and the "illimitable Broads." Through the pylons of Euston station, passengers eventually reached Scotland. And chaotic Waterloo launched travelers toward Wessex. To Forster, railways also represented the infinite subjectivity derived from individual passenger experiences and expectations. He shares the example of Italian waiters in Berlin who called the *Anhalt*

Bahnhof station in Germany the *Stazione d'Italia* because, despite its location, it transported them home. Leaving Wickham Place for Howards End, Aunt Juley carried Margaret Schlegel's note in a mundane chore rendered as a timeless and limitless mission on the railway. Although just a one-hour journey to the Wilcox estate, Aunt Juley was "gone irrevocably" through "innumerable tunnels" and crossed the "immense viaduct over Tewin Water toward the endless Great North Road." Aboard the train, she adjusted her windows "again and again," napped for "a hundred years," and reached the "indeterminate" Hilton station. Forster commented optimistically, not during the Victorian era when railways were experimental and new, but in the Edwardian era when the world understood their unlimited potential as entryways to infinity. T. S. Eliot echoed this lesson in 1941: "Fare forward travellers! not escaping from the past/Into different lives, or into any future; You are not the same people who left the station/Or who will arrive at any terminus, While the narrow rails slide together behind you."[5]

This four-volume collection of historical documents traces the cultural production of Victorian and Edwardian worldviews of railways and examines their reproduction in other parts of the globe. Together they reveal the emergence of world railway cultures – transcultural local receptions, adaptations, and representations of steam locomotion that were both similar to and different from their European and American predecessors. The collection profiles material representations of railways in metonyms and metaphors used throughout the world. Each volume is arranged according to historical geography, and selections are presented chronologically within subject areas to reflect changes over time. The selected timeframe spans from the advent of the first modern railway in 1830 to 1930, when the automobile and internal combustion engine began displacing passenger traffic by train. After WWII, affordable air travel further decreased railway traffic due to the growing need to reach intercontinental and transoceanic destinations. The relevance of historical research about railways continues, however, due to the resurgence of interest in high-speed train transport as an alternative to the soaring costs of fossil fuels and the environmental problems associated with car emissions. Experiments with full automation – namely, remote operation of Australian juggernauts using Global Positioning Systems technology through telecommunication satellites – have resulted in railway companies hauling iron ore through 1,000 miles of desert without a single human aboard the train. Still, major cities throughout the world are converting old tracks to walking trails and bicycle paths and commuter traffic outside of major cities has declined.

This collection captures nineteenth- and early-twentieth-century railway experiences by focusing on writers in various genres who recorded them firsthand for posterity. Railways have been described as sources of wonder and despair, tools of progress and weapons of destruction, and transformational vehicles that promoted both liberation and segregation, equality and inequality, and mutual understanding and racism. Of course, what period observers, historians, novelists, poets, and other literary figures generally described were often filtered through the limited ideological constructs of humans, specifically Eurocentric and ethnocentric worldviews that narrowed Forster's infinite universe into the one-way tunnels of triumphal imperial and national histories. Few studies have balanced and historicized railways from the standpoint of the human cultures they created and destroyed. Whereas Pendleton used news stories and Forster drew upon life experiences to construct their narratives, *A World History of Railway Cultures* turns to period sources that include: railway reports, parliamentary papers, government documents, police reports, public health records, engineering reports, technical papers, medical surveys, memoirs, diaries, letters, travel narratives, ethnographies, newspaper articles, editorials, pamphlets, broadsides, paintings, engravings, cartoons, photographs, ephemera, and extracts from novels and poetry collections. Of these documentary sources, the nineteenth-century travel narrative reigned supreme in the origination and propagation of railway metonyms. The editor's five original essays and forty headnotes on the cultural hegemony that railways reproduced introduces over 300 carefully selected and edited primary and period sources. Students and researchers come to understand railways not as static engineering marvels and applied technologies of industrial capitalism, but as powerful, fluid, and idiosyncratic historical constructs and cultural systems that reflected the societies into which they were introduced and helped all peoples negotiate the promises and perils of modernity. The production and reproduction of railway cultures mirrored modernity itself as the product of contradictory historical processes.

Inception

Why has the steam locomotive become the most enduring image of the nineteenth and early twentieth centuries? The answer has much to do with what railways came to represent. By the time George Stephenson and his son Robert introduced the *Rocket* at the Rainhill Trials in 1829, their steam-powered locomotive engines were already operating at the Stockton & Darlington Railway (S&D, 1825) in England. From 1803–1824, George, the engineer-inventor, had constructed fifty-five steam engines and sixteen steam locomotives. Stephenson's engine outperformed all others at the Lancashire competition, and the Liverpool and Manchester Railway (L&M, 1830) hired him to engineer and build its line, provide a fleet of engines, and ultimately to end the practice of using mixed forms of traction, including horses, cables, and stationary engines in favor of a track fully dedicated to the newest source of industrial energy. Other railways permitted individually owned vehicles of all types of traction to access their lines. The L&M discontinued this practice and developed a timetable for freight, passenger, and mixed trains pulled exclusively by steam locomotives. The company had a paid staff. It owned and maintained all bridges, viaducts, tunnels, and track without government oversight. It built and managed stations, halts, workshops, offices, sheds, restaurants, and hotels. To assist the transshipment of goods and the transfer of passengers, the L&M acquired canals, docks, warehouses, and other interests to serve as transition points. For these reasons, historians consider the L&M the first modern railway and its inauguration date of September 15, 1830 as the dawn of the railway era. Estimates vary, but between 50,000 and 400,000 spectators stood alongside the track in a festive atmosphere that momentarily suspended working-class anger with the government on the eve of the Reform Act (1832).[6] The great railway historian C. F. Dendy Marshall explained the metamorphosis from the S&D old colliery line to the "epoch-making" L&M as "analogous to that between a grub and a butterfly."[7] Within years the Dundee & Newtyle (1831), London and Birmingham (1833), Grand Junction (1833), London and Southampton (1834), Dublin and Kingstown (1834), and the Great Western (London to Bristol, 1835) offered similar services. Many of the old stagecoach lines went out of business. Within a decade, more than 2,000 miles of trunk lines radiated from London, and a century later (1914), 20,000 track miles spread over the British Isles. In the two decades between 1890 and 1910, the imperial powers of Europe and the United States constructed more than 600,000 miles of railroad track over the planet's surface.[8] Among the greatest understatements in railroad literature is that the new transportation technology improved upon the carrying capacity of passengers in horse-drawn carriages and bullocks wagons for overland freight. In fact, since their introduction at collieries and mines, steam-operated railways annihilated animal competition as surely as their speed shortened the time to reach overland distances. Speed soon became the second immeasurable bonus of steam-powered locomotion. Within a single generation of its debut, the train's velocity accelerated from that of the carthorse to the racehorse.[9] By 1850, railways achieved rates of fifty miles per hour, increasing the tempo of modern life.

It is no wonder that the first animal that came to mind to describe and even name steam locomotives was the horse.[10] Maritime traditions for ships influenced naming practices in the railway industry, but the train as analog of the horse preoccupied Britons for a century. Every horse that pulled a carriage and every reputable stagecoach had names. Some, like the *Tantivy*, *Bang up*, *Hark Forward*, and *Taglioni*, seemed one of a kind,[11] whereas others such as *Defiance*, *Eclipse*, *Lightning*, *Rattler*, and *Soho* represented entire fleets of the stagecoach lines.[12] In the gentile world of the 1830s, the sport of kings – horse racing – featured equestrian names that inspired confidence in riders, spectators, and bettors, not unlike the appellations bandied about by the Stephensons at Killingworth and in the factory at Newcastle-upon-Tyne. With proper names such as *Rocket*, *Meteor*, *Comet*, *Arrow*, and *Dart*, Stephenson locomotives outpaced the fastest and most powerful horses, won the £500 prize at Rainhill, and captured the public imagination. In 1837, William Jerdan invented the new term "Hippothanasia" to suggest that steam locomotives rendered horses obsolete, effectively euthanizing the horse-breeding business: "the whole Equestrian order had been destroyed at a blow." Although his list of railways and allusions to Jonathan Swift's satirical classic *Gulliver's Travels* reveals a humorous tone, serious concerns arose over the future of the horse.[13] Nevertheless, the R. Stephenson Company and the Galloway Company of Manchester inspired confidence in an unproven technology by using names like the *Northumbrian* and *Caledonian* for their locomotive engines. Thoroughbreds and Stephenson engines alike also featured the Roman names of gods and planets: *Mercury*, *Mars*, *Jupiter*, and *Saturn*. Still other locomotives like *Vesuvius* and *Etna* shook the ground, erupted, and flowed over landscapes like their volcano namesakes. The popular children's fiction writer Helen C. Knight ascribed equine characteristics to the locomotives that galloped across the English landscape: "These noble *steam-horses* panting, prancing, snorting, puffing, blowing, shooting through tunnels, dashing across bridges, coursing high embankments, and racing over the fields and far away. England and the world never saw before a sight like that."[14] Victorian literature went a long way toward educating readers about the relative speed and agility of the "iron horse," the locomotive's first metonym.

The steam locomotive as horse exemplifies how an innocuous metaphor is reproduced with distinct meanings in different historical settings and contexts. In England and the U.S., people originally viewed trains with glowing admiration and terrible suspicion. Emily Dickinson's poem "The Railway Train" clarified her point of view with complimentary metaphors of a horse:

> I like to see it lap the Miles,
> And lick the valleys up,
> And stop to feed itself at tanks;
> And then, prodigious, step
>
> Around a pile of mountains,
> And, supercilious, peer
> In shanties by the sides of roads;
> And then a quarry pare
>
> To fit its sides, and crawl between,
> Complaining all the while
> In horrid, hooting stanza;
> Then chase itself down a hill
>
> And neigh like Boanerges;
> Then, punctual as a star,
> Stop – docile and omnipotent –
> At its own stable door.[15]

Like Helen Knight's book, the poem compared the train to a mighty but gentle horse. The animal possessed advanced human and godlike characteristics such as prodigious, supercilious, punctual, docile, and omnipotent. Dickinson's biblical reference to Boanerges, Jesus Christ's name for brothers James and John in the New Testament, meant "the son of thunder," or alluded to any thunderous sermon of a nineteenth-century preacher. Although there is not enough allegory in the rest of the poem to draw a definitive conclusion, references in the last stanza to Jesus's epithet for the Apostles, a star, a stable, and the pairing of "docile" and "omnipotent" subtly induces thoughts of the Christ savior and his birth in a stable in Bethlehem. The steam locomotive as Messiah remains one of the most studied metonyms in world railway history.

Terms that Europeans and Americans coupled with "horse" to describe the locomotive always said something about the popular receptivity of the technology. For example, references to the "iron steed" simply seemed imitative of "iron horse," but "steam-horses," as used above by Knight, and "fire-horses," which riddled Victorian-era newspapers, innovated by identifying the new power source of engines. Other equine metaphors for the locomotive included the warhorse and charger. In Ellen Clayton's novel *Cruel Fortune*, a "war-charger" rushed under a brick arch and made "a sound as if drawing a mighty sword from a steel scabbard."[16] In Germany, positive references to the knight's steed or charger implied noble characteristics, while hell stallions rendered locomotives evil.[17] According to Paul Youngman, novelist Peter Rosegger's *The Steamhorse my Pegasus* (1896) delivered "unequivocal and fulsome praise of the railway as a means of poetic enhancement." An Austrian realist, Rosegger might have portrayed railways as a winged horse, but Germans apprised of Greek mythology also knew the dark side of Pegasus as an uncontrollable protean force and fallen angel.[18] Characters in German literature called the train *schwarzer Teufel*, or "black Devil," so often that peasants likely used the term to describe wild horses and ill-behaved mules, then transferred their exasperation to the train.

Whether or not scholars accept Michel Foucault's post-structural term *heterotopia*, his conceptualization and contextualization of trains as "other places" captures the nineteenth-century spatial significance of railways. Foucault stated that

> a train is an extraordinary bundle of relations because it is something through which one goes, it is also something by means of which one can go from one point to another, and then it is also something that goes by.[19]

More important than Foucault's wordplay is its conceptual applicability to the complex semiotics and epistemologies of different world cultures that tried to make sense of the transportation revolution's "extraordinary bundle of relations" in specific temporal and geographical contexts. Deconstructing such relations moves beyond the basic symbolism attached to the "iron horse" metaphor to variegated analogies of trains as 1) spacious objects that emulated the home, church, synagogue, mosque, temple, castle, barn, factory, courthouse, prison, or town hall "through which one goes"; 2) a means of transportation like a ship on open water used to "go from one point to another"; and 3) vehicles such as the stagecoach seen traversing human social spaces, or "something that goes by." Foucault attributes the emergence of "other places" to the scientific discoveries of Galileo, whose seventeenth-century theories unlocked the possibility of an infinite universe. Neither Galileo nor Foucault was the first to observe that Europeans in sailing vessels claimed ownership of their geographical discoveries by renaming every new territorial possession after the old, thereby reproducing neo-Europes (New Spain, New England, New France, New Holland).[20] Foucault connected the spatial dimensions of trains to the human reordering of space, which is often reflected in mnemonic traditions.

The English came closest to achieving what Foucault called *rational utopias* by creating names and designating the purposes for railway spaces that fit in with the "hierarchic ensemble" of known sacred places. Railways were not initially designed as "counter-sites" or heterotopias. The English railways owed their nomenclature to the familiar horse-drawn carriage business that preceded them. Britons called engineers "drivers," conductors "guards," cars "carriages," waiting facilities "stations," and ticket offices "booking offices."[21] In terms of spatial relationships, the actual road was a Euclidean line called the "permanent way," and steam-locomotive engines originally pulled private carriages or mounted them by crane or ramp on larger "trucks" or "drays." First-class railway carriages – with all their woodwork, padding, and embroidery – resembled Victorian living rooms, third-class cars approximated wagons, and railway station architecture was based on cathedrals, abbeys, and palaces that complimented boroughs like the "fairy-tale citadel" of St Pancras.[22] Ideally, passengers in "cabins" could sit "in perfect comfort" next to friends and family, read, and retire to a "sleeper." American railways, which emerged about the same time, anointed new staff positions and technologies with names specific to the scientific field of mechanical engineering, the specific locale, or the inventor. They borrowed less from the stagecoach and turnpike tradition, but many U.S. travelers compared their spacious coaches, center aisles, and rows of benches to church pews, courthouses, and schoolhouses. U.S. railway companies imitated the amenities that steamboat companies introduced to make voyages luxurious. Sleeping berths, cabins, and parlors for playing cards, smoking cigars and pipes, listening to musical entertainment, and dancing were a few examples that predated George M. Pullman's pioneering architectural makeover of luxury sleeping cars on the Chicago and Alton railway since 1859. Thirty-five years passed before trains had enough horsepower to pull carriages across continents, and thus the "palace-car" was born.[23] Owing something to steamboat travel, Americans aboard the transcontinentals got "seasick" on the endless undulating plains of the Midwest, which resembled oceans to them.[24]

As this collection will demonstrate, trains failed as rational utopias when an infinite number of spatial, social, and cultural variables influenced their inception and reception in all parts of the world, at which point they became in every setting the equivalents of Foucault's heterotopias, or counter-sites where all other real sites "are simultaneously represented, contested, and inverted."[25] Six examples suffice to clarify the relevance of Foucault's concepts to the formation of world railway cultures and their "extraordinary bundle of relations." The English originated the class system on trains by designating individual carriages and entire trains as first-, second-, and third-class, Parliamentary, and Workmen's; middle-class passengers complained about the filth and smell of third-class trains, but the working class resented the bourgeoisie for taking advantage of the reduced fares. Actual railways to Chicago and Canada assisted the Underground Railroad in Antebellum America. Catholics, Hindus, and Muslims prayed on trains during pilgrimages that reinforced religious traditions. The Congolese referred to Henry Morton Stanley, the British, the British ability to shatter African resistance, and the railway alike as "Bula Matadi" (stone breaker). Mexican railways once represented foreign control of the economy under a U.S.-backed dictator until revolutionaries turned them against the very state that built them, whereby trains became symbols of the Mexican Revolution. Diverse ethnic groups and material representations of Siberia's austere geography made their way into the passenger cabins of trans-Siberian trains, significant among them Russian horsemen who rode trains to expand their nomadism. All of these examples, "represented, contested, and inverted" the original meanings and uses of railways beyond steam-powered transport.

To take Foucault's notions further, much of the world's reception of railways entailed understandings couched in relational terms. Anthropologist Inga Clendinnen explained that when Spanish *conquistadores* reintroduced the horse to the Americas, the Maya referred to the animal as the "tapir of Castile." The culture borrowed selectively and stretched the meaning of their own words to incorporate new concepts.[26] Such adaptations were hardly suggestive of an inferior indigenous culture. Nineteenth-century communities with little or no immediate reference points for railway technology similarly started with the familiar and moved outward to the new and imaginary. Natives in Madras, India called all forms of vehicles "bandy." After hauling thousands of tons of what their English supervisors called "ballast," the workers began to refer to locomotives as *Ballaster Bandy*, a name which stuck into the twentieth century.[27] The Guarani of South America, who named the majestic waterfalls Iguazu (Big), nicknamed the only train in Paraguay the *Maquina-Guazu*, or Big Machine.[28] Patterns of local appropriation transcend names to include other spaces. Mongols likened railway carriages to yurts. South Asians described them to Englishmen as a "couch borne on the wind with the speed of lightning."[29] And railway history furnishes scores of examples of people conducting standard domestic chores in trains. Women in India and Russia carried kitchen items aboard trains. Long pilgrimages to sacred shrines required Hindu women to cook meals and perform religious rituals with certain foods on Indian railways. Every family member boarded carrying pots, pans, cooking utensils, and railway rugs for sleeping. The Russian *samovar* (tea urn), wicker baskets, sugar boxes filled with pots, pans, and crockery, bundles of bedding, and sled-runners, all varied in size and quantity to reflect the number of travelers and the distance, especially on emigrant trains. Russian peasants knew train timetables accommodated one-hour stops for the other passengers to eat at buffets, so they unpacked their baskets at the stations, cooked meals, and listened for the second whistle before boarding again.[30] Bourgeois travelers dined as well. Norma Lorimer was on the Oasis Railway between Cairo and Libya:

> We ate our lobster cutlets to the accompaniment of Arab songs . . . and sipped our liqueurs and black coffee in rocking chairs on the wide verandah, under the opulence of a desert moon and the splendor of a night-blue sky ablaze with stars.[31]

The Egyptian railways were literally and metaphorically oases in the North African deserts.

Forster and Foucault both acknowledged the formation of infinite subjectivities with the coming of the railway. Early riders on steam locomotives almost uniformly felt exhilaration from the train's speed, but whether the experience was uplifting or harrowing was left to the individual. The actress Fanny Kemble enjoyed her time in the engine compartment with George Stephenson and felt the sensation of "flight" on her first railway journey.[32] To travel on the earliest trains often meant crossing long bridges, viaducts, and embankments, which enhanced the sensation of flight. One of the world's first roller-coasters, the 200-foot-long Grand Centrifugal Railway or Flying Railway, appeared in London in 1842. The ride featured a single-passenger car that descended a steep decline and relied on speed and centrifugal force to conquer gravity so that the "Lady or Gentleman" rider passed through a loop safely upside down. It was, of course, constructed in line with railway engineering principles.[33] In the early days of railway travel, companies loaded private carriages onto railway trucks for long journeys with their occupants still seated inside. Marianne North recalled "the great delight" of sitting next to her father on the rumble seat atop the carriage as the train chugged along south of York. She bit down hard on her lip and shut her eyes whenever the train passed through tunnels and over bridges.[34] Thomas Creevy, who opposed railway expansion, found his first ride "*frightful*: it is really flying, and it is impossible to divest yourself of the notion of instant death to all upon the least accident happening. It gave me a headache which has not left me yet."[35] Creevy also noted that sparks from the engine that flew into the passenger compartment burned one woman's cheek and another's clothing.[36] In 1842, England's great novelist Charles Dickens – who was ambivalent toward trains even before surviving a train wreck at Staplehurst – penned that second-class carriages without doors on either side exposed riders to the elements: "and how the wind does rush through a railway-carriage, as if angry at the almost windlike rapidity with which man, when steam is his ally, can dart along the earth!"[37] Another passenger approaching Liverpool by train for the first time wrote:

> down we dived into the long tunnel, emerging from the darkness at a pace that made my hair sensibly tighter and hold on with apprehension. Thirty miles in the hour is pleasant going when one is a little accustomed to it. It gives one such a contempt for time and distance! The whizzing past of the return trains, going in the other direction with the same velocity, making you recoil in one second, and a mile off the next was the only thing which, after a few minutes, I did not take to very kindly.[38]

Outside Berlin, an American aboard a railway carriage enjoyed the "fleeting" and calm pleasure of "sitting like a philosopher, and . . . flying over the beautiful earth, like a spirit."[39] In the 1880s, the Bengali writer Purna Chandra Basu, already unnerved by the rattling noise of his train, crossed the Sone Bridge: "the chasm below and the velocity with which we were moving almost made my brain dizzy."[40] In the high 1890s, Mexicans entering the chasm-crossing Metlac Bridge felt the sensation of detachment from the land because they could no longer view terrain immediately beside the train.[41]

Equally significant about early railway "flight" was that few passengers likened the sensation to four-in-one stagecoaches, mails, post-chaises, and wagons because they no longer felt the road beneath them. Leave it to Thomas Carlyle to pass down to posterity the archetypical description of the rite of passage that one's first train ride represented:

> The whirl through the confused darkness on those steam wings, was one of the strangest things I have experienced – hissing and dashing on, one knew not whither. We saw the gleam of towns in the distance – unknown towns. We went over the tops of houses – one town or village I saw clearly, with its chimney heads vainly stretching up towards us – under the stars; not under the clouds, but among them. Out of one vehicle into another, snorting, roaring we flew: likest thing to a Faust's flight on the Devil's mantle; or as if some huge steam night-bird had flung you on its back, and was sweeping through unknown space with you.[42]

As Carlyle alluded, railway travel completely changed the point of view of the traveler, who in pedestrian, horse-drawn, or water transportation modes never occasioned to rise above or dip below the land's surface. In 1839, a passenger recorded this significant impression:

> The novelty of the scene is delightful; now, where the natural surface of the ground is highest, we travel embosomed in deep recesses; and then, where the ordinary course of the road would lead through a valley, we ride above the tops of the trees, and look down upon the surrounding country. The reflecting traveller probably falls into a pleasing vision, arising out of the triumph of human art.

The same writer saw railway engineering as creative artistic expression and later stated that railways represented works of peace. Many early riders lauded railways as an engineered mechanical road with a constant speed and without the unpredictable nature of horses and declivities. An American stated his preferences for the railway by recounting everything that he hated about stagecoaches: "I like to travel fast. I dread vicious horses; I feel for distressed horses. I hate going down hill; chain-breaking, coach upsetting and coachman dying."[43]

Surely a carriage the size of a small bungalow and packed with men could not move without draft animals? William Douglas attended the inauguration of the Bombay to Panwell branch of the Great Indian Peninsular Railway. Dozens packed themselves into carriages and were sitting when the train lurched ahead. Douglas wrote:

> they began to feel uneasy, a tremor ran through them, and a half belief crept into their minds that the devil had got them in hand; so being already startled, it required very little more to move them, and when the shrill shriek of the whistle was heard, it acted upon them like an electric shock – they instantly jumped headlong out, over one another, through the doors and windows, and way out into the open air on to solid ground, where the whole assembly dispersed to the four winds of heaven, whilst turbans and slippers, beetle-nut and chinam boxes, strewed to the ground. After the panic had abated, what a spree it was to see them looking each for his own things! Some with two pairs of slippers and no turban, others with two turbans and an odd slipper, not their own, and such shouting and screaming.

Douglas's most important observation followed after the men gathered themselves, entrained for the second time, rode thirty minutes to their destination, and jumped down casually from the cars while the train slowed. To the man they exclaimed "Wa wah! Ka-Khoob!" which Douglas translated as "Bravo! Beautiful!"[44] The immutability of the Indian people was disproved every morning in the late 1850s.

Early critics of the railway viewed the speed and spatial limits of the carriages as a form of industrialized transport, with humans relegated to the role of freight. An editorial in the *Quarterly Review* (1824), objecting to travel at twenty miles per hour, predicted that the people of Woolwich will neither want "to be fired off upon one of Congreve's ricochet rockets, as trust themselves to the mercy of such a machine, going at such a rate."[45] Just as factory machinery increased production by restricting the roles and spatial mobility of workers while subjecting them to unrelenting time discipline, trains reduced passengers to compartmentalized stationary objects carried according to precise timetables. Train carriages in England and the U.S. originally featured hard, narrow, and low seats with stiff backs. Whatever flew outside of the cars (dust, ash, snow, rain) infiltrated the compartment through open windows without panes and begrimed the passengers. Under a microscope, the iron components of railway dust contaminants taken as samples from passenger coaches looked like metal slivers that one author compared to "tenpenny nails."[46] Enclosed in cars sealed from inclement weather, passengers ingested this filth and often reported feeling short-of-breath: "conversation was a luxury that could be indulged in only by those of recognized superiority in lung power."[47] Shuttling human cargo efficiently from one part of the country to another depersonalized travel. John Ruskin remarked that the train transformed the traveler "into a living parcel."[48] Dickens felt "'forced' like a cucumber, or a melon, or a pine-apple," into a crowded train.[49] Japanese passengers said *sushi-zume no densha*, which meant the train was packed like sushi.[50] In *The Practice of Everyday Life*, Michel de Certeau likened the "closed and autonomous insularity" of railways to traveling imprisonment, an experience of enclosure within a grid of rationalized cells akin to an "incarceration-vacation."[51] Michel Chevalier noted that trains appealed to the Americans' twin passions for movement and mechanization, but like the elevator or Ferris wheel, there were always limits to that agency.[52] Forster wrote in *A Passage to India* that the locomotive was a "coffin from the scientific north which troubled the scenery four times a day."[53] The coffin metaphor extended to sleeper cars in the U.S.[54] A German writer referred to the train as the "funeral car of absolutism" in Wilhelmine, Germany.[55] Walking through the central corridor of Russian fourth-class trains, the English traveler Annette Meakin felt like she was passing great cupboards of shelves packed with "grimy humanity."[56] Third-class trains in the U.S., the so-called immigrant sleepers, were completely wooden and devoid of any upholstery so that a hose could be turned on them.[57] As time passed, and railway companies offered first-, second-, and third-class carriage service to reflect social hierarchies, every class complained when only one type of service was available.

Steam locomotives were always first seen by people from afar, sometimes even in period illustrations, before passengers actually drew close and boarded them. At first glance, the traction of locomotives remained a mystery to pedestrian spectators. If people all over the world were confused about how railways worked, they joined literary giants no less brilliant than Alfred Tennyson, who observed the L&M train from behind a packed nighttime crowd and thought the wheels ran in grooves carved into the road rather than atop rails. The L&M inauguration inspired in Tennyson one of the most hallowed lines about the locomotive's transformative role: "Forward, forward let us range,/Let the great world spin for ever down the ringing grooves of change." The lines appeared in his poem "Locksley Hall" in 1842, the same year that Queen Victoria rode the rails for the first time. It took the young Tennyson a dozen years to commit to paper the fading memory of a misunderstanding of his youth. He later explained: "It was a black night . . . and there was such a vast crowd round the train at the station that we could not see the wheels."[58] The confusion of the great poet was a widespread one within an early-nineteenth-century context when engineers experimented with diverse forms of surfaces, track, and traction to move freight. These inventions included granite roads, "L," "I," "T," and inverted "U"-shaped rails with flanges that gave the appearance of grooves, wooden rails, elevated tracks set on posts, horse- and cable-drawn suspension railways, and stationary steam engines that used ropes to pull cars down the line. To optimize traction, George Stephenson moved the flange, originally called "creases," from the rails to the wheels, which sometimes gave the impression of concave rims rolling over flat surfaces. From a distance, onlookers could not tell if the track was raised or recessed under an oncoming train. Many early illustrations of seventeenth- and eighteenth-century colliery railways also showed laden trucks moving down rails that appeared flattened into the ground.[59]

Tennyson's misperception held fast in the earliest popular images of the locomotive, which showed trains hugging the ground, crossings, and platforms. Before the age of photography, period illustrators who captured the introduction of trains all over the world performed a public disservice in rudimentary depictions of moving trains. Others deliberately altered images to make them appear safer. Because steam locomotives were controversial and perceived as imminently combustible, R. Ackermann's early engravings intentionally disguised the engines by truncating the chimney, showing slight steam emissions, and hiding the cylindrical boiler within a box frame to appear truck-like. To diminish the locomotive's reputation as a danger to the public, T. T. Bury's "Edge Hill Station" exaggerated the monumentality of the surrounding architecture to cast shadows over diminutive trains.[60] Moreover, wheels were optional to many of the illustrators and engravers of the 1830s. Artists depicted in line drawings masterfully engineered bridges and viaducts, which appeared in exact proportion to the surrounding still landscapes, while graphically miniaturized and spatially imprecise trains steamed ahead. Some of their attention to detail can be attributed to the artist honoring the intent of the architects and engineers, who earnestly sought to adapt stations, bridges, and tunnels to the local environment.[61] One might generously interpret the blurred lines and lack of verticality of squat trains as artistic efforts to capture the engines in motion within an immutable landscape. But these early drawings were rather the product of haste as artists of varying skill levels quickly sketched a series of wooden and metallic boxes that passed by at twenty miles per hour, then reconstructed the image from memory in an engraving with permanent symmetrical infrastructure supported by pillars and arches but dwarfed trains. Painters and illustrators rendered trains at halt in stations more accurately relative to their surroundings than to moving trains. By the late nineteenth century, precisely rendered locomotives dominated oil-based modern-life and landscape paintings largely because as objects in the real world, they were perceived as safer.

Certainly landscape paintings, as well as the turbulent and abstract oil-on-canvas *Rain, Steam, and Speed* (1844) by J. M. W. Turner, were suggestive of Wordsworth's primary critique of the railway. It was in reference to the railways' disfigurement of tranquil valleys that the poet laureate of Rydal Mount queried, "Is there no nook of England ground secure/ from rash assault?"[62] Before a single steam locomotive crossed over tracks, teams of railway navigators, or navvies, scarred the English landscape with picks and shovels. Mechanization via the steam shovel and dredge further marred the landscapes of England. Historians who have downplayed the effects of rural mechanization have imposed a presentist aesthetic of partially defacing nature that distorts the attitudes of eighteenth- and nineteenth-century landowners who raised hell over a torn hedge, felled tree, or missing cobblestone. Parliamentarian Berkeley of Cheltenham belted out disdainfully that the echo of hissing railroad engines destroyed the once-noble sport of hunting.[63] In *Praeterita*, John Ruskin admitted his "native disposition" for quiet countrysides unadulterated by railways and the people they poured forth. To Ruskin, railways and their bridges spoiled vistas and cast shadows that ruined sunlit streams. During the Crystal Palace Exhibition (1851), he noticed that excursion trains brought "expatiating roughs," who toppled fences, shouted at the cows, and tore up blossoming foliage. Within the same pages, Ruskin reminisced about the joys of sightseeing in the Italian Alps, Venice, and the "old cities" when there were no railway stations to obstruct the views.[64] Ruskin was "appalled by the way railroads brutally amputated every hill in their path and raised mounds of earth across meadows vaster than the walls of Babylon."[65] Carlyle, who reminisced of childhood visits to the Roman ruins at Birrens (Middlebie), noted in 1866, that the site was now subjected to the "screams and shudders" of the Caledonian Railway.[66] To Mark Twain, the idea of a train service to the ashes of Pompeii "was as strange a thing as one could imagine."[67] Aristocratic landowners in England predicted that the very bridges and culverts built by railway companies would someday be antiquarian relics.[68]

Once railway gangs arrived in countrysides, there was no guarantee they would leave anytime soon. The British and Americans may have owned the engineering blueprints and schedules, but native workers insisted on upholding local customs and pre-modern methods to construct railways. Asking non-European wage laborers to embrace western technology and save time required consistent cajoling from impatient supervisors, who usually gave up. Laborers all over the world shunned the western wheelbarrow and tilt-cart because neither existed in the rural settings of their upbringing. In India and Mexico, balancing the cart on a single wheel so perplexed workers that they hoisted fully laden wheelbarrows on their heads and carried them to their destination. South Asian excavators hauled heavy loads in woven baskets also on their heads. Mexicans bore sacks full of rocks on their backs or loaded bags on each side of a burro. Japanese coolies believed that filling two equally weighted baskets full of rocks and slinging each on one end of a bamboo shoulder pole was more efficient than the wheelbarrow.[69] Three thousand Chinese coolies deployed this method in the Hingan mountain section between Mongolia and Manchuria on the Siberian Railway.[70] Yet others used cloth or wooden stretchers to move dirt. In many parts of the world, railway companies hired not only local laborers but also their entire families including wives and kids. Men, women, and children in India carved their way through the Ghat Mountains.[71] Japanese land surveyors who carried the ranks of samurai wore their steel blades, which interfered with the accuracy of western survey instruments. To avoid faulty readings, foreign advisors entered complex negotiations with the samurai to set aside their swords while measurements were taken.[72] One of the more insightful commentaries on labor in Northwest India came from a *sahib* engineer Victor Bayley, who wrote several books based on his experiences building the Khyber Railway. He hired Pathans and Shinwaris to provide for his security and in exchange loyal Muslim and Hindu subordinates repeatedly warned and saved him from hostile tribes and ill-intentioned *dacoits*.[73]

When critics from all nations and social classes were not complaining about the machines or workforces themselves, they deplored the impact railways and their rolling stock had on the natural environment, farmlands, and livestock herds.

In America, John Orvis, Nathaniel Hawthorne, and Henry David Thoreau all resented industrialism's machine-based intrusions in the countryside.[74] Contrary to all the paintings that showed trains passing through idyllic surroundings with stationary cows and horses, a correspondent with the *Cincinnati Enquirer* set the record straight in 1846:

> herds of cattle, sheep, and horses, stand for a few seconds and gaze at the passing train, then turn and run for a few rods with all possible speed, stop and look again with eyes distended, and head and ears erect, seemingly so frightened at the tramp of the iron horse as to have lost the power of locomotion.[75]

Farmers retaliated against the Michigan Central for the loss of healthy cattle by deliberately tethering sick and dying cows near rail lines – and indeed tied them in between the rails themselves – so that the railroad company had to compensate them for their lost stock. When the company got wise to it and started paying half as much per cow, incensed farmers placed obstacles on the lines, burned stations, and threw stones at passing trains. A dozen or so conspirators were jailed.[76] In Mexico, railways crushed the sacred plants of the Tarahumara, and in India a train rolled mercilessly over hundreds of gray monkeys.[77] Sometimes nature attacked the railways. In India, where railways and telegraph lines were built in tandem, telegraph poles were fitted with spiked collars to prevent wild elephants from uprooting them like trees. When one pole came down, so did a mile's worth due to an entangled elephant. Bull elephants "frolicking on the track" prevented railways from operating at night.[78] Swarms of grasshoppers stopped trains in Nebraska.[79] What became of old rolling stock was almost universal. Locals purchased carriages and engines for cottages, outhouses, garden and yard decorations, tool and storage sheds, and chicken coops.[80] A French cartoon published in *L'Assiette au Beurre* (1907) showed old four-wheeled train carriages equipped with gas lamps and stove pipes serving as homes in the Paris suburbs.[81] All would become rusty eyesores in good time. At least one British traveler expressed gratitude that the western seaport of Granville in France was "not (as in England) strewn with the wrecks of abandoned railways – ruins which, by some strange fatality, never look picturesque."[82]

The Victorian landscape aesthetic of a picturesque countryside, ruined by railways in the 1830s, was enhanced by the timely appearance of the vintage steam locomotive in the 1840s.[83] This was an early example of the train's alterity, whereby through deliberate human action the destroyer of nature transforms into its opposite, the creator of nature. Victorian attitudes shifted quickly with the appearance of mechanically reproduced engravings, lithographs, illustrated magazines, and landscape paintings that featured trains in harmony with their natural surroundings. Passengers also soon enjoyed the experience of passing through and gazing at pastoral farmlands between cities and towns, and seeing return trains gliding through seas of green pastures and meadows full of wildflowers. From the summit of Long Cliff in 1842, Thomas Potter described the uninterrupted Midland Counties train as "a pleasing object darting across the grand panorama."[84] This sentiment emerged also in America, where transcendentalist Ralph Waldo Emerson famously compared the iron rails to the magician's rod and asserted that "Nature adopts them very fast . . . and the gliding train of cars she loves like her own."[85] From 1857–1907, the Currier and Ives company sold inexpensive colored lithographs that showed trains in rural areas. British and American railway companies hired artists, photographers, and writers to travel on their trains to depict what they saw in promotional literature for tourist excursions.[86] All sorts of collectible printed train ephemera embellished the walls of the poorest cottages.[87] The visual and literary imagery helped market railway tourism. By the 1890s, aesthetes and literary figures on both sides of the Atlantic no longer considered railways ruinous, so much as harmonious with quaint rural scenery. Lynne Kirby argued that railways "trained" spectator-audiences of early silent films by preparing them for the anticipated "shock of temporal disorientation in relation to speed, acceleration, and simultaneity."[88]

Once railways settled in and showed signs of decay, railway companies began promoting them as nostalgic remnants of the distant past or an "invented tradition," even though they had been around for only 20 years.[89] Station architecture was carefully planned to fit into cityscapes and town blueprints as if they had always been there. As older models of locomotives passed ruined castles, crumbling churches, stone bridges, and rustic cottages, modern travel writers upheld the pretense that scenic railways had always belonged to the sublime and antiquated "country."[90] Locomotives somehow seemed less threatening when they expired after a known life cycle. German author Berthold Auerbach promoted the *eisenbahn* as a purveyor of all things good, including physical movement through old landscapes newly set in motion by excavations, embankments, ballasting, and tracks.[91] Henry James, no lover of railways, could not help but comment on their confidence and dominance of the American countryside. To James, "the great straddling, bellowing railway" distracted attention from the shade of elms and freshly painted white homes of New England, as if the country exists for the railways, not the railways for the country. In contrast to the proper size of rural dirt roads, railway cars descended like a conquering army and altered the "old felicity of proportion."[92] Railways "sat enthroned" like no other, and Americans submitted to a "monotony of acquiescence" to their dominion, despite the "pomp and circumstance, the quickened pace, the heightened fever, the narrowed margin" of "*our* ugly era."[93] In the final chapter of James's *The American Scene*, the railroad station in Savannah yielded to a party of "bare-headed and vociferous" young women who boarded the train and treated it like their own public gathering place or home. The moralizing writer listened to the "innocently immodest ventilation of their puerile privacies" that convinced him that the "great moving proscenium of the Pullman" was in fact the brusque America that adopted him as son.[94] All the terms that he used to describe the railway were metonyms for the U.S. as well as characteristics that shaped American national identity.

Reception

Until recently, historians and literary critics of the past have provided a lopsided view of railways as an exclusively benign force in history. Since most railways were introduced from without, like agriculture, this collection adopts the alternative view that host peoples and subordinate cultures continually shaped and redefined railways as agents of different forms of modernity. By redressing the extreme imbalance of uncritical narratives and biographies, scholars and popular historians have begun to contextualize and historicize the overall impact of the world's railways. The oft-retold sensational account of the roles that the railway and telegraph played in apprehending the murderer John Tawall in January 1845 provided Victorian-era melodrama for over a century. After he killed his paramour and fled to London by railway, a timely telegraphic alert to authorities at Paddington station led to his arrest at the station. The press extolled the railway police, London police, telegraphers, and railway that foiled Tawall's escape, and he was hanged in March.[95] Press coverage overshadowed the grim realities of the technology's history. In the years before the Tawall arrest, forty-one passengers and an undisclosed number of employees were killed by railways in England due to human and mechanical error. In 1844, several hundred were injured by an industrial technology that never promoted safety first in its 100-year history. Passenger deaths due to railway accidents on UK trains peaked at ninety in 1870.[96] Moreover, several recent studies have established the death toll for world railway construction as a human life or two for every track mile, which amounted to 600,000 to 1.2 million deaths by 1910. This meant that in the year of Tawall's capture, a minimum average of 7,500 workers died during worldwide railway construction. Victorian-era periodicals covered many of these terrible accidents and published the statistics that suggested to the public that railways were still safer than other forms of transportation due to the ratio of double-digit deaths to the millions of passengers carried in a year. Historians wrote around the issue because only safe railways met standards of historical progress. In an important study that shows why railway companies in England were commercially unsuccessful and not particularly well-liked in the 1850s and 1860s, R. W. Kostal argued that it was never just railway officials, but also "smash-and-grab joint-stock promoters," "bubble" lawyers, and litigation attorneys who dashed and dawdled forward without regard to public safety. A powerful consensus emerged between a capitulating Parliament and an impatient public that victimized everyone through hegemonic legal processes that kept railway laws years behind the industry. Mercenary speculators, parliamentary lawyers, and personal injury litigators siphoned railway earnings and ruined investors of middling income.[97] Similarly, Richard White exposed the seedy underbelly of corporate monopoly, greed, and failure in his book *Railroaded*.[98] The sheer lack of consideration for what the unregulated industry did to taxpayers, coolies, employees, and entire Native American tribes typifies western attitudes toward new technologies in general. The systems that Kostal and White examined led to persistent legacies of public distrust of railways, in terms of economic development, financial investment, and public safety, first embodied in England and America as "manias" then evolving toward the "ruinous railways" metonym worldwide.

Indeed, the history of world railways is a greater story when it is told as an industry overcoming challenging problems. To address this history requires researchers to wade through the collective amnesia about its sordid episodes and work them back into narratives. Railways projected and reflected human shortcomings, as well as genius, and as flawed constructs they place in relief the perennial struggles that societies have with themselves. L. T. C. Rolt explained in four editions that human fallibility was responsible for railway accidents, which happened just often enough to remind people that the possibility of industrialized death lay just around the corner. As Rolt argued, the railway accident revealed the contrast between trivial human error and terrible consequence. When accidents increased in the 1860s and 1870s, railway inspection offices under H. W. Tyler began publishing annual statistical reports as a compromise to prevent government intervention. Pedestrians originally had trouble estimating the careless speeds of trains, which blew past crowds with little acknowledgement of their vulnerability. Company by-laws forbade passengers from riding on train roofs as if they were continuing the longstanding practice of riding atop stagecoaches. The incidents of travelers jumping off trains to reclaim their hats led companies to lock passengers inside the carriages, a practice later condemned when a fire consumed an entire carriage full of trapped people at Versailles in 1842.[99]

The L&M nevertheless shattered all doubts that the British people would embrace railways as an alternative to the next best form of transport regardless of the risks.[100] In many ways, the postmodern term "alterity" is a concept rooted in the eighteenth-century Enlightenment, which sprouted in nineteenth-century industrialism, and grew uncontrollably in the early twentieth century's altered reality of extremism and two world wars. Victorians validated steam transportation in Messianic terms. After the L&M's debut, Lord Brougham exclaimed: "I beheld a kind of miracle exhibited before my astonished eyes."[101] In a progressive time and place where a Christian leader could also be a socialist, Charles Kingsley was moved to tears by a seemingly supernatural event: the Great Exhibition of 1851. With such sentiments swelling in him, he delivered a sermon for the ages:

> If these forefathers of ours could rise from their graves this day they would be inclined to see in our hospitals, in our railroads, in the achievements of our physical science, confirmation of that old superstition of theirs, proofs of the kingdom of God, realizations of the gifts which Christ received for men, vaster than any of which they had dreamed.[102]

Why should Europeans have been so surprised when the hill tribes of Bombay embraced the fire horse as a manifestation of a god or devil? Tribal elders asked for permission to propitiate it with garlands of fragrant flowers, bowls of honey, ghee, and sugar, and daubs of red paint. After negotiating with railway officials, they settled for painting the buffers.[103]

In an age of great transition, Victorians fought a daily battle between appreciation for everything modern and anxieties wrought by the kaleidoscopic changes that surrounded them. Modernists expected rail transport to unify the human races. For Lord Macaulay, improvements in transportation brought moral, intellectual, and material benefits to humankind because they bound together "the great human family."[104] French thinker Benjamin Gastineau proclaimed that the railway would father all future peoples due to its role in intermingling the races.[105] As Walter Benjamin discovered, Gastineau also originated the metonym of railways as "godlike animators."[106] Scottish novelist R. B. Cunninghame Graham thought railways made "the whole world more common than all the international pilgrimages of all past times."[107] A more representative turn-of-the-century view was that of Colombian President Rafael Reyes. In a statement influenced by positivism and social Darwinism, he said:

> In times past it was the Cross or the Koran, the sword or the book that accomplished the conquests of civilization; today it is the powerful locomotive, flying over the shining rail, breathing like a volcano, that awakens peoples to progress, well-being and liberty . . . and those who do not conform to that progress it crushes beneath its wheels.

Reyes viewed the railroads as a "panacea for all the nation's ills."[108]

Yet the masses never accepted locomotives as a cure-all. The most prevalent word used by those who encountered trains for the first time was "monster." The term was employed in both its terrifying and playful meanings in England and the U.S. after 1830, France and Germany after 1840, Austria and India after 1850, Australia and Japan after 1870, Russia and China after 1880, Mexico and Ecuador after 1890, Turkey and Uruguay after 1910. Steam locomotives towered over people, hissed and clanked, breathed fire, belched smoke, and screeched. They caught fire, exploded in fiery infernos, jumped their tracks, and collided head-on with one another, during which carriages on both trains "telescoped," one within the other from the deadly impact. In the U.S., these single-track head-on collisions were called "cornfield meetings" because they occurred too far from civilization for anyone to render assistance. In the industrial novels of the late 1840s and early 1850s, machines in general "obtrude[d] into the narrative . . . like monstrous anomalies,"[109] yet, when their accident record worsened, writers began to grant the iron monsters human personal characteristics that made them appear as if they had lives of their own. Because trains and streetcars earned such fiendish reputations for killing and maiming railway employees and pedestrians, everyday onlookers remained wary at first sightings.

Science fiction author Ray Bradbury once described a frightful traveling carnival with a line from Shakespeare's *Macbeth*: "something wicked this way comes." People worldwide uttered comparable forebodings upon the coming of the locomotive. Popular apprehension was reflected in periodical literature, fiction, and the arts. George Cruikshank's famous cartoon *The Railway Dragon* featured the train monster reversing into a family's dining room with the threatening chant "I come to dine, I come to sup, I come, I come, to eat you up," while a woman cries "Oh the Monster!"[110] Theater and literature followed suit. In the first scene of Act 3 in Dion Boucicault's sensational drama *After Dark* (1868), Old Tom observes the incapacitated Captain Chumley lying helplessly on the tracks of London's underground railway and remarks, "See, it comes, the monster comes."[111] The young pastor of Torwald, Wolfgand Wieser, in Rosegger's epistolary novel *The Eternal Light* (1896), wrote about a premonition in his diary: "at times something frightens me, as if something monstrous were fluttering in the air. As if something unheard of were to come over our valley of Torwald." He later sees the "black monster," as villagers cry: "Pray that it doesn't come!"[112] Rosegger viewed the train as both savior and destroyer of the Austrian alpine village that raised him. Writing in the 1880s, Australian journalist and travel writer Hume Nisbet felt accosted by the streetcar in Sydney:

> What an awful monster that is which comes roaring along the main street, vomiting out clouds of dirty smoke over this fair sunlit city a ruthless monster, which demands its weekly sacrifice, either unwary man, woman, or child who may trip and fall before its approach; as ugly and remorseless a malformation as ever Frankenstein raised up and let loose – the steam tramcar.[113]

Travel writer Louisa Jebb Wilkins described the Anatolian Railway as a monster that ran his fangs into desolation and shot you into the desert "like a ball out of a cannon's mouth."[114]

Art historian Michael Freeman noted that Victorians who saw trains for the first time drew comparisons to Frankenstein's monster. Not far removed from the publication of Mary Shelley's *Frankenstein* (1818, and reissued in 1830), writers and artists seemed concerned that an aberration of science might destroy humankind.[115] The India-born journalist and author of *Vanity Fair*, William Makepeace Thackeray poked fun at the "cast-iron Frankenstein" in his early account of railway travel.[116] Train enthusiast Thomas Roscoe called the Fire Fly class of engine on the Grand Junction Railway a "Centaur" and "a huge monster in mortal agony, whose entrails are like burning coals!"[117] Descriptions of mechanical monsters abounded in the news dailies and weeklies. The *Gloustershire Chronicle* related a Mechanics' Institution excursion to Birmingham aboard a "monster train" with a "living freight" of members.[118] A surviving passenger in an accident on the Great Western reported:

> On looking out the window, I shall never forget the sight I beheld – the other carriages, which were before us one within the other, like a

telescope; and what with the great monster roaring, the groaning of the poor sufferers, and the stillness of the night, it was a most dreadful and horrifying scene.[119]

The German poet-engineer Max Eyth, who authored a novel about the British railway accident at Tay Bridge (*Berufstragik*), described the ill-fated train as a "black, dripping monster with its two eyes of fire."[120] Journalists livened up their stories about railway schedules that violated the Sabbath with allusions to unstoppable mechanized beasts: "onward went the monster with puff and snort, and rattle of wheels."[121] John Davidson, the prolific Scottish playwright and poet, referred to the train as a "monster taught/ To come to hand."[122] Across the Atlantic, Mexican elites deemed the locomotives "centaurs of progress." Historian of Mexico, Michael Matthews, found this poem in a Mexican magazine in 1896: "Look at it swallowing up the distance/ It barely seems to touch the ground/ bloated by nausea/ it belches clouds through its burning maw!"[123] At the heights of Railway Mania in the mid-1840s, "monster" was synonymous with "giant," as in the Great Western's monster engine, or as a negative term for the "devouring, monopolising monster" – the London and Northwestern.[124] Dickens described Staggs' Garden as the product of the "monster train."[125] Novelist Margaret Oliphant dubbed one passing train "the red-eyed ogre" and conjured another with this imagery:

> The roar and rustle with which some one-eyed monster, heard long before seen, came plunging and snorting out of the darkness, all the rapid, shifting phantasmagoria of that new fashion of the picturesque which belongs to modern times.[126]

Locomotives took a while to shake off their reputation as inhospitable iron brutes compared to livery services. Horse-drawn coaches, while more dangerous both to drivers and riders, were difficult to eliminate, foreshadowing not their lingering death so much as their replacement by the omnibus and motor car. The earliest issues of *The Railway Times* and the *Daily News* promoted the railway industry by emphasizing the safety of locomotive travel. They also reported accidents and boiler explosions culled from British newspapers. In 1841, a writer in the *Brighton Herald* expressed regret for the passing of horse carriage service and the arrival of the impersonal London and Brighton Railway to Castle Square. "In the progress of the world towards perfection," he stated, "we are obliged to resign many pleasures." He listed nostalgic things lost to the senses: the sight of four-in-hand coaches and their bounding steeds; the rousing journeys through free country and rural roads; the salutations of onlookers and fellow passengers; the sharp sounds of horns and clinking of metal harnesses at top speeds; the tempting smells of wines and cakes sold by wayside cottages; the comical scenes, jests, and practical jokes of friends; and the pleasant hours of conversation, cigars, and brandy sitting alongside the coachman, who, with "rubicund visage" always turned and said: "Now, Sir, we're off directly." Of late, passengers exchanged the excitement of coach travel for the "dull routine of the stationhouse." The Brighton editorialist aired regret:

> One is of no consequence in a railroad – every body is reduced to the same level – there is no forming a connection with a train – it has the same regard to a man who goes the first time as to one who has been all his life; there is no solicitation, no patronage, no thanks – every thing is done by rule, by mechanism. You feel you are dealing, not with flesh and blood, but with some new body into which humanity does not enter – a monster-creature of mighty power, but no heart – a company, that offers you greater advantages than could any individual, but does it out of no regard to your simple self, but for some other monster, called the Public, of which you are so insignificant an atom that whether you go with it or hold aloof from it is all the same – in the casting up of the great account, you will not be noticed.

Train passengers "sacrifice all the kindly virtues at the shrine of order."[127]

Worldwide reports of railway trains behaving monstrously proliferated. Military historians have commented about instances when a technological apparatus destroyed itself and others by means of its own power. When the safety valves of highly pressurized steam cylinders were stuck shut, just one human, mechanical, or environmental error caused tubes to burst, drop onto fire bars, ignite the boiler, and literally detonate the engine like a bomb. In 1829, two such explosions killed railway personnel on the S&D.[128] The train as bomb also went off in North Wales (1868), when the Irish Mail struck a petroleum wagon and sent passengers to kingdom come.[129] Steam locomotives also endangered pedestrians. During the L&M inauguration, an engine struck and killed the parliamentarian railway advocate and president of the Board of Trade William Huskisson, who stepped off one train and was run over by the next at Parkside. Since then, the train's perceived appetite for destruction grew disproportionate to reality, even though two accounts of train wrecks in the UK (Rolt) and U.S. (Mark Aldrich) together surpass 700 pages.[130] Since most of the world's railways were single-track rather than double-track lines, increasing railway density combined with an inadequate number of passing loops and signals made accidents structurally inevitable. It turns out, however, that the primary cause of train accidents in the early days of railroad transportation were drunk or colorblind engineers. The combination of the two was absolutely lethal. Poorly constructed track often left consecutive rails overlapping, with one jutting upward with each passing train. Eventually the spikes sprung from the ground, and one upended rail rose high enough for the train's wheels to run under it and impale the carriage and anyone in it. This was called a "snake's head" in the U.S.[131]

In his article "Getting the Traffic Through," Edward Hungerford of *Harper's Magazine* explored further the theme of the iron monster as a benign force of nature:

> The railroad is a monster – his feet are dipped into the navigable seas and his many arms reach into the uplands. His fingers clutch the treasures of

the hills – coal, iron, timber – all the wealth of Mother Earth. His busy hands touch the broad prairies – corn, wheat, fruits – the yearly produce of the land. With ceaseless activity he brings the raw products that they may be made into the finished. He centralized industry. He fills the ships that sail the seas. He brings the remote town in quick touch with the busy city. He stimulates life. He makes life. . . . The railroad is life itself!

Hungerford's anatomical metaphors denoted the monster's extensive reach. Its arms stretched and its tireless hands burrowed until the rivers, hills, valleys, prairies, unknown country, and great tracts of land yielded its bounty. Towns sprung to life where no human had ever lived. Hungerford wrote about the dominant American theme of the railway as agent of economic opportunity.[132] In June 1876, America's Centennial year, a train ran from New York to San Francisco in less than 84 hours. Hungerford's monster covered 3,317 miles at an average speed of forty miles per hour and surmounted four mountain ranges, including a summit of 8,000 feet.[133] Only a "fire-Titan" with "iron muscles that never tire" achieved this feat. As historian Leo Marx wrote: "The locomotive is the perfect symbol because its meaning is inherent in its physical attributes."[134]

World peoples also likened trains to giant mythical dragons and serpents. From Dorset, a protestor cursed the railways with allegory as "monstrous serpents that wind their hideous *trains* through the length and breadth of the land, and, like the rod of Aaron, swallowed up all other channels of communication and industry." The locomotive had opened Pandora's Box, unleashed a plague on humanity, and destroyed local economies: the "dragon monster whose fiery wings have scorched and burnt up industry and commerce to the very roots" also ruined the "labor, profit, wealth, and comfort of the community."[135] Cunninghame Graham wrote in *Scottish Stories*: "the train slipped past Watford, swaying round the curves like a gigantic serpent," and carried the metaphor to describe the locomotive's movements as it "steals through corries and across moors," "slackening" at its stop, and "slid[ing] almost imperceptibly away as the passengers upon the platform looking after it with that half foolish half astonished look with which men watch a disappearing train."[136] Prevalent images in German writing were locomotives as "fiery dragons," "hellish dragons," and "seed of dragon's teeth," their smokestacks emitting "snake-like clouds."[137] South Australian Aborigines believed a giant snake named *Gandba* or *Jeedarra* inhabited the desert of Nullarbor (Latin for "no trees"). Capable of swallowing travelers, the mighty serpent terrified natives until it was overshadowed by the sinister man-eating metal snake called *Meletna* (the transcontinental railway). Daisy Bates, the Irish-born ethnologist of Ooldea, South Australia, observed that whenever aborigines sighted the train for the first time, they exclaimed "Irr! Irr! Irr!"[138]

References to steam locomotive as "devils" in all parts of the world depended on context. For two decades after 1830, Europeans and Americans cornered the market not only in railways, but negative associations of them as evil serpents in the Garden of Eden. Literary figures and everyday folk referred to them as "devils," the "devil's mantle," "devil's transport," "demons," "the demon king in pantomime," and "abominations."[139] The rustic peoples of the French countryside thought locomotives were vehicles from hell.[140] "Spanked along the road to Liverpool," Lord Shaftesbury wrote in 1839, "It is quite a just remark that the Devil, if he travelled, would go by train."[141] Tolstoy believed the devil invented the locomotive and pronounced Russian trains hellspawn; he famously died at a railway station in Astapovo but not in the way of his unforgettable heroine Anna Karenina.[142] The Muslim Bokhariot horsemen of the Russian trans-Caspian region referred to trains, foreigners, and enemy Cossacks interchangeably as devils. Thus, their term for the railway – *Shaitan arba* – meant "the Devil's wagon," "the foreign Devil's wagon," or the "Cossack Devil's wagon" in different circumstances.[143] From centers and peripheries worldwide, native peoples referred to trains and trollies as "dark angels," "killers," and their onslaught as "demonic" and "terrorizing." One member of a school board in Ohio called the railroad "a device of Satan to lead immortal souls to hell."[144] Japanese political dissidents in Tokyo voiced outrage over the prospect of importing an "abominable alien machine."[145] In the earliest days of railway travel, looking out windows at the passing scenery elicited comparisons to literary passages they once read. An American passenger on a train from misty Berlin compared the rush of scenery as "something like Milton's description of the voyage of Satan to Earth."[146]

In most parts of the world, the railway monster was believed to have otherworldly origins. Railway manager Joseph Tatlow recalled that Robert Stephenson's first fleet of steam locomotives "appeared like the realization of fabled powers or the magician's wand."[147] Thoreau likened them to the arrival of a new race worthy to inhabit the earth.[148] Historian William Cronon cites a Chicago resident's description of locomotives as "talismanic wands" that "draw upon a mysterious creative energy that was beyond human influence or knowledge."[149] Japanese peasants, already fearful of the fires caused by trains, also blamed them for supernatural invasions. In Suye Mura, farmers believed that railway construction destroyed so many foxholes that the trains were haunted and possessed by vengeful fox spirits that could be seen at night as a series of hazy lights.[150] Similarly, a Jesuit Priest in Icaiche, Yucatán (1894) related the Mayan belief that the train's desecration of sacred burial mounds released demons upon earth.[151] The train's perceived mystical powers to animate held fast well into the twentieth century. One amazed observer in Riobamba, Ecuador remarked: "I imagine, in sum, that even corpses could be resuscitated by the heat expended by that blessed monster."[152] To a wide-eyed journalist in Montevideo, Uruguay, the streetcar was "something like the coming of the Messiah, the passage of a monster, the revelation of a phenomenon."[153] The Mexican Indian workforce that excavated the colossal Pyramid of the Sun at Teotihuacán nicknamed the train that relieved them of carting dirt by hand the "Quetzalcoatl," after the Aztec feathered-serpent god.[154] The monstrous engine hauled away 100 tons of earth every hour for a total of 1.6 million cubic feet. The amount of dirt excavated for this pyramid matched that for many railways.

World peoples also referred to locomotives as minor deities. At a time when high-speed express trains crisscrossed all of Europe, Michel de Certeau described the quotidian scene of a train crawling to a stop at a station: "the immobile machine suddenly seems monumental and almost incongruous in its mute, idol-like inertia, a sort of god undone."[155] The nineteenth-century Bengali travel writer Bholanauth Chunder asserted that the railway's inventor was entitled to the same recognition as Bhaghiruth, the Hindu god that carried the Ganges down from Heaven. Chunder also argued that the railway beat Hercules in feats of strength; Hercules merely altered the course of a river, the "Rail" turned "the courses of men, merchandise, and mind, all into new channels."[156] Railway scholars Ian Kerr and Harriet Bury wrote about the powerful imagery of Indian poet Radhacharan Goswami, who described railways as a demon "towering over the corpse of India." Goswami's poem *Relwey Stotra* from 1884 conveys the railroads' monstrous subcontinental presence through corporeal metaphor:

[The feet of the railroad] are in both Delhi and Karachi/ Your hands are the Avadh Rohilkhand Railway and the Rajputana Railway/ Your arse is the Great Indian Peninsula Railway and the rest are all the hairs on your body/ You lie down and crush the contents of Bharatvarsh/ On the day when you receive your oblation of rupees, you lift it up like a demon cow and devour Hindustan.[157]

Kerr, Bury, and Marian Aguiar all find that the people of India met railways with ambivalence. Goswami's poem appeared in print long before Mahatma Gandhi's nationalist criticism in which he deemed railways as "evil."

Themes in Goswami's poem recurred in Emile Zola's *The Human Beast* (1890) and Frank Norris's *The Octopus* (1901). Zola portrayed railways as "a huge body, a gigantic being lying across the earth, his head in Paris, his vertebrae all along the line, his limbs stretching out into branch lines, with feet and hands on Le Havre and the other terminals."[158] Norris's railroad evolved from a simple octopus into a terrifying cephalopod:

From Reno on one side to San Francisco on the other, ran the plexus of red, a veritable system of blood circulation, complicated, dividing, and reuniting, branching, splitting, extending, throwing out feelers, offshoots, taproots, feeders – diminutive little bloodsuckers that shot out from the main jugular and went twisting up into some remote country, laying hold upon some forgotten village or town, involving it into one of a myriad branching coils, one of a hundred tentacles, drawing it, as it were, toward that center from which all this system sprang.[159]

Many firsthand observers from interior regions, who never saw large oceanic vessels from the coastlines, possessed no conceptual framework for the railway juggernaut. Surely, native accounts of the first sightings of European steamers and naval vessels are instructive. When the aboriginal Australian Yalgunga, father of Joobaitch in the Wordungmat tribe, first saw a European boat spill its human cargo onto the banks of the Swan River in 1829, his initial reaction was to grip the outreached hand of Lieutenant Irwin. His second response was to gather his family and belongings and withdraw to swampy Goobabbilup never to return.[160] Villagers in India accustomed to watching country boats float down the Surma gathered on the banks when steamer service began in the 1870s:

> [They] literally rendered *puja* or worship to the boat. The women cried out *ulu; ulu,* the cry which is made by them on all auspicious occasions, and prostrated themselves devoutly on the ground, taking the apparently self-moving boat to be some sort of manifestation of the Deity. Sometimes they would bring flowers and vermillion and other materials of worship, and throw these in the direction of the boat to the intense amusement of the European captain and his crew.[161]

In another region of India, Chunder paralleled the railway's fulfilment of a Hindu prophecy with the Burmese who first saw the steamship:

> The first sight of a steamer no less amazed than alarmed the Burmese, who had a tradition that the capital of their empire would be safe, until a vessel should advance up the Irrawady without oars and sails! Similarly does the Hindoo look upon the Railway as a marvel and miracle – a novel incarnation for the regeneration of Bharat-versh [India].[162]

When "fire vehicles" of the British Raj tore through the Indian subcontinent, mothers in the Western Ghats Mountains (Southwest India) hurried out of their homes bearing their babies to trackside just to set eyes on passing locomotives.[163] In contrast, when the people of San José de Gracia in Michoacán, Mexico saw a locomotive for the first time, their legs trembled and some even "took to their heels."[164]

Other large animals of nonthreatening, imaginary, or ancient character came to mind upon sight of the steam locomotive. The French compared them to the flying dragons and magical talismans that transported protagonists in the fantasy genre of fiction.[165] In 1860, Scottish writer William Edmondstoune Aytoun wrote of "resonant steam-eagles."[166] To Mrs. Aeneas Gunn of Darwin, Australia, the train mimicked a prehistoric animal:

> as the train zig-zagged through jungle and forest and river-valley – stopping now and then to drink deeply at magnificent rivers ablaze with water-lilies [sic.] – it almost seemed as though it were some kindly Mammoth creature, wandering at will through the bush.[167]

One traveler compared the spider-web patterns on railway maps to early cartographic renditions of sea monsters. To Henry Blackburn, the map of Normandy that showed the outstretched tentacles of France's railway network in the 1890s resembled the devil-fish from Victor Hugo's *Travailleurs de la Mer*.[168]

Even when fear and doubt subsided, people were still left with the imposing spectacle of the machine that stood before them. Some were inspired with wonder, others wondered how trains moved without animal traction. Ronald Ross, the scientist who discovered the mosquito vector of malaria, remarked in his memoirs that British children in India where he grew up were "fired with curiosity as to how it [the locomotive] could move by itself."[169] In the late 1890s, the two Chinese servants Esau and Lassoo, who accompanied Captain M. S. Wellby on a train from Tientsin to Tongku, asked him how it moved.[170] Captain H. H. P. Deasy trekked across the "roof of the world" in Tibet and Chinese Turkestan. He recorded this anecdote about his servants:

> Two of my Ladakis told me that they had never been further south than Kashmir, and they were as innocent of modern improvements as were the men of Tir, who had never been beyond their own valleys. They might possibly have heard of railway trains, but that these were driven by steam they could not believe. Bullocks or ponies hidden by the carriages might, they thought, somehow drag them along, but beyond this perfectly rational position these children of Nature would not go. While they rejected my statements, their looks said more plainly their words, "Do you suppose that we are fools?"[171]

After native line workers in Madras completed a track segment, they excitedly gathered around a locomotive. When an opportunistic driver unleashed the screaming demons of steam: "the unsuspecting coolies . . . scattered like a bursting rocket."[172] In Brazil, Caripuna tribesmen paddled canoes long distances from Bolivia up the Madeira River just to set eyes on the "Devil's Railroad." An American railroad employee for the Madeira-Mamoré line, infamously named the "Mad Mary," recorded their response.

> Convinced that the thing couldn't move, after all, they all turned and marched in single file back toward the river. Just then the engine gave three shrill toots of its whistles. It was worth an admission fee to see that bunch whirl round and gaze in excited expectation toward the train.[173]

Following the Caste War in Mexico, Romualdo Chable, a captured Maya rebel sent by train to Mexico City to meet with President Porfirio Díaz, marveled over this strange and mysterious machine powered by "fire" and "candles." When asked if he was afraid of the train, Chable remarked, "When I saw so many enter it, why should I be afraid?"[174]

When critics did not describe railways in negative terms, they issued warnings, voiced opposition, or expressed confusion with the technology. French railway manuals promised uninitiated readers help in negotiating the dangers lurking around the corner at railway stations, which they equated to mazes, dungeons, prisons, and hell. Some recommended that women remain vigilant against rapists armed with chloroform and that men carry swordsticks or pistols to protect themselves against madmen.[175] To prevent fatalities from passengers falling from the unsteady platforms between coaches, a New Jersey company painted pictures of graves and tombstones on the cars. Whenever railways in Great Britain failed to pay dividends, stockholders renamed them according to their initials. The Manchester, Sheffield, and Liverpool became the Money, Sunk, and Lost, and the Great Central was Gone Completely.[176] Critics in Japan similarly ridiculed the Meiji government's railway program by splitting apart and altering the characters for "railway" – *tetsudō*, or "iron road" – into a character that read "the way to lose money."[177] Japanese woodblock artists of the Meiji period produced fine graphic representations of trains, except for one detail – the square wheels. In this conception, the track moved the train or the train moved not at all. Railroad scholars have shared the story of Japanese passengers boarding for the first time and leaving their sandals on the railway platform, as they did traditionally when entering a home.[178] Expecting the sandals to be there when they returned, they were effectively without footwear until they completed the round trip.

Superstitions accompanied railway history, and the unproven technology engendered harebrained fears. These phobias contrasted with sensible concerns that the railways would put out of business bargemen, carters, stagecoach drivers, horse trainers, and innkeepers along traditional roadways. In England, shepherds swore that the soot of trains would turn their sheep's wool black. Farmers suspected cows would stop producing milk. And virtually every anxious person worried that pregnant ladies would miscarry.[179] Women in George Eliot's *Middlemarch* insisted that cows and horses would prematurely cast their calves and foals.[180] Pamphlets and testimony cautioned that railways would prevent hens from laying eggs and cows from grazing. Conservation of fox and pheasant habitats would be futile.[181] The "baleful breath" of locomotives would cause crops to wither and die, and its velocity would asphyxiate passengers. Anyone who followed too closely would "be whirled straight to death and damnation."[182] Homeowners worried that the sparks from train chimneys would turn their fields into ash. The smoke would kill birds, and boilers might "blow passengers to atoms."[183] If German realist novels lived up to their billing, then German peasants thought that the train's arrival would stop fields from producing, kill trees, and burn villages to the ground.[184] Some of this nonsense felt akin to common sense because country folk also predicted that railways would collide with livestock, cause horses to bolt, and burn homes to the ground – and they did.

Railways were perceived worldwide as dangerous loci for women. This remains a great irony since women's travel writing is invaluable precisely because they proved more sociable than men. Anne Green wrote about the regret expressed by nineteenth-century French women who preferred the amorous comfort and personal security of coach travel over distasteful modern travel on crowded trains and omnibuses, where men groped and otherwise assaulted them.[185] Women worldwide nonetheless rode trains forewarned and forearmed against sexual brutality and abhorrent male behavior. In preparation of tunnels, where couples who sat together commonly kissed, German women kept needles between their lips to "check familiarity."[186] A woman from St. Petersburg and the Mayor of Vladivostok, both of whom carried pistols on trains, advised two Englishwomen on the Trans-Siberian Railway to purchase small revolvers at Omsk to guarantee their personal security.[187] Between the 1880s and 1920s in New Zealand's history, "ladies cars" were attached to trains on the Christchurch to Dunedin line of the South Island Express to protect women from "tanked up" male passengers. The line had earned its nickname as the "Royal Soaks Express" because men from Port Chalmers drank whiskey and other alcoholic beverages day and night at railway station bars and accosted women on the trains. During the prohibition decade, the Women's Christian Temperance Union pressured the railway to enforce laws against the sale of liquor and accommodate women with their own cars up through 1926.[188] Women travel writers also commented on the gentlemanly behavior of men on trains, which reinforced both gender identities. According to Amy Richter, "[F]inding femininity in a setting steeped in the values of manly achievement offers an opportunity to reconsider the separate spheres ideal as an agent of change."[189] Richter argued that American women pressed railways to achieve greater "public domesticity" in providing safer, more comfortable, and private places for all passengers.

Railways and their stations in extreme environments harbored everyone from tourists to the dispossessed. In the 1860s, trains out of Cairo were akin to iron camels: they lurched slowly through the desert heat, required lots of stored water, and carried few passengers and less freight. They also derailed in sand storms.[190] After decades of humdrum service, Egyptian railways earned a new metonym from travel writer Norma Lorimer, who anointed them as the new oases. The Oasis Railway cut travel time over a distance of 120 miles in northeastern Africa from six days to twenty-four hours. Aboard the *train-de-luxe*, Lorimer noted the anachronism of picturesque natives in *jebbas* and turbaned heads beside Englishmen in tweed suits, as a gramophone played Madame Melba's famous song from *La bohème*. It sounded "as perfect as in the opera-house at Covent Garden." In the engineer's car she enjoyed an almost panoramic view of the desert, "as though we had been travelling on camels the old way."[191] In Russia, the train protected travelers in Siberia from certain death due to the harsh elements of winter.

Incursion

To nineteenth-century observers, railways not only instilled fear and uncertainty, but their construction and operation assaulted the senses and altered traditional lifestyles in an instant. In 1888, the French cartoonist Albert Robida predicted that "an indigestion" of the iron, steel, chemicals, and explosives of scientific barbarism was to result in the last gasp of the nineteenth century.[192] Dynamite and blasting powder explosions, cave-ins and landslide accidents, fires caused by sparks near coal, and epidemic diseases all cost thousands of lives. The loud hum of cranes, noisy steam shovels, and the shrill sounds of steam engines operating pumps, dredges, and tracklayers terrified frontier peoples. The ear-splitting clatter of whistles and horns introduced the concept of noise pollution to rural peoples and animals unaccustomed to high decibels. George Stephenson had raised his horse alongside his workshops so whenever a locomotive engine screeched, the indifferent "Bobby" walked toward it and rubbed his nose against it.[193] While Ida Pfeiffer traveled through the suburbs in Lima, she wondered why there were no barriers between the trains and playing children. Before she left, a donkey wandered onto the rail, the train hit it and derailed, injuring several and killing another.[194] French railway history has left two of the most horrifying railway images, one real and another fictional. The first was the aforementioned incident at Versailles where passengers who had been locked into their railway carriages from the outside perished within the burning train. In *The Human Beast*, Émile Zola described the ultimate catastrophe of a runaway train hurtling oblivious troops to their end:

> And what did they matter, the victims crushed on the road by the locomotive? Was it not going into the future, careless of spilt blood? Without a master, through the blackness, a blind, deaf beast, unleashed with death, it sped on, and on, loaded with cannon-fodder, with soldiers stupid with exhaustion, drunk, singing.[195]

By equating the runaway train and railway accident with the disaster of war, Zola commented on the Franco-Prussian War and anticipated WWI as the "Great Train Wreck" of Europe.

Among the earliest proponents of railways were military generals who promoted them as tools for national defense. At first, railways aided states that turned guns on their own people. During the Chartist uprising in Great Britain (1842), the royal army used railways to occupy key strategic positions within London to prepare a defense. In 1844, Sir James Willoughby Gordon, quarter-master general in England, calculated that marching 1,000 soldiers from London to Manchester took an exhausting seventeen days. The L&M transported the same unit in nine hours, and the troops arrived fresh.[196] Monarchies quickly mobilized barracks by train and captured railway stations during the revolutions of 1848. Modernizing states soon deployed railways as weapons of pacification. Railways then entered strategic design as troop movers, arms transporters, tactical vehicles, and lifelines of logistical support in war. Nations that never completed lines risked defeat at the hands of those that did. The British and French tested their applicability in the Crimea (1854) against the Russians. The Great Indian Rebellion, or "Indian Mutiny" of 1857, exposed the weaknesses of Great Britain's grip on the Indian subcontinent for lack of industrial transport. Railways subsequently played decisive roles in wars since 1860, including the U.S. Civil War, the Wars of German Unification (1866–1871), the Paraguayan War (1870), the War of the Pacific (1879–1882), the Spanish-American War (1898), the Boer War (1899–1902), the Russo-Japanese War (1904–1905), the Mexican Revolution (1910–1920) and Russian Revolution (1917), and World Wars I and II (1914–1918, 1939–1945). In addition, railways helped "hammer" Africans into submission, subjugate Native America, and subordinate China to Europe and Japan.[197] Railway cultures emerged out of the fire, ashes, and death of war and conquest.

The theme of failing technology, running the gamut from minor travel nuisances to the national catastrophe of the Franco-Prussian War, informed French literature for much of the nineteenth century. Flaubert, Baudelaire, Nerval, and Viennet all blamed the railways for the frustrating disappointments of the century.[198] It is true that Pellerin produced a painting of Jesus driving a steam locomotive but, from one perspective, this suggests that operating the machine without a breakdown or surviving the miserable conditions of travel in France required divine intervention. The ten-minute train ride from St. Denis to Paris still took 45 additional minutes to reclaim baggage and hail a coach.[199] During the inauguration of the Havre and Rouen Railway in March 1847, so many dignitaries were on site to occupy the train's carriages that the railway company improvised with cattle wagons for everyone else. In incomparable impudence, each passenger who boarded the wagon uttered a "moo"; the human cargo soon "mooed" in concert, and when detraining "mooed" again in unison. When the stationmaster took hold of one of the offenders, the rest of the herd stampeded against him, and the official fled for his life.[200] Marcel Proust's "Within a Budding Grove," a chapter from his *Remembrance of Things Past*, expressed forcefully that railways reinforced the incessant instability of modern life by subjecting humans to an "uninterrupted series of partial deaths."[201]

The introduction of new transport technologies provoked widespread concerns of health risks. Early passengers who felt disoriented during railway travel often complained of health problems. Train rides were deafening, dizzying, and believed to impair physiological and cognitive function. Railway companies fought off claims of spinal disfigurement, heart and lung ailments, and psychological disorders. Trains have been blamed for just about every human malady that exists, but buried deep in the human psyche were reasons why they supposedly induced the "ABCs" of scariest health conditions: apoplexy, blindness, catarrhs, colds, consumption, deafness, depression, epilepsy, heart failure, hemorrhage, miscarriage, neurological disorders, nerve damage, palpitation, paralysis, pathological nervousness, pneumonia, rheumatism, spinal injuries, suicidal delirium, and toothaches.[202] The original names for these so-called maladies were truly terrifying: railway neurosis, railway blindness, and railway spine.[203] Passing through pitch-black tunnels or industrial areas lighted up at night with coal fires reminded passengers of Dante's Inferno and induced hallucinations and psychological trauma. Many of these ailments had nothing to do with locomotive travel.

The combination of physical and mental maladies, however, gave rise to a burgeoning medical literature on railway afflictions that grew less scientific every day. Reports of the Commission on the *Influence of Railway Travelling on Public Health* (1862) by Lord Shaftesbury and articles by Thomas Buzzard published in *The Lancet* in 1866, coincided with the appearance of William Camp's essay "Railway Accidents or Collisions," and John Eric Erichsen's book *On Railway and Other Injuries of the Nervous System*. Railway spine evolved from a physical injury to psychological trauma, as exemplified by professional prognoses of "railway shock," "railway brain," or even "traumatic neurosis."[204] During WWI, shell shock was easily diagnosed in part because of fundamental understandings of shock induced by railway trauma.[205] Passengers and pedestrians inhaled noxious fumes and smoke, choked on coke dust and ash, and ingested and coughed up pollutants. Hot cinders from the engine and smokestacks drifted through windows and burned passengers so often that railway stations had to install medical facilities. Passengers worldwide faced the difficult choice between opening the car windows and risking burn marks on their clothing and skin from floating ash, or closing the windows and suffering heat exhaustion.[206] Railway authorities often made senseless decisions to discomfort passengers. In order to downgrade second-class accommodations to third-class cars, Japanese companies removed the insulating layer of a double-roof which subjected passengers to intense summer heat.[207] In Mexico, Indian peasants rode second-class and henequen fiber bundles for export traveled first-class.

Experiments with locomotives within city limits proved abortive since residents could not stomach the stench, the noise, or the costs of steam power. English literary figure George Augustus Sala toured New York City during the Civil War and referred to the horse-drawn railway carriages along Broadway and Fifth Avenue as "monstrous Noah's Arks on wheels."[208] After initial trial runs, European cities returned to horse-drawn trams, and Asian cities embraced the rickshaw once again.[209] Following a collision involving a train and a horse-drawn tram, Malayan authorities determined that steam-powered locomotives were too dangerous for Penang. The double-decker passenger trains were removed to a nearby forest only to rust away beneath the palms.[210] American companies introduced electricity to street railways in the 1880s and cut energy costs in half. The cheaper form of mass transit soon reached Europe.[211]

Travel in subterranean railways (later shortened to "subways") initially provoked disbelief, but millions soon sung their praises. The pace by which engineers and construction crews built London's first underground railway was phenomenal. The City of London and Great Western Railway each pledged funds to the project. In late 1861, *The Times* reported that the Metropolitan Railway Company attained enough finance capital for its chief engineer Thomas Fowler to start excavating a giant 4.5-mile tunnel through London's underground as a means of diverting traffic from the overcrowded surface streets.[212] Crews worked night and day to dig the giant hole from west to east. Fowler was careful not to disrupt the water and sewer service of businesses and residents. Just over a year later, on January 10,

1863, 30,000 passengers rode the Metropolitan Subterranean Railway for the first time. By early 1864, the railway accommodated 9.5 million travelers; by 1892, 90 million.[213] Later known as the Metropolitan, the first line ran from Paddington to Farringdon Street. Victoria Station later became an important stop. At the time, the underground system was hailed as an impressive engineering achievement.

The speed of the Met's construction left little time for the public to contemplate the absurdity of traveling underground like foxes and moles. Surface transportation on omnibuses was cheap, even though thick traffic resulted in long commutes. Hanging outside a Paddington 'bus was still a reliable way to get across town. As *The Times* stated prior to the subway project's start, Londoners only knew one kind of underground, the one of sewers, gas tubes, water mains, rats, poisonous vapors, and above all darkness. The other dangers – rapists, serial murderers, and the occult – did not materialize in the public imagination until people actually had reason to brave the passages underground. A subterranean rail system also belonged to that species of futuristic propositions that belonged to the imagination, which *The Times* listed as: "flying machines, warfare by balloons, tunnels under the Channel." English engineers, however, knew how to fortify tunnels, in this case with concrete and rows of brick rings, all sealed with asphalt to provide a tight water seal. Building an oversized tunnel – wide, spacious, clean, and well-lit – and platforms and stairways no different from those above ground won over the public. None of this, however, prevented William Morris from characterizing an underground railway carriage as a "vapour-bath of hurried and discontented humanity."[214] Travelers booked trips from Edinburgh, Liverpool, and Manchester to Dover and Southampton that ran right through London's underground railway. Over twenty-three million passengers, up to 100,000 commuters per day, used it in 1867. The main trunk lines of the Great Western, Midland, Great Northern, and the London, Chatham, and Dover all tapped into the Metropolitan. The latter company connected it to its newest suburban lines.[215]

The arrival of city railways was not lost on urban populations. City dwellers noticed, watched in awe, and increased their walking speed. Above all, the size, speed, and unpredictability of the steam-powered or electric tramcars caused anxiety, danger, and death. Parisians referred to the Paris Metro's streetcar system as the *Necropolitain* because of its reputation for electrocution, asphyxiation, and pickpockets.[216] Mexico City residents, many of them newly arrived peasants looking for work, described the electric trolleys as the new Yellow Fever and their drivers as *mataristas* or killers, a play on the word *motoristas* (motorists).[217] The trolleys were susceptible to power surges that suddenly increased their speeds, killing over 1,000 people in the late 1890s alone. More precise figures are known for 1904 to 1906: 134 dead and 657 injured.[218] The satirical newspaper *El Chango* once featured a cartoon entitled "Death in Electric Form" showing mutilated victims of the streetcars and the impersonal cruelty of mechanized death.[219] As tramcars rattled through the dusty streets of the bucolic *La Piedad*, women called to their children and hoisted them off far away from the lines in fear of unregulated voltage and careless drivers. Older residents shook their heads in disapproval and crossed themselves piously.[220] To commoners, the electric trams had no visible power source. At night, the sparks that radiated from their roofs where they contacted overhead wires and the smell of fire and brimstone suggested satanic origins.[221] Some trams were eventually fitted with cattle guards to reduce the number of human fatalities. The world-renowned painter Frida Kahlo was a passenger in a streetcar accident that beset her with a lifelong limp and robbed her of the ability to have children. In response to popular fears, Mexican President Porfirio Díaz temporarily prohibited trolleys using an "occult force" from carrying funeral corteges or coffins (1900).[222] For a limited time, horse dung once again littered the streets of Porfirian Mexico City.

In Montevideo, Uruguay, urban electrification brought not only contested notions of modernity but also the first general workers' strike in 1911. German and British electric streetcar companies sold 40,000 tickets on the day inaugurating the first trolley lines in 1906. As historian Anton Rosenthal explained, however, the public's fear of electrocution, fires, and traffic accidents turned the symbol of progress into a case of oppressive foreign technology. In early 1909, seven such accidents occurred daily as the quiet approach of speedy electric streetcars killed unsuspecting children, pedestrians, and passengers. The windows in some trolleys fell shut so suddenly that the public called them *guillotinas*. Meanwhile, the streetcar companies blamed their own conductors, motormen, line men, and machine men for every problem. If anarchist workers were involved in a streetcar accident, the company fined, suspended, or fired them outright. Any violation of the *reglamento*, even having tuberculosis, gave the companies the excuse to dismiss a syndicalist or send them to jail. Worker grievances culminated in a streetcar workers' strike in May 1911. Streetcar men and citizens threw stones and tar at the moving vehicles, cut their cables, and set one trolley down the track at high speed, whereby it struck another streetcar and destroyed both. As Rosenthal concludes, the *eléctrico* became the preferred target of May Day protestors and strikers alike.[223]

Trends involving trains in the late-1800s changed African American perspectives in the U.S. Railroad mania swept through America, with over $1 billion invested in more than 200 railroad lines by the 1860s. Civil War historian James McPherson commented on the fears that arose not only by unreceptive African American onlookers but also white passengers riding the loud "smoke-puffing iron contraption." To combat anxiety, the West Point train line linked up a flatbed barrier car between the engine and the passenger cars. The car was piled with cotton bales so that African American bands could play on the moving "stage" to drown out the noisy engine. Other railroads employed skilled black musicians to play on barrier cars, granting them opportunities otherwise denied to them in either slave or wage economies. African Americans accepted the locomotives as symbols of movement, opportunity, and progress, but also rebellion and the unfulfilled promises of freedom, equality, and power before the Civil War. Since many of the routes of the Underground Railroad utilized actual trains, McPherson upholds the traditional abolitionist view that railroads signified freedom.[224]

Scholar of African American literature Darcy A. Zabel has examined how trains as symbols of freedom granted Harriet Tubman and John Henry greater stature as historical figures.[225]

During Reconstruction, however, the views of southern blacks toward railroads devolved from symbols of emancipation to vehicles of oppression. Jim Crow Laws and Black Codes made it possible for black men to be arrested and convicted for minor criminal infractions such as poaching and loitering. The standard sentence of five years' hard labor gave Northern railroad companies expanding into the New South an inexpensive labor pool of incarcerated African Americans that numbered in the tens of thousands. Black convicts were leased, for example, to the New Orleans Northeastern Railroad to experience slave-like working conditions on railroad gangs. They were chained, sometimes with metal spurs riveted to their feet, and suffered through heat exhaustion, pneumonia, malaria, dysentery, frostbite, and something called shackle poisoning. They were also severely punished by the whip.[226] At the turn of the twentieth century, trains and streetcars – originally the only public space where blacks and whites had equal access – became symbols of segregation. In 1889, the Interstate Commerce Commission enacted an "equity of accommodation" ruling that allowed streetcars and railroad cars to be exclusively white or black so long as their counterparts were of equal quality. The *Plessy v. Ferguson* (1896) case tested its legality.[227] The U.S. tendency toward legal separation of races contrasted greatly with integration on the French omnibus. French art in the 1890s, such as Théophile-Alexandre Steinlen's "In the Omnibus" (*Gil Blas*, 1894) and Maurice Delondre's oil painting of the same title (1890), shows Parisians of all classes and races riding together and genuinely representing the equality and rights of citizens.[228]

Much of the work railway companies did was to diffuse, resolve, or otherwise overcome the public's fear and misgivings of railways. This lawyering, marketing, and public relations work started in England long before the L&M. "Gladstone's Railway Bill" was so comprehensive and unexpected that workmen hailed it as "an accommodation of the public" and the railway version of a Reform Act.[229] William Edmondstoune Aytoun later quipped that railway interests "disarmed the hostility of their opponents."[230] Whenever popular opinion identified railways as sordid vehicles of gain, they reduced fares and improved comfort.[231] Railways once portrayed as environmental nuisances and health threats became picturesque additions to the landscape and a means to reach the relaxation of the coast in a matter of hours. Instead of killing livestock or turning white sheep as black as coal, they carried animals to slaughter for a fraction of the original costs to drive them overland. The French loved how railways leveled the price of grain and wine, and American consumers continually praised the railways for bringing fresh meat, dairy products, vegetables, and fish to dinner tables.[232] Ten years after Russians in Siberia starved in the 1891 famine, Annette Meakin wrote about the new international division of labor: "A large amount of the butter consumed by our London poor is made by Siberian peasants."[233]

Despite the mixed experiences of inception, reception, and incursion, railways soon eased human toil for whomever purchased the relief. Hegemonic rather than democratic processes produced most of the unforeseen positive effects of railways mostly because few nations practiced democracy in the long nineteenth century, and railways always reflected the societies in which they operated. To summarize the positive effects, we turn to seven great railway historians, each representing a significant world region.[234] Railways integrated national and international markets in food grains, dairy products, meat proteins, fresh vegetables and fruits, and other comestible commodities, enabling the peoples of this planet to feed themselves at affordable prices. Integrated trading and railway networks allowed for much more mobile labor markets, creating ever greater demand for manufactured goods and services. As a new industry in transportation that required both heavy outlays of finance capital and corollary infrastructural development, railways became the single largest employers in many countries, and the second or third biggest employers in advanced industrial nations. Backward and forward linkages ensured in most, but not all, cases, railway-led growth of other industries and commercial agriculture. Real estate prices increased due to railway expansion. The emergence of boom towns proved that cities no longer needed to form on the coasts or at the confluence of rivers. Railways also played important roles in urbanization, especially with the emergence of commuter trains that ran to and from suburban areas of major cities. Although railways initially spread germs and exacerbated epidemics, they eventually were deployed to stop diseases in their tracks through quarantine, inspections, and fumigation on one hand, and circulation of medicines, medical personnel, and armed forces on the other. Although not foolproof, railways helped to alleviate, if not relieve, famines by moving grain to regions experiencing scarcity and offering jobs to the unemployed in famine-stricken areas. They transported religious pilgrims to sacred sites, children to schools, and tourists to major landmarks. Railways granted women customary rights to access and exercise new forms of domesticity in public spaces. Railway expansion facilitated national-state formation, as citizens previously unknown to one another met face to face at common destinations. For good and for worse, railways contributed to national defense, aided the rapid deployment of national, imperial, and colonial armies, and assisted rebel forces in overthrowing oppressive regimes. In sum, railways and their metonyms aided the transition of world cultures to industrial capitalism in the modern age.

Notes

1 John Pendleton, *Our Railways: Their Origin, Development, Incident and Romance*, 2 vols. (London: Cassell and Company, 1894), I: vii.
2 Schivelbusch, *The Railway Journey* (Berkeley: University of California Press, 1986); Freeman, *Railways and the Victorian Imagination* (New Haven: Yale University Press, 1999).
3 Ian J. Kerr, ed., *27 Down: New Departures in Indian Railway Studies* (Delhi: Orient Longman, 2007); Kerr, *Building the Railways of the Raj, 1850–1900* (London:

Oxford University Press, 1995); Kerr, ed., *Railways in Modern India* (New York: Oxford University Press, 2001); Kerr, *Engines of Change: The Railroads that Made India* (Westport, Conn.: Praeger, 2007); John Hurd, "Railways and the Expansion of Markets in India, 1861–1921," *Explorations in Economic History* 12 (1975), 263–288; John Hurd II and Ian J. Kerr, eds., *India's Railway History: A Research Handbook* (Boston: Brill, 2012); Manu Goswami, *Producing India: From Colonial Economy to National Space* (Chicago: University of Chicago Press, 2004); Laura Bear, *Lines of the Nation: Indian Railway Workers, Bureaucracy, and the Intimate Historical Self* (New York: Colombia, 2007); Marian Aguiar, *Tracking Modernity: India's Railway and the Culture of Mobility* (Minneapolis: University of Minnesota Press, 2011); Ritika Prasad, *Tracks of Change: Railways and Everyday Life in Colonial India* (Cambridge: Cambridge University Press, 2015).

4 *Howards End* (London: E. Arnold, 1910), 12–13.

5 "The Dry Salvages," in *Collected Poems, 1909–1962* (New York: Harcourt, Brace, 1963), 210.

6 Robert E. Carlson, *The Liverpool and Manchester Railway Project, 1821–1831* (New York: Augustus M. Kelley, 1969), 70, 231; Jack Simmons, *The Railways of Britain: An Historical Introduction* (London: Macmillan, 1968; New York: St. Martin's, 1968), 1–3; Freeman, 30.

7 Marshall, *A History of British Railways down to the Year 1830* (London: Oxford University Press, 1938; Oxford reprint edition, 1971), 199.

8 O. S. Nock, *World Atlas of Railways* (London: Mitchell Beazley, 1978), 8; Ronald E. Robinson, "Introduction: Railway Imperialism," in Clarence B. Davis and Kenneth E. Wilburn, Jr., eds., *Railway Imperialism* (New York: Greenwood Press, 1991), 5 fn.1; Christian Wolmar, *Blood, Iron, and Gold: How the Railroads Transformed the World* (New York: Public Affairs, 2010), xiv.

9 Marshall, 199.

10 Horace Porter, "Railway Passenger Travel," *Scribner's Magazine* 4 (July–Dec. 1888), 298.

11 Robert Colton, *Pedestrian and Other Reminiscences at Home and Abroad, with Sketches of Country Life, by Sylvanus* (London: Longman, Brown, Green, and Longmans, 1846), 187–190.

12 W. Edmondstoune Aytoun, *Norman Sinclair*, 3 Vols. (Edinburgh: William Blackwood and Sons, 1861), I: 251.

13 "Hippothanasia; Or, the Last of Tails," *Bentley's Miscellany* 1 (1837), 319–324.

14 Helen C. Knight, *The Rocket* (New York: American Travel Society, 1860), 103, emphasis mine. This "book for the boys" went through several editions in both the U.S. and the British Isles. In England, expanded versions appeared as *"Puffing Billy" and the Prize "Rocket;" or the Story of the Stephensons* (London: Patridge, n.d.), and *The Rocket: The Story of the Stephensons, Father and Son* (London: T. Nelson and Sons, 1894).

15 "The Railway Train," in *Emily Dickinson, Poems: 2d Series*, Ed. T. W. Higginson and Mabel Loomis Todd, Tenth ed. (Boston: Little, Brown, 1904), 39.

16 Ellen C. Clayton, *Cruel Fortune* (London, 1865), III, 10. Quoted in Myron F. Brightfield, "The Coming of the Railroad to Early Victorian England as Viewed by Novels of the Period (1840–1870)," *Technology and Culture*, Vol. 3, No. 1 (Winter, 1962), 54.

17 Paul A. Youngman, *Black Devil and Iron Angel: The Railway in Nineteenth-Century German Realism* (Washington D.C.: Catholic University of American Press, 2005), 41, 46.

18 *Ibid.*, 62–63.

19 Michel Foucault, "Dos Espace Autres," in *Architecture/Mouvement/Continuité* (Oct. 1984), Trans. Jay Miskowiec as "Of Other Spaces: Utopias and Heterotopias," *Diacritics* 16: 1 (Spring 1986), 22–27.

20 Alfred Crosby, *Ecological Imperialism: The Biological Expansion of Europe, 900–1900* (Cambridge: Cambridge University Press, 1986), 3–4.
21 Porter, 298.
22 Jeffrey Richards and John M. MacKenzie, *The Railway Station: A Social History* (New York: Oxford University Press, 1986), 3.
23 Porter, 303–304.
24 Leland, 305.
25 Foucault, 24.
26 *Ambivalent Conquests: Maya and Spaniard in Yucatan, 1517–1570* (Cambridge: Cambridge University Press, 1987), 137.
27 C. O. Burge, *The Adventures of a Civil Engineer: Fifty Years on Five Continents* (London: Alston Rivers, 1909), 99.
28 R. B. Cunninghame Graham, *Thirteen Stories* (London: Heinemann, 1901), 78.
29 Sir Richard Temple, *The Story of My Life*, 2 vols. (London: Cassell, 1896), I: 273.
30 William Digby, *Unknown Siberia: From Tigers, Gold, and Witch Doctors* (np: np, n.d), 14.
31 Norma Lorimer, *By the Waters of Egypt* (London: Methuen, 1909), 427.
32 See her invaluable letter in Section 3 of this volume. It is also partly reproduced in Pendleton, I: 64.
33 Freeman, 38–40.
34 Marianne North, *Recollections of a Happy Life*, ed. Mrs. John Addington Symonds, 2 vols. (Second ed.: New York and London: Macmillan, 1892), 12.
35 *The Creevy Papers: A Selection from the Correspondence & Diaries of the Late Thomas Creevy.* Ed. Sir Herbert Maxwell (New York: E. P. Dutton, 1904), 546.
36 Carlson, 226.
37 *American Notes* (New York: Harper & Bros., 1842), 9.
38 Nathaniel Parker Willis, *Pencillings by the Way* (New York: Morris & Willis, 1844), 216.
39 John W. Corson, *Loiterings in Europe* (New York: Harper & Brothers, 1848), 263.
40 Harriet Bury, "Novel Spaces, Transitional Moments: Negotiating Text and Territory in Nineteenth-Century Hindi Travel Accounts," in Ian J. Kerr, ed., *27 Down*, 7–8 fn22.
41 Michael Matthews, "De Viaje: Elite Views of Modernity and the Porfirian Railway Boom," *Mexican Studies/Estudios Mexicanos* 26: 2 (Summer 2010), 259–260; Matthews, *The Civilizing Machine: A Cultural History of Mexican Railroads, 1876–1910* (Lincoln: University of Nebraska Press, 2013), 60–61.
42 Humphery Jennings, *Pandaemonium: The Coming of the Machine as Seen by Contemporary Observers* (New York: Free Press, 1985), 212; Freeman, 38.
43 Quoted in John Fraser, *English Railways: Statistically Considered* (London: E. Wilson, 1903), 13–15.
44 William Douglas, *Soldiering in Sunshine and Storm* (Edinburgh: A. and C. Black, 1865), 6–8.
45 Vol. 31 (1824–1825), 362.
46 Porter, 299–300.
47 *Ibid.*, 300.
48 Ruskin quoted in Schivelbusch 54, fn.8; Nicholas Daly, "Railway Novels: Sensation Fiction and the Modernization of the Senses," *ELH* 66 (1999), 479.
49 "A Flight," in *Reprinted Pieces* (New York: University Society, 1908), 151–161.
50 Paul H. Noguchi, *Delayed Departures, Overdue Arrivals: Industrial Familialism and the Japanese National Railways* (Honolulu: University of Hawai'i Press, 1990, 44.
51 Michel de Certeau, *The Practice of Everyday Life*, Trans. Steven F. Randell (Berkeley: University of California Press, 1984), 111.
52 *Society, Manners and Politics in the United States*. Cited in Mark Seltzer, *Bodies and Machines* (New York: Routledge, 1992), 18.

53 *A Passage to India* (New York: Meier, 1978).
54 E. H. Carbutt, *Six Months' Fine Weather in Canada, Western U.S., and Mexico* (London: S. Low, Marston, Searle, Rivington, 1889), 119.
55 Youngman, 30.
56 Annette M. B. Meakin, *A Ribbon of Iron* (Westminster: A. Constable, 1901), 13.
57 Porter, 311, 318.
58 Tennyson quoted in Christopher Ricks, ed., *Tennyson: A Selected Edition* (London: Longman, 1969), 192; Matthew Beaumont and Michael J. Freeman, *The Railway and Modernity: Time, Space, and the Machine Ensemble* (Oxford: Peter Lang, 2007), 43.
59 Marshall, 13–108 *passim*; David Haward Bain, *Empire Express: Building the First Transcontinental Railroad* (New York: Penguin, 1999), 17–18.
60 Marshall, 204, and fig. 93 on 205.
61 Philip Pacey, "The Picturesque Railway," *Visual Resources* 18: 4 (Jan. 2002), 291.
62 Jacques Barzun, *From Dawn to Decadence: 500 Years of Cultural Life, 1500–Present* (New York: Harper Collins, 2000), 541.
63 Pendleton, I: 90.
64 John Ruskin, *Praeterita: Outlines of Scenes and Thoughts, Perhaps Worthy of Memory in My Past Life* (Boston: D. Estes, [1890]), 42–43, 68, 100, 237, 330.
65 C. Barman, *Early British Railways* (London, 1950), 25. Quoted in Freeman, 44.
66 Thomas Carlyle, *Reminiscences*. Ed. James Anthony Froude. 2 vols. (London: Longmans, Green, 1881), I: 167.
67 *The Innocents Abroad* (Hartford: American Publishing Company, 1875), 335.
68 Frederick S. Williams, *Our Iron Roads Their History, Construction, and Social Influences* (London: Ingram, Cooke, and Co., 1852), 39; Freeman, 33.
69 Dan Free, *Early Japanese Railways, 1853–1914: Engineering Triumphs that Transformed Meiji-Era Japan* (Rutland, VT.: Tuttle Publishing, 2008), 74.
70 John Foster Fraser, *The Real Siberia* (London: Cassell, 1902), 244–245.
71 Wolmar, *Blood, Iron, and Gold*, 59.
72 Free, 74.
73 Victor Bayley, *Permanent Way through the Khyber* (London: Jarrolds, 1939), 15–16, 59–61. Bayley also wrote *Dangerous Derelict, House of Hatred, Dynamite, North-West Mail, City of Fear, Khyber Contraband, Pathan Treasure, Frontier Fires, Liquid Fury, Carfax of the Khyber, Indian Artifex, and Nine-Fifteen from Victoria*.
74 Leo Marx, *The Machine in the Garden: Technology and the Pastoral Ideal in America* (New York: Oxford University Press, 1964; 2nd ed. with new Afterword, 2000), 215–217; Michael Adas, *Dominance by Design: Technological Imperatives and America's Civilizing Mission* (Cambridge and London: Belknap Press of Harvard University Press, 2006), 80; Pacey, 285–309.
75 Quoted in Leo Marx, 195.
76 Stewart H. Holbrook, *The Story of American Railroads* (New York: Crown, 1947), 88.
77 Paul Vanderwood, *Disorder and Progress: Bandits, Police, and Mexican Development* (Wilmington: Scholarly Resources, 1992), 94; Alan Knight, *The Mexican Revolution*, 2 vols. (Cambridge: Cambridge University Press, 1986), I: 118; John W. Mitchell, *The Wheels of Ind* (London: Thornton Butterworth, 1934), 89–90.
78 John W. Mitchell, 42–43, 82.
79 Leland, *Traveling Alone: A Woman's Journey around the World* (New York: American News Company, 1890), 303.
80 Pacey, 293.
81 Eugen Weber, *France: Fin de Siècle* (Cambridge: The Belknap Press of Harvard University, 1986), 55.
82 Henry Blackburn, *Artistic Travel* (London: S. Low, Marston, 1892), 30–31.
83 Pacey, 285.

84 Michael Robbins, "Railways and Landscapes," in *The Railway Lovers' Companion*, ed. Bryan Morgan (London: Eyre and Spottiswood, 1963), 219–222; Pacey, 289, 294. On these themes see also Ian Carter, *Railways and Culture in Britain: The Epitome of Modernity* (Manchester: Manchester University Press, 2001).
85 Leo Marx, 234; Emerson quoted in Pacey, 288.
86 *Ibid.*, 297–298. Hundreds of these brochures, guides, and posters are accessible online in metadata searches on railways.
87 Clare Pettitt, "'The Annihilation of Space and Time,' Literature and Technology," in "Part IV: Matters of Debate," *Cambridge History of Victorian Literature*, ed. Kate Flint, (Cambridge: Cambridge University Press, 2012), 554. Foreign traveler E. L. Butcher noticed pictures of trains in the homes of Muslim families in Egypt. See *Things Seen in Egypt* (London: Seeley, Service and Co., 1914), 178.
88 *Parallel Tracks: The Railroad and Silent Cinema* (Durham: Duke University Press, 1997), 7.
89 Hobsbawm and Ranger, "Introduction," *The Invention of Tradition* (Cambridge: Cambridge University Press, 1983), 1–2.
90 Pacey, 291, 297.
91 Youngman, 47–48.
92 Henry James, *The American Scene* (London: Chapman and Hall, 1907), 27.
93 *Ibid.*, 42, 44, 156.
94 *Ibid.*, 433.
95 Pettitt, 560–561.
96 R. W. Kostal, *Law and English Capitalism, 1825–1875* (Oxford: Oxford University Press, 1994), 281, Table 3.
97 Kostal, 179–180, 368–372.
98 Richard White, *Railroaded: The Transcontinentals and the Making of Modern America* (New York: W. W. Norton, 2011).
99 *Red for Danger: A History of Railway Accidents and Railway Safety*. Fourth ed. (London: David & Charles, 1982), 15–16, 19, 22.
100 Williams, 29.
101 *Ibid.*, 27.
102 *Letters and Memories*, I: 239–240 (Unabridged ed.), I: 280–281; Walter E. Houghton, *The Victorian Frame of Mind* (New Haven: Yale University Press, 1957), 43.
103 C. F. Gordon Cumming, *In the Himalayas and on the Indian Plains* (London: Chatto & Windus, 1884), 44–45.
104 Houghton, 1, 3, 21–23, 54. Quote on 41.
105 Cited in Anne Green, *Changing France: Literature and Material Culture in the Second Empire* (London: Anthem, 2011), 36 fn5.
106 This theme is developed in Volume 3. Benjamin Gastineau, *La vie en chemin de fer* (Paris: E. Dentu, 1861), 50. Cited in Walter Benjamin, *The Arcades Project* (Cambridge: Belknap Press of Harvard University), 588.
107 Cunninghame Graham, "The Colonel," in *Scottish Stories* (London: Duckworth, 1914), 1.
108 *La opinion*, February 10, 1902, quoted in Bergquist, *Coffee and Conflict in Colombia* (Durham: Duke University Press, 1986), 221–222.
109 Pettitt, 557.
110 Carter, 63, 65.
111 Dion Boucicault, *After Dark; or A Drama of London Life* (1868). Nicholas Daly, "Blood on the Tracks: Sensation Drama, the Railway, and the Dark Face of Modernity," *Victorian Studies* 42: 1 (Autumn, 1998–Autumn 1999), 60.
112 Youngman, 81.
113 Hume Nisbet, *A Colonial Tramp: Travels and Adventures in Australia and New Zealand*, 2 vols. (London: Ward & Downey, 1891), 233.

114 *By Desert Ways to Baghdad* (London: T. Nelson & Sons, 1912), 55.
115 Freeman, 13–15.
116 William Makepeace Thackeray, *The Paris Sketchbook of Mr. M.A. Titmarsh; The Irish Sketch Book; & Notes of a Journey from Cornhill to Grand Cairo* (New York: Caxton, 1840), 266.
117 *The Grand Junction Railway* (London: 1939), 43.
118 Reprinted in *The Railway Times* 176 (Vol. 4, no. 20), May 15, 1841, No. 528.
119 *The Times* (London) reprinted in *The Railway Times* 196 (Vol. 4, no. 40), Saturday October 2, 1841, 1038.
120 Quoted in Youngman, 147.
121 *The Railway Times* 206 (Vol. 4, no. 50), December 11, 1841, No. 1294.
122 "Song of a Train," in *Selected Poems* (London: J. Lane, 1905), 98–99.
123 Matthews, *The Civilizing Machine*, 59; Matthews, "De Viaje: Elite Views of Modernity," 258; Translation mine.
124 *The Railway Times* 443 (Vol. 9, no. 26), June 27, 1846, 902; 458 (Vol. 9, no. 41), October 10, 1846, 1469.
125 *Dombey and Son* (New York: John Wiley, 1848), 241.
126 Mrs. Margaret Oliphant, *The House on the Moor* (New York: Harper and Brothers, 1861), 164. Quoted in Brightfield, 65.
127 Reprinted in *The Railway Times*, No. 196 (Vol. 4: no. 40), Saturday October 2, 1841, 1039–1040.
128 Marshall, 192 and 196.
129 Freeman, 84.
130 See Rolt, *Red for Danger* and Aldrich, *Death Rode the Rails: American Railroad Accidents and Safety, 1828–1965* (Baltimore: Johns Hopkins University Press, 2006).
131 Porter, 301.
132 Edward Hungerford, "Getting the Traffic Through," *Harper's Magazine* 119 (1909), 876.
133 Porter, 311.
134 Leo Marx, 191, 207.
135 Reprinted from the *Dorset Chronicle* in *The Railway Times* 302 (Vol. 4, no. 41), Saturday October 14, 1843, 1123.
136 "Beattock for Moffat," in *Scottish Stories*, 56, 59, 64.
137 Youngman, 10, 21, 30.
138 Daisy Bates, *The Passing of the Aborigines* (New York: Praeger, 1967), 132, 172, 191–192, 222. Bates writes that tribal peoples responded similarly whenever they first saw "houses, the white women and babies, paper, pannikins, tea, sugar and all the mystifying belongings of the 'waijela,'" (192). See also David Burke, *Road through the Wilderness: The Story of the Transcontinental Railway, the First Great Work of Australia's Federation* (Kensington, Australia: New South Wales Press, 1991), 28.
139 *The Railway Magazine*, January 1836, 293; Freeman, 13, 27, 31, 38–39, 49, and 52; Youngman, 29–30; A. Kim Clark, *The Redemptive Work: Railways and Nation in Ecuador, 1895–1930* (Wilmington, DE: Scholarly Resources, 1998), 55; Rolt, *Red for Danger*, 21.
140 Weber, 68.
141 Quoted in Jennings, 212.
142 Barzun, 543.
143 George Dobson, *Russia's Railway Advance into Central Asia; Notes of a Journey from St. Petersburg to Samarkand* (London: W. H. Allen, 1890), 197, 240.
144 John F. Stover, *American Railroads* (Chicago: University of Chicago Press, 1961), 17; Wolmar, *Blood, Iron, and Gold*, 78.
145 Cited in Steven John Ericson, "State and Private Enterprise: Railroad Development in Meiji Japan" (Ph.D. dissertation, Harvard University, 1985), 16–17.

146 Corson, 263.
147 Tatlow, *Fifty Years of Railway Life in England, Scotland and Ireland* (London: The Railway Gazette, 1920), 14.
148 Quoted in Leo Marx, 252.
149 *Nature's Metropolis: Chicago and the Great West* (New York: Norton, 1991), 72.
150 John Embree, *Suye Mura* (Chicago: University of Chicago Press, 1939), 258. Cited in Paul Hideyo Noguchi, "The 'One Railroad Family' of the Japanese National Railways: A Cultural Analysis of Japanese Industrial Familialism" (Ph.D. dissertation, University of Pittsburgh, 1977), 41; Noguchi, *Delayed Departures*, 44–45.
151 Grant D. Jones, "Levels of Settlement Alliance among the San Pedro Maya of Western Belize and Eastern Petén, 1857–1936," in Grant D. Jones, ed., *Anthropology and History in Yucatán* (Austin and London: University of Texas Press, 1977), 183, fn. 113.
152 Cited in Clark, *The Redemptive Work*, 45.
153 Anton Rosenthal, "The Arrival of the Electric Streetcar and the Conflict over Progress in Early Twentieth-Century Montevideo," *Journal of Latin American Studies* 27, no. 2 (May 1995), 330.
154 Christina Bueno, *The Pursuit of Ruins: Archaeology, History, and the Making of Modern Mexico* (Albuquerque: University of New Mexico Press, 2016), 199–200.
155 de Certeau, 111 and 114.
156 Chunder, *The Travels of a Hindoo to Various Parts of Bengal and Upper India* (London: Trubner, 1869), 140, 162.
157 Kerr, *Engines of Change*, 108. See also Harriet Bury, 14 fn40.
158 Kern, *The Culture of Time and Space, 1880–1918* (Cambridge: Harvard University Press, 1983), 213.
159 Norris cited in *Ibid*.
160 Daisy Bates, 62–63, 69. Bates heard this story presumably from Joobaitch and white settlers.
161 Bipin Chandra Pal, *Memories of My Life and Times*, 2 vols. (Calcutta: Ugayatri Prakshak, 1932–1951), I: 188.
162 Chunder, 140; Marian Aguiar, *Tracking Modernity*, 36.
163 Michael Adas, *Machines as the Measure of Men*, 223.
164 Luis González, *San José de Gracia: Mexican Village in Transition*, Trans. John Upton (Austin: University of Texas Press, 1974), 96.
165 Green, 38.
166 *Norman Sinclair*, 3 Vols. (Edinburgh: William Blackwood and Sons, 1861), I: 250.
167 Quoted in Patsy Adam-Smith, *When We Rode the Rails* (Sydney: Lansdowne, 1983), 138.
168 *Artistic Traveler* (London: S. Low, Marston, 1892), 34.
169 Ronald Ross, *Memoirs: With a Full Account of the Great Malaria Problem and its Solution* (London: John Murray, 1923), 20.
170 M. S. Wellby, *Through Unknown Tibet* (T. Fisher Unwin, 1898), 417.
171 H. H. P. Deasy, *In Tibet and Chinese Turkestan, Being the Record of Three Years' Exploration* (London: T. Fisher Unwin, 1901), 270.
172 Burge, 100.
173 Kravigny, *The Jungle Route* (New York: Orlin Tremaine Company, 1940), 115, 169, 48–49.
174 Nelson Reed, *The Caste War of Yucatán* (Stanford: Stanford University Press, 1964), 285.
175 Green, 39–42.
176 John R. Kellett, *The Impact of Railways on Victorian Cities* (London: Routledge & Kegan Paul, 1969), 80.

177 Cited in Ericson, "State and Private," 6.
178 *Ibid.*, 5. See also Tom Richards and Charles Rudd, *Japanese Railways in the Meiji Period, 1868–1912* (Uxbridge: Brunel University and Central Japan Railway Company, 1991), 7.
179 Williams, 39; Margaret Armstrong, *Fanny Kemble: A Passionate Victorian* (London: Macmillan, 1938), 106; Carlson, 72.
180 *Middlemarch*, New ed. (Edinburgh and London: W. Blackwood, 1874), 408–409.
181 Pendleton, I: 42; Carlson, 72.
182 Rolt, 21.
183 Pendleton, I: 42–43; Carlson, 72.
184 Youngman, 29–30.
185 Green, 42, 44.
186 J. H. Clapham, *The Economic Development of France and Germany*, Fourth ed. (Cambridge: Cambridge University Press, 1968), 151.
187 Meakin, 23–24.
188 Graham Hutchins, *Last Train to Paradise: Journeys from the Golden Age of New Zealand Railways* (Auckland: Exisle, 2011), 158, 164–165.
189 Richter, *Home on the Rails: Women, the Railroad, and the Rise of Domesticity* (Raleigh: University of North Carolina Press, 2005), 7.
190 James Hingston, *The Australian Abroad on Branches from the Main Routes Round the World* (Melbourne: W. Inglis, 1885), 348; E. L. Butcher, *Egypt as We Know It* (London: Mills & Bonn, 1911), 9.
191 Lorimer, 427.
192 Cited in Weber, 67–68.
193 Smiles, 264.
194 Ida Pfeiffer, *A Lady's Second Voyage Round the World* (New York: Harper, 1856), 344.
195 Emile Zola, *The Human Beast*, Trans. Louis Colman (New York: United Book Guild, 1948), 384. See also Green, 48.
196 *Family Herald*, II: (1844–1845), 189.
197 See E. J. Hobsbawm, *The Age of Capital, 1848–1875* (New York: Scribner, 1975) and *The Age of Empire*, 1875–1914 (New York: Pantheon, 1987).
198 Green, 51–56 fn79.
199 *Ibid.*, 54.
200 *The Railway News* in Pendleton, II: 77–78.
201 Paul Souday on Marcel Proust, *Within a Budding Grove*; William H. Gass, "Marcel Proust at 100: Proust," *New York Times Review of Books*, July 11, 1971, 1–2, 12.
202 Williams, 39; Greene, 44–45.
203 John Eric Erichsen, *Railway and Other Injuries of the Nervous System* (Philadelphia: Henry C. Lea, 1867); Schivelbusch, 134–144.
204 Erichsen, 57–62; Schivelbusch, 139, 143; Daly, "Railway Novels," 468–469.
205 Daly, "Railway Novels," 469.
206 Lady Howard, *Journal of a Tour in the United States, Canada, and Mexico* (London: S. Low, Marston, 1897), 8; Marianne North, *Recollections of a Happy Life*, Second ed. (London: MacMillan, 1892), I: 200–201.
207 Richards and Rudd, 12.
208 *My Diary in America in the Midst of War* (London: Tinsley Brothers, 1865), 86–87. Sala apprenticed with Dickens, wrote for *Household Words*, and earned a huge readership with his "Echoes of the Week" column for *Illustrated London News*. He later contributed to *Cornhill* and the *Daily Telegraph*, and edited *Temple Bar*. See Peter Blake, *George Augustus Sala and the Nineteenth-Century Periodical Press: The Personal Style of a Public Writer* (Burlington, VT: Ashgate, 2015), 2–3.

209 John P. McKay, *Tramways and Trollies* (Princeton: Princeton University Press, 1976), 29–33.
210 *Pinang Gazette*, May 4, 1899. Cited in Francis, *Penang Trams*, 13. See the photograph on page 14.
211 Weber, 70.
212 "The Metropolitan Subterranean Railway," *The Times* (London), 30 November 1861, 5.
213 Walter Thornbury, *Old and New London: A Narrative of its History, its People, and its Places*, Six Vols. (London: Cassell, Petter & Galpin, [1872–1878], V and VI: 225–226; Pendleton, I: 520.
214 *News from Nowhere* (Boston: Roberts Brothers, 1890), 8.
215 "New Works on The Metropolitan Railway," *Illustrated London News*, Supplement, 8 February 1868, 141–142.
216 Weber, 70.
217 Pablo Piccato, *City of Suspects: Crime in Mexico City, 1900–1931* (Durham: Duke University Press, 2001), 24–25.
218 Ariel Rodríguez Kuri, *La experiencia olvidada. El Ayuntamiento de México: Política y gobierno, 1876–1912* (Mexico City: El Colegio de México, Centro de Estudios Históricos, Universidad Autónoma Metropolitana, Atzcapotzalco, 1996), 172.
219 Robert Buffington and William E. French, "The Culture of Modernity," in *The Oxford History of Mexico*, Ed. Michael C. Meyer and William H. Beezley (New York: Oxford University Press, 2000), 400.
220 Mary Barton, *Impressions of Mexico with Brush and Pen* (New York: Macmillan, 1911), 45–46; Mary Elizabeth Blake and Margaret Francis Buchanan Sullivan, *Mexico: Picturesque, Political, and Progressive* (Boston: Lee and Shepard Publishers, 1888), 90–91; *El Imparcial*, 9 November 1899: 2; Matthew D. Esposito, *Funerals, Festivals, and Cultural Politics in Porfirian Mexico* (Albuquerque: University of New Mexico Press, 2010), 29–31.
221 Moisés González Navarro, *El Porfiriato: La vida social*, in *Historia Moderna de México*, IX: 695; Tony Morgan, "Proletarians, Politicos, and Patriarchs: The Use and Abuse of Cultural Customs in the Early Industrialization of Mexico City, 1880–1910," in *Rituals of Rule, Rituals of Resistance: Public Celebrations and Popular Culture in Mexico*, Ed. William H. Beezley, Cheryl English Martin, and William E. French (Wilmington, DE: SR Books, 1994), 153; Patrick Frank, *Posada's Broadsheets: Mexican Popular Imagery, 1890–1910* (Albuquerque: University of New Mexico Press), 190–191.
222 Moisés González Navarro, *El Porfiriato: La vida social*, in *Historia Moderna de México*, Ed. Daniel Cosío Villegas, 9 vols. (Mexico: Editorial Hermes, 1955–1968), IX: 695.
223 Quotes from *La Tribuna Popular*, March 6, 1909, 6, June 23, 1907, 1. Cited in Anton Rosenthal, "The Arrival of the Electric Streetcar and the Conflict Over Progress in Early Twentieth-Century Montevideo," *Journal of Latin American Studies* 27, no. 2 (May 1995), 329–331. See also Rosenthal, "Streetcar Workers and the Transformation of Montevideo: The General Strike of May 1911," *The Americas* 51, no. 4 (April 1995), 471–494.
224 James McPherson and Miller Williams, ed., *Railroads: Trains and Train People in American Culture* (New York: Random House, 1976), 5–9.
225 Darcy A. Zabel, *The (Underground) Railroad in African American Literature* (New York: Peter Lang, 2004).
226 Leon Litwack, *Trouble in Mind: Black Southerners in the Age of Jim Crow* (New York: Knopf, 1998), 272; Darcy A. Zabel, "Impact of the Railroad on African American Life," (unpublished paper), 11–12.

227 Edward Ayers, *Southern Crossing: A History of the American South, 1877–1906* (New York: Oxford University Press, 1995), 97.
228 Weber, 72–73.
229 "New Railway Regulations," *The Illustrated London Almanack* (1845), 57, and (1852), 57.
230 *Norman Sinclair*, 3 Vols. (Edinburgh: William Blackwood and Sons, 1861), I: 271.
231 Williams, 39.
232 Allan Mitchell, *The Great Train Race: Railways and the Franco-German Rivalry, 1815–1914* (New York: Berghahn Books, 2000), 30.
233 Meakin, 114.
234 John Coatsworth, *Growth Against Development: The Economic Impact of Railroads in Porfirian Mexico* (DeKalb: Northern Illinois University Press, 1981); Steven J. Ericson, *The Sound of the Whistle: Railroads and the State in Meiji Japan* (Cambridge: Harvard University Asia Center, 1996); Abigail Green, *Fatherlands: State-Building and Nationhood in Nineteenth-Century Germany* (Cambridge: Cambridge University Press, 2011), 223–266; Ian Kerr, ed., *Railways in Modern India*, 10; Robert Lee, *The Railways of Victoria, 1854–2004* (Carlton, Victoria: Melbourne University Publishing, 2007); Steven G. Marks, *Road to Power: The Trans-Siberian Railroad and the Colonization of Asian Russia, 1850–1917* (Ithaca: Cornell University Press, 1991; Amy G. Richter, *Home on the Rails: Women, the Railroad, and the Rise of Public Domesticity* (Chapel Hill: University of North Carolina Press, 2005).

Volume I

THE UNITED KINGDOM

ENGLAND AS EPICENTER OF RAILWAY CULTURES AND THE *PAX BRITANNICA*

> As to the neighborhood which had hesitated to acknowledge the railroad in its struggling days, that had grown wise and penitent as any Christian might in such a case, and now boasted of its powerful and prosperous relation. There were railway patterns in its drapers' shops, and railway journals in the windows of its newsmen. There were railway hotels, coffee-houses, lodging-houses, boarding-houses; railway-plans, maps, views, wrappers, bottles, sandwich-boxes, and time-tables; railway hackney-coach and cab-stands; railway omnibuses, railway streets and buildings, railway hangers-on and parasites, and flatterers out of all calculation. There was even railway time observed in clocks, as if the sun itself had given in. Among the vanquished was the master chimney sweeper, whilom incredulous at Staggs's Gardens, who now lived in a stuccoed house three stories high, and gave himself out, with golden flourishes upon a varnished board, as contractor for the cleansing of the railway chimneys by machinery.
> Charles Dickens, *Dombey and Son* (1848), 241.

Every new generation of railway researcher profitably reconsiders Dickens' passage in light of their own eras. Staggs' Gardens of the 1840s still has relevance as a locus of timeless reinvention: of neighborhoods, religion, relations of power and wealth, journals, hotels, cafes, the list of material representations of railway culture goes on. Dickens' memorable imagery of the railway's omnipresence in England and the sun's surrender to the clock is analyzed below. For now, it is the final sentence that embodied nineteenth-century world railway cultures. Ever the brilliant wordsmith, Dickens played with a keyword conspicuous in its archaism even in 1847. Hiding in plain sight is "whilom," meaning "up until now" or "in the past." In shorthand, Dickens referred to the cultural aptitude of Britons in Staggs' Gardens to set aside their collective uncertainty and disbelief with the rapidity of change and *adapt*. This mutability toward progress explains the chimney sweeper's agility within the shifting milieu. The sun gave in, but he "gave himself out." Modernity vanquished unbelievers, but the resilient chimney sweep persevered "with golden flourishes upon a varnished board." He mastered a machine to clean the chimneys of trains and reinvented himself into a three-story home. Dynamic societies with fluid relations of production adjusted nimbly to change and left many others behind.

In some of his characters, Dickens narrates the English parable of John Bull, the fictional Englishman who symbolizes the inventiveness of the factory engineer and whose historico-spatial analogues were indeed the two great cities of the industrial north in Lancashire, Manchester and Liverpool, and also London. Victorian culture worshiped the anti-intellectual of Carlyle, Froude, Kingsley, and Hughes, the Man of Practice admired for his industrial achievements and exalted for his imperial conquests. Stolid, earnest, hard-working, willfully ignorant, and tenacious, he prized and practiced rule of thumb, machines, and empiricism over scientific theory. The builder of railways, fleets, and empires had access to capital to invest in action and the use of force.[1] From 1800–1821, Lancashire's population grew 56 percent. Manchester rose to prominence as the cotton manufacturing center of the world. Liverpool imported raw cotton, exported cotton goods, and demanded 1,200 tons of coal per day by 1825.[2] London was the financial capital of the world. On December 4, 1830, after conveying over 50,000 passengers on nearly 1,000 round-trips, L&M crews loaded eighteen railway wagons with 135 bales and bags of cotton, 200 barrels of flour, sixty-three sacks of oatmeal, and thirty-four sacks of malt. The locomotive engine that hauled the fifty-one-ton load from Liverpool to Manchester was Stephenson's significantly named Number One engine *Planet*.[3]

Great Britain never needed railways to achieve a global empire, nor even a capitalist world. London and Liverpool had been ports of call for international shipping traffic for two centuries prior to steam-locomotive railways. By 1830, a world market already existed, and Great Britain controlled ten ports that regulated trade within the main oceanic systems. London on the Thames and Liverpool on the Mersey exercised hegemony over trade in the Atlantic, and with it the North Sea and Mediterranean. British control of Calcutta (1760s) and the Straits Settlements of Penang (1786), Singapore (1819), and Malacca (1824), as well as Cape Colony (1814), granted access to the Indian Ocean system. Malacca, the new colonies of Australia (1788) and New Zealand (1788, 1840), and later the treaty port of Hong Kong (1842) provided windows on the Asiatic Pacific. Equally important was the control of shipping lanes through the smaller straits and seas. The partition of Africa, the race for the Pacific, and competition for the Southeast Asian mainland and Indonesia were all secondary to Great Britain's primary goal of paramountcy, not just over the Indian subcontinent but the entire southern half of Asia. British Prime Ministers, the Foreign Office, and Parliament never sought to challenge the Tsars for all of Asiatic Russia. But what Kipling called the "Great Game" in the late nineteenth century was in fact the Anglo-Russian rivalry over an imaginary north-south dividing line of Asia in the Crimea and Black Sea area, the trans-Caspian region and Persia, the Khyber Pass and Sind of northwestern India (now Afghanistan and Pakistan), and China before the rise of Japan.[4] Great

Britain withstood tests of its colonial policy and military might in the Crimean War and Indian Mutiny. Railways, canals, telegraphs, submarine cables, shipping lines, Reuters, and the Suez Canal all produced a greater British Empire by 1870. Railways played the largest roles in accelerating imperial expansion and integrating territorial possessions. The twenty-first-century resurgence of China and India, the continuing development of the globally networked economies of the "Asian tigers," and restoration of a multipolar world greatly clarifies the priorities of British foreign policy decisions in the late nineteenth century.

Inception

Victorian railway cultures originated in London and radiated throughout England, then the world. Even before 1830, oceanic steamers and clipper ships had transformed London into the most visited and internationalized city in the world, especially after the French Revolution and Napoleonic period. Once London was linked by rail to Liverpool, Manchester, Birmingham, Leeds, Sheffield, Bristol, Nottingham, Bradford, Hull, Newcastle, Brighton, and Edinburgh, England became the undisputed center of capitalism, the heart of the *Pax Britannica*, and the epicenter of railway culture. Marx understood the significance of the L&M railway as a signpost that confirmed that Great Britain had achieved the highest form of capitalist production. In *Grundrisse* (1857–1858), a collection of then-unpublished writings produced between *The Communist Manifesto* (1848) and *Capital* (1867), Marx singled out the L&M as a "necessity of production for the Liverpool cotton brokers and even more for the Manchester manufacturers."[5] Importantly, Marx understood the presuppositions that informed the railway's construction as a *road*. The limitations of freight carriage were well known. The cotton industry had maximized its profitability with no discernable improvements in circulating its goods given extant modes of transport. The exchange value of the two primary products of cotton and coal threatened to eliminate their surplus value due to rising transportation costs. This was especially true for the Lancashire merchants who sold surplus production in the distant markets of India. Surplus capital and labor were readily available. There was no interruption in production or circulation of commodities during railway construction. Capitalists even presumed that railways would acquire what Marx later described as "surplus time," the acquisition of more productive labor resulting from reductions in the labor and material costs associated with horse and barge modes (carters, horses, fodder, tolls, transshipment, barges, and canal fees). Hence, Marx asked: Can capital squeeze surplus value out of the costs of transportation?[6] The L&M Board of Directors had answered in the affirmative, acquiring surplus time by building a mechanical road that moved by itself. The physical conditions of exchange required the annihilation of space by time.[7]

Like canal construction and other massive excavations, railways destroyed in order to create. Contrary to the way railway promoters depicted other modes of transportation as archaic vestiges of the feudal past, every transportation system prior to the onset of railways underwent widespread material improvements based on the influence of industrialism.[8] Railway companies devastated their rival canal companies by promoting the increasing efficiencies of steam-powered ground communications while exposing the defects of canal systems. Early treatises on railway technology privileged the word "celerity" to assert that steam power offered to overland routes what canals could never guarantee: speed, reliability, and cost efficiency.[9] The proponents of railways educated different segments of society about the universal applicability of the technology as overland transport surmounted every geographical, topographical, geological, and climatological obstacle. Once again, the L&M experiment under the supervision of George Stephenson proved engineers and workmen capable of cutting their way through uneven hills, erecting embankments, bridging and diverting water, conquering the wetlands of Chat Moss, and even tunneling outside of Liverpool. All told, engineers and workers erected sixty-three bridges, extended the Olive Mount excavation for two miles, moved three million cubic yards of earth, and built each of the nine arches of the Sankey Viaduct seven stories high.[10] Canals served only those riverine communities with ample natural water supplies, and the costs of canal excavation and locks to surmount inclines were astronomical. Railways ascended hills effortlessly and adapted to preexisting roads in ways that eliminated the troublesome labor inefficiencies of loading and carting, carting and uncarting, shipping, unshipping, and transshipping. For example, river and canal vessels, such as shallow-draft barges and steam-paddle ships, were unsafe in open seas, and large clipper ships struggled with impassable depths, bends, and obstacles in rivers. In both instances, freight had to be loaded and unloaded from ships and wagons. In addition, canal companies were not carriers. In order to ship anything from Wolverhampton to Hull, for example, the freight had to be transshipped four times by different carriers, all of whom charged fees: Wolverhampton to Shardlow, Shardlow to Gainsborough, Gainsborough to Hull, and Hull to destination.[11] Unlike canals, railway construction did not "interpose so formidable a barrier between the contiguous portions of an estate."[12] Whereas railways operated rain or shine year-round, canal companies limited or discontinued service during summer droughts when water levels were low or the winter months when ice impeded traffic. Ice flows had always threatened barges from the Mersey River and Bridgewater Canal in Liverpool to Lake Baikal in Siberia. When railways broke down in poor weather, repairs delayed traffic for a few hours or days, while canal defects shut down traffic for entire seasons. In addition, engineers praised railways for connecting two points by direct lines through space, as opposed to the circuitous routes of canal systems, which inevitably tied into equally serpentine natural river systems. Horse-drawn colliery lines that moved coal from point A to point B had proven the geometrical simplicity of trains for decades. Railway experts also rolled out the golden actuarial scroll of overland carriage for one-third the expense – an oft-repeated list of cost savings in railway construction, maintenance, and repairs that required one-third the financial outlay of canals. Tolls were cheaper, if levied at all, and freight charges per mile were one-third the prices that canal companies charged. They predicted freight rates for railways to drop further with high-volume shipments and mechanical improvements. The same benefits of technological modifications did not apply to "stationary" canal systems. The time-savings of transporting freight and passengers by rail also justified switching to railways. Canal transport by paddle-wheel propulsion topped out at four miles per hour due to water resistance, while steam locomotives routinely ran at twenty miles per hour in the 1830s.[13] In the end, capitalists used standard industrial-age arguments related to time savings, work discipline, economies of scale, and spatial and mechanical efficiency to promote railway systems over its closest competitor.

Critics of canal systems also cited their poor environmental and public health record as rationale for modernization. By the 1830s, farmers in the UK, U.S., and even India filed complaints that canal leakages waterlogged their fields and pastures on one side and desiccated lands on the other. All over the world, the rise in subsoil water tables caused by canal construction rendered groundwater availability unpredictable, thereby defeating the purpose of canal-fed irrigation. Medical health professionals and even engineers began to implicate canals and other large-scale excavation projects as sources of infectious diseases that were injurious and often deadly to nearby workers, settlers, and residents.[14] The coincidence of massive earthworks, canal building, and malaria in Europe (English fens), the Americas (Mississippi Valley), and India (Indo-Gangetic plains), for example, led to theories about the release of toxic miasmas or poisonous "animalcules" that caused marsh fevers in workforces. Not until the microbiological discoveries of the 1890s was malaria properly understood as a disease caused by a germ borne and transmitted by the *Anopheles* mosquito. Public health officials began to condemn canal, railway, and road-building companies, not for originating malaria – which was well-known for decades – but for inadvertently producing mosquito hatcheries in "borrow pits" and irrigation ditches along their lines and exposing laborers and nearby settlements to epidemics. "Railway malaria" was a significant killer of railroad workers and the rural poor in India, Italy, the U.S. South, and many other world regions. Canal and irrigation projects also shouldered some of the blame for water-borne illnesses, such as cholera, typhoid fever, and dysentery, that infected work camps.

England's main trunk lines extended between a handful of important cities that eventually linked to the industrialized port cities of London and Liverpool. Regional clusters centered on Manchester, Leeds, Derby, Birmingham, and York, Sheffield, Bradford, Hull, Newcastle, Brighton, Southampton, and Bristol. Norwich, Exeter, Cardiff, and Chester either began their own lines or were linked into existing ones by the early 1850s. The cities of Dublin and Belfast began their expansions in Ireland. In Scotland, Edinburgh connected with Glasgow. Railways urbanized the United Kingdom. By 1851, Great Britain became the first modern nation in which more people lived in cities and towns (51 percent) than in rural areas (49 percent).[15] From over 100 railway companies, eight principal lines emerged and dominated passenger and freight traffic in the 1870s. If

London was the center of a clock, the Great Northern ran in the direction of the hour hand at noon, the Great Eastern to two o'clock, the London, Chatham, and Dover to four, the London and South Western to eight, the Great Western at nine, the London and Northwestern at ten, and the Midland at eleven. The only main line that did not end in London was the Lancashire and Yorkshire Railway, which connected Liverpool and Hull. To take the clock metaphor a step further, the Railways Act of 1921 amalgamated British railways by combining the numbers of the clock into four three-hour blocks: the Great Northern was noon to three, the Southern three to six, the Great Western six to nine, and the London and North Eastern nine to twelve. Removing the face of the clock reveals the regional gears and sprockets of a complex communications and transportation system that ran of its own device.

The machine that moved itself, like the clock, was powered by an invisible source of energy. Period illustrations reproduced that hiddenness in the silent pages of *Mechanic's Magazine*, in Isaac Shaw's striking engravings of the L&M inauguration, and the many lithographic prints, reproductions, and aquatints of J. C. Bourne, R. Ackermann, and T. T. Bury.[16] Illustrated newspapers, histories, and magazines featured the woodcut engravings of George Dodgson, William and Edward Radclyffe, T. Creswick, D. Wilson, H. Griffith, D. R. Hill, I. H. LeKuex, L. Wrightson, and Newton Fielding. The first product of the transportation revolution to arrive to major cities throughout England, Scotland, Wales, and Ireland were the noisy, smoking locomotive engines themselves, pulling a "train" of carriages full of passengers. Eventually, however, those railways reached the townsfolk of distant settlements like the Dartmoor of Sara Marsh's novel:

> [T]hese people have spoken this patois from century to century – ay, and they would still go on from century to century, ignorant of the wonders outside their beloved moor, if it were not for the arrival of the great iron horse. That famous horse, which in the last thirty years has brought about more changes, and been the cause of more innovations, than have taken place in hundreds of years previously – that horse will, at length, link this moor to the rest of the world; the people will mix with others, civilization will come to them here, and then they may, in the course of a few generations, learn to speak English![17]

Comparative world history offers a unique perspective on the waves of change emanating from the North Atlantic. One of the most important revisions in the history of industrialism and railway historiography in recent decades is the recognition that social changes did not happen overnight. In *Masters and Workmen*, Irish novelist Frederick Richard Chichester (Earl of Belfast) acknowledged this when he wrote:

> Yonder flying vehicles, smoking and groaning along the railroad to the magnificent station of one of England's dark cities of industry, though

a minister of good, yet bears within itself the evidence, that joy and sorrow, vice and virtue, wealth and poverty must continue to travel on together to the grave, as long as society exists. In those carriages, as in life, there is a first, a second, and a third class, all profitting [sic], in a certain degree, by the inventions of the age, yet all retaining unchanged their early destination.[18]

Heeding structural continuities as well as changes are important, but comparative world history illuminates a second critical point that links Dickens' Staggs' Garden, Sara Marsh's Dartmoor, and Chichester's *Masters and Workmen* to the world at large: railway imperialism began with Great Britain's conquest of itself. Historian Ronald Robinson's criteria for railway expansion was reminiscent of British history. Railway imperialism spread the influence of industrialism, converted isolated agricultural towns into food producers for growing markets, conjoined local and national markets, integrated countries, regions, and towns into the world economy, provided investment opportunities for capitalists, combined military forces at a single point, staked out territories and spheres of influence, littered the landscape with Gothic and Classical Cathedral-like stations, and shrank time and space.[19] Although Robinson used specific examples (Prussia, the German principalities, the Raj), the processes and functions of railway expansion and integration, empire-building and military control, and revolutionizing overland transport challenged Britons to submit to universal progress. Railway imperialists sought to produce industrial workmen from Staggs' Garden who spoke impeccable English.

English submission to universal progress did not start well. Of all the newfangled changes that railways introduced throughout the world, the most controversial was the adoption of standard time. Like industrialism in general, standard time in England was neither accepted overnight nor embraced after sixty years (1780–1840). Capitalist enterprise and the factory system depended on gaslight to increase the length of the working day, breaking with the natural cycles that marked seasonal, daily, and hourly change. In factory towns, precise public clocks began competing with church bells in town squares. In 1775, there were only twenty steam engines in all England; by 1888, the number reached 110,000.[20] Many of these stationary engines operated on time-regulated factory floors day and night. In 1792, the English adopted a longitudinal standard called meridian time, when clocks in Bristol were set at ten minutes before London.[21] In 1840, railway stations throughout England designated London time as "Railway Time" to set train schedules. Just weeks after the Great Exhibition closed its doors, the public announcement for a proposed zero meridian at Greenwich appeared in the *Illustrated London News* (1852). The telegraph was to regulate all public clocks in the realm. By June, the Electric Telegraph Company, Astronomer Royal, and South-Eastern Railway Company were connected by wire to the Greenwich Observatory and a chronometrical device in London's west end. Designed by engineer Edwin

Clarke, the towering apparatus looked like a gilded weather vane 110 feet above the Thames, under which floated a giant zinc ball painted black with a visible white stripe. Synchronized by electric signal with Greenwich, the ball descended slowly, controlled by an air cylinder to indicate the exact time to London and river vessels below the bridge.[22]

The effects of standardized time and railway timetables can easily be exaggerated. Fourteen major towns and all of east and west England ignored the Greenwich clock.[23] Long after the installation of Big Ben in 1859, the quotidian rhythms of pastoral communities remained guided by nature rather than the British Empire's magnificent timepiece. Sundials remained objects worth their weight in stone. Towns like Dorchester rejected the new "London Time" or maintained clocks at railway stations that kept two different times. In 1879, Sanford Fleming, the Canadian builder of the Inter-Colonial Railway, recommended the global adoption of universal time to synchronize world commerce and standardize international travel. Greenwich Mean Time was brokered at a Washington D.C. conference. In the U.S., seventy time zones fell to just four. The English, Welsh, Scots, and Irish became more conscious about preserving their own local times. Well into the 1880s, trains ran on Greenwich Time while rural folk still conducted business according to local clocks. Districts held fast to the accuracy of their own clocks and looked askance at any timepiece introduced from without.[24] Lack of respect for train timetables continued to interrupt train service until the mobilization of troops at the onset of WWI. Not until the 1920s did Greenwich Mean Time become internationally accepted as universal time.

Railways nonetheless standardized distance and drastically reduced travel time between London and the rest of England. Agrarian communities along the tracks began adhering to the new time-consciousness since the products of their harvests had to be loaded onto trains before departure in order to reach expanding markets. Farmers tied their workdays not only to the agricultural seasons but also to cycles of production and consumption dictated by standardized public time, industrial interests, and market capitalism. Charles Dickens' quip that the adoption of railway time was "as if the sun itself had given in," applied to London more than anywhere else.[25] Literary critics tie his devotion to time pieces (watches, clocks), as well as a healthy respect for time-thrift in his novels, to the author's own experiences as a journalist and serialized writer with strict publishing deadlines.[26] Others regard Dickens as Victorian society's master teacher, whose sensation novels trained readers to process the transformations wrought by modern technology and time.[27] The novels of Thomas Hardy also appealed to contemporary readers by exploring the tensions between pre-industrial rural life and modern urban living, especially in a timeless Wessex. "In creating this chronotope of Wessex," Trish Ferguson explains, "Hardy captured . . . the sense of rupture and nostalgia for the pre-mechanical age before time discipline was enforced by industrial capitalism."[28] *Return of the Native* also distanced Edgon Heath from modernity, as time passes only through seasonal celebrations, and there were no references to railways or their timetables. In *Jude the Obscure*, Hardy introduces Fawley's son as "Little Father Time," a child automaton not unlike a human clock who has been alienated by the "mechanization of human perception."[29] Hardy witnessed the dawn of the industrial age, commented on the frenetic pace of modern life, and criticized the dislocating effects of labor discipline and regulated time.

Dickens may have been overtly conscientious about time management, the world of factory production, and rapid communications,[30] but like his friend Wilkie Collins, he developed a distaste for railway transport. Dickens had survived a train accident at Staplehurst (1865), which killed ten people and injured forty others. Experts on the preeminent Victorian novelist noted his ambivalence toward railway technology and his oscillation between narratives of phantasmagoric journeys (*Dombey and Son*) and social critiques of a dystopic world in which science and technology sanitized the creative imagination (*Hard Times*).[31] Other scholars of Victorian literature have closely examined the immediate impact of railways on nineteenth-century fiction in several subgenres, such as industrial, sensation, detective, horror, and science fiction novels.[32] A moral imperative inspired Victorian writers to understand the radical changes of the period.[33] Railway technology so transformed storytelling that some experts viewed the novel itself as technology that produced new narrative meanings.[34] If Dickens reported on the middle-class fetish with time, Lewis Carroll's *Alice in Wonderland* (1865) rejected outright the new time regime as wage slavery.[35] Victorian novels surely commented on railway travel's conflict with traditional notions of time, but after the 1860s, middle-class complaints emerged that centered on the railways' failure to meet the expectations of modern passengers in terms of punctuality and safety. Victorian aspirations far surpassed Dickens' references to oppressive clocks. Within one generation, overlapping and competing railway networks heralded a new awareness of time constraints and scheduling conflicts largely related to the new passenger densities on railways. More significant perhaps than references to train wrecks were the nervous ticks of modern life captured in the behaviors of the novels' characters, especially as it relates to their modern obsessions.[36] Anxiety of missing trains due to a broken timepiece recur mostly in sensation novels. Temporal displacement and what David Harvey called time-space compression caused a world of problems identified and deconstructed by novelists and scholars of railway cultures.[37] Alfred Haviland's *Hurried to Death* (1868) was addressed to railway travelers and suggested a newfound phobia of arriving late, exemplified by watch-toting passengers who made it their priority to synchronize them with the clocks at railway stations and pout when trains were late.[38] A certain moral economy developed of what was fair in terms of train delays since the companies' claims of rapid transport were reflected both in the prices of tickets and expectations that passengers subordinate their own schedules to the timetables by arriving to the stations early and undergoing the rituals of boarding.[39] The primary "machine" of the

Enlightenment, the clock, finally became an irreplaceable object upon which depended new modes of perception.[40]

Reception

The new railway cultures compensated for radical changes in time by arresting the rapid movement of trains at points along the permanent way. The classes empowered by industrialism – middle classes and to lesser extent the working classes – stood to benefit from railways most by creating spaces that matched the material conditions of their lifestyles. Railway cultures in the UK were historically produced and reproduced through architectural, literary, aesthetic, and linguistic means, all of which converged in the carriages and at railway stations. The earliest architectural inspirations for railway stations were those fixed and often spectacular objects of every English and American community – cathedrals. Church architecture in the form of domes, pillars, and gothic spires were hallmarks of station architecture. This is not to say that the covered railway platforms along the tracks gave any impression of ecclesiastical permanence. To the contrary, the cheap roofing materials of boarding platforms coupled with the size of crowds awaiting trains suggested improvisational sites of mobility and transition. Railway station buildings, however, were built to last. Railway architecture at Euston, King's Cross, St Pancras, Charing Cross, Manchester, Liverpool, Normanton, Leeds, York, Carlisle, Edinburgh, and Glasgow expressed the Eurocentric persuasions and ambitions of a global bourgeoisie.[41]

As a product of middle-class sensibilities, railway stations symbolized the transition to modern industrial life. The station represented every possible place that served mobile people as transitional loci: a port of call, harbor, way station, depot, an island refuge, market, restaurant, book shop, public sleeping area for the weary, stimulant for the restless, and a terrible inconvenience for modern passengers. It is illustrative of the unintended consequences of modernity to identify the functions that railway stations were *not* originally expected to perform and the peoples who they were *not* intended to serve. During subsistence crises such as famines and droughts, the Irish in Dublin, Indians in the Deccan, and Aborigines in Australia all sought food assistance at stations. Railway stations all over the planet became magnets for panhandling, loitering, scam artists, and thieves. Siberian peasants descended from the hills to railway stations for relief whenever forest fires consumed their fields; one European traveler saw a string of makeshift camps along twelve miles of track.[42] At every station of the Trans-Australian Railway, white travelers rubbed shoulders with Aborigines, some of whom begged for change, others sought food and water, and not a few rode the railways just for the thrill of it.[43]

G. K. Chesterton addressed this theme obliquely in two insightful short essays entitled "The Prehistoric Railway Station" and "The Lost Railway Station." The first of the two appears in the present volume. In the second, written three months before his death, Chesterton recalled fond memories of his favorite north of

London station, where he "once dreamed a dream." He never named the station, but he references the nearby suburbs of Harrow and Ealing and revealed clues about its whereabouts with several other details for anyone who cared to guess: 1) it was as quiet and comfortable as the courtyard of an old *inn*; 2) it had the usual *bookstall* and *refreshment bars*; 3) a *fountain* stood at its center; 4) a *model of an ocean liner* was on display; and 5) *hostelries* reminded him of 6) the *market-place of a village*. Chesterton remarked that he could imagine a village maiden filling her jug at the fountain and a boy dreaming of seafaring adventures to the ends of the earth in the toy boat. He then contemplated what might happen if the railway station was detached from its foundations, cast out on its own, and "left to live its own simple life, like a *farm* surrounded by floods, or a *hamlet* snowed up in the mountains." By the time the train arrived well into the future, "the little *commonwealth* ought to have a whole tangle of traditions ultimately to be traced back to the lost idea of a train." After Judgment Day, if the people forgot it was a train station at "a date centuries hence," the ticket office will serve as something like a confessional box, the bookstall the Bodleian or Alexandria Library, the fountain a religious center. "[A]ll society is like that strange railway station," Chesterton affirmed. He would name the imagined future station something prosaic and religious like nearby Marylebone.

Chesterton intended to write a moral for his daydream, but his train arrived. He described modern society as essentially unmoored from traditions like a rudderless ship. "The Lost Station" was the ultimate Foucauldian heterotopia, a spatial representation of "Other Places" known to British railway passengers. Travelers used stations as a surrogate for the inn, bookstall, bar, fountain, ocean liner, hostelry, marketplace, farm, hamlet, and commonwealth, and combination thereof. Chesterton's spatial references transport us to the countryside with Christian allusions to the Eden paradise in Ealing, a suburban market garden, and everlasting life in Heaven (Harrow) on the greenbelt in greater London.[44] A brief anecdote highlights by comparison the British heterotopic theme of returning to the quiet pleasures of the countryside. Japanese appreciation for their high-speed railways is matched by popular disdain for crowded Tokyo subways that require employees to push and pull passengers in and out of jam packed cars at every stop. But scholars of Japan have described railways as the umbilical cord that ties urban dwellers to their maternal origins in the countryside. The train stations themselves, especially public areas, are filled with reminders of pastoral beginnings: *bonsai* plants (dwarf trees), *ikebana* (arranged flowers), and even koi ponds. At Shinjuku Station, one railway employee earned widespread acclaim for broadcasting the sounds of *suzumushi* insects that "sing" like crickets over the public address system. When interviewed, the worker said that the hearts of Tokyo people still reside in the country, and the sounds linked them to simpler days in the rural past.[45]

Stations and trains were also surrogate centers of book and experiential learning, if not formal education. The Industrial Revolution created the conditions for greater global literacy through machine production of cheaper paper, printing, and bound and unbound reading materials.[46] The combined use of the steam press, binding and composing machinery, and the railway led to the mass production and distribution of books. Trains and steamers not only spread various forms of literature rapidly throughout the world, but they were also sites of recreational reading for a growing market of mobile passengers who read serialized novels. Although Dickens' *Pickwick Papers* (1836–1837) initially sold more copies, *Oliver Twist* (1837–1838) is widely considered the first major work of Victorian fiction, a genre originally serialized in monthly journals or published in two or more volumes before being compiled into single or multi-volume editions called "novels." It has been estimated that Victorians published no fewer than 25,000 journals, of which *Bentley's Miscellany*, *Household Words*, and *All Year Round* are just a few preeminent examples. To cater to the tastes of middle-class travelers, publishers mass-produced pocket-sized "railway novels," which were sold at train stations. Famous among booksellers were the circulating libraries of Edward Mudie and W. H. Smith, which left English ports in boxes to reach readers in the overseas colonies.[47] While the works of historians such as Thomas Carlyle, Edward Bulwer Lytton, and R. H. Horne dominated reading lists prior to mid-century, the English novelists began to capture the market in the high Victorian period (1848–1870). Middle-class consumers read both, and supplemented their reading appetites with heavy servings of biographies, religious tracts, and magazines with large circulations. The promotional literature for railways and locomotive travel was vast beyond compare. By 1846, there were twenty-six railway journals alone, and popular publications like *The Family Herald* ran "Scientific and Useful" sections that publicized the latest products that railways transported throughout the British Isles.

Trains and railways inspired drama. The dramatic theatrical and cinematic scene in which an evildoer ties a damsel in distress to a railway track while the steam-powered monster bears down on her was a product of Victorian-era sensibilities that swept through the interconnected world. Play and film directors held audiences in suspense until the providential arrival of a hero saved the defenseless captive at the last possible moment.[48] In the original version of American playwright Augustin Daly's *Under the Gaslight* (1867), the protagonist was a woman, Laura, who rescued a one-armed Civil War veteran named Snorkey. Similar train rescue scenes appeared in England the following year. In Dion Boucicault's *After Dark* (*A Drama of London Life*, 1868), villains rendered Captain Gordon Chumley "insensible" with liquor and

> laid [him] across the rails of the Metropolitan line to be crushed by the coming train . . . but he is perceived and snatched up at the right moment by the ever-ready Old Tom, and then the train sweeps across the stage, raising the audience to a perfect fever of excitement.[49]

In Watts Phillips' *Land Rats and Water Rats*, peril awaited a fair maiden in distress:

> For Hetty Calvert, as the lovely florist is named, threatening to be an inconvenient witness of certain atrocities, is fastened across a railway

just as the express train is about to arrive, and is only rescued in the nick of time by the carpenter.[50]

Here again, the "ultra-realism" and "pre-eminence of the English in the art of stage decoration" thrilled theater crowds that would not give a horse-drawn carriage crossing Blackfriars Bridge a second glance unless an "exact *facsimile*" appeared on stage.[51]

To stage the "sensation scene," theaters constructed tracks and used large wooden flats to capture the imposing dimensions of trains. Play productions suspended the disbelief of audiences by artfully capturing the train's menace – derivative of the inability to stop due to its velocity – with whistles, sounds, lighting, and smoke effects that alternately terrified and excited audiences.[52] Sometimes the effects backfired, as in the first showing of *Under the Gaslight* when technical difficulties split the train in two and revealed the legs of the train operator to the audience, suggesting locomotion by human instead of stage machinery.[53] When an on-stage train underwhelmed an audience in 1900, a reviewer wondered what would happen to the train if it hit the actor.[54] Would-be victims always lied prostrate and incapacitated to reach the maximum dramatic potential. Often it was the squirming, groaning, and faint cries for help from innocents facing mutilation that brought audiences to the edge of their seats. Since the trains were animated in such a way as to grant them mythical characteristics and mystical force, they resembled for modern audiences the dragons that once preyed on princesses and devoured sidekicks. Some of the engines even had lighted eyes, fiery innards, and smoke emanating from their "nostrils." Hence, the themes of impending carnage are ancient, but nineteenth-century sets also emphasized the perils of modernity. No longer imaginary magical creatures, these machines killed people, as exemplified by the notorious Abergele, Armagh, Staplehurst, Shrewsbury curve, and Quintinshill railway disasters. On stage, locomotives were presented as relentless and remorseless mechanical accomplices to diabolical murderers everywhere. To the Victorian-era reviewer who detailed the villains' foiled plans, the passing *train* represented death incarnate: "with a shriek, the baffled death rushes by."[55]

Scholars have revealed significant things about nineteenth-century Victorian culture in their close readings of railway rescue scenes. Nicholas Daly analyzed the scenes beyond the laughable cheap-thrill entertainment that it later became in twentieth-century cinema to reveal underlying anxieties rooted in the Victorian imagination. In 1868 alone, at least five theaters in London ran some version of the scene in four different plays.[56] Audiences craved representations of all new modern technologies in an era that commodified and industrialized spectacular visual imagery. Clare Pettitt has suggested that sensation fiction on stage deployed new technologies to repackage old melodramatic plots, but now "the process of unmasking and the climatic recognition scenes are speeded up by the penny post, the railway, and the telegraph."[57] Dramatic renditions of burning houses, steamboats, fire engines, hot air balloons, and the coaches of the Messageries Royal all stood center stage. In a fascinating witticism of the modern, the great Victorian dramatist Boucicault, known for his sensational stage effects in nearly 150 plays, once remarked "I can spin out these rough-and-tumble dramas as a hen lays eggs. It's a degrading occupation, but more money has been made out of guano then out of poetry."[58] Boucicault's *After Dark*, which first appeared at the Princess's Theater on August 12, 1868, went on to achieve critical acclaim in fashionable and cheap theaters alike. Boucicault's family history reflected the tragedies and triumphs of railway technology, as Dion lost his oldest son in a train accident, and his father, the self-proclaimed early expert in the steam engine and locomotive technology Dionysius Lardner, rather recklessly tested the safety of early track networks.[59] Unique about Boucicault's rescue scene was that it was staged to take place in the recently inaugurated underground railway in London. Not so exceptional about *After Dark* was that the crowded subterranean line harbored antagonists such as Dicey Morris, the stereotypical Jewish villain who ran a criminal underworld of gambling, money-lending, and prostitution. Daly illustrated how the middle-class audiences who watched in suspense rode to the theater district in trains, omnibuses, and the underground railway fully aware of the Abergele train wreck, as well as anti-Semitic themes.[60] This is not, however, what made railway rescue scenes thrilling for audiences. Victorian dramatists "envision[ed] scenarios in which a human agent can beat a mechanical agent, in which for a moment, the human comes to enter and master the temporal world of the machine."[61] The accelerated pace and mechanical dangers of industrial life introduced into factory settings for the working class also unnerved middle-class railway travelers, who read sensation fiction and attended plays that exposed them to the heightened sensory experiences of quotidian life.[62] For example, Daly regards the sensation novel as a form of technology that helped readers negotiate modern feelings of shock and displacement that accompanied railway travel. The emergence of railway pathologies, especially in the medical literature after 1860, reveals a society coming to terms with the effects of industrialized travel. The railway rescue scene's popularity derived from the triumphant human ability to thwart the industrial accident caused by "machine time."[63] For a while, even Vaudeville and burlesque performers, minstrels, sketch artists, and variety acts poked fun at the railroad scene.[64] The bound-to-the-tracks trope has since been serialized in early cinema and countless examples of visual entertainment featuring a narrow escape from machine-based mutilation.

American scholarly interpretations of the railroad rescue scene focused on the role reversal of women from actual heroines to distressed damsels. Early versions often featured women outracing the trains to save men. Amy Hughes argued that the downgraded roles reflected late-nineteenth-century reactions to the radical politics partly represented in *Under the Gaslight*, as the rescued Snorkey remarks about his axe-wielding savior: "And these are the women who ain't to have a vote!"[65] Women had it worse inside passenger compartments. Some railways provided separate ladies' compartments to prevent "outrages," such as sexual assault.[66]

Railways promoted other forms of entertainment that relied on the presentation of spectacular, realistic, and often exotic displays. Travelling circuses and shows reached overland destinations quicker than ever. Generations of Latin Americans saw live elephants for the first time, and crowds greeted Buffalo Bill's Wild West Show in the major cities of Europe. Sometimes the tragedies associated with dying races were all too realistic. In 1845, George Catlin, an American folklorist, brought an exhibition of artifacts, live grizzly bears, and actual Chippewa and Ioway Indians to Liverpool, Manchester, London, and Newcastle. The bears traveled by train in cages covered with tarps, and they howled and tore up the flooring and grounds beneath the cage wherever they stayed overnight. As usual, the Native Americans proved more adept than their promoter as ambassadors of goodwill. Catlin's record of English perceptions of the Indians and vice versa appears in this volume. When one of the elderly Indians died in Liverpool, family and friends were disappointed that locals buried him in a grave with two additional coffins.[67]

Trains rendered habitual what was once extraordinary even during holidays: getting out of town. Consistent with the railway's pattern of alterity, railway companies soon found an immediate remedy for industrial toil, railway-induced illnesses, or any other malady, in the weekend and holiday excursion to "the country" and seaside resorts. The Victorian era's "Age of Sensation" (1860–1890) was really exported as Ages of Sensations to other parts of the world (1830–1930). Since railway service often lacked adventure of any kind, its first customers were railway employees. Joseph Tatlow, Director of the Midland Great Western Railway (Ireland) and Dublin and Kingstown Railway, invoked Charles Lamb to describe his first railway office job in England as a tall stool and "the dry drudgery at the desk's dead wood."[68] Tourist retreats to seaside resorts began on the British and French railways in the 1840s, and by the end of the twentieth century, the American transcontinentals gave birth to the extended vacation through remote wildernesses. The English sought escapes to the country and seaside resorts at Brighton, Southampton, and Bristol.[69] The French streamed to vacation wonderlands on the Channel Coast and Norman Coast as well as to the Alps, the Vosges, the Pyrenees, and the Massif Central. These places were the first to set up tourist information bureaus. The only folks left in Paris during holidays were those not able to leave.[70] Eugen Weber argued that the popular classes partook of the same culture by combining it with their holy days and pilgrimages. In France, this included the pilgrimages of Catholics to shrines at Lourdes, La Salette, and Lisieux. These sacred sites and their healing springs drew 300,000–400,000 pilgrims annually.

Railway companies ran headlong into Sabbatarians who claimed that Sunday rail service violated Christian teachings and created diversions for parishioners who should attend church. In the 1870s and early 1880s, railway companies began to respond to public demand for faster excursion trains to run on weekends, especially on Bank Holidays. The companies did not want to offend the customer base of churchgoers who commuted during the remainder of the week and tried to schedule departure times early and late on Sundays to accommodate church services. An incident occurred on June 3, 1883, when a shipment of herring arrived from Scotland's Isle of Sky to Strome Ferry, the western terminus of the Highland Railway. The railway had arranged a special train to deliver the fresh cargo to Inverness, but during transshipment 150 fishermen from Lewis and nearby villages armed with clubs and sticks met the fishing boats, shut down the pier, and captured the train station in protest of its Sunday operations. Police and railway officials intervened, but violence ensued and local villagers "smote the Sabbath-breakers hip and thigh."[71] Ten men were later convicted of "mobbing and rioting" and sentenced to four months in prison. After eight weeks at Calton Gaol in Edinburgh, Home Secretary William Harcourt took mercy on them and set them free. Various Christian religious denominations in the U.S., Canada, Australia, and New Zealand challenged Sunday train service.

Incursion

Sabbatarianism represented symptoms of a deeper illness between city-based capitalist interests and the rural countryside. Historians who have focused only on the greed of landowners who accepted one-time payoffs worth five times the value of their lands miss the point of rural conservatism and traditional reactions toward trespassing. A century's worth of canal and macadamized roadbuilding preconditioned these classes to the notion that they were powerless to stop it. Rural agrarians almost never stood by railway construction without traditional forms of protest. In some areas of the world, such as England, Mexico, and Ecuador, farmers did not even wait for tracks to be laid to sabotage their arrival. In the 1820s, no fewer than 150 petitions opposed the L&M railway bill. English tenant farmers and gamekeepers threw stones at survey teams to defend the lands of the Earls of Sefton and Derby. George Stephenson's survey crew faced barricaded entryways and was driven off at Knowsley. Near St. Helens, colliers threatened to throw the trespassers down a coal pit. On the Duke of Bridgewater's property, Stephenson "was threatened to be ducked in the pond." At one point, the L&M board of directors hired a prizefighter to defend its engineers and surveying equipment from angry colliers and farmers, who were seen carrying guns, pitchforks, sticks, and stones. Bridgewater's agent Mr. Bradshaw directed his men to discharge guns at night, and they threatened to carry off Stephenson to Worsley. Stephenson retaliated by producing false documents and having his men fire off guns at a distance far from the surveyors to create a diversion for his survey work. It was only after Charles Blacker Vignoles routed a new line that opposition in Lancashire relented.[72]

Conditions did not improve on other lines. Surveyors for the London and Birmingham Railway worked with lanterns at night and during religious services to avoid the ire of the "lords of the soil" and Anglican clergy.[73] Closer to mid-century, large groups of navvies were called upon, provided with pay and drink, and asked to intimidate anyone who threatened the surveyors.[74] English literature is filled with examples of active resistance against the railway companies. At the Warwickshire of George Eliot's fictional *Middlemarch*, farm laborers turned their hayforks on railway agents.[75] English comparisons to the behaviors of people in other parts of the world justify a fuller explanation of rural reaction beyond the narrow corporate interests of a landed elite that held their property in ransom. English Engineer Victor Bayley wrote of the tendency of hill tribesmen in the Khyber Pass to obliterate survey marks within hours of a crew's measurements. Railway men risked sniper fire from the hills whenever they showed up on the camp's parade grounds to play soccer or field hockey. Anything of value, including dynamite, was pilfered from camp stores, forcing superintendents to build *burjis*, or manned lookout towers (by the end the railway had hired 570 riflemen). None of Bayley's explanations on the great benefits of trains worked with his Pathan audience until he learned the culture's appreciation for humor and Rabelaisian themes. Adopting a new persona he called his "imp of mischief," he turned to Sher Ali Khan and his followers and grinned: "The gradient will be steep and the trains will travel slowly. They will be carrying rich merchandise and will pass close to your doors. The Sultan Khel are notorious robbers and raiders. Think of the opportunities for looting the trains." After translation, the crowd roared: "Build the railway and loot the trains."[76] In Ecuador, Andean peasants secretly pulled survey stakes and ran off with instruments and equipment in retaliation against survey teams for trampling their fields and irrigation works.[77]

English landowners and their tenants set an example for the world, but armed opposition against railways almost never reached the levels of popular violence and plebian insolence levied against other transport systems in England such as canals, turnpikes, and toll-roads. Horse-drawn coaches received comparatively little protest, but when canals and locks undercut the carters who supplied London with grain, malt, and provisions, they petitioned Lord Burghley to end construction and the barge trade. In 1581, the carters rioted and set fire to the locks, and any number of them dug channels into riverbanks to disrupt the water flow into canals and interrupt the river trade.[78] Bands of armed men gathered at night to set fire to toll-gates, as well as the homes of English toll collectors. In the early 1700s, moneylenders stopped issuing loans for road improvements in fear of retaliation. In 1728, an Act was passed that jailed offenders for three months if convicted of destroying turnpike gates, with seven years' incarceration for a repeat offense. This really angered the arsonists, and after years of nighttime attacks, Parliament issued the death sentence for convicted offenders in 1735. This hardly dissuaded the "good people" of Ledbury-Turnpike in Hereford, who bore axes and guns in their marches, and those of Somersetshire in Bristol as they armed themselves with rusty swords, pitchforks, axes, guns, pistols, and clubs. Lives were lost. In contrast, stagecoach service evolved so gradually in Early Modern England that they avoided controversy, and the best that one dissident could do was publish a pamphlet arguing that stagecoaches would put innkeepers out of business because patrons would spend more time in carriages than drinking beer at the inns. William T. Jackman asserted that vested interests always rose up in hatred against their competition.[79] But not every rioter represented monopolists. The scale of resistance against early modern modes of transport in England happened against railways elsewhere in the nineteenth century.

Popular anxiety over the onset of railways was not always owed to the arrival of unknown technologies but sometimes to hordes of foreign laborers. Railway historiography sings the praises of the hard-working and good-natured "navvies," the railway "navigators" who built some of England's most troublesome lines.[80] They hailed from "the country" as the sons of farmers who lacked educations and jobs. Unskilled and mobile, many gained experience as day laborers draining the fens in Lincolnshire, digging canals in Lancashire or Yorkshire, and constructing roads in the Eastern Counties. Some "petty breach of the peace" in their own county may have resulted in a move to the railways in another district.[81] Others had acquired railway building experience on the Northumberland and Durham coalfield lines.[82] Their nicknames often reflected their county of origin, such as "Lincoln Jack" and "Norfolk." Since many men were young and single, they invested little in their own temporary housing, which consisted of huts with sodden walls, clay floors, and no restrooms.[83] In *The Life of George Stephenson*, Samuel Smiles glorified the navvies and the honorable works they accomplished on the L&M. He listed their prodigious achievements and explained how they "worked hard and lived hard," endangered themselves daily, competed in "horse-barrow runs," and received pay at "unusually long intervals."[84]

Navvies earned reputations as disruptive forces all their own. John Pendleton claimed that the counties of Bridgewater preferred an invasion of Danish warriors to a horde of navvies.[85] Scholar-librarian of English literature Myron Brightfield found a passage illustrative of Victorian attitudes toward navvies in the anonymously written novel *Yesterday* (1859):

> A railway was in progress near at hand, and bands of navigators were quartered in that quiet place, working mightily, drinking as hard as they worked or harder, disturbing the familiar stillness of the neighbourhood by brawl and revel, frightening some of the inhabitants, corrupting others. Poor Mabel scarcely knew her old favourite spots, now that they were haunted by these red-capped gnomes, who seemed never quiet except when they lay on a bank in a drunken sleep, who played rough tricks, like sailors ashore, and startled the holy quiet of a Sunday afternoon by hoarse songs of ruffian mirth, or hoarser bellowings of ruffian fury.[86]

Mabel was not the only person to criticize their reckless and immoral behavior. In Stephen W. Fullom's *The Great Highway*, Irish and English navvies fought each other and then picked up brick bats and rioted against the superintendents for picking sides.[87] Property owners dreaded their appearance *en masse*, which simulated peasant rebellions: "From their huts to that part of the railway at which they worked, over corn or grass, tearing down embankments, injuring young plantations, making gaps in hedges, on they went, in one direct line without regard to damage done."[88] Navvies stole game off sacred preserves, defied game-keepers, threw stones at passers-by, and left worksites like "dogs released from a week's confinement."[89] They also robbed and brutalized one another with impunity. No one praised them for their thrift; one historian likened them to sailors who "work for their money like horses and spend it like asses."[90] Paydays invited drunken sprees. Beer, gin, and whiskey, which they called "white beer," motivated physical and verbal abuses of women, constables, neighbors, and one another. Reverends chastised them for their amoral conduct and spiritual destitution. The navvies earned high enough wages, but they were often left penniless once they completed a railway.[91] In any given year, 50,000 navvies and unskilled workers were engaged in railway construction. At the height of railway mania in 1847, more than 250,000 worked the lines.[92]

Although contemporary middle-class observers depicted navvies as a raucous bunch, scholars who have studied their culture confirm several of the themes rendered so realistically in the poetry and autobiographical novels of Irish navvy-poet Patrick MacGill. Navvies like Dermond Flynn (MacGill) and Moleskin Joe of the novel *Children of the Dead End* were forced out of their cottages in their early teens to join the workforce and help pay for family household expenses. They fell victim to capitalist exploitation and bounced from odd jobs to railway gangs in the most depressed economic conditions. Just when their daily and weekly wages began to make a difference, railway employers changed to monthly pay. Some rode out the storm between paydays but many returned to vagrancy. Other period sources described the "truck system" of "company stores" that was designed to saddle navvies with debt. Few railway workers possessed the savings to last a month without pay, so they turned to subsistence tickets, called "subs," which were used to purchase goods only at Tommy Shops or "tally-shops." Even *The Railway News* called the system "grossly absurd" because the shopkeepers were in league with the contractors to sell inferior goods to the men for inflated prices – 10 percent above market by some estimates.[93] At the end of the month, the amount spent in sub tickets was deducted from the borrowers' pay. Navvies exchanged sub tickets at half their value, sometimes risking them in games of chance, as a means to accumulate enough of the script to buy tobacco and alcohol on credit. Disagreements over sub tickets escalated to drunken brawls.[94] Railway contractors often paid workers at the very hovels that sold beer to the men.[95] The truck system and Tommy Shops perpetuated a cycle of navvy debt, which reinforced tendencies toward alcoholism, gambling, and physical violence. The system perpetuated lifestyles that led to debt bondage and the continued degradation of the "English Condition" of the working class.

Ethnic conflict often pitted one group of navvies against another. When Irish navvies killed a policeman at Gorebridge, near Dalkeith, Scotland in 1846, one thousand Scots and Englishmen drove them out and burned their huts and possessions.[96] Benjamin Disraeli's poignant didactic novel *Sybil or The Two Nations* portrays the Chartist Uprising in 1842 from the perspective of working-class men and women who took up arms against every institution and social class arrayed against them, especially the Tommy Shops.[97] Railway magnate Samuel Morton Peto waged campaigns against the vices that tempted workers. Peto selected good contractors who cared about their men, paid workers weekly, built housing for them, distributed Bibles, and hired clergy to read the scriptures to them.[98] His paternalistic style inspired British contractors all over the world to find alternatives to wage slavery. Social reformers like Edwin Chadwick criticized the government and railway companies for not providing for the public health of residents and workforces. After a deadly typhus epidemic swept through London, Chadwick famously indicted the water distribution and sewerage systems as the culprits for horrid mortality rates, poor urban health, and dreadful sanitation practices. A champion of the navvies, Chadwick targeted railway companies for ignoring the health needs of their workforce. The railway companies later offered better housing accommodations and sanitary facilities. Navvies organized "Butty gangs" of specialists who agreed to do piecework for a price, then divided the earnings among all members. They took up collections when one of their penniless comrades was "on tramp," needed medicine or a doctor, or died in an accident.[99] Contractors encouraged them to form "sick-clubs" to guarantee mutual assistance during epidemics. Reforms such as the Truck Acts, revisions of the Poor Laws, the Public Health Act (1848), laws requiring worker's compensation and employer liability, and organizations such as the Navvy Mission Society (1876) provided some societal protection to the working class, but English companies were merely the first to exploit its railway workers deliberately. The sight of navvy funeral processions to cemeteries was much too frequent to deny the dangers of railway construction in the UK.

The engineer and entrepreneur Robert Stephenson's "Résumé of the Railway System and its Results," an exemplary discourse of its times (1858), never credits navvies for any of the extraordinary achievements he listed. Wages were their reward, even though thousands perished on the job in Great Britain and more than one million workers died building the world's railways. Patterns established during the high Victorian era in Great Britain were repeated on every continent. Although navvies, coolies, and convicts belonged to different social classes in distinct settings, the ideas that railway workers were expendable, that they misbehaved, and that they posed a threat to the communities through which they passed persisted well into the twentieth century. Stephenson was a Member of Parliament and the President of the Institution of Civil Engineers when he provided an impressive snapshot of the Empire's material progress in railways. The figures, statistics, and analogies that he used to illustrate the magnitude of 25 years' worth of engineering achievements imply the sheer magnitude of the navvies' underappreciated labor. One wonders if the rate of excavating 550 million cubic yards every 25 years would have leveled all England by 1900.[100]

John Kellett has argued that Victorian-era railway company managers, engineers, consultants, and contractors had more influence over changes in urban landscapes than any other municipal authority or business concern. Their decisions to sink millions into landmark stations and reduce fares for the working class altered the fabric of city life. To railway entrepreneurs, the social and environmental impact of steam-locomotive transport on cities was peripheral to the immediacy of raising business capital and earning profits from increasingly competitive passenger services. One of the problems that the companies faced when competing for urban commuter traffic was that only a small percentage of the workforce could afford daily fares, even on the low-cost "parliamentary trains." The population of London, for example, approached 6.5 million, but only 250,000 people used the trains to get to work.[101] Most workers chose meals over train fare and supplemented long walks to their workplaces with the occasional cheap ride on an overcrowded omnibus. Working folks perceived trains as city-to-city people movers over longer distances than the average daily commute to worksites. In the 1860s, the best way for railway companies to compete was to win the price competition against rivals by lowering fares for third-class passengers and advertising the new prices until commuters could no longer afford other forms of transport. The decision to make mass transportation to the suburbs affordable led to the Cheap Trains Act (1844), which some railway managers opposed. The London, Brighton, and South Coast railway had just spent £2 million to widen Victoria station. Its manager, William Forbes, objected to overrunning their new glorious facilities with workmen's trains: "It will turn Victoria into an Elysium for workers and a Hades for the rest of the community."[102] The Act required railways to run at least one workmen's train daily at 12 miles per hour or faster, charging no more than a penny per mile. The act required seats in carriages that were protected by the weather. London remained a tale of two cities. Well-to-do passengers who travelled on workmen's trains to save money could barely stand the filth, stench, and disgusting habits of their brethren. Workmen spat on the train floor, lit up pipes, cursed like sailors, insulted women, and cooked herrings in the waiting rooms. Likewise, workmen argued that well-healed shopkeepers, clerks, and salesmen had no right to take advantage of the low fares on workmen's trains.[103] It is important to emphasize here, in anticipation of the unlimited number of complaints worldwide, that the first to object to riding with and accommodating the budgets of workers on third-class trains were railway officials and middle-class passengers in Victorian England. Likewise, the first proletarian fare dodgers to treat the railway carriages like extensions of their worksites and factory floors were also Victorians.

William Powell Frith achieved in his iconic social panoramas of English crowds quintessential hegemonic images of class leveling in the industrial age. *The Railway Station* (1862), *Life at the Seagate (Ramsgate Sands)*, which Queen Victoria actually purchased, and *Derby Day*, a mainstay at Royal Academy exhibitions, still stand as Victorian group portraits. The modern-life paintings were so popular that iron railings and police guards had to be installed to protect them from adoring publics.[104] Art critic Caroline Arscott wrote about Frith's sensationalized groupings of travelers who complimented modernity by synchronizing their movements with the steam-powered train: "A picture such as *The Railway Station* offered a compendium of observation, social commentary, comedy, pathos, adventure and moral reflection that perfectly fitted the appetites and expectations of the middle-class viewing public."[105] Frith was an avid theater-goer and admirer of his patron Charles Dickens. He certainly knew the difference between sober fact and Dickensonian fiction. He hired a photographer to help him frame scenes and visualize passengers, and sketched social groupings based on the observations of his apprentices. But he also painted for his livelihood, which included support for two households, a wife and mistress, and seventeen surviving children between them. A market in illustrated magazines and engravings popularized Frith's works in artful reproductions that compensated the painter for his adopted commercial style. The extent of realism in his paintings still divides scholars. Both Frith and his critics cited as influences the painter William Hogarth and cartoonist George Cruikshank. Sally Woodcock found Frith's panoramas to be a "benchmark of normality against which to judge the immoderation of nineteenth-century materiality," and Mary Cowling regards his paintings as "a veritable mirror of their own times."[106] Historian Harold Perkins called attention to one significant departure from his bourgeois themes – the realism of the working-class cluster in the background to the left. Laborers no longer left their homes for good to find work but commuted to distant workplaces and returned by dusk.[107]

On April 1, 1872, England moved toward greater inclusivity by eliminating second-class carriage service, running third-class carriages on all trains, and extending first-class amenities to all. Some of the old parliamentary trains were removed from service. Interestingly, the law passed shortly after Liberal parliamentarian John Lubbock introduced legislation that became the first Bank Holiday Act in 1871. With Easter Sunday and three Mondays declared official holidays, the railways started scheduling excursion trains to destinations far from the big cities. The Midland Railway led by James Allport began to admit third-class passengers to express trains with corridors, comfortable upholstery, lavatories, and refreshment cars. The Great Eastern also upgraded its trains and rebounded from perennial debt by developing a reputation as the "Poor Man's Line." The Cheap Trains Act of 1883 made workmen's trains even more affordable. For Whit Monday in 1892, the Great Eastern alone carried 135,000 passengers from London during the weekend. That very weekend, thousands visited Epping Forest and Southend-on-Sea.[108] Businesses in Blackpool and Brighton advertised with posters in London railway stations and thousands of handbills placed in the carriages of trains. The Isle of Man became the vacation grounds of Liverpudlians, and Douglas grew into a fashionable resort.

Part 1: the *Rocket*, Rainhill Trials, and early promotion of railways

Capitalist competition motivated the earliest efforts of railway companies to challenge canal firms in hauling freight, specifically the carriage of cotton and coal. Steam engines depended on the bituminous mineral to fire its furnaces, and early locomotives pulled tenders full of both coal and water. The illustrations and articles that appeared in *Mechanics' Magazine* reached thousands of interested readers – engineers, industrialists, inventors, investors, and laypersons alike in the United Kingdom, continental Europe, and the United States. These pages collected the earliest technical descriptions of the most famous engine, Stephenson's *Rocket*, as well as an account of the Rainhill competition that pitted it against several other engines. Whereas the editors of *The Times* clearly favored the London-based engine of John Braithwaite and John Ericsson called the *Novelty*, *Mechanics'* offered a more balanced appraisal of each engine's performances. Shortly after the death of William Huskisson at the Liverpool & Manchester inauguration, railway promoters hired engravers, lithographers, painters, and illustrators like R. Ackermann, J. C. Bourne, and T. T. Bury to produce prints that depicted the iron horse as a passenger-friendly and safe mode of transport. These men represented the railway companies' earliest publicists for their roles in altering public perceptions of the iron monster. Few people believed that a ten-ton rolling steam engine that ate coal, belched smoke, and ran at twenty miles per hour could remain harmless for long. Some of the earliest artistic prints were exhibited at railway stations, while others found their way into the living rooms and studies of avid consumers. Independent of any railway company's payroll was the engraver Isaac Shaw, who created some of the first prints that presented side views of freight and passenger trains. Less-successful prints followed in books and periodicals of the 1830s, but they all met public relations objectives of promoting the safety of trains and normalizing railway travel. Charles Maclaren's influential treatise comparing railways favorably to canal barges appeared in multiple journals, including *The Scotsman* and *The Pamphleteer* in 1824–1825. Many of his conclusions were also examined in the editorial pages of *The Edinburgh Review* and *Herapath's Railway Journal*. Of special interest to the formation of railway cultures was the gradual transition of arguments that promoted economies in freight transport to assertions of cheaper and faster passenger travel. Once passenger traffic eclipsed the business in goods, railways were here to stay.

Part 2: engineering enemies

Railway expansion met with formidable resistance all over the world in the nineteenth century. In England, widespread opposition arose first from powerful men of the propertied classes who defended their estates and financial interests against the potential violations of the "infernal machines." Landowners, such as the Earls of Derby and Sefton, as well as the owners of canal works like the Duke of Bridgewater, summoned allies in Parliament and rallied farmers on their landholdings to wield every possible weapon from pens and rhetoric to pitchforks and curses against the L&M railway company and its survey teams. Horse-drawn passenger carriage lines and overland freight companies on the turnpikes and tollways also stood to lose business to cheaper railway transport. Innkeepers and shopkeepers along highways worried that an alternative railway route would divert traffic from their storefronts. John Ruskin and William Wordsworth were only the best-known intellectuals to oppose railways on the basis of environmental despoliation. Their writings appealed to the sensibilities of those who appreciated the unscathed landscapes of pre-industrial England, not to mention privacy from city folk and the urban blight of industrial factory towns. Wordsworth's protest materialized in sonnets and a letter to Prime Minister Gladstone. Ruskin published his opinions in *Precious Thoughts* and *The Seven Lamps of Architecture*. The people of George Eliot's *Middlemarch* possessed attitudes about railways that were remarkably accurate for the times. The cantankerous Thomas Creevy expressed contempt for the actual mode of transport and opposed railway acts in Parliament. Conservative forces on every continent rose to protect the status quo against economic competition and threats to conservation. Such hostility toward railways in the UK provoked the L&M's Director Joseph Sandars to publish a scathing indictment against the monopolistic practices of canal companies in *A Letter on the Subject of the Projected Rail Road between Liverpool and Manchester*. When five editions of this antagonistic "Letter" failed to secure a Railway Act in Parliament, the L&M board of directors set a historic precedent in its "Second Prospectus of the Liverpool and Manchester Railway Company." The private company negotiated with their rivals and broadened the appeal of locomotive transport beyond purely economic rationale to moderate the cultural misgivings of traditional underclasses. While focusing on the landowners and their tenants produces facile explanations of a middle-class struggle against the conservative and reactionary aristocracy and peasantry, Sanders and Stephenson faced the stiffest opposition from direct capitalist competitors. To overcome enmity required a temporary transference of powers to more compromising men on the L&M Board, engineering staff, and the land survey. Conciliatory stock offerings, horse-trading, compensatory settlements to landowners, and other appeals diminished opposition in Parliament. Likewise, in the interest of public safety, the L&M subjected itself to Parliamentary oversight regarding the controversial use of steam engines. This complex process of accommodation, evident in the collection's sources, preceded railway construction on Great Britain's lines. Those railway companies that practiced diplomacy to mediate conflict won consent; those that did not failed.

Part 3: cultures of railway construction

Railways in nineteenth-century England borrowed their laborers and even the name for them from canal construction crews. Canal workers were called "navigators," or "navvies" for short, and they had won recognition as a group excavating canals long before railways ran alongside or over them. Railway navvies emerged as one of the first distinct railway cultures. The earliest writers about navvies, such as John Francis and Stephen W. Fullom, were informed about their subjects by period newspapers, which romanticized these hard-working groups that deposited themselves and the railways on the doorstep of Britons. These authors referred to navvies as ill-mannered brutes but argued that their reputations reflected their rural upbringing, lower-class status, lack of education, and arduous labors. The authors rationalized even the rudest behavior of cussing, drinking, fighting, womanizing, and thieving as forms of stress relief, coping, and entertainment during the dreary transition to industrial discipline. *A History of the English Railway* by Francis regards the navvies as both constructive and destructive forces, and reports on the felonies and misdemeanors they committed. In addition, Francis details the abuses of the "truck system" that kept workers dependent on company credit to survive. Their accumulated debts tied them to their jobs. Fullom's novel *The Great Highway* situates a navvy riot in the context of the day-to-day grind of their supervisors, which included refereeing disputes between feuding Irish and English workers. In one chapter the main characters find themselves under siege and fearful of losing their lives. Benjamin Disraeli's novel *Sybil or The Two Nations* (1845) explores the "English Condition" question of an industrial nation irrevocably divided into two classes at war. This selection highlights the attitudes of the working class and its politicization during the Chartist revolt in 1842. Although the riotous masses incorporate workers from all sectors, they identify common enemies.

By the 1860s, the tone had changed. Characters in novels and periodical literature depict the navvies as ruffians, hooligans, punks, miscreants, foreigners, strangers, outsiders, and aliens who threatened quiet towns and the idyllic country. The invasive and transient nature of the railway business produced much of the notoriety, but so did navvy conduct. The novels of Irish navvy-poet Patrick MacGill meet the criteria of great world literature because they redefined the railway navigator by humanizing him at the turn of the twentieth century. Navvies grew up dirt poor to families with absentee, underemployed, and alcoholic fathers. Desperate single mothers worried incessantly about their ill children, and circumstances forced the oldest among them to earn wages. *Children of the Dead End: The Autobiography of a Navvy* and *Gleanings from a Navvy's Scrapbook* are incomparable sources about the navvy's sad life.

Part 4: novel impressions: early Victorian railway cultures

"The wheels were placed upon the iron bands." So started Fanny Kemble in her letter to Margaret describing her first ride on Stephenson's machine. Controversy attended the introduction of railways in England. Machines were usually hidden behind the doors of the great factories and ironmongeries, not screaming their way in and out of workshops and stations. Firsthand accounts of the railway's debut by Fanny Kemble and an anonymous contributor to *Buck's Gazette* (reprinted in *Herapath's Journal*) convey the thrill of the railway journey in the 1830s. Perhaps appropriately for an actress, Kemble narrated her experience with a flair for the dramatic. She detailed the characteristics that made steam-powered locomotives such fairy tales and mysteries to spectators. The "magical machine" with "flying white breath" and "rhythmical unvarying pace" had no visible motive force. The people atop viaducts who looked down at her from so far away looked like pygmies. As the train reached thirty-five miles per hour, she drank the air, and the wind weighed her eyelids down. She had no fear of flying through openings in the sheer rock walls of cuttings, which she described as descending below the surface. The author of the next entry from *Herapath's* equated locomotives with the series of enchantments found in the Arabian Nights. Still searching for descriptors, the writer refers to the train as an automaton that emits a series of explosions that sound like a lion or tiger panting. References to lightning, thunder, and hurricane winds do not apply to the weather outside. The passing of trains were called "meetings." In his memoirs from 1837, Charles Greville relates the new experience of traveling from Knowsley to Liverpool, and by train from Liverpool to Birmingham and back, all in time to learn about election outcomes.

The satirical press in London and other major cities throughout the world published humorous and often biting criticism of the early railways. No issue escaped their eye, and their editorial views often addressed daily shortcomings that were truly universal but not always significant enough to be reported in the daily newspapers. The editor of the satirical magazine *Punch*, William Makepeace Thackeray, was an astute and often hilarious critic of railways. In his piece "Two Days in Wicklow," from *The Irish Sketch Book*, he introduces the world to the "railroad dandies" of Ireland. In the following selections from *Punch* in the 1840s, Thackeray takes on the "Railway Idlers" of the provincial countryside, who overcame the nuisances of modern railway travel to sightsee in London. Along with providing social commentary on the rural-urban divide, *Punch* abhors the parsimony of railway companies and the parents who hold rather large children on their laps to avoid paying train fare. Thackeray comments on the exorbitant charges at railway hotels (e.g. in Southampton): "The bill is always made out on the principle of never seeing the visitor again." The *London Charivari* also lampoons the builders of extravagant railway stations as the "architects of their own fortune."

In the 1840s, railway travel was by no means outmoded or commonplace. Travelers described the novel experience of approaching industrial and mining towns in trains only to see smoke-filled skies from the factories and chimneys, as well as from steam engines at the coal mines. The characters in Albert Richard Smith's novel, *The Struggles and Adventures of Christopher Tadpole at Home and Abroad*, demonstrate their local knowledge of railway culture. Smith describes third-class carriages as "rattling open pig-pens on wheels." Charles Dickens left some of the most memorable impressions of the railway as a symbol of early Victorian England. Excerpts from *Mugby Junction*, *Dombey and Son*, and *Our Mutual Friend* compliment many of the shorter vignettes discussed in previous essays.

Part 5: timetables, calendars, and stations: mid-Victorian railway cultures, 1848–1870

In 1830, Henry Booth identified the need to understand how railways will affect human notions of time and space. Many of Booth's corollary observations that time is money, cost savings derive from economies of scale, and humans will have greater control of their spatial environments have all become commonplaces associated with railways. A generation later in 1852, Europe and the U.S. agreed to recognize "Railway Time," also called "Uniform Time," to begin at the zero meridian of Greenwich, England. One year later, George Measom published his travel book *The Official Illustrated Guide to the Brighton and South Coast Railways and All Their Branches, including a Description of the Crystal Palace at Sydenham, and a Topical Account of the Isle of Wight*. Railway publications of all sorts exploded. *Bradshaws* guides containing railway timetables and advertisements galore appeared in public newsstands and the shops of private booksellers everywhere. The weekend getaway industry was born, and Easter excursions, Bank Holidays (after 1871), and other traditions grew so popular that the "crush" of Hamstead Heath or Paddington station became a more widespread phenomenon.

William Powell Frith's panorama of locomotive transportation captured the bustling multitude at Paddington Station, recording various social types who found themselves on the railway platform. Captivating for its time and highly popular to date, it is an unlikely composition resplendent with colorful costumed subjects instead of the hodge-podge of scrambling humanity in muted hue commonly found on the Great Western line. The simultaneity of dramatic events on Frith's stage-like platform appealed to the Victorian imagination, but it is as improbable as a present-day filmmaker's telescoping a Victorian novel into a two-hour motion picture. Frith nevertheless renders comprehensible in one image many material representations of railway cultures in the early Victorian age. The Yorkshire-born London transplant was so confident in the realism of his creation that he features himself and his family at center-left.

In circus-like fashion, American painter, author, and entertainer George Catlin escorted Ioway and Ojibbeway Indians and two grizzly bears on a tour through England, France, and Belgium in 1843. His account describes terrible ordeals for the company he kept. *The Illustrated London News* covered the story in December that year. On his trip to London for the Great Exhibition of 1851, John Overton Choules toured the Greenwich Fair, Woolwich naval yard, and Bristol and Bath on the Great Western Railway. This highly praised line is both the subject and setting of a chapter in Miss Julia Pardoe's *Reginald Lyle*. In "Mischances," a chapter of Elizabeth Gaskell's *North and South*, the author explores the railway station as a site of painful farewells and frightening encounters for young Margaret. When her father asks to take her brother Frederick to the Milton station, the dutiful girl knew that the dangerous Leonards was after him, but she replied in the affirmative anyway, "I am getting very brave and very hard. It is a well-lighted road all the way home if it should be dark. But I was out last week much later."

Railway stations such as Charing Cross, Victoria, and Waterloo drew enormous attention in the 1840s and 1850s. In Frances Eleanor Trollope's novel *Veronica* and Miss Muloch's *A Life for a Life*, the novelists explore the cold loneliness of vacuous cathedral-like spaces that alienated the people who architects rarely thought about. Despite lacking a university education, George Augustus Sala completed an apprenticeship with Dickens for *Household Words*. Sala's "The Art of Sucking Eggs," a commentary on the modern railway station, appeared in the first issue of his own publication *Temple Bar* 1 (1861). G. K. Chesterton's "The Prehistoric Railway Station" was published in his work *Tremendous Truffles*. He found railway stations peaceful public sites that contrasted with the private spaces that money could buy. He enjoyed their automatic machines that dispensed chocolate, cigarettes, toffee, and scents and used a nearby scale to weigh himself. To Chesterton, the list of railway stations read like a litany of solemn and saintly memories, if not saints, and the bookstalls therein made accessible a space similar to the Vatican or Bodleian Library. He expressed interest in the title of the book: *Get on or Get Out*.

Part 6: subterranean railways and the underground: high Victorian railway cultures

The famous railway rescue scene moved underground to the subway system in Dion Boucicault's sensational play *After Dark* (1868). The theme of a dark London underground originated in medieval times when the labyrinth of drainage canals and sewers became home for all kinds of imaginary monsters, demons, ghosts, and madmen. During the Victorian era, even Jack the Ripper was believed to reside there. Early reports of the subterranean or underground railway system, however, show engineering efforts to manufacture modern subway terminals into transitional social spaces. Builders were not deluded into thinking they could replicate the utopian railway stations of the surface hundreds of feet underground, but they worked diligently to connect them thematically and aesthetically to the stations above ground. The earliest reports of *The Times* and *Illustrated London News* represented efforts to persuade the public that the subway was cheap, safe, and fast. Gustave Doré's timeless illustrations show very little difference between the dystopic railways above and below ground.

Although the underground railway system was a hallmark achievement of the mid-Victorian era, period literature called attention to several other important developments in railway cultures, especially for women. When novelist Mortimer Collins published *The Vivian Romance* in 1870, Europeans and Americans were already speculating about air transportation and the advantages of flight. The bourgeoisie, however, also yearned for the bygone days of pleasant travel by mail carriage. Collins' narrator did both, merging past and future with retrospection and prospection, suggesting that balloon travel might somehow restore the carriage's "wholesome travel with wind on your face." The character also considered locomotive travel as an abomination, and railways were as common in the British landscape as clotheslines. Author of sensation novels M. E. Braddon and Lady Margaret Majendie, a fiction writer of the high Victorian era, explored the wholly different theme of women's liberation. Elizabeth Braddon's *Henry Dunbar* presented the reality of train rides as a mundane chore, involving long stints of overnight travel wrapped in a railway rug and interminable waiting in railway stations. These periods of mind-numbing stasis were nonetheless interspersed with moments of refreshing nourishment, restorative sunshine, and reunions with familiar people. In Braddon's *The Lovels of Arden*, young women like Clarissa Lovel, who knew very few people beyond her immediate family, took railways to visit distant relatives, picnic, draw, paint, and otherwise engage in the "divine amusement" and "glorious profession" of art and, of course, participate in more public forms of courtship. Similarly, in "A Railway Journey," Lady Margaret Majendie explored the new freedoms that young women experienced, including the freedom to ride trains with complete strangers and fall victim to practical jokes. Edith's eventful railway journey from Euston Station to Hatton involved the train's near miss at a cattle crossing and the unforgettable image of a fellow passenger weighed down with baskets, which included a brace of hares and a lone rabbit hanging by a snare around his neck. But her youthful companion "Uncle George" ended the journey with the biggest surprise.

Part 7: netherworlds and nostalgia: late Victorian and Edwardian railway cultures

The turn-of-the-century decades in the United Kingdom were one of the most prolific times of imaginative literary production. E. M. Forster's masterpiece, *Howards End*, published toward the end of this period, introduced the notion of railway stations, most notably King's Cross, as gateways to "Infinity." The author was fascinated that these gateways led to infinite destinations but always returned home. As such, railway stations became the initial settings for the infinite directions that a fictional novel might take. George Gissing proved this in *The Nether World*, where an innocent wedding day turned into a bleak bout of bacchanalia for newly married couple Pennyloaf and Bob, Clem Peckover, Jack Bartley, and Suke Jollop. It began as a train departed from Holburn Viaduct and flew over the rooftops of South London destined for the carnival at the Crystal Palace. Elizabeth Robbins Pennell updated a new generation of *Harper's* readers on London's Underground Railway. Readers of this collection will recognize the railway's influence on H. G. Wells, especially in his descriptions of the pilot and his fictional machine, the aeropile, in *When the Sleeper Wakes* (1899): "How great the monster seemed, so swift and steady!" *The Spectator*, a daily newspaper published in London, speculated about the future of "The Motor Car." That one of the infinite pathways led England into WWI and the eventual decline of Europe was one of history's great tragedies.

The period was also one of retrospection and reflection. Selections of James John Hissey, an overlooked travel writer who was often as perceptive as Henry James but without the literary flourish, detailed various points of interest in the British Isles. Outside Berkhampstead, for example, he pointed out anachronisms and the juxtaposition of three modes of transport – ancient, preindustrial, and industrial – in one setting. Picturesque Lincolnshire was the star attraction in his travel account *Over Fen and Wold*. The two short stories of "Q," Sir Arthur

Quiller-Couch, glisten eyes for taking readers back to very simple times when railway trains were privileged sites for people-watching and people-helping. Scholars of Victorian literature credit Thomas Hardy (*Under the Greenwood Tree, The Return of the Native, Jude the Obscure*) and George Whyte-Melville (*The Brookes of Bridlemere*) for writing poignant novels about bygone eras. To Whyte-Melville the act of riding trains at top speeds bred confidence and a spirit of competition in passengers. To one of Hardy's characters, the railway station displaced the cathedral as the center of town. Trains also threatened towns by bringing hordes of out-of-towners during annual fairs. Henry James provided accounts of two very different places, London and the Isle of Wight, during the Edwardian era. The world-famous Railway Children save the day in Edith Nesbit's version of the "railway rescue" scene. E. M. Forster joins Quiller-Couch, Hardy, and Whtye-Melville in uncovering a more innocent and infinitely curious English past.

Part 8: the railway accident, public health, and military deployment

Railway accidents at Wolverhampton (1838) and Armagh (1889) distressed the public for generations. *The Spectator* and other newspapers provided immediate coverage of the shocking events, with several follow-up articles every time investigations produced a new piece of information. Serial publications also routinely revisited the episodes in morbid detail, and the place names became synonymous with the great train disasters. These two accidents joined the annals of others that included Staplehurst (1865), Abergele (1868), Abbots Ripton (1876), the Tay Bridge (1879), Shrewsbury curve (1907), and Quintinshill (1915). In the 1860s, *The Lancet* ran a series of articles entitled "The Influence of Railway Travelling on Public Health" (1862), and John Charles Hall published his book *Medical Evidence in Railway Accidents* (1868), which was based on his experiences as a Senior Physician at the Sheffield Public Hospital. The short extracts from *The Lancet* illustrated the speculative nature of medicine in the high Victorian period. Hall's anatomy lesson in Chapter 3, "Railway Accidents," supplements the statistics of the era that demonstrated a general lack of employee and passenger safety. When trains collided with every other imaginable vehicle, passengers paid the price with concussions and other forms of head trauma. The railway companies were liable and required to compensate passengers for their injuries. "In the Temple Gardens" is a heart-wrenching fictional story of the kind of railway accident that preoccupied the minds of Victorian-era parents.

British periodicals always reported on the uses of trains for wartime mobilization, communications, and transport. The *Illustrated London News* was a rich source of reliable information about the prosecution of the Crimean War from the time troops set down in the Crimea in 1854 to the Russian surrender on March 30, 1856. Great Britain sent railway navvies to Balaclava to construct a portable rail system to facilitate the shipment of troops and arms to the front at Sebastopol. In 1855, French president and soon-to-be emperor Louis Napoleon Bonaparte crossed the English Channel on a railway tour through England. *The Spectator* announced the invasion of the Free State in its issue of March 17, 1900. A most exceptional source on the Second Boer War, the personal diary of Eyre Lloyd related the story of a brave and earnest member of the 2nd Coldstream Guards killed in action during the winter of 1901. An Assistant Staff Officer, Lloyd kept a diary, in which he commented regularly about the use and abuse of railways. The diary was privately published with a small circulation.

Part 9: the great war and interwar railway cultures

Long before the nationalization of British Railways, amalgamation facilitated mobilization for war and national defense. Since the onset of the railway system to 1914, Great Britain had never been engaged in national defense or a war in Europe. Any wars were fought far from its shores. British railways were nonetheless built to instantly concentrate troops at the port cities and on the populated coasts. The National Defense Act (1888) provided for railways to be turned over to the state during wartime, but the law did not preclude private railway companies from retaining civilian personnel, administration, and operations during the war. The Engineer and Railway Volunteer Staff Corps in wartime comprised the general managers of the leading railways. In 1915, *The Times* news publications issued its sixth volume of its *History of the War* series, which included a chapter entitled "Railways and the War." The article referred often to the Second Boer War as a model after which the British deployed, rehabilitated, and protected French railways. The construction of blockhouses, placement of quick-fire artillery, maxim guns, barbed-wire fencing, and search lights all worked in combination. The chapter provided ample coverage of the German, French, Russian, and Belgian uses of railways in WWI. For the final entry on WWI, we turn to Edwin A. Pratt, whose book *British Railways and the Great War* still serves as required reading for students and scholars of WWI. Immediately after thousands of railway men were called to duty, women joined the war effort by serving on the railway as booking clerks, ticket collectors, waitresses on dining cars, and cleaners of engines and carriages. As the documents in this section attest, women transcended their traditional roles in clerical positions on the railway to embrace ever-greater responsibilities. After the war, Parliament extended voting rights to 8.4 million women over the age of 30 who qualified as property owners, householders, women married to homeowners, and university graduates and empowered women to run for election to the House of Commons. Ten years later, voting rights extended to women over the age of 21.

Thomas Hardy's poignant and mysterious poem, "Midnight on the Great Western," represents Great Britain's return to normalcy after WWI. Along with Lord Monkswell's "neo-Victorian" piece "Making up Lost Time," it ushered in the 1920s, when time was again of the essence, commercial flight began, and the *Flying Scotsman* broke the British record for the longest non-stop service from King's Cross to Edinburgh (392.5 miles). *Railway Magazine* noted a return to pre-war standards in the artistic railway posters that appeared in the early 1920s. In *Harper's* Frank Parker Stockbridge anticipated Charles Lindbergh's flight by denoting a new era in commercial aerial navigation with the arrival of transoceanic airplanes. Of particular note to railway history is the pattern Stockbridge had identified, which followed in the footsteps of railways. First, he notes, planes will carry international mail; second, newspapers and light manufacturing goods, such as essences of perfumes; third, passengers. For all intents and purposes, Winston Churchill, the Secretary of State for Aviation, controlled, if not militarized, the skies over Great Britain, enforcing laws related to air navigation by all airplanes, seaplanes, dirigibles, and anchored balloons. Aircraft had to pass government inspections, and early airports, called aerodromes, had to meet government regulations. Pilots were to be trained, required to pass physical and technical examinations, and licensed. Stockbridge ends, "This is not a dream of the year 2000 – it is the sober, present."

Part 10: railway cultures of Scotland and Ireland

The final section on the United Kingdom demonstrates local patterns of adjustment and resistance to time, work discipline, and railways in Scotland and Ireland. The Scottish journalist David Croal published his memoirs *Early Recollections of a Journalist* anonymously in 1898. Prior to the railways, the people of Edinburgh eagerly anticipated the daily mail coach from the south. Croal related efforts to accelerate the service for the final 120 miles from the northernmost railway terminus at Morpath, Northumberland, England to Edinburgh, Scotland. Since letters and newspapers were not particularly heavy, the Post Office deployed light-weight, two-wheeled carriages with a single driver pulled by two horses called a curricle. Despite the omnipresence of trains in the 1890s, the speedy curricle "with its red-coated guard" stood out in Croal's memory. Charles Richard Weld spent two months in the Scottish highlands, Orcadia, and the Isle of Skye in 1860. Weld shipped his heavy baggage by sea and caught the Great Northern train from London to Aberdeen, when he felt the "agonising uncertainty" of receiving a telegram at a stop along the way. The telegraph was still used sparingly for emergencies and important announcements. Weld admitted as much when his railway itinerary was interrupted by a dispatch from a "Laird" – the axiomatic expression for a landed estate owner in Scotland – who happened to be a member of his hunting and fishing party. Transferring to the North Western, Weld commented on a commercial traveler stowing packages of every shape throughout the cabin, a reference worth comparing to the practices of passengers throughout the world. William Edmondstoune Aytoun's title character in *Norman Sinclair* wondered what happened to all the stagecoaches that "carried you into the very heart of the country." Did someone round them up and sacrifice them in "a magnificent holocaust"? The novel's characters and themes fit so clearly into the high Victorian period with its metaphors and metonyms for the train – the "steam-eagle," "screaming metallic competitors," "magical carpets," and "screaming engine."

The real gem to examine at length is found in Chapter 7, "Railway Morals," in which Aytoun mocks the Parliamentary inquiries that wore down George Stephenson in the 1820s and comments on the effects of the railway mania in Scotland. C. F. Gordon Cumming's travels in the Hebrides coincided with one of the storied local events of late Victorian Scotland she called "The Sunday War." Gordon Cumming's insights add much to the interpretation of events at Strome Ferry, where Sabbatarians with clubs occupied by force the port works and train station to prevent a load of kippered herring from leaving on a Sunday. She suggested that the economic motives of local fishermen lay behind the Puritanical reaction. In another excerpt from *In the Hebrides* (1883), Gordon Cumming lamented that the mountains of the Hebrides echo the shrieks of trains, which now empty their full carriages of people from the Strand and Picadilly. "You breakfast one morning in sight of the great Skye hills, and the next finds you at Euston square – a process so simple that life becomes one incessant railway journey, for ever whirling to and fro!" In *Memories* (1904), the Scottish native corroborates Croal's recollections about stagecoach service and remarks that among the many things railways brought to Scotland were bridges!

The issues of the *Dublin Penny Journal* introduced here reveal that Ireland treaded the same path as England in the early development of railways. The Dublin and Kingstown Railway opened four years after the L&M. Railway engineers, inventors, promoters, and early enthusiasts engaged in the same debates and actively pursued railway expansion. In May 1845, American travel writer J. Jay Smith strolled down Sackville Street in Dublin and rode the Atmospheric Railway to its terminus at Dalkey. The Earl of Belfast (Frederick Richard Chichester) began his novel *Masters and Workmen* with an epigram from Wordsworth's verse "Old things have been unsettled." Published in 1851, Chichester's work explores opportunities for the poor to scale the social ladder as iron workers in industrial factories. Science and industry ushered in greater economic security and moral betterment but proved once again by way of England's railways to dark cities that change brings both good and bad to new generations; the result in a capitalist society is continuity in different forms. Andrew Dickinson considered Europe a vast mine from which he excavated priceless gems. When he visited Chichester's Emerald Isle in 1850, he witnessed abject poverty, whereby the train station became a source of relief for peddlers. Train passengers threw coins out of carriage windows like feed for pigeons. "Half-starved, hatless tatterdemalions" in rags scrambled and some remained penniless even after chasing the train for two miles from Castle Blaney to Armagh. If poverty was a social disease, Ireland has been "doctored almost to death" and railways have not improved their lot. At mid-century, Sir Francis Bond Head toured Ireland with an improvised itinerary along the railway between Dublin and Galway. He chose Athlone, the halfway point between the Irish Channel and the Atlantic, as well as the center of the island, for further exploration. He detrained amidst a sea of travelers, walked for a while, and, among the "paroxysms of convulsive grins" of Irish locals, caught a ride to Tuam. He passed sunburnt threshers and reapers – not the machines – but men and women wielding handheld farming tools during harvest. The speed of overland transport became obvious when they overcame horse-drawn canal boats that appeared to be moving backward. George Foxcroft Haskins provides a vivid description of both the rural surroundings and city of Cork after years of famine. In his memoirs, written when he was a political prisoner in Australia, General Thomas Francis Meagher discussed his rebel activity against England in 1848, when Great Britain suspended Habeas Corpus in Ireland. Meagher's plans included urban warfare with barricades and disruption of train service in Waterford, Kilkenny, and Tipperary, while insurgents rallied Irish populations as far and wide as Glasgow to foment dissent. C. O. Burge's remembrances adopted the structure of an endless train, with story after story of his encounters with nineteenth-century locomotives in Ireland. Three extracts by J. M. Synge finds the inveterate traveler and novelist in West Kerry, Galway, Gorumna, and the Aran Islands. The theme of overloaded aisles in third-class trains recurred in Ireland as Synge reported the contents of the passenger car as flour sacks, cases of porter, chairs, and other household goods. Commenting on the relationship between the homespuns of natural wool and dreaded political reforms that weaken their individuality, Synge states with a touch of melancholy: "it is part of the misfortune of Ireland that nearly all the characteristics which give colour and attractiveness to Irish life are bound up with a social condition that is near to penury." During the same week of Gladstone's death, a drunk porter met Synge at Galway to carry off his baggage toward town. Synge deposited his belongings at a local hotel and intermingled with the railway stations crowd, where he catches a third-class carriage from Connaught to Ballinasloe and finally to the Parnell celebrations in Dublin. Singers sang, sailors and soldiers fought, the pleasant girl in the seat next to him listened to his guided tour, and the rowdy carriage next to him roared above the din. He concluded that the train's tumult reflected wild West Ireland. Railway man Joseph Tatlow helped introduce Ireland's first golf course. In *The Road Round Ireland*, master storyteller Padraic Colum taught the world how to pronounce words in the Cork dialect by inflecting the last word of a sentence like a "bursting bud." As the last word of Volume I on the United Kingdom, Colum's excerpt from "On the Train" bursts from the pages for capturing in charming and inimitable prose the greatest pastime on trains: eavesdropping!

Notes

1 Walter E. Houghton, *The Victorian Frame of Mind: 1830–1870* (New Haven: Yale University Press, 1985), 113, 121–123, 174, 198–199.
2 R. E. Carlson, *The Liverpool and Manchester Railway Project, 1821–1831* (New York: Augustus M. Kelley, 1969), 17–19.
3 *Ibid.*, 239–240.
4 Gregory Blue, "Introduction," in Gregory Blue, Martin Bunton, and Ralph Croizier, eds., *Colonialism and the Modern World: Selected Studies* (New York: M. E. Sharpe, 2002), 6–7; Thomas R. Metcalf, "India in the Indian Ocean Arena," in *Ibid.*, 27.

5 Marx, *Grundrisse: Foundations of the Critique of Political Economy*, Trans. Martin Nicolaus (London: Penguin, 1973), 530.
6 *Ibid.*, 516–533, Question on 522.
7 *Ibid.*, 524.
8 Carlson, 17–26, 41.
9 See, for instance, Charles Maclaren, *Railways Compared with Canals & Common Roads, and Their Uses and Advantages Explained* (Edinburgh: Constable, 1825), 49; George W. Smith, "Rail-Roads and Canals," in Nicholas Wood, *A Practical Treatise on Rail-Roads, and Interior Communications in General* (Philadelphia: Carey and Lea, 1832), 471–473.
10 Samuel Smiles, *The Life of George Stephenson, Railway Engineer* (New York: Harper, 1868), 258; Frederick S. Williams, *Our Iron Roads Their History, Construction, and Social Influences* (London: Ingram, Cooke, and Co., 1852), 26; Carlson, 187–190.
11 William T. Jackman, *The Development of Transportation in Modern England*, 2 vols. (Cambridge: The University Press, 1916), I: 441.
12 Maclaren, 49–51, quote on 49.
13 Maclaren, 48–54; Smith, 471–473.
14 Smith, 471–472.
15 Michael G. Mulhall, *The Dictionary of Statistics* (London: George Routledge and Sons, 1892), 445.
16 John Bourne and John Britton, *Drawings of the London and Birmingham Railway with an Historical and Descriptive Account* (London: J. C. Bourne, 1839).
17 Mrs. Sara Marsh, *Chronicles of Dartmoor* 2 vols. (London, 1866), I: 267. Quoted in Brightfield, 69–70.
18 Frederick Richard Chichester [Earl of Belfast], *Masters and Workmen: A Tale Illustrative of the Social and Moral Condition of the People*, 3 Vols. (London: Newby, 1851), I: 11.
19 Ronald Robinson in Clarence B. Davis and Kenneth E. Wilburn, Jr., eds. with Ronald Robinson, *Railway Imperialism* (New York: Greenwood Press, 1991), 1–2.
20 Mulhall, (1892), 546.
21 Louis James, *The Victorian Novel* (Oxford: Blackwell, 2006), 97.
22 *Illustrated London News*, January 3, 1852, 10; June 26, 1852, 516.
23 *Ibid.*, January 3, 1852, 10. They were Norwich, Yarmouth, Cambridge, Ipswich, Colchester, Harwich, Oxford, Bristol, Bath, Portsmouth, Exeter, Dorchester, Launceston, and Falmouth.
24 Derek Howse, *Greenwich Time and the Discovery of Longitude* (Oxford: Oxford University Press, 1980), 109; C. A. Schott, "Standard Railway Time," *Nature* 29 (15 Nov 1883), 70; Trish Ferguson, "Hardy's Wessex and the Birth of Industrial Subjectivity," in *idem.*, ed., *Victorian Time: Technologies, Standardizations, Catastrophes* (London: Palgrave Macmillan, 2013), 57.
25 Charles Dickens, *Dombey and Son* (New York: John Wiley, 1848), 241.
26 Ferguson, "Introduction," 5; Daragh Dawes, "The Best of Time, the Worst of Time: Temporal Consciousness in Dickens," in Ferguson, ed., *Victorian Time*, 17–18.
27 Nicholas Daly, *Literature, Technology, and Modernity, 1860–2000* (Cambridge: Cambridge University Press, 2004), 46.
28 Ferguson, "Hardy's Essex," 58.
29 *Ibid.*, 73.
30 Dawes, 16–37.
31 Ferguson, "Introduction," 2, 5.
32 Herbert Sussman, *Victorians and the Machine: The Literary Response to Technology* (Cambridge: Harvard University Press, 1968); Myron F. Brightfield, "The Coming of

the Railroad to Early Victorian England as Viewed by Novels of the Period (1840–1870)," *Technology and Culture* 3: 1 (Winter 1962), 45–72; Brightfield, *Victorian England in its Novels* (1840–1870), 4 vols. (1967–1968); Richard Altick, *Deadly Encounters: Two Victorian Sensations* (Philadelphia: University of Pennsylvania, 1986); Altick, *The Presence of the Present: Topics of the Day in the Victorian Novel* (Columbus: Ohio State University Press, 1991); Daly, *Literature, Technology, and Modernity*; Daly, "Railway Novels: Sensation Fiction and the Modernization of the Senses," *ELH* 66 (1999), 483–509; Michael Freeman, *Railways and the Victorian Imagination* (New Haven: Yale University Press, 1999); Adrian E. Gavin and Andrew F. Humphries, *Transport in British Fiction: Technologies of Movement, 1840–1940*; Anna Despotopoulou, *Women and the Railway, 1850–1915* (Edinburgh: Edinburgh University Press, 2015); Tamara Ketabgian, *The Lives of Machines: The Industrial Imaginary in Victorian Literature and Culture* (Ann Arbor: University of Michigan Press, 2011; Trish Ferguson, ed., *Victorian Time*; Diedre Coleman and Hilary Fraser, eds., *Minds, Bodies, Machines, 1770–1930* (New York: Palgrave, 2011); Charlotte Mathieson, *Mobility in the Victorian Novel* (New York: Palgrave, 2015); Clare Pettitt, "'The Annihilation of Space and Time,' Literature and Technology," in "Part IV: Matters of Debate," *Cambridge History of Victorian Literature*, Ed. Kate Flint (Cambridge: Cambridge University Press, 2012), 550–572.
33 James, 30.
34 Pettitt, 551. See also Nicholas Dames, *The Physiology of the Novel: Reading, Neural Science, and the Form of Victorian Fiction* (Oxford: Oxford University Press, 2007), 57–58.
35 Ferguson, "Introduction," 5–6.
36 Daly, "Railway Novels," 461–487.
37 *The Condition of Postmodernity: An Enquiry into the Origins of Cultural Change* (Oxford: Blackwell, 1990).
38 *Hurried to Death: or, A Few Words of Advice on the Dangers of Hurry and Excitement Especially Addressed to Railway Travellers* (London: Henry Renshaw, 1868).
39 Daly, "Railway Novels," 473.
40 Leo Marx, *The Machine in the Garden: Technology and the Pastoral Ideal in America* (New York: Oxford University Press, 1964; 2nd ed. with new Afterword, 2000), 248.
41 See Jeffrey Richards and John M. MacKenzie, *The Railway Station: A Social History* (New York: Oxford University Press, 1986), Chapter 1.
42 John Foster Fraser, *The Real Siberia* (London: Cassell, 1902), 19.
43 Bates, *passim*.
44 "The Lost Railway Station," in *The Spice of Life*, ed. Dorothy Collins (Beaconsfield: Darwen Finlayson, 1964), 132–135. Italics mine for emphasis.
45 Paul Hideyo Noguchi, "The 'One Railroad Family' of the Japanese National Railways: A Cultural Analysis of Japanese Industrial Familialism" (Ph.D. diss., University of Pittsburgh, 1977), 41–42; Noguchi, *Delayed Departures, Overdue Arrivals: Industrial Familialism and the Japanese National Railways* (Honolulu: University of Hawai'i Press, 1990), 45.
46 On these themes, see the opening chapters of Houghton; James, 1–7, 12.
47 James, 12.
48 Nicholas Daly, "Blood on the Tracks: Sensation Drama, the Railway, and the Dark Face of Modernity," *Victorian Studies* 42: 1 (Autumn, 1998–Autumn, 1999), 47–76. Scholars have traced the tangled origins of the railway scene to *Under the Gaslight* (1867). It is possible that Daly, who won an injunction to prevent American managers from performing his "scene" in productions of Boucicault's *After Dark* in New York, copied a similar story that was published in *The Galaxy Magazine* (March 1867).

But since the connection had not been clearly established, *Daly v. Palmer* found that the dramatists in New York violated Daly's copyright. Daly's play had long runs in U.S. cities, and the playwright used profits to open his own theater on Fifth Avenue in 1869. But no other creator derived as much fame as Boucicault, who wrote *After Dark* by choosing the Metropolitan subterranean railway in London as the setting, plotting back from the harrowing sensation scene of the American Daly, and gaining permission from French playwrights D'Ennery and Grangé to use their storyline. In this sense, *After Dark* was a truly cosmopolitan (re)production. See Daly, "Blood on the Tracks," 47–48; Richard Fawkes, *Dion Boucicault: A Biography* (London: Quartet, 1979), 172–173; and George Pate, "Totally Original:" Daly, Boucicault, and Commercial Art in Late Nineteenth Century Drama," *Theatre Symposium* 32: 1 (2014), 9–21; Seldon Faulkner, "The Great Train Scene Robbery," *Quarterly Journal of Speech* 50: 1 (1964), 24–28.

49 "Princess's Theatre," *Times* (London), 17 Aug. 1868: 4.
50 "Surrey Theatre," *Times* (London), 14 Sept. 1868: 6.
51 *Ibid.* Italics in the original.
52 Daly, "Blood on the Tracks," 47–48.
53 Pate, "Totally Original," 9–21.
54 Daly, "Blood on the Tracks," 48, 69.
55 *Era* 16 August 1868: 11; 3 Sept. 1868: 11. Cited in *Ibid.*, 48.
56 The theaters included the Victoria, Surrey, East London, New Standard, Princess's, Sadler's Wells, the Whitechapel Pavilion, and the Grecian Saloon in Hoxton. After initial successes, several others in Highby, Greenock, Brighton, Dublin, Hull, and Leeds featured railway rescue scenes. The individual productions that featured "the scene" were *The Scamps of London* (1843), *Land Rats and Water Rats* (1868), *Danger* (1868), and *After Dark* (1868). See Daly, "Blood on the Tracks," p. 70 fn2.
57 Pettitt, 561.
58 Quoted in Townsend Walsh, *The Career of Dion Boucicault* (New York: The Dunlap Society, 1915), 95–96; Fawkes, 148.
59 Fawkes, 197–200; Daly, "Blood on the Tracks," 53–58.
60 Daly, 61–68
61 *Ibid.*, 60.
62 Wolfgang Schivelbusch, *The Railway Journey* (Berkeley: University of California Press, 1986), 122; Daly, "Railway Novels: Sensation Fiction and the Modernization of the Senses," *ELH* 66: 2 (Summer 1999), 461–487, especially 468–471.
63 Daly, 69.
64 Pate, 9–21.
65 *Ibid.*, 20–21 fn17; Pettit, 561.
66 Daly, "Railway Novels," 470.
67 George Catlin, *Adventures of the Ojibbeway and Ioway Indians in England, France, and Belgium*, Third ed. (London: n.p., 1852); *Family Herald* 3 (1845–46), 13.
68 "Work" in *The Poetical Works of Charles Lamb* (London: E. Moxon, 1838), 93; *Fifty Years of Railway Life in England, Scotland and Ireland* (London: The Railway Gazette, 1920), 56.
69 John Pendleton, *Our Railways: Their Origin, Development, Incident and Romance*, 2 vols. (London: Cassell and Company, 1894), II: 92–98.
70 Weber, *France: Fin de Siècle*, 179–180, 190–192.
71 Pendleton, II: 72–74; C. F. Gordon Cumming, *In the Hebrides* (London: Chatto & Windus, 1883), 201–204. Quote in Pendleton.
72 John Francis, *A History of the English Railway: Its Social Relations and Revelations*, 2 vols. (London: Longman, Brown, Green, & Longmans, 1851), I: 118; Smiles, 191–193; Pendleton, I: 41–42; Carlson, 45, 71–72, 112, 143–145; Freeman, 31.

73 Thomas Roscoe, *The London and Birmingham Railway* (London: Charles Tilt, 1839), 13, 15; Williams, 74–75; Freeman, 33; David Cannadine, *Aspects of Aristocracy: Grandeur and Decline in Modern Britain* (New Haven: Yale University Press, 1994), 15, 56.
74 Williams, 74.
75 *Middlemarch*, New edition (Edinburgh and London: W. Blackwood, 1874), 408–413.
76 Victor Bayley, *Permanent Way through the Khyber* (London: Jarrolds, 1939), 22–23, 34, 38, 55, quote on 39.
77 Clark, *The Redemptive Work*, 172.
78 Jackman, I: 165–167.
79 *Ibid.*, I: 71–73 fn5, 123–124, 167.
80 Francis, II: 67–91; Smiles, 258–261.
81 Williams, 130.
82 Smiles, 258–259.
83 J. T. Middleton, "The Railway Navvy: Past and Present," in *The Jubilee of The Railway News: 50 Years of Railway Progress* (London: The Railway News, 1914), 26–27.
84 *Ibid.*, 258–261.
85 Pendleton, I: 74.
86 Anonymous, *Yesterday* (London, 1859), 260ff. Quoted in Myron F. Brightfield, "The Coming of the Railroad to Early Victorian England, as Viewed by Novels of the Period (1840–1870)," *Technology and Culture* 3: 1 (Winter, 1962), 47.
87 *The Great Highway: A Story of the World's Struggles*, Third ed. (London: G. Routledge & Co., 1854), 126–133.
88 Francis, II: 73.
89 *Ibid.*, 73–74.
90 Williams, 134.
91 Francis, II: 85; Williams, 136.
92 Harold Perkins, *The Age of the Railway* (Newton Abbot, Devon: David & Charles, 1970), 92.
93 Middleton, 26; Perkins, 91.
94 Middleton, 26.
95 Williams, 134.
96 *Ibid.*, 136.
97 Benjamin Disraeli, *Sybil or The Two Nations* (London: Longmans, Green, and Co., 1913).
98 Francis, II: 83; Williams 137–138.
99 Middleton, 26–27.
100 Robert Stephenson, "Résumé of the Railway System and its Results," in Samuel Smiles, *The Life of George Stephenson, Railway Engineer*, Fifth ed. (London: J. Murray, 1858), 515–550.
101 John R. Kellett, *The Impact of Railways on Victorian Cities* (London: Routledge & Kegan Paul, 1969), 60, 65, 69, 72, 95.
102 *Ibid.*, 95.
103 *Ibid.*, 97–98.
104 Vivien Knight, "The Private Life of William Powell Frith," in Mark Bills and Vivien Knight, eds., *William Powell Frith: Painting the Victorian Age* (New Haven and London: Yale University Press, 2006), 1, 5, 17–18.
105 Arscott, "William Powell Frith's *The Railway Station*: Classification and the Crowd," in Bills and Knight, eds., *William Powell Frith*, 79–81, quote on 79.

106 Woodcock, "'Very Efficient as a Painter': The Painting Practice of William Powell Frith, 145–156, and Cowling "Frith and his Followers: Painters and Illustrators of London 'Life'," in *Ibid*, 67–68. See also chapters by Mark Bills and David Trotter.
107 Perkins, 118.
108 Jack Simmons, *The Railways of Britain: An Historical Introduction* (London: Macmillan, 1968; New York: St. Martin's, 1968), 25–26; G. Kitson Clark, *The Making of Victorian England* (New York: Atheneum, 1976), 145–146; Pendleton, II: 82.

Part 1

THE *ROCKET*, RAINHILL TRIALS, AND EARLY PROMOTION OF RAILWAYS

1

EARLY ILLUSTRATIONS OF THE *ROCKET* AND LIVERPOOL AND MANCHESTER TRAINS

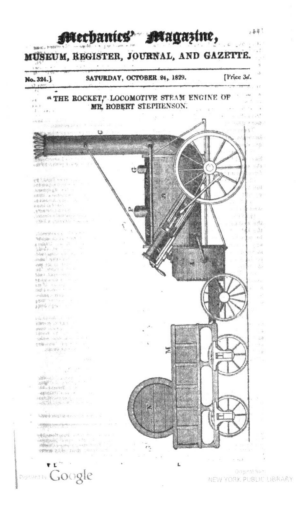

Figure 1.1 The *Rocket* with wagon car from the cover of *Mechanics' Magazine*, 24 October, 1829.

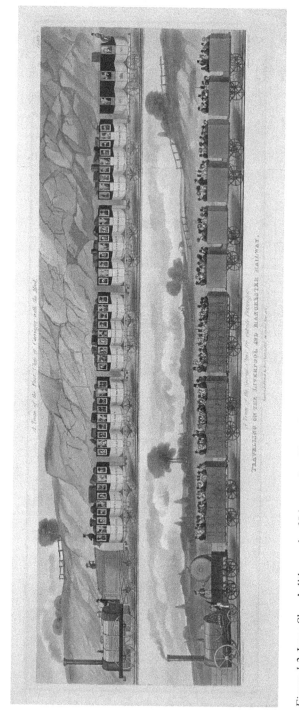

Figure 1.2 Isaac Shaw's lithograph of Liverpool and Manchester passenger train. S. G. Hughes aquatint (1831). Yale Center for British Art, Paul Mellon Collection.

Figure 1.3 Isaac Shaw's lithograph of Liverpool and Manchester freight train. S. G. Hughes aquatint (1831). Yale Center for British Art, Paul Mellon Collection.

2

THE RAINHILL TRIALS AND INAUGURATION OF THE LIVERPOOL & MANCHESTER RAILWAY, 'ACCOUNT OF THE COMPETITION OF LOCOMOTIVE STEAM-CARRIAGES ON THE LIVERPOOL AND MANCHESTER RAILWAY', IN *MECHANICS' MAGAZINE* 12: 322 (OCTOBER 10, 1829), 114–116; 12: 323 (OCTOBER 17, 1829), 135–141; 12: 324 (OCTOBER 24, 1829), 146–147; 12: 325 (OCTOBER 31, 1829), 161; 14: 372 (SEPTEMBER 25, 1830), 64–69

Grand mechanical competition – rail-road race for £500

The great rail-road between Liverpool and Manchester being now nearly completed, the directors of the undertaking sometime ago announced that they would give a premium of £500. for the locomotive engine, which should, at a public trial to be made on the 1st of the present month of October, (afterwards postponed to the 6th) draw on the railway a given weight with the greatest speed at the least expence. The offer of so handsome a premium, and the brilliant professional prospects which the winning of it presented to mechanical men, naturally exerted a very lively spirit of competition among them. In almost every quarter of the country, engine makers and engine inventors set themselves to work to secure the prize, and the result, we are happy to say, has been such as to furnish a lasting example of the wisdom of calling into action, and giving fair play to *the general talent of a country*, when any great public object has, as in the present instance, to be accomplished.

At all hands, the directors of the Liverpool and Manchester railway, deserve thanks for their conduct on this occasion, from their constituents, for the good sense and liberality which dictated a competition by which the capability of the railway, to do all that was promised, and much more, has been at once placed beyond all doubt, and the chances of a profitable return for the money invested in it increased at least tenfold; from the owners of the competing engines, for the liberal encouragement by which they were induced to *start for the plate*, and the impartial spirit, (divested of all local and personal influences) in which the competition has been conducted, and from the nation at large, for the powerful impulse which this demonstration of the extraordinary celerity with which carriages may be propelled on railways, must give to the more extensive adoption of this mode of conveyance throughout the kingdom.

The principal conditions on which the prize was offered were these:—1st. That each engine entered for the competition should weigh not more than six tons, and be capable of drawing after it, day by day, on a level plain, a train of carriages of a gross weight, equal to three times the weight of the engine itself, at a rate of not less than ten miles per hour, with a pressure of steam in the boiler not exceding 50lb. on the square inch. 2. That the engine and boiler should be supported on springs, and rest on six wheels, and the height from the ground to the top of the chimney should not exceed 15 feet. 3. That the engine should "effectually consume its own smoke;" and 4. That there should be two safety-valves, one of which should be completely out of the reach of the engine-man's interference.

The gentlemen appointed by the directors to act as judges on the occasion, were J. U. Rastrick, Esq., of Stourbridge, civil engineer, Nicholas Wood, Esq., of Killingworth, civil engineer, (author of the excellent work on railways) and John Kennedy, Esq., of Manchester.

The portion of the railway chosen for the "running ground" was on the Manchester side of Rainhill Bridge, (about nine miles from Liverpool) where the railway runs for two or three miles on a dead level.

Early on Tuesday, the day of competition, great crowds of people were assembled from all parts, to witness the sight. There were many individuals who had come hundreds of miles for no other purpose; and, as may readily be supposed, these were not idle spectacle hunters, but chiefly engineers and men of science capable of appreciating, in its full extent, the great importance of the exhibition.

The number of competitors was at first reported to be ten, and we have reason to know there was at least as many engines as this in preparation. In this new sort of race, however, as in others, there were some withdrawn, and some prevented by accidents from making their appearance; and the number was reduced on the morning of trial, to five, who were thus described in the official list of *the running coaches:*—

No. 1 Messrs. Braithwaite and Erickson, of London; "The Novelty;" copper and blue; weight, 2 tons 15 cwt.

2 Mr. Ackworth, of Darlington; "The Sans Pareil;" green, yellow, and black; weight, 4 tons, 8 cwt. 2 qrs.

THE *ROCKET*, RAINHILL TRIALS, AND EARLY PROMOTION OF RAILWAYS

3. Mr. Robert Stephenson, Newcastle-upon-Tyne; "The Rocket;" yellow and black; white chimney; weight, 4 tons, 3 cwt.
4. Mr. Brandreth, of Liverpool; "The Cycloped;" weight, 3 tons; worked by a horse.
5. Mr. Burstall, Edinburgh; "The Perseverance;" red wheels; weight, 2 tons, 17 cwt.

The engine which made the first trial, was the "Rocket" of Mr. Robert Stephenson (the son, we believe, of Mr. George Stephenson, the engineer of the railway.) It is a large and strongly-built engine, and went with a velocity, which, as long as the spectators had nothing to contrast it with, they thought surprising enough. It drew a weight of twelve tons, nine cwt. at the rate of ten miles four chains in an hour, (just exceeding the stipulated maximum,) and, when the weight was detached from it, went at a speed of about eighteen miles an hour. The faults most perceptible in this engine, were a great inequality in its velocity, and a very partial fulfilment of the condition that it should "effectually consume its own smoke."

The next engine that exhibited its powers was "The Novelty" of Messrs. Braithwaite and Erickson. The great lightness of this engine, (it is about one half lighter than Mr. Stephenson's) its compactness, and its beautiful workmanship, excited universal admiration; a sentiment speedily changed into perfect wonder, by its truly marvelous performances. It was resolved to try first its speed merely; that is at what rate it would go, carrying only its compliment of coke and water, with Messrs. Braithwaite and Erickson to manage it. Almost at once, it darted off at the amazing velocity of twenty-eight miles an hour, and it actually did one mile in the incredibly short space of one minute and 53 seconds! Neither did we observe any appreciable falling off in the rate of speed; it was uniform, steady, and continuous. Had the railway been completed, the engine would, at this rate, have gone nearly the whole way from Liverpool to Manchester within the hour; and Mr. Braithwaite has, indeed, publicly offered to stake a thousand pounds, that as soon as the road is opened, he will perform the entire distance in that time.

It was now proposed to make a trial of the "Novelty," with three times its weight attached to it; but through some inattention as to the supply of water and coke, a great delay took place in preparing it for its second trip, and by the time all was ready, the day was drawing so near to a close, that the directors thought it proper to defer the prosecution of the competition till the following day.

Second day, 7th October

"The Novelty" engine of Messrs. Braithwaite and Ericsson was this day tried with a load of three times its weight attached to it, or 11 tons, 5 cwt.; and it drew this with ease at the rate of 20¾ miles per hour: thus proving itself to be equally good for speed as for power. We took particular notice to-day of its power of consuming its own smoke, and did not any time observe the emission of the smallest particle from the chimney.

The weather now became wet, and the rail-ways clogged with mud, which made it necessary to suspend the prosecution of the experiments before the day had half elapsed. The attendance of spectators this morning was by no means so numerous as on the preceding day; but there were few of those absent—the engineers, men of science, &c.—whose presence was most desirable.

Third day, 8th October

Before the commencement of the experiments to-day, it was announced that the judges on reconsidering the card of "Stipulations and Conditions" originally issued, and of which we gave the substance last week, had considered them so defective as to make it necessary to substitute the following:—

"TRIAL OF THE LOCOMOTIVE ENGINES.
LIVERPOOL AND MANCHESTER RAILWAY.

"The following is the Ordeal which we have decided each Locomotive Engine shall undergo, in contending for the Premium of £500, at Rainhill.

"The weight of the locomotive engine, with its full complement of water in the boiler, shall be ascertained at the weighing machine, by eight o'clock in the morning, and the load assigned to it shall be three times the weight thereof. The water in the boiler shall be cold, and there shall be no fuel in the fire-place. As much fuel shall be weighed, and as much water shall be measured and delivered into the tender-carriage, as the owner of the engine may consider sufficient for the supply of the engine for a journey of thirty-five miles. The fire in the boiler shall then be lighted, and the quantity of fuel consumed for getting up the steam shall be determined, and the time noted.

"The tender-carriage, with the fuel and water, shall be considered to be, and taken as a part of the load assigned to the engine.

"Those engines that carry their own fuel and water, shall be allowed a proportionate deduction from their load, according to the weight of the engine.

"The engine, with the carriages attached to it, shall be run by hand up to the starting-post; and as soon as the steam is got up to fifty pounds per square inch, the engine shall set out upon its journey.

"The distance the engine shall perform each trip, shall be one mile and three-quarters each way, including one-eighth of a mile at each end for getting up the speed, and for stopping the train; by this means the engine with its load will travel one and a half mile each way at full speed.

"The engine shall make ten trips, which will be equal to a journey of thirty-five miles; thirty-miles whereof shall be performed at full speed, and the average rate of travelling shall not be less than ten miles per hour.

"As soon as the engine has performed this task, (which will be equal to the travelling from Liverpool to Manchester,) there shall be a fresh supply of fuel and water delivered to her; and as soon as she can be got ready to set out again, she shall go up to the starting-post, and make ten trips more, which will be equal to the journey from Manchester back again to Liverpool.

"The time of performing every trip shall be accurately noted, as well as the time occupied in getting ready to set out on the second journey.

"Should the engine not be enabled to take along with it sufficient fuel and water for the journey of ten trips, the time occupied in taking in a fresh supply of fuel and water, shall be considered and taken as a part of the time in performing the journey.

J. U. RASTRICK, Esq. Stourbridge, C. E.
NICHOLAS WOOD, Esq. Killingworth, C. E. } Judges.
JOHN KENNEDY, Esq. Manchester.
"Liverpool, Oct. 6th, 1829."

Having set these preliminary matters to right, we now proceed with our narrative of the experiments.

The engine which exhibited on this the third day was "The Rocket" of Mr. Stephenson. The trial was conducted in the manner laid down in the "Ordeal" we have just quoted; and it was understood on all hands that this trial should be considered decisive of its merits.

The engine, with its complement of water in the boiler, weighed 4 tons 5 cwt. and the load attached to it was 12 tons 15 cwt., or including a few persons who rode, about 13 tons. The journey was 1½ mile each way, with an additional length of 220 yards at each end to stop the engine in, making in one journey 3½ miles. The first experiment was for 35 miles, which is exactly 10 journeys, and, including all the stoppages at the ends, was performed in 3 hours and 10 minutes, being upwards of 11 miles an hour. After this a fresh supply of water was taken in, which occupied 16 minutes, when the engine again started, and ran 35 miles in 2 hours and 52 minutes, which is upwards of 12 miles an hour, including all stoppages. The speed of the engine, with its load, when in full motion, was, at different times, 13, 13½, 14, and 16 miles an hour; and, had the whole distance been in one continued direction, there is little doubt but the result would have been 15 miles an hour. The consumption of coke was on an average about half a ton in the 70 miles.

Fourth day, 9th October

To-day a public notice appeared from Messrs. Braithwaite and Ericsson, stating, that in consequence of the alterations made in the conditions of the competition, the trial of their engine in the manner prescribed by the new "Ordeal," had, with the approbation of the judges, been deferred till the following day. The 9th became thus a *dies non* in the competition.

Fifth day, 10th October

At the appointed hour this morning "The Novelty" was weighed, and three times its weight assigned to it by the judges. The steam was got up in 54 minutes from the time of lighting the fire. The engine then went one trip by way of rehearsal, when a small pipe accidentally gave way, and it was found necessary to send to Prescot, a distance of two miles, to have it repaired.[1]

In the interval, Mr. Stephenson's locomotive engine was run twice down the course and back, making in all 7 miles, but with the whole load taken off from behind, including even the tender-carriage with the water-tank and fuel. Thus *stripped for the race*, "The Rocket" performed the seven miles in the space of 14 minutes 14 seconds, being at the rate of 30 miles an hour! This was a rate of speed nearly equal to the utmost which "The Novelty" had achieved; but as it carried with it neither fuel nor water, it is not a speed which it could have long sustained.

"The Novelty," having now had its broken pipe repaired, made several trips, but solely for the gratification of the spectators, who were to-day extremely numerous, and not with any view to a decisive exhibition of its powers.

Another carriage, with seats for the accommodation of passengers, was now substituted for the loaded waggons attached to "The Novelty," and about forty-five ladies and gentlemen ascended to enjoy the great novelty of a ride by steam. We can say for ourselves that we never enjoyed any thing in the way of travelling more. We flew along at the rate of a mile and a half in three minutes; and though the velocity was such, that we could scarcely distinguish objects as we passed by them, the motion was so steady and equable, that we could manage not only to read, but write.

Sixth day, 13th October

Mr. Acworth's engine, "The Sans Pareil," was pronounced to be this day ready to exhibit its powers. We were informed that, on weighing it, the judges found it to exceed by two or three hundred-weight the maximum of six tons; it was, nevertheless, allowed to start to do 70 miles, in the same manner as "The Rocket," with three times its great weight attached to it—that is, upwards of 1800 tons. It was soon manifest that a very powerful competitor had entered the field. For two hours "The Sans Pareil" kept going with great regularity, and during that time completed upwards of 25 miles. It went occasionally, when at its utmost speed, a mile in 4' 10" and 4' 17", being at the rate of nearly 15 miles an hour. While thus bidding fair—if not to win the prize, at least to come in second best—a similar accident happened to it as befel "The Novelty;" one of the feed pipes burst, and it was rendered for the time incapable of proceeding.

We understand the judges subsequently resolved that "The Sans Pareil" should have another trial on Friday, the 16th.

Seventh day, 14th October

It being generally understood that this was to be the day of a more decisive trial of Messrs. Braithwaite and Ericsson's engine—that is, according to the new conditions named by the judges—there was almost as numerous an assemblage of spectators as on the first day of the competition.

A fresh pipe had, it appeared, been substituted for the one which failed on the preceding trial; one or two other parts of the machinery that were in a faulty state, had also been renovated; but the engine, with the exception of some of the flanges of the boiler being as Mr. Ericsson expressed it, rather *green*, was pronounced in a working state.

The steam was on this occasion got up to a pressure of 50lbs. in somewhat less than 40 minutes, and at an expenditure of about 15lbs. of coke.

The engine now started to do the 70 miles for a continuance; but just as it had completed its second trip of three miles, when it was working at the rate of 15 miles an hour, the new cement of some of the flanges of the boiler, yielded to the high temperature to which it was exposed, and the spectators had again the mortification to hear it announced that it was, under these circumstances, impossible the trial could go on.

Mr. Burstall's engine, "The Perseverance," which had met with an injurious accident on its way to Liverpool, but been since repaired, was now allowed to make some experimental trials. We left it returning from a third or fourth trip; but if we may judge from the degree of speed which it then exhibited—not more, certainly, than five miles an hour—it has no chance.

We were informed that, early on Wednesday morning, before we reached the course, an experiment had been made with Mr. Stephenson's engine on a part of the railway which runs with an inclination of 1 in 96, and that it drew up this plane a carriage containing 25 passengers, with great ease.

Seventh day, 14th October

It appears that after we left the railway on Wednesday se'nnight, and took our departure for town, Messrs. Braithwaite and Ericsson intimated to the judges, that as the joints of "The Novelty" which had given way, could not be restored to a working state before the lapse of at least eight days, and the prolongation of the competition was likely to be attended with great inconvenience to many parties, they would withdraw their engine from any further trial, and "leave it to be judged of by the performances it had already exhibited."

Now, though we are of opinion that "The Novelty" is the sort of engine that will be found best adapted to the purposes of the railway, and are inclined to think that "The Sans Pareil" is at least as good an engine as "The Rocket;" yet as neither the one nor the other has equalled "The Rocket" in a performance, which had the winning of the prize of £500 expressly for its object, we do not see how the Directors can in justice do otherwise than award that prize to Mr. Stephenson. Besides, whatever may be the merits of "The Rocket," as contrasted with either of its rivals, it is so much superior to all the old locomotive engines in use, as to entitle Mr. Stephenson to the most marked and liberal consideration, for the skill and ingenuity displayed in its construction.

Opening of the railway, 15th September, 1830

The arrangements made for the important ceremonial of finally opening the railway for public traffic, were extremely judicious, and reflected great credit on all concerned. All the loose stones and rubbish which lay at the mouths of the tunnels, and on different parts of the line, were removed; the rails had been well swept; and strong paling was erected along the high ground on each side of the deep cuttings for several miles, to protect the spectators from the danger of falling over, in their eagerness to witness the procession. There were also constables and soldiers in abundance to assist in keeping the railway clear, and impressing on the multitude some regard for their lives and limbs. The persons to whom places were assigned in the procession were requested to assemble at the company's station in Crownstreet, not later than half-past nine in the morning. Each engine and its train of carriages had distinguishing flags; the colours of the admission-cards corresponded with those of the flags, and every card bore the number of the seat which was allotted to its fortunate possessor. The business of marshalling the company was thus literally rendered of a self-acting description. Each person had only to do as he was directed, and all chance of confusion was sure to be avoided.

The number of locomotive engines employed on the occasion was eight, named as follows:—The Northumbrian, the Phœnix, the North Star, the Rocket, the Dart, the Comet, the Arrow, the Meteor. The whole of these engines have been built by Messrs. Stephenson and Co., of Newcastle. The Rocket our readers will at once recognise as an old acquaintance; the rest are constructed on a similar plan, differing from it only in dimensions and in some indifferent matters of arrangement. It was expected that three engines, constructed by Messrs. Braithwaite and Ericsson, on their patent principle, would have been also in readiness, namely, the far-famed Novelty, and two new engines which Messrs. B. and E. had contracted to build for the Railway Company, not exceeding five tons weight, and capable of drawing 40 tons gross, at the rate of 15 miles an hour—the consumption of coke not to exceed half a pound weight per ton per mile. But these engines not having arrived from London early enough to be subjected to a preliminary trial, the directors thought it would not be prudent to allow them to make part of a procession which it was of the utmost consequence should be exposed to as few risks of failure as possible. The whole of Messrs. Stephenson and Co.'s engines had, we believe, been repeatedly tried, and with success, several weeks before.

The Northumbrian was appointed to take the lead of the procession, drawing a splendid carriage, appropriated to the reception of the Duke of Wellington, Sir Robert Peel, and about thirty other distinguished individuals, who honoured the ceremony with their presence. Each of the other locomotives drew four carriages, containing between eighty and ninety persons. So that the total number of individuals accommodated with seats in the procession, must have been about 600. It fell to our lot to make part of the train of the Arrow, the seventh engine in the line of procession.

At twenty minutes to eleven o'clock the procession commenced its progress towards Manchester, the Northumbrian taking exclusively one of the two lines of rail, and the rest of the engines the other. The brilliancy of the *cortege*—the novelty of the sight—considerations of the almost boundless advantages of the stupendous power about to be put in operation—gave to the spectacle an interest unparalleled. On every side the tumultuous voice of praise was heard, and countless thousands waved their hats to cheer on the sons of enterprise in this their crowning effort. The engines proceeded at a moderate speed towards Wavertree-lane, when increased power having been added, they went forward with great swiftness, and thousands fell back, whom all the previous efforts of a formidable police could not move from the road. Numerous booths and vehicles lined the various roads, and were densely crowded. After passing Wavertree-lane, the procession entered the deep ravine at Olive Mount, and the eye of the passenger could scarcely find time to rest on the multitudes that lined the roads, or admire the various bridges thrown across this great monument of human labour. Shortly afterwards Rainhill bridge was neared, and the inclined plane of Sutton began to be ascended at a more slackened rate. The summit was soon gained, and twenty-four miles an hour became the maximum of the speed. About noon the procession passed over the Sankey viaduct. The scene at this part was particularly striking. The fields below were occupied by thousands, who cheered us as we passed over the stupendous edifice: carriages filled the narrow lanes, and vessels in the water had been detained, in order that their crews might gaze up at the gorgeous pageant passing far above their mast heads. Shortly after we passed the borough of Newton, and reached Parkside, 17 miles from Liverpool Here the engines stopped to take in a supply of water and fuel, and many of the company having alighted in the interval, were walking about congratulating each other on the truly delightful treat they were enjoying, all hearts bounding with joyous excitement, and every tongue eloquent in the praise of the gigantic work now completed, and the advantages and pleasures it afforded. A murmur and an agitation at a little distance now betokened something alarming, and too soon we learnt the particulars of an accident which has justly created the deepest sorrow throughout the Empire.

The Phœnix and North Star having taken in their supplies of water and fuel, had resumed their journey, and passed the Northumbrian, which remained stationary on the other line, in order that the whole train of carriages might here pass in review before the Duke of Wellington and his party. Several gentlemen embraced the opportunity to alight from the state carriage, and were walking about on the road; among the number was Mr. Huskisson, who caught the eye of the Duke of Wellington. A recognition immediately followed, when the duke extended his hand, which Mr. Huskisson advanced to take. At this moment the Rocket came rapidly forward upon the other line, and a cry of danger was raised. Several gentlemen succeeded in regaining the state carriage, but Mr. Huskisson, who was in a weak state of health, and one of whose limbs was somewhat tender, became flurried, and, after making two attempts to cross the road upon which the Rocket was moving, ran back, in a state of great agitation, to the side of the duke's carriage. White, the engineer, saw the unfortunate gentleman, as the engine approached, in a position of imminent danger, and immediately endeavoured to arrest its progress, but without success. Mr. Holmes, M.P., who had not been able to get into the carriage, stood next to Mr. Huskisson, and, perceiving that he had altogether lost his presence of mind, seeming like a man bewildered, cried out, "For God's sake, Mr. Huskisson, be firm!"—The space between the two lines of rails is just four feet; but, the state car being eight feet wide, extended two feet beyond the rail on which it moved, thus diminishing the space to *two feet* between its side and the rail on which the Rocket was moving. The engine, besides, projected somewhat over the rail on which it ran, still farther diminishing the standing room to not more, perhaps, than *one foot and a half*, when the vehicles were side by side on the opposite rails. To make matters worse the door of the state car happened to be *three feet* broad, and, when on the full swing, extended *one foot beyond* the rail on which the Rocket moved; so that it was impossible for that engine to pass without striking it. Of this door Mr. Huskisson had grasped hold, when he stepped back, after his vain attempts to cross the road, when warned of the approach of the Rocket. Mr. Littleton, M.P. for Staffordshire, who had sprung into the state car, had just "pulled in" (to use his own expression) Prince Esterhazy, when he saw Mr. Huskisson, alarmed and agitated, with his hand on the door, which he seemed to grasp with a kind of trembling or convulsive hold. At this moment the Rocket struck the door, and Mr. Huskisson was thrown to the ground, across one of the rails of the line on which the engine was advancing, the wheels of which went over his leg and thigh, and fractured them in so dreadful a manner as to produce death, before the lapse of many hours.

The Duke of Wellington and Sir Robert Peel now with great propriety of feeling, expressed a wish that the procession, instead of going forward to Manchester, should return to Liverpool, and the directors acquiesced in the proposition. The directors, however, on reconsideration, thought the policy of this course doubtful. Another consultation was accordingly held, in the midst of which, Mr. Hulton, of Hulton, a magistrate, came up, and stated to his grace, that if the procession did not reach Manchester, where an unprecedented concourse of people would be assembled, and would wait for it, he should be fearful of the consequences to the peace of the town. The duke remarked, "There is something in that." Sir Robert Peel then said, "Where are these directors? Let us see them;" and his grace and the right honourable baronet moved to the spot where the directors were in deliberation. A circle was formed round the group, and the point was discussed at much length. Some of the directors observed, that they were but trustees for property to an immense amount; that the value of that property might be affected, if the procession did not go on, and thus demonstrate the practicability of locomotive travelling on an extensive scale: and that, though the illustrious duke and his *cortége* might not deem it prudent to proceed, it was the duty of the directors to complete the ceremony of opening the road. The Boroughreeve of Manchester repeated and enforced the arguments respecting the difficulty of preserving the public peace, if the assembled thousands were not gratified by a sight of the procession at Manchester. This reasoning having great weight, the Duke of Wellington acquiesced in the opinion of the directors. His grace then proposed, that the whole party should proceed, but return as soon as possible, and refrain from all festivity at Manchester.

The procession accordingly resumed its onward progress, and reached Manchester at a quarter before three. Neither the Duke of Wellington nor any of his party alighted, but the greater portion of the company in the other carriages descended as they arrived, and were shown into the large upper rooms of the company's warehouses, where they hastily partook of a cold collation.

After a delay of more than two hours at Manchester—a delay, the cause of which every one felt at a loss to comprehend—it turned out that the van of the procession, including the state carriage containing the Duke of Wellington and his friends, and one train of four carriages, had taken their departure an hour before, and that the detention of the remainder was owing to the absence of three of their engines, which had gone forward to Eccles to obtain a fresh supply of water and fuel, but missed their way back. The twenty-four vehicles thus left behind were now formed into one continuous line, with the three remaining engines at their head; and at twenty minutes past five o'clock we set out on our return to Liverpool. The engines not having the power, however, to drag along the double load that had devolved upon them at a faster rate than from five to ten miles an hour (once or twice only, and that but for a few minutes, did it reach the rate of twelve miles an hour), it was past eight o'clock before we reached Parkside, the scene of Mr. Huskisson's melancholy accident, Here the engines again stopped to water, and a good deal of time was wasted in the operation. Proceeding onwards, we were met on the Kenyon embankment by two of the missing engines, which were immediately attached to the three which had drawn us from Manchester. It would be superfluous to inquire how it was that we happened to be deprived of the assistance of these engines, since, instead of now accelerating our progress, they seemed actually to retard it. We went still slower than before—stopping continually to take in water (query, to take breath), and creeping along at a snail's pace, till we reached Sutton inclined plane; to get up which the greater part of the company were under the necessity of alighting, and making use of their own legs. On reaching the top of the plane, we once more took our seats, and at ten o'clock we found ourselves again at the company's station in Crownstreet, having accomplished the distance of 33 miles in 4 hours and 40 minutes.

The accident

While we lament the fate of Mr. Huskisson, we cannot but inquire how it happened that the steam-carriage which caused the dreadful accident was not stopped before it had come in contact with the unfortunate gentleman? In all the accounts which we have seen, a great deal is said about the alarm created in the mind of Mr. Huskisson, and of the persons in whose company he was, at the sight of the Rocket coming on with portentous velocity, while they were standing on the railway, near the carriage of the Duke of Wellington. We are told of the various ways in which the persons who were so circumstanced endeavoured to escape from the threatened danger; some of them getting into the carriage, some scrambling round it, and others clinging to the frame-work; but all leaving the unhappy Mr. Huskisson to his fate, although an invalid, who had lately risen from a bed of sickness, and could not be supposed to possess either the vigour of Mr. Holmes or the activity of Mr. Calcraft, to enable him to escape the approaching ruin. While this was going on, and while among those admirers of mechanical enterprise, *sauve que peut* was the principle of motion, why did not the person in command of the Rocket put an end to their apprehensions and to the danger at once, by instantly stopping the machine? Could he do it, or could he not? The writers who describe the engines praise them no less for their power than their *manageableness*. One of our correspondents said they were as easily managed as ponies, and he could hardly believe but they were endued with animal life. Another said they more deserved the name of creatures than of machines—meaning thereby, we presume, that their action seemed rather the effect of volition than of any mechanical arrangement. Why, then, was not this *manageable quality* displayed under circumstances so well calculated to call it forth? What would be said of a coachman who, on seeing the alarm that the swiftness of his horses caused to a group of persons so circumstanced as Mr. Huskisson and his friends were, did not stop them before one of the party was crushed under his wheels? We observe, that the finding of the coroner's jury does not attribute blame to any person, and we are willing to believe that the engineer did all that lay in his power; but it makes us have no very high idea of the control under which these steam-carriages are, which we were told were as manageable as ponies! The living creatures that draw carriages, not being machines, sometimes run away, and become more furious by the attempt to restrain them; but steam-carriages, if once the principle of immediate control over their action be obtained, are always, of course, capable of being instantly stopped. Now, as it was some time, according to all the published statements of this melancholy affair, before any mischief was done, that Mr. Huskisson and his friends saw the Rocket approach, and exhibited by their actions the sense of great peril, why, if it were only to prevent confusion and quiet their apprehensions, did not the Rocket, we again ask, immediately stop? This wants explanation, and that explanation was not given on the coroner's inquest, where it appears only one witness, and he a nobleman, was examined. There were, we apprehend, many plain mechanics who could have given a better explanation of the matter than the Earl of Wilton; but we suppose the coroner considered aristocratic evidence of so much more value than plebeian testimony, that, in a case of which ten or twelve commoners would have been examined, their information was rendered unnecessary by the statement of a solitary lord. But it may turn out that all the published accounts of the accident and the report of the inquest are incorrect, and instead of Mr. Huskisson having seen the Rocket, and the conductor of the Rocket having seen him some time before the fatality, it may have been that the whole thing happened without any previous time for preparation, in which case, indeed, no blame could rest either on the conductor, or the machine which he was appointed to guide and control.— *Morning Herald.*

The preceding observations are evidently intended, and it is to be feared are but too well calculated to excite a prejudice against the employment of steam carriages at a high rate of speed. It is of importance, therefore, to ascertain how the matter of fact really stands. The writer in the *Morning Herald* asks, apparently in a tone of defiance, whether the engine *could* have been stopped in time to prevent the melancholy accident? If the fact be, as we have been informed, it is—that the *sauve qui peut* movements of the gentlemen round the car of the Duke of Wellington were noticed by the engineer and other persons on the Rocket, at a distance of at least fifty yards, we have no hesitation in saying decidedly that it must have been owing to a fault somewhere, that the engine was not stopped. The gear of an engine can be reversed almost instantaneously, and the momentum of any weight attached to it can be checked by what is technically called a break; and if there had been a due use of these expedients in the present instance, no accident would have occurred. We have seen an engine of more power than the Rocket brought, while going at a rate of 18 miles an hour, to a standstill, within a space of less than twenty yards, and the Rocket is stated to have been going at the rate of no more than 8 or 10 miles. Whether it was owing to any defectiveness in the arrangements for reversing the gear of the Rocket, and applying the break, or to want of attention in the engineer and breaksman, that the engine was not stopped, we are not prepared to say; and we agree with the *Herald*, that these were points which it fell peculiarly within the province of the coroner's inquest to ascertain, and which it is much to be regretted they did not ascertain. We are inclined to think that it must have been the reversing gear, and not the engineer, which was in fault; an opinion which we formed on what we observed of another accident caused on a subsequent day by a fellow engine of the Rocket's, and which only great good luck prevented from being still more disastrous. On Tuesday night last, the Phœnix was exercising at the Manchester end of the line, and running at great velocity, when it came into contact with one of the railway waggons, which had, through some inadvertence, been left on the same line, and such was the force of the concussion, that the waggon, though weighing at least a couple of tons, was lifted bodily off the rails and projected to a distance of, at least, fifty yards! Crowds of people were looking on, and but that the waggon took the direction of an unoccupied space of ground, a great many lives must have been lost. The engineer was asked—"Why he had not reversed the gear of his engine when he perceived the waggon before him?" His answer was, that "he had reversed it, but that it was of no use—the engine could not be stopped." We saw good reason to believe that this was really the fact; and we think it probable, that if a similar question had been put to the engineer of the Rocket, we should have had a similar answer.

But is it to be permitted, that there should be a possibility of such destructive accidents occurring from a mere inefficiency of machinery? Why should not the power of the reversing gear of every engine be tested before it is allowed to run? It seems to us that Parliament would do well to pass a law, enacting that no locomotive-carriage shall run on a public railway which is not provided with machinery sufficient to stop it when going at any velocity within a space of twenty or thirty yards; and a regulation which it would be wise in Parliament to enact, it would not be discreditable to a public-spirited body of individuals like the directors of the Liverpool and Manchester Railway alone to adopt of their own accord.

Commencement of traffic on the railway

On the Thursday morning after the opening of the railway, the Northumbrian left Liverpool with 130 passengers, and arrived at Manchester in one hour and fifty minutes. In the evening it returned with 120 passengers and 3 tons of luggage in one hour and forty-eight minutes. This was the first journey performed for hire; the fare charged was 7*s.* each.

On Friday, the 17th, six carriages commenced running regularly between the two towns; one starting from each place at the hours of seven in the morning, twelve at noon, and four in the afternoon. On Sunday the mid-day trip is dispensed with, that it may not interfere with the hours of Divine Service. The time occupied in the journey is seldom more than two hours, and often less.

Note

1 Things should have been better ordered. In any future competition, we would recommend that there should be a forge at hand, with all the necessary tools and materials, for repairing instantly any accident of this sort.

3

CHARLES MACLAREN, *RAILWAYS COMPARED WITH CANALS & COMMON ROADS, AND THEIR USES AND ADVANTAGES EXPLAINED* (EDINBURGH: CONSTABLE, 1825), PP. 48–54

TIBERIUS travelled 200 miles in two days, and this was reckoned an extraordinary effort. But in our times a shopkeeper or mechanic travels twice as fast as the Roman Emperor, and twenty years hence he may probably travel with a speed that would leave the fleetest courser behind. Such a new power of locomotion cannot be introduced without working a vast change in the state of society. With so great a facility and celerity of communication, the provincial towns of an empire would become so many suburbs of the metropolis—or rather the effect would be similar to that of collecting the whole inhabitants into one city. Commodities, inventions, discoveries, opinions, would circulate with a rapidity hitherto unknown, and above all, the intercourse of man with man, nation with nation, and province with province, would be prodigiously increased.

Hitherto the superiority of the railway has been deduced chiefly from the facilities it affords for employing a high velocity. But we should err widely if we supposed that its advantages depend solely on this circumstance.

1   The railway has this very great advantage over the canal, that it can generally be made at one-third of the expense. Hence the means are easier raised; the undertaking is less hazardous; and where a miscalculation occurs, failure is less ruinous. The railway also is less destructive to property. It does not interfere with drains, or load the neighbouring grounds with an excess of moisture; or interpose so formidable a barrier between the contiguous portions of an estate. It is practicable in a much greater variety of situations. It does not, like the canal, require a supply of water; it can be carried through bogs, beds of gravel, rocks full of fissures, and even quick sands. It can at all times dispense with a perfect level, and if necessary, it may ascend a hill. Its inclined planes, even with stationary engines, will probably be less expensive than canal locks, and will be passed with less loss of time.

2   In two points the canal may be allowed to have some superiority. It is not shut by snow; and the pathway not being confined to distinct lines, but extending over every foot of its surface, the passing and repassing of a throng of boats presents less difficulty than that of waggons on a railway. On the other hand, the navigation of the canal is obstructed or closed by ice in winter, and droughts in summer; and when thorough repairs are wanted at a single spot, the communication between its extremities is entirely interrupted. These disadvantages do not apply to the railway.

3   In the canal a more rapid rate of motion than 4 miles an hour is impracticable, or at least is very destructive, and hence it scarcely admits of the application of steam power. Even though an extravagant scale of expense were adopted, and the breadth and depth so much enlarged that steam-power might be employed, it has been shewn that, from the nature of the resisting medium, a high velocity could not be obtained without a prodigious waste of power. The great superiority of the railroad in this point has been already explained. Here, too, it may be observed, that though the indefinite breadth of the waterway in the open sea, renders the resistance perhaps one-third or one-fourth less than in a canal, yet the advantage is more than counterbalanced by the inequality of action in the paddle-wheels, produced by the winds and waves.

4   Railways have this grand advantage, that they may either be usefully combined with the ordinary roads of a country, or be substituted for them, and expanded into a general system of internal communication. Canals, on the other hand, though they facilitate the transportation of commodities between distant parts greatly, are only applicable in peculiar situations, and they incorporate but imperfectly with the ordinary channels of communication. They are rather something foreign and extrinsic introduced for a special purpose, than a constituent part of the general system by which the familiar intercourse between district and district is carried on. Though canal carriage, for instance, is but one-fourth of the expense of carting, a farmer who has produce to send twenty miles, of which a canal would carry it eighteen, will rather send his carts the whole distance, than take the use of the boat, with the trouble and loss of time attending shipping and unshipping. Railways, partly from their comparative cheapness, and still more because they are practicable in all situations, and upon inclined as well as level ground, may be ramified over a whole country, and become the universal medium of communication. Not only every town and village, but every considerable farm, may have its branch. And although in the extreme branches the inclination should be unfavourable, and the road of a ruder and cheaper kind, it will still correspond in its scale with the main trunk; and the waggon loaded at the farm, though it may require an additional horse in the first and less perfect part of its course, will proceed to the distant market town, without the necessity of transferring its load to another vehicle. The expense and time are thus saved, and the chances of injury avoided, arising from the transference of commodities

from one vehicle to another. Let us take an instance. Coals are brought to Edinburgh by the Union Canal, from a distance of 27 miles. They are conveyed from the pit in waggons, along a road or railway. From the waggon they are transferred to the boat; from the boat, after completing the voyage, to the wharf; from the wharf to the cart; and from the cart to the cellar of the consumer. To say nothing of the injury done to the great coal in these numerous shiftings (though that is very considerable), let us look to the expense. The loading and unloading of the boat costs about 8d. per ton; the loading of the cart and the carting, 1s.—in all 1s. 8d., which is nearly one-fifth of the price to the consumer. This extra expense might be avoided by the railroad, for the same waggon which received the coals at the pit, would pass along the branch and main trunk to the city; and when it arrived there, by slipping on different wheels, or covering its proper wheels with a circular case, it could be made to traverse the streets, and carry its load to the consumer's door. But when railways become general, it is probable that all the principal streets of a city will be fitted with tracts of smooth stone, along which a single horse will be able to drag two or three tons. Produce or goods sent to town from a farm or manufactory in the country, could be loaded in the owner's own waggon, then driven with horses along a branch railway, and when it arrived at the main trunk, the horses might return; the waggon could be attached with a train of others to the locomotive engine, and so conveyed to the city under the care of the owner's servant, if he chose. By this means the chances of breakage to which delicate articles are exposed in unloading and reloading, and the chances of theft when property is committed to the care of the servants of third parties, would be avoided.

In laying down Railroads, it is desirable to keep circumstances of this kind in view, for two reasons. 1. That lines may not be chosen which are merely adapted to some local or limited object—such as the transportation of coal or iron, but such as, without sacrifising objects of this kind, would be calculated to serve the purpose of general thoroughfares for every species of internal intercourse. 2. That the Railroad, by its form, breadth, strength, and other qualities, should be adapted for such an extended and general system of communication. 3. And what is of very great importance, *that Railroads designed to serve as commercial thoroughfares, should in every part of the country be made upon one uniform scale,* that the vehicles which ply upon one may be capable of plying upon all. Unless this is attended to, the waggons and steam coaches adapted to one Railroad will be of as little use when brought to another, as a cart is when its load is to be carried on a Canal. Counties and districts would in truth be isolated by this want of system, and each, though provided with the most perfect railroads, would be impervious to the travelling machines of the county or district adjoining.

Nothing but experience can tell us correctly the form and proportions of a railroad best calculated for a great system of internal communication. But as we must start upon some plan, in order that this provisional plan may be as perfect as possible, it is extremely desirable that we should anticipate, as far as we can, the future results of extensive practice, by experiments skilfully made upon a large scale. To render these experiments satisfactory, they should not be confided to mere practical men. A person who is not thoroughly instructed in the powers and properties of matter, and the principles of mechanics, cannot devise experiments so as to meet all the difficulties of the subject; and in the results to which they lead, truths will escape his eye, which would be obvious to the man of science.

4

NINETEENTH-CENTURY ENGRAVINGS, LITHOGRAPHS, AND PRINTS

Figure 4.1 "View of the Entrance to the Liverpool and Manchester Railway." *Mechanics' Magazine* XIV: 342 (September 25, 1830).

Figure 4.2 Isaac Shaw. "View on the Liverpool and Manchester Railway with the Locomotive "Twin Sisters" in a Siding." (1830). Yale Center for British Art, Paul Mellon Collection.

Figure 4.3 Isaac Shaw. "Opening of the Liverpool and Manchester Railway," (1830). Yale Center for British Art, Paul Mellon Collection.

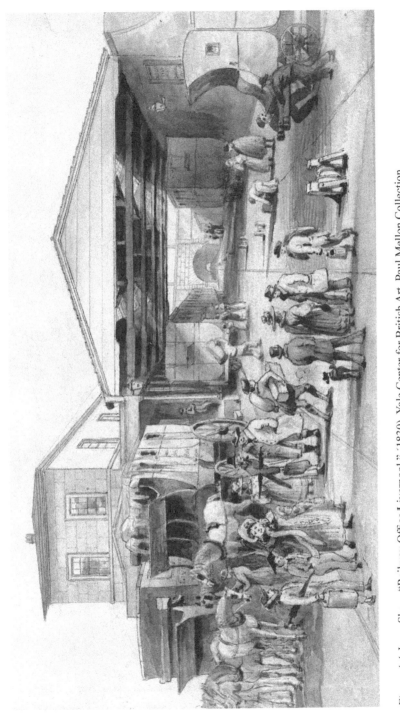

Figure 4.4 Isaac Shaw. "Railway Office Liverpool," (1830). Yale Center for British Art, Paul Mellon Collection.

Figure 4.5 "Metropolitan Railway." *The Wonders of the Universe: A Record of Things Wonderful and Marvelous in Nature, Science, and Art* (New York: Cassell & Co., 1885), 53.

Part 2

ENGINEERING ENEMIES

5

JOSEPH SANDARS, *A LETTER ON THE SUBJECT OF THE PROJECTED RAIL ROAD BETWEEN LIVERPOOL AND MANCHESTER*. SECOND ED. (LONDON: W. WALES, 1824), PP. 3–32

> *To the Members of both Houses of Parliament, and to the Merchants, Manufacturers, and Others, interested in the Conveyance of Goods between Liverpool and Manchester.*

My Lords and Gentlemen,

At a period when the profits of Trade, Commerce, and Manufactures are almost entirely dependant on economy, the enormous charge for the freight of goods between this port and Manchester is become quite insufferable, and its reduction so intimately connected with the general prosperity of the country, that I do not deem any apology necessary for drawing your attention to the subject.

I have chosen the present moment as the most proper, because I believe an application will be made to Parliament in the ensuing Session, for an Act to form a Rail-way between this town and Manchester, a measure which was contemplated two years ago; and after you have read what I shall submit to your consideration, you will perhaps have less difficulty in coming to a decision whether such a project is entitled to your support.

In endeavouring to unmask a monopoly, and to penetrate into the contrivances which 60 years cunning experience have suggested, I presume allowance will be conceded for any immaterial errors. It is almost impossible that *perfect* accuracy should be attained on such subjects; and I make this declaration the more readily, because those errors may possibly pass uncontradicted; for it is by no means difficult to imagine the impolicy of entering on a defence, where what has been exposed bears no proportion to that which has escaped detection.

It is perhaps unnecessary to state to you, that the two principal lines of Water conveyance between this port and Manchester, pass under the names of the "Duke of Bridgewater's Canal," and the "Old Quay" or "Mersey and Irwell Navigation;"

the first enters the Mersey at Runcorn, 16 miles above Liverpool; the latter making nearly the whole passage by the rivers Mersey and Irwell; but it will be quite necessary to our investigation to inquire when the parties concerned obtained the Acts of Parliament, and what were the conditions which they undertook to perform.[1]

The Duke obtained his Acts in 1760, 1762, and 1766, and the Old Quay Proprietors, only 39 in number, in 1733.

To such persons as have not perused the Acts of Parliament obtained by the Duke, I must set out with informing them, that his Grace is bound not to charge more than 2s. 6d. per ton for Canal dues, and for this charge of 2s. 6d. he is bound to find all persons carrying goods on his Canal with wharfage or warehouse room for a certain period. He also bound himself not to charge more than 6s. per ton, tonnage included, for any goods which he may carry by his own vessels. *(See note a.)* Now, how far his Grace and the Trustees named in his will have fulfilled these engagements, I will endeavour to show.

Shortly after the Duke obtained his Acts, the Trent and Mersey or Grand Trunk Proprietors obtained an Act for making a Canal to connect the Trent and Mersey Rivers.[2] It happened that the Engineer of his Grace was appointed Engineer for the Trent and Mersey Canal Company; and as he was surveying the line for this Company, from Preston Brook to Runcorn, he discovered that it would be the very best which the Duke could adopt for his. His Grace, therefore, entered into an arrangement with the Trent and Mersey Company, by which the two Canals were to unite at Preston Brook; and his Grace contracted to cut from thence to Runcorn, under the Trent and Mersey Act, at his own expense, for which he was to receive, as a consideration, a tonnage duty of 6d. per ton on all goods which were destined to enter the Trent and Mersey at Preston Brook. This sum, however, his Grace exacts on all goods which are conveyed from Liverpool to Manchester, in addition to the 2s. 6d. allowed by his own Acts, although it is evident that he must have brought his Canal to Runcorn, even if he had not made that advantageous arrangement with the Trent and Mersey Company, and for no greater compensation than that allowed by his own Acts. He thus converted an arrangement, in all respects beneficial to himself, into a pretext for exacting a greater sum than by law allowed. By this device the tonnage duty, between Liverpool and Manchester, was raised from 2s. 6d. to 3s. But this was not all. His Grace bound himself to the Trent and Mersey Company, that if he ever found it necessary to deviate from the line specified in their Act, or had occasion to make increased accommodation at Runcorn, still no more than 6d. per ton should be charged. His Grace soon found that the Lock which connects the Canal with the tide-way of the Mersey was quite inadequate to pass one-fourth of the vessels which appeared; but, instead of fulfilling the true meaning of the Act, he constructed a large Reservoir, into which vessels, destined to enter his Canal, were admitted at tide time. This he pretended to construct for the convenience and despatch of his own vessels; but he has had the kindness to permit those of other carriers, on the condition that they pay him 1s. per ton for the privilege, and this he collects on goods passing along his *own* Canal as well as on those destined for the Trent and Mersey. By this second device he raised his tonnage dues to 4s. per ton. It is very true that vessels may pass by the Old Lock if they choose; but it is also true, that, if he choose to block up the passage with one or two of his own, he can compel every carrier to enter his Reservoir; and I may assert, without fear of contradiction, that in point of fact it is impossible for a carrier to resist the exaction without a great sacrifice of time. But the third and last device, for adding 1s. 2d. more to the tonnage dues, remains to be pointed out. At the time the Rochdale Canal Company obtained their Act for cutting a line from Rochdale to Manchester, his Grace obtained permission to make the Lock which now connects his Canal with the Rochdale; and for this he was empowered to levy 1s. 2d. on all goods which passed his Lock, for the avowed purpose of indemnifying himself from the loss which his warehouse property might sustain by the junction in question: but, in consideration of this, he was bound to find warehouse room, gratis, for a certain limited time. (*b*) It will scarcely be believed, that instead of all this he exacts the 1s. 2d. per ton on all goods which are carried between Liverpool and Manchester, whether they pass the Junction Lock or not. Thus, you will observe, his Grace, by one manœuvre or another, contrives to exact 5s. 2d. per ton on all goods that are navigated on his line, although it is perfectly clear that the Legislature never intended that he should have more than 2s. 6d. It will be asked, how does it happen that these unjust and unlawful exactions are not resisted? I believe that in one instance only has resistance been successful. A few years since, a merchant in Manchester tendered 6s. per ton for the carriage of goods; the Trustees of the Duke refused it, and brought their action, but submitted to a nonsuit.

There is, however, a very sufficient reason why this example was not followed. The Trustees possess all the warehouses, and have bought all the land on the banks of the Canal on which others could conveniently construct them at Manchester, so that they can exact their own terms, or nearly so. In 1810 a company of carriers between Liverpool and Manchester was established, called the Manchester Grocers' Company. They were fortunate enough to obtain a warehouse on the banks of the Rochdale Canal, and were, therefore, independent of the Duke; but the Rochdale Canal Proprietors unwisely became jealous of this new Company, and gave them notice to quit. They were then thrown on the mercy of the Trustees, and, in open defiance of law, they extort from them £600 a-year for a warehouse, and make them pay the 1s. 2d. per ton on all the goods they carry from Liverpool to Manchester, although they do not pass the Junction Lock at all. This, I presume, is, to use the words of his Act, "a compensation for the diminution in the profits of his wharfage as aforesaid." These Gentlemen, however, seem very well satisfied, for their shares have advanced 200 per cent.; they have obtained a slice of the monopoly, though at a very high rate, and have sunk silently into the old leaven.

There yet remains another exaction on the part of the Duke to be pointed out.

All goods which pass up from Liverpool to Runcorn, to enter the Trent and Mersey navigation, pay above twice the freight which they ought, owing to the Trustees of the Duke having monopolised nearly the whole of the land and warehouses at Runcorn. At the present moment, they charge 5s. per ton on grain, while bye-carriers, in abundance, would be found to contract at 2s. But, if a bye-carrier arrive, the owner of the goods, who thought to save a few shillings a ton, finds that he has not only to pay the 2s. but also the 5s.; for say the Trustees, what will you do with the goods? ours are the only warehouses, and your goods shall not be landed without your paying us as much as if we had carried them ourselves. Pay us the 5s. and your goods shall be received and forwarded. I ask the Trustees of the Duke whether, in 1818, they did not make Fowler, Brothers, pay 6s. 8d. per ton for landing the goods which a bye-carrier had brought, and for which they paid him 6s. 8d. freight; and whether it was not more than twelve months, and after repeated applications and interviews, before any restitution was submitted to, and then only one half of what had been so unjustly exacted.

So much for that line of conveyance called the Duke of Bridgewater's Canal.

With regard to the Old Quay Company, of which the Duke was an original proprietor, and I believe has ever since remained so, they were established by Act of Parliament in 1733, and are entitled to levy 3s. 4d. per ton for tonnage duties, but are not restricted as to the rate of freight. They have adhered faithfully to the charge of tonnage, but as they have for a long time, and till lately, possessed nearly all the warehouses in Manchester, on the banks of their navigation, they were enabled to make much more money by freight; and common sense, therefore, points out that a bye-carrier on their line would meet with all sorts of impediments. In fact they almost monopolized the carrying trade, for of what use is a navigation without warehouses? What could have induced the Grocers' Company to establish themselves on the Duke's line, where they are subject to 5s. 2d. tonnage, when they would only have been liable to 3s. 4d. on the Old Quay, the navigation of which is in some respects much preferable to that of the Duke? It may be said that the Duke's line was preferred on account of its connection with the Rochdale Canal; and that consideration might have some influence, but it is beyond question that the Grocers' Company did apply to the Old Quay Company, and that they either could not or would not afford the facilities which the Grocers required. I am aware that it is not imperative on the Old Quay Company to find warehouse room, but if the accommodation which they have had to offer has not kept pace with their increasing trade, the bye-carrier had no chance with them, because although the rate of freight at any given time might be sufficient to induce him to look out for accommodation in some less eligible situation, he was deterred from doing it by the conviction that if he became troublesome to them by his competition, they could reduce the freight whenever they pleased, and destroy his prospects. They have therefore controlled opposition, and have virtually established something very like a monopoly.

Though the Old Quay Proprietors have not violated their own laws, they have become parties to the proceedings of the Duke's Trustees, byopenly joining them to raise the rate of freight. Whatever difference might exist before, they entered into a combination with them in 1810; and by public advertisement[3] announced the advance which had been mutually agreed upon. Each advertisement bears the signature of the respective Agents, one is a verbatim copy of the other, and each occupies a column. It was this extraordinary advance of freight which gave existence to the Grocers' Company; the extravagance of the charge could no longer be endured, and the Grocers sought for refuge on the banks of the Rochdale Canal.

Having thus shown the powers and conduct of the two great carrying concerns, I shall proceed to examine into the charges now actually made by them for the carriage of goods from this port to Manchester. Heavy goods, such as corn, pay 12s. 6d. per ton, and light, such as cotton, pay 15s. This is a very moderate advance from 6s. 8d.; but it seems that, in the year 1810, they exacted nearly one-third more than they now do, and nearly three times what they exacted in 1795.

I have before me freight notes of the following dates:—

	Cwt.	qrs.	lbs.	Charge in 1795. s. d.	Charge in 1810. £. s. d.	Charge in 1822. £. s. d.
July 4, 1 Chest of Starch,	3	0	4—	1 3—0	2 10—0	2 4
Sept. 17, 2 Hhds. Sugar...	38	2	26—	11 0—1	16 3—1	5 10
Oct. 8, 1 Hhd. Lump do.	6	0	15—	2 3—0	5 7—0	4 1
1796.						
Jan. 2, 1 Hhd. Tobacco,	5	2	20—	2 1—0	5 4—0	4 3
April 19, 6 Boxes Soap....	12	0	0—	4 5—0	9 0—0	7 6
May 31, 12 Baskets Fruit,	9	3	21—	3 7—0	9 2—0	7 6

That the Trustees of the Duke have refused to make any reduction in their charges I can testify, for I have now before me a letter written by Captain Bradshaw, in reply to a Memorial, on the part of the Corn Merchants of Liverpool, for a reduction of freight, in which he says to their Chairman:—

Runcorn, 9th April, 1822

SIR,

I am directed by Mr. Bradshaw to acquaint you, for the information of the Merchants connected with the Grain trade of the port of Liverpool, that, having taken into full consideration the allegations contained in their Memorial, and all the information he is in possession of on the subject, he does not feel himself justified in making any alteration in the Trustees' present rate of freights.—I remain, Sir,

Your obedient servant,
JAMES BRADSHAW.

Robert Greenham, Esq. Chairman of the Committee of the Liverpool Corn Exchange

Here, then, we have a flat denial to a request to reduce the rate of freight from 12s. 6d. to 10s. per ton. I have not now a copy of the memorial before me, but I know, that if it were not stated in that document, it was most distinctly pointed out, when Capt. Bradshaw favoured the Committee with an interview, that such a reduction would then satisfy them.

From what I have stated, it will appear that freights in 1810 were nearly three times what they were in 1795; and that even now they are double the rate then paid. It is computed that nearly 1000 tons of goods pass daily between the towns of Liverpool and Manchester;[4] but calculating the quantity at only 600 tons, and reckoning the average charge of freight at 14s. the daily amount will be £420, so that £210 per day is paid in addition to what was paid for the same weight in 1795, £1260 per week, and the enormous sum of £65,520 per annum! From whence and from whom is this immense revenue raised? In the first place, from the merchants and manufacturers, and for no other purpose than to enrich a few individuals, originally only 40 in number, who are daily violating Acts of Parliament—Acts which, by a long course of cunning policy, they have contrived to convert into the most oppressive and unjust monopoly known to the trade of this kingdom,—a monopoly which there is every reason to believe compels the public to pay, in one shape or other, £100,000 more per annum than they ought to pay.

Having shown that the two Companies are deaf to all remonstrances, to all entreaties; that they are actuated solely by a spirit of monopoly and extortion, permit me to point out that the only remedy the public has left, is to go before Parliament, and ask for permission to establish a new line of conveyance. I am very far from thinking, however, that the necessity for this depends solely on the extravagant charges of the two Companies; if it did, that necessity might be superseded by a reduction of charges. But the necessity depends on the fact, that the present means of conveying goods are not adequate to discharge the business of the port, and that another line of conveyance has become requisite. It is requisite to give due facility to trade, and without it there will never be any permanent reduction in the rates of carriage, and no security against future combinations to advance them. It is quite clear that, if another line of conveyance is to be adopted, it must be a Railroad, for another Canal could not be formed, because the existing establishments have engrossed all the water. They possess just such a monopoly as all the water mills of the kingdom would have done, if the steam engine had never been discovered. It is this monopoly on the part of the Canals that the projectors of the Rail-road wish to do away: and they will accomplish it by the power of steam, as soon as an Act of Parliament can be obtained. Independently of these considerations, the Railroad possesses decided intrinsical advantages over a Canal conveyance, a few of which I will endeavour to point out.

It is computed that goods could be carried for considerably less than is *now* charged, and for one-half of what *has* been charged; and that they would be conveyed in one-sixth of the time. Canals in Summer are often short of water, and in Winter are obstructed by frost;—a Rail-way would not have to encounter these impediments. The goods by a Rail-way are not exposed to the risk of the voyage by water, and this is no trivial consideration. Manufacturers are little aware of the risks they run; and in proof of this I need say nothing more than refer them to the public papers for the detail of losses in the Mersey occasioned by the storms of the 30th November, 1821, and 5th December, 1822, when upwards of 50 vessels of one description or other were lost or stranded. I will also suggest to the Underwriters, both of Liverpool and London, that a Rail-way will be no trifling saving to them. Instead of their risks commencing in Liverpool as declared by their policies, they do, in point of fact, commence at Manchester. It is notorious, that goods coming down the Canals and Rivers frequently receive damage; but the packages are polished up in Liverpool previous to shipment, and pass inspection. On being opened in a Foreign market the secret is discovered, and an average is the result. The Underwriters are, therefore, called upon to pay a loss against which they never insured, and for which they received no premium.

It is well known to commercial men, and particularly to those connected with corn and timber, that great difficulty has been found in getting vessels to convey goods to Manchester. Timber has frequently been detained in Liverpool a month for want of vessels,[5] and corn and other commodities 8 or 10 days. This is a serious evil, for men will not resort to a market from whence they have such a difficulty in getting their goods. This would be remedied by a Rail-way. Vessels are too expensive to be built and kept in repair to answer any sudden press of business, for they would receive more injury in slack times, when laid up, than when employed; but a few hundred waggons, kept under cover, would at all times be in readiness to act at a few moments' notice, and the expense would be comparatively trifling.

A Rail-way would enable the people of Liverpool and other parts to buy coals several shillings per ton below the price they now pay. It would open all the collieries on the line to the sea, and would render this a very considerable shipping-port; and yet it is on this account that the Proprietors of the Leeds Canal are about to oppose it.

The distance between Liverpool and Manchester, by the three lines of Water conveyance, is upwards of 50 miles—by a Rail-road it would only be 33. Goods conveyed by the Duke and Old Quay are exposed to the storms, the delays from adverse winds, and the risk of damage, during a passage of 18 miles, in the tide-way of the Mersey. For days together it frequently happens, that when the wind blows very strong either south or north, their vessels cannot move against it. It is very true that when the winds and tide are favourable, they can occasionally effect a passage in 14 hours; but the average is certainly 30. However, notwithstanding all the accommodation they can offer, the delays are such that the spinners and dealers are frequently obliged to cart cotton on the public high road, a distance of 36 miles, for which they pay four times the price which would be charged by a Rail-road, and they are three times as long in getting it to hand. The same observation applies to manufactured goods which are sent by land carriage daily, and for which the rate paid is five times that which they would be subject to by the Rail-road. This enormous sacrifice is made for two reasons—sometimes because conveyance by water cannot be promptly obtained, but more frequently because speed and certainty, as to delivery, are of the first importance. Packages of goods sent from Manchester, for immediate shipment at Liverpool, often pay two or three pounds per ton, and yet there are those who assert that the difference of a few hours in speed can be no object. The merchants know better.

A Rail-road will enable passengers to travel between Liverpool and Manchester at the rate of 10 or 12 miles an hour, at one-half the price they pay now. A Rail-road will prevent any future combination to raise freights, and it would make the Trustees of his Grace of Bridgewater as anxious to let and sell warehouses and land, as they have been to grasp and retain them.

I trust I have made it appear that the advantages of a Rail-way over a Water conveyance, are quite sufficient of themselves to warrant an application to Parliament. Of its success no doubt can be entertained; for if I can show the Legislature that his late Grace bound himself not to charge more than 2s. 6d. per ton, canal dues, for the navigation of the whole length of his line, surely the grounds of his charging 5s. 2d. will be minutely examined into. In the first place, if his Grace found it convenient or necessary to alter his line, and to cut a part of it under the Trent and Mersey Act, ought he, in common fairness, to be entitled to the 6d. per ton which he charges under that act, on all goods which go to Manchester. If I show the Legislature, from the Duke's own record, that he is entitled to no more than 2s. 6d. tonnage, will they not demand the reason of the charge of 1s. per ton for entering the Trent and Mersey Canal through his reservoir? I know the Trustees will meet me on this point by saying, "the parliamentary line is open to you;" but when I explain to the Legislature that his Grace himself is an extensive carrier, and that the parliamentary lock, from the circumstance of its having no receiving basin, is not capable of admitting even the vessels belonging to the Trustees during the short time the tide will permit vessels to pass; and that from this cause his Grace has the power at any time to impede other vessels for days together—would they not see the necessity for remedying this? I ask for the parliamentary line only, and if the carrying trade has increased so as to require its being enlarged, his Grace is bound so to enlarge it.

If the Legislature granted his late Grace an Act to pull down houses, to remove all obstructions, and to compel people to sell their land to enable him to complete his Canal, and all for the public good, surely the Legislature will examine on what authority his successors refuse to accommodate the public with warehouses, and on what Act of Parliament it is that they exact the

1s. 2d. per ton on goods which never pass the Junction Lock at Manchester. Finally, the Legislature will narrowly examine into the reasons why, at one time, freights should have been exacted at the rate of 16s. 8d. per ton, and why they should now average 14s. when by law only 6s. can be demanded.

In short, it appears to me that the application for a Rail-road would be irresistible. That the two Companies will endeavour to rouse every sort of opposition there can be no question: they will endeavour to alarm the whole body of Canal Proprietors of the kingdom; but if the Canal Proprietors are wise they will never lend themselves and their influence to support such a monopoly and extortion as I have set forth. The very foundation of all their own Acts is the "public good," and if they step forward to support such exactions as I have endeavoured to describe, they will only prove to that public that the very moment they have the power they will commit the same injustice. The Canal Proprietors are too wary thus to be inveigled; they will reply, abate the nuisance complained of—offer to abide by the laws of your own seeking, by the laws which gave you existence, and then your opposition will be marked by a penitent and reasonable disposition. As to the landed proprietors there is not an individual who will not be immensely benefited by the Rail-way passing upon or within a mile or two of his grounds; and I confess I am at a loss to imagine how the two Companies can contrive to persuade any gentleman that opening his estate for the sale of its produce in either the Liverpool or Manchester market can possibly prejudice his interest. Time and distance are convertible terms; if by opening better roads and providing a quicker conveyance, 36 miles are performed in the same time that 18 were, I will venture to say that every farmer in the neighbourhood of Warrington or Newton will find his condition greatly benefited. The Rail-way will enable him to fertilize his land with the lime-stone of Wales and Derbyshire, at a considerable reduction on the present cost; it will enable him to get manure from the large towns at a cheaper rate than he now obtains it.

The only class of men who would sustain any injury are the Proprietors of the two Canals; and it is very true that their profits would be diminished, but I am very far from thinking that they would be destroyed, for there will be business enough for all. They have, however, had their day, and must be satisfied to put up with such competition as the course of time and improvements force upon them. I can assert, without affectation, that I am not so enamoured of the rage for improvement as to lose all respect for vested rights, for vested interests; but there is a wide difference between an invention which has superseded an old machine which has paid its owners thirty times over, and an invention which supersedes a machine which has not returned the Proprietor first cost. The Proprietors of the two Canals have not the slightest claim to talk about vested rights—the 39 original Proprietors of the Old Quay have been paid every other year, for nearly half a century, the total amount of their investment: and as to those who have recently paid £1250 for that which cost only £70, I can only state my regret that they did not thoroughly apprise themselves of the means by which this species of property was so unjustly enhanced in value. There is good reason to believe that the nett income of the Duke's Canal has, for the last twenty years, averaged nearly £100,000 per annum. The Trustees of his Grace may flatter themselves that they have a vested right to exact this income in perpetuity; but I apprehend the public will be of a very different opinion.

It is not likely that such a measure as the establishment of a Rail-road will pass without opposition. Every improvement has been opposed by some one, and yet improvements have gone on. The inhabitants in the vicinity of London at one time petitioned Parliament to prevent the extension of Turnpike-roads:—they wanted to continue in possession of the monopoly of supplying that city with their own produce. Nevertheless Turnpike-roads have multiplied. About the year 1765, when Canals were projected, numerous pamphlets were published to show their danger and impolicy. The Turnpike Trustees and the owners of Pack Horses saw danger to their interest, and they made the landed proprietors believe that Canals would supersede the use of horses, and thereby diminish the consumption of hay and oats. The parties joined, and by their representation that internal navigation would destroy the coasting trade, and consequently the nursery for seamen, succeeded for a year or two in preventing several important undertakings which were contemplated, and amongst the rest, the Trent and Mersey Navigation. What has been the effect of Canals? They have increased trade, commerce, and manufactures—they have increased turnpike-roads—they have increased the number of horses and the growth of hay and corn—they have increased both the coasting trade and the number of seamen. Canals have done well for the country, just as high roads and pack horses had done before Canals were established; but the country has now presented to it, in this instance, a cheaper and more expeditious mode of conveyance, and the attempt to prevent its adoption is utterly hopeless. The Steam Engine has raised the productive powers of this country to an extent which even to ourselves appears wonderful, but which our ancestors would have regarded as the idle dream of some visionary. It enabled us to carry on the war, and it will be the chief means of paying off our debts. Till lately its powers have been confined to manufactories and other stationary employments—but now they are employed in navigation, and steam-boats, have superseded all the coasting packets in the kingdom:—The public reap the benefit. It has been ascertained that its powers may now be applied to the propelling or dragging of goods and passengers on a Rail-road, and this too at a cheaper, safer and much more expeditious rate than goods and passengers are at present subject to between this town and Manchester. How monstrous is the idea that the Canal Proprietors should be protected from the consequences of such a discovery. Are the powers of the human mind to be controlled—are its efforts to be restrained by a small body of men, for the protection of their own comparatively insignificant interest? Are their pools of water to form the boundary beyond which science and art shall not be applied in the carrying trade? He who thinks that the march of improvement can thus be stopped,—that the interest of the whole nation can thus be sacrificed—would be a very likely person to make experiments in screwing down safety valves. Were it possible to prevent the establishment of Rail-roads in England, a severe blow would be struck at our boasted superiority in commerce and manufactures; for the rest of the world will adopt them, and embrace the full benefit of the discovery. The Emperor of Russia has obtained a model of the Loco-motive Engine, and at the present moment he has a professional agent investigating the Rail-roads of the north. The Americans, too, are alive to the subject, and at the seat of Government it is undergoing discussion. Letters just received from Washington are full of inquiries upon it.

Those who consider the measure as one of local interest take a very erroneous view of it. To Ireland, as presenting a much cheaper and more expeditious medium of conveyance for its agricultural products to the great manufacturing districts, it is of the utmost importance, for every reduction is a direct bonus to that country. To Ireland such a measure is indispensable, now that by the late extension of the Ayr and Calder navigation vessels of 200 tons can come nearly to Leeds and Wakefield with the corn, the flax, and the butter of the Continent, and of course at much less expense than heretofore. The Proprietors of this establishment have joined the Canal league against the project; and, therefore, it behoves the Irish Members to bestir themselves. The Proprietors know that it will reduce the rate at which the corn, the flax, the linen, and the butter of Ireland can be conveyed into Yorkshire; and that, therefore, it will circumscribe the sale of Continental produce, and diminish the amount of their tonnage. It is only necessary to mention one fact to show what friends these Proprietors are to every thing connected with Ireland. For the tonnage of bulky raw sugar, on their line, they charge only 4s. 8d.; but for Irish provisions they exact the enormous price of 7s. per ton. Before long we shall see Dutch butter introduced into Lancashire by means of this navigation, and nothing can keep it out but a reduction of freight on Irish between Liverpool and Manchester. Ireland is bound by still more powerful considerations to support it, for by means of the Rail-road and Steamboats, the passage from Manchester to Dublin will be reduced to 16 or 18 hours. The cheap labour of Ireland will undoubtedly be put in requisition by the manufacturers of this country. During the last two years a transit of goods has been taking place for this purpose, and it is rapidly increasing:—there is nothing wanted but the Rail-road to ensure to the Irish peasantry a considerable share of employment from this source.

Phillips, in his History of Inland Navigation, states, that according to Du Halde, the Canals of China, by far the most extensive in the world, "are cut through any kind of property, gardens, plantations, or pleasure grounds; not even the gardens of the Emperor or any of his governors are exempted; but when the work arrives at the garden or pleasure ground, the governor or even the Emperor himself digs the first spade of earth, and pronounces with an audible voice, 'this is to let those of inferior stations know that no private pleasure shall obstruct the public good.'"

If their Celestial Majesties arrived at this point of true wisdom some centuries ago, it only proves that knowledge travels from east to west slower than might have been expected, and that the liberal and enlightened opinions of Mr. Ricardo and Mr. Huskisson possess less originality than has been claimed for them. If the gentlemen and noblemen through whose estates the line of road is intended to pass, should oppose any objections, I would beg to quote the words of Phillips, who says, "that the good of a part must always give way to the good of the whole, when they happen to interfere, is one of the most essential principles of civil association; but it is at all times reasonable that the great interest of the community should be pursued and supported with as little injury to individuals as possible."—In this latter sentiment I most cordially concur. I would defer to my Lord Derby, my Lord Sefton, or to Lord Stanley, on all points affecting their substantial comforts and convenience, and I am convinced that they possess feelings of a character too liberal and patriotic to urge speculative, frivolous, or fanciful objections. It may be very pleasant for noblemen to exclude from the precincts of their domains the industrious classes of society—they may derive a morning's entertainment from visiting a manufacturing or sea-port town, as they would from a view on the Lakes, or from inspecting a community of bees in a glass hive;—but these feelings, and these times, are fast wearing away—there is a feeling of mutual good, of mutual dependance, before which both aristocratic and democratic tendencies subside to their just and healthful level. Where the general good is concerned, society knows nothing of privileged classes. There is no man, now, who would wield his rich inheritance against the comfort and the necessities of the community, in which he lives and moves and has his being. Such an attempt would be as visionary and as unjust as an Agrarian law.

Parliament is too discreet to suffer narrow views of policy to predominate. It is now fully sensible of the injurious effects of restrictions and monopolies, and of the importance of a free and cheap trade, both at home and abroad: it has encouraged and supported improvements of every description,—it has preferred the interest of the many to the advantage of the few, and it cannot, for a moment, be doubted but that it will extend its protection to this projected undertaking, and give the requisite authority for its completion. The case is too strong to admit of either compromise or vacillation.

The country requires the aid of this and of every other improvement which can be suggested;—it is loaded with an immense debt—it is heavily taxed, and Ireland is surcharged with a population of several millions, existing in a state of misery unknown to any other people in the world.

Economy in time and expense, the adoption of new machinery, and industry, and talent, will doubtless enable us to triumph over all these difficulties, and to place a population, now fit for treason or for spoil, in a state of comfort and content. Such powers, applied to our inexhaustible, but hitherto imperfectly developed mineral treasures,—to our trade, commerce, and agriculture, cannot fail to elevate this nation still higher in the scale of wealth and importance, and to show the world that she is not less dominant in peace than she was powerful and irresistible in war.

I have the honour to be,
My Lords and Gentlemen,
Your obedient and faithful servant,
JOSEPH SANDARS.

Liverpool, Oct. 6, 1824.

P. S. Since the greater part of the foregoing statements was written, a new Company of Carriers have established themselves on the Old Quay line; and in consequence of this, and the dread of the Rail-road, freights have been reduced to 10s. for corn; but cotton still remains at 15s. The exactions of the Trustees of the Duke have of necessity thrown this Company on the Old Quay Navigation. The Trustees have discovered that they cannot do these things with impunity, and they have at last withdrawn that part of their charges which relates to the 1s. per ton, for entering the reservoir at Runcorn; but the other exactions remain unmitigated. The public, however, have no security whatever against the resumption of this charge, nor against future combination to restore freights to a higher level, but the establishment of a Rail-road, and nothing short of this ought to satisfy them. The formation of the New Company has had no sensible effect in increasing the facilities of conveyance, in proof of which, I submit the following document:—

"We, the undersigned Merchants and Brokers resident in the port of Liverpool, do hereby declare, that we have for a long time past experienced great difficulty in obtaining vessels to convey goods from this place to Manchester; and that the delay is highly prejudicial to the trading and manufacturing interest at large.

"That we consider the present establishments for the transport of goods quite inadequate; and that a new line of conveyance has become absolutely necessary to conduct the increasing trade of the country with speed, certainty, and economy."

This document has been signed within the last few days by upwards of 150 of the most respectable merchants in the town, not one-third of whom are Share-holders in the Rail-road. Perhaps the fact of many Proprietors of the Leeds and Sankey Canals, as well as of the Old Quay Company, having either signed this document, or become Share-holders, is the strongest proof which could be offered, that a Rail-road is necessary, and that its adoption is considered certain and indispensable.

October 29th

I avail myself of a second edition to lay before the public a statement of the losses which took place on the 26th instant, in the River Mersey, in consequence of the gale of wind which occurred between twelve and one at noon:—

Sunk. . . . . . .Old Quay flat Fox; a full cargo of grain for Manchester: two men and one boy lost—both men have left families.
Sunk. . . . . . .Duke's flat Ellesmere; a cargo of wheat for Preston Brook: three hands lost—two of them have left families.
Ashore. . . . . Duke's flat Robert; timber laden for Manchester.
Ashore. . . . . Clare's flat William; grain laden for Warrington.
Ashore. . . . . Shanklin's flat Overton; cargo of grain for Chester.

So much for the perils of the River Navigation.

Within the last fourteen days, the difficulty of getting grain conveyed from Liverpool to the interior has been attended with very great expense. Cargoes sold have been obliged to be landed; of course, the expense falls upon the Irish Consignor.

J. S.

(*a.*) Extracts from the third and last Act obtained by the Duke, still restricting the charge for tonnage and carriage to the rate granted by the first and second.

"Provided always, and be it enacted by the authority aforesaid, that no person or persons whatsoever, shall have, take, or receive any greater or larger sum or sums of money than six shillings per ton, each ton to consist of twenty hundred weight, and so in proportion for any greater or less quantity for the freight and tonnage of any goods, wares, or merchandize whatsoever, to be navigated or conveyed upon any part of the Canal to be made by virtue of this Act, for the conveyance of such goods, wares, and merchandize, upon all or any part of the said navigable Cuts or Canals by this or the said recited Acts authorised to be made between Manchester and Liverpool aforesaid. And if any person or persons whatsoever shall take or receive any greater price or sum than as aforesaid, every person so offending, shall, for every such offence, forfeit and pay the sum of Five Pounds, to be recovered, levied, and applied in such manner as the penalties and forfeitures are by this and the said first recited Acts authorised, to be recovered, levied, and applied, any thing herein, or in the said recited Acts contained to the contrary thereof in any wise notwithstanding."

"And be it further enacted by the authority aforesaid, that in consideration of the great charges and expense, the said Francis, Duke of Bridgewater, his heirs and assigns, must necessarily bear and sustain in the making, maintaining, and supplying with water the said Cut or Canal, and all the other works hereby authorised to be erected and made, it shall be lawful for any person or persons as the said Francis, Duke of Bridgewater, his heirs or assigns shall, by writing under his or their hand or hands, appoint from time to time, and at all times hereafter, to ask, demand, take and recover for the proper use of the said Francis, Duke of Bridgewater, his heirs or assigns, for tonnage and wharfage for all coal, stone, timber, and other goods, wares and merchandizes, and commodities whatsoever, which shall be navigated, carried, or conveyed, upon or through the said Cut or Canal, Trenches, Sluices, or Passages, such rates and duties as the said Francis, Duke of Bridgewater, his heirs or assigns, shall think fit, not exceeding two shillings and sixpence per ton. Provided also that nothing in this Act contained, shall empower the said Duke of Bridgewater, his heirs or assigns, to take any higher tonnage rate or duty, throughout the whole or any part of *all* the said navigation than is authorised by the said former Acts to be taken upon the said Cuts or Canals therein mentioned."

(*b.*) Extract from the Rochdale Canal Act relating to the Junction Lock at Manchester.

"And whereas the said Francis, Duke of Bridgewater, hath expended a considerable sum of money in making Wharfs for the convenience of the public adjoining or near to his Canal at the town of Manchester, and when the proposed junction is made with his Canal, the profits arising from those Wharfs will be considerably diminished; nevertheless, the said Francis, Duke of Bridgewater, is consenting to such junction being made upon being authorised to build a Lock upon the said Rochdale Canal, near to the said junction, and to collect certain rates hereinafter mentioned, as a compensation for the diminution in the profits of his Wharfage as aforesaid.

"For every ton of coal, stone, timber, and other goods, wares, merchandize, and commodities whatsoever, (except flags) which shall be navigated, carried, or conveyed from the said Rochdale Canal, into or upon the said Canal belonging to the said Francis, Duke of Bridgewater, or from his said Canal into or upon the said Rochdale Canal, the sum of fourteen pence.—Flags, 2d.

"Provided always, and be it further enacted, that all persons who shall have paid the respective rates herein before mentioned, for the passing of any goods, wares, merchandize, or other things through the Lock, to be built at or near Castlefield, as aforesaid, shall have free liberty to land such goods, wares, merchandize, or other things, at *any Wharf,* and to lodge the same in *any warehouse* belonging to the said Francis, Duke of Bridgewater, his heirs or assigns, and to continue such goods, wares, merchandize, or other things, upon any such Wharf, and in any such warehouse as aforesaid, for any time not exceeding six days, without being liable to pay any rate or payment for the same."

Printed by W. Wales and Co. Liverpool.

Notes

1 The Leeds Canal, which is a third, but more circuitous route of conveyance, may surely be omitted, when the bare charge of tonnage amounts to 9s. 2d. per ton.
2 I have not been able to procure a copy of this Act, but I am assured that my statements are substantially correct.
3 See Liverpool Advertiser, September 29, 1810.
4 It is true that what are called "down Goods," that is, such as pass from Manchester to Liverpool, were reduced a short time ago to 10s., but they form only a small portion of the whole.
5 Messrs. Duncan and Fletcher, Messrs. Brereton and Newsham, and other Timber Merchants, can certify this fact; and Messrs. Cannon and Miller have, within the last two months, been fined £69. by the Corporation, in small fines of 10s. to 25s. for suffering timber to remain on the Quays. These Gentlemen were promised vessels by the carriers from day to day, and it was cheaper for them to incur the fines than to remove it to their yards. Are trades thus to be taxed for the benefit of the Duke and the Old Quay?

6

'SECOND PROSPECTUS OF THE LIVERPOOL AND MANCHESTER RAILWAY COMPANY', *LIVERPOOL MERCURY* XV, DECEMBER 30, 1825, 203

LIVERPOOL AND MANCHESTER RAILWAY COMPANY.

NEW LINE.

COMMITTEE.

CHARLES LAWRENCE, Esq. Chairman.

ROBERT GLADSTONE, Esq.
JOHN MOSS, Esq.   } Deputy Chairmen.
JOSEPH SANDARS, Esq.

Robert Benson, Liverpool,
H. H. Birley, Manchester,
Joseph Birley, Ditto,
Henry Booth, Liverpool,
Thos. S. Brandreth, Ditto,
John Ewart, Ditto,
Peter Ewart, Manchester,
Robert H. Gregg, Ditto,
Richard Harrison, Liverpool,
Thomas Headlam, Ditto,
Adam Hodgson, Ditto,

Isaac Hodgson, Liverpool,
Joseph Hornby, Ditto,
John Kennedy, Manchester,
Aaron Lees, Ditto,
Wellwood Maxwell, Liverpool,
William Potter, Ditto,
William Rathbone, Ditto,
William Rotheram, Ditto,
John Ryle, Manchester,
Thomas Sharpe, Ditto,
John Wilson, Liverpool.

Parliamentary Agent—Thomas M. Sherwood, Esq.
Engineers—Messrs. George and John Rennie.
Solicitors—Messrs. Pritt and Clay.
Bankers—Messrs. Moss, Rogers, and Moss, Liverpool.

CAPITAL . . . . . £510,000.

Prospectus

THE Committee of the Liverpool and Manchester Railway, before entering upon the labours which a renewed application to Parliament will impose upon them, are desirous to advert to the causes which led to the unsuccessful termination of their late efforts: and, at the same time, briefly to explain the grounds upon which they rest their anticipations of success, in the ensuing Session.

A very prominent objection taken by the opponents of the Bill, was founded on the errors in the Section and Levels, as exhibited before Parliament. These errors the Committee at once acknowledged, and regretted; and to avoid all chance of similar complaint, in future, they have engaged the professional services of most eminent Engineers, aided by assistants of undoubted talents and activity, whose combined efforts justify the fullest assurance, not only of the correctness of the Plans and Sections, but that the whole Line will be laid down and arranged with that skill and conformity with the rules of mechanical science, which will equally challenge approbation, whether considered as a national undertaking of great public utility, or as a magnificent specimen of art.

A second objection to the measure (which, however, was insisted upon, out of doors, more than in Parliament) was the interruption and inconvenience anticipated from the Line of Road crossing various streets in Liverpool and Manchester. This difficulty has been completely obviated. In the New Line, recommended by Messrs. Rennie, the Railway enters Liverpool by means of a Tunnel and inclined Plane, thus effecting a direct and most desirable communication, with the King and Queen's Docks, without interfering with a single street. It does not enter the town of Manchester at all; the Line terminating near the New Bailey Prison, in the township of Salford.

A third objection to the measure was taken by the Old Quay Company, on the ground that the Railway interfered with their navigation, by reason of a bridge in the neighbourhood of Manchester over the River Irwell. The Committee are happy to state that this difficulty is avoided, in as much as the New Line does not cross the Irwell at all.

A fourth manifestation of opposition was on the part of the Leeds and Liverpool Canal Company, on the ground that the Railway passed *under* their Canal, in its way to the Prince's Dock. However futile such an objection, it is satisfactory to be enabled to state, that even this assumed ground of opposition is altogether avoided, as the Line does not go near the Canal in question.

Another and more plausible objection was founded on the employment of the Locomotive Engine. It was contended in the *first* place, that this new and peculiar power was incompetent to perform the task assigned to it; in the *second* place, that it was unsafe; and lastly, that in its operation it would prove a public nuisance. By the evidence, however, it was proved, that it was perfectly competent to perform all that was proposed to be accomplished; and, before the evidence was closed, the Counsel for the opponents of the Bill admitted that it was *safe*. Upon the third point of objection, the Committee are confident such improvements will be made in the construction and application of this effective Machine, as will obviate all objection on the score of nuisance, and as a guarantee of their good faith towards the public, they will not require any Clause empowering them to use it—or they will submit to such restrictions in the employment of it as Parliament may impose for the satisfaction and ample protection both of Proprietors on the Line of Road, and of the Public at large.

The last, but not the least important objection which the Railway had to encounter, was on the part of several Landowners on the Lines. Amongst their opponents, on this ground, the Committee regret they were obliged to number the Noble Earls of Derby and Sefton, whose Estates the Railway crossed for a considerable distance, as well as others, whose Property the Line also unavoidably intersected.

The Committee most fully admit that the opinions and personal convenience of Proprietors on the Line of Road are entitled to every consideration, and they have been most anxious, by all practicable means, to meet the wishes, or to remove the objections, of every Landowner on the Road. They are happy to be able to state, that they can no longer, in this respect, find an opponent in Lord Sefton, as they do not, on the Line of Road they are about to apply for, cross any portion of his Lordship's Estate. And with reference to the Earl of Derby, they conceive they are entitled to apply the same observation, inasmuch as the New Line crosses only a few detached fields of his Lordship's Property, far removed from the Knowsley Domain, and the great Turnpikeroad from Liverpool to Manchester intervening.

With reference to the Landowners, generally, upon the New Line, the Committee have to state, that they have spared no pains to accommodate the exact route to the wishes of Proprietors whose Estates they cross; whether, on the one hand, by removing the Road to a distance from the Mansions of Proprietors, and from those portions of Estates more particularly appropriated to Game Preserves; or, on the other hand, by introducing it more immediately into the vicinity of districts abounding in Coal, which, by this means, will be brought into a cheap and expeditious communication with the Liverpool and Manchester Markets. And they are happy to state, that their efforts, in these respects, have been, in a great measure, successful. In an important national undertaking, where a Road has to be carried through a populous country for [Illegible Text] miles, it will hardly be expected that every Proprietor will assent, or that no individual will consider himself aggrieved. The Committee have used every effort to render the measure not only unobjectionable, but advantageous to every Landowner on the Line. In all cases they are prepared to give a full value for the Land they may require; and should there be instances where unavoidable inconvenience is occasioned, they are most anxious to admit that peculiar damage must be met by peculiar compensation.

In regard to the existing means of conveyance, the Committee are desirous to state, that they are actuated by no hostile feeling to their interest and prosperity. They have felt that the increased and increasing trade of the two great towns of Manchester and Liverpool, and the rapidly increasing intercourse with Ireland, demanded additional facilities in the means of transit; and the professed and sincere desire of the Committee has been confined to supply this want. – The Committee have the satisfaction of being able to state, that, in accordance with this feeling, the opposition of the most powerful of the existing establishments has been removed by the Marquis of Stafford having for himself, and those of his family, who are beneficially interested in the profits of the Duke of Bridgewater's Canal, become a Subscriber to the Railway to the extent of 1000 shares. Being satisfied that the proceedings of last Session of Parliament have removed the misapprehensions which existed, both in regard to the nature and the management of the Bridgewater Canal, they felt it would be unfit to continue their opposition to the proposed measure in its improved form.

Having thus disposed of the objections and difficulties which the Committee have had to encounter, they will briefly advert to those prominent and unequivocal advantages of the measure, upon which they rest their claim to the favour of the Public, and the sanction of Parliament.

In their Prospectus of last year, the Committee stated "the total quantity of Merchandise passing between Liverpool and Manchester at *one thousand tons per day*." This quantity, it would seem, is underrated, the whole traffic being admitted, on all hands, in a Committee of the House of Commons, to be 1200 tons per diem; which immense aggregate tonnage is at present subject to all the delays incidental to the River Navigation.

The Committee of the Railway propose to effect the transit of Merchandise in a few hours, with uniform regularity, and at such reduced rates as will secure to the towns of Liverpool and Manchester a pecuniary saving, which, whether estimated in proportion to the expenditure upon which it is effected, or with reference to the aggregate amount, has seldom been equalled in any scheme of improvement submitted to the Public.

Neither is the immediate pecuniary saving to the towns of Liverpool and Manchester to be estimated with reference merely to the cost of conveying Merchandise between the respective towns. The *travelling* between Liverpool and Manchester is upon the most extensive scale; and the economy to be effected in this branch of expenditure, though impossible to be estimated with accuracy, must be considered as most important, and, of itself, no small recommendation of the undertaking.

The advantages, however, above enumerated, are only a part of the beneficial results which this scheme proposes.—The line of Railway, as now laid down, passes through a rich and extensive Coal district, in full working, for the supply of Liverpool, and requiring only a facility of transport to be brought into requisition for the supply of Manchester. As a moderate computation, Liverpool requires for its local consumption 900 tons of Coal per day, besides what is required for Foreign Commerce, and for the numerous Steam-packets which sail daily through the season between Liverpool and various ports [Illegible Text] Ireland, Scotland, and Wales. An aggregate consumption of 500,000 tons per annum may be taken as under the mark. Of this large quantity a considerable proportion is brought to market by Land Carriage; extensive fields of Coal in the direct line of the Railway having no other means of access to Liverpool. With reference to Manchester, the ordinary consumption for domestic purposes may be considered the same as in Liverpool, and the quantity used in the extensive Factories of that town may be computed as equivalent to the demand for the Steam-vessels, and for the Export Trade at Liverpool, the aggregate consumption, therefore, of the two towns, may be estimated, with sufficient accuracy, at ONE MILLION of tons per annum.

The importance to the community of a moderate price to be paid for an article of such extensive and universal consumption is immediately apparent, and some idea of the benefit to be derived from such a facility of transport as may insure a more enlarged and effectual competition, may be formed from the circumstance that in Manchester the price of Coals was advanced 1s. 6d. per ton immediately upon the Railway Bill being withdrawn in the last Session of Parliament;—while in Liverpool, within the last 35 years, the price of the best Coal has been advanced upwards of 7s. per ton—that is, clearly 100 per cent. But estimating the reduction in the price of this article at 2s. per ton, here is a saving of £100,000 per annum (an amount equal to the whole Assessed Taxes of the two towns) effected upon a single article, not of luxury, and confined to the higher and mercantile classes of the community, but an article of the first necessity—of daily and hourly consumption, and forming no small item in the expenditure of every poor man's family.

Moreover, it would be to take a very narrow and imperfect view of the great question now under discussion to limit our consideration to the immediate accommodation of the mercantile classes—to the pecuniary saving proposed to the travelling community—or even to the still more important saving to the consumers of Coals, and of every description of Goods conveyed between Liverpool and Manchester. The question demands a wider survey, and the consideration of more distant results. We must contemplate the important effects upon the commerce of the nation, which are to be anticipated, on the one hand, from *affording*, or, on the other hand, from *denying*, facilities to the commercial operations of this great county. Above all, we must look to Ireland, the natural Granary of the manufacturing districts of this country. To the sister kingdom, a facility of intercourse and conveyance between Liverpool and the interior of Lancashire and Yorkshire is of paramount importance: in the first place, for the cheap and regular transport of her agricultural produce; and, secondly, for the rapid transit of Cotton and Woollen Goods in different stages of their manufacture, which alone seems wanting to foster the growing industry of Ireland; to give to her some proportionate advantage for her cheap labour, and thus render her an auxiliary and a helpmate to the more stable manufacturing establishments of this country.

But the subject does not end here. It becomes a question of serious import, whether this country, which is indebted for so much of her wealth, and power, and greatness, to the bold and judicious application of mechanical science, shall now pause in the career of improvement, while it is notorious that other nations will adopt the means of aggrandisement which we reject; whether England shall relinquish the high vantage ground she at present possesses, not more with a reference to the direct operations of Commerce and Manufactures, than, generally, in the successful application of the most important principles of science and of art.

The Committee feel that it is unnecessary to dwell at greater length on the question they have thus brought before the public. They are about to apply for the sanction of the Legislature; and they are determined to relax no efforts on their part to bring about the honourable and speedy accomplishment of the great work in which they have engaged.

CHARLES LAWRENCE, Chairman.

Liverpool, December 26, 1825.

7

GEORGE ELIOT, *MIDDLEMARCH*. NEW EDITION. (EDINBURGH AND LONDON: W. BLACKWOOD, 1874), PP. 407–414

Dorothea's confidence in Caleb Garth's knowledge, which had begun on her hearing that he approved of her cottages, had grown fast during her stay at Freshitt, Sir James having induced her to take rides over the two estates in company with himself and Caleb, who quite returned her admiration, and told his wife that Mrs Casaubon had a head for business most uncommon in a woman. It must be remembered that by "business" Caleb never meant money transactions, but the skilful application of labour.

"Most uncommon!" repeated Caleb. "She said a thing I often used to think myself when I was a lad:—'Mr Garth, I should like to feel, if I lived to be old, that I had improved a great piece of land and built a great many good cottages, because the work is of a healthy kind while it is being done, and after it is done, men are the better for it.' Those were the very words: she sees into things in that way."

"But womanly, I hope," said Mrs Garth, half suspecting that Mrs Casaubon might not hold the true principle of subordination.

"Oh, you can't think!" said Caleb, shaking his head. "You would like to hear her speak, Susan. She speaks in such plain words, and a voice like music. Bless me! it reminds me of bits in the 'Messiah'—'and straightway there appeared a multitude of the heavenly host, praising God and saying;' it has a tone with it that satisfies your ear."

Caleb was very fond of music, and when he could afford it went to hear an oratorio that came within his reach, returning from it with a profound reverence for this mighty structure of tones, which made him sit meditatively, looking on the floor and throwing much unutterable language into his outstretched hands.

With this good understanding between them, it was natural that Dorothea asked Mr Garth to undertake any business connected with the three farms and the numerous tenements attached to Lowick Manor; indeed, his expectation of getting work for two was being fast fulfilled. As he said, "Business breeds." And one form of business which was beginning to breed just then was the construction of railways. A projected line was to run through Lowick parish where the cattle had hitherto grazed in a peace unbroken by astonishment; and thus it happened that the infant struggles of the railway system entered into the affairs of Caleb Garth, and determined the course of this history with regard to two persons who were dear to him.

The submarine railway may have its difficulties; but the bed of the sea is not divided among various landed proprietors with claims for damages not only measurable but sentimental. In the hundred to which Middlemarch belonged railways were as exciting a topic as the Reform Bill or the imminent horrors of Cholera, and those who held the most decided views on the subject were women and landholders. Women both old and young regarded travelling by steam as presumptuous and dangerous, and argued against it by saying that nothing should induce them to get into a railway carriage; while proprietors, differing from each other in their arguments as much as Mr Solomon Featherstone differed from Lord Medlicote, were yet unanimous in the opinion that in selling land, whether to the Enemy of mankind or to a company obliged to purchase, these pernicious agencies must be made to pay a very high price to landowners for permission to injure mankind.

But the slower wits, such as Mr Solomon and Mrs Waule, who both occupied land of their own, took a long time to arrive at this conclusion, their minds halting at the vivid conception of what it would be to cut the Big Pasture in two, and turn it into three-cornered bits, which would be "nohow;" while accommodation-bridges and high payments were remote and incredible.

"The cows will all cast their calves, brother," said Mrs Waule, in a tone of deep melancholy, "if the railway comes across the Near Close; and I shouldn't wonder at the mare too, if she was in foal. It's a poor tale if a widow's property is to be spaded away, and the law say nothing to it. What's to hinder 'em from cutting right and left if they begin? It's well known, *I* can't fight."

"The best way would be to say nothing, and set somebody on to send 'em away with a flea in their ear, when they came spying and measuring," said Solomon. "Folks did that about Brassing, by what I can understand. It's all a pretence, if the truth was known, about their being forced to take one way. Let 'em go cutting in another parish. And I don't believe in any pay to make amends for bringing a lot of ruffians to trample your crops. Where's a company's pocket?"

"Brother Peter, God forgive him, got money out of a company," said Mrs Waule. "But that was for the manganese. That wasn't for railways to blow you to pieces right and left."

"Well, there's this to be said, Jane," Mr Solomon concluded, lowering his voice in a cautious manner—"the more spokes we put in their wheel, the more they'll pay us to let 'em go on, if they must come whether or not."

This reasoning of Mr Solomon's was perhaps less thorough than he imagined, his cunning bearing about the same relation to the course of railways as the cunning of a diplomatist bears to the general chill or catarrh of the solar system. But he set about acting on his views in a thoroughly diplomatic manner, by stimulating suspicion. His side of Lowick was the most remote from the village, and the houses of the labouring people were either lone cottages or were collected in a hamlet called Frick, where a water-mill and some stone-pits made a little centre of slow, heavy-shouldered industry.

In the absence of any precise idea as to what railways were, public opinion in Frick was against them; for the human mind in that grassy corner had not the proverbial tendency to admire the unknown, holding rather that it was likely to be against the poor man, and that suspicion was the only wise attitude with regard to it. Even the rumour of Reform had not yet excited any millennial expectations in Frick, there being no definite promise in it, as of gratuitous grains to fatten Hiram Ford's pig, or of a publican at the "Weights and Scales" who would brew beer for nothing, or of an offer on the part of the three neighbouring farmers to raise wages during winter. And without distinct good of this kind in its promises, Reform seemed on a footing with the bragging of pedlars, which was a hint for distrust to every knowing person. The men of Frick were not ill-fed, and were less given to fanaticism than to a strong muscular suspicion; less inclined to believe that they were peculiarly cared for by heaven, than to regard heaven itself as rather disposed to take them in—a disposition observable in the weather.

Thus the mind of Frick was exactly of the sort for Mr Solomon Featherstone to work upon, he having more plenteous ideas of the same order, with a suspicion of heaven and earth which was better fed and more entirely at leisure. Solomon was overseer of the roads at that time, and on his slow-paced cob often took his rounds by Frick to look at the workmen getting the stones there, pausing with a mysterious deliberation, which might have misled you into supposing that he had some other reason for staying than the mere want of impulse to move. After looking for a long while at any work that was going on, he would raise his eyes a little and look at the horizon; finally he would shake his bridle, touch his horse with the whip, and get it to move slowly onward. The hour-hand of a clock was quick by comparison with Mr Solomon, who had an agreeable sense that he could afford to be slow. He was in the habit of pausing for a cautious, vaguely-designing chat with every hedger or ditcher on his way, and was especially willing to listen even to news which he had heard before, feeling himself at an advantage over all narrators in partially disbelieving them. One day, however, he got into a dialogue with Hiram Ford, a waggoner, in which he himself contributed information. He wished to know whether Hiram had seen fellows with staves and instruments spying about: they called themselves railroad people, but there was no telling what they were, or what they meant to do. The least they pretended was that they were going to cut Lowick Parish into sixes and sevens.

"Why, there'll be no stirrin' from one pla-ace to another," said Hiram, thinking of his waggon and horses.

"Not a bit," said Mr Solomon. "And cutting up fine land such as this parish! Let 'em go into Tipton, say I. But there's no knowing what there is at the bottom of it. Traffick is what they put for'ard; but it's to do harm to the land and the poor man in the long-run."

"Why, they're Lunnon chaps, I reckon," said Hiram, who had a dim notion of London as a centre of hostility to the country.

"Ay, to be sure. And in some parts against Brassing, by what I've heard say, the folks fell on 'em when they were spying, and broke their peep-holes as they carry, and drove 'em away, so as they knew better than come again."

"It war good foon, I'd be bound," said Hiram, whose fun was much restricted by circumstances.

"Well, I wouldn't meddle with 'em myself," said Solomon. "But some say this country's seen its best days, and the sign is, as it's being overrun with these fellows trampling right and left, and wanting to cut it up into railways; and all for the big traffic to swallow up the little, so as there shan't be a team left on the land, nor a whip to crack."

"I'll crack *my* whip about their ear'n, afore they bring it to that, though," said Hiram, while Mr Solomon, shaking his bridle, moved onward.

Nettle-seed needs no digging. The ruin of this country-side by railroads was discussed, not only at the "Weights and Scales," but in the hay-field, where the muster of working hands gave opportunities for talk such as were rarely had through the rural year.

One morning, not long after that interview between Mr Farebrother and Mary Garth, in which she confessed to him her feeling for Fred Vincy, it happened that her father had some business which took him to Yoddrell's farm in the direction of Frick: it was to measure and value an outlying piece of land belonging to Lowick Manor, which Caleb expected to dispose of advantageously for Dorothea (it must be confessed that his bias was towards getting the best possible terms from railroad companies). He put up his gig at Yoddrell's, and in walking with his assistant and measuring-chain to the scene of his work, he encountered the party of the company's agents, who were adjusting their spirit-level. After a little chat he left them, observing that by-and-by they would reach him again where he was going to measure. It was one of those grey mornings after light rains, which become delicious about twelve o'clock, when the clouds part a little, and the scent of the earth is sweet along the lanes and by the hedgerows.

The scent would have been sweeter to Fred Vincy, who was coming along the lanes on horseback, if his mind had not been worried by unsuccessful efforts to imagine what he was to do, with his father on one side expecting him straightway to enter the Church, with Mary on the other threatening to forsake him if he did enter it, and with the working-day world showing no eager need whatever of a young gentleman without capital and generally unskilled. It was the harder to Fred's disposition because his father, satisfied that he was no longer rebellious, was in good humour with him, and had sent him on this pleasant ride to see after some greyhounds. Even when he had fixed on what he should do, there would be the task of telling his father. But it must be admitted that the fixing, which had to come first, was the more difficult task:—what secular avocation on earth was there for a young man (whose friends could not get him an "appointment") which was at once gentlemanly, lucrative, and to be followed without special knowledge? Riding along the lanes by Frick in this mood, and slackening his pace while he reflected whether he should venture to go round by Lowick Parsonage to call on Mary, he could see over the hedges from one field to another. Suddenly a noise roused his attention, and on the far side of a field on his left hand he could see six or seven men in smock-frocks with hay-forks in their hands making an offensive approach towards the four railway agents who were facing them, while Caleb Garth and his assistant were hastening across the field to join the threatened group. Fred, delayed a few moments by having to find the gate, could not gallop up to the spot before the party in smock-frocks, whose work of turning the hay had not been too pressing after swallowing their mid-day beer, were driving the men in coats before them with their hay-forks; while Caleb Garth's assistant, a lad of seventeen, who had snatched up the spirit-level at Caleb's order, had been knocked down and seemed to be lying helpless. The coated men had the advantage as runners, and Fred covered their retreat by getting in front of the smock-frocks and charging them suddenly enough to throw their chase into confusion. "What do you confounded fools mean?" shouted Fred, pursuing the divided group in a zigzag, and cutting right and left with his whip. "I'll swear to every one of you before the magistrate. You've knocked the lad down and killed him, for what I know. You'll every one of you be hanged at the next assizes, if you don't mind," said Fred, who afterwards laughed heartily as he remembered his own phrases.

The labourers had been driven through the gateway into their hay-field, and Fred had checked his horse, when Hiram Ford, observing himself at a safe challenging distance, turned back and shouted a defiance which he did not know to be Homeric.

"Yo're a coward, yo are. Yo git off your horse, young measter, and I'll have a round wi' ye, I wull. Yo daredn't come on wi'out your hoss an whip. I'd soon knock the breath out on ye, I would."

"Wait a minute, and I'll come back presently, and have a round with you all in turn, if you like," said Fred, who felt confidence in his power of boxing with his dearly-beloved brethren. But just now he wanted to hasten back to Caleb and the prostrate youth.

The lad's ankle was strained, and he was in much pain from it, but he was no further hurt, and Fred placed him on the horse that he might ride to Yoddrell's and be taken care of there.

"Let them put the horse in the stable, and tell the surveyors they can come back for their traps," said Fred. "The ground is clear now."

"No, no," said Caleb, "here's a breakage. They'll have to give up for to-day, and it will be as well. Here, take the things before you on the horse, Tom. They'll see you coming, and they'll turn back."

"I'm glad I happened to be here at the the right moment, Mr Garth," said Fred, as Tom rode away. "No knowing what might have happened if the cavalry had not come up in time."

"Ay, ay, it was lucky," said Caleb, speaking rather absently, and looking towards the spot where he had been at work at the moment of interruption. "But—deuce take it—this is what comes of men being fools—I'm hindered of my day's work. I can't get along without somebody to help me with the measuring-chain.

However!" He was beginning to move towards the spot with a look of vexation, as if he had forgotten Fred's presence, but suddenly he turned round and said quickly, "What have you got to do to-day, young fellow?"

"Nothing, Mr Garth. I'll help you with pleasure—can I?" said Fred, with a sense that he should be courting Mary when he was helping her father.

"Well, you mustn't mind stooping and getting hot."

"I don't mind anything. Only I want to go first and have a round with that hulky fellow who turned to challenge me. It would be a good lesson for him. I shall not be five minutes."

"Nonsense!" said Caleb, with his most peremptory intonation. "I shall go and speak to the men myself. It's all ignorance. Somebody has been telling them lies. The poor fools don't know any better."

"I shall go with you, then," said Fred.

"No, no; stay where you are. I don't want your young blood. I can take care of myself."

Caleb was a powerful man and knew little of any fear except the fear of hurting others and the fear of having to speechify. But he felt it his duty at this moment to try and give a little harangue. There was a striking mixture in him—which came from his having always been a hard-working man himself—of rigorous notions about workmen and practical indulgence towards them. To do a good day's work and to do it well, he held to be part of their welfare, as it was the chief part of his own happiness; but he had a strong sense of fellowship with them. When he advanced towards the labourers they had not gone to work again, but were standing in that form of rural grouping which consists in each turning a shoulder towards the other, at a distance of two or three yards. They looked rather sulkily at Caleb, who walked quickly with one hand in his pocket and the other thrust between the buttons of his waistcoat, and had his everyday mild air when he paused among them.

"Why, my lads, how's this?" he began, taking as usual to brief phrases, which seemed pregnant to himself, because he had many thoughts lying under them, like the abundant roots of a plant that just manages to peep above the water. "How came you to make such a mistake as this? Somebody has been telling you lies. You thought those men up there wanted to do mischief."

"Aw!" was the answer, dropped at intervals by each according to his degree of unreadiness.

"Nonsense! No such thing! They're looking out to see which way the railroad is to take. Now, my lads, you can't hinder the railroad: it will be made whether you like it or not. And if you go fighting against it, you'll get yourselves into trouble. The law gives those men leave to come here on the land. The owner has nothing to say against it, and if you meddle with them you'll have to do with the constable and Justice Blakesley, and with the handcuffs and Middlemarch jail. And you might be in for it now, if anybody informed against you."

Caleb paused here, and perhaps the greatest orator could not have chosen either his pause or his images better for the occasion.

"But come, you didn't mean any harm. Sombody told you the railroad was a bad thing. That was a lie. It may do a bit of harm here and there, to this and to that; and so does the sun in heaven. But the railway's a good thing."

"Aw! good for the big folks to make money out on," said old Timothy Cooper, who had stayed behind turning his hay while the others had been gone on their spree;—"I'n seen lots o' things turn up sin' I war a young un—the war an' the peace, and the canells, an' the oald King George, an' the Regen', an' the new King George, an' the new un as has got a new ne-ame—an' it's been all aloike to the poor mon. What's the canells been t' him? They 'n brought him neyther me-at nor be-acon, nor wage to lay by, if he didn't save it wi' clemmin' his own inside. Times ha' got wusser for him sin' I war a young un. An' so it'll be wi' the railroads. They'll on'y leave the poor mon furder behind. But them are fools as meddle, and so I told the chaps here. This is the big folks's world, this is. But yo're for the big folks, Muster Garth, yo are."

Timothy was a wiry old labourer, of a type lingering in those times—who had his savings in a stocking-foot, lived in a lone cottage, and was not to be wrought on by any oratory, having as little of the feudal spirit, and believing as little, as if he had not been totally unacquainted with the Age of Reason and the Rights of Man. Caleb was in a difficulty known to any person attempting in dark times and unassisted by miracle to reason with rustics who are in possession of an undeniable truth which they know through a hard process of feeling, and can let it fall like a giant's club on your neatly-carved argument for a social benefit which they do *not* feel. Caleb had no cant at command, even if he could have chosen to use it; and he had been accustomed to meet all such difficulties in no other way than by doing his "business" faithfully. He answered—

"If you don't think well of me, Tim, never mind; that's neither here nor there now. Things may be bad for the poor man—bad they are; but I want the lads here not to do what will make things worse for themselves. The cattle may have a heavy load, but it won't help 'em to throw it over into the roadside pit, when it's partly their own fodder."

"We war on'y for a bit o' foon," said Hiram, who was beginning to see consequences. "That war all we war arter."

"Well, promise me not to meddle again, and I'll see that nobody informs against you."

"I'n ne'er meddled, an' I'n no call to promise," said Timothy.

"No, but the rest. Come, I'm as hard at work as any of you today, and I can't spare much time. Say you'll be quiet without the constable."

"Aw, we wooant meddle—they may do as they loike for oos"—were the forms in which Caleb got his pledges; and then he hastened back to Fred, who had followed him, and watched him in the gateway.

They went to work, and Fred helped vigorously. His spirits had risen, and he heartily enjoyed a good slip in the moist earth under the hedgerow, which soiled his perfect summer trousers. Was it his successful onset which had elated him, or the satisfaction of helping Mary's father? Something more. The accidents of the morning had helped his frustrated imagination to shape an employment for himself which had several attractions. I am not sure that certain fibres in Mr Garth's mind had not resumed their old vibration towards the very end which now revealed itself to Fred. For the effective accident is but the touch of fire where there is oil and tow; and it always appeared to Fred that the railway brought the needed touch.

8

THE CREEVY PAPERS: A SELECTION FROM THE CORRESPONDENCE & DIARIES OF THE LATE THOMAS CREEVY. ED. SIR HERBERT MAXWELL. (NEW YORK: E. P. DUTTON, 1904), PP. 429–431, 545–546

Mr. Creevey to Miss Ord

"London, March 16, 1825.

" . . . Sefton and I have come to the conclusion that our Ferguson is *insane*. He quite foamed at the mouth with rage in our Railway Committee in support of this infernal nuisance—the loco-motive Monster, carrying *eighty tons* of goods, and navigated by a tail of smoke and sulphur, coming thro' every man's grounds between Manchester and Liverpool. He was supported by Scotchmen only, except a son of Sir Robert Peel's, and against every landed gentleman of the county—his own particular friends, who were all present, such as Ld. Stanley, Ld. Sefton, Ld. Geo. Cavendish, &c."

"25th March.

" . . . I get daily more interested about this railroad—on its own grounds, to begin with, and the infernal, impudent, lying jobbing by its promoters . . . . "

"31st May.

" . . . This railway is the devil's own—from 12 till 4 daily is really too much. We very near did the business to-day; we were 36 to 37 on the Bill itself. I led for the Opposition in a speech of half an hour . . . . "

"June 1.

" . . . Well—this devil of a railway is strangled at last. I was sure that yesterday's division had put him on his last legs, and to-day we had a clear majority in the Committee in our favour, and the promoters of the Bill withdrew it, and took their leave of us . . . . We had to fight this long battle against an almost universal prejudice to start with—interested shareholders and perfidious Whigs, several of whom affected to oppose us upon *conscientious* scruples. Sefton's ecstacies are *beyond*, and he is pleased to say it has been all my doing; so it's all mighty well."

"6th.

It was not amiss to hear bold York congratulating Sefton and the Countess upon *their victory over the railway.*

Mr. Creevey to Miss Ord

"Knowsley, Nov. 1st, 1829.

" . . . You have no doubt in your paper reports of Huskisson's return to office. Allow me to mention a passage which Lord Derby read to me out of a letter to himself from Lady Jane Houston, who lives very near Huskisson . . . . 'Houston saw Huskisson yesterday, who talked to him of his return to office as of a thing quite certain, and of Edward Stanley doing so too. Indeed he spoke of the latter as quite the Hope of the Nation!' As the Hope of the Nation was present when this was read, it would not have been decent to laugh; but the little Earl gave me a look that was quite enough."

"14th.

" . . . To-day we have had a *lark* of a very high order. Lady Wilton sent over yesterday from Knowsley to say that the Loco Motive machine was to be upon the railway at such a place at 12 o'clock for the Knowsley party to ride in if they liked, and inviting this house to be of the party. So of course we were at our post in 3 carriages and some horsemen at the hour appointed. I had the satisfaction, for I can't call it *pleasure*, of taking a trip of five miles in it, which we did in just a quarter of an hour—that is, 20 miles an hour. As accuracy upon this subject was my great object, I held my watch in my hand at starting, and all the time; and as it has a second hand, I knew I could not be deceived; and it so turned out there was not the difference of a second between the coachee or conductor and myself. But observe, during these five miles, the machine was occasionally made to put itself out or *go it;* and then we went at the rate of 23 miles an hour, and just with the same ease as to motion or absence of friction as the other reduced pace. But the quickest motion is to me *frightful:* it is really flying, and it is impossible to divest yourself of the notion of instant death to all upon the least accident happening. It gave me a headache which has not left me yet. Sefton is convinced that some damnable thing must come of it; but he and I seem more struck with such apprehension than others . . . . The smoke is very inconsiderable indeed, but sparks of fire are abroad in some quantity: one burnt Miss de Ros's cheek, another a hole in Lady Maria's silk pelisse, and a third a hole in some one else's gown. Altogether I am extremely glad indeed to have seen this miracle, and to have travelled in it. Had I thought worse of it than I do, I should have had the curiosity to try it; but, having done so, I am quite satisfied with my *first* achievement being my *last.*"

9

WILLIAM WORDSWORTH, 'ON THE PROJECTED KENDEL AND WINDERMERE RAILWAY', 147, 'LETTERS ON THE KENDAL AND WINDERMERE RAILWAY, 301–311', FROM VOL. 8 OF *THE POETICAL WORKS OF WILLIAM WORDSWORTH*. ED. WILLIAM ANGUS KNIGHT. (EDINBURGH: W. PATERSON, 1888–1889), PP. 147, 301–311

Is then no nook of English ground secure
From rash assault? Schemes of retirement sown
In youth, and 'mid the busy world kept pure
As when their earliest flowers of hope were blown,
Must perish;—how can they this blight endure?
And must he too the ruthless change bemoan
Who scorns a false utilitarian lure
'Mid his paternal fields at random thrown?
Baffle the threat, bright Scene, from Orrest-head
Given to the pausing traveller's rapturous glance:
Plead for thy peace, thou beautiful romance
Of nature; and, if human hearts be dead,
Speak, passing winds; ye torrents, with your strong
And constant voice, protest against the wrong.
October 12*th*, 1844.

Kendal and Windermere Railway

To the Editor of the 'Morning Post.'

Sir,

Some little time ago you did me the favour of inserting a sonnet expressive of the regret and indignation which, in common with others all over these Islands, I felt at the proposal of a railway to extend from Kendal to Low Wood, near the head of Windermere. The project was so offensive to a large majority of the proprietors through whose lands the line, after it came in view of the Lake, was to pass, that, for this reason, and the avowed one of the heavy expense without which the difficulties in the way could not be overcome, it has been partially abandoned, and the terminus is now announced to be at a spot within a mile of Bowness. But as no guarantee can be given that the project will not hereafter be revived, and an attempt made to carry the line forward through the vales of Ambleside and Grasmere, and as in one main particular the case remains essentially the same, allow me to address you upon certain points which merit more consideration than the favourers of the scheme have yet given them. The matter, though seemingly local, is really one in which all persons of taste must be interested, and, therefore, I hope to be excused if I venture to treat it at some length.

I shall barely touch upon the statistics of the question, leaving these to the two adverse parties, who will lay their several statements before the Board of Trade, which may possibly be induced to refer the matter to the House of Commons; and, contemplating that possibility, I hope that the observations I have to make may not be altogether without influence upon the public, and upon individuals whose duty it may be to decide in their place whether the proposed measure shall be referred to a Committee of the House. Were the case before us an ordinary one, I should reject such an attempt as presumptuous and futile; but it is not only different from all others, but, in truth, peculiar.

In this district the manufactures are trifling; mines it has none, and its quarries are either wrought out or superseded; the soil is light, and the cultivateable parts of the country are very limited; so that it has little to send out, and little has it also to receive. Summer Tourists, (and the very word precludes the notion of a railway) it has in abundance; but the inhabitants are so few and their intercourse with other places so infrequent, that one daily coach, which could not be kept going but through its connection with the Post-office, suffices for three-fourths of the year along the line of country as far as Keswick. The staple of the district is, in fact, its beauty and its character of seclusion and retirement; and to these topics and to others connected with them my remarks shall be confined.

The projectors have induced many to favour their schemes by declaring that one of their main objects is to place the beauties of the Lake district within easier reach of those who cannot afford to pay for ordinary conveyances. Look at the facts. Railways are completed, which, joined with others in rapid progress, will bring travellers who prefer approaching by Ullswater to within four miles of that lake. The Lancaster and Carlisle Railway will approach the town of Kendal, about eight or nine miles from eminences that command the whole vale of Windermere. The Lakes are therefore at present of very easy access for *all* persons; but if they be not made still more so, the poor, it is said, will be wronged. Before this be admitted let the question be fairly looked into, and its different bearings examined. No one can assert that, if this intended mode of approach be not effected, anything will be taken away that is actually possessed. The wrong, if any, must lie in the unwarrantable obstruction of an attainable benefit. First, then, let us consider the probable amount of that benefit.

Elaborate gardens, with topiary works, were in high request, even among our remote ancestors, but the relish for choice and picturesque natural *scenery* (a poor and mean word which requires an apology, but will be generally understood), is quite of recent origin. Our earlier travellers—Ray, the naturalist, one of the first men of his age—Bishop Burnet, and others who had crossed the Alps, or lived some time in Switzerland, are silent upon the sublimity and beauty of those regions; and Burnet even uses these words, speaking of the Grisons—'When they have made up estates elsewhere they are glad to leave Italy and the best parts of Germany, and to come and live among those mountains of which the very sight is enough to fill a man with horror.' The accomplished Evelyn, giving an account of his journey from Italy through the Alps, dilates upon the terrible, the melancholy, and the uncomfortable; but, till he comes to the fruitful country in the neighbourhood of Geneva, not a syllable of delight or praise. In the *Sacra Telluris Theoria* of the other Burnet there is a passage—omitted, however, in his own English translation of the work—in which he gives utterance to his sensations, when, from a particular spot he beheld a tract of the Alps rising before him on the one hand, and on the other the Mediterranean Sea spread beneath him. Nothing can be worthier of the magnificent appearances he describes than his language. In a noble strain also does the Poet Gray address, in a Latin Ode, the *Religio loci* at the Grande Chartruise. But before his time, with the exception of the passage from Thomas Burnet just alluded to, there is not, I believe, a single English traveller whose published writings would disprove the assertion, that, where precipitous rocks and mountains are mentioned at all, they are spoken of as objects of dislike and fear, and not of admiration. Even Gray himself, describing, in his Journal, the steeps at the entrance of Borrowdale, expresses his terror in the language of Dante:—'Let us not speak of them, but look and pass on.' In my youth, I lived some time in the vale of Keswick, under the roof of a shrewd and sensible woman, who more than once exclaimed in my hearing, 'Bless me! folk are always talking about prospects; when I was young there was never sic a thing neamed.' In fact, our ancestors, as everywhere appears, in choosing the site of their houses, looked only at shelter and convenience, especially of water, and often would place a barn or any other out-house directly in front of their habitations, however beautiful the landscape which their windows might otherwise have commanded. The first house that was built in the Lake district for the sake of the beauty of the country was the work of a Mr English, who had travelled in Italy, and chose for his site, some eighty years ago, the great island of Windermere; but it was sold before his building was finished, and he showed how little he was capable of appreciating the character of the situation by setting up a length of high garden-wall, as exclusive as it was ugly, almost close to the house. The nuisance was swept away when the late Mr Curwen became the owner of this favoured spot. Mr English was followed by Mr Pocklington, a native of Nottinghamshire, who played strange pranks by his buildings and plantations upon Vicar's Island, in Derwentwater, which his admiration, such as it was, of the country, and probably a wish to be a leader in a new fashion, had tempted him to purchase. But what has all this to do with the subject?— Why, to show that a vivid perception of romantic scenery is neither inherent in mankind, nor a necessary consequence of even a comprehensive education. It is benignly ordained that green fields, clear blue skies, running streams of pure water, rich groves and woods, orchards, and all the ordinary varieties of rural Nature, should find an easy way to the affections of all men, and more or less so from early childhood till the senses are impaired by old age and the sources of mere earthly enjoyment have in a great measure failed. But a taste beyond this, however desirable it may be that every one should possess it, is not to be implanted at once; it must be gradually developed both in nations and individuals. Rocks and mountains, torrents and wide-spread waters, and all those features of Nature which go to the composition of such scenes as this part of England is distinguished for, cannot, in their finer relations to the human mind, be comprehended, or even very imperfectly conceived, without processes of culture or opportunities of observation in some degree habitual. In the eye of thousands and tens of thousands, a rich meadow, with fat cattle grazing upon it, or the sight of what they would call a heavy crop of corn, is worth all that the Alps and Pyrenees in their utmost grandeur and beauty could show to them; and notwithstanding the grateful influence, as we have observed, of ordinary Nature and the productions of the fields, it is noticeable what trifling conventional prepossessions will, in common minds, not only preclude pleasure from the sight of natural beauty, but will even turn it into an object of disgust. 'If I had to do with this garden,' said a respectable person, one of my neighbours, 'I would sweep away all the black and dirty stuff from that wall.' The wall was backed by a bank of earth, and was exquisitely decorated with ivy, flowers, moss, and ferns, such as grow of themselves in like places; but the mere notion of fitness associated with a trim garden-wall, prevented, in this instance, all sense of the spontaneous bounty and delicate care of Nature. In the midst of a small pleasure-ground, immediately below my house, rises a detached rock, equally remarkable for the beauty of its form, the ancient oaks that grew out of it, and the flowers and shrubs which adorn it. 'What a nice place would this be,' said a Manchester tradesman, pointing to the rock, 'if that ugly lump were but out of the way.' Men as little advanced in the pleasure which such objects give to others are so far from being rare, that they may be said fairly to represent a large majority of mankind. This is a fact, and none but the deceiver and the willingly deceived can be offended by its being stated. But as a more susceptible taste is undoubtedly a great acquisition, and has been spreading among us for some years, the question is, what means are most likely to be beneficial in extending its operation? Surely that good is not to be obtained by transferring at once uneducated persons in large bodies to particular spots, where the combinations of natural objects are such as would afford the greatest pleasure to those who have been in the habit of observing and studying the peculiar character of such scenes, and how they differ one from another. Instead of tempting artisans and labourers, and the humbler classes of shopkeepers, to ramble to a distance, let us rather look with lively sympathy upon persons in that condition, when, upon a holiday, or on the Sunday, after having attended divine worship, they make little excursions with their wives and children among neighbouring fields, whither the whole of each family might stroll, or be conveyed at much less cost than would be required to take a single individual of the number to the shores of Windermere by the cheapest conveyance. It is in some such way as this only, that persons who must labour daily with their hands for bread in large towns, or are subject to confinement through the week, can be trained to a profitable intercourse with Nature where she is the most distinguished by the majesty and sublimity of her forms.

For further illustration of the subject, turn to what we know of a man of extraordinary genius, who was bred to hard labour in agricultural employments, Burns, the poet. When he had become distinguished by the publication of a volume of verses, and was enabled to travel by the profit his poems brought him, he made a tour, in the course of which, as his companion, Dr Adair, tells us, he visited scenes inferior to none in Scotland in beauty, sublimity, and romantic interest; and the Doctor having noticed, with other companions, that he seemed little moved upon one occasion by the sight of such a scene, says—'I doubt if he had much taste for the picturesque.' The personal testimony, however, upon this point is conflicting; but when Dr Currie refers to several local poems as decisive proofs that Burns' fellow-traveller was mistaken, the biographer is surely unfortunate. How vague and tame are the poet's expressions in those few local poems, compared with his language when he is describing objects with which his position in life allowed him to be familiar! It appears, both from what his works contain, and from what is not to be found in them, that, sensitive as they abundantly prove his mind to have been in its intercourse with common rural images, and with the general powers of Nature exhibited in storm and in stillness, in light or in darkness, and in the various aspects of the seasons, he was little affected by the sight of one spot in preference to another, unless where it derived an interest from history, tradition, or local associations. He lived many years in Nithsdale, where he was in daily sight of Skiddaw, yet he never crossed the Solway for a better acquaintance with that mountain; and I am persuaded that, if he had been induced to ramble among our Lakes, by that time sufficiently celebrated, he would have seldom been more excited than by some ordinary Scottish stream or hill with a tradition attached to it, or which had been the scene of a favourite ballad or love song. If all this be truly said of such a man, and the like cannot be denied of the eminent individuals before named, who to great natural talents added the accomplishments of scholarship or science, then what ground is there for maintaining that the poor are treated with disrespect, or wrong done to them or any class of visitants, if we be reluctant to introduce a railway into this country for the sake of lessening by eight or nine miles only, the fatigue or expense of their journey to Windermere?—And wherever any one among the labouring classes has made even an approach to the sensibility which drew a lamentation from Burns when he had uprooted a daisy with his plough, and caused him to turn the 'weeder-clips aside' from the thistle, and spare 'the symbol dear' of his country, then surely such a one, could he afford by any means to travel as far as Kendal, would not grudge a two hours' walk across the skirts of the beautiful country that he was desirous of visiting.

The wide-spread waters of these regions are in their nature peaceful; so are the steep mountains and the rocky glens: nor can they be profitably enjoyed but by a mind disposed to peace. Go to a pantomime, a farce, or a puppet-show, if you want noisy pleasure—the crowd of spectators who partake your enjoyment will, by their presence and acclamations, enhance it; but may those who have given proof that they prefer other gratifications continue to be safe from the molestation of cheap trains pouring out their hundreds at a time along the margin of Windermere; nor let any one be liable to the charge of being selfishly disregardful of the poor, and their innocent and salutary enjoyments, if he does not congratulate himself upon the especial benefit which would thus be conferred on such a concourse.

> O, Nature, a' thy shows an' forms,
> To feeling pensive hearts hae charms!

So exclaimed the Ayrshire ploughman, speaking of ordinary rural Nature under the varying influences of the seasons, and the sentiment has found an echo in the bosoms of thousands in as humble a condition as he himself was when he gave vent to it. But then they were feeling, pensive hearts; men who would be among the first to lament the facility with which they had approached this region, by a sacrifice of so much of its quiet and beauty, as, from the intrusion of a railway, would be inseparable. What can, in truth, be more absurd, than that either rich or poor should be spared the trouble of travelling by high roads over so short a space according to their respective means, if the unavoidable consequence must be a great disturbance of the retirement, and in many places a destruction of the beauty of the country, which the parties are come in search of? Would not this be pretty much like the child's cutting his drum to learn where the sound came from?

Having, I trust, given sufficient reason for the belief that the imperfectly educated classes are not likely to draw much good from rare visits to the Lakes performed in this way, and surely on their own account it is not desirable that the visits should be frequent, let us glance at the mischief which such facilities would certainly produce. The directors of railway companies are always ready to devise or encourage entertainments for tempting the humbler classes to leave their homes. Accordingly, for the profit of the shareholders and that of the lower class of innkeepers, we should have wrestling matches, horse and boat races without number, and pot-houses and beer-shops would keep pace with these excitements and recreations, most of which might too easily be had elsewhere. The injury which would thus be done to morals, both among this influx of strangers and the lower class of inhabitants, is obvious; and, supposing such extraordinary temptations not to be held out, there cannot be a doubt that the Sabbath day in the towns of Bowness and Ambleside, and other parts of the district, would be subject to much additional desecration.

Whatever comes of the scheme which we have endeavoured to discountenance, the charge against its opponents of being selfishly regardless of the poor, ought to cease. The cry has been raised and kept up by three classes of persons—they who wish to bring into discredit all such as stand in the way of their gains or gambling speculations; they who are dazzled by the application of physical science to the useful arts, and indiscriminately applaud what they call the spirit of the age as manifested in this way; and, lastly, those persons who are ever ready to step forward in what appears to them to be the cause of the poor, but not always with becoming attention to particulars. I am well aware that upon the first class what has been said will be of no avail, but upon the two latter some impression will, I trust, be made.

To conclude. The railway power, we know well, will not admit of being materially counteracted by sentiment; and who would wish it where large towns are connected, and the interests of trade and agriculture are substantially promoted, by such mode of intercommunication? But be it remembered, that this case is, as has been said before, a peculiar one, and that the staple of the country is its beauty and its character of retirement. Let then the beauty be undisfigured and the retirement unviolated, unless there be reason for believing that rights and interests of a higher kind and more apparent than those which have been urged in behalf of the projected intrusion will compensate the sacrifice. Thanking you for the judicious observations that have appeared in your paper upon the subject of railways,

                I remain, Sir,
                    Your obliged,
                        WM. WORDSWORTH.

Part 3

CULTURES OF RAILWAY CONSTRUCTION

10

JOHN FRANCIS, *A HISTORY OF THE ENGLISH RAILWAY: ITS SOCIAL RELATIONS AND REVELATIONS.* 2 VOLS. (LONDON: LONGMAN, BROWN, GREEN, & LONGMANS, 1851). VOL. 2, CHAPTER 3 PP. 67–91

A CHAPTER devoted to the railway labourer may be regarded as intrusive by some, and as gossipping by others; by a third class it may be considered as repulsive. But the "navigator" is necessary to the rail. He is an important portion of this new system of political economy. He risks life and limb to form the works which we admire. He braves all weather, he dares all danger, he labours with a power and a purpose which demand attention. For years he was disregarded by those who, availing themselves of his strength and skill, left him, when his daily task was done, to his own pleasures and his own resources. Rude, rugged, and uncultivated, possessed of great animal strength, collected in large numbers, living and working entirely together, they are a class and a community by themselves. Before the time of that great duke who called inland navigation into existence, this class was unknown; and in the works which bear witness to his forethought, the "navigator" gained his title. The canal manias which ensued created a demand and increased the body; the great architectural works of the kingdom continued it; and when the rail first began to spread its iron road through England, the labourer attracted no attention from politician or philosopher, from statistician or from statesman; he had joined no important body, he had not made himself an object of dread. Rough alike in morals and in manners, collected from the wild hills of Yorkshire and of Lancashire, coming in troops from the fens of Lincolnshire, and afterwards pouring in masses from every county in the empire; displaying an unbending vigour and an independent bearing; mostly dwelling apart from the villagers near whom they worked; with all the strong propensities of an untaught, undisciplined nature; unable to read and unwilling to be taught; impetuous, impulsive, and brute-like; regarded as the pariahs of private life, herding together like beasts of the field, owning no moral law and feeling no social tie, they increased with an increased demand, and from thousands grew to hundreds of thousands. They lived only for the present; they cared not for the past; they were indifferent to the future. They were a wandering people, who only spoke of God to wonder why he had made some so rich and others so poor; and only heard of a coming state to hope that there they might cease to be railway labourers. They were heathens in the heart of a Christian people; savages in the midst of civilisation: and it is scarcely an exaggeration to say, that a feeling something akin to that which awed the luxurious Roman when the Goth was at his gates, fell on the minds of those English citizens near whom the railway labourer pitched his tent.

"A perfect dread," said one witness before a committee of the House of Commons, "was on the minds of the people of the town near which the railway labourer was expected." Nor was it until this period, when they became an element of the power of England; when their numbers made them feared by the rich who avoided them, and a curse to the poor who associated with them, that the Chadwicks of the nineteenth century could compel the attention they deserved

The inquiry instituted by parliament elicited information which surprised some and revolted all. The mode in which they herded together was melancholy; and if the homes of the people be an index to their civilisation, the home of the railway labourer was significant enough. They earned high wages, and they spent them. They worked hard, and they lived well. The waste of power which their daily labour necessitated, was supplied by an absorption of stimulant and nourishment perfectly astounding. Bread, beef, bacon, and beer, were the staple of their food. They drank ardent spirits if they had money, credit, or craft to procure it; for "there was not an atom's worth of honesty among them." They devoured as earnestly as they worked; they drank whisky by the tumbler, and called it "white beer:" and they proved what open air and hard labour would do in the disposal of their food. They were in a state of utter barbarism. They made their homes where they got their work. Some slept in huts constructed of damp turf, cut from the wet grass, too low to stand upright in; while small sticks, covered with straw, served as rafters. Barns were better places than the best railway labourer's dwellings. Others formed a room of stones without mortar, placed thatch or flags across the roof, and took possession of it with their families, often making it a source of profit by lodging as many of their fellow-workmen as they could crowd into it. It mattered not to them that the rain beat through the roof, and that the wind swept through the holes. If they caught a fever, they died; if they took an infectious complaint, they wandered in the open air, spreading the disease wherever they went. In these huts they lived; with the space over-crowded; with man, woman, and child mixing in promiscuous guilt; with no possible separation of the sexes; in summer wasted by unwholesome heats, and in winter literally hewing their way to their work through the snow. In such places from nine to fifteen hundred men were crowded for six years. "Living like brutes, they were depraved, degraded, and reckless. Drunkenness and dissoluteness of morals prevailed. There were many women, but few wives; loathsome forms of disease were universal. Work often went on without intermission on Sundays as well as on other days."

"Possessed of all the daring recklessness of the smuggler," says Mr. Roscoe, and it is necessary to quote other opinions to confirm the writer's picture, so serious is the nature of his assertions, "their ferocious behaviour can only be equalled by the brutality of their language. It may be truly said their hand is against every man's, and before they have been long located, every man's hand is against theirs. From being long known to each other, they generally act in concert, and put at defiance any local constabulary force; consequently crimes of the most atrocious character were common, and robbery without any attempt at concealment was an every-day occurrence." Attention was rarely paid to the day of rest, excepting to make it a day of debauchery. Many of them lived in a state of intoxication until their money was spent, and they were again obliged to have recourse to labour, to the loan ticket and the truck system.

 The dread which such men as these spread throughout a rural community, was striking; nor was it without a cause. Depredation among the farms and fields of the vicinity were frequent. They injured everything they approached. From their huts to that part of the railway at which they worked, over corn or grass, tearing down embankments, injuring young plantations, making gaps in hedges, on they went, in one direct line, without regard to damage done or property invaded. Game disappeared from the most sacred preserves; game-keepers were defied; and country gentlemen who had imprisoned rustics by the dozen for violating the same law, shrunk in despair from the railway "navigator." They often committed the most outrageous acts in their drunken madness. Like dogs released from a week's confinement, they ran about and did not know what to do with themselves. They defied the law; broke open prisons; released their comrades, and slew policemen. The Scotch fought with the Irish, and the Irish attacked the Scotch; while the rural peace-officers, utterly inadequate to suppress the tumult, stood calmly by and waited the result. When no work was required of them on the Sunday, the most beautiful spots in England were desecrated by their presence. Lounging in highways and byeways, grouping together in lanes and valleys, insolent and insulting, they were dreaded by the good, and welcomed by the bad. They left a sadness in the homes of many whose sons they had vitiated and whose daughters they had dishonoured. Stones were thrown at passers-by; women were personally abused; and men were irritated. On the week day, when their work was done, the streets were void of all save their lawless visitors and of those who associated with them. They were regarded as savages; and when it is remembered that large bodies of men armed with pitchforks and scythes went out to do battle with those on another line a few miles off, the feeling was justified by facts. Crime of all description increased, but offences against the person were most common. On one occasion, hundreds of them were within five minutes' march of each other, ere the military and the magistrates could get between them to repress their daring desires.

 Their presence spread like a pestilence. Tempted by the high wages they received, the hind left his master to join them. Occasionally the inhabitants of the district received the labourer as a lodger, and paid for it in the impurity of character and conduct it engendered. The females of his family left their home to join the wild encampment, and were in their turn left by those who had betrayed them. Their boys aped the vices of men. They fought, smoked, swore, and reeled along the streets at an age when, in other classes, they are scarcely left by themselves. The "navigators," wanderers on the face of the earth, owning no tie and fearing no law; "were," said the Rev. St. George Sargent, "the most neglected and spiritually destitute people I ever met; ignorant of Bible religion and Gospel truth, infected with infidelity, and prone to revolutionary principles."

And for all these things were railway companies responsible. Letting large portions of their works to contractors, the latter divided their respective portions among others with smaller capital, who again subletting their part of the works to a minor class—as much labourers as contractors—engaged the workmen, assisted their operations, shared in their toils, and disregarded their welfare when the work was over. In many cases the men were paid their wages monthly; in some not so often. When new men were engaged, they could only live by assistance from their employers. This led to the truck system, the advances being made by orders on a shop, in exchange for which, the labourer received inferior provisions at an extravagant price. Against each man an account was kept, and on the pay day he received the balance due. This balance being necessarily small was soon dissipated; and the "navigator" had no other resource. The same demand for advances arose, the same issue of tickets occurred, the same extortion followed. The man was maintained by credit, and improvident habits were continued.

The carelessness of the contractor for the welfare of the employed is to be accounted for when it is remembered that he often sprung from the ranks. It has been said in the previous volume, that the railway contractor forms a feature of the present period. The first directors of railway companies committed the great mistake of letting small contracts to irresponsible men, who made large profits if they succeeded, or left the directors without a remedy if they failed. Thus a small success led to larger efforts; the careful "navigator" became first an underganger and then a ganger; the ganger changed into a contractor; and at this time there are many men who, twenty years since, delved and dug, and gained their bread by the sweat of their brow, are now in possession of most valuable estates. They have bought the places which railway speculation often sent into the market; they possess capital to invest in the landed property which the operation of the corn laws may yet throw open to the highest bidder; they possess shrewdness which enables them to imitate the conventional manners of society; they educate their family for the position they have acquired, and their children will probably occupy an important place in the great landed power of the country. There was, therefore, in too many cases no sympathy between the employer and the employed. There was no confidence between the contractor and the labourer; the system of subletting, handing the latter over to uneducated and reckless people, who, choosing them only for their skill and power, looked after them but to see that their work was done. From such as these the "navigator" found a difficulty even in procuring his wages. Law was of no avail to him. "There is no law," said the Rev. Robert Wilson, a magistrate, "which will enforce it; if the employer has no goods on which to levy the amount, there is no remedy." Nor was this an uncommon circumstance. The above gentleman stated that he had as many as twenty-eight or thirty cases in one morning; that within two and a-half years he had adjudicated on a hundred; and that it frequently arose, not from misapprehension, but because the ganger "did not choose to pay." Sometimes a different movement was tried. "Two labourers," said Mr. Wilson, "complained to me that they had been paid £1 short in their wages. It was on a pay-night, the room very much crowded, a small room; and the ganger read from a book the sum to be paid to them; it was £2 9s., and one of them took up the money and went away to the other end of the table to count it with his comrade; directly the money is down, they are hurried away to make room for others. When he got to the other end of the table he counted the money and found £1 9s. instead of £2 9s. He counted it over in the presence of his comrade and they returned to the ganger to be paid the other £1. He said, 'I paid you £2 9s.' The complaint was laid before me, and the evidence on the part of the labourer was this, that one had taken up the money and gone to the table and counted it in the presence of the other. The comrade said, 'I saw him count the money;' but of course he could not say that he had slipped away one pound. The ganger merely said, in his defence, he had ordered the £2 9s. to be paid. The time-keeper, who pays the money from a basin, said he had put down £2 9s.; and another person, also in the employ of the ganger, said he was sitting near the table, and he could see that £2 9s. was put on the table and taken up by the labourer."

The truck system, originated one hundred years ago, was maintained on the greater number of the lines in formation. Under the pretence that the works were too far from the town to be supplied by its shopkeepers, the contractor often arranged with some person to open a shop near the works, where the men might have their wants supplied; and as the labourer was not paid his wages weekly, he was obliged to go to these shops, knowing that the goods he received were very dear and very bad. The feeling was strong on the subject, and many men made it a rule never to work on lines where there was a "tommy-shop." So sensible of the imposition were those who were obliged to take the tickets that they would often sell them at any discount. The plan led to every sort of knavery. It was disadvantageous also to the peace of the works. It was contrary to the peace of the men. It prevented the circulation of money in the villages near which the "navigators" worked. It created quarrels with the shopkeepers. It produced exorbitant charges for an inferior quality. It caused frequent disputes on the night of settlement. "The men get drunk," said one witness, "lose their tickets, and say they have not had them; or they sell a two shilling ticket for half its value, spend the money, and declare they were not paid." They never were satisfied with what they received. Unable to keep accounts, and miscalculating the value of the goods they had taken, they were paid less than they imagined their due, leaving the place angry, excited, and fit for any wild or wicked work. Bad feelings were thus produced between the employer and the employed. Additional scenes of drunkenness, riot, and disorder marked the monthly payments. Mr. Jackson said the men complained with great reason of the truck system; they were most cruelly used. The Rev. Robert Wilson added that the railway labourers were induced to behave ill to their employers from the treatment they received. Mr. Speirs was of opinion that it was disadvantageous to the works, and contrary to the interests of the men.

The reverend Mr. Thompson said it led to every sort of trickery; while, in addition to these opinions, Mr. Brunel believed it to be "a very bad system." Nor can it be sufficiently denounced. Its evils on the railway may not be so great as in Manchester. Mr. D'Israeli, in his fine story of "Sybil," has developed with great power the mode in which the principle worked there. Nor can there be a doubt that in an inferior degree the same evils were felt by the large body of men concerning whom this chapter treats. Even if the labourer, wishing to be economical, applied for cash, he could only procure it at the rate of one hundred per cent. per annum.

"If they are not unfairly dealt with," said the report of the committee, "the men suspect they are over-reached, and this engenders ill-will and distrust towards their employers. They have little or no means of checking the account of advances made to them, or of ascertaining whether the balance paid is really correct; and hence the monthly payment seems frequently an occasion for dispute, riot, and discontent. The contractor, being interested in the large expenditure of the men, has a strong motive to encourage their extravagance and wastefulness, and to induce them to anticipate their wages. In some instances, the men cannot get employment unless they will deal at their master's shop. Those who live on credit are apt to be more profuse and improvident than those who pay their way; the less frequently the men are paid, the longer they must live on credit; and thus the employer is induced to pay his men at long intervals."

It must be added that all contractors were not patrons of truck shops. To the honour of Mr. Peto, by whom thousands of this class were employed, some attempt was made to humanise them. He was careful in his selection of overseers. He always paid his wages weekly in money, and boldly avowed that no contracter who understood his own interest or his obligations to the men, would act otherwise. Attention was paid to their religious instruction. Clergymen and scripture-readers were induced to visit them. He provided them with barracks to lodge in; he introduced habits of thrift and carefulness; he encouraged them in joining sick-clubs, and gave large sums to induce them. No one who could read was without a Bible. The consequence was, that men staid with him fourteen or fifteen years; that drunkenness was uncommon; and that, though dissoluteness of mind and manner was impossible utterly to prevent, there was but little among the large number employed by Mr. Peto.[1] Nor was this gentleman alone in his endeavours. Mr. Jackson, also a large railway contractor, always paid in money. "I find," said he, "setting aside any reference to feeling as to the comfort and condition of the men, and looking at it in a business point of view, that it is much more profitable, much more comfortable, and much better in every respect, that the men should be taken care of." He looked after the morals of the men employed by him; he provided for their comfort and accommodation; he built sixty or seventy wooden cottages; and although the erection of these places might not pay in a pecuniary light, they far more than repaid in the purer feeling they created, and in the development of a moral effect previously unknown.

Mr. Chadwick first drew the attention of the public to this class; and in a paper read before the statistical society of Manchester, made some statements so startling, that the House of Commons deemed it necessary to appoint a committee to inquire into the condition of the railway labourer; "who," said Mr. Chadwick, "has been detached from the habits and influence of his home and his village, and set to work amongst promiscuous assemblages of men attracted from all parts; has received double his ordinary amount of wages, and has been surrounded by direct inducements to spend them in drink and debauchery. If he were a married man, little or none of his earnings have been returned to his wife and family, who in his absence have commonly obtained parochial relief, on the ground either of 'desertion by the husband,' or of his 'absence in search of work.' Whether he were married or single, the whole of the excess of money earned beyond his ordinary rate of wages has been expended under the inducements to which he has been subjected, and at the completion of the works, he has been discharged penniless, and has returned discontented, reckless, deteriorated in bodily and mental condition, or he has, with others of the same class, entered the ranks of the dangerous swarm of able-bodied mendicants, vagrants, and depredators, of whom the committals within the last few years have been so largely increased. The employment is transitory, but the evil effects have been permanent. The extra labourers available for such undertakings, the loose men unattached to any place of working, could not be expected to be of the best description of labourers; but from the absence of proper regulations, the good have been deteriorated, the indifferent made positively bad, and the bad worse."

The ills arising from the endeavour of the capitalist to employ his capital, should be counteracted as much as possible by the same agency. Instead of being an evil, the collection of these men might be made a benefit. They might be taught their responsibility; they might be shown the use of uniting; they might be introduced into the social scale which they injure; they might be raised from material to moral life; they might be educated and taught their true position; they might be treated like men, and not left to themselves, like beasts.

At war with all civilised society, the great mass glorying in Chartism, they are to be dreaded: for their thews and sinews would form no trifling element of success. It is the duty of every railway company to watch over their interests; it is the duty of every contractor to provide for them mentally as well as physically; and it is the duty of every good government to see that the power which calls them into existence also places them in that position in the state which their welfare as men demands.

No legal enactment followed the inquiry of the committee of the House of Commons; and with the following extract the present chapter is concluded:—

"The class of the labouring population, to the state of which the inquiries of your committee have been addressed, is already large, and is likely to become very much more numerous. The rapid growth of the railway system of communication will be necessarily accompanied, for several years to come, by a vast expenditure of capital in mere construction, giving employment, probably, to not much less than 200,000 of the effective labouring population of the country.

"The great amount of outlay already thus made, its suddenness, and its temporary concentration at particular localities—often spots before but thinly inhabited—have created or developed evils, touching both the welfare of the labourers employed and the interests of society, the taint of which seems not unlikely to survive their original cause.

"It does not seem altogether unreasonable to expect that the steady employment and the high wages attained by the men engaged on railway works, added to the opportunities for their instruction, for their acquiring habits of order, of systematic industry, and of economy, as well as for bringing favourable influences to bear on them, which are afforded by the collection of large bodies of these men together, under an organised system of labour, should serve most usefully in effecting a valuable and permanent improvement of their state. Good wages, or at least such wages as secure those dependent thereon from constantly balancing on the verge of destitution, seem to be one element essential to the improvement of the labouring classes. With reference to the class your committee has had under their consideration, this element undoubtedly exists; but, besides high wages, other circumstances must be favourable, before improvement of social condition can be looked for; and if they are unfavourable, increased means of gratification may become positively harmful to the recipient as well as to society. Even the disposition and habits of the individual, the main elements in considering the prospects of improving his condition, must greatly depend on the external circumstances in which he exists; on the treatment he experiences; on the kind of life he has no choice but to lead.

"As regards the class of labourers under consideration, your committee cannot but conclude, on the evidence they have received from various parts of the country, that the circumstances under which their labour is carried on are too generally of a deteriorating kind. They are brought hastily together in large bodies; no time is given for that gradual growth of accommodation which would naturally accompany the gradual growth of numbers; they are, therefore, crowded into unwholesome dwellings, while scarcely any provision is made for their comfort or decency of living; they are released from the useful influences of domestic ties and from the habits of their former routine of life, (influences and habits the more important, in proportion to their want of education); they are hard worked; they are exposed to great risk of life and limb; they are too often hardly treated; and many inducements are presented to them to be thoughtless, thriftless, and improvident. Under these circumstances, your committee fears that intemperance, disorder, and demoralisation run a better chance of growth than decency, frugality, and improvement;

and they cannot wonder at the feelings of dislike and dismay with which the permanent inhabitants of a neighbourhood often view the arrival of these strangers among them.

"Your committee begs to suggest that every railway company, before employing more than a small given number of labourers together, in the construction of any part of their work, should be required to notify their intention to the public board, which may be charged with the general supervision of railways, and to state the number of men likely to be employed thereupon. A competent officer should then be required by the board to proceed to the place named, and to ascertain whether there was already adequate decent lodging to be obtained for the work-people, within a reasonable distance, and to report accordingly to the board. If it should be sufficient, that then the company should be allowed at once to proceed; otherwise, not until they have provided lodging to the satisfaction of such officer, certified by him to the board; and these proceedings should be at the expense of the company, the exercise of whose powers might be made dependent on their being taken. The inspecting officer should be required, from time to time, to visit the works and the lodgings, and to report thereon to the board, with a power to make sanitary regulations respecting them to be observed by the company, on approval by the board.

"Facilities for instruction are little worth wherever the men are incited by their treatment to wastefulness, drunkenness, and disorder, are unjustly dealt with, defrauded, and crowded together in places where a 'humane person would hardly put a pig.' No teaching can be of much avail to counteract the ceaseless operation of such degrading and deteriorating influences."

Note

1 In the endeavours of Mr. Peto to ameliorate the evils of the railway labourer, he met with an earnest and willing assistant in his partner, Mr. Grissell who, under the same auspices as Mr. Peto, has realised a large fortune by similar means. On the dissolution of partnership with the latter, Mr. Grissell retired from business—excepting with the contract for the Houses of Parliament—has become a landed proprietor, and co-operating with his late partner and friend, is a favourable specimen of the great railway contractor of the nineteenth century.

Mr. Grissell relates with great zest the difficulties which Mr. Peto and himself experienced in commencing as contractors. To those who know Mr. Bidder, the engineer, it need not be said that he was the last person to whom most men would have applied for information and assistance on the subject. However, to him did Mr. Peto address himself, and for a long time in vain; nor was it until the charms or the chance of a conservatory, built in the best style of the firm, had warmed the very inaccessible Mr. Bidder, that Mr. Peto succeeded in his object.

11

BENJAMIN DISRAELI, *SYBIL OR THE TWO NATIONS* (LONDON: LONGMANS, GREEN, AND CO., 1913), PP. 433–441

A Chartist leader had been residing for some time at Wodgate, ever since the distress had become severe, and had obtained great influence and popularity by assuring a suffering and half-starving population that they were entitled to four shillings a-day and two pots of ale, and only eight hours' work. He was a man of abilities and of popular eloquence, and his representations produced an effect; their reception invested him with influence, and as he addressed a population who required excitement, being slightly employed and with few resources for their vacant hours, the Chartist, who was careful never to speak of the Charter, became an important personage at Wodgate, and was much patronised by Bishop Hatton and his Lady, whose good offices he was sedulous to conciliate. At the right moment, everything being ripe and well prepared, the Bishop being very drunk and harassed by the complaints of his subjects, the Chartist revealed to him the mysteries of the Charter, and persuaded him not only that the Five Points would cure everything, but that he was the only man who could carry the Five Points. The Bishop had nothing to do; he was making a lock merely for amusement: he required action; he embraced the Charter, without having a definite idea what it meant, but he embraced it fervently, and he determined to march into the country at the head of the population of Wodgate, and establish the faith.

Since the conversion of Constantine, a more important adoption had never occurred. The whole of the north of England and a great part of the midland counties were in a state of disaffection; the entire country was suffering; hope had deserted the labouring classes; they had no confidence in any future of the existing system. Their organisation, independent of the political system of the Chartists, was complete. Every trade had its union, and every union its lodge in every town and its central committee in every district. All that was required was the first move, and the Chartist emissary had long fixed upon Wodgate as the spring of the explosion, when the news of the strike in Lancashire determined him to precipitate the event.

The march of Bishop Hatton at the head of the Hell-cats into the mining districts was perhaps the most striking popular movement since the Pilgrimage of Grace. Mounted on a white mule, wall-eyed and of hideous form, the Bishop brandished a huge hammer with which he had announced that he would destroy the enemies of the people: all butties, doggies, dealers in truck and tommy, middle masters and main masters. Some thousand Hell-cats followed him, brandishing bludgeons, or armed with bars of iron, pick-handles, and hammers. On each side of the Bishop, on a donkey, was one of his little sons, as demure and earnest as if he were handling his file. A flowing standard of silk, inscribed with the Charter, and which had been presented to him by the delegate, was borne before him like the oriflamme. Never was such a gaunt, grim crew. As they advanced, their numbers continually increased, for they arrested all labour in their progress. Every engine was stopped, the plug was driven out of every boiler, every fire was extinguished, every man was turned out. The decree went forth that labour was to cease until the Charter was the law of the land: the mine and the mill, the foundry and the loomshop, were, until that consummation, to be idle: nor was the mighty pause to be confined to these great enterprises. Every trade of every kind and description was to be stopped: tailor and cobbler, brush-maker and sweep, tinker and carter, mason and builder, all, all; for all an enormous Sabbath, that was to compensate for any incidental suffering which it induced by the increased means and the elevated condition that it ultimately would insure: that paradise of artizans, that Utopia of Toil, embalmed in those ringing words, sounds cheerful to the Saxon race: 'A fair day's wage for a fair day's work.'

DURING the strike in Lancashire the people had never plundered, except a few provision shops chiefly rifled by boys, and their acts of violence had been confined to those with whom they were engaged in what, on the whole, might be described as a fair contest. They solicited sustenance often in great numbers, but even then their language was mild and respectful, and they were easily satisfied and always grateful. A body of two thousand persons, for example (the writer speaks of circumstances within his own experience), quitted one morning a manufacturing town in Lancashire, when the strike had continued for some time and began to be severely felt, and made a visit to a neighbouring squire of high degree. They entered his park in order, men, women, and children, and then, seating themselves in the immediate vicinity of the mansion, they sent a deputation to announce that they were starving and to entreat relief. In the instance in question, the lord of the domain was absent in the fulfilment of those public duties which the disturbed state of the country devolved on him. His wife, who had a spirit equal to the occasion, notwithstanding the presence of her young children, who might well have aggravated feminine fears, received the deputation herself; told them that of course she was unprepared to feed so many, but that, if they promised to maintain order and conduct themselves with decorum, she would take measures to satisfy their need. They gave their pledge and remained tranquilly encamped while preparations were making to satisfy them. Carts were sent to a neighbouring town for provisions; the keepers killed what they could, and in a few hours the multitude were fed without the slightest disturbance, or the least breach of their self-organised discipline. When all was over, the deputation waited again on the lady to express to her their gratitude; and, the gardens of this house being of celebrity in the neighbourhood, they requested permision that the people might be allowed to walk through them, pledging themselves that no flower should be plucked and no fruit touched. The permission was granted: the multitude, in order, each file under a chief and each commander of the files obedient to a superior officer, then made a progress through the beautiful gardens of their beautiful hostess. They even passed through the forcing houses and vineries. Not a border was trampled on, not a grape plucked; and, when they quitted the domain, they gave three cheers for the fair castellan.

The Hell-cats and their followers were of a different temper from these gentle Lancashire insurgents. They destroyed and ravaged; sacked and gutted houses; plundered cellars; proscribed bakers as enemies of the people; sequestrated the universal stores of all truck and tommy shops; burst open doors, broke windows; destroyed the gas-works, that the towns at night might be in darkness; took union workhouses by storm, burned rate-books in the marketplace, and ordered public distribution of loaves of bread and flitches of bacon to a mob; cheering and laughing amid flames and rapine. In short, they robbed and rioted; the police could make no head against them; there was no military force; the whole district was in their possession; and, hearing that a battalion of the Coldstreams were coming down by a train, the Bishop ordered all railroads to be destroyed, and, if the Hell-cats had not been too drunk to do his bidding and he too tipsy to repeat it, it is probable that a great destruction of these public ways might have taken place.

Does the reader remember Diggs' tommy shop? And Master Joseph? Well, a terrible scene took place there. The Wodgate girl, with a back like a grasshopper, of the Baptist school religion, who had married Tummas, once a pupil of the Bishop, and still his fervent follower, although he had cut open his pupil's head, was the daughter of a man who had worked many years in Diggs' field, had suffered much under his intolerable yoke, and at the present moment was deep in his awful ledger. She had heard from her first years of the oppression of Diggs, and had impressed it on her husband, who was intolerant of any tyranny except at Wodgate. Tummas and his wife, and a few chosen friends, therefore, went out one morning to settle the tommy-book of her father with Mr. Diggs. A whisper of their intention had got about among those interested in the subject. It was a fine summer morning, some three hours from noon; the shop was shut, indeed it had not been opened since the riots, and all the lower windows of the dwelling were closed, barred, and bolted.

A crowd of women had collected. There was Mistress Page and Mistress Prance, old Dame Toddles and Mrs. Mullins, Liza Gray and the comely dame, who was so fond of society that she liked even a riot.

'Master Joseph, they say, has gone to the North,' said the comely dame.

'I wonder if old Diggs is at home?' said Mrs. Mullins.

'He won't show, I'll be sworn,' said old Dame Toddles.

'Here are the Hell-cats,' said the comely dame. 'Well, I do declare, they march like reglars; two, four, six, twelve; a good score at the least.'

The Hell-cats briskly marched up to the elm-trees that shaded the canal before the house, and then formed in line opposite to it. They were armed with bludgeons, crowbars, and hammers. Tummas was at the head, and by his side his Wodgate wife. Stepping forth alone, amid the cheering of the crowd of women, the pupil of the Bishop advanced to the door of Diggs' house, gave a loud knock, and a louder ring. He waited patiently for several minutes: there was no reply from the interior, and then Tummas knocked and rang again.

'It's very awful,' said the comely dame.

'It's what I always dreamt would come to pass,' said Liza Gray, 'ever since Master Joseph cut my poor baby over the eye with his three-foot rule.'

'I think there can be nobody within,' said Mrs. Prance.

'Old Diggs would never leave the tommy without a guard,' said Mrs. Page.

'Now, lads,' said Tummas, looking round him and making a sign; and immediately some half dozen advanced with their crowbars and were about to strike at the door, when a window in the upper story of the house opened, and the muzzle of a blunderbuss was presented at the assailants.

The women all screamed and ran away.

''Twas Master Joseph,' said the comely dame, halting to regain her breath.

''Twas Master Joseph,' sighed Mrs. Page.

''Twas Master Joseph,' moaned Mrs. Prance.

'Sure enough,' said Mrs. Mullins, 'I saw his ugly face.'

'More frightful than the great gun,' said old Dame Toddles.

'I hope the children will get out of the way,' said Liza Gray, 'for he is sure to fire on them.'

In the meantime, while Master Joseph himself was content with his position and said not a word, a benignant countenance exhibited itself at the window, and requested in a mild voice to know, 'What his good friends wanted there?'

'We have come to settle Sam Barlow's tommy-book,' said their leader.

'Our shop is not open to-day, my good friends: the account can stand over; far be it from me to press the poor.'

'Master Diggs,' said a Hell-cat, 'canst thou tell us the price of bacon to-day?'

'Well, good bacon,' said the elder Diggs, willing to humour them, 'may be eightpence a pound.'

'Thou art wrong, Master Diggs,' said the Hell-cat, ''tis fourpence and long credit. Let us see half a dozen good flitches at fourpence, Master Diggs; and be quick.'

There was evidently some controversy in the interior as to the course at this moment to be pursued. Master Joseph remonstrated against the policy of concession, called conciliation, which his father would fain follow, and was for instant coercion; but age and experience carried the day, and in a few minutes some flitches were thrown out of the window to the Hell-cats, who received the booty with a cheer.

The women returned.

"'Tis the tenpence a pound flitch,' said the comely dame, examining the prize with a sparkling glance.

'I have paid as much for very green stuff,' said Mrs. Mullins.

'And now, Master Diggs,' said Tummas, 'what is the price of the best tea a-pound? We be good customers, and mean to treat our wives and sweethearts here. I think we must order half a chest.'

This time there was a greater delay in complying with the gentle hint; but, the Hell-cats getting obstreperous, the tea was at length furnished and divided among the women. This gracious office devolved on the wife of Tummas, who soon found herself assisted by a spontaneous committee, of which the comely dame was the most prominent and active member. Nothing could be more considerate, good-natured, and officious, than the mode and spirit with which she divided the stores. The flitches were cut up and apportioned in like manner. The scene was as gay and bustling as a fair.

'It is as good as grand tommy-day,' said the comely dame, with a self-complacent smile, as she strutted about, smiling and dispensing patronage.

The orders for bacon and tea were followed by a popular demand for cheese. The female committee received all the plunder and were active in its distribution. At length, a rumour got about that Master Joseph was entering the names of all present in the tommy-books, so that eventually the score might be satisfied. The mob had now much increased. There was a panic among the women, and indignation among the men: a Hell-cat advanced and announced that, unless the tommy-books were all given up to be burnt, they would pull down the house. There was no reply: some of the Hell-cats advanced; the women cheered; a crowbar fell upon the door; Master Joseph fired, wounded a woman and killed a child.

There rose one of those universal shrieks of wild passion which announce that men have discarded all the trammels of civilisation, and found in their licentious rage new and unforeseen sources of power and vengeance. Where it came from, how it was obtained, who prompted the thought, who first accomplished it, were alike impossible to trace; but, as it were in a moment, a number of trusses of straw were piled up before the house and set on fire, the gates of the timber-yard were forced, and a quantity of scantlings and battens soon fed the flame. Everything indeed that could stimulate the fire was employed; and every one was occupied in the service. They ran to the water side and plundered the barges, and threw the huge blocks of coal upon the enormous bonfire. Men, women, and children were alike at work with the eagerness and energy of fiends. The roof of the house caught fire: the dwelling burned rapidly; you could see the flames like the tongues of wild beasts, licking the bare and vanishing walls; a single being was observed amid the fiery havoc, shrieking and desperate; he slung convulsively to a huge account-book. It was Master Joseph. His father had made his escape from the back of the premises and had counselled his son instantly to follow him, but Master Joseph wished to rescue the ledger as well as their lives, and the delay ruined him.

'He has got the tommy-book,' cried Liza Gray.

The glare of the clear flame fell for a moment upon his countenance of agony; the mob gave an infernal cheer; then, some part of the building falling in, there rose a vast cloud of smoke and rubbish, and he was seen no more.

12

STEPHEN W. FULLOM, 'THE BRAWL VIADUCT', 'ENGLISH AND IRISH', AND 'THE REWARD OF MERIT', IN *THE GREAT HIGHWAY: A STORY OF THE WORLD'S STRUGGLES.* THIRD ED. (LONDON: G. ROUTLEDGE & CO., 1854), PP. 119–146

The Brawl viaduct

THE viaduct and embankment progressed steadily, though slowly, and meanwhile, Ernest, with work of all kinds going on around him, enjoyed a thousand opportunities of augmenting his practical efficiency. In a short time he learnt levelling and the use of the theodolite, and was able to draw a plan of a bridge, and estimate the cost of its construction. Parkyns and Blouser readily instructed him in all they knew, and he found the same willingness in the agents and superintendents of the contractors; but Wormwood, while he made no end of friendly professions, uniformly evaded giving any information. Soon, however, he found himself in the background and was often glad to seek aid from the more alert judgment of Ernest.

But it was not in engineering alone that Ernest enlarged his fund of knowledge. The colossal embankment which was now fast closing on the viaduct, an Alps of art, had been dug up from as vast a cutting, and in this excavation he found leisure to pursue the interesting researches of geology. In the mines of Wales he had looked into the limestone and the coal: here, in the broader light of day, he beheld the diluvium, the clays, and the chalk. Often he stood in rapt contemplation of this marvellous and most terrible history. Full of suggestion indeed was its half-faded writing, and, from the wreck of worlds, he turned with a calmer spirit to the littleness of his own occupations, elevated and refined in his views, and impressed alike by the solemn inspiration of religion, and the beautiful lessons of philosophy.

Gradually his task at the viaduct drew to a completion. The arches, which from their great span had excited no little apprehension, were now well set, and the centres being lowered, the massive structure stood exposed to view, a rare combination of elegance and solidity. In honour of the event, the contractors gave their' workmen a holiday, and for one day, operations were suspended on that portion of the line.

It was a bright morning, as if Nature, too, made holiday, and Ernest enjoyed, as only those who are constantly occupied can, the luxury of an idle day. But as evening came on, with thoughts still clinging to his duty, he strolled along by the side of the works, in proud contemplation of their appearance. The spectacle was one that might well excite interest, and suggest reflection. A noble achievement of science, a wondrous result of labour, it was, at the same time, a grand revelation of human progress. Soon that lofty causeway, constructed under his eye, would traverse the country like an artery, disseminating a new stream of wealth, like fresh blood, through the length and breadth of the land. The miraculous element of steam would draw along its road of iron a whole host of travellers, carrying the beneficent influences of civilization to the remotest nooks—a comet with its train of light! Far more swiftly would the electric wire, the girdle of the new highway, diffuse, on lightning wings, the same benign effects, annihilating time and space, and uniting all men in a common bond of brotherhood.

If we looked back with wonder at the Appian roads of the Romans, which remain among the proudest monuments of their enterprise and genius, how would posterity, in the lapse of ages, regard this triumph of later times? Here was a road towering over valleys and tunnelled through mountains, which would only perish, as far as human judgment could foresee, with the soil on which it rested. The thought was suggestive, and instinctively Ernest's eye turned on the ground, wandering over it with a half-abstracted glance. Suddenly light gleamed in his look, kindling his face with startled interest. He stooped down, and remained a moment with his eyes fixed on the turf: THE GROUND WAS SLIPPING! He traced a crack, as yet but imperfectly marked, alongside the whole length of the embankment. The mighty fabric of earth, as it acquired cohesion, was pressing out the natural soil, driving away its own foundation: the subsidence would soon be felt at its junction with the viaduct; as the embankment slipped down, it would tear away the buttresses; and in a few hours the stately achievement of the builder, to which he had just attributed a more than Egyptian stability, would be a heap of ruins.

For a moment, Ernest was confounded at this unexpected casualty. But it was not a time to hesitate, and he quickly decided on the course he should pursue. Flying to the inn, he despatched expresses to Mr. Colville and Mr. Hammer, briefly stating what he had discovered, at the same time sending for Parkyns, Wormwood, and Blouser, that he might have the advantage of their assistance and advice in such a great emergency. He also addressed a note to the agent of the contractor, requiring his immediate presence at the works.

The agent, Mr. Shorter, a plain, precise-looking man, the very embodiment of a practical idea, even his whiskers being adjusted in a matter-of-fact way, promptly attended, and learnt the critical situation of the viaduct.

"What you say, is no doubt correct, sir," he observed, in reply to Ernest's statement, "but that is no business of mine. Our people engaged to build the viaduct, and they have built it: if the embankment breaks away the brickwork, the fault does not rest with us."

"But you're bound to lend me your aid to preserve it," rejoined Ernest.

"I am willing to do so."

"You recognise my authority?"

"Certainly. You are the representative of the Company here."

"And you concur with me, that nothing can be done, unless we take measures to arrest the slip at once?"

"I am quite of that opinion."

"Then I order you to clear out the earth from the buttresses of the viaduct, and to lighten the top of the embankment, by throwing the earth down on the subsiding side, so as to extend the slope beyond where the ground has slipped. You must instantly put on your whole force, and work all night."

"You will please to give me these instructions in writing, sir, stating you take upon yourself the whole responsibility of the proceeding."

"That is but reasonable. You shall have it at once."

"Then, your orders shall be obeyed."

Night was coming on, but, through the untiring efforts of Ernest, scarcely an hour had elapsed, ere a large body of men were on the works, carrying out his energetic measures. Fires blazed along the bank, illuminating the surrounding country, and throwing a lurid glare, like the reflection of a volcano, on the dark and lowering sky. Teams of horses moved to and fro, dragging along the rugged tramway heavy loads of earth from the interior of the buttresses, which were shot rapidly over the bank, while hundreds of navvies, under their several gangers, worked away with their picks, and heaped up a fresh supply. Ernest stood in the midst of the brickwork, the point of greatest importance, stimulating the workmen, as they cleared away the earth, by his presence and example. Here, at length, when the night had far waned, he was joined by the other three assistants.

"Why, Glynn, my boy, what's all this?" cried Parkyns.

"Who ordered it?" demanded Wormwood, his eyes preparing for a spring.

Ernest hastily explained.

"What a go!" observed Blouser.

"I hope you all approve of what I have done?" said Ernest.

"Egad, I don't know what to say to it, my dear fellow," answered Parkyns, "and that's the truth. I hope I. C. will bear you out."

"I don't think he will," said Wormwood. "I wouldn't stand in Glynn's shoes for a trifle."

"What do *you* think of it, Blouser?" asked Ernest.

"Stunnin!" said Blouser.

"You approve?"

"Whole hog," said Blouser, emphatically.

"It's a great satisfaction for me to know you do," returned Ernest, "as I value your opinion, and it confirms me in my own."

"Put on the steam," said Blouser.

"I hope it's all right," observed Parkyns, a little ashamed; "but I once got into a tremendous scrape with a similar thing on the Grand Trunk Line, where I saved a superb bridge, and got the bullet the next day. I then determined never to originate anything again."

"Why, this is something new," observed Wormwood, incredulously. "How is it you've never told us of it before?"

"*Mister* Wormwood," answered Parkyns, turning very red, "I beg you'll keep your observations to yourself. There are many things I've done which I have never told you, and never shall. As a gentleman, I can only be understood by gentlemen. But you're Glynn's friend: why don't you stand by him now, when your friendship may be useful?"

"Because I don't approve of what he's done," answered Wormwood, pertly.

"And is that acting like Gisippus?" asked Parkyns.

"Good!" said Blouser. "Sold again!"

"It's no matter," observed Ernest. "I take the whole onus of the thing on myself: I'm only glad to have Blouser's opinion that I've acted right."

"And have you sent for I. C. and the Yellow-hammer?" asked Parkyns.

"Yes."

"Then, let's have some refreshments—Riley!"

"Here you are, your honour," answered Riley, producing his can.

"What, have you got some?"

"Sure, I knew your honours couldn't do without mixtur," replied Pat: "and so I brought some up wid me, good luck to it! By the same token—"

"Never mind the token," observed Parkyns, "but run down to the King's Head, and tell them to send up supper for four, and put it down to the Company."

"Ay, ay, your honour," answered Pat. And he muttered as he moved off—"Sure I may as well say for *five* while I'm about it, so I might! Arrah! So I will, too!"

The supper, which was not only enough for five, but for a dozen (the G H R being in high odour at the inn), soon made its appearance, and Parkyns, Wormwood, and Blouser at once set to, and regaled themselves. Ernest, too conscientious to feast at the expense of the Company, and thinking only of the work in hand, declined to participate in the repast, remaining immovable at his post.

Suddenly there was a lull among the workmen, and the party at supper jumped up, not without a hint, dexterously telegraphed by Riley, as to who was approaching. It was Mr. Hammer.

In a moment he was under the arch of the buttress, confronting Ernest.

"Is Mr. Colville here?" he inquired, quickly.

"No, sir."

"Then what are you doing? Who has ordered all this?"

"I have, sir."

"You?"

"Yes, sir. I was afraid of the viaduct being torn down before I could receive your instructions, and I ventured to act on my own responsibility."

"*Your* responsibility. Who gave *you* any responsibility?"

"I thought—"

"You'd no business to think, sir," cried the Yellow-hammer, with the look of a kite.

"Mr. Glynn, I told you," observed Wormwood, in a very gentle voice, "I was afraid that—"

"I really am surprised, Mr. Wormwood," cried Mr. Hammer, "that this proceeding should be sanctioned by you."

"By me, sir!" said Wormwood, fixing his eyes. "Not by me, I assure you. I told Mr. Glynn, I did not, and could not sanction it."

"Then who has?"

"Name of Blouser," said Blouser, stepping forward.

"I think it right to state, sir, that I alone am responsible," observed Ernest. "Mr. Blouser, though he believed I had acted for the best, has in no way interfered, and the contractor has but obeyed my orders. I saw the crack in the ground, and thought the only way to arrest the slip was to clear out the buttresses, and lighten the embankment."

"And you thought right," said a loud, clear voice. "You have saved the viaduct, and I highly approve of your conduct."

There was a moment's pause, when a loud cheer rang along the bank, as the workmen recognised Mr. Colville.

English and Irish

THE measures originated by Ernest effectually arrested the landslip, and gave the embankment permanence and stability. This result, however, was not the work of a day, or a few hours, but though the effect, to a certain extent, was immediate, occupied a considerable time, and was frequently interrupted by minor difficulties, not easily comprehended by unprofessional minds. At length, all obstacles were overcome, and the undertaking completed.

Ernest was now removed to another part of the line, where the work of construction being finished, Mr. Colville had commenced the operation of laying down the rails. Such a task, to one of any experience, might seem simple enough, but in this case it was really far otherwise, the rails being laid on a new principle, on longitudinal sleepers, and requiring, from various causes, unremitted attention on the part of the engineer. Wormwood was joined with Ernest in the duty, and they relieved each other night and day, sometimes remaining up together all night, when, from any unforeseen circumstance, the work called for an extraordinary degree of vigilance. Blouser and Parkyns superintended an adjoining tract, and an old tiled hovel, by the side of a canal, the deserted lair of a brickmaker, served as an office for all.

Ernest was now brought into much closer contact with the navvies, and saw more of them, as a class, in a few days, than he had ever seen before. Familiar as he was with the low moral condition of the miners and ironworkers of the West, the desperate character and demoralized habits of these reckless men took him completely by surprise, and he could not but wonder that, in the nineteenth century, in the midst of a community foremost in every good work, such ignorance and barbarism could exist. Melancholy, indeed, it was to see a peasantry so brutalized and degraded, retaining nothing of humanity but its form. Among them the name of God was never pronounced but in execration and blasphemy; the mind recognised no scruple of morality or religion; and, in domestic life, the sacred tie of marriage was unknown. Every base passion, every pernicious habit, every low, grovelling, and debasing vice by which human nature can be tainted and defiled, here stood forth in its most hideous aspect, unreproved and unchecked; and the very labour which, under proper direction, might have been made a means of elevation, became an additional cause of debasement, being pursued without intermission night and day, even on Sunday, under the stimulus of beer and gin, till the men were constantly either stupified or intoxicated, and threw off alike restraint and shame.

Among the various gangs were many Irishmen, and, to the other causes of quarrel which were continually arising, that of nationality, the most bitter of all, was soon added. The Irish working under price, were naturally regarded as intruders, and a bad feeling grew up, which, pervading both parties, was always ready to break out on the slightest provocation. Sometimes the Irish, sometimes the English, were the agressors, and the result was always a fight, embittering the combatants still further against each other, and rendering the breach wider and wider. On one of these occasions Ernest had been appealed to, and had decided in favour of the Irish, who, as it happened, were at the moment in the right, though an hour afterwards he might have given a verdict against them; but no one paused to inquire whether his decision was just and impartial: they only cared to know which side he was on. From that day, he was adopted as a champion by the Irish, and, unknown to himself, became the object of all those feelings of devotion so readily excited in the Irish heart, while, on the other hand, he was cordially detested by the English, who looked upon him, through the distorted medium of their prejudices, as the patron of the Irish, and a betrayer and persecutor of his own countrymen.

One night Ernest and Wormwood were both on duty, and had retired for a few moments to the office, to consult on some point of difficulty, when a tremendous uproar was heard without, and Pat Riley, for once without his can, rushed in breathless, exhibiting unmistakable marks of punishment.

"Och, run for your life, Mr. Glynn, dear!" he cried. "They're comin' down on us like mad, swearin' vengance, and they'll take it sure enough. Hear to 'em!"

"What is it!" cried Wormwood, turning pale, and half making for the door.

"Sure it's Mr. Glynn they're after," cried Pat. "And, whist! how he sits there, as if it was a wake we was at. And maybe it 'ull end in a wake, yet. Och! run for your life, your honour, will you?"

"Now take your breath, and then tell me quietly what is the matter, Pat," replied Ernest.

"Tell you quietly, do you say? Arrah, then, I'm in a pretty state to be quiet, aint I, and with them roarin' villins comin' on, too. And here they are upon us, faix! and now we are as good as kilt entirely."

There was indeed a rush of feet in the passage, and, before Ernest could interpose, half a dozen men had entered, their heads streaming with blood; and shut and secured the door. A glance showed that they were Irish, and a fearful yell without, bursting at once from hundreds of voices, indicated the close proximity of their enemies. The Irish, however, had the advantage of great experience in such affrays, and in a moment they so barricaded the door and lower window of the hovel, with desks, chairs, and stools, that the assailants, with all their combined strength, were unable to force an entrance.

Ernest now learnt from Riley the origin of the disturbance, from which it appeared, that the English had come to the resolution of driving the Irish off the line, at the same time subjecting them, in revenge for past affronts, to the grossest ill-usage, and denouncing summary vengeance against all who had supported them. In this category Ernest was included, and in fact many of the assailants were calling upon him by name, to stand forth and show himself, that they might tear his heart out—a shocking threat, coming from such men, who were not only brutal enough to tear out his heart, but almost savage enough to eat it.

The first attack was followed up by a volley of brickbats, which the door and window-shutters, in themselves very crazy defences, would have been unable to resist, if they had not been so effectually barricaded.

"We can't stand this long," said Ernest, to Wormwood. "What is to be done?"

"I—I don't know," answered Wormwood, who was suffering from a tremor in his fangs. "I—I wish I could get out, and—and run."

"But you can't. You'd be caught, and most likely be severely handled. But we must get some one out, and send for assistance, or we shall be murdered."

"You're not—not goin' yourself," stammered Wormwood, who, ever suspecting treachery, thought Ernest wished to secure his own retreat, and leave him in the lurch. "I—I won't—won't hear of it, Mis—Mister Glynn."

"Don't be alarmed," returned Ernest. "I've no intention of running away, even if it were possible, which it does not appear to be. The thing is, can we apprise our friends of our situation? I think we might."—He turned to Riley, and asked if he could swim.

"Like a duck, yer honour, no less," returned Riley.

"Then you must get out at the back of the house, and drop into the canal," rejoined Ernest—"when you can make over the brickfield to Drayland, and knock up Mr. Shorter. Let him know the extremity we are in, and he'll do something to assist us."

"Troth, I wisht he was here now, yer honour," returned Riley, as another furious assault was made on the door, "but it's myself that'll give him no paice till he's on the road."

There was no door at the back of the hovel, which, as already observed, stood on the brink of the canal; but about midway between the ground and roof, there was a small fan-light, for the purpose of lighting the stairs; and it was through this outlet that Riley was to make his egress. The poor fellow devoted himself to the enterprise with a resolution approaching the heroic, and submitted in silence to the operation of being worked through the small aperture, though it occasioned him no little suffering. But a party were watching the back of the house, from the bank higher up, and his descent from the casement, after clinging for a moment to the sill, was a signal for a shower of brickbats, one of which struck him a violent blow as he fell with a splash in the water. A fearful yell announced his flight to the mob in front, who, supposing that all the inmates were attempting to escape, redoubled their efforts to gain an entrance, while two or three of the rearward party threw off their smocks, and followed Riley into the water. The Irishman scarcely ventured to appear on the surface, but struck out below, and a few efforts brought him to his feet, when he scrambled up the bank, and darted away. He had not gone many steps, however, when he tumbled headlong into a stagnant pool, and before he could extricate himself his pursuers had gained the bank, and were close upon him. A loud halloo betrayed their presence, and consciousness of his proximity; but Riley doubled round a brick-kiln, and got a start. He then made a dash for the road, hotly pursued by the navvies.

While this was proceeding outside, Ernest, foreseeing that the door must soon be forced, was strengthening his defences within, by erecting a second barricade at the foot of the stairs. Having previously used all the furniture, he would now have been at a loss for material, but his Irish garrison, with the help of their pickaxes, tore up the flooring of the upper room, and pulled out the grates, forming with these accessories an impassable barrier. They then raised the bricks which composed the floor of the passage, heaping them up behind the barricade, to serve as missiles, and finally, under Ernest's direction, took up their position on the stairs, and awaited the enemy.

The door withstood its assailants longer than they expected, but, at last, it broke in with a crash, throwing down the rampart of chairs and stools, which fell in fragments in the passage. A swarm of navvies poured in, brandishing pickaxes and shovels, and made a rush at the inner barricade; but were received, as they advanced, with such a shower of bricks, that they fell back over each other, blocking up the way, and causing a frightful scene of confusion—heightened, if possible, by the darkness, Ernest having extinguished the light. Still the mob behind, more and more infuriated, pushed on, trampling over their own accomplices, and uttering the most appalling yells, mingled with threats too horrible to be repeated. Missiles could no longer keep them back, and a struggle commenced over the barricade, in which Ernest, now fighting for his life, took a foremost part. A gigantic navvie at length seized him by the throat, and was dragging him over the barricade, when a blow from an Irishman's shovel drove him back, and set Ernest free. But in the encounter, one of the planks broke down, greatly weakening the defence, and the assailants, pushing forward in a body, gained a footing on the stairs. All now seemed lost, but at this critical moment there was a loud cry of "War-ork," used on the line to denote the approach of a constable, and presently it arose from without as from one voice. Cheered by the hope of succour, the defendants made a desperate effort to maintain their ground, and as the cry of "War-ork" again rose, the assailants fell back, rushing from the house as other shouts were heard, followed by the trampling of horse. In fact, as they poured forth, a troop of cavalry galloped up to the hovel, scattering the mob in all directions.

Riley, it turned out, had made his way to Mr. Shorter's; but the riot had already spread along the line, and knowing that no ordinary force could repress it, the overseer had gone off at once to—, and brought down the military, whose timely appearance secured the safety of Ernest and his companions. For some moments they were in great alarm about Wormwood, who had mysteriously disappeared; but, at last he was found in the upper room, concealed in a cupboard, and half dead with fear.

The reward of merit

THE ferment caused by the riot, extending for some distance along the line, did not subside for several days. Many on both sides were severely injured, and not a few were apprehended by the police, and afterwards, as the most active of the rioters, brought to trial at the assizes. Ernest, having fought in the dark, was unable to identify any of the parties, but the case was made out against several, and they were sentenced to transportation, while others, guilty in a less degree, were adjudged various terms of imprisonment.

On the morning following the riot, Parkyns and Blouser, hearing what had occurred, paid an early visit to the office, impatient to learn the real facts; and found Ernest already at work.

"Here's a game!" cried Blouser, as he came upon the wreck in the passage.

"Faix, it's true for you, yer honour," observed Pat Riley, who had just appeared with his can. "It bate Donnybrook holler, you may take yer oath."

"Where did you make your great stand?" asked Parkyns of Ernest.

"Just here," replied Ernest, "at the foot of the stairs."

"Sitch a gettin' up stairs I never did see," remarked Blouser.

"By dad, yer honour's a good judge," remarked Riley.—"It was a beautiful skrimmage, no doubt; and you'd give the two eyes of your head to see sitch another!"

"Over here," said Blouser, pointing significantly over his left shoulder.

"It was a good position, and well chosen," remarked Parkyns, with the air of a general. "A barricade here, and the rise of the stairs behind, with the narrow passage in front, gave you a great advantage, and you might hold out a long time. How many of you were there?"

"Half a dozen in all," answered Ernest.

"Of those half-dozen I ask but three, to make a new Thermopylæ," said Parkyns.

"Good!" cried Blouser. "Bravo Rouse!"

"I've no doubt Parkyns would have distinguished himself," said Ernest; "but still I can't help thinking we did pretty well, and I'm quite satisfied to have got off as we did. But what's become of Wormwood?"

"Hooked it," replied Blouser.

"Not he," said Parkyns. "I called round at his place, and found he'd set off at daylight for Markford, no doubt to report his exploits to the Yellow-hammer, and you'll find, when the cat comes out, that it was Wormwood who did everything, and that our worthy friend Glynn was a mere cipher in the affair."

"And so it proved; for, about half an hour afterwards, Mr. Hammer, thus accurately informed, appeared on the line, walking arm-in-arm with Wormwood, in the most friendly and confidential manner—a condescension which seemed almost too much for his *protégé*, who, in the words of Mr. Blouser, looked "staggered" on the occasion. They were attended by two of the mounted patrol, as a guard of honour, neither gentleman being yet thoroughly satisfied that all was safe.

Mr. Hammer scowled at Ernest as he entered the office.

"A good night's work you have made, sir, meddling with the men," he said. "What business have you with their quarrels?"

"I really don't understand you, sir," replied Ernest, indignant at this affront. "Surely Mr. Wormwood, if he has told you anything of what has occurred, must have let you know that we acted here last night in self-defence, and had nothing whatever to do with the quarrels of the men."

"I can answer for myself, that I had not, most certainly," said Wormwood, with a glare at his patron.

"Don't drag in Mr. Wormwood, I beg, sir," cried Mr. Hammer. "For his part in this occurrence, both the Company and Mr. Colville are greatly indebted to him, and, in their name, I take this opportunity to tender him publicly their thanks. I am not imputing blame to him, but to you. I am told you have been interfering in the disputes of the work-people, and from this all the disturbance has originated."

"Then, I can only say, sir, your informant has wilfully misled you," replied Ernest.

"What do you say?"

"What I am prepared to prove. I have never interfered with the work-people in any way, except when appealed to, and then only so far as was necessary to prevent the stoppage of the works."

"That's enough, sir. I don't want to hear any more."

"Pardon me, Mr. Hammer. You have brought a charge against me—a charge of the most serious description, and I must be heard in refutation of it. If not, I shall appeal to Mr. Colville."

"Enough, I tell you," said Mr. Hammer, turning purple with rage.

"Are you satisfied of my innocence, sir?" pursued Ernest, "because here is Mr. Shorter"—the overseer entered at this instant—"who knows all the circumstances, and you must permit me to request an investigation. You are acquainted with the whole history of this disturbance among the workmen, Mr. Shorter?"

"Yes."

"What has been my conduct in the matter?"

"Extremely proper."

"Have I ever shown a disposition to interfere unnecessarily?"

"Quite the reverse. You have abstained from interfering as long as possible."

"Have I ever done anything to warrant an imputation of favouritism or partiality?"

"On the contrary, your conduct has always been characterised by forbearance, moderation, and a spirit of justice."

"For he's a jolly good fellow," broke out Blouser. "*Hem!*—beg pardon."—And he blew his nose violently, in the utmost confusion.

"I hope, sir, you are now convinced I have been misrepresented to you," said Ernest to Mr. Hammer.

"Very well, sir—very well," returned Mr. Hammer. "Let it be a warning to you not to interfere again—that's all."—And before Ernest could reply, he marched out of the office, followed by Wormwood.

"This is too bad," exclaimed Ernest. "He pretends to give me a reprimand, though I have disproved the charge. But I will ask him to produce my accuser."—And he made a movement towards the door.

"Stop where you are," said Parkyns, arresting him. "You've said quite enough to vindicate your character as a gentleman, and as a gentleman I applaud you for it. But a word more would do harm."

"Mild," observed Blouser, "mild's the word. Let off the steam, my boy."

But the impetuous young man, irritated at treatment so undeserved, and smarting under Mr. Hammer's reproof, broke from them, and rushed out.

Mr. Hammer had just got into his gig, which, on alighting to walk up the line, he had directed to be brought round to the office by the road, and Ernest only encountered Wormwood.

"I am indebted to you, I presume, for this unprovoked attack," he said, with a look of scorn. "If you have anything to allege against me, state it openly and fairly, and I will meet it."

"What can have put this into your head?" replied Wormwood. "I can have nothing to say of you, Mr. Glynn, but what is to your advantage."

"You know you have misrepresented me to Mr. Hammer, and that I have in consequence been censured, when my conduct deserved approbation."

"You accuse me of this! Where is your proof?"

"Proof!"

"Yes," said Wormwood, his eyes protruding. "I ask—I demand your proof. On what evidence do you charge me with so base an action?"

Ernest was confounded by the question. He had, indeed, acted only on suspicion—a suspicion dictated equally by an instinct in his own breast (too often a blind guide), and by several concurring circumstances; but a moment's reflection showed him that, however he might suspect, he had no right to condemn on such slender and inconclusive grounds.

"I have always acted towards you as a friend," resumed Wormwood. "With me, friendship is a sacred sentiment, and the ruling principle of my life. But there are some people—people whom I have shrined in my heart, and defended behind their backs, who are incapable of friendship, and always suspecting and doubting. I ought to know there is no such thing as friendship in the world—it's too sacred: it's always on one side. Gisippus sacrificed himself to his friend: and Cæsar thought he had a friend in Brutus, but Brutus stabbed him. That was the unkindest cut of all."

"If you were my friend," said Ernest, "why didn't you attest what I said when I appealed to you?"

"So I did."

"I understood you to speak only for yourself."

"Then it was a mistake, for I meant to speak clearly and decisively."

"I'm glad to hear you say so. I've been too hasty, perhaps, in accusing you, and am sorry for it. I hope we shall really be friends in future."

They shook hands, Wormwood declaring he had no object in life but friendship, and that, regarded as a moral influence, friendship was the most pure and noble that could animate the bosom of man.

"I drink to that sentiment," cried Parkyns, appearing at the office-door, "Riley, the mixture! Mr. Wormwood's sentiment, Blouser!—friendship."—Parkyns had become very satirical on the subject of Wormwood's attachment,—"not forgetting absent friends, Mr. Hammer to wit."

"Hammer and tongs," said Blouser. "Go ahead!"

Peace being established, matters proceeded in their usual course. The work of laying the rails progressed rapidly, and, as it advanced, was regarded with the greatest interest in the scientific world. Soon a run of about three miles was complete, and presented, in its structure and general features, an appearance so different from other railways, that it might well excite curiosity and attract universal attention.

On this tract it was determined to experimentalize, and accordingly an engine was brought down from London by the road, with half a dozen carriages, for the purpose of running a train on the new-fashioned rails.

And here it may be necessary to explain the principle on which the rails were put down, which, fortunately for the reader, can be done in a few words. On most lines, the rails are laid at intervals of a few feet, on transverse sleepers, to which they are secured by iron grooves, called chairs, causing at times a jolting, and often a vibratory motion, very far from agreeable. To get rid of such a drawback, and secure a perfectly easy motion, the rails on the Hirlemdown line were laid without chairs, on longitudinal sleepers, running the whole length of the rail, and supported, at short distances, by cross beams, fastened on piles. To render this massive framework still more stable, as well as to insure steadiness under the pressure of a train, the sleepers were packed, as it was called, with sifted gravel—that is, every stone was thrown aside, and the sand of the gravel beaten underneath the sleeper in a mass, affording, it was supposed, a uniformly level base, which would resist any amount of pressure, and consequently prevent the least vibration.

Great was the excitement when the engine, so long expected, made its appearance at Drayland, mounted on a colossal truck, drawn by a whole stud of horses. Chains of iron and massive wedges, strengthened by bolts, were necessary to secure its huge frame to the vehicle, as if it were a monster instinct with life, ready to bear down at once on everything in the road. And it required but a draught of water in its tubes, inflating its iron lungs with a little vapour, to snap its chains as Samson did the threads of flax—leap from its lofty car, and dart on its course uncontrolled, though a stone wall stood in the way.

The whole country turned out, as one man, to view the first trip on the line. Scientific men from every part of the kingdom, including the most eminent engineers of the day, came down in troops, and filled all the carriages. The controversy which had been raging from the first projection of the line was now about to be decided, and a great scientific principle negatived or affirmed. Isaac Colville, after seeing that everything was in order, himself mounted the engine—it might be with a shade of anxiety perceptible in his face, but still with the decision of a hero, and all the confidence of genius. The hour was at hand when his days of ceaseless toil, his sleepless nights, his untiring energy, vigilance, and exertion, would be rewarded, and the object of his ambition achieved. After reviling him in every possible way, so bitterly and so long, his enemies had come to be present at his defeat, and would have to bear witness to his triumph. Yet, in truth, he did not think of their discomfiture, but of his own success.

With a shriek of joy the engine felt the vivifying steam circulating in its veins. It drew along the stately train, peopled with human beings, as if it were a feather, gliding over the rails with the swiftness of thought. Nothing could be easier than the motion—nothing more smooth, steady, or agreeable. Mr. Colville's detractors began to look serious; his friends to exult. In a moment there was but one opinion as to the result of the experiment: its success was complete.

But the return trip, though the line of rails was the same, excited a misgiving: once or twice there had been a sensible vibration. The sceptics took heart again, and suggested another trial. This, to their surprise, no less than Mr. Colville's, was more decisive, showing a marked unsteadiness in the motion. There was a general exclamation of wonder, and, as the train drew up, every one sprang from the carriages to see how such a change could have arisen. The cause was but too clear: the weight of the train, as it flew over the rails, had driven out the packing, and the sleepers being unsupported, except at the cross beams, undulated under pressure, and imparted a vibratory motion to the train.

But the Colvillites contended that this was one of those little incidents which always occur at first experiments, and which, therefore, could not be regarded as a result. The defect would be remedied by a little fresh packing, and, accordingly, fresh packing was immediately resorted to. Further experiments, however, produced the same effect, and for several days they were renewed with consequences precisely similar, till, at length, the conviction began to spread, among the chiefs of both parties, that Isaac Colville's great scheme was a FAILURE.

An ardent admirer of Mr. Colville, Ernest, nevertheless, early perceived, from a careful examination of the sleepers, that it was not the packing, but the *quality* of the packing that led to this result. He observed that the fine gravel, though beaten in a mass beneath the sleeper, yet possessing in itself no binding property, pulverized under pressure, and flew out like dust. It then became clear to him that what the packing required was the power of cohesion, and as this could not be imparted where there was no natural capability, he came to the conclusion that some new material, which was not open to such an objection, must be used, and the sifted gravel discarded. What if he tried the gravel UNSIFTED! No sooner did the idea occur to him, than he proceeded, with characteristic promptitude, to put it in execution, and, with his own hands, packed the coarse gravel under two sleepers, awaiting the passage of the train to test its powers of resistance.

How high his heart beat when—stooping down as the train passed, to watch, with eager eyes, the effect of the enormous pressure—he saw the two sleepers remain immovable! Again and again the train passed and repassed, in every other spot driving out the packing like chaff; but here, for the few paces resting on the new material, the rails stood firm as a rock—all the more firm, indeed, the more they were pressed.

A strange revulsion of feeling came over Ernest, and he turned from the spot, at the very moment that his hopes were realized, with a sickening sensation of diffidence. He had made an important discovery, but to what purpose? How could he turn it to account? how communicate it to Mr. Colville? The world would scoff, indeed, at such a tyro as he was, with his experience of twelve months, presuming to offer a suggestion to the great engineer. No; better bury his discovery in oblivion than expose himself, by such a step, at once to derision and disgrace.

He thought over the subject all night, and all the next day; but at length ambition triumphed over discretion, and he determined to write to Mr. Colville, informing him of the experiment he had made, and its result.

It will readily be understood, by those who have acquired any perception of his character, how carefully every word of his letter was weighed and considered, and how sensible its writer was of the difficulty of alluding to Mr. Colville's failure, and his own success. With all his pains, he would, perhaps, a year later, when his pen had acquired greater felicity of expression, have written an epistle much less open to misconstruction, and more to the point. But probably he would not then have written it at all.

Not till after long hesitation was the momentous composition finally consigned to the Post-office—that bourne whence no letter returns. And now that the Rubicon was passed, Ernest's misgivings became intolerable. He flew to the Post-office to withdraw the letter, but it was too late: Mercury had gone.

The experiments on the line had been suspended for a day or two, and next morning, Ernest was walking down the works, in company with Parkyns, longing to tell him what he had done, but not knowing how to open the subject, when the latter, who had been carefully examining the road, suddenly stopped at the spot where Ernest had been operating.

"Hilloa, how's this?" he said. "Look here!"

"Well?" said Ernest.

"Well, don't you see?" resumed Parkyns. "The packing here hasn't given way."—He jumped up and down on the two sleepers—first on one, and then on the other. "By Jove, they're as firm as the ground itself. I can't make it out."

"Shall I tell you how it is?" said Ernest.

"Why, you haven't been up to anything yourself, have you?"

"Yes. As an experiment, I packed these two sleepers with unsifted gravel, and you see how they've stood."

Parkyns turned very red at this announcement—so difficult is it, even when we are not destitute of good-nature, to hear without vexation of the success of another.

"You've hit the nail on the head there, and no mistake," he said. "It's very odd, I've thought of the same thing myself, several times, and intended to try it in a day or two."—Parkyns always had a foreshadowing of every one's discoveries, but invariably after the event—"What are you going to do about it?"

"I've written to Mr. Colville, mentioning what led me to the discovery, and how it has answered."

"The deuce you have! 'Pon my word, Glynn, the size of your cheek is alarming."

"You think I've acted wrong?"

"I don't say wrong, but foolishly—desperately. Don't you know that I. C. thinks his own conceptions immaculate? Don't you see he never gives in—that though every one else is convinced, he goes on, day after day, testing and experimenting, when his best friends acknowledge it's all up? And you've had the audacity to tell him so!"

"You take a wrong view of his character. All this is only the decision and perseverance of genius, which will not tamely be conquered. But I shall be sorry if he misconstrues my motives."

"Misconstrues! I tell you I see 'sack' written on your face as plain as if the word was already spoken."

"You had much the same apprehensions about the Brawl viaduct."

"Ah! there the case was different. A casualty occurred, and you acted with promptitude and decision, and acted right. It was impossible not to approve of what you had done. But even in that case, what good did you ever get by it?"

"None, I confess."

"And depend upon it, you'll get still less by this move."

Such remarks were not calculated to raise Ernest's spirits, and, as Parkyns said no more, they walked on to the office in silence. A letter was lying there for Ernest, in the handwriting of Mr. Hammer, and, conjecturing its purport, he tore it open, and read as follows:—

"Sir,

"I am requested by Mr. Colville to inform you that he has no further occasion for your services.

"Your obedient servant,
"I. I. Hammer."

"Well, what news?" asked Parkyns.

Ernest handed him the letter.

"I told you so," said Parkyns, running his eye over the contents. "My dear fellow, NEVER TEACH YOUR GRANDMOTHER!"

13

PATRICK MACGILL, *CHILDREN OF THE DEAD END: THE AUTOBIOGRAPHY OF A NAVVY* (LONDON: H. JENKINS, 1914), PP. 129–145, 209–212, 225–229, 254–262

A dead man's shoes

"In the grim dead-end he lies,
With passionless filmy eyes,
English Ned, with a hole in his head,
Staring up at the skies.

"The engine driver swore, as often he swore before:
'I whistled him back from the flamin' track,
And I couldn't do no more!'

"The ganger spoke through the 'phone: 'Platelayer seventy-one
Got killed to-day on the six-foot way
By a goods on the city run.

" 'English Ned is his name, no one knows whence he came;
He didn't take mind of the road behind,
And none of us is to blame.' "
—From *Songs of the Dead End.*

THE law has it that no man must work as a platelayer on the running lines until he is over twenty-one years of age. If my readers look up the books of the— Railway Company, they'll find that I started work in the service of the company at the age of twenty-two. My readers must not believe this. I was only eighteen years of age when I started work on the railway, but I told a lie in order to obtain the post.

One day, five weeks following my return from the Argyllshire moors, and long after all my money had been expended on the fruitless search for Norah Ryan,

I clambered up a railway embankment near Glasgow with the intention of seeking a job, and found that a man had just been killed by a ballast engine. He had been cut in two; the fingers of his left hand severed clean away were lying on the slag. The engine wheels were dripping with blood. The sight made me sick with a dull heavy nausea, and numberless little blue and black specks floated before my eyes. An almost unbearable dryness came into my throat; my legs became heavy and leaden, and it seemed as if thousands of pins were pricking them. All the men were terror-stricken, and a look of fear was in every eye. They did not know whose turn would come next.

A few of them stepped reluctantly forward and carried the thing which had been a fellow-man a few minutes before and placed it on the green slope. Others pulled the stray pieces of flesh from amidst the rods, bars, and wheels of the engine and washed the splotches of blood from the sleepers and rails. One old fellow lifted the severed fingers from the slag, counting each one loudly and carefully as if some weighty decision hung on the correct tally of the dead man's fingers. They were placed beside the rest of the body, and prompted by a morbid curiosity I approached it where it lay in all its ghastliness on the green slope with a dozen men or more circled around it. The face was unrecognisable as a human face. A thin red sliver of flesh lying on the ground looked like a tongue. Probably the man's teeth in contracting had cut the tongue in two. I had looked upon two dead people, Dan and Mary Sorley, but they might have been asleep, so quiet did they lie in their eternal repose. This was also death, but death combined with horror. Here and there scraps of clothing and buttons were scrambled up with the flesh, but all traces of clothing were almost entirely hidden from sight. The old man who had gathered up the fingers brought a bag forward and covered up the dead thing on the slope. The rest of the men drew back, quietly and soberly, glad that the thing was hidden from their eyes.

"A bad sight for the fellow's wife," said the old man to me. "I've seen fifteen men die like him, you know."

"How did it happen?" I asked.

"We was liftin' them rails into the ballast train, and every rail is over half a ton in weight," said the man, who, realising that I was not a railway man, gave full details. "One of the rails came back. The men were in too big a hurry, that's what I say, and I've always said it, but it's not their fault. It's the company as wants men to work as if every man was a horse, and the men daren't take their time. It's the sack if they do that. Well, as I was a-sayin', the rail caught on the lip of the waggon, and came back atop of Mick—Mick Deehan is his name—as the train began just to move. The rail broke his back, snapped it in two like a dry stick. We heard the spine crack, and he just gave one squeal and fell right under the engine. Ugh! it was ill to look at it, and, mind you, I've seen fifteen deaths like it. Fifteen, just think of that!"

Then I realised that I had been saved part of the worst terror of the tragedy. It must have been awful to see a man suddenly transformed into that which lay under the bag beside me. A vision came to me of the poor fellow getting suddenly caught in the terrible embrace of the engine, watching the large wheel slowly revolving downwards towards his face, while his ears would hear, the last sound ever to be heard by them, the soft, slippery movement of that monstrous wheel skidding in flesh and blood. For a moment I was in the dead man's place, I could feel the flange of the wheel cutting and sliding through me as a plough slides through the furrow of a field. Again my feelings almost overcame me, my brain was giddy and my feet seemed insecurely planted on the ground.

By an effort I diverted my thoughts from the tragedy, and my eyes fell on a spider's web hung between two bare twigs just behind the dead man. It glistened in the sunshine, and a large spider, a little distance out from the rim, had its gaze fixed on some winged insect which had got entangled in the meshes of the web. When the old man who had seen fifteen deaths passed behind the corpse, the spider darted back to the shelter of the twig, and the winged insect struggled fiercely, trying to free itself from the meshes of death.

On a near bough a bird was singing, and its song was probably the first love-song of the spring. In the field on the other side of the line, and some distance away, a group of children were playing, children bare-legged, and dressed in garments of many colours. Behind them a row of lime-washed cottages stood, looking cheerful in the sunshine of the early spring. Two women stood at one door, gossiping, no doubt. A young man in passing raised his hat to the women, then stopped and talked with them for a while. From far down the line, which ran straight for miles, an extra gang of workers was approaching, their legs moving under their apparently motionless bodies, and breaking the lines of light which ran along the polished upper bedes of the rails. The men near me were talking, but in my ears their voices sounded like the droning of bees that flit amid the high branches of leafy trees. The coming gang drew nearer, stepping slowly from sleeper to sleeper, thus saving the soles of their boots from the contact of the wearing slag. The man in front, a strong, lusty fellow, was bellowing out in a very unmusical voice an Irish love song. Suddenly I noticed that all the men near me were gazing tensely at the approaching squad, the members of which were yet unaware of the tragedy, for the rake of ballast waggons hid the bloodstained slag and scene of the accident from their eyes. The singer came round behind the rear waggon, still bellowing out his song.

> "I'll leave me home again and I'll bid good-bye to-morrow,
> I'll pass the little graveyard and the tomb anear the wall,
> I have lived so long for love that I cannot live for sorrow
> By the grave that holds me cooleen in a glen of Donegal."

Every eye was turned on him, but no man spoke. Apparently taking no heed of the splotches of blood, now darkly red, and almost the colour of the slag on which they lay, he approached the bag which covered the body.

"What the devil is this?" he cried out, and gave the bag a kick, throwing it clear of the thing which it covered. The bird on the bough atop of the slope trilled louder; the song of the man died out, and he turned to the ganger who stood near him, with a questioning look.

"It's Mick, is it?" he asked, removing his cap.

"It's Micky," said the ganger.

The man by the corpse bent down again and covered it up slowly and quietly, then he sank down on the green slope and burst into tears.

"Micky and him's brothers, you know," said a man who stood beside me in a whisper. The tears came into my eyes, much though I tried to restrain them. The tragedy had now revealed itself in all its horrible intensity, and I almost wished to run away from the spot.

After a while the breakdown van came along; the corpse was lifted in, the brother tottered weakly into the carriage attached to the van, and the engine puffed back to Glasgow. A few men turned the slag in the sleeper beds and hid the dark red clotted blood for ever. The man had a wife and several children, and to these the company paid blood money, and the affair was in a little while forgotten by most men, for it was no man's business. Does it not give us an easy conscience that this wrong and that wrong is no business of ours?

When the train rumbled around the first curve on its return journey I went towards the ganger, for the work obsession still troubled me. Once out of work I long for a job, once having a job my mind dwells on the glories of the free-footed road again. But now I had an object in view, for if I obtained employment on the railway I could stop in Glasgow and continue my search for Norah Ryan during the spare hours. The ganger looked at me dubiously, and asked my age.

"Twenty-two years," I answered, for I was well aware that a man is never taken on as a platelayer until he has attained his majority.

There and then I was taken into the employ of the—Railway Company, as Dermod Flynn, aged twenty-two years. Afterwards the ganger read me the rules which I had to observe while in the employment of the company. I did not take very much heed to his droning voice, my mind reverting continuously to the tragedy which I had just witnessed, and I do not think that the ganger took very much pleasure in the reading. While we were going through the rules a stranger scrambled up the railway slope and came towards us.

"I heard that a man was killed," he said in an eager voice. "Any chance of gettin' a start in his place?"

"This man's in his shoes," said the ganger, pointing at me.

"Lucky dog!" was all that the man said, as he turned away.

The ganger's name was Roche, "Horse Roche" – for his mates nicknamed him "Horse" on account of his enormous strength. He could drive a nine-inch iron spike through a wooden sleeper with one blow of his hammer. No other man on the railway could do the same thing at that time; but before I passed my twenty-first birthday I could perform the same feat quite easily. Roche was a hard swearer, a heavy drinker, and a fearless fighter. He will not mind my saying these things about him now. He is dead over four years.

Books

"For me has Homer sung of wars,
Æschylus wrote and Plato thought,
Has Dante loved and Darwin wrought,
And Galileo watched the stars."
—From *The Navvy's Scrap Book*.

UP till this period of my life I had no taste for literature. I had seldom even glanced at the daily papers, having no interest in the world in which I played so small a part. One day when the gang was waiting for a delayed ballast train, and when my thoughts were turning to Norah Ryan, I picked up a piece of paper, a leaf from an exercise book, and written on it in a girl's or woman's handwriting were these little verses:

"No, indeed! for God above
Is great to grant, as mighty to make,
And creates the love to reward the love,—
I claim you still, for my own love's sake!
Delayed it may be for more lives yet,
Through worlds I shall traverse, not a few—
Much is to learn and much to forget
Ere the time be come for taking you.

"I have lived (I shall say) so much since then,
Given up myself so many times,
Gained me the gains of various men,
Ransacked the ages, spoiled the climes;
Yet one thing, one, in my soul's full scope,
Either I missed or itself missed me:
And I want and find you, Evelyn Hope!
What is the issue? let us see!"

While hardly understanding their import, the words went to my heart. They expressed thoughts of my own, thoughts lying so deeply that I was not able to explain or express them. The writer of the verse I did not know, but I thought that he, whoever he was, had looked deep into my soul and knew my feelings better than myself. All day long I repeated the words to myself over and over again, and from them I got much comfort and strength, that stood me in good stead in the long hours of searching on the streets of Glasgow for my luckless love. Under the glaring lamps that lit the larger streets, through the dark guttery alleys and sordid slums I prowled about nightly, looking at every young maiden's face and seeing in each the hard stare of indifference and the cold look of the stranger. Round the next corner perhaps she was waiting; a figure approaching reminded me of her, and I hurried forward eagerly only to find that I was mistaken. Oh! how many illusions kept me company in my search! how many disappointments! and how many hopes. For I wanted Norah; for her I longed with a great longing, and a dim vague hope of meeting her buoyed up my soul.

"And I want and find you, Evelyn Hope!
What is the issue? let us see!"

Such comforting words, and the world of books might be full of them! A new and unexplored world lay open before me, and for years I had not seen it, or seeing, never heeded. I had once more the hope that winged me along the leading road to Strabane when leaving for a new country. Alas! the country that raised such anticipations was not what my hopes fashioned, but this newer world, just as enticing, was worthy of more trust and greater confidence. I began to read eagerly, ravenously. I read Victor Hugo in G— Tunnel. One day a falling rail broke the top joint of the middle finger of my left hand. Being unable for some time to take part in the usual work of the squad I was placed on the look-out when my gang worked on the night-shift in the tunnel at G—. When the way was not clear ahead I had to signal the trains in the darkness, but as three trains seldom passed in the hour the work was light and easy. When not engaged I sat on the rail beside the naphtha lamp and read aloud to myself. I lived with Hugo's characters, I suffered with them and wept for them in their troubles. One night when reading *Les Miserables* I cried over the story of Jean Valjean and little Cosette. Horse Roche at that moment came through the darkness (in the tunnel it is night from dawn to dawn) and paused to ask me how I was getting along.

"Your eyes are running water, Flynn," he said. "You sit too close to the lamp smoke."

I remember many funny things which happened in those days. I read the chapter on *Natural Supernaturalism*, from *Sartor Resartus*, while seated on the footboard of a flying ballast train. Once, when Roche had left his work to take a drink in a near public-house, I read several pages from *Sesame and Lilies*, under shelter of a coal waggon, which had been shunted into an adjacent siding. I read Montaigne's *Essays* during my meal hours, while my mates gambled and swore around me.

I procured a ticket for the Carnegie Library, but bought some books, when I had cash to spare, from a second-hand bookseller on the south side of Glasgow. Every pay-day I spent a few shillings there, and went home to my lodgings with a bundle of books under my arm. The bookseller would not let me handle the books until I bought them, because my hands were so greasy and oily with the muck of my day's labour. I seldom read in my lodgings. I spent most of my evenings in the streets engaged on my unsuccessful search. I read in the spare moments snatched from my daily work. Soon my books were covered with iron-rust, sleeper-tar and waggon grease, where my dirty hands had touched them, and when I had a book in my possession for a month I could hardly decipher a word on the pages. There is some difficulty in reading thus.

I started to write verses of a kind, and one poem written by me was called *The Lady of the Line*. I personified the spirit that watched over the lives of railway men from behind the network of point-rods and hooded signals. The red danger lamp was her sign of power, and I wrote of her as queen of all the running lines in the world.

I read the poem to my mates. Most of them liked it very much and a few learned it by heart. When Horse Roche heard of it he said: "You'll end your days in the madhouse, or"—with cynical repetition—"in the House of Parliament."

On Sunday afternoons, when not at work, I went to hear the socialist speakers who preached the true Christian Gospel to the people at the street corners. The workers seldom stopped to listen; they thought that the socialists spoke a lot of nonsense. The general impression was that socialists, like clergymen, were paid speakers; that they endeavoured to save men's bodies from disease and poverty as curates save souls from sin for a certain number of shillings a day. From the first I looked upon socialist speakers as men who had an earnest desire for justice, and men who toiled bravely in the struggle for the regeneration of humanity. I always revolted against injustice, and hated all manner of oppression. My heart went out to the men, women, and children who toil in the dungeons and ditches of labour, grinding out their souls and bodies for meagre pittances. All around me were social injustices, affecting the very old and the very young as they affected the supple and strong. Social suffering begins at any age, and death is often its only remedy. That remedy is only for the individual; the general remedy is to be found in Socialism. Industry, that new Inquisition, has thousands on the rack of profit; Progress, to millions, means slavery and starvation; Progress and Profit mean sweated labour to railway men, and it meant death to many of them, as to Mick Deehan, whose place I had filled. I had suffered a lot myself: a brother of mine had died when he might have been saved by the rent which was paid to the landlord, and I had seen suffering all around me wherever I went; suffering due to injustice and tyranny of the wealthy class. When I heard the words spoken by the socialists at the street corner a fire of enthusiasm seized me, and I knew that the world was moving and that the men and women of the country were waking from the torpor of poverty, full of faith for a new cause. I joined the socialist party.

For a while I kept in the background; the discussions which took place in their hall in G— Street made me conscious of my own lack of knowledge on almost any subject. The members of the party discussed Spencer, Darwin, Huxley, Karl Marx, Ricardo, and Smith, men of whom I had never even heard, and inwardly I chafed at my own absolute ignorance and want of the education necessary for promoting the cause which I advocated. Hours upon hours did I spend wading through Marx's *Capital*, and Henry George's *Progress and Poverty*. The former, the more logical, appealed to me least.

I had only been two months in the socialist party when I organised a strike among the railway men, the thirty members of the Flying Squad on which I worked.

We were loading ash waggons at C—engine shed, and shovelling ashes is one of the worst jobs on the railway. Some men whom I have met consider work behind prison walls a pleasure when compared with it. As these men spoke from experience I did not doubt their words. The ash-pit at C—was a miniature volcano. The red-hot cinders and burning ashes were piled together in a deep pit, the mouth of which barely reached the level of the railway track. The Flying Squad under Horse Roche cleared out the pit once every month. The ashes were shovelled into waggons placed on the rails alongside for that purpose. The men stripped to the trousers and shirt in the early morning, and braces were loosened to give the shoulders the ease in movement required for the long day's swinging of the shovel. Three men were placed at each waggon and ten waggons were filled by the squad at each spell of work. Every three wrought as hard as they were able, so that their particular waggon might be filled before the others. The men who lagged behind went down in the black book of the ganger.

On the day of the strike the pit was a boiling hell. Chunks of coal half-burned and half-ablaze, lumps of molten slag, red-hot bricks and fiery ashes were muddled together in suffocating profusion. From the bottom of the pit a fierce impetus was required to land the contents of the shovel in the waggon overhead. Sometimes a brick would strike on the rim of the waggon and rebound back on the head of the man who threw it upwards. "Cripes! we'll have to fill it ourselves now," his two mates would say as they bundled their bleeding fellow out of the reeking heat. A shower of fine ashes were continuously falling downwards and resting upon our necks and shoulders, and the ash-particles burned the flesh like thin red-hot wires. It was even worse when they went further down our backs, for then every move of the underclothing and every swing of the shoulders caused us intense agony. Under the run of the shirt the ashes scarred the flesh like sand-paper. All around a thick smoke rested and hid us from the world without, and within we suffered in a pit of blasting fire. I've seen men dropping at the job like rats in a furnace. These were usually carried out, and a bucket of water was emptied on their face. When they recovered they entered into the pit again.

Horse Roche stood on the coupling chains of the two middle waggons, timing the work with his watch and hastening it on with his curses. He was not a bad fellow at heart, but he could do nothing without flying into a fuming passion, which often was no deeper than his lips. Below him the moke was so thick that he could hardly see his own labourers from the stand on the coupling chain. All he could see was the shovels of red ashes and shovels of black ashes rising up and over the haze that enveloped the pit beneath. But we could hear Roche where we wrought. Louder than the grinding of the ballast engine was the voice of the Horse cursing and swearing. His swearing was a gift, remarkable and irrepressible; it was natural to the man; it was the man.

"God's curse on you, Dan Devine, I don't see your shovel at work at all!" he roared. "Where the hell are you, Muck MaCrossan? Your waggon isn't nearly water-level yet, and that young whelp, Flynn, has his nearly full! If your chest was as broad as your belly, MacQueen, you'd be a danged sight better man on the ash-pile! It's not but that you are well enough used to the ashes, for I never yet saw a Heelin man who didn't spend the best part of his life before a fire or before grub! Come now, you men on the offside; you are slacking it like hell! If you haven't your waggon up over the lip, I'll sack every God-damned man of you on the next pay day! Has a brick fallen on Feeley's head? Well, shove the idiot out of the pit and get on with your work! His head is too big, anyhow, it's always in the road!"

This was the manner in which Horse Roche carried on, and most of the men were afraid of him. I felt frightened of the man, for I anticipated the gruelling which he would give me if I fell foul of him. But if we had come to blows he would not, I am certain, have much to boast about at the conclusion of the affair. However, I never quarrelled with Roche.

On the day of the strike, about three o'clock in the afternoon, when fully forespent at our work, the ballast engine brought in a rake of sixteen-ton waggons. Usually the waggons were small, just large enough to hold eight tons of ashes. The ones brought in now were very high, and it required the utmost strength of any one of us to throw a shovelful of ashes over the rim of the waggon. Not alone were the waggons higher, but the pile in the pit had decreased, and we had to work from a lower level. And those waggons could hold so much! They were like the grave, never satisfied, but ever wanting more, more. I suggested that we should stop work. Discontent was boiling hot, and the men scrambled out of the pit, telling Roche to go to hell, and get men to fill his waggons. Outside of the pit the men's anger cooled. They looked at one another for a while, feeling that they had done something that was sinful and wrong. To talk of stopping work in such a manner was blasphemy to most of them. Ronald MacQueen had a wife and a gathering of young children, and work was slack. Dan Devine was old, and had been in the service of the company for twenty years. If he left now he might not get another job. He rubbed the fine ashes out of his eyes, and looked at MacQueen. Both men had similar thoughts, and before the sweat was dry on their faces they turned back to the pit together. One by one the men followed them, until I was left alone on the outside. Horse Roche had never shifted his position on the coupling chains. "It'll not pain my feet much, if I stand till you come back!" he cried when we went out. He watched the men return with a look of cynical amusement.

"Come back, Flynn," he cried, when he saw me standing alone. "You're a fool, and the rest of the men are cowards; their spines are like the spines of earth worms."

I picked up my shovel angrily, and returned to my waggon. I was disgusted and disappointed and ashamed. I had lost in the fight, and I felt the futility of rising in opposition against the powers that crushed us down. That night I sent a letter to the railway company stating our grievance. No one except myself would sign it, but all the men said that my letter was a real good one. It must have been too good. A few days later a clerk was sent from the head of the house to inform me that I would get sacked if I wrote another letter of the same kind.

Then I realised that in the grip of the great industrial machine I was powerless; I was a mere spoke in the wheel of the car of progress, and would be taken out if I did not perform my functions there. The human spoke is useful as long as it behaves like a wooden one in the socket into which it is wedged. So long will the Industrial Carriage keep moving forward under the guidance of heavy-stomached Indolence and inflated Pride. There is no scarcity of spokes, human and wooden. What does it matter if Devine and MacQueen were thrown away? A million seeds are dropping in the forest, and all women are not divinely chaste. The young children are growing. Blessings be upon you, workmen, you have made spokes that will shove you from the sockets into which your feet are wedged, but God grant that the next spokes are not as wooden as yourselves!

Again the road was calling to me. My search in Glasgow had been quite unsuccessful, and the dull slavery of the six-foot way began to pall on me. The clerk who was sent by the company to teach me manners was a most annoying little fellow, and full of the importance of his mission. I told him quietly to go to the devil, an advice which he did not relish, but which he forbore to censure. That evening I left the employ of the—Railway Company.

Just two hours before I lifted my lying time, the Horse was testing packed sleepers with his pick some distance away from the gang, when a rabbit ran across the railway. Horse dropped his pick, aimed a lump of slag at the animal and broke its leg. It limped off; we saw the Horse follow, and about a hundred paces from the point where he had first observed it Roche caught the rabbit, and proceeded to kill it outright by battering its head against the flange of the rail. At that moment a train passed us, travelling on the down line. Roche was on the up line, but as the train passed him we saw a glint of something bright flashing between the engine and the man, and at the same moment Roche fell to his face on the four-foot way. We hurried towards him, and found our ganger vainly striving to rise with both arms caught in his entrails. The pick which he had left lying on the line got caught in the engine wheels and was carried forward, and violently hurled out when the engine came level with the ganger. It ripped his belly open, and he died about three minutes after we came to his assistance. The rabbit, although badly wounded, escaped to its hole. That night I was on the road again.

By instinct I am a fighter. I never shirk a fight, and the most violent contest is a tonic to my soul. Sometimes when in a thoughtful mood I said to myself that fighting was the pastime of a brute or a savage. I said that because it is fashionable for the majority of people, spineless and timid as they are, to say the same. But fighting is not the pastime of a brute; it is the stern reality of a brute's life. Only by fighting will the fittest survive. But to man, a physical contest is a pastime and a joy. I love to see a fight with the bare fists, the combatants stripped naked to the buff, the long arms stretching out, the hard knuckles showing white under the brown skin of the fists, the muscles sliding and slipping like live eels under the flesh, the steady and quick glance of the eye, the soft thud of fist on flesh, the sharp snap of a blow on the jaw, and the final scene where one man drops to the ground while the other, bathed in blood and sweat, smiles in acknowledgment of the congratulations on the victory obtained.

Gambling was another manner of fighting, and brim full of excitement. In it no man knew his strength until he paid for it, and there was excitement in waiting for the turn-up. Night after night I sat down to the cards, sometimes out in the open and sometimes by the deal plank on the floor of Red Billy's shack. Gambling was rife and unchecked. All night long the navvies played banker and brag; and those who worked on the night-shift took up the game that the day labourers left off. One Sunday evening alone I saw two hundred and fifty banker schools gathered in a sheltered hollow of the hills. That Sunday I remembered very well, for I happened to win seven pounds at a single sitting, which lasted from seven o'clock on a Saturday evening until half-past six on the Monday morning. I finished the game, went out to my work, and did ten hours' shift, although I was half asleep on the drill handle for the best part of the time.

One day a man, a new arrival, came to me and proposed a certain plan whereby he and I could make a fortune at the gambling school. It was a kind of swindle, and I do not believe in robbing workers, being neither a thief nor a capitalist. I lifted the man up in my arms and took him into the shack, where I disclosed his little plan to the inmates. A shack some distance off was owned by a Belfast man named Ramsay, and several Orangemen dwelt in this shack. Moleskin proposed that we should strip the swindler to the pelt, paint him green, and send him to Ramsay's shack. Despite the man's entreaties, we painted him a glorious green, and when the night came on we took him under cover of the darkness to Ramsay's shack, and tied him to the door. In the morning we found him, painted orange, outside of ours, and almost dead with cold. We gave him his clothes and a few kicks, and chased him from the place.

I intended, when I came to Kinlochleven, to earn money and send it home to my own people, and the intention was nursed in good earnest until I lifted my first day's pay. Then Moleskin requested the loan of my spare cash, and I could not refuse him, a pal who shared his very last crumb of bread with me time and again. On the second evening the gamble followed the fight as a matter of course; and on the third evening and every evening after I played—because I was a gambler by nature. My luck was not the best; I lost most of my wages at the card-table, and the rest went on drink. I know not whether drink and gambling are evils. I only know that they cheered many hours of my life, and caused me to forget the miseries of being. If drunkenness was a vice, I humoured it as a man might humour sickness or any other evil. But drink might have killed me, one will say. And sickness might have killed me, I answer. When a man is dead he knows neither hunger nor cold; he suffers neither from the cold of the night nor the craving of the belly. The philosophy is crude, but comforting, and it was mine. To gamble and drink was part of my nature, and for nature I offer no excuses. She knows what is best.

I could not save money, I hated to carry it about; it burned a hole in my pocket and slipped out. I was no slave to it; I detested it. How different now were my thoughts from those which buoyed up my spirit on first entering Kinlochleven! those illusions, like previous others, had been dispelled before the hard wind of reality. I looked on life nakedly, and henceforth I determined to shape my own future in such a way that neither I, nor wife, nor child, should repent of it. Although passion ran riot in my blood, as it does in the blood of youth, I resolved never to marry and bring children into the world to beg and starve and steal as I myself had done. I saw life as it was, saw it clearly, standing out stark from its covering of illusions. I looked on love cynically, unblinded by the fumes off the midden-heap of lust, and my life lacked the phantom happiness of men who see things as they are not.

The great proportion of the navvies live very pure lives, and women play little or no part in their existence. The women of the street seldom come near a model, even when the navvies come in from some completed job with money enough and to spare. The purity of their lives is remarkable when it is considered that they seldom marry. "We cannot bring children into the world to suffer like ourselves," most of them say. That is one reason why they remain single. Therefore the navvy is seldom the son of a navvy; it is the impoverished and the passionate who breed men like us, and throw us adrift upon the world to wear out our miserable lives.

I write for the papers

"'Awful Railway Disaster,'
The newspapers chronicle,
The men in the street are buying.
My! don't the papers sell.
And the editors say in their usual way,
'The story is going well.'"
—From *Songs of the Dead End*.

DAY after day passed and the autumn was waning. The work went on, shift after shift, and most of the money that I earned was spent on the gambling table or in the whisky store. Now and again I wrote home, and sent a few pounds to my people, but I never sent them my address. I did not want to be upbraided for my negligence in sending them so little. The answers to my letters would always be the same: "Send more money; send more money. You'll never have a day's luck if you do not help your parents!" I did not want answers like that, so I never sent my address.

One night towards the end of October I had lost all my money at the gambling school, although Moleskin had twice given me a stake to retrieve my fallen fortunes. I left the shack, went out into the darkness, a fire in my head and emptiness in my heart. Around me the stark mountain peaks rose raggedly against the pale horns of the anæmic moon. Outside the whisky store a crowd of men stood, dark looks on their faces, and the wild blood of mischief behind. Inside each shack a dozen or more gamblers sat cross-legged in circles on the ground, playing banker or brag, and the clink of money could be heard as it passed from hand to hand. Above them the naphtha lamps hissed and spluttered and smelt, the dim, sickly light showed the unwashed and unshaven faces beneath, and the eager eyes that sparkled brightly, seeing nothing but the movements of the game. Down in the cuttings men were labouring on the night-shift, gutting out the bowels of the mountain places, and forcing their way through the fastness steadily, slowly and surely. I could hear the dynamite exploding and shattering to pieces the rock in which it was lodged. The panting of weary hammermen was loud in the darkness, and the rude songs which enlivened the long hours of the night floated up to me from the trough of the hills.

I took my way over the slope of the mountain, over the pigmies who wrought beneath, fighting the great fight which man has to wage eternally against nature. Down in the cuttings I could see my mates toiling amidst the broken earth, the sharp ledges of hewn rock, and the network of gang-planks and straining derricks that rose all around them. The red glare of a hundred evil-smelling torches flared dismally, and over the sweltering men the dark smoke faded away into the rays of the pallid moon. With the rising smoke was mingled the steam of the men's bent shoulders and steaming loins.

Above and over all, the mystery of the night and the desert places hovered inscrutable and implacable. All around the ancient mountains sat like brooding witches, dreaming on their own story of which they knew neither the beginning nor the end. Naked to the four winds of heaven and all the rains of the world, they had stood there for countless ages in all their sinister strength, undefied and unconquered, until man, with puny hands and little tools of labour, came to break the spirit of their ancient mightiness.

And we, the men who braved this task, were outcasts of the world. A blind fate, a vast merciless mechanism, cut and shaped the fabric of our existence. We were men flogged to the work which we had to do, and hounded from the work which we had accomplished. We were men despised when we were most useful, rejected when we were not needed, and forgotten when our troubles weighed upon us heavily. We were the men sent out to fight the spirit of the wastes, rob it of all its primeval horrors, and batter down the barriers of its world-old defences. Where we were working a new town would spring up some day; it was already springing up, and then, if one of us walked there, "a man with no fixed address," he would be taken up and tried as a loiterer and vagrant.

Even as I thought of these things a shoulder of jagged rock fell into a cutting far below. There was the sound of a scream in the distance, and a song died away in the throat of some rude singer. Then out of the pit I saw men, red with the muck of the deep earth and redder still with the blood of a stricken mate, come forth, bearing between them a silent figure. Another of the pioneers of civilisation had given up his life for the sake of society.

I returned to the shack, and, full of the horror of the tragedy, I wrote an account of it on a scrap of tea-paper. I had no design, no purpose in writing, but I felt compelled to scribble down the thoughts which entered my mind. I wrote rapidly, but soon wearied of my work. I was proceeding to tear up the manuscript when my eye fell on a newspaper which had just come into the shack wrapped around a chunk of mouldy beef. A thought came to me there and then. I would send my account of the tragedy to the editor of that paper. It was the *Dawn*, a London halfpenny daily. I had never heard of it before.

I had no envelope in my possession. I searched through the shack and found one, dirty, torn, and disreputable in appearance. Amongst all those men there was not another to be found. I did not rewrite my story. Scrawled with pencil on dirty paper, and enclosed in a dirtier envelope, I sent it off to Fleet Street and forgot all about it. But, strange to say, in four days' time I received an answer from the editor of the *Dawn*, asking me to send some more stories of the same kind, and saying that he was prepared to pay me two guineas for each contribution accepted.

The acceptance of my story gave me no great delight; I often went into greater enthusiasm over a fight in the Kinlochleven ring. But outside a fight or a stiff game of cards, there are few things which cause me to become excited. My success as a writer discomfited me a little even. I at first felt that I was committing some sin against my mates. I was working on a shift which they did not understand; and men look with suspicion on things beyond their comprehension. A man may make money at a fight, a gaming table or at a shift, but the man who made money with a dirty pencil and a piece of dirty paper was an individual who had no place in my mates' scheme of things.

For all that, the editor's letter created great stir amongst my mates. It passed round the shack and was so dirty on coming back that I couldn't read a word of it. Red Billy said that he could not understand it, and that I must have copied what I had written from some other paper. Moleskin Joe said that I was the smartest man he had ever met, by cripes! I was. He took great pleasure in calling me "that mate of mine" ever afterwards. Old Sandy MacDonald, who had come from the Isle of Skye, and who was wasting slowly away, said that he knew a young lad like me who went from the Highlands to London and made his fortune by writing for the papers.

"He had no other wark but writin', and he made his fortune," Sandy asserted, and everyone except myself laughed at this. It was such a funny thing to hear old Sandy make his first joke, my mates thought. A man to earn his living by writing for the papers! Whoever heard of such a thing?

In all I wrote five articles for the *Dawn*, then found that I could write no more. I had told five truthful and exciting incidents of my navvying life, and I was not clever enough to tell lies about it. Ten guineas came to me from Fleet Street. Six of these I sent home to my own people, and for the remainder I purchased many an hour's joy in the whisky store and many a night's life-giving excitement at the gaming table.

I sent my address home with the letter, and when my mother replied she was so full of her grievances that she had no time to enquire if I had any of my own. Another child had been born, and the family in all now consisted of thirteen.

A new job

"The more you do, the more you get to do."
—*Cold Clay Philosophy*.

WHEN we arrived in Glasgow I parted company with Moleskin Joe. I told him that I was going to work on the railway if I got an opening, but my mate had no liking for a job where the pay could be only lifted once a fortnight; he wanted his sub. every second day at least. He set out for the town of Carlisle. There was a chance of getting a real job there, he said.

"Mind you, if there's a chance goin' for another man, I'll let you know about it," he added. "I would like you to come and work along with me, matey, for me and you get on well together. Keep clear of women and always stand up to your man until he knocks you out—that's if you're gettin' the worst of the fight."

We parted without a handshake, as is the custom with us navvy men. He never wrote to me, for I had no address when he left, and he did not know the exact model to which I was going. Once out of each other's sight, the link that bound us together was broken, and being homeless men we could not correspond. Perhaps we would never meet again.

I got a job on the railway and obtained lodgings in a dismal and crooked street, which was a den of disfigured children and a hothouse of precocious passion, in the south side of Glasgow. The landlady was an Irishwoman, bearded like a man, and the mother of several children. When indoors, she spent most of her time feeding one child, while swearing like a carter at all the others. We slept in the one room, mother, children and myself, and all through the night the children yelled like cats in the moonshine. The house was alive with vermin. The landlady's husband was a sailor who went out on ships to foreign parts and always returned drunk from his voyages. When at home he remained drunk all the time, and when he left again he was as drunk as he could hold. I had no easy job to put up with him at first, and in the end we quarrelled and fought. He accused me of being too intimate with his wife when he was away from home. I told him that my taste was not so utterly bad, for indeed I had no inclination towards any woman, let alone the hairy and unkempt person who was my landlady. I struck out for him on the stair head. Three flights of stairs led from the door of the house down to the ground floor. I threw the sailor down the last flight bodily and headlong; he threw me down the middle flight. Following the last throw, he would not face up again, and I had won the fight. Afterwards the woman came to her husband's aid. She scratched my face with her fingers and tore at my hair, clawing like an angry cat. I did not like to strike her back, so I left her there with her drunken sailor and went out to the streets. Having no money I slept until morning beside a capstan on Glasgow quay. Next day I obtained lodgings in Moran's model, and I stopped there until I went off to London eleven months afterwards.

I did not find much pleasure in the company of my new railway mates. They were a spineless and ignorant crowd of men, who believed in clergycraft, psalm-singing, and hymn-hooting. Not one of them had the pluck to raise his hands in a stand-up fight, or his voice in protest against the conditions under which he laboured. Most of them raised their caps to the overseers who controlled their starved bodies and to the clergy who controlled their starved souls. They had no rational doctrine, no comprehension of a just God. To them God took on the form of a monstrous and irritable ganger who might be pacified by prayers instead of by the usual dole of drink.

Martin Rudor was the name of my new ganger. He was very religious and belonged to the Railway Mission (whatever that is). He read tracts at his work, which he handed round when he finished perusing them. These contained little stories about the engine-driver who had taken the wrong turning, or the signalman who operated the facing points on the running line leading to hell. Martin took great pleasure in these stories, and he was an earnest supporter of the psalm-singing enthusiasts who raised a sound of devilry by night in the back streets of Glasgow. Martin said once that I was employed on the permanent way that led to perdition. I caught Martin by the scruff of the neck and rubbed his face on the slag. He never thought it proper to look out my faults afterwards. Martin ill-treated his wife, and she left him in the end. But he did not mind; he took one of his female co-religionists to his bosom and kept her in place of his legal wife, and seemed quite well pleased with the change. Meanwhile he sang hymns in the street whenever he got two friends to help and one to listen to him.

What a difference between these men and my devil-may-care comrades of Kinlochleven. I looked on Martin Rudor and his gang with inexpressible contempt, and their talk of religion was a source of almost unendurable torment. I also looked upon the missions with disgust. It is a paradox to pretend that the thing called Christianity was what the Carpenter of Galilee lived and died to establish. The Church allows a criminal commercial system to continue, and wastes its time trying to save the souls of the victims of that system. Christianity preaches contentment to the wage-slaves, and hob-nobs with the slave drivers; therefore, the Church is a betrayer of the people. The Church soothes those who are robbed and never condemns the robber, who is usually a pillar of Christianity. To me the Church presents something unattainable, which, being out of harmony with my spiritual condition, jars rather than soothes. To me the industrial system is a great fraud, and the Church which does not condemn it is unfaithful and unjust to the working people. I detest missions, whether organised for the betterment of South Sea Islanders or unshaven navvies. A missionary canvasses the working classes for their souls just in the same manner as a town councillor canvasses them for their votes.

I have heard of workers' missions, railway missions, navvies' missions, and missions to poor heathens, but I have never yet heard of missions for the uplifting of M.P.'s, or for the betterment of stock exchange gamblers; and these people need saving grace a great deal more than the poor untutored working men. But it is in the nature of things that piety should preach to poverty on its shortcomings, and forget that even wealth may have sins of its own. Clergymen dine nowadays with the gamblers who rob the working classes; Christ used the lash on the gamblers in the Temple.

I heard no more of Norah Ryan. I longed to see her, and spent hours wandering through the streets, hoping that I would meet her once again. The old passion had come back to me; the atmosphere of the town rekindled my desire, and, being a lonely man, in the midst of many men and women, my heart was filled with a great longing for my sweetheart. But the weary months went by and still there was no sign of Norah.

When writing home I made enquiries about her, but my people said that she had entirely disappeared; no Glenmornan man had seen Norah Ryan for many years. My mother warned me to keep out of Norah's company if ever I met her, for Norah was a bad woman. My mother was a Glenmornan woman, and the Glenmornan women have no fellow-feeling for those who sin.

Manual labour was now becoming irksome to me, and eight shillings a week to myself at the end of six days' heavy labour was poor consolation for the danger and worry of the long hours of toil. I did not care for money, but I was afraid of meeting with an accident, when I might get maimed and not killed. It would be an awful thing if a man like me got deprived of the use of an arm or leg, and an accident might happen to me any day. In the end I made up my mind that if I was to meet with an accident I would take my own life, and henceforth I looked at the future with stoical calm.

I have said before that I am very strong. There was no man on the railway line who could equal me at lifting rails or loading ballast waggons. I had great ambitions to become a wrestler and go on the stage. No workman on the permanent way could rival me in a test of strength. Wrestling appealed to me, and I threw the stoutest of my opponents in less than three minutes. I started to train seriously, bought books on physical improvement, and spent twelve shillings and sixpence on a pair of dumb-bells. During meal hours I persuaded my mates to wrestle with me. Wet weather or dry, it did not matter! We went at it shoulder and elbows in the muddy fields and alongside the railway track. We threw one another across point-rods and signal bars until we bled and sweated at our work. I usually took on two men at a time and never got beaten. For whole long months I was a complete mass of bruises, my skin was torn from my arms, my clothes were dragged to ribbons, and my bones ached so much that I could hardly sleep at night owing to the pain. I attended contests in the music-halls, eager to learn tips from the professionals who had acquired fame in the sporting world.

The shunter of our ballast train was a heavy-shouldered man, and he had a bad temper and an unhappy knack of lifting his fists to those who were afraid of him. He was a strong rung of a man, and he boasted about the number of fights in which he had taken part. He was also a lusty liar and an irrepressible swearer. Nearly everyone in the job was afraid of him, and to the tune of a wonderful vocabulary of unprintable words he bullied all Martin Rudor's men into abject submission. But that was an easy task. He felt certain that every man on the permanent way feared him, and maybe that was why he called me an Irish cur one evening. We were shovelling ashes from the ballast waggons on one line into the four-foot way of the other, and the shunter stood on the foot-board of the break-van two truck lengths away from me. I threw my shovel down, stepped across the waggons, and taking hold of the fellow by the neck and waist I pulled him over the rim of the vehicle and threw him headlong down the railway slope. I broke his coupling pole over my knee, and threw the pieces at his head. The breaking of the coupling pole impressed the man very much. Few can break one over their knees. When the shunter came to the top of the slope again, he was glad to apologise to me, and thus save himself further abuse.

That evening, when coming in from my work, I saw a printed announcement stating that a well-known Japanese wrestler was offering ten pounds to any man whom he could not overcome in less than five minutes in a ju-jitsu contest. He was appearing in a hall on the south side of the city, and he was well-known as an exponent of the athletic art.

I went to the hall that evening, hoping to earn the ten pounds. The shunter was four stone heavier than I was, yet I overcame him easily, and the victory caused me to place great reliance on myself.

I took a threepenny seat in the gallery, and waited breathless for the coming of the wrestler. Several artists appeared, were applauded or hissed, then went off the stage, but I took very little heed of their performances. All my thoughts were centred on the pose which I would assume when rising to accept the challenge.

Sitting next to me was a fat foreigner, probably a seller of fish-suppers or ice-cream. I wondered what he would think of me when he saw me rise to my feet and accept the challenge. What would the girl who sat on the other side of me think? She kept eating oranges all the evening, and giggling loudly at every indecent joke made by the actors. She was somewhat the worse for liquor, and her language was far from choice. She was very pretty and knew it. A half-dressed woman sang a song, every stanza of which ended with a lewd chorus. The girl beside me joined in the song and clapped her hands boisterously when the artiste left the stage.

The wrestler was the star turn of the evening, and his exhibition was numbered two on the programme. When the number went up my heart fluttered madly, and I felt a great difficulty in drawing my breath.

The curtain rose slowly. A man in evening dress, bearing a folded paper in his hand, came out to the front of the stage. One of the audience near me applauded with his hands.

"That's nae a wrestler, you fool!" someone shouted. "You dinna ken what you're clappin' about."

"Silence!"

The audience took up the word and all shouted silence, until the din was deafening.

"Ladies and gentlemen," began the figure on the stage, when the noise abated.

Everyone applauded again. Even the girl beside me blurted out "Hear! hear!" through a mouthful of orange juice. Those who pay threepence for their seats love to be called ladies and gentlemen.

"Ladies and gentlemen, I have great pleasure in introducin' U— Y—, the well-known exponent of the art of ju-jitsu."

A little dark man with very bright eyes stepped briskly on the stage, and bowed to the audience, then folded his arms over his breast and gazed into vacancy with an air of boredom. He wore a heavy overcoat which lay open at the neck and exposed his chest muscles to the gaping throng.

"Everybody here has heard of U— Y—, no doubt." The evening dress was speaking again. "He is well known in America, in England, and on the continent. At the present time he is the undefeated champion of his weight in all the world. He is now prepared to hand over the sum of ten pounds to any man in the audience who can stand against him for five minutes. Is there any gentleman in the audience prepared to accept the challenge?"

"I could wrestle him mysel'," said the girl of the orange-scented breath in a whisper. Apart from that there was silence.

"Is any man in the audience prepared to accept the offer and earn the sum of ten pounds?" repeated the man on the stage.

"I am."

Somehow I had risen to my feet, and my words came out spasmodically. Everyone in front turned round and stared at me. My seat-mate clapped her hands, and the audience followed her example.

There is no need to give an account of the contest. Suffice to say that I did not collar the ten-pound note, and that I had not the ghost of a chance in the match. It only lasted for forty-seven seconds. The crowd hissed me off the stage, and I got hurriedly into the street when I regained my coat in the dressing-room. I went out into the night, sick at heart, a defeated man, with another of my illusions dashed to pieces. I took no interest in wrestling afterwards.

14

PATRICK MACGILL, 'A PLATELAYER'S STORY' AND 'THE NAVVIES' SUNDAY' AND FROM *GLEANINGS FROM A NAVVY'S SCRAPBOOK*. SECOND ED. (DERRY, NORTH IRELAND: DERRY JOURNAL, 1911), PP. 52–53, 55

A Platelayer's Story

Jimmy an' me were mates, sir, to me he was all in all,
Our work it wus weary and heavy, an' our wages was awfully small—
'Tis there on the railway line, sir, I laboured along with Jim—
But 'tis now I am feeling lonely, for to-day we have buried him:
None better upon the surface as hammersman I'll go bail,
A good 'un to work a shovel, a man at the end of a rail;
Weren't what some call pious, never at church or prayer,
But the greatest rogues I know, sir, goes every Sunday there.
Fond of his pint? Well, rather, an' hated the boss by creed,
But never refused a penny to cumfort a pal in need.

'Twas the evenin' to lift the pay, sir, an' min' you the boys were glad,
Every one of the twenty that worked in the Flyin' Squad.
The gaffer said, "That will do, lads;" we flung our tools away,
An' made for the ticket office, where we would receive our pay.
The boys were all in a hurry, the evenin' was nice an' fine,
An' the road wus far to the office, two miles along the line.
The pay day comes but seldom, the money has much to do,
But still there is always for pleasure an extra shillin' or two,
That's if you aren't marri'd, but this much I'd like to say,
The labourers on the railway could do with a bigger pay.

We sighted the level crossin', that lies by the Old Road End,
Just at that selfsame crossin' the line has a sudden bend,
An' there in the fourfoot sittin', what do you think did we see,
But a fair little child of seven, content as a child could be.
The signal stick above us fell down with a crash; we knew'

Been workin' so long on the surface, the City Express was due;
Some of the fellows shouted, but the baby gave no sign,
An' sudden we heard the injin a-coming along the line;
But Jim never spoke a word, sir, but took to his heels and ran,
An' what with wettin's an' sweatin's, it's more nor some of us can;
Hard on his heels came rushin' an' roarin' the big express,
An' it happened all in a minute, a minute or maybe less.
He reached where the child was sittin' an' paused, for he seemed to know
The injin was cryin' for some one, an' one of the two must go—
He thought as he would, poor fellow, his life was a useless one,
Many another to labour when he was buried an' gone,
Men were so very plenty, an' work was so sparin', or
Since life had so little to give him, what was he livin' for;
An' the child might have brighter prospects, if any thoughts came to Jim
Of which of the two was for livin' his duty was clear to him.

He paused for the flash of an eyelid; then lifted the child and threw
It out on the grassy pathway, where daisies and violets grew,
Safe an' unhurt—but Jimmy; for the first time in thirty years,
I looked on a mangled body, with my eyes filled up with tears:

There was blood on the mighty injin, an' blood on the runnin' train,
But they carried none better with them that day than the gallant lad they'd slain.
So warm hearted wus Jimmy, an' the clay is so cold beneath—
The boys collected among them, an' placed on his grave a wreath.
The clergymen say that prayin' God's favour forever wins,
But I think that the death he died, sir, will cancel a lot of sins.
Some say that his life wus evil, religious folks I know,
But Christ has a word in the matter, that Judgment Day will show.

The Navvies' Sunday

Some swear at the dirty sleeper, some curse the frosty guage;
The sun hangs o'er the city, but seems afraid to shine,
The rails are heavy and rusty, the gangers are in a rage—
'Tis Sunday. When gods are resting the navvies repair the line.
'Tis Sunday. The pious people are going to church to pray,
They see the weary workers, and wonder why they're there,
They talk of the far-off savage, who rests on the Sabbath day,
But here the freeborn Britons forget themselves and swear.

Six days a week shalt thou labour for ordinary wage,
The seventh, thy pay is doubled, and work is trebled. Well,
Better to handle the hammer and bring the crossing to gauge
And earn the six and eightpence that sends you down to hell.
Sunday. The hymns are rising up to the far-off skies,
The churches are filled with mortals, who walk on the narrow road,
But, hark! from the busy railway the sounds of the hammers rise—
Oh, they who labour on Sunday must move on a pathway broad.

But why should I talk of their sorrows? Why should I wail their woes?
After a day of hurry, think of the joys of rest—
Why they hold that dignity labour only knows,
And if their wages are little—only the poor are blest.
Aren't their homes in England, England that rules the waves?
Sailors and soldiers gallant, to guard them night and day—
Their duty is clear as Britons, Britons that are not slaves,
To work for their country's welfare, e'en on the Sabbath day.

Part 4

NOVEL IMPRESSIONS
Early Victorian railway cultures

15

FRANCES ANN KEMBLE, *RECORDS OF A GIRLHOOD*. SECOND ED. (NEW YORK: H. HOLT, 1884), PP. 278–284

While we were acting at Liverpool an experimental trip was proposed upon the line of railway which was being constructed between Liverpool and Manchester, the first mesh of that amazing iron net which now covers the whole surface of England and all the civilized portions of the earth. The Liverpool merchants, whose far-sighted self-interest prompted them to wise liberality, had accepted the risk of George Stephenson's magnificent experiment, which the committee of inquiry of the House of Commons had rejected for the government. These men, of less intellectual culture than the Parliament members, had the adventurous imagination proper to great speculators, which is the poetry of the counting-house and wharf, and were better able to receive the enthusiastic infection of the great projector's sanguine hope that the Westminster committee. They were exultant and triumphant at the near completion of the work, though, of course, not without some misgivings as to the eventual success of the stupendous enterprise. My father knew several of the gentlemen most deeply interested in the undertaking, and Stephenson having proposed a trial trip as far as the fifteen-mile viaduct, they, with infinite kindness, invited him and permitted me to accompany them; allowing me, moreover, the place which I felt to be one of supreme honor, by the side of Stephenson. All that wonderful history, as much more interesting than a romance as truth is stranger than fiction, which Mr. Smiles's biography of the projector has given in so attractive a form to the world, I then heard from his own lips. He was a rather stern-featured man, with a dark and deeply marked countenance; his speech was strongly inflected with his native Northumbrian accent, but the fascination of that story told by himself, while his tame dragon flew panting along his iron pathway with us, passed the first reading of the "Arabian Nights," the incidents of which it almost seemed to recall. He was wonderfully condescending and kind in answering all the questions of my eager ignorance, and I listened to him with eyes brimful of warm tears of sympathy and enthusiasm, as he told me of all his alternations of hope and fear, of his many trials and disappointments, related with fine scorn how the "Parliament men" had badgered and baffled him with their book-knowledge, and how, when at last they thought they had smothered the irrepressible prophecy of his genius in the quaking depths of Chatmoss, he had exclaimed, "Did ye ever see a boat float on water? I will make my road float upon Chatmoss!" The well-read Parliament men (some of whom, perhaps, wished for no railways near their parks and pleasure-grounds) could not believe the miracle, but the shrewd Liverpool merchants, helped to their faith by a great vision of immense gain, did; and so the railroad was made, and I took this memorable ride by the side of its maker, and would not have exchanged the honor and pleasure of it for one of the shares in the speculation.

LIVERPOOL, August 26th.

MY DEAR H—,

A common sheet of paper is enough for love, but a foolscap extra can alone contain a railroad and my ecstasies. There was once a man, who was born at Newcastle-upon-Tyne, who was a common coal-digger; this man had an immense constructiveness, which displayed itself in pulling his watch to pieces and putting it together again; in making a pair of shoes when he happened to be some days without occupation; finally—here there is a great gap in my story—it brought him in the capacity of an engineer before a committee of the House of Commons, with his head full of plans for constructing a railroad from Liverpool to Manchester. It so happened that to the quickest and most powerful perceptions and conceptions, to the most indefatigable industry and perseverance, and the most accurate knowledge of the phenomena of nature as they affect his peculiar labors, this man joined an utter want of the "gift of the gab;" he could no more explain to others what he meant to do and how he meant to do it, than he could fly; and therefore the members of the House of Commons, after saying, "There is rock to be excavated to a depth of more than sixty feet, there are embankments to be made nearly to the same height, there is a swamp of five miles in length to be traversed, in which if you drop an iron rod it sinks and disappears: how will you do all this?" and receiving no answer but a broad Northumbrian "I can't tell you how I'll do it, but I can tell you I *will* do it," dismissed Stephenson as a visionary. Having prevailed upon a company of Liverpool gentlemen to be less incredulous, and having raised funds for his great undertaking, in December of 1826 the first spade was struck into the ground. And now I will give you an account of my yesterday's excursion. A party of sixteen persons was ushered into a large court-yard, where, under cover, stood several carriages of a peculiar construction, one of which was prepared for our reception. It was a long-bodied vehicle with seats placed across it, back to back; the one we were in had six of these benches, and was a sort of uncovered *char à banc*. The wheels were placed upon two iron bands, which formed the road, and to which they are fitted, being so constructed as to slide along without any danger of hitching or becoming displaced, on the same principle as a thing sliding on a concave groove. The carriage was set in motion by a mere push, and, having received this impetus, rolled with us down an inclined plane into a tunnel, which forms the entrance to the railroad.

This tunnel is four hundred yards long (I believe), and will be lighted by gas. At the end of it we emerged from darkness, and, the ground becoming level, we stopped. There is another tunnel parallel with this, only much wider and longer, for it extends from the place which we had now reached, and where the steam-carriages start, and which is quite out of Liverpool, the whole way under the town, to the docks. This tunnel is for wagons and other heavy carriages; and as the engines which are to draw the trains along the railroad do not enter these tunnels, there is a large building at this entrance which is to be inhabited by steam-engines of a stationary turn of mind, and different constitution from the traveling ones, which are to propel the trains through the tunnels to the terminus in the town, without going out of their houses themselves. The length of the tunnel parallel to the one we passed through is (I believe) two thousand two hundred yards. I wonder if you are understanding one word I am saying all this while! We were introduced to the little engine which was to drag us along the rails. She (for they make these curious little fire-horses all mares) consisted of a boiler, a stove, a small platform, a bench, and behind the bench a barrel containing enough water to prevent her being thirsty for fifteen miles,—the whole machine not bigger than a common fire-engine. She goes upon two wheels, which are her feet, and are moved by bright steel legs called pistons; these are propelled by steam, and in proportion as more steam is applied to the upper extremities (the hip-joints, I suppose) of these pistons, the faster they move the wheels; and when it is desirable to diminish the speed, the steam, which unless suffered to escape would burst the boiler, evaporates through a saefty-valve into the air. The reins, bit, and bridle of this wonderful beast is a small steel handle, which applies or withdraws the steam from its legs or pistons, so that a child might manage it. The coals, which are its oats, were under the bench, and there was a small glass tube affixed to the boiler, with water in it, which indicates by its fullness or emptiness when the creature wants water, which is immediately conveyed to it from its reservoirs. There is a chimney to the stove, but as they burn coke there is none of the dreadful black smoke which accompanies the progress of a steam vessel. This snorting little animal, which I felt rather inclined to pat, was then harnessed to our carriage, and, Mr. Stephenson having taken me on the bench of the engine with him, we started at about ten miles an hour. The steam-horse being ill adapted for going up and down hill, the road was kept at a certain level, and appeared sometimes to sink below the surface of the earth, and sometimes to rise above it. Almost at starting it was cut through the solid rock, which formed a wall on either side of it, about sixty feet high. You can't imagine how strange it seemed to be journeying on thus, without any visible cause of progress other than the magical machine, with its flying white breath and rhythmical, unvarying pace, between these rocky walls, which are already clothed with moss and ferns and grasses; and when I reflected that these great masses of stone had been cut asunder to allow our passage thus far below the surface of the earth, I felt as if no fairy tale was ever half so wonderful as what I saw. Bridges were thrown from side to side across the top of these cliffs, and the people looking down upon us from them seemed like pigmies standing in the sky. I must be more concise, though, or I shall want room. We were to go only fifteen miles, that distance being sufficient to show the speed of the engine, and to take us on to the most beautiful and wonderful object on the road. After proceeding through this rocky defile, we presently found ourselves raised upon embankments ten or twelve feet high; we then came to a moss, or swamp, of considerable extent, on which no human foot could tread without sinking, and yet it bore the road which bore us. This had been the great stumbling-block in the minds of the committee of the House of Commons; but Mr. Stephenson has succeeded in overcoming it. A foundation of hurdles, or, as he called it, basket-work, was thrown over the morass, and the interstices were filled with moss and other elastic matter. Upon this the clay and soil were laid down, and the road *does* float, for we passed over it at the rate of five and twenty miles an hour, and saw the stagnant swamp water trembling on the surface of the soil on either side of us. I hope you understand me. The embankment had gradually been rising higher and higher, and in one place, where the soil was not settled enough to form banks, Stephenson had constructed artificial ones of wood-work, over which the mounds of earth were heaped, for he said that though the wood-work would rot, before it did so the banks of earth which covered it would have been sufficiently consolidated to support the road.

We had now come fifteen miles, and stopped where the road traversed a wide and deep valley. Stephenson made me alight and led me down to the bottom of this ravine, over which, in order to keep his road level, he has thrown a magnificent viaduct of nine arches, the middle one of which is seventy feet high, through which we saw the whole of this beautiful little valley. It was lovely and wonderful beyond all words. He here told me many curious things respecting this ravine: how he believed the Mersey had once rolled through it; how the soil had proved so unfavorable for the foundation of his bridge that it was built upon piles, which had been driven into the earth to an enormous depth; how, while digging for a foundation, he had come to a tree bedded in the earth fourteen feet below the surface of the ground; how tides are caused, and how another flood might be caused; all of which I have remembered and noted down at much greater length than I can enter upon it here. He explained to me the whole construction of the steam-engine, and said he could soon make a famous engineer of me, which, considering the wonderful things he *has* achieved, I dare not say is impossible. His way of explaining himself is peculiar, but very striking, and I understood, without difficulty, all that he said to me. We then rejoined the rest of the party, and the engine having received its supply of water, the carriage was placed behind it, for it cannot turn, and was set off at its utmost speed, thirty-five miles an hour, swifter than a bird flies (for they tried the experiment with a snipe). You cannot conceive what that sensation of cutting the air was; the motion is as smooth as possible, too. I could either have read or written; and as it was, I stood up, and with my bonnet off "drank the air before me." The wind, which was strong, or perhaps the force of our own thrusting against it, absolutely weighed my eyelids down. [I remember a similar experience to this, the first time I attempted to go behind the sheet of the cataract of Niagara; the wind coming from beneath the waterfall met me with such direct force that it literally bore down my eyelids, and I had to put off the attempt of penetrating behind the curtain of foam till another day, when that peculiar accident was less directly hostile to me in its conditions.] When I closed my eyes this sensation of flying was quite delightful, and strange beyond description; yet, strange as it was, I had a perfect sense of security, and not the slightest fear. At one time, to exhibit the power of the engine, having met another steam-carriage which was unsupplied with water, Mr. Stephenson caused it to be fastened in front of ours; moreover, a wagon laden with timber was also chained to us, and thus propelling the idle steam-engine, and dragging the loaded wagon which was beside it, and our own carriage full of people behind, this brave little she-dragon of ours flew on. Farther on she met three carts, which, being fastened in front of her, she pushed on before her without the slightest delay or difficulty; when I add that this pretty little creature can run with equal facility either backward or forward, I believe I have given you an account of all her capacities.

Now for a word or two about the master of all these marvels, with whom I am most horribly in love. He is a man of from fifty to fifty-five years of age; his face is fine, though careworn, and bears an expression of deep thoughtfulness; his mode of explaining his ideas is peculiar and very original, striking, and forcible; and although his accent indicates strongly his north-country birth, his language has not the slightest touch of vulgarity or coarseness. He has certainly turned my head.

Four years have sufficed to bring this great undertaking to an end. The railroad will be opened upon the 15th of next month. The Duke of Wellington is coming down to be present on the occasion, and, I suppose, what with the thousands of spectators and the novelty of the spectacle, there will never have been a scene of more striking interest. The whole cost of the work (including the engines and carriages) will have been eight hundred and thirty thousand pounds; and it is already worth double that sum. The directors have kindly offered us three places for the opening, which is a great favor, for people are bidding almost anything for a place, I understand.

16

'RAILROAD TRAVELLING', *HERAPATH'S RAILWAY JOURNAL* (THE RAILWAY MAGAZINE) 1 (MAR.–DEC. 1836), 110–112

Although the whole passage between Liverpool and Manchester is a series of enchantments, surpassing any in the "Arabian Nights," because they are realities, not fictions, yet there are certain epochs in the transit, which are peculiarly exciting. These are the startings, the ascents and descents, the tunnels, the Chat Moss, and the meetings. At the instant of starting, or rather before, the automaton belches forth an explosion of steam, and seems for a second or two, quiescent. But quickly the explosions are reiterated, with shorter and shorter intervals, till they become too rapid to be counted, though still distinct. These belchings or explosions, more nearly resemble the pantings of a lion or tiger, than any sound that has ever vibrated on my ear. During the ascent they become slower and slower, till the automaton actually labours like an animal out of breath, from the tremendous efforts to gain the highest point of the elevation. The progression is proportionate; and before the said point is gained, the train is not moving faster than a horse could pace, with the slow motion of the animated machine, the breathing becomes more laborious, the growl more distinct, till, at length the animal appears exhausted, and groans like the tiger, when nearly overpowered in contest by the buffalo.

The moment that the height is reached, and the descent commences, the pantings rapidly increase; the engine, with its train, starts off with an augmenting velocity; and in a few seconds it is flying down the declivity like lightning, and with a uniform growl or roar, like a continuous discharge of distant artillery. At this period, the whole train is going at the rate of about 35 or 40 miles an hour! I was on the outside, and in front of the first carriage, just over the engine. The scene was magnificent, I had almost said terrific. Although it was a dead calm, the wind appeared to be blowing a hurricane, such was the velocity with which we darted through the air. Yet all was steady; and there was something in the precision of the machinery, that inspired a degree of confidence over fear—of safety over danger. A man may travel from the pole to the equator, from the Straits of Malacca to the

Isthmus of Darien, and he will see nothing so astonishing as this. The pangs of Etna and Vesuvius excite feelings of horror, as well as of terror; the convulsion of the elements during a thunder storm, carries with it nothing of pride, much less of pleasure, to counteract the awe inspired by the fearful workings of perturbed nature; but the scene which is here presented, and which I cannot here adequately describe, engenders a proud consciousness of superiority in human ingenuity, more intense and convincing than any effort or product of the poet, the painter, the philosopher, or the divine. The projections, or transits of the train through the tunnels or arches, are very electrifying. The deafening peal of thunder, the sudden immersion in gloom, and the clash of reverberated sounds in confined space, combine to produce a momentary shudder, or idea of destruction—a thrill of annihilation, which is instantly dispelled on emerging into the cheerful light.

The meetings or crossings of the steam trains, flying in opposite directions, are scarcely less agitating to the nerves than the transits through the tunnels. The velocity of their course, the propinquity or identity of the iron orbits along which these meteors move, call forth the involuntary but fearful thought of a possible collision, with all its threatening consequences. The period of suspense, however, though exquisitely painful, is but momentary; and in a few seconds the object of terror is far out of sight behind.

The first-class or train is the most fashionable, but the second and third are the most amusing. I travelled one day from Liverpool to Manchester in the lumber train. Many of the carriages were occupied by the "swinish multitude," and others by a multitude of swine. These last were "neat as imported," from the Emerald Isle, and therefore were naturally vociferous, if not eloquent. It was evident that the other passengers would have been considerably annoyed by the orators of this last group, had there not been stationed in each carriage, an officer somewhat analagous to the Usher of the Black Rod, but whose designation on the railroad I found to be "Comptroller of the Gammon." No sooner did one of the long faced gentlemen raise his note too high, or wag his jaw too long, than the "Comptroller of the Gammon" gave him a whack over the snout with the but end of his shillelagh; a snubber that never failed to stop his oratory for the remainder of the journey.

17

CHARLES GREVILLE, *MEMOIRS (SECOND PART): A JOURNAL OF THE REIGN OF QUEEN VICTORIA FROM 1837 TO 1852*. 3 VOLS. ED. HENRY REEVE. (NEW YORK: D. APPLETON AND CO., 1885), I, P. 11

July 25*th*.—I remained at Knowsley till Saturday morning, when I went to Liverpool, got into the train at half-past eleven, and at five minutes after four arrived at Birmingham with an exact punctuality which is rendered easy by the great reserved power of acceleration, the pace at which we traveled being moderate and not above one half the speed at which they do occasionally go; one engineer went at the rate of forty-five miles an hour, but the Company turned him off for doing so. I went to Kenilworth, and saw the ruins of Leicester's Castle, and thence to Warwick to see the Castle there, with both of which I was very much delighted, and got to town on Sunday to find myself in the midst of all the interest of the elections, and the sanguine and confident assertions and expectations of both parties. The first great trial of strength was in the City yesterday; and though Grote beat Palmer at last, and after a severe struggle, by a very small majority, it is so far consolatory to the Conservative interest that it shows a prodigious change since the last general election, when the Conservative candidate was 2,000 behind his opponents.

18

WILLIAM MAKEPEACE THACKERAY, 'TWO DAYS IN WICKLOW', IN *THE PARIS SKETCH BOOK OF MR. M.A. TITMARSH, THE IRISH SKETCH BOOK, & NOTES OF A JOURNEY FROM CORNHILL TO GRAND CAIRO* (NEW YORK: CAXTON, 1840), PP. 491–493

THE little tour we have just been taking has been performed, not only by myriads of the "car-drivingest, tay-drinkingest, say-bathingest people in the world," the inhabitants of the city of Dublin, but also by all the tourists who have come to discover this country for the benefit of the English nation. "Look here!" says the ragged, bearded genius of a guide at the Seven Churches. "This is the spot which Mr. Henry Inglis particularly admired, and said it was exactly like Norway. Many's the song I've heard Mr. Sam Lover sing here—a pleasant gentleman entirely. Have you seen my picture that's taken off in Mrs. Hall's book? All the strangers know me by it, though it makes me much cleverer than I am." Similar tales has he of Mr. Barrow, and the Transatlantic Willis, and of Crofton Croker, who has been everywhere.

The guide's remarks concerning the works of these gentlemen inspired me, I must confess, with considerable disgust and jealousy. A plague take them! what remains for me to discover after the gallant adventurers in the service of Paternoster Row have examined every rock, lake, and ruin of the district, exhausted it of all its legends, and "invented new" most likely, as their daring genius prompted? Hence it follows that the description of the two days' jaunt must of necessity be short; lest persons who have read former accounts should be led to refer to the same, and make comparisons which might possibly be unfavorable to the present humble pages.

Is there anything new to be said regarding the journey? In the first place, there's the railroad: it's no longer than the railroad to Greenwich, to be sure, and almost as well known; but has it been *done?* that's the question; or has anybody discovered the dandies on the railroad?

After wondering at the beggars and carmen of Dublin, the stranger can't help admiring another vast and numerous class of inhabitants of the city—namely, the dandies. Such a number of smartly-dressed young fellows I don't think any town possesses: no, not Paris, where the young shopmen, with spurs and stays, may be remarked strutting abroad on fête-days; nor London, where on Sundays, in the Park, you see thousands of this cheap kind of aristocracy parading; nor Liverpool, famous for the breed of commercial dandies, desk and counter D'Orsays and cotton and sugar-barrel Brummels, and whom one remarks pushing on to business with a brisk determined air. All the above races are only to be encountered on holidays, except by those persons whose affairs take them to shops, docks, or counting-houses, where these fascinating young fellows labor during the week.

But the Dublin breed of dandies is quite distinct from those of the various cities above named, and altogether superior: for they appear every day, and all day long, not once a week merely, and have an original and splendid character and appearance of their own, very hard to describe, though no doubt every traveller, as well as myself, has admired and observed it. They assume a sort of military and ferocious look, not observable in other cheap dandies, except in Paris perhaps now and then; and are to be remarked not so much for the splendor of their ornaments as for the profusion of them. Thus, for instance, a hat which is worn straight over the two eyes costs very likely more than one which hangs upon one ear; a great oily bush of hair to balance the hat (otherwise the head no doubt would fall hopelessly on one side) is even more economical than a crop which requires the barber's scissors oft-times; also a tuft on the chin may be had at a small expense of bear's-grease by persons of a proper age; and although big pins are the fashion, I am bound to say I have never seen so many or so big as here. Large agate marbles or "taws" globes terrestrial and celestial, pawnbrokers' balls,—I cannot find comparisons large enough for these wonderful ornaments of the person. Canes also should be mentioned, which are sold very splendid, with gold or silver heads, for a shilling on the Quays; and the dandy not uncommonly finishes off with a horn quizzing-glass, which being stuck in one eye contracts the brows and gives a fierce determined look to the whole countenance.

In idleness at least these young men can compete with the greatest lords; and the wonder is, how the city can support so many of them, or they themselves; how they manage to spend their time: who gives them money to ride hacks in the "Phaynix" on field and race days; to have boats at Kingstown during the summer; and to be crowding the railway-coaches all the day long? Cars go whirling about all day, bearing squads of them. You see them sauntering at all the railway-stations in vast numbers, and jumping out of the carriages, as the trains come up, and greeting other dandies with that rich large brogue which some actor ought to make known to the English public: it being the biggest, richest, and coarsest of all the brogues of Ireland.

I think these dandies are the chief objects which arrest the stranger's attention as he travels on the Kingstown railroad, and I have always been so much occupied in watching and wondering at them as scarcely to have leisure to look at anything else during the pretty little ride of twenty minutes so beloved by every Dublin cockney. The waters of the bay wash in many places the piers on which the railway is built, and you see the calm stretch of water beyond, and the big purple hill of Howth, and the lighthouses, and the jetties, and the shipping. Yesterday was a boat-race, (I don't know how many scores of such take place during the season,) and you may be sure there were tens of thousands of the dandies to look on. There had been boat-races the two days previous: before that, had been a field day—before that, three days of garrison races—to-day, to-morrow, and the day after, there are races at Howth. There seems some sameness in the sports, but everybody goes: everybody is never tired; and then, I suppose, comes the punch-party, and the song in the evening—the same old pleasures, and the same old songs the next day, and so on to the end. As for the boat-race, I saw two little boats in the distance tugging away for dear life—the beach and piers swarming with spectators, the bay full of small yachts and innumerable row-boats, and in the midst of the assemblage a convict-ship lying ready for sail, with a black mass of poor wretches on her deck—who, too, were eager for pleasure.

19

WILLIAM MAKEPEACE THACKERAY, 'PHYSIOLOGY OF THE LONDON IDLER', *PUNCH* 3 (1842), P. 102, 'RAILWAY PARSIMONY', *PUNCH* 13 (1847), 150, 'NATURAL PHENOMENON', *PUNCH* 14 (1848), 87, AND 'RAILWAY CHARGES', *PUNCH* 14 (1848), 218

Chapter X.—Of the visitor to London

ALTHOUGH the visitor is a provincial by birth, yet he ranks as one of the London Idlers the instant he arrives in town; indeed, the more remote his country residence may be, the more entitled is he to be classed as such.

When alone, his head quarters are merely coach-office inns and Piazza hotels; but if married, he takes furnished lodgings for himself, wife, and (according to circumstances) daughters, in Arundel or Norfolk Street, which a friend has probably engaged for him.

An author has stated that the pleasure of travelling consists not so much in the enjoyment of the present, as the retrospection of the past; and this is possibly the idea upon which the visitor acts, since his whole journey is a series of nuisances from beginning to end. The first discomfort begins at the terminus of the railway, where he cannot remember which locker his luggage was put into, and, consequently, losing the omnibus during the search, is compelled to hire a cab at a quadruple fare. The lost bag, portmanteau, or whatever it may be, is at last found under the seat he had been occupying; after the railway porters, in their strenuous exertions to discover the property, have concealed themselves successively in every locker, with only their legs visible, like so many bees half-way up a train of bell-flowers, or, more correctly, like Mr. W. H. Payne when that eccentric gentleman shuts himself into a door or enchanted helmet, in a Covent Garden pantomime.

At length the visitor arrives at his apartment, after encountering dangers on his journey, to which the perils of the Khyber Pass were but minor annoyances; and then the usual first-night-in-a-new-lodging discomforts crowd upon him.

There is no tea, no bread, no candles, salt, or lump-sugar; everything has to be purchased, and when purchased, to be stowed away in various chiffoniers of that shabby-genteel appraisement-looking build which one only encounters in furnished lodgings, with creaking hinges, faded curtains in front, rusty keys, and ricketty locks that only the landlady can open. And there is a sad cheerless air in lodgings. The very furniture has a sharp and famished appearance, although rubbed up to the last point of friction, and the carpet is brushed until it is threadbare. The hundred insignificant objects that made home HOME—those remote appealers to our feelings, although only books, pictures, or children's toys littered about, are nowhere visible. The very chairs have an expression of outline which seems to say "I am only yours whilst you pay for me;" the fire-irons and fender look cold and formal; and the round mirror, with its frame of gilt knobs and distorted candelabra, has an air of attempted gaiety, that is perfectly distressing to contemplate.

And when the visitor awakes on the first morning of his sojourn in town—which he does at an early hour, after a slumber broken at intervals of every twenty minutes by the never-dying murmur of the London streets—his first business at breakfast is to spread the map of London widely open before him, and commence a deep investigation of the nearest practicable road from one point to another. Short cuts proverbially take up the most time to accomplish; and for this reason the visitor spends half his day in losing himself in a labyrinth of courts and alleys. Having decided upon the first sight that he shall visit, he sallies forth, and commences the undertaking by discovering the residence of a friend, to whom he has given two days' shooting last year, and upon whom he reckons, to run about with him all day long, and show him the Lions of the Metropolis.

Railway parsimony

WE don't know whether the tightness in the Money Market is to be pleaded by way of excuse, but the fact is, that the parsimony of the South-Eastern Railway Company is rapidly reaching its very deepest bathos. The lamps in the first-class carriages have long been on such a miserable scale of dinginess that they suffice only to render "darkness visible;" and, as we have come to the conclusion that it is useless to try and get the Company to trim the lamps, we have determined to set to work, and trim the Company. Sometimes an attempt is made to avoid the lighting altogether, under the pretence of a *lapsus memoriæ* on the part of the guard, who, when appealed to, promises the lamp at the next Station, but fails to keep his promise, unless a clamour is kept up with sufficient vigour by the unenlightened passenger.

The intelligent librarian, who we believe pays a liberal rent for his privilege of book-vending, ought to have a compensation for the loss he must incur; for it is quite evident that it is useless to buy books and newspapers at night, if the directors will not allow sufficient light to read them by. If the wretched farthing rushlight system is pursued, it will be necessary to sell a candle and candlestick with each number of a new periodical. Perhaps, as the librarian is very obliging, he will lend this little article of accommodation to any of his customers who will undertake to leave it at the Station where he alights—though, by the way, a-lighting will soon become a misnomer on the South-Eastern, for the platforms after dark are in such a state of obscurity, that dogs, similar to those who act as convoys to blind beggars, ought to be provided at all the Stations for the guidance of nocturnal travellers.

Among the other pieces of paltriness the Directors have resorted to, is the refusal to part with a single copy of their time-table without the charge of one halfpenny. This halfpenny wisdom, added to the more than pound foolishness of constructing a line to Margate 104 miles in length, when seventy would have been sufficient, must, we should think, prove anything but beneficial to the prospects of this Company. One should be endowed with the feline faculty of seeing in the dark, to travel in comfort on the South-Eastern at night; and, by the way, the cat-like possession of nine lives would be advantageous to a frequenter of railways.

Invaluable advice to railway directors

IF the morning is wet, you should issue orders to have all the third-class carriages thrown open instantly; but if the morning is fine, then have them closed as fast as you can. By this arrangement you will have the second and first-class carriages very nicely filled—and your pockets also.

Natural phenomenon

ONE of the most remarkable of natural phenomena is the wonderful effect produced upon the age of a child by its becoming a passenger by a railway or on board a steam-boat. In the earlier stages of juvenility it is a singular fact that infants who have for some time maintained a respectable footing, relapse suddenly into the position of children in arms, for whom, it will be remembered, no fare is payable. Perhaps, however, the most astounding result is shown in the variableness of the human stature amongst children under ten years of age, as exemplified by the payment of half fares at railway stations and on steamboats. It is of course impossible to doubt the assertions made by the parties on these occasions; but we think it might be made a *sine quâ non* with every boy under ten, whose height is above five feet, to produce the register of the date of his birth, before being entitled to travel as a half-price passenger.

There ought really to be some Statute of Limitations passed in favour of steamboat and railway Directors, so that the half-fare regulation should be confined to individuals not exceeding a certain height; or the Company—like the cabmen—might have the option of charging either by time or by measurement. Some arrangement of the kind is imperatively called for, now that the season for locomotion is coming on, or the traffic accounts will suffer by the deception of those who, from their high standing, ought to be above a practice worthy only of littleness.

Railway charges

CHARGES on a railway for scalding yourself with a cup of tea or a basin of soup are extraordinary, but still we think they lag far behind those of the railway hotels. The bill is always made out on the principle of never seeing the visitor again. He is therefore charged as much as his patience or his purse will bear, which is a sure plan of never inducing him to return. Our feelings towards Southampton, for instance, are anything but friendly, and the next time we visit that inhospitable town, we shall walk up and down the pier all night, or go to bed in the boiler of the engine, sooner than submit to the atrocious impositions of the railway hotels. We were in one for five minutes, during which time the waiter exchanged just three words with us, when we were asked at the door for "one shilling." "What for?" we indignantly exclaimed. "Attendance, Sir, one shilling." It is true we might have stopped all the night conversing with the same attendant for the same amount; still, we thought that fourpence a word was a trifle too dear, even to converse with a waiter at Southampton.

We beg to draw up a small scale of prices, moderate too, for the general use of railway hotels.

	s.	d.
For asking to look at *Bradshaw's*	1	0
For looking at same	1	0
For a wax candle to read the same	1	0
Attendance	1	0
	4	0

This would do capitally for a casual visitor; but if a person slept there, immense ingenuity might be shown in the high valuation of each separate item, recollecting always that it is not very likely you will ever see the visitor again. The following would not be a poor specimen of its kind: –

	s.	d.
Taking off your boots	1	0
Attendance, lighting you up to bed	1	0
Bed	2	6
Sheets and towels	1	6
Pair of slippers	1	0
Shaving water	1	0
Breakfast, with water-cresses	5	0
The *Times*, at ditto	1	0
Cleaning your boots	1	0
Attendance	1	0
Cigar, and light for the same	1	0
Attendance	1	0
	18	0

This would not be very bad for one bed and breakfast; but still the thing may be better done. We just throw out the crude hint; and railway hotel proprietors are quite clever enough to improve upon it. What extraordinary notions, by the bye, a railway hotel bill will give an antiquarian of the next century, of the dearness of provisions at the present period!

20

ALBERT RICHARD SMITH, *THE STRUGGLES AND ADVENTURES OF CHRISTOPHER TADPOLE AT HOME AND ABROAD* (LONDON: WILLOUGHBY, 1847), PP. 481–483

AFTER a hurried dinner in the coffee-room of the Golden Cross—ordered rather for the good of the house than his own—Christopher prepared to start, with his companion, to Arden Court.

But his astonishment was very great, almost matching his delight, when upon entering the dusty office in the street running out of the Strand, he encountered no less a person than Mr. Blandy.

"I dare say you are surprised to see me," said the good gentleman; "but I could not stay at home a minute longer. I found, after you went, so much more information about your affairs, and such a number of papers, that I got here as soon as I could. What are you going to do?"

Christopher explained that it was his intention to set off at once to Arden Court.

"The very thing I was going to propose, if our friend here had not given me a hint about the matter. If Gudge is there we cannot have a better opportunity than the present; so—I am your man."

They were soon ready, and rattling in a cab towards the railway terminus, where the steam from many impatient engines was gleaming in the gas-lights. At the station all was bustle for the mail-train. The passengers were crowding up to the apertures by which the clerks are so strongly fortified; and the clerks themselves were jamming the tickets into those wonderful machines between coffee-pots and nutcrackers, over which they hold unlimited control, and distributing them as fast as their pair of arms could do it.

Mr. Blandy took second class tickets, which he always made a point of doing, saying that they would get there quite as soon as the others. And beyond the knowledge of the fact, he was learned in railway travelling; and preferred the second class for various reasons.

For although comfortable enough, he was wont to remark, there is little sociability in a first class carriage on a railway. Everybody seems to have an idea that he is the only one who is really entitled, by payment and position, to a seat therein: and so is afraid of compromising his dignity by speaking, There is consequently no conversation: the heads of the four corner occupants are usually looking out of the windows by day, or leaning against them by night; and the centre ones look at one another. By the same rule, however, that you rarely see a pretty woman in an omnibus, so, somehow or other, you scarcely ever meet with ordinary ones in a first class carriage. And this fact Mr. Blandy would also insist upon.

The second class travellers are all deep fellows. They come early to get a back seat—or at all events to sit with their back to the engine. They will watch the weather-cocks well, and make their selection of place according to the wind. In warm weather they are chatty and communicative enough, since many of them are in the habit of meeting every day in the train; and they are given to facete observations, which end in drawing parallels between the engine and a horse; except perhaps on Monday afternoons, when the talk is purely agricultural, and about the state of the fields on the side of the line, carried on by farmers returning from Mark Lane. But in cold weather they talk but little. They insist upon closing all the windows to suffocation; and after a few exchanged courtesies—taking their parcels out of each other's way, or spreading a cloak over two or three pairs of knees, they are heard of no more.

As for the rattling open pig-pens upon wheels, which were formerly surnamed third class carriages, Mr. Blandy only looked upon them as wonderful machines, possessing the property of always meeting the rain, no matter from what quarter the wind might be blowing—horizontal shower baths, from whose searching power there was no escape. A wet steaming dripping coach used to be a melancholy object enough, swaying through a village with its compact hood of umbrellas, looking for all the world like a large green tortoise lying over the top: but it was nothing in forlorn appearance to an open car. There was no escaping the rain. If you turned your back to it, it filled the nape of your neck; if you faced it, you had overflowing pockets, with an additional cataract from the front rim of your hat, which before long was as limp as wet brown paper. Some rash people used to cover their heads with their handkerchiefs, but it came all the same: it was only prolonging the misery, as you did not know next where to put your handkerchief when you removed it. Everything was ruined, from your health downwards.

The bell rang: the door slammed: the last evening newspaper was sold to some sanguine person who expected to be able to read it by the light of the illuminated finger-glasses in the roof of the carriages, and the train moved off—a few friends walking by the side of the carriages, smiling and nodding, to the end of the platform, and then having, for the hundredth time, said "You'll write soon, wont you?" retiring.

Nobody of any singularity travelled with them, except an old lady, of the family you always meet in second class carriages. They had first found her in great distress about a box, as one of the omnibuses came up to the door—a box unlike any ever seen before. Then, being found, it was a source of the deepest trouble to her on arriving at the train, because it would not go into any locker or under any of the seats; and it was finally put into a remote van, where the old lady would liked to have gone as well, to be near it, had she not been so nervous. Like Mrs. Grittles, and old ladies generally, her ideas of steam-power were very limited. She looked upon the engine as something between clock-work and gunpowder, which kept her in perpetual dread: and whenever they met a train, she gave herself up for lost. Indeed on these occasions her agony was terrible to witness, and some time always elapsed before Mr. Blandy could assure her that some dreadful accident had not happened, and that nobody was crushed. At every stoppage she made great confusion by having the window down (which stuck as fast as second-class windows do generally), and inquiring of the local policeman or attendant time-keeper if the box was safe: or else she looked sharply after every passenger that got out, for fear he, or she, should walk off with it. And when finally she reached her destination, she so nearly shut herself in by her own umbrella, which she got in some marvellously inextricable manner across the door, that she was all but carried away from her box, after all.

Christopher, Mr. Blandy, and the agent, alighted at the next station: and immediately went to the first inn to procure some means of conveyance to Arden Court. It was a new building, run up upon the speculation of the traffic that there might be, at some future time, when the adjacent common had become a peopled and flourishing town. Everything had been provided against such a period. There was a blue board, with letters that absolutely dazzled by their brightness, running all across the hotel and flauntingly blazoning forth the names of the brewers whose "entire" was retailed on the premises. There were also announcements of beds, and lock-up coach-houses and post-horses; and there was too a coffee-room, on the tables of which a waiter regularly laid a number of cloths every day to entice travellers, and as regularly folded them all up again at night, nobody having come. For there was a chillness about the coffee-room that made people shiver, even in the dog-days. It was just the sort of place at which, you knew by foresight, that if you had ordered mutton chops, there would have been great delay and confusion, and over the blind you would have seen the pot-boy run to the butchers; and the waiter would have brought you musty pale ale, and the pickles would have been confined to cabbage, if indeed you got that: and finally, you would have been strenuously recommended to try eggs and bacon, and perchance have been compelled to do it.

As Christopher and his companions walked over the loose gravel and broken bottles that formed the new road, over what a year ago had been a furze field, the landlord rang an imposing bell—which was in the habit of frightening procrastinating travellers into an idea that the up-train was off—and answered it himself by coming to the door: for the waiter had left that day, to better himself.

"Can we have a chaise and horses to Arden Court?" asked Christopher.

"Yes sir—directly sir," said the landlord.

And he rang the same bell very violently, again, to get up a little excitement; but this time nobody answered it.

"Please to walk into the bar gentlemen," he said. He had not expected anybody else that night, and the fire had long gone out in the coffee-room. The guests went into the bar, to the discomfiture of the landlady who was mending socks, and the wife of the man at the station who had brought her work for the evening, whilst the landlord ran round to the stables.

21

CHARLES DICKENS, 'PAUL'S SECOND DEPRIVATION', IN *DOMBEY AND SON*. 2 VOLS. (NEW YORK: HARPER & BROS, 1852), I: 70–72

POLLY was beset by so many misgivings in the morning, that but for the incessant promptings of her black-eyed companion, she would have abandoned all thoughts of the expedition, and formally petitioned for leave to see number one hundred and forty-seven, under the awful shadow of Mr. Dombey's roof. But Susan, who was personally disposed in favor of the excursion, and who (like Tony Lumpkin), if she could bear the disappointments of other people with tolerable fortitude, could not abide to disappoint herself, threw so many ingenious doubts in the way of this second thought, and stimulated the original intention with so many ingenious arguments, that almost as soon as Mr. Dombey's stately back was turned, and that gentleman was pursuing his daily road towards the city, his unconscious son was on his way to Staggs's Gardens.

This euphonious locality was situated in a suburb, known by the inhabitants of Staggs's Gardens by the name of Camberling Town; a designation which the Strangers' Map of London, as printed (with a view to pleasant and commodious reference) on pocket-handkerchiefs, condenses, with some show of reason, into Camden Town. Hither the two nurses bent their steps, accompanied by their charges; Richards carrying Paul, of course, and Susan leading little Florence by the hand, and giving her such jerks and pokes from time to time, as she considered it wholesome to administer.

The first shock of a great earthquake had, just at that period, rent the whole neighborhood to its centre. Traces of its course were visible on every side. Houses were knocked down; streets broken through and stopped; deep pits and trenches dug in the ground; enormous heaps of earth and clay thrown up; buildings that were undermined and shaking, propped by great beams of wood. Here, a chaos of carts, overthrown and jumbled together, lay topsy-turvy at the bottom of a steep unnatural hill; there, confused treasures of iron soaked and rusted in something that had actually become a pond. Everywhere were bridges that led nowhere; thoroughfares that were wholly impassable; Babel towers of chimneys, wanting' half their height; temporary wooden houses and enclosures, in the most unlikely situations; carcases of ragged tenements, and fragments of unfinished walls and arches, and piles of scaffolding, and wildernesses of bricks, and giant forms of cranes, and tripods straddling above nothing. There were a hundred thousand shapes and substances of incompleteness, wildly mingled out of their places, upside down, burrowing in the earth, aspiring in the air, mouldering in the water, and unintelligible as any dream. Hot springs and fiery eruptions, the usual attendants upon earthquakes, lent their contributions of confusion to the scene. Boiling water hissed and heaved within dilapidated walls; whence, also, the glare and roar of flames came issuing forth: and mounds of ashes blocked up rights of way, and wholly changed the law and custom of the neighborhood.

In short, the yet unfinished and unopened Railroad was in progress; and, from the very core of all this dire disorder, trailed smoothly away, upon its mighty course of civilisation and improvement.

But as yet, the neighborhood was shy to own the Railroad. One or two bold speculators had projected streets; and one had built a little, but had stopped among the mud and ashes to consider farther of it. A bran new Tavern, redolent of fresh mortar and size, and fronting nothing at all, had taken for its sign The Railway Arms; but that might be rash enterprise—and then it hoped to sell drink to the workmen. So, the Excavators' House of Call had sprung up from a beer shop; and the old established Ham and Beef Shop had become The Railway Eating House, with a roast leg of pork daily, through interested motives of a similar immediate and popular description. Lodging-house keepers were favorable in like manner; and for the like reasons were not to be trusted. The general belief was very slow. There were frowzy fields, and cowhouses, and dunghills, and dustheaps, and ditches, and gardens, and summer-houses, and carpet-beating grounds, at the very door of the Railway. Little tumuli of oyster shells in the oyster season, and of lobster shells in the lobster season, and of broken crockery and faded cabbage leaves in all seasons, encroach upon its high places. Posts, and rails, and old cautions to trespassers, and backs of mean houses, and patches of wretched vegetation, stared it out of countenance. Nothing was the better for it, or thought of being so. If the miserable waste ground lying near it could have laughed, it would have laughed it to scorn, like many of the miserable neighbors.

Staggs's Gardens was uncommonly incredulous. It was a little row of houses, with little squalid patches of ground before them, fenced off with old doors, barrel staves, scraps of tarpaulin, and dead bushes; with bottomless tin kettles and exhausted iron fenders, thrust into the gaps. Here, the Staggs's Gardeners trained scarlet beans, kept fowls and rabbits, erected rotten summer houses (one was an old boat), dried clothes, and smoked pipes. Some were of opinion that Staggs's Gardens derived its name from a deceased capitalist, one Mr. Staggs, who had built it for his delectation. Others, who had a natural taste for the country, held that it dated from those rural times when the antlered herd, under the familiar denomination of Staggses, had resorted to its shady precincts. Be this as it may, Staggs's Gardens was regarded by its population as a sacred grove not to be withered by railroad; and so confident were they generally of its long outliving any such ridiculous inventions, that the master chimney-sweeper, at the corner, who was understood to take the lead in the local politics of the Gardens, had publicly declared that on the occasion of the Railroad opening, if it ever did open, two of his boys should ascend the flues of his dwelling, with instructions to hail the failure with derisive jeers from the chimney pots.

22

CHARLES DICKENS, 'MUGBY JUNCTION', IN *STORIES FROM THE CHRISTMAS NUMBERS OF "HOUSEHOLD WORDS" AND "ALL YEAR ROUND."* (NEW YORK: MACMILLAN AND CO., 1896), PP. 464–465, 500–512

He took up his hat and walked out, just in time to see, passing along on the opposite side of the way, a velveteen man, carrying his day's dinner in a small bundle that might have been larger without suspicion of gluttony, and pelting away towards the Junction at a great pace.

"There's Lamps!" said Barbox Brothers. "And by the bye—"

Ridiculous, surely, that a man so serious, so self-contained, and not yet three days emancipated from a routine of drudgery, should stand rubbing his chin in the street, in a brown study about Comic Songs.

"Bedside?" said Barbox Brothers testily. "Sings them at the bedside? Why at the bedside, unless he goes to bed drunk? Does, I shouldn't wonder. But it's no business of mine. Let me see. Mugby Junction, Mugby Junction. Where shall I go next? As it came into my head last night when I woke from an uneasy sleep in the carriage and found myself here, I can go anywhere from here. Where shall I go? I'll go and look at the Junction by daylight. There's no hurry, and I may like the look of one Line better than another."

But there were so many Lines. Gazing down upon them from a bridge at the Junction, it was as if the concentrating Companies formed a great Industrial Exhibition of the works of extraordinary ground spiders that spun iron. And then so many of the Lines went such wonderful ways, so crossing and curving among one another, that the eye lost them. And then some of them appeared to start with the fixed intention of going five hundred miles, and all of a sudden gave it up at an insignificant barrier, or turned off into a workshop. And then others, like intoxicated men, went a little way very straight, and surprisingly slued round and came back again. And then others were so chock-full of trucks of coal, others were so blocked with trucks of casks, others were so gorged with trucks of ballast, others were so set apart for wheeled objects like immense iron cotton-reels: while others were so bright and clear, and others were so delivered over to rust and ashes and idle wheelbarrows out of work, with their legs in the air (looking much like their masters on strike), that there was no beginning, middle, or end to the bewilderment.

Barbox Brothers stood puzzled on the bridge, passing his right hand across the lines on his forehead, which multiplied while he looked down, as if the railway Lines were getting themselves photographed on that sensitive plate. Then was heard a distant ringing of bells and blowing of whistles. Then, puppet-looking heads of men popped out of boxes in perspective, and popped in again. Then, prodigious wooden razors, set up on end, began shaving the atmosphere. Then, several locomotive engines in several directions began to scream and be agitated. Then, along one avenue a train came in. Then, along another two trains appeared that didn't come in, but stopped without. Then, bits of trains broke off. Then, a struggling horse became involved with them. Then, the locomotives shared the bits of trains, and ran away with the whole.

"I have not made my next move much clearer by this. No hurry. No need to make up my mind to-day, or to-morrow, nor yet the day after. I'll take a walk."

It fell out somehow (perhaps he meant it should) that the walk tended to the platform at which he had alighted, and to Lamps's room. But Lamps was not in his room. A pair of velveteen shoulders were adapting themselves to one of the impressions on the wall by Lamps's fire-place, but otherwise the room was void. In passing back to get out of the station again, he learnt the cause of this vacancy, by catching sight of Lamps on the opposite line of railway, skipping along the top of a train, from carriage to carriage, and catching lighted namesakes thrown up to him by a coadjutor.

"He is busy. He has not much time for composing or singing Comic Songs this morning, I take it."

The direction he pursued now was into the country, keeping very near to the side of one great Line of railway, and within easy view of others. "I have half a mind," he said, glancing around, "to settle the question from this point, by saying, 'I'll take this set of rails, or that, or t'other, and stick to it.' They separate themselves from the confusion, out here, and go their ways."

No. 1 Branch line.—The signal-man

"HALLOA! Below there!"

When he heard a voice thus calling to him, he was standing at the door of his box, with a flag in his hand, furled round its short pole. One would have thought, considering the nature of the ground, that he could not have doubted from what quarter the voice came; but instead of looking up to where I stood on the top of the steep cutting nearly over his head, he turned himself about, and looked down the Line. There was something remarkable in his manner of doing so, though I could not have said for my life what. But I know it was remarkable enough to attract my notice, even though his figure was foreshortened and shadowed, down in the deep trench, and mine was high above him, so steeped in the glow of an angry sunset, that I had shaded my eyes with my hand before I saw him at all.

"Halloa! Below!"

From looking down the Line, he turned himself about again, and, raising his eyes, saw my figure high above him.

"Is there any path by which I can come down and speak to you?"

He looked up at me without replying, and I looked down at him without pressing him too soon with a repetition of my idle question. Just then there came a vague vibration in the earth and air, quickly changing into a violent pulsation, and an oncoming rush that caused me to start back, as though it had force to draw me down. When such vapour as rose to my height from this rapid train had passed me, and was skimming away over the landscape, I looked down again, and saw him refurling the flag he had shown while the train went by.

I repeated my inquiry. After a pause, during which he seemed to regard me with fixed attention, he motioned with his rolled-up flag towards a point on my level, some two or three hundred yards distant. I called down to him, "All right!" and made for that point. There, by dint of looking closely about me, I found a rough zigzag descending path notched out, which I followed.

The cutting was extremely deep, and unusually precipitate. It was made through a clammy stone, that became oozier and wetter as I went down. For these reasons, I found the way long enough to give me time to recall a singular air of reluctance or compulsion with which he had pointed out the path.

When I came down low enough upon the zigzag descent to see him again, I saw that he was standing between the rails on the way by which the train had lately passed, in an attitude as if he were waiting for me to appear. He had his left hand at his chin, and that left elbow rested on his right hand, crossed over his breast. His attitude was one of such expectation and watchfulness that I stopped a moment, wondering at it.

I resumed my downward way, and stepping out upon the level of the railroad, and drawing nearer to him, saw that he was a dark sallow man, with a dark beard and rather heavy eyebrows. His post was in as solitary and dismal a place as ever I saw. On either side, a dripping-wet wall of jagged stone, excluding all view but a strip of sky; the perspective one way only a crooked prolongation of this great dungeon; the shorter perspective in the other direction terminating in a gloomy red light, and the gloomier entrance to a black tunnel, in whose massive architecture there was a barbarous, depressing, and forbidding air. So little sunlight ever found its way to this spot, that it had an earthy, deadly smell; and so much cold wind rushed through it, that it struck chill to me, as if I had left the natural world.

Before he stirred, I was near enough to him to have touched him. Not even then removing his eyes from mine, he stepped back one step, and lifted his hand.

This was a lonesome post to occupy (I said), and it had riveted my attention when I looked down from up yonder. A visitor was a rarity, I should suppose; not an unwelcome rarity, I hoped? In me, he merely saw a man who had been shut up within narrow limits all his life, and who, being at last set free, had a newly-awakened interest in these great works. To such purpose I spoke to him; but I am far from sure of the terms I used; for, besides that I am not happy in opening any conversation, there was something in the man that daunted me.

He directed a most curious look towards the red light near the tunnel's mouth, and looked all about it, as if something were missing from it, and then looked at me.

That light was part of his charge? Was it not?

He answered in a low voice,—"Don't you know it is?"

The monstrous thought came into my mind, as I perused the fixed eyes and the saturnine face, that this was a spirit, not a man. I have speculated since, whether there may have been infection in his mind.

In my turn, I stepped back. But in making the action, I detected in his eyes some latent fear of me. This put the monstrous thought to flight.

"You look at me," I said, forcing a smile, "as if you had a dread of me."

"I was doubtful," he returned, "whether I had seen you before."

"Where?"

He pointed to the red light he had looked at.

"There?" I said.

Intently watchful of me, he replied (but without sound), "Yes."

"My good fellow, what should I do there? However, be that as it may, I never was there, you may swear."

"I think I may," he rejoined. "Yes; I am sure I may."

His manner cleared, like my own. He replied to my remarks with readiness, and in well-chosen words. Had he much to do there? Yes; that was to say, he had enough responsibility to bear; but exactness and watchfulness were what was required of him, and of actual work—manual labour—he had next to none. To change that signal, to trim those lights, and to turn this iron handle now and then, was all he had to do under that head. Regarding those many long and lonely hours of which I seemed to make so much, he could only say that the routine of his life had shaped itself into that form, and he had grown used to it. He had taught himself a language down here,—if only to know it by sight, and to have formed his own crude ideas of its pronunciation, could be called learning it. He had also worked at fractions and decimals, and tried a little algebra; but he was, and had been as a boy, a poor hand at figures. Was it necessary for him when on duty always to remain in that channel of damp air, and could he never rise into the sunshine from between those high stone walls? Why, that depended upon times and circumstances. Under some conditions there would be less upon the Line than under others, and the same held good as to certain hours of the day and night. In bright weather, he did choose occasions for getting a little above these lower shadows; but, being at all times liable to be called by his electric bell, and at such times listening for it with redoubled anxiety, the relief was less than I would suppose.

He took me into his box, where there was a fire, a desk for an official book in which he had to make certain entries, a telegraphic instrument with its dial, face, and needles, and the little bell of which he had spoken. On my trusting that he would excuse the remark that he had been well educated, and (I hoped I might say without offence), perhaps educated above that station, he observed that instances of slight incongruity in such wise would rarely be found wanting among large bodies of men; that he had heard it was so in workhouses, in the police force, even in that last desperate resource, the army; and that he knew it was so, more or less, in any great railway staff. He had been, when young (if I could believe it, sitting in that hut,—he scarcely could), a student of natural philosophy, and had attended lectures; but he had run wild, misused his opportunities, gone down, and never risen again. He had no complaint to offer about that. He had made his bed, and he lay upon it. It was far too late to make another.

All that I have here condensed he said in a quiet manner, with his grave dark regards divided between me and the fire. He threw in the word, "Sir," from time to time, and especially when he referred to his youth,—as though to request me to understand that he claimed to be nothing but what I found him. He was several times interrupted by the little bell, and had to read off messages, and send replies. Once he had to stand without the door, and display a flag as a train passed, and make some verbal communication to the driver. In the discharge of his duties, I observed him to be remarkably exact and vigilant, breaking off his discourse at a syllable, and remaining silent until what he had to do was done.

In a word, I should have set this man down as one of the safest of men to be employed in that capacity, but for the circumstance that while he was speaking to me he twice broke off with a fallen colour, turned his face towards the little bell when it did NOT ring, opened the door of the hut (which was kept shut to exclude the unhealthy damp), and looked out towards the red light near the mouth of the tunnel. On both of those occasions, he came back to the fire with the inexplicable air upon him which I had remarked, without being able to define, when we were so far asunder.

Said I, when I rose to leave him, "You almost make me think that I have met with a contented man."

(I am afraid I must acknowledge that I said it to lead him on.)

"I believe I used to be so," he rejoined, in the low voice in which he had first spoken; "but I am troubled, sir, I am troubled."

He would have recalled the words if he could. He had said them, however, and I took them up quickly.

"With what? What is your trouble?"

"It is very difficult to impart, sir. It is very, very difficult to speak of. If ever you make me another visit, I will try to tell you."

"But I expressly intend to make you another visit. Say, when shall it be?"

"I go off early in the morning, and I shall be on again at ten to-morrow night, sir."

"I will come at eleven."

He thanked me, and went out at the door with me. "I'll show my white light, sir," he said, in his peculiar low voice, "till you have found the way up. When you have found it, don't call out! And when you are at the top, don't call out!"

His manner seemed to make the place strike colder to me, but I said no more than, "Very well."

"And when you come down to-morrow night, don't call out! Let me ask you a parting question. What made you cry, 'Halloa! Below there!' to-night?"

"Heaven knows," said I. "I cried something to that effect—"

"Not to that effect, sir. Those were the very words. I know them well."

"Admit those were the very words. I said them, no doubt, because I saw you below."

"For no other reason?"

"What other reason could I possibly have?"

"You had no feeling that they were conveyed to you in any supernatural way?"

"No."

He wished me good night, and held up his light. I walked by the side of the down Line of rails (with a very disagreeable sensation of a train coming behind me) until I found the path. It was easier to mount than to descend, and I got back to my inn without any adventure.

Punctual to my appointment, I placed my foot on the first notch of the zigzag next night, as the distant clocks were striking eleven. He was waiting for me at the bottom, with his white light on. "I have not called out," I said, when we came close together; "may I speak now?" "By all means, sir." "Good night, then, and here's my hand." "Good night, sir, and here's mine." With that we walked side by side to his box, entered it, closed the door, and sat down by the fire.

"I have made up my mind, sir," he began, bending forward as soon as we were seated, and speaking in a tone but a little above a whisper, "that you shall not have to ask me twice what troubles me. I took you for some one else yesterday evening. That troubles me."

"That mistake?"

"No. That some one else."

"Who is it?"

"I don't know."

"Like me?"

"I don't know. I never saw the face. The left arm is across the face, and the right arm is waved,—violently waved. This way."

I followed his action with my eyes, and it was the action of an arm gesticulating, with the utmost passion and vehemence, "For God's sake, clear the way!"

"One moonlight night," said the man, "I was sitting here, when I heard a voice cry, 'Halloa! Below there!' I started up, looked from that door, and saw this Some one else standing by the red light near the tunnel, waving as I just now showed you. The voice seemed hoarse with shouting, and it cried, 'Look out! Look out!' And then again, 'Halloa! Below there! Look out!' I caught up my lamp, turned it on red, and ran towards the figure, calling, 'What's wrong? What has happened?

Where?' It stood just outside the blackness of the tunnel. I advanced so close upon it that I wondered at its keeping the sleeve across its eyes. I ran right up at it, and had my hand stretched out to pull the sleeve away, when it was gone."

"Into the tunnel?" said I.

"No. I ran on into the tunnel, five hundred yards. I stopped, and held my lamp above my head, and saw the figures of the measured distance, and saw the wet stains stealing down the walls and trickling through the arch. I ran out again faster than I had run in (for I had a mortal abhorrence of the place upon me), and I looked all round the red light with my own red light, and I went up the iron ladder to the gallery atop of it, and I came down again, and ran back here. I telegraphed both ways, 'An alarm has been given. Is anything wrong?' The answer came back, both ways, 'All well.' "

Resisting the slow touch of a frozen finger tracing out my spine, I showed him how that this figure must be a deception of his sense of sight; and how that figures, originating in disease of the delicate nerves that minister to the functions of the eye, were known to have often troubled patients, some of whom had become conscious of the nature of their affliction, and had even proved it by experiments upon themselves. "As to an imaginary cry," said I, "do but listen for a moment to the wind in this unnatural valley while we speak so low, and to the wild harp it makes of the telegraph wires."

That was all very well, he returned, after we had sat listening for a while, and he ought to know something of the wind and the wires,—he who so often passed long winter nights there, alone and watching. But he would beg to remark that he had not finished.

I asked his pardon, and he slowly added these words, touching my arm, –

"Within six hours after the Appearance, the memorable accident on this Line happened, and within ten hours the dead and wounded were brought along through the tunnel over the spot where the figure had stood."

A disagreeable shudder crept over me, but I did my best against it. It was not to be denied, I rejoined, that this was a remarkable coincidence, calculated deeply to impress his mind. But it was unquestionable that remarkable coincidences did continually occur, and they must be taken into account in dealing with such a subject. Though to be sure I must admit, I added (for I thought I saw that he was going to bring the objection to bear upon me), men of common sense did not allow much for coincidences in making the ordinary calculations of life.

He again begged to remark that he had not finished.

I again begged his pardon for being betrayed into interruptions.

"This," he said, again laying his hand upon my arm, and glancing over his shoulder with hollow eyes, "was just a year ago. Six or seven months passed, and I had recovered from the surprise and shock, when one morning, as the day was breaking, I, standing at the door, looked towards the red light, and saw the spectre again." He stopped, with a fixed look at me.

"Did it cry out?"

"No. It was silent."

"Did it wave its arm?"

"No. It leaned against the shaft of the light, with both hands before the face. Like this."

Once more I followed his action with my eyes. It was an action of mourning. I have seen such an attitude in stone figures on tombs.

"Did you go up to it?"

"I came in and sat down, partly to collect my thoughts, partly because it had turned me faint. When I went to the door again, daylight was above me, and the ghost was gone."

"But nothing followed? Nothing came of this?"

He touched me on the arm with his forefinger twice or thrice, giving a ghastly nod each time:

"That very day, as a train came out of the tunnel, I noticed, at a carriage window on my side, what looked like a confusion of hands and heads, and something waved. I saw it just in time to signal the driver, Stop! He shut off, and put his brake on, but the train drifted past here a hundred and fifty yards or more. I ran after it, and, as I went along, heard terrible screams and cries. A beautiful young lady had died instantaneously in one of the compartments, and was brought in here, and laid down on this floor between us."

Involuntarily I pushed my chair back, as I looked from the boards at which he pointed to himself.

"True, sir. True. Precisely as it happened, so I tell it you."

I could think of nothing to say, to any purpose, and my mouth was very dry. The wind and the wires took up the story with a long lamenting wail.

He resumed. "Now, sir, mark this, and judge how my mind is troubled. The spectre came back a week ago. Ever since, it has been there, now and again, by fits and starts."

"At the light?"

"At the Danger-light."

"What does it seem to do?"

He repeated, if possible with increased passion and vehemence, that former gesticulation of, "For God's sake, clear the way!"

Then he went on. "I have no peace or rest for it. It calls to me, for many minutes together, in an agonised manner, 'Below there! Look out! Look out!' It stands waving to me. It rings my little bell—"

I caught at that. "Did it ring your bell yesterday evening when I was here, and you went to the door?"

"Twice."

"Why, see," said I, "how your imagination misleads you. My eyes were on the bell, and my ears were open to the bell, and if I am a living man, it did NOT ring at those times. No, nor at any other time, except when it was rung in the natural course of physical things by the station communicating with you."

He shook his head. "I have never made a mistake as to that yet, sir. I have never confused the spectre's ring with the man's. The ghost's ring is a strange vibration in the bell that it derives from nothing else, and I have not asserted that the bell stirs to the eye. I don't wonder that you failed to hear it. But *I* heard it."

"And did the spectre seem to be there, when you looked out?"

"It WAS there."

"Both times?"

He repeated firmly: "Both times."

"Will you come to the door with me, and look for it now?"

He bit his under lip as though he were somewhat unwilling, but arose. I opened the door, and stood on the step, while he stood in the doorway. There was the Danger-light. There was the dismal mouth of the tunnel. There were the high, wet stone walls of the cutting. There were the stars above them.

"Do you see it?" I asked him, taking particular note of his face. His eyes were prominent and strained, but not very much more so, perhaps, than my own had been when I had directed them earnestly towards the same spot.

"No," he answered. "It is not there."

"Agreed," said I.

We went in again, shut the door, and resumed our seats. I was thinking how best to improve this advantage, if it might be called one, when he took up the conversation in such a matter-of-course way, so assuming that there could be no serious question of fact between us, that I felt myself placed in the weakest of positions.

"By this time you will fully understand, sir," he said, "that what troubles me so dreadfully is the question, What does the spectre mean?"

I was not sure, I told him, that I did fully understand.

"What is its warning against?" he said, ruminating, with his eyes on the fire, and only by times turning them on me. "What is the danger? Where is the danger? There is danger overhanging somewhere on the Line. Some dreadful calamity will happen. It is not to be doubted this third time, after what has gone before. But surely this is a cruel haunting of *me*. What can *I* do?"

He pulled out his handkerchief, and wiped the drops from his heated forehead.

"If I telegraph Danger, on either side of me, or on both, I can give no reason for it," he went on, wiping the palms of his hands. "I should get into trouble, and do no good. They would think I was mad. This is the way it would work,—Message: 'Danger! Take care!' Answer: 'What Danger? Where?' Message: 'Don't know. But, for God's sake, take care!' They would displace me. What else could they do?"

His pain of mind was most pitiable to see. It was the mental torture of a conscientious man, oppressed beyond endurance by an unintelligible responsibility involving life.

"When it first stood under the Danger-light," he went on, putting his dark hair back from his head, and drawing his hands outward across and across his temples in an extremity of feverish distress, "why not tell me where that accident was to happen,—if it must happen? Why not tell me how it could be averted,—if it could have been averted? When on its second coming it hid its face, why not tell me, instead, 'She is going to die. Let them keep her at home'? If it came, on those two occasions, only to show me that its warnings were true, and so to prepare me for the third, why not warn me plainly now? And I, Lord help me! A mere poor signal-man on this solitary station! Why not go to somebody with credit to be believed, and power to act?"

When I saw him in this state, I saw that for the poor man's sake, as well as for the public safety, what I had to do for the time was to compose his mind. Therefore, setting aside all question of reality or unreality between us, I represented to him that whoever thoroughly discharged his duty must do well, and that at least it was his comfort that he understood his duty, though he did not understand these confounding Appearances. In this effort I succeeded far better than in the attempt to reason him out of his conviction. He became calm; the occupations incidental to his post as the night advanced began to make larger demands on his attention: and I left him at two in the morning. I had offered to stay through the night, but he would not hear of it.

That I more than once looked back at the red light as I ascended the pathway, that I did not like the red light, and that I should have slept but poorly if my bed had been under it, I see no reason to conceal. Nor did I like the two sequences of the accident and the dead girl. I see no reason to conceal that either.

But what ran most in my thoughts was the consideration how ought I to act, having become the recipient of this disclosure? I had proved the man to be intelligent, vigilant, painstaking, and exact; but how long might he remain so, in his state of mind? Though in a subordinate position, still he held a most important trust, and would I (for instance) like to stake my own life on the chances of his continuing to execute it with precision?

Unable to overcome a feeling that there would be something treacherous in my communicating what he had told me to his superiors in the Company, without first being plain with himself and proposing a middle course to him, I ultimately resolved to offer to accompany him (otherwise keeping his secret for the present) to the wisest medical practitioner we could hear of in those parts, and to take his opinion. A change in his time of duty would come round next night, he had apprised me, and he would be off an hour or two after sunrise, and on again soon after sunset. I had appointed to return accordingly.

Next evening was a lovely evening, and I walked out early to enjoy it. The sun was not yet quite down when I traversed the field-path near the top of the deep cutting. I would extend my walk for an hour, I said to myself, half an hour on and half an hour back, and it would then be time to go to my signal-man's box.

Before pursuing my stroll, I stepped to the brink, and mechanically looked down, from the point from which I had first seen him. I cannot describe the thrill that seized upon me, when, close at the mouth of the tunnel, I saw the appearance of a man, with his left sleeve across his eyes, passionately waving his right arm.

The nameless horror that oppressed me passed in a moment, for in a moment I saw that this appearance of a man was a man indeed, and that there was a little group of other men, standing at a short distance, to whom he seemed to be rehearsing the gesture he made. The Danger-light was not yet lighted. Against its shaft, a little low hut, entirely new to me, had been made of some wooden supports and tarpaulin. It looked no bigger than a bed.

With an irresistible sense that something was wrong,—with a flashing self-reproachful fear that fatal mischief had come of my leaving the man there, and causing no one to be sent to overlook or correct what he did,—I descended the notched path with all the speed I could make.

"What is the matter?" I asked the men.

"Signal-man killed this morning, sir."

"Not the man belonging to that box?"

"Yes, sir."

"Not the man I know?"

"You will recognise him, sir, if you knew him," said the man who spoke for the others, solemnly uncovering his own head, and raising an end of the tarpaulin, "for his face is quite composed."

"O, how did this happen, how did this happen?" I asked, turning from one to another as the hut closed in again.

"He was cut down by an engine, sir. No man in England knew his work better. But somehow he was not clear of the outer rail. It was just at broad day. He had struck the light, and had the lamp in his hand. As the engine came out of the tunnel, his back was towards her, and she cut him down. That man drove her, and was showing how it happened. Show the gentleman, Tom."

The man, who wore a rough dark dress, stepped back to his former place at the mouth of the tunnel.

"Coming round the curve in the tunnel, sir," he said, "I saw him at the end, like as if I saw him down a perspective-glass. There was no time to check speed, and I knew him to be very careful. As he didn't seem to take heed of the whistle, I shut it off when we were running down upon him, and called to him as loud as I could call."

"What did you say?"

"I said, 'Below there! Look out! Look out! For God's sake, clear the way!'"

I started.

"Ah! it was a dreadful time, sir. I never left off calling to him. I put this arm before my eyes not to see, and I waved this arm to the last; but it was no use."

Without prolonging the narrative to dwell on any one of its curious circumstances more than on any other, I may, in closing it, point out the coincidence that the warning of the engine-driver included, not only the words which the unfortunate signal-man had repeated to me as haunting him, but also the words which I myself—not he—had attached, and that only in my own mind, to the gesticulation he had imitated.

23

CHARLES DICKENS, *OUR MUTUAL FRIEND* (NEW YORK: MACMILLAN, 1907), P. 720

Then, the train rattled among the house-tops, and among the ragged sides of houses torn down to make way for it, and over the swarming streets, and under the fruitful earth, until it shot across the river: bursting over the quiet surface like a bomb-shell, and gone again as if it had exploded in the rush of smoke and steam and glare. A little more, and again it roared across the river, a great rocket: spurning the watery turnings and doublings with ineffable contempt, and going straight to its end, as Father Time goes to his. To whom it is no matter what living waters run high or low, reflect the heavenly lights and darknesses, produce their little growth of weeds and flowers, turn here, turn there, are noisy or still, are troubled or at rest, for their course has one sure termination, though their sources and devices are many.

24

CHARLES DICKENS, 'A FLIGHT', IN *REPRINTED PIECES* (NEW YORK: UNIVERSITY SOCIETY, 1908), PP. 151–161

W<small>HEN</small> Don Diego de—I forget his name—the inventor of the last new Flying Machines, price so many francs for ladies, so many more for gentlemen—when Don Diego, by permission of Deputy Chaff Wax and his noble band, shall have taken out a Patent for the Queen's dominions, and shall have opened a commodious Warehouse in an airy situation; and when all persons of any gentility will keep at least a pair of wings, and be seen skimming about in every direction; I shall take a flight to Paris (as I soar round the world) in a cheap and independent manner. At present, my reliance is on the South Eastern Railway Company, in whose Express Train here I sit, at eight of the clock on a very hot morning, under the very hot roof of the Terminus at London Bridge, in danger of being "forced" like a cucumber or a melon, or a pine-apple—And talking of pine-apples, I suppose there never were so many pine-apples in a Train as there appear to be in this Train.

Whew! The hot-house air is faint with pine-apples. Every French citizen or citizeness is carrying pine-apples home. The compact little Enchantress in the corner of my carriage (French actress, to whom I yielded up my heart under the auspices of that brave child, "M<small>EAT</small>-<small>CHELL</small>," at the St. James's Theatre the night before last) has a pine-apple in her lap. Compact Enchantress's friend, confidante, mother, mystery, Heaven knows what, has two pine-apples in her lap, and a bundle of them under the seat. Tobacco-smoky Frenchman in Algerine wrapper, with peaked hood behind, who might be Abd-el-Kader dyed rifle-green, and who seems to be dressed entirely in dirt and braid, carries pine-apples in a covered basket. Tall, grave, melancholy Frenchman, with black Vandyke beard, and hair close-cropped, with expansive chest to waistcoat, and compressive waist to coat: saturnine as to his pantaloons, calm as to his feminine boots, precious as to his jewellery, smooth and white as to his linen: dark-eyed, high-foreheaded, hawk-nosed—got up, one thinks, like Lucifer or Mephistopheles, or Zamiel, transformed into a highly genteel Parisian—has the green end of a pine-apple sticking out of his neat valise.

Whew! If I were to be kept here long, under this forcing-frame, I wonder what would become of me—whether I should be forced into a giant, or should sprout or blow into some other phenomenon! Compact Enchantresss is not ruffled by the heat—she is always composed, always compact. O look at her little ribbons, frills, and edges, at her shawl, at her gloves, at her hair, at her bracelets, at her bonnet, at everything about her! How is it accomplished! What does she do to be so neat? How is it that every trifle she wears belongs to her, and cannot choose but be a part of her? And even Mystery, look at *her!* A model. Mystery is not young, not pretty, though still of an average candle-light passability; but she does such miracles in her own behalf, that, one of these days, when she dies, they'll be amazed to find an old woman in her bed, distantly like her. She was an actress once, I shouldn't wonder, and had a Mystery attendant on herself. Perhaps, Compact Enchantress will live to be a Mystery, and to wait with a shawl at the side-scenes, and to sit opposite to Mademoiselle in railway carriages, and smile and talk subserviently, as Mystery does now. That's hard to believe!

Two Englishmen, and now our carriage is full. First Englishman, in the monied interest—flushed, highly respectable—Stock Exchange, perhaps—City, certainly. Faculties of second Englishman entirely absorbed in hurry. Plunges into the carriage, blind. Calls out of window concerning his luggage, deaf. Suffocates himself under pillows of great-coats, for no reason, and in a demented manner. Will receive no assurance from any porter whatsoever. Is stout and hot, and wipes his head, and makes himself hotter by breathing so hard. Is totally incredulous respecting assurance of Collected Guard, that "there's no hurry." No hurry! And a flight to Paris in eleven hours!

It is all one to me in this drowsy corner, hurry or no hurry. Until Don Diego shall send home my wings, my flight is with the South Eastern Company. I can fly with the South Eastern, more lazily, at all events, than in the upper air. I have but to sit here thinking as idly as I please, and be whisked away. I am not accountable to anybody for the idleness of my thoughts in such an idle summer flight; my flight is provided for by the South Eastern and is no business of mine.

The bell! With all my heart. It does not require *me* to do so much as even to flap my wings. Something snorts for me, something shrieks for me, something proclaims to everything else that it had better keep out of my way,—and away I go.

Ah! The fresh air is pleasant after the forcing-frame, though it does blow over these interminable streets, and scatter the smoke of this vast wilderness of chimneys. Here we are—no, I mean there we were, for it has darted far into the rear— in Bermondsey where the tanners live. Flash! The distant shipping in the Thames is gone. Whirr! The little streets of new brick and red tile, with here and there a flagstaff growing like a tall weed out of the scarlet beans, and, everywhere, plenty of open sewer and ditch for the promotion of the public health, have been fired off in a volley. Whizz! Dust-heaps, market-gardens, and waste grounds. Rattle! New Cross Station. Shock! There we were at Croydon. Bur-r-r-r! The tunnel.

I wonder why it is that when I shut my eyes in a tunnel I begin to feel as if I were going at an Express pace the other way. I am clearly going back to London now.

Compact Enchantress must have forgotten something, and reversed the engine. No! After long darkness, pale fitful streaks of light appear. I am still flying on for Folkestone. The streaks grow stronger—become continuous—become the ghost of day—become the living day—became I mean—the tunnel is miles and miles away, and here I fly through sunlight, all among the harvest and the Kentish hops.

There is a dreamy pleasure in this flying. I wonder where it was, and when it was, that we exploded, blew into space somehow, a Parliamentary Train, with a crowd of heads and faces looking at us out of cages, and some hats waving. Monied Interest says it was at Reigate Station. Expounds to Mystery how Reigate Station is so many miles from London, which Mystery again develops to Compact Enchantress. There might be neither a Reigate nor a London for me, as I fly away among the Kentish hops and harvest. What do *I* care?

Bang! We have let another Station off, and fly away regardless. Everything is flying. The hop-gardens turn gracefully towards me, presenting regular avenues of hops in rapid flight, then whirl away. So do the pools and rushes, haystacks, sheep, clover in full bloom delicious to the sight and smell, corn-sheaves, cherry-orchards, apple-orchards, reapers, gleaners, hedges, gates, fields that taper off into little angular corners, cottages, gardens, now and then a church. Bang, bang! A double-barrelled Station! Now a wood, now a bridge, now a landscape, now a cutting, now a—Bang! a single-barrelled Station—there was a cricket-match somewhere with two white tents, and then four flying cows, then turnips—now the wires of the electric telegraph are all alive, and spin, and blur their edges, and go up and down, and make the intervals between each other most irregular: contracting and expanding in the strangest manner. Now we slacken. With a screwing, and a grinding, and a smell of water thrown on ashes, now we stop!

Demented Traveller, who has been for two or three minutes watchful, clutches his great-coats, plunges at the door, rattles it, cries "Hi!" eager to embark on board of impossible packets, far inland. Collected Guard appears. "Are you for Tunbridge, sir?" "Tunbridge? No. Paris." "Plenty of time, sir. No hurry. Five minutes here, sir, for refreshment." I am so blest (anticipating Zamiel, by half a second) as to procure a glass of water for Compact Enchantress.

Who would suppose we had been flying at such a rate, and shall take wing again directly? Refreshment-room full, platform full, porter with watering-pot deliberately cooling a hot wheel, another porter with equal deliberation helping the rest of the wheels bountifully to ice cream. Monied Interest and I re-entering the carriage first, and being there alone, he intimates to me that the French are "no go" as a Nation. I ask why? He says, that Reign of Terror of theirs was quite enough. I ventured to inquire whether he remembers anything that preceded said Reign of Terror? He says not particularly. "Because," I remark, "the harvest that is reaped, has sometimes been sown." Monied Interest repeats, as quite enough for him, that the French are revolutionary,—"and always at it."

Bell. Compact Enchantress, helped in by Zamiel, (whom the stars confound!) gives us her charming little side-box look, and smites me to the core. Mystery eating sponge-cake. Pine-apple atmosphere faintly tinged with suspicions of sherry.

Demented Traveller flits past the carriage, looking for it. Is blind with agitation, and can't see it. Seems singled out by Destiny to be the only unhappy creature in the flight, who has any cause to hurry himself. Is nearly left behind. Is seized by Collected Guard after the Train is in motion, and bundled in. Still, has lingering suspicions that there must be a boat in the neighbourhood, and *will* look wildly out of window for it.

Flight resumed. Corn-sheaves, hop-gardens, reapers, gleaners, apple-orchards, cherry-orchards, Stations single and double-barrelled, Ashford. Compact Enchantress (constantly talking to Mystery, in an exquisite manner) gives a little scream; a sound that seems to come from high up in her precious little head; from behind her bright little eyebrows. "Great Heaven, my pine-apple! My Angel! It is lost!" Mystery is desolated. A search made. It is not lost. Zamiel finds it. I curse him (flying) in the Persian manner. May his face be turned upside down, and Jackasses sit upon his uncle's grave!

Now fresher air, now glimpses of unenclosed Down-land with flapping crows flying over it whom we soon outfly, now the Sea, now Folkestone at a quarter after ten. "Tickets ready, gentlemen!" Demented dashes at the door. "For Paris, sir?" No hurry.

Not the least. We are dropped slowly down to the Port, and sidle to and fro (the whole Train) before the insensible Royal George Hotel, for some ten minutes. The Royal George takes no more heed of us than its namesake under water at Spithead, or under earth at Windsor, does. The Royal George's dog lies winking and blinking at us, without taking the trouble to sit up; and the Royal George's "wedding party" at the open window (who seem, I must say, rather tired of bliss) don't bestow a solitary glance upon us, flying thus to Paris in eleven hours. The first gentleman in Folkestone is evidently used up, on this subject.

Meanwhile, Demented chafes. Conceives that every man's hand is against him, and exerting itself to prevent his getting to Paris. Refuses Consolation. Rattles door. Sees smoke on the horizon, and "knows" it's the boat gone without him. Monied Interest resentfully explains that *he* is going to Paris too. Demented signifies that if Monied Interest chooses to be left behind, *he* don't.

"Refreshments in the Waiting-Room, ladies and gentlemen. No hurry, ladies and gentlemen, for Paris. No hurry whatever!"

Twenty minutes' pause, by Folkestone clock, for looking at Enchantress while she eats a sandwich, and at Mystery while she eats of everything there that is eatable, from pork-pie, sausage, jam, and gooseberries, to lumps of sugar. All this time, there is a very waterfall of luggage, with a spray of dust, tumbling slant-wise from the pier into the steamboat. All this time, Demented (who has no business with it) watches it with starting eyes, fiercely requiring to be shown *his* luggage. When it at last concludes the cataract, he rushes hotly to refresh—is shouted after, pursued, jostled, brought back, pitched into the departing steamer upside down, and caught by mariners disgracefully.

A lovely harvest day, a cloudless sky, a tranquil sea. The piston-rods of the engines so regularly coming up from below, to look (as well they may) at the bright weather, and so regularly almost knocking their iron heads against the cross beam of the skylight, and never doing it! Another Parisian actress is on board, attended by another Mystery. Compact Enchantress greets her sister artist—Oh, the Compact One's pretty teeth!—and Mystery greets Mystery. *My* Mystery soon ceases to be conversational—is taken poorly, in a word, having lunched too miscellaneously—and goes below. The remaining Mystery then smiles upon the sister artists (who, I am afraid, wouldn't greatly mind stabbing each other), and is upon the whole ravished.

And now I find that all the French people on board begin to grow, and all the English people to shrink. The French are nearing home, and shaking off a disadvantage, whereas we are shaking it on. Zamiel is the same man, and Abd-el-Kader is the same man, but each seems to come into possession of an indescribable confidence that departs from us—from Monied Interest, for instance, and from me. Just what they gain, we lose. Certain British "Gents" about the steersman, intellectually nurtured at home on parody of everything and truth of nothing, become subdued, and in a manner forlorn; and when the steersman tells them (not exultingly) how he has "been upon this station now eight year, and never see the old town of Bullum yet," one of them, with an imbecile reliance on a reed, asks him what he considers to be the best hotel in Paris?

Now, I tread upon French ground, and am greeted by the three charming words, Liberty, Equality, Fraternity, painted up (in letters a little too thin for their height) on the Custom-house wall—also by the sight of large cocked hats, without which demonstrative head-gear nothing of a public nature can be done upon this soil. All the rabid Hotel population of Boulogne howl and shriek outside a distant barrier, frantic to get at us. Demented, by some unlucky means peculiar to himself, is delivered over to their fury, and is presently seen struggling in a whirlpool of Touters— is somehow understood to be going to Paris—is, with infinite noise, rescued by two cocked hats, and brought into Custom-house bondage with the rest of us.

Here, I resign the active duties of life to an eager being, of preternatural sharpness with a shelving forehead and a shabby snuff-coloured coat, who (from the wharf) brought me down with his eye before the boat came into port. He darts upon my luggage, on the floor where all the luggage is strewn like a wreck at the bottom of the great deep; gets it proclaimed and weighed as the property of "Monsieur a traveller unknown;" pays certain francs for it, to a certain functionary behind a Pigeon Hole, like a pay-box at a Theatre (the arrangements in general are on a wholesale scale, half military and half theatrical); and I suppose I shall find it when I come to Paris—he says I shall. I know nothing about it, except that I pay him his small fee, and pocket the ticket he gives me, and sit upon a counter, involved in the general distraction.

Railway station. "Lunch or dinner, ladies and gentlemen. Plenty of time for Paris. Plenty of time!" Large hall, long counter, long strips of dining-table, bottles of wine, plates of meat, roast chickens, little loaves of bread, basins of soup, little caraffes of brandy, cakes, and fruit. Comfortably restored from these resources, I begin to fly again.

I saw Zamiel (before I took wing) presented to Compact Enchantress and Sister Artist, by an officer in uniform, with a waist like a wasp's, and pantaloons like two balloons. They all got into the next carriage together, accompanied by the two Mysteries. They laughed. I am alone in the carriage (for I don't consider Demented anybody) and alone in the world.

Fields, windmills, low grounds, pollard-trees, windmills, fields, fortifications, Abbeville, soldiering and drumming. I wonder where England is, and when I was there last—about two years ago, I should say. Flying in and out among these trenches and batteries, skimming the clattering drawbridges, looking down into the stagnant ditches, I become a prisoner of state, escaping. I am confined with a comrade in a fortress. Our room is in an upper story. We have tried to get up the chimney, but there's an iron grating across it, imbedded in the masonry. After months of labour, we have worked the grating loose with the poker, and can lift it up. We have also made a hook, and twisted our rugs and blankets into ropes. Our plan is, to go up the chimney, hook our ropes to the top, descend hand over hand upon the roof of the guard-house far below, shake the hook loose, watch the opportunity of the sentinel's pacing away, hook again, drop into the ditch, swim across it, creep into the shelter of the wood. The time is come—a wild and stormy night. We are up the chimney, we are on the guard-house roof, we are swimming in the murky ditch, when lo! "Qui v'là?" a bugle, the alarm, a crash! What is it? Death? No, Amiens.

More fortifications, more soldiering and drumming, more basins of soup, more little loaves of bread, more bottles of wine, more caraffes of brandy, more time for refreshment. Everything good, and everything ready. Bright, unsubstantial-looking, scenic sort of station. People waiting. Houses, uniforms, beards, moustaches, some sabots, plenty of neat women, and a few old-visaged children. Unless it be a delusion born of my giddy flight, the grown-up people and the children seem to change places in France. In general, the boys and girls are little old men and women, and the men and women lively boys and girls.

Bugle, shriek, flight resumed. Monied Interest has come into my carriage. Says the manner of refreshing is "not bad," but considers it French. Admits great dexterity and politeness in the attendants. Thinks a decimal currency may have something to do with their despatch in settling accounts, and don't know but what it's sensible and convenient. Adds, however, as a general protest, that they're a revolutionary people—and always at it.

Ramparts, canals, cathedral, river, soldiering and drumming, open country, river, earthenware manufactures, Creil. Again ten minutes. Not even Demented in a hurry. Station, a drawing-room with a verandah: like a planter's house. Monied Interest considers it a band-box, and not made to last. Little round tables in it, at one of which the Sister Artists and attendant Mysteries are established with Wasp and Zamiel, as if they were going to stay a week.

Anon, with no more trouble than before, I am flying again, and lazily wondering as I fly. What has the South Eastern done with all the horrible little villages we used to pass through, in the *Diligence?* What have they done with all the summer dust, with all the winter mud, with all the dreary avenues of little trees, with all the ramshackle postyards, with all the beggars (who used to turn out at night with bits of lighted candle, to look in at the coach windows), with all the long-tailed horses who were always biting one another, with all the big postilions in jackboots—with all the mouldy cafés that we used to stop at, where a long mildewed tablecloth, set forth with jovial bottles of vinegar and oil, and with a Siamese arrangement of pepper and salt, was never wanting? Where are the grass-grown little towns, the wonderful little market-places all unconscious of markets, the shops that nobody kept, the streets that nobody trod, the churches that nobody went to, the bells that nobody rang, the tumble-down old buildings plastered with many-colored bills that nobody read? Where are the two-and-twenty weary hours of long long day and night journey, sure to be either insupportably hot or insupportably cold? Where are the pains in my bones, where are the fidgets in my legs, where is the Frenchman with the nightcap who never *would* have the little coupé-window down, and who always fell upon me when he went to sleep, and always slept all night snoring onions?

A voice breaks in with "Paris! Here we are!"

I have overflown myself, perhaps, but I can't believe it. I feel as if I were enchanted or bewitched. It is barely eight o'clock yet—it is nothing like half-past—when I have had my luggage examined at that briskest of Custom-houses attached to the station, and am rattling over the pavement in a hackney-cabriolet.

Surely, not the pavement of Paris? Yes, I think it is, too. I don't know any other place where there are all these high houses, all these haggard-looking wine shops, all these billiard tables, all these stocking-makers with flat red or yellow legs of wood for signboard, all these fuel shops with stacks of billets painted outside, and real billets sawing in the gutter, all these dirty corners of streets, all these cabinet pictures over dark doorways representing discreet matrons nursing babies. And yet this morning—I'll think of it in a warm-bath.

Very like a small room that I remember in the Chinese baths upon the Boulevard, certainly; and, though I see it through the steam, I think that I might swear to that peculiar hot-linen basket, like a large wicker hour-glass. When can it have been that I left home? When was it that I paid "through to Paris" at London Bridge, and discharged myself of all responsibility, except the preservation of a voucher ruled into three divisions, of which the first was snipped off at Folkestone, the second aboard the boat, and the third taken at my journey's end? It seems to have been ages ago. Calculation is useless. I will go out for a walk.

The crowds in the streets, the lights in the shops and balconies, the elegance, variety, and beauty of their decorations, the number of the theatres, the brilliant cafés with their windows thrown up high and their vivacious groups at little tables on the pavement, the light and glitter of the houses turned as it were inside out, soon convince me that it is no dream; that I am in Paris, howsoever I got here. I stroll down to the sparkling Palais Royal, up the Rue de Rivoli, to the Place Vendôme. As I glance into a print-shop window, Monied Interest, my late travelling companion, comes upon me, laughing with the highest relish of disdain.

"Here's a people!" he says, pointing to Napoleon in the window and Napoleon on the column. "Only one idea all over Paris! A monomania!" Humph! I THINK I have seen Napoleon's match? There was a statue, when I came away, at Hyde Park Corner, and another in the City, and a print or two in the shops.

I walk up to the Barrière de l'Etoile, sufficiently dazed by my flight to have a pleasant doubt of the reality of everything about me; of the lively crowd, the overhanging trees, the performing dogs, the hobby-horses, the beautiful perspectives of shining lamps: the hundred and one enclosures, where the singing is, in gleaming orchestras of azure and gold, and where a star-eyed Houri comes round with a box for voluntary offerings. So, I pass to my hotel, enchanted; sup, enchanted; go to bed, enchanted; pushing back this morning (if it really were this morning) into the remoteness of time, blessing the South Eastern Company for realising the Arabian Nights in these prose days, murmuring, as I wing my idle flight into the land of dreams, "No hurry, ladies and gentlemen, going to Paris in eleven hours. It is so well done, that there really is no hurry!"

Part 5

TIMETABLES, CALENDARS, AND STATIONS
Mid-Victorian railway cultures

25

HENRY BOOTH, 'CONSIDERATIONS, MORAL, COMMERCIAL, ECONOMICAL', *AN ACCOUNT OF THE LIVERPOOL AND MANCHESTER RAILWAY* (LIVERPOOL: WALES AND BAINES, 1830), PP. 85–94

Before concluding our account of the Railway, we shall take a single glance at the position we occupy, and the probable changes, whether for good or evil, which may be expected to occur (as the consequence of our operations) in the state and circumstances of the community around. The first and most obvious result must needs be a great revolution in the established modes of conveyance, both for merchandise and passengers, between Liverpool and Manchester; and consequently in the private interests of a large class of persons, who have been engaged, directly or indirectly, in the coaching or carrying business. An undertaking like the Liverpool and Manchester Railway, completed at a cost, including its machinery and carriages, of upwards of £800,000. for a line of thirty-one miles, and professing to be decidedly superior to existing establishments, cannot be brought imperceptibly or silently into operation. But though a great change must take place in the application of capital, and the distribution of revenue, amongst large companies and wealthy proprietors, the effect on the whole, with reference to the employment of the labouring classes, may be considered as decidedly favourable. It has frequently been matter of regret, that in the progress of mechanical science, as applicable to trade and manufactures, the great stages of improvement are too often accompanied with severe suffering to the industrious classes of society. The machinery of the present day continually supersedes that of a few years back; and as the substitution of mechanism for manual labour is the object generally aimed at, immediate privation to the labouring community seems the inevitable result. It has consequently been a subject of speculation, how far the rapid extension of manufactures, by the instrumentality of successive improvements in machinery, is advantageous to a country, as regards its moral and social condition. I recollect that, during the progress of the Railway Bill through Parliament, when some members of the Railway Committee waited on Lord Harewood, and urged the advantages to trade and manufactures to be anticipated from the facilities of communication to be afforded by the Railway, his Lordship demurred at once to our proposition, that any new impetus to manufactures *would* be advantageous to the country. And before this point can be settled, we must determine the broader and more general question, whether it be desirable that a nation should continue in the quiet enjoyment of pastoral or agricultural life, or that it should be launched into the bustle and excitement of commerce and manufactures. We must refer to the history of the world, and compare the characters and capabilities for happiness, of different ages and nations. We must decide between qualities of different kinds and claims of opposite characters—between the simple and the refined; between the passive and the active; between a state of society presenting fewer temptations, and adorned by humbler virtues, and one where, amidst the collision of interests and the excitements of passion, there is room at least for the exercise of the highest qualities, both moral and intellectual. We must determine in what happiness consists: whether in the cultivation and exercise of all the active powers and faculties which belong to us as men, and citizens, and freemen; or whether it be wise to limit our ambition to more sober and tranquil enjoyments, to a state of society, where, if there be fewer pleasures there are also fewer pains, and where, at least, may be realized the poet's definition of contentment—"Health, peace, and competence." Fortunately, we are not required to make choice between two conditions of society, separated, in the history of man, and in the ordinary course of events, by centuries of gradual and imperceptible transition. It must be admitted that the golden age is past, and it is to be feared the iron age has succeeded; that, with reference to many of us, our lines are fallen amidst eternal rivalries and jealousies—agricultural, manufacturing, and commercial. The stern principle of competition is prominent in every department of industry. The most strenuous activity is hardly sufficient, in the present day, to secure to the artizan, or his employer, a scanty return for his labour or capital. Every invention, by which time is saved and business expedited, is seized with avidity, and in self-defence. Every increased facility of production, though its inevitable tendency be to glut the market and to lower prices, yet, as it affords immediate gain to its possessor, is eagerly resorted to. If profit be reduced to the smallest per centage on capital, every one is active to realize this minimum, as expeditiously as possible: one step diminished in the process of a manufacture, or the saving of a few hours in the period of conveyance from one town to another, forms part of a nice calculation, every small item in which must be attended to, in order to secure a very moderate remuneration. Hence all the contrivances for abridging labour, for shortening distances, and expediting returns. Every one is on the alert in his own department, or he is left behind; the most active exertion being barely sufficient to enable a man to maintain his station in the world. The race of competition is universal and unceasing—every manufacture striving against every other; cotton and silk and woollen reciprocally against each other, and against themselves, and iron against iron, in all its multifarious branches. Every class, and every individual, in every department of industry, hurrying along, struggling with fortune and the times, and jostling his fellow-sufferers; while the Land-owner boldly enters the list against the field—"Protection" his motto—viewing with complacency the desperate efforts of the rival competitors, and especially the never-ceasing race of population against subsistence—the great first mover in the busy drama.

But how little soever to the taste of the contemplative mind may be the present condition and aspect of society, as constituting a vast trading community, the Liverpool and Manchester Railway presents one great object for our admiration, almost unalloyed by any counteracting or painful consideration. We behold, at once, a new theatre of activity and employment presented to an industrious population, with all the indications of health and energy and cheerfulness which flow from such a scene. Or if we take a wider range, and anticipate the extension of Railways throughout the country, intersecting the island in every direction where the interchange of commodities, or the communication by travelling, will warrant the cost of their establishment; if we look to the construction of only one hundred Railways, equal in extent to the Liverpool and Manchester, comprising a line of three thousand miles, in various situations, and absorbing a capital of fifty or sixty millions of pounds sterling, what a source of occupation to the labouring community! what a change in the facility of giving employment to capital, and consequently in the value of money!

But perhaps the most striking result produced by the completion of this Railway, is the sudden and marvellous change which has been effected in our ideas of time and space. Notions which we have received from our ancestors, and verified by our own experience, are overthrown in a day, and a new standard erected, by which to form our ideas for the future. Speed—despatch—distance—are still relative terms, but their meaning has been totally changed within a few months: what was quick is now slow; what was distant is now near; and this change in our ideas will not be limited to the environs of Liverpool and Manchester—it will pervade society at large. Our notions of expedition, though at first having reference to locomotion, will influence, more or less, the whole tenor and business of life. In the commercial world, the first successful attempt to introduce fresh energy and despatch into the system of our foreign trade was the institution of Packet Ships, a few years ago, to sail between New York and Liverpool, on stated days, whether fully loaded or not. The convenience, both to passengers and shippers of goods, from knowing precisely the day of sailing, soon made the Packet Ships the favourite conveyance, and accordingly their numbers and destinations rapidly multiplied. But this improvement, though great, was less open to general observation, and its effects, therefore, less striking than what may be expected from the establishment of Railway conveyance and Locomotive Engines. A transition in our accustomed rate of travelling, from eight or ten miles an hour, to fifteen or twenty (not to mention higher speeds), gives a new character to the whole internal trade and commerce of the country. A saving of time is a saving of money. For the purposes of locomotion, about half the number of carriages will suffice, if you go twice the speed; or the aggregate travelling of the country may be doubled, or more than doubled, without any additional expense to the community. The same may be said of the number of waggons for the conveyance of merchandise. The saving of capital, therefore, in this department of business is considerable, from expedition alone. A great part of the inland trade of the country is conducted by the agency of travellers; and here, what a revolution in the whole system and detail of business, when the ordinary rate of travelling shall be twenty miles instead of ten, per hour. The traveller will live double times: by accomplishing a prescribed distance in *five* hours, which used to require *ten*, he will have the other five at his own disposal. The man of business in Manchester will breakfast at home—proceed to Liverpool by the Railway, transact his business, and return to Manchester before dinner. A hard day's journeying is thus converted into a morning's excursion. It has been well observed, in our public journals, that Manchester is thus brought as near to Liverpool as the east to the west end of London, whether we estimate vicinity by the cost of conveyance, or the time not unfrequently spent in effecting it. Gradually, the whole internal traffic of the country, with all the varieties of local intercourse, will assume a new character. Already a Railway, on a grand scale, is advertised from London to Birmingham, and from Birmingham to Liverpool; and thus is commenced that grand trunk, which will unite the north and the south, and bring into closer communication the Capitals of England, Scotland, and Ireland. The rapid transit of intelligence, from one end of the country to the other, will not be the least important of the results to be accomplished; while the quick conveyance of merchandise will infuse new life into trade and manufactures. The grocer in Birmingham will receive his ponderous hogsheads of sugar or coffee with the celerity of a parcel by the post-coach; and the *warehouseman* in the Metropolis will be supplied with his bales of spring goods, from Manchester, in less time than he has been accustomed to receive his patterns by the flying van.

But we must not confine our views to London, or Liverpool, or Manchester: there can be no question that foreign countries will adopt the Railway communication, as one great step in mechanical improvement and commercial enterprise. France and Germany and America have already their Railways; and the Pasha of Egypt may be expected to follow close on the heels of his brother potentates. The country of the Pyramids, of Memphis, and of Thebes, shall then be celebrated for Railways and Steam Carriages; the land of the proud Mameluke or the wandering Arab, of Sphynxes and Mummies, will become the theatre of mechanical invention, science and the arts. The stately Turk, with his turban and slippers, will quit his couch and his carpet, to mount his Engine of fire and speed, that he may enjoy the delight of modern locomotion. So long is it, since a reward was offered to the inventor of a new pleasure, that some scepticism were excusable as to the possibility of any great and novel excitement. But the Locomotive Engine and Railway were reserved for the present day. From west to east, and from north to south, the mechanical principle, the philosophy of the nineteenth century, will spread and extend itself. The world has received a new impulse. To the fortunate few, who are independent of times and circumstances, the present moment is a period of more than ordinary interest; to the world at large, it continues, as it was wont to be, a season of labour and difficulty. Whether the period will ever arrive when a whole community shall enjoy the pleasures and satisfactions to be expected from that happy combination of the powers and capabilities of the human race, which is conceivable, but has hitherto been realized only by the Utopian theorist;—whether we shall ever see united, the energy, activity, and enterprise of a refined and commercial people, with the simplicity and quiet enjoyment of philosophical life, in its most favoured aspects;—whether the period will sometime come, when the fervour of an earnest enthusiasm—religious, moral, social—shall not be inconsistent with the calculations of the merchant, or the speculations of the political economist;—when science and literature, commerce and the arts, and all the stirring influences of man's nature, in the highest state of wealth and civilization, shall be enlisted to promote the improvement and well-being of the whole community;—when, by a happy alchemy, the iron and the golden age shall be amalgamated, and man be allowed to enjoy the benefits of two states of society, hitherto deemed incompatible, or at least separated, in our experience, by intervening centuries, if indeed either counterpart has ever been realised.—These are speculations which we may glance at, for a moment, in passsing, and forget when the vision is gone. But the world and its inhabitants are constantly before us; and here we find no pause or resting place—no period of uninterrupted enjoyment or repose, for the million. The genius of Watt, or Davy, or Stephenson, may improve the state of nations, or the fortunes of individuals, but it affects not the condition of the great mass of the human race: for this consummation we must look to other sciences than chemistry and mechanics; to the tardy overthrow of prejudice, and the slow progress of unpopular truth; to the diffusion of that knowledge which teaches the laws and principles on which depend the moral, physical, and political condition, the subsistence, and well-being of mankind.

Meanwhile, the genius of the age, like a mighty river of the new world, flows onward, full, rapid, and irresistible. The spirit of the times must needs manifest itself in the progress of events, and the movement is too impetuous to be stayed, were it wise to attempt it. Like the "Rocket" of fire and steam, or its prototype of war and desolation—whether the harbinger of peace and the arts, or the Engine of hostile attack and devastation—though it be a futile attempt to oppose so mighty an impulse, it may not be unworthy our ambition, to guide its progress and direct its course.

26

'EASTER TRAVELLING', *ILLUSTRATED LONDON NEWS*, APRIL 29, 1905, 626

The London and North-Western Railway Company announces that the ticket offices at Euston, Broad Street, Victoria (Pimlico), Kensington, and Willesden Junction will be open throughout the day, from Monday, April 17, to Monday, April 24, inclusive, so that passengers wishing to obtain tickets can do so at any time of the day prior to the starting of the trains, and so avoid the crush at the stations. Tickets, dated to suit the convenience of passengers, can also be obtained at any time (Sundays and Bank Holidays excepted) at the town receiving-offices of the company. Additional express trains will be run and special arrangements made in connection with the London and North-Western passenger trains for the Easter holidays.

The Great Western Railway Company has made complete arrangements for the conveyance in comfort of the holiday passengers travelling at Easter. Many of the principal expresses will be run in two parts, and several additional expresses will be run on the days preceding Good Friday. The Great Western Railway Company has also issued a forty-page pamphlet giving details of excursions from London to about five hundred towns and seaside and inland resorts for periods varying from half-day and day to fifteen days, at low fares, thus affording countrymen in London an opportunity of visiting their homes at small cost, and Londoners are enabled to take a holiday at some of the most delightful pleasure resorts in the United Kingdom. The pamphlet can be obtained gratis at the company's stations.

Quaint and ingenious advertising characterises the age we live in—a fact that the Great Northern Company has not been slow to recognise. In the shape of an Easter egg, a coloured pictorial announcement issued by the Great Northern Railway Company displays a third-class return ticket with the words "King's Cross to Anywhere." One has but to turn over the pages of this pamphlet to realise that splendid opportunities for travel are being offered by the company. A letter or a call at any station or Great Northern office throughout the entire system, asking for further information, will be promptly attended to. A speciality is being made of week-end tickets, which will be issued on the Thursday, Good Friday, or Saturday, and available for return up to and including the following Tuesday.

The Midland Railway Company announces that on Good Friday, Easter Sunday, Monday, and Tuesday, day excursion tickets will be issued to Southend and Westcliffe-on-Sea, in addition to the week-end tickets, as announced on special bills. Half-day and week-end tickets will be issued every Saturday, until further notice, to Flitwick, Ampthill, Turvey, Olney, Piddington, Bedford, Wellingborough, and Kettering. Week-end tickets will be issued on Thursday, April 20, as well as on Friday and Saturday, April 21 and 22, from London (St. Pancras) to the principal seaside and inland holiday resorts, including the Peak District of Derbyshire, Morecambe, Lake District, Yorkshire, the North-East Coast, and Scotland, available for return on any day (where train service permits) up to and including the following Tuesday, April 25, except day of issue. Tickets, bills, etc., may be had at St. Pancras and other Midland stations and City booking-offices, and from Thomas Cook and Son, Ludgate Circus and branch offices.

The Great Central Railway Company is offering ample and admirable facilities to those desirous of spending Easter at places reached by its comfortable and picturesque route. Excursions are announced from London (Marylebone), Woolwich, Greenwich, and Metropolitan stations, to all the principal towns and holiday resorts in the Midlands, North of England, North-East and North-West Coast watering-places, Douglas (Isle of Man), Scotland, and Ireland. The information has been concisely tabulated in the form of an A.B.C. programme.

For visiting Holland and Germany during the Easter holidays, the Great Eastern Railway's Royal British Mail Hook of Holland route offers exceptional facilities. Passengers leaving London in the evening and the Northern and Midland counties in the afternoon arrive at the chief Dutch cities the following morning. A corridor-train with vestibuled carriages, dining and breakfast cars, is run on the Hook of Holland service between London and Harwich. From the Hook of Holland through-carriages and restaurant-cars run in the North and South German express-trains to Cologne, Bâle, and Berlin, reaching Cologne at noon, Bâle and Berlin in the evening. Special cheap tickets have been arranged by the Harwich-Antwerp route for passengers wishing to visit Brussels for the Field of Waterloo, also to Liége for the Universal Exhibition.

The Great Eastern Railway will issue tourist, fortnightly, and Thursday, Friday, or Saturday to Monday or Tuesday tickets to Yarmouth, Gorleston-on-Sea, Lowestoft, Mundesley-on-Sea, Cromer, Clacton-on-Sea, Walton-on-Naze, Dovercourt, Harwich, Felixstowe, Aldeburgh, Southwold, and Hunstanton, by all trains from Liverpool Street, also from Great Eastern suburban stations at same fares as from Liverpool Street; also from St. Pancras (Midland Station) and Kentish Town to Hunstanton, Yarmouth, Gorleston-on-Sea, Lowestoft, Mundesley-on-Sea, and Cromer (except on Good Friday).

The South-Eastern and Chatham Railway announces special excursion tickets to Paris, viâ Folkestone and Boulogne, by the service leaving Charing Cross at 2.20 p.m. on April 19, 21, and 22, and by trains leaving Charing Cross at 10 a.m., 2.5 and 2.20 p.m. on Thursday, April 20. They will also be issued by the night mail service leaving Charing Cross at 9 p.m. and Cannon Street at 9.5 p.m., from April 19 to 22, inclusive, viâ Dover and Calais.

The splendid programme of excursions arranged by the London and South Western Railway Company for the Easter Holidays is well worth the consideration of any in doubt as to the best place to spend an enjoyable time. No difficulty will be experienced in making a selection from the numerous delightful resorts reached by this company on the sunny south and southwest coasts, the most lovely of which will be found between Southsea and Plymouth, and include the Isle of Wight, Bournemouth, Swanage, Weymouth, Lyme Regis, Seaton, Sidmouth, Budleigh Salterton, Exmouth, etc. Fast excursion trains will run direct from Waterloo Station in a few hours; the cheap fares, comfortable carriages, and smooth running over a well-laid track all combine to make a pleasant journey. Many will be spending Easter on the Continent: for such the company has made ample arrangements. Fourteen-day excursion tickets will be issued from Waterloo to the French coast for Paris, Normandy, Brittany, etc.

At Easter it is now quite the fashion to flit across the Channel to Dieppe, Rouen, or Paris, where, on foreign soil, amidst unfamiliar scenery and surroundings, it is not difficult to dismiss from the mind all business worries; and, to enable the journey to be performed economically, the Brighton Railway Company has arranged to run special fourteen-day excursions, viâ the Newhaven-Dieppe Royal Mail route, through the charming scenery of Normandy and the Valley of the Seine. The tickets will be issued on Thursday, April 20, by the morning express service and by a special afternoon service, also by the express night service on Wednesday, Thursday, Friday, and Saturday evenings, April 19 to 22.

27

WILLIAM POWELL FRITH, 'THE RAILWAY STATION', (PADDINGTON STATION) (1862)

Figure 27.1 Frith, "The Railway Station", 1862

28

GEORGE CATLIN, *ADVENTURES OF THE OJIBBEWAY AND IOWAY INDIANS IN ENGLAND, FRANCE, AND BELGIUM.* THIRD ED. (LONDON: N.P., 1852), PP. 15, 17, 20–26, 34–35, 123–127, 129, 145–146

The grizly bears being thus comfortably and safely quartered in the immediate charge of my man Daniel, who had taken an apartment near them, and my collection being lodged in the Custom-house, I started by the railway for London to effect the necessary arrangements for their next move. I had rested in and left Liverpool in the midst of rain, and fog, and mud, and seen little else of it; and on my way to London I saw little or nothing of the beautiful country I was passing through, travelling the whole distance in the night. The luxurious carriage in which I was seated, however, braced up and embraced on all sides by deep cushions; the grandeur of the immense stations I was occasionally passing under; the elegance and comfort of the cafés and restaurants I was stumbling into with half-sealed eyes, with hundreds of others in the middle of the night, with the fat, and rotund, and ruddy appearance of the night-capped fellow-travellers around me, impressed me at once with the conviction that I was in the midst of a world of comforts and luxuries that had been long studied and refined upon.

I opened my eyes at daylight at the terminus in the City of London, but could see little of it, as I was driven to Ibbotson's Hotel, in Vere-street, through one of the dense fogs peculiar to the metropolis and to the season of the year in which I had entered it. To a foreigner entering London at that season, the first striking impression is the blackness and gloom that everywhere shrouds all that is about him. It is in his hotel—in his bed-chamber—his dining-room, and if he sallies out into the street it is there even worse; and added to it dampness, and fog, and mud, all of which, together, are strong inducements for him to return to his lodgings, and adopt them as comfortable, and as a luxury.

I succeeded quite well in wending my way down the Haymarket, the Strand, and Fleet-street, slipping and sliding through the mud, until I was in front or in the rear (I could not tell which) of the noble St. Paul's, whose black and gloomy walls, at the apparent risk of breaking my neck, I could follow up with my eye, until they were lost in the murky cloud of fog that floated around them. I walked quite round it, by which I became duly impressed with its magnitude below, necessarily leaving my conjectures as to its elevation, for future observations through a clearer atmosphere.

I used the rest of this gloomy day in obtaining from the Lords of the Treasury the proper order for passing my collection through the Customs, which has been before mentioned, arranging my letters of credit, &c., and returned by the evening's train to Liverpool, to join my collection again, and Daniel and the grizly bears.

On my return to that city I found poor Daniel in a sad dilemma with the old lady about the bears, and the whole neighbourhood under a high excitement, and in great alarm for their safety. The bears had been landed in the briefest manner possible; exempted from the usual course that almost everything else takes through the Queen's warehouse; and, though relieved from the taxes of the customs, I soon found that I had duties of a different character accumulating that required my attention in another quarter. The agreement made by the old lady with Daniel to keep them in her yard for so much per day, and for as long a time as he required, had been based upon the express and very judicious condition that they were to do no harm. From the moment of their landing they had kept up an almost incessant howling, so Rocky-Mountain-ish and so totally unlike any attempts at music ever heard in the country before, that it attracted a crowd night and day about the old lady's door, that almost defeated all attempts at ingress and egress. A little vanity, however, which she still possessed, enabled her to put up with the inconvenience, which she was turning to good account, and counting good luck, until it was ascertained, to her great amazement as well as alarm, that the bears were passing their huge paws out of the cage, between the iron bars, and lifting up the round stones of her pavement for the pleasure of once more getting their nails into the dirt, their favourite element, and which they had for a long time lost sight of.

In their unceasing pursuit of this amusement, by night and by day, they had made a sad metamorphosis of the old lady's pavement, as, with the strength of their united paws, they had drawn the cage around to different parts of the yard, totally unpaving as they went along. At the time of the poor old lady's bitterest and most vehement complaint, they were making their move in the direction of her humble tenement, the walls of which were exceedingly slight; and her alarm became insupportable. The ignorant crowd outside of the inclosure, who could get but a partial view of their operations now and then, had formed the most marvellous ideas of these monsters, from the report current amongst them that they were eating the paving-stones; and had taken the most decided and well-founded alarm from the fact that the bears had actually hurled some of the paving-stones quite over the wall amongst their heads, which were calling back an increased shower of stones and other missiles, adding fresh rage and fears to the growling of the bears, which altogether was threatening results of a more disastrous kind.

In this state of affairs I was very justly appealed to by the old lady for redress and a remedy, for it was quite evident that the condition of her agreement with Daniel had been broken, as the bears were now decidedly doing much harm to her premises; destroying all her rest, and (as she said) "her appetite and her right mind;" and I agreed that it was my duty, as soon as possible, to comply with her urgent request that they should be removed. She insisted on its being done that day, as "it was quite impossible to pass another night in her own bed, when there was such howling and groaning and grunting in her yard, by the side of her house." Daniel took my directions and immediately went through the town in search of other quarters for them, and was to attend to their moving whilst I was to spend the day in the Custom-house, attending to the examination of my collection of 600 paintings and many thousand Indian costumes, weapons and other curiosities, which were to be closely inspected and inventoried, for duties.

Immersed in this mystery of difficulties and vexations at the customs during the day, I had lost sight of Daniel and his pets until I was free at night, when I was assailed with a more doleful tale than ever about the bears. Troubles were gathering on all sides. Poor Daniel had positively arranged in several places for them, but when "their characters were asked from their last places," he met defeat in every case, and was obliged to meet, at last, the increased plaints of his old landlady, whose rage and ranting were now quite beyond control. She had made complaint to the police, of whom a *posse* had been sent to see to their removal. Daniel in the mean time had dodged them, and was smiling amidst the crowd at the amusing idea of their laying hold of them, or of even going into the yard to them. The police reported on the utter impossibility of removing them to any other part of the town, their "character" having been so thoroughly published already to all parts; and it was advised, to the utter discomfiture of the old lady, that it would be best for them to remain there until they should be removed to London, and that I should pay for all damages. The poor old lady afterwards had a final interview with Daniel in the crowd, when she very judiciously resolved that if the bears did not move, *she must*—which she did that night, and placed Daniel in her bed, as the guardian of her property and of his pets, until the third or fourth day afterwards, when they were moved to the railway, and by it (night and day, catching what glimpses they could of the country they were serenading with their howls and growls as they passed through it under their tarpaulin) they were conveyed to the great metropolis.

Owing to the multiplicity of articles to be examined and inventoried in the customs, and the great embarrassment of the clerks in writing down their Indian names, my labours were protracted there to much tediousness; but when all was brought to a close by their proposing, most judiciously, to count the number of curiosities instead of wasting paper and time and paralysing my jaws by pronouncing half a dozen times over, and syllable by syllable, their Indian names, my collection of eight tons weight was all on the road and soon at the Euston station in London, where we again recognised the mournful cries of the grizlies, who had arrived the night before.

On arriving at the station, I found Daniel at a small inn in the vicinity, where he seemed highly excited by some unpleasant altercation he had had with the landlord and inmates of the house, growing out of national and political prejudices, which had most probably been too strongly advanced on both sides. Daniel had suddenly raised a great excitement in the neighbourhood by his arrival with the grizly bears, whose occasional howlings had attracted crowds of people, curious to know the nature of the strange arrival; and all inquirers about the station being referred to their keeper, who was at the inn, brought Daniel and his patience into notoriety at once.

At Liverpool he had had great difficulty in getting permission to travel by the luggage train, to keep company with the bears, the necessity of which he urged in vain, until he represented that, unless he was with them to feed them, their howlings and other terrific noises and ravings would frighten their hands all out of the stations, and even add probabilities to their breaking loose from the cage in which they were confined, to feed upon the human flesh around them, and of which they were peculiarly fond. Upon these representations, he was allowed the privilege of a narrow space, to stand or to sit, in the corner of one of the luggage-trains, and thus bore the bears company all the way.

When they entered the first tunnel on their way, they raised a hideous howl, which they continued until they were through it, which might have been from a feeling of pleasure, recognizing in it something of the character of the delightful gloominess of their own subterranean abodes; or their outcries might have been from a feeling of dread or fear from those narrow and damp caverns, too much for their delicate tastes and constitutions. This, however, is matter for the bears to decide. At Birmingham, where they rested on the truck for the greater part of a day, their notification to the town had called vast crowds of spectators around them; and though their tarpaulin prevented them from being seen, many, very many, drew marvellous accounts of them from one another, and from the flying reports which had reached them several days before from Liverpool, of "two huge monsters imported from the Rocky Mountains, that had scales like alligators, with long spears of real flint at the ends of their tails; that they made nothing of eating paving-stones when they were hungry, and that in Liverpool they had escaped, and were travelling to the north, and demolishing all the inhabitants of Lancashire as they went along," &c. Their occasional howls and growls, with, once in a while, a momentary display of one of their huge paws, exhibited from under the tarpaulin, riveted the conviction of the gaping multitude as to the terror and danger of these animals, while it put at rest all apprehensions as to their being at large and overrunning the country. Poor Daniel had to stand between the crowd and his pets, to save them from the peltings and insults of the crowd, and at the same time, to muster every talent he had at natural history, to answer the strange queries and theories that were raised about them. He was assailed on every side with questions as to the appearance and habits of the animals, and at last, about "the other animals," as they called them, "running on two legs, in America;" for many of them, from his representations, had come fresh from the coal-pits and factories, with ideas that Americans were a sort of savages, and that savages, they had understood, were "a sort of wild beastises, and living on raw meat." These conjectures and queries were answered amusingly for them, by Daniel; and, after he had a little enlightened them by the information he gave them, their conversation took a sort of political turn, which, I have before said, he was prone to run into; and thus, luckily, the time was whiled away, without any *set-to* to bother the bears and himself, which he had seen evidently preparing, until the whistle announced them and him on their way again for the metropolis.

The next morning he found himself and the bears safe landed at the terminus in London, where I have already said that I found him and released him from a medley of difficulties he had worked himself into.

MY business now, and all my energies, were concentrated at the Egyptian Hall, where my collection was arranged upon the walls. The main hall was of immense length, and contained upon its walls 600 portraits and other paintings which I had made during eight years' travels amongst forty-eight of the remotest and wildest tribes of Indians in America, and also many thousands of articles of their manufacture, consisting of costumes, weapons, &c. &c., forming together a pictorial history of those tribes, which I had been ambitious to preserve as a record of them, to be perpetuated long after their extinction. In the middle of the room I had erected also a wigwam (or lodge) brought from the country of the Crows, at the base of the Rocky Mountains, made of some twenty or more buffalo skins, beautifully dressed and curiously ornamented and embroidered with porcupine quills.

My friend the Honourable C. A. Murray, with several others, had now announced my collection open to their numerous friends and such others as they chose to invite during the three first days when it was submitted to their private view, and by whom it was most of the time filled; and being kindly presented to most of them, my unsentimental and unintellectual life in the atmosphere of railroads and grizly bears was suddenly changed to a cheering flood of soul and intellect which greeted me in every part of my room, and soon showed me the way to the recessed world of luxury, refinements, and comforts of London, which not even the imagination of those who merely stroll through the streets can by any possibility reach.

During this private view I found entered in my book the names of very many of the nobility, and others of the most distinguished people of the kingdom. My friend Mr. Murray was constantly present, and introduced me to very many of them, who had the kindness to leave their addresses and invite me to their noble mansions, where I soon appreciated the elegance, the true hospitality and refinement of English life. Amongst the most conspicuous of those who visited my rooms on this occasion were H. R. H. the Duke of Cambridge, the Duke and Duchess of Sutherland, the Duke and Duchess of Buccleuch, Duke of Devonshire, Duke of Wellington, the Bishop of London, the Bishop of Norwich, Sir Robert and Lady Peel, Lord Grosvenor, Lord Lennox, Duke of Richmond, Duke of Rutland, Duke of Buckingham, Countess-Dowager of Dunmore, Countess-Dowager of Ashburnham, Earl of Falmouth, Earl of Dunmore, Lord Monteagle,

Lord Ashley, Earl of Burlington, Sir James and Lady Clark, Sir Augustus d'Este, Sir Francis Head, and many others of the nobility, with most of the editors of the press, and many private literary and scientific gentlemen, of whose kindness to me while in London I shall have occasion to speak in other parts of this work.

The kindness of my friend Mr. Murray on this occasion can never be forgotten by me. He pointed out to my illustrious visitors the principal chiefs and warriors of the various tribes, with many of whom he was personally acquainted; explaining their costumes, weapons, &c., with all of which his rambles in the Indian countries beyond the Mississippi and Missouri had made him quite familiar.

The exhibitions at night were progressing much as I have above described—the hall invariably full, and the Indians, as well as the public, had their own amusement in the room, and also amusing themes for conversation after retiring to their own quarters.

In the midst of our success and of their amusement and enjoyment, an occurrence took place that was near getting us into difficulty, as it raised a great excitement in the neighbourhood and no little alarm to many old women and little children.

As I was leaving my exhibition-rooms one morning, I met, to my great surprise, an immense crowd of people assembled in front, and the streets almost completely barricaded with the numbers that were rapidly gathering, and all eyes elevated towards the roof of my building. I asked the first person I met what was the matter?—supposing that the house was on fire—to which he replied, "I believes, sir, that the Hob-jib-be-ways has got loose; I knows that some on em is hout, for I seed one on em runnin hover the tops of the ouses, and they'l ave a ard matter to catch em, hin my hopinion, sir."

It seems that the poor fellows had found a passage leading from their rooms out upon the roof of the house, and that, while several of them had been strolling out there for fresh air, and taking a look over the town, a crowd had gathered in the street to look at them, and amongst the most ignorant of that crowd the rumour had become current that they "had broke loose, and people were engaged in endeavouring to take them."

I started back to my room as fast as I could, and to the top of the house, to call them down, and stop the gathering that was in rapid progress in the streets. When I got on the roof, I was as much surprised at the numbers of people assembled on the tops of the adjoining houses, as I had been at the numbers assembled in the streets. The report was there also current, and general, that they had "broke out," and great preparations were being made on the adjoining roofs, with ropes and poles, &c., to "take them," if possible, before any harm could be done. About the time I had got amongst them, and was inviting them down, several of the police made their appearance by my side, and ordered them immediately into their room, and told me that in the excited state of the town, with their mills all out, such a thing was endangering the peace; for it brought a mob of many thousands together, which would be sure not to disperse without doing some mischief. I was ordered by the police to keep them thereafter in the rooms, and not to allow them to show themselves at the windows, so great were their fears of a riot in the streets, if there was the least thing to set it in motion. As an evidence of the necessity of such rigour, this affair of about fifteen minutes' standing had already brought ten or fifteen thousand people together, and a large body of the police had been ordered on to the ground, having the greatest difficulty during the day to get rid of the crowd.

For our passage to London we had chartered a second-class carriage to ourselves, and in it had a great deal of amusement and merriment on the way. The novelty of the mode of travelling and the rapidity at which we were going raised the spirits of the Indians to a high degree, and they sang their favourite songs, and even gave their dances, as they passed along. Their curiosity had been excited to know how the train was propelled or drawn, and at the first station I stepped out with them, and forward to the locomotive, where I explained the power which pulled us along. They at once instituted for the engine, the appellation of the "Iron-horse;" and, at our next stopping-place, which was one where the engine was taking in water, they all leaped out *"to see the Iron-horse drink."*

Their songs and yells set at least a thousand dogs barking and howling on the way, and as we came under the station at Birmingham, called up a fat old gentleman, who opened our door and very knowingly exclaimed, "What the devil have you got here? some more of them damned grisly bears, have you?" He was soon merged in the crowd that gathered around us, and, with doors closed, the Indians sat out patiently the interval, until we were under weigh again. Arrived at the Euston station, in London, an omnibus conveyed them suddenly to apartments in George-street, which had been prepared for them. They were highly excited when they entered their rooms, talking about the Queen, whom they believed had just passed in her carriage, from seeing two footmen with gold-laced hats and red breeches and white stockings, standing up and riding on a carriage behind, with large gold-headed canes in their hands: it proved, however, to have been the carriage of Lady S—n, familiarly known in that neighbourhood; and the poor fellows seemed wofully disappointed at this information.

The good landlady, who took a glance of them as they came in, was becoming alarmed at the bargain she had made for the rooms, and came to Mr. Rankin, expressing her fears that the arrangement would never answer for her, as "she did not expect such wild, black-looking savages from the Indies." Mr. Rankin assured her that they were quite harmless, and much more of gentlemen than many white men she might get in her house, and he would be responsible for all damage that they would ever do to her property, even if she left the whole of it unsecured by lock and key. So she said she would venture to try them for a week, and see how they behaved. They were now in the midst of the great city of London, which they had been so anxious to see; and, upon putting their heads out of the windows to take a first peep, the smoke was so dense that they could see but a few rods, when they declared that the "prairies must be on fire again."

After one of their first drives about the City, when they had been passed through Regent Street, the Strand, Cheapside, Oxford Street and Holborn, I spent the evening in a talk with them in their rooms, and was exceedingly amused with the shrewdness of their remarks upon what they had seen. They had considered the "prairies still on fire," from the quantity of smoke they met; one of the women had undertaken to count the number of carriages they passed, but was obliged to give it up; "saw a great many fine houses, but nobody in the windows; saw many men with a large board on the back, and another on the breast, walking in the street—supposed it was some kind of punishment; saw men carrying bags of coal, their hats on wrong side before; saw fine ladies and gentlemen riding in the middle of the streets in carriages, but a great many poor and ragged people on the sides of the roads; saw a great many men and women drinking in shops where they saw great barrels and hogsheads; saw several drunk in the streets. They had passed two *Indians* in the street with brooms, sweeping away the mud; they saw them hold out their hands to people going by, as if they were begging for money

On my return from London I had joined the Indians at Leeds, where they had been exhibiting for some days, and found them just ready to start for York. I was their companion by the railway, therefore, to that ancient and venerable city; and made a note or two on an occurrence of an amusing nature which happened on the way. When we were within a few miles of the town the Indians were suddenly excited and startled by the appearance of a party of fox-hunters, forty or fifty in number, following their pack in full cry, having just crossed the track ahead of the train.

This was a subject entirely new to them and unthought of by the Indians; and, knowing that English soldiers all wore red coats, they were alarmed, their first impression being that we had brought them on to hostile ground, and that this was a "war-party" in pursuit of their enemy. They were relieved and excessively amused when I told them it was merely a fox-hunt, and that the gentlemen they saw riding were mostly noblemen and men of great influence and wealth. They watched them intensely until they were out of sight, and made many amusing remarks about them after we had arrived at York. I told them they rode without guns, and the first one in at the death pulled off the tail of the fox and rode into town with it under his hatband. Their laughter was excessive at the idea of "such gentlemen hunting in open fields, and with a whip instead of a gun; and that great chiefs, as I had pronounced them, should be risking their lives, and the limbs of their fine horses, for a poor fox, the flesh of which, even if it were good to eat, was not wanted by such rich people, who had meat enough at home; and the skin of which could not be worth so much trouble, especially when, as everybody knows, it is good for nothing when the tail is pulled off."

29

JOHN OVERTON CHOULES, *YOUNG AMERICANS ABROAD* (BOSTON: GOULD AND LINCOLN, 1853), PP. 48–52, 92–95

As to accidents in travel, we, no doubt, have our full share; but since our arrival in England the railroad trains have had some pretty rough shakings, and the results in loss of life and limb would have passed for quite ugly enough, even had they happened in the west. I very much wish you could have been with us on Easter Monday, when we passed the day at Greenwich, and were at the renowned Greenwich Fair, which lasts for three days. The scene of revelry takes place in the Park, a royal one, and really a noble one. Here all the riffraff and bobtail of London repair in their finery, and have a time. You can form no notion of the affair; it cannot be described. The upper part of the Park, towards the Royal Observatory, is very steep, and down this boys and girls, men and women, have a roll. Such scenes as are here to be witnessed we cannot match. Nothing can exceed the doings that occur. All the public houses swarm, and in no spot have I ever seen so many places for drinking as are here. The working-men of London, and apprentices, with wives and sweethearts, all turn out Easter Monday. It seems as though all the horses, carts, chaises, and hackney coaches of the city were on the road. We saw several enormous coal wagons crammed tightly with boys and girls. On the fine heath, or down, that skirts the Park, are hundreds of donkeys, and you are invited to take a halfpenny, penny, or twopenny ride. All sorts of gambling are to be seen. One favorite game with the youngsters was to have a tobacco box, full of coppers, stuck on a stick standing in a hole, and then, for a halfpenny paid to the proprietor, you are entitled to take a shy at the mark. If it falls into the hole, you lose; if you knock it off, and away from the hole, you take it. It requires, I fancy, much adroitness and experience to make any thing at "shying" at the "bacca box." At night, Greenwich is all alive—life is out of London and in the fair. But let the travel-ler who has to return to town beware. The road is full of horses and vehicles, driven by drunken men and boys; and, for four or five miles, you can imagine that a city is besieged, and that the inhabitants are flying from the sword. O, such weary-looking children as we saw that day! One favorite amusement was to draw a little wooden instrument quick over the coat of another person, when it produces a noise precisely like that of a torn garment. Hundreds of these machines were in the hands of the urchins who crowded the Park. Here, for the first time, I saw the veritable gypsy of whose race we have read so much in Borrow's Zincali. The women are very fine looking, and some of the girls were exquisitely beautiful. They are a swarthy-looking set, and seem to be a cross of Indian and Jew. Those we saw were proper wiry-looking fellows. One or two of the men were nattily dressed, with fancy silk handkerchiefs. They live in tents, and migrate through the midland counties, but I believe are not as numerous as they were thirty years ago. You will not soon forget how we were pleased with the memoirs of Bamfield Moore Carew, who was once known as their king in Great Britain. I wonder that book has never been reprinted in America. I am pretty sure that Greenwich Park would please your taste. I think the view from the Royal Observatory, and from whence longitude is reckoned, is one of the grandest I have ever seen. You get a fine view of the noble palace once the royal residence, but now the Sailor's Home. You see the Thames, with its immense burden, and, through the mist, the great city. As to the Hospital, we shall leave that for another excursion: we came to Greenwich at present merely to witness Easter Fair, and it will not soon be forgotten by any of us.

Yours, &c.,   James.

BRISTOL.

DEAR CHARLEY:—

As we had a few days to spare before the exhibition opened, we proposed to run down to Bristol and Bath, and pass a week. We took the Great Western train first-class cars, and made the journey of one hundred and twenty miles in two hours and forty minutes. This is the perfection of travelling. The cars are very commodious, holding eight persons, each having a nicely-cushioned chair. The rail is the broad gage; and we hardly felt the motion, so excellent is the road. The country through which we passed was very beautiful, and perhaps it never appears to more advantage than in the gay garniture of spring. We left Windsor Castle to our left, and Eton College, and passed by Reading, a fine, flourishing town; and at Swindon we made a stay of ten minutes. The station at this place is very spacious and elegant. Here the passengers have the only opportunity to obtain refreshments on the route; and never did people seem more intent upon laying in provender. The table was finely laid out, and a great variety tempted the appetite. The railroad company, when they leased this station, stipulated that every train should pass ten minutes at it. But the express train claimed exemption, and refused to afford the time. The landlord prosecuted the company, obtained satisfactory damages, and now even the express train affords its passengers time to recruit at Swindon. This place has grown up under the auspices of the railroad, and one can hardly fancy a prettier place than environs the station. The cottages are of stone, of the Elizabethan and Tudor style, and are very numerous; while the church, which is just finished, is one of the neatest affairs I have yet seen in England. The town of Swindon is about two miles from the station, and I expect to visit it in the course of my journey. You know, my dear Charley, how long and fondly I have anticipated my visit to my native city, and can imagine my feelings on this route homewards. We passed through Bath, a most beautiful city, (and I think as beautiful as any I ever saw,) and then in half an hour we entered Bristol. The splendid station-house of the railroad was new to me, but the old streets and houses were all familiar as if they had been left but yesterday.

LONDON.

DEAR CHARLEY:—

Ever since we reached London, I have wanted to go to Woolwich, the great naval arsenal and dockyard, because I expected I should obtain a pretty good idea of the power of the British navy; and then I like to compare such places with our own; and I have often, at Brooklyn Navy Yard, thought how much I should like to see Woolwich. Woolwich is on the Thames, and about ten miles from the city. You can go at any hour by steamer from London Bridge, or take the railway from the Surrey side of the bridge. We were furnished with a ticket of admission from our minister; but unfortunately, we came on a day when the yard was closed by order. We were sadly disappointed, but the doorkeeper, a very respectable police officer, told us that our only recourse was to call on the commanding officer, who lived a mile off, and he kindly gave us a policeman as a guide. On our way, we met the general on horseback, attended by some other officers. We accosted him, and told our case. He seemed sorry, but said the yard was closed. As soon as we mentioned that we came from America, he at once gave orders for our admission, and was very polite. Indeed, on several occasions we have found that our being from the United States has proved quite a passport.

We had a special government order to go over all the workshops and see the steam power, &c., &c. I think I shall not soon forget the wonderful smithery where the Nasmyth hammers are at work, employed in forging chain cables and all sorts of iron work for the men-of-war. We went in succession through the founderies for iron and brass, the steam boiler manufactory, and saw the planing machines and lathes; and as to all the other shops and factories, I can only say, that the yard looked like a city.

We were much pleased with the ships now in progress. One was the screw steamer, the Agamemnon, to have eighty guns. There, too, is the Royal Albert, of one hundred and twenty guns, which they call the largest ship in the world. Of course, we think this doubtful. It has been nine years in progress, and will not be finished for three more. It is to be launched when the Prince of Wales attains the rank of post captain. We saw, among many other curiosities, the boat in which Sir John Ross was out twenty-seven days in the ice. We went into an immense building devoted to military stores, and in one room we saw the entire accoutrements for ten thousand cavalry, including bridles, saddles, and stirrups, holsters, &c.

The yard is a very large affair, containing very many acres; it is the depository of the cannon belonging to the army and navy for all the region, and there were more than twenty thousand pieces lying upon the ground. Some were very large, and they were of all varieties known in war.

After a delightful hour spent in listening to the best martial music I ever heard played, by the band, we took steamboat for Greenwich, and, landing there, walked to Blackheath, where we had an engagement to dine at Lee Grove with a London merchant. Here we had a fine opportunity to witness the luxury and elegance of English social life. This gentleman, now in the decline of life, has an exquisitely beautiful place, situated in a park of some sixty acres. The railroad has been run through his estate, and, of course, has made it very much more valuable for building; but as it injures the park for the embellishment of the mansion, it was a fair subject for damages, and the jury of reference gave its proprietor the pretty verdict of eleven thousand pounds. At the table we had the finest dessert which the hothouse can furnish. Our host gave us a very interesting account of his travels in America more than forty years ago. A journey from New York to Niagara, as related by this traveller, was then far more of an undertaking than a journey from New Orleans to New York, and a voyage thence to England, at the present time.

In the evening, we took the cars for London, and reached our comfortable hotel, the Golden Cross, Charing Cross, at eleven o'clock.

30

MISS (JULIA) PARDOE, 'ON THE RAIL', *REGINALD LYLE* (NEW YORK: BURGESS & DAY, 1854), PP. 103–106

"NOTHING could have been more pleasant or more fortunate!" exclaimed a wiry-haired, green-spectacled man, with a snub nose, and very dilapidated teeth, as he labored to make himself thoroughly comfortable in one of the first-class carriages on the Great Western Railway; and who, while speaking, tucked in the rug which he had spread over his knees with a minute and jealous care, that proved his perfect appreciation of his own personal value. "To think that you should have chosen this very day, and this very train; you, who so seldom venture beyond the Bills of Mortality. And here we are too, likely to have the carriage to ourselves; for we shall start within two minutes, and the rush seems pretty nearly over."

"It is fortunate, truly, Mr. Ravensdale; and I equally congratulate myself upon the circumstance—particularly as yon mentioned that you were anxious to see me."

"So I was—so I am. Not on any matter of business, however; although I am going to ask your advice. But there's the bell. We're off, sure enough, without any intrusion; all snug and comfortable."

There was a slamming of doors, a shouting of hoarse voices, a hurried fall of feet, as porters and guards ran to their respective posts along the platform. A heavy panting, a shrill shriek, a slight movement, accompanied by an under-current of motion, which seemed as though the pulses of the mighty machine were throbbing with impatience; an accelerated impulse, a few parting injunctions pealed out from iron lungs, a dull echo from the lofty roof of the building, a plunge into the open air—and the steam-fiend, breathing fire, and snorting smoke, was driving a long column of heated spray over fair meadows and pleasant gardens, sprinkling the hedge-rows with unwholesome dew, and dimming cottage windows with its unclean moisture.

On—on—suspended in mid-air; startling the cattle from their quiet rest in the low-lying fields; rushing, like a brobdignagian arrow, under viaducts; roaring over rivers, rattling through ravines, tearing through tunnels, skirting leafless woods, and rustic villages, and princely parks; looking down upon the spires of sequestered churches and humble grave-yards, fighting with the wind, and lashing the hailstorm into powder.

On—on—the mighty monster pursues its headlong course, mindless and merciless, destroying alike time and space; devouring both; and still roaring and rattling on its way; leaving in its dark wake long lines of sullen metal, clutching the earth, and girding nature with fetters riveted into her very bosom.

But what avails words? Only a century ago the passage of a railway-train would have been a marvel and a mystery; while in the present age it is a mere every-day affair; and men, with a stopwatch in their hands, querulously cavil for five lost minutes.

The train had, as we stated before we indulged in this digression, left the station, and was rushing at full speed upon its way; while the carriage into which our readers have already looked was occupied only by three travellers; who, as we have shown, were not strangers to each other.

"I suppose," said the gentleman in the green spectacles; "that as there are no women here we may venture upon a cigar?"

"If we open a window, I see no objection."

"But I see fifty to do doing so. Let them disinfect the carriage, if they consider it infected, when we have left it. The breath of a pure manilla is worth all the perfume that was ever wasted at a court-ball. Try them."

"Thank you. I shall not refuse, for I left home hastily, and am not provided. They look well, indeed."

"And you, Mr. Trevor?"

"I follow the example of Mr. Brunton, Sir, and accept your offer with gratitude. One had need create a peculiar and personal atmosphere such a day as this."

"Well said; I have little faith, and place less confidence in a man who affects no care for the 'creature-comforts;' fellows who talk of 'roughing it,' as though it were either commendable or gentlemanlike to be as happy amid disorder and privation, as when surrounded by comfort and luxury. Of all pitiful and paltry conceits this appears to me to be the most odious. One reason why I always travel by rail is of course for the sake of speed—that point requires no explanation; for in whatever else profusion may be praiseworthy, there is nothing more desirable than to economise time. Time, after all, is every man's great capital. It may be a mere theory, to be sure, as some strange logician once attempted to prove, at least to his own satisfaction; but in spite of such would-be philosophers, I hold that Time is a real, even although an untangible possession, and to be valued accordingly. But the main cause of my preference for the rail is its comfort; no stopping to change, or to bait horses; no tough steaks or four-year-old chicken at a wayside house of call; no bad ale and worse wine; no unbuttoning of great-coats and double-breasted waistcoats to fee guards and coachmen, in a hard frost, or under a pouring rain; none, in short, of those minor miseries that wear a man to death in spite of himself. Here we are in a good, well-padded carriage, air-tight and water-tight, so long as we see fit to leave it so; with nothing to do but to make ourselves comfortable, read our paper, smoke our cigar, or talk over our affairs with a friend. Nevertheless, however, it is true that at times we are not altogether able to—"

And a glance at Trevor finished the imperfect sentence.

"If you allude to the presence of my companion, in making the remark," observed the lawyer, who had at once understood the meaning of the look; "you may speak freely before him. He is to me a second self, from whom I have no secrets; and I can pledge myself for his discretion."

"Good; then I shall stand upon no ceremony in troubling you on the subject to which I some time ago alluded. You are aware that I have a daughter; an only daughter. Her mother died while she was quite a child, and I never married again. I found that the position of a family man interfered with my habits, and consequently with my comfort. Not that I had any reason to complain of Mrs. Ravensdale during the three years of our married life; but she never thoroughly understood me, and had certain ideas of her own, which occasionally interfered with my notions, and consequently unhinged my nerves. So, warned by past experience, I resolved to remain a widower. Well, the child was no trouble, as I found a home for her without any difficulty, until she was old enough to be sent to a fashionable school, where she still remains: although she begins to think herself old enough to take her place in the world. I have been anxious on this point for many months, truly and deeply anxious: for what could I do with a flighty girl under my roof? When lo!—and this is just the point on which I want to consult you—the young lady herself quietly terminates all my difficulty by writing to inform me that she has provided a home for herself, and a husband into the bargain, if I will only consent to make her happy."

"Such a communication must have relieved your mind, under the circumstances," observed the lawyer, withdrawing the cigar from his mouth, and half-filling the carriage with its perfumed vapor.

"Why, I confess that it is the very thing of all others that I should rejoice to do," was the reply of Mr. Ravensdale: "if it can be accomplished without any interference with my own comfort, for she is a good girl, and deserves all the indulgence that I can show her. But, how now!" he pursued angrily; "I do believe that there is a ventilator in the roof, for I felt a cold blast about my shoulders, even through my great-coat. This is really too bad; and on my return to town I shall make a complaint to the directors."

"And so the young lady has already made her selection of a companion for life," said Mr. Brunton, smiling at the egotism of his companion. "Well, since it seems that she could not so thoroughly in any other way have met your wishes, it appears to me that I am called upon to congratulate rather than to counsel you."

31

ELIZABETH GASKELL, 'MISCHANCES', *NORTH AND SOUTH* (LONDON: OXFORD UNIVERSITY PRESS, 1908), PP. 312–317

> What! remain to be
> Denounced—dragged, it may be, in chains.
> WERNER.

ALL the next day they sat together—they three. Mr. Hale hardly ever spoke but when his children asked him questions, and forced him, as it were, into the present. Frederick's grief was no more to be seen or heard; the first paroxysm had passed over, and now he was ashamed of having been so battered down by emotion; and though his sorrow for the loss of his mother was a deep real feeling, and would last out his life, it was never to be spoken of again. Margaret, not so passionate at first, was more suffering now. At times she cried a good deal; and her manner, even when speaking on indifferent things, had a mournful tenderness about it, which was deepened whenever her looks fell on Frederick, and she thought of his rapidly approaching departure. She was glad he was going, on her father's account, however much she might grieve over it on her own. The anxious terror in which Mr. Hale lived lest his son should be detected and captured, far outweighed the pleasure he derived from his presence. The nervousness had increased since Mrs. Hale's death, probably because he dwelt upon it more exclusively. He started at every unusual sound; and was never comfortable unless Frederick sat out of the immediate view of anyone entering the room. Towards evening he said:

'You will go with Frederick to the station, Margaret? I shall want to know he is safely off. You will bring me word that he is clear of Milton, at any rate?'

'Certainly,' said Margaret. 'I shall like it, if you won't be lonely without me, papa.'

'No, no! I should always be fancying some one had known him, and that he had been stopped, unless you could tell me you had seen him off. And go to the Outwood station. It is quite as near, and not so many people about. Take a cab there. There is less risk of his being seen. What time is your train, Fred?'

'Ten minutes past six; very nearly dark. So what will you do, Margaret?'

'Oh, I can manage. I am getting very brave and very hard. It is a well-lighted road all the way home, if it should be dark. But I was out last week much later.'

Margaret was thankful when the parting was over—the parting from the dead mother and the living father. She hurried Frederick into the cab, in order to shorten a scene which she saw was so bitterly painful to her father, who would accompany his son as he took his last look at his mother. Partly in consequence of this, and partly owing to one of the very common mistakes in the 'Railway Guide' as to the times when trains arrive at the smaller stations, they found, on reaching Outwood, that they had nearly twenty minutes to spare. The booking-office was not open, so they could not even take the ticket. They accordingly went down the flight of steps that led to the level of the ground below the railway. There was a broad cinder-path diagonally crossing a field which lay along-side of the carriage-road, and they went there to walk backwards and forwards for the few minutes they had to spare.

Margaret's hand lay in Frederick's arm. He took hold of it affectionately.

'Margaret! I am going to consult Mr. Lennox as to the chance of exculpating myself, so that I may return to England whenever I choose, more for your sake than for the sake of anyone else. I can't bear to think of your lonely position if anything should happen to my father. He looks sadly changed—terribly shaken. I wish you could get him to think of the Cadiz plan, for many reasons. What could you do if he were taken away? You have no friend near. We are curiously bare of relations.'

Margaret could hardly keep from crying at the tender anxiety with which Frederick was bringing before her an event which she herself felt was not very improbable, so severely had the cares of the last few months told upon Mr. Hale. But she tried to rally as she said:

'There have been such strange unexpected changes in my life during these last two years, that I feel more than ever that it is not worth while to calculate too closely what I should do if any future event took place. I try to think only upon the present.' She paused; they were standing still for a moment, close on the field side of the stile leading into the road; the setting sun fell on their faces. Frederick held her hand in his, and looked with wistful anxiety into her face, reading there more care and trouble than she would betray by words. She went on:

'We shall write often to one another, and I will promise—for I see it will set your mind at ease—to tell you every worry I have. Papa is'—she started a little, a hardly visible start—but Frederick felt the sudden motion of the hand he held, and turned his full face to the road, along which a horseman was slowly riding, just passing the very stile where they stood. Margaret bowed; her bow was stiffly returned.

'Who is that?' said Frederick, almost before he was out of hearing.

Margaret was a little drooping, a little flushed, as she replied: 'Mr. Thornton; you saw him before, you know.'

'Only his back. He is an unprepossessing-looking fellow. What a scowl he has!'

'Something has happened to vex him,' said Margaret, apologetically. 'You would not have thought him unprepossessing if you had seen him with mamma.'

'I fancy it must be time to go and get my ticket. If I had known how dark it would be, we wouldn't have sent back the cab, Margaret.'

'Oh, don't fidget about that. I can take a cab here, if I like; or go back by the railroad, when I should have shops and people and lamps all the way from the Milton station-house. Don't think of me; take care of yourself. I am sick with the thought that Leonards may be in the same train with you. Look well into the carriage before you get in.'

They went back to the station. Margaret insisted upon going into the full light of the flaring gas inside to take the ticket. Some idle-looking young men were lounging about with the station-master. Margaret thought she had seen the face of one of them before, and returned him a proud look of offended dignity for his somewhat impertinent stare of undisguised admiration. She went hastily to her brother, who was standing outside, and took hold of his arm. 'Have you got your bag? Let us walk about here on the platform,' said she, a little flurried at the idea of so soon being left alone, and her bravery oozing out rather faster than she liked to acknowledge even to herself. She heard a step following them along the flags; it stopped when they stopped, looking out along the line and hearing the whizz of the coming train. They did not speak; their hearts were too full. Another moment, and the train would be here; a minute more, and he would be gone. Margaret almost repented the urgency with which she had entreated him to go to London; it was throwing more chances of detection in his way. If he had sailed for Spain by Liverpool, he might have been off in two or three hours.

Frederick turned round, right facing the lamp, where the gas darted up in vivid anticipation of the train. A man in the dress of a railway porter started forward; a bad-looking man, who seemed to have drunk himself into a state of brutality, although his senses were in perfect order.

'By your leave, miss!' said he, pushing Margaret rudely on one side, and seizing Frederick by the collar.

'Your name is Hale, I believe?'

In an instant—how, Margaret did not see, for everything danced before her eyes—but by some sleight of wrestling, Frederick had tripped him up, and he fell from the height of three or four feet, which the platform was elevated above the space of soft ground, by the side of the railroad. There he lay.

'Run, run!' gasped Margaret. 'The train is here. It was Leonards, was it? oh, run! I will carry your bag.' And she took him by the arm to push him along with all her feeble force. A door was opened in a carriage—he jumped in; and as he leant out to say, 'God bless you, Margaret!' the train rushed past her; and she was left standing alone. She was so terribly sick and faint that she was thankful to be able to turn into the ladies' waiting-room, and sit down for an instant. At first she could do nothing but gasp for breath. It was such a hurry; such a sickening alarm; such a near chance. If the train had not been there at the moment, the man would have jumped up again and called for assistance to arrest him. She wondered if the man had got up: she tried to remember if she had seen him move; she wondered if he could have been seriously hurt. She ventured out; the platform was all alight, but still quite deserted; she went to the end, and looked over, somewhat fearfully. No one was there; and then she was glad she had made herself go and inspect, for otherwise terrible thoughts would have haunted her dreams. And even as it was, she was so trembling and affrighted that she felt she could not walk home along the road, which did indeed seem lonely and dark, as she gazed down upon it from the blaze of the station. She would wait till the down train passed and take her seat in it. But what if Leonards recognized her as Frederick's companion! She peered about, before venturing into the booking-office to take her ticket. There were only some railway officials standing about; and talking loud to one another.

'So Leonards has been drinking again!' said one, seemingly in authority. 'He'll need all his boasted influence to keep his place this time.'

'Where is he?' asked another, while Margaret, her back towards them, was counting her change with trembling fingers, not daring to turn round until she heard the answer to this question.

'I don't know. He came in not five minutes ago, with some long story or other about a fall he'd had, swearing awfully; and wanted to borrow some money from me to go to London by the next up-train. He made all sorts of tipsy promises, but I'd something else to do than listen to him; I told him to go about his business; and he went off at the front door.'

'He's at the nearest vaults, I'll be bound,' said the first speaker. 'Your money would have gone there too, if you'd been such a fool as to lend it.'

'Catch me! I knew better what his London meant. Why, he has never paid me off that five shillings'—and so they went on.

And now all Margaret's anxiety was for the train to come. She hid herself once more in the ladies' waiting-room, and fancied every noise was Leonards' step—every loud and boisterous voice was his. But no one came near her until a train drew up; when she was civilly helped into a carriage by a porter, into whose face she durst not look till they were in motion, and then she saw that it was not Leonards.

32

GEORGE AUGUSTUS SALA, 'THE ART OF SUCKING EGGS', IN *TEMPLE BAR* 1 (1861), 558–564

THERE are many admirable essays upon deportment, upon the art of standing upon one leg, upon the art of making a little knowledge go a long way, and upon most of the "habits of good society." There are profound treatises upon the tying of cravats, upon the fluke considered as an element of social progress, and the true principles of currency. There are "hand-books" upon dining, and treatises showing us how to live without dinners; with "ten minutes' advice about keeping a banker," or about making a banker keep us. All these guides to the art of living, with thousands more of a similar character, are very excellent things in their way, and they show us how well supplied we are with teachers. Almost every man we pass in the street is prepared to direct us in the matter of food, of habits, of morals, or religion; to tell us what *he* considers to be best; to lay bare his little experience before us; and, if need be, to convert us to his peculiar mode of living. I am not free myself from this weakness of human nature, and I therefore speak with little hesitation as a guide upon travelling. I have ridden in many omnibuses, many cabs, and many railway carriages (not to mention many other more eccentric conveyances), and am consequently fully qualified to teach my grandmothers and grandfathers how to suck these particular social eggs.

The first qualification necessary to form a perfect railway traveller is some little knowledge of his subject. He must be familiar with the leading characteristics of the different main lines; the plans of their termini; the number and position of their different junctions; the peculiar local pronunciation of their porters; the chief towns or ports they run down to; and the character of their ordinary passenger traffic. No man, for instance, who travels second-class in a night-train between London and Portsmouth, or between Bristol and Plymouth, or between Birmingham and Liverpool, must complain if he finds his carriage turned into the hold of a ship, and himself surrounded by noisy, mutinous mariners. He must not complain if he is choked with the fumes of strong cavendish; if he is jammed up with tar-smelling bundles of naval bedding; if he is asked to sing a song about poor Tom Bowling; to join a score of excited, brown-faced, blue-shirted pirates in a lusty chorus; or forced to drink raw brandy out of enormous stone bottles.

A railroad is little more than a common highway; and those who *will* go to Portsmouth, Plymouth, or Liverpool in second-class carriages, must do as Portsmouth, Plymouth, or Liverpool does. On the other hand, a traveller who rises early, and takes a "market-train" from Peterborough to Northampton, must not complain if he finds himself amongst agriculturalists and cattle-dealers, who breathe an atmosphere of ale, and cheese, and onions. As he has selected his travelling-bed, so he must lie upon it; and the best thing he can do is to imitate Locke, the philosopher, and cross-examine his neighbours with a view of extracting valuable information.

A knowledge of stations, routes, and junctions is most essential to the perfect railway traveller, because without it there can be none of that well-grounded self-reliance which is one of the few luxuries of travelling. There is hardly a more pitiable object to be met with in a railway carriage of any class, than a man who scarcely knows where he has come from, where he is going to, what line he is on, whether Manchester is in Lancashire, Kent, or the Eastern Counties, and who cannot find his way through the mazes of "Bradshaw." Such a man is not a living, thinking, independent human being; he is a band-box, a portmanteau, a carpet-bag. He lies at the mercy of every fellow-passenger, every ticket-collector, every guard or porter. He wears out the patience of those who have the misfortune to sit in the same carriage; he thrusts his head out of the window at every station, under the notion that he is being whirled away from his destination, or has already arrived at it; he loses his ticket on the platform, or puts it in some part of his clothes where he cannot find it; and generally leaves a comforter, an umbrella, or a hat-box under the seat behind him. There are thousands of such helpless wanderers always roaming about the country for some mysterious purpose, who either cannot learn the art of travelling, or will not submit to be taught. They belong to the class who are always too late for trains, and who spend half a day at some lonely hermitage of a station. They get out at great junctions, where ten minutes are allowed for refreshment, pay for soups and sandwiches which they never find time to eat, forget the position of their carriage (its number they never think of noting), are pushed hurriedly from door to door by unceremonious officials, and are haunted for hours with a dreadful suspicion that they have given a sovereign at the refreshment-counter in mistake for a shilling.

For far more intelligent and observant travellers than these there are also many traps and pitfalls. Swindon, on the Great Western Line, is a refreshment-station so constructed, that, unless you are careful, you may go out at a door exactly like the one you came in at, get into a train that is waiting for you exactly like the one you have just left, lean back on your comfortable seat for about an hour, and find yourself at Gloucester instead of Bristol. Leeds, Manchester, or any other towns or junctions which form a meeting-point for many converging lines, are even more bewildering to those who have not cool heads, inquiring tongues, and some little experience. Roadside stations, again, as announced by the ordinary run of porters, are dialect puzzles, only to be unravelled by such curious inquirers into the Lancashire, Yorkshire, Dorset, and West Country languages as Prince Lucien Bonaparte and kindred linguists. Apart from local or imported peculiarities of pronunciation, there is a general drawling, sing-song, professional twang, which must be specially contrived to hide the names of such stations from railway passengers. This may, perhaps, be defended on the same ground as the Jew clothesman defended his "O' clo' " abbreviation when attacked by Samuel Taylor Coleridge,—viz. that any one who had to pronounce a particular word an infinite number of times would soon fall into a like habit of adulterating language. This may be a good answer from a street-hawker, who must starve if he cannot make himself understood; but is hardly so good when coming from men whose faults are paid for by others.

A railway porter whose mind is not given to his work, whose thoughts are above and beyond the dull level of his surroundings, or who has fallen into a certain habit from long familiarity with a certain place—may be a very troublesome guide on a busy platform. I have accosted such public servants gently and civilly, and have once or twice observed them gazing over me or through me into the dim future,—thinking, it may be, of fate, free-will, and foreknowledge absolute; drunk, it may be, with reading intoxicating accounts of "self-made men" (price one shilling, at the railway book-stall), and feeling themselves already budding into chairmen and directors. I have observed that nothing but the glitter of a sixpence will ever break this reverie of ambition; and without blaming those who first introduced the old coaching system of bribing upon railroads, I am content to accept it as an established fact, and not only to bribe porters myself, but to recommend every traveller to do so. The loss of time in standing out against this "imposition," as it is called, upon purity principles is greater than the gain, and these sixpences are now a part of the recognised cost of a journey.

An eccentric, weak, or really absent-minded porter, or official, who has been suddenly transplanted from a large to a small station, or a small to a large station, is much more difficult to deal with. A station-master who is not strong enough for his place, who is easily flurried by an extra excursion-train, or an unexpected cargo of luggage, hunting-dogs, or horses, is apt to forget that attention to "points" and signals which is necessary to prevent accidents. Carefully as our wonderful network of railways is managed, a few officers of this kind will always creep in, from some error of judgment on the part of superintendents. Luckily their shortcomings are not observed by the general public; and until a collision does occur, the travellers repose in the bliss of ignorance. There are a few railway officers, however, who have no skill in concealing their defects, and the public either laugh at or censure them, according to the humour of the moment. A porter who has not been long promoted from following the plough, and who may have been an excellent servant at one of those little washhouse-looking stations near a bridge, which is happy in attending to its four or five trains a-day, may be almost driven mad by the bustle of a great inland terminus like Birmingham, with its scores of trains always rattling in from the east, west, north, and south. He may miss that little plot of sloping earth at the side of the station where he trained his scarlet-runners, grew his enormous potatoes and gooseberries, and raised the name of his beloved dwelling-place in oyster-shell-relievo. He may pine to return to that rural quiet, which was never broken by more than a dozen daily passengers, with familiar faces, whose Christmas-boxes were a certain annuity to him, and who never bullied him like hasty commercial travellers overburdened with luggage.

On the other hand, a porter removed from the noise and excitement of Birmingham to one of these rail-side hermitages, would hardly do his work in a cheerful spirit, and might probably take to drinking in the intervals of business. There are porters of both these kinds to be met with,—humble, would-be useful, but misplaced and discontented men, and happy is the traveller who is not dependent on them for assistance or information. I have heard of one who had somehow drifted from the north into the south-west, and who daily drove weak-minded, ignorant passengers frantic by shouting out "Birmingham" instead of Balham. Upon being remonstrated with, he excused himself by saying he had been calling out the name of the first town for fifteen years; and he put it to any man whether it was easy to throw off, in a few days, or even weeks, such a long-settled habit.

The morals of railway travelling—the higher etiquette proper to be observed in railway carriages—form a most important part of this subject. It is not alone sufficient to avoid treading on a fellow-passenger's toes, or sitting on his hat, or incommoding him with gusts of wind from the open window. The social amenities of railway intercourse should embrace many acts far more thoughtful and unselfish than these, and opposed to the first-come-first-served principle which governs so many travellers. It is very delightful for two or more intimate friends to be able to retain a whole compartment to themselves during a long journey, without paying the company for such a luxury; but they should not grasp at this unfair privilege by filling each seat in their carriage with portmanteaus and rugs, or by acting the old rather exploded game of the lunatic and his keepers. They should not attempt to block up the carriage-windows at the side of the platform; nor should they commit themselves so far as to say that several seats are engaged by passengers who have just gone to purchase a newspaper. Such tricks and misrepresentations are sure to be exposed by some determined station-superintendent before the starting of the train, and they often lead to constraint and unpleasantness. The travellers who are forced into such carriages by the arm of authority are not likely to prove very agreeable companions on the journey, while the greedy first-comers can never remove the impression caused by their deliberate lies. The softest seat, in such cases, becomes hard and unbearable, and the carriage is turned into a cage, a round-house, or a dungeon.

The nature and amount of conversation fit for travelling companions must be left, in a great measure, to the taste and discretion of travellers. It is not well, perhaps, to turn a carriage into a "discussion forum," nor is it well to venture upon no remarks to your neighbour beyond the level of commonplace. The description of personal diseases and their symptoms, of family and professional matters, may at once be struck out of the list of allowable topics; and it is a little out of date to make any remarks about the wonders of steam, or the once miraculous fact—now no longer miraculous—that a man may breakfast in London, dine at Manchester, and sup in Edinburgh. It is not well to persist in addressing observations, either profound or simple, to a fellow-passenger who is evidently averse to conversation, because many men are often travelling on anxious and important business that requires sustained thought and reflection. Some economists of time are fond of studying, or arranging future operations in the hours of travelling, and they soon show, by their answers, that their minds are fully occupied.

With regard to the almost universal custom of smoking in railway carriages in defiance of bye-laws and regulations, it may be a nuisance or not, according as it is persisted in. In a carriage where ladies are present it is never proposed; and in a carriage containing none but gentlemen it is put to the vote. The minority of one, who is not a smoker, gives in out of politeness to the wishes of his companions, and is never strong-minded enough to protest against the encroachment. Combination proves too much for the non-smokers, and very properly so. Until the latter have a sufficient regard for their own comfort and interest to invent and use a retaliative nuisance,—say an assafœtida pastile, for example,—they must suffer in silence. There is no help for those men, especially travellers, who will not help themselves.

Slumber is an excellent aid to the impatient traveller in helping him through his journey, but it must be used with care and moderation. Like all good things, it is liable to be indulged in too freely, and then it often interferes with the object it was intended to assist. I have known travellers carried past their destinations again and again, because they thought themselves capable of opening their closed eyes at a certain time. I have heard of one man who left London by a night-train to reach a particular spot in Kent, who was carried past this spot to Dover sound asleep, who started back by an early morning mail, who was again carried past his station fast asleep, and who awoke to find himself once more at the London terminus. This may be a travelling joke, but it is founded in some degree upon fact, and it conveys a useful lesson.

Those who are not familiar with the railway stations of their country, and are good sleeping travellers, should be warned of a few other shocks that may easily come upon them. A sleeping passenger, on his way from Glasgow to Loch Lomond, may be roused from his dreams by a Scotch porter, and told that he has arrived at Alexandria! A similar passenger, on his road from Ayr to Dalmellington, may be similarly bewildered by hearing the name of Patna; and, rubbing his eyes, he may wonder whether he is in Egypt or the East, or whether Egypt and the East have removed to Scotland. In other parts of the United Kingdom he may be similarly bewildered with the Danish-sounding stations of Elsenham and Goathland; with the French-sounding stations of St. Devereux and Plessy; with the Russian-sounding stations of Ulleskelf and Dromkeen; with the Spanish-sounding stations of Clonsilla, Torre, and Pontardulais; with the German-sounding stations of Helensburgh and Droylsden; with the Hungarian or Polish-sounding stations of Piel and Magerhafelt; and with the Italian-sounding stations of Eastrea, Aspatria, and Etruria. These are only a few out of many philological nightmares that may arouse the sleeping traveller at any moment, supposing the different local pronunciations to be tolerably intelligible.

The art of travelling in cabs is a much more simple matter, and it consists mainly in selecting a horse that will stand, a driver who does not look likely to become abusive, and in undoing all the work of meddling legislation. The whole rolling stock of the cab interest is rotting under Government protection. While the mileage rate is fixed by Act of Parliament, there is no legislative limit, on the other side, to the price of hay and corn, and no allowance made for the violent changes in the weather. Rain, snow, fog, may come and go, and still the paternal Government ordains that we shall travel for sixpence a-mile. Pentonville Hill, and other metropolitan mountains, shall be ascended at the same price, according to distance, as we pay for traversing a level, uncrowded road in the outskirts; and the passage from Holborn Bridge to the Brighton Railway, which goes up Snow Hill, through Newgate Street, Cheapside, and over London Bridge,—the four most crowded thoroughfares in the world,—is measured out under the same unbending scale of charges. The chief labour of the traveller in cabs is to discover and allow for these inequalities of the London streets and the London weather, and to make his peace with the over-regulated drivers. In Manchester, and other large towns, he gets a better vehicle, under free-trade, at about the same fares, and is saved all this terrible trouble of thinking.

The art of travelling in omnibuses requires a certain knowledge of localities, and a certain nimbleness in ascending and descending the roofs of these vehicles. In Paris, at the back of the "knife-board," you are told, in dismounting, which foot to put down first; but this is another instance of a paternal Government watching over the smallest things, which I do not wish to see copied in England. There are not many steps from the regulation of omnibuses and their passengers, to the regulation of newspapers and periodicals; and social reform, as Milton would have said, becomes nothing but old despotism "writ large."

A traveller who rides much in London omnibuses will find them remarkably like certain lines of railway. He will see that the character of the vehicle is governed very much by the neighbourhood it runs to, and that the passengers vary with the different hours of the day. Coming from Hornsey, Highgate, Clapham, or Putney, in the morning about nine, he will find himself amongst men of business, rolling down to the City, and talking, it may be, of the treaty, or the Bank rate of discount. Going to Stamford Hill, or Highbury, in the middle of the day, he will find himself amongst rather serious middle-aged ladies, returning home from shopping, or other town duties. Coming from Brompton, about noon, he may join a few actors, rolling down to rehearsal; and going to Stepney, or Blackwall, about the same hour, he may find himself amongst sailors, captains, and ship-chandlers. Going to Greenwich, by the way of the Old Kent Road, about nine or ten o'clock at night, he may find himself in the middle of a few drunken pensioners, whose wooden legs are stuck across the vehicle, like the bars of hurdles. A wooden leg is a very difficult article to manage in a crowded omnibus—so is a warming-pan—a dragoon's sabre-sword, fixed uniform fashion—a basket of clothes going home from the wash—a wet umbrella—a spoiled child with gingerbread—an oilskin waterproof cape—and a large French clock. All these things, however, have to be tolerated at different times, with conductors who seem to keep all their small change in their mouths, and whose legs are so protected with many wrappers, that that they can hardly feel the blows which warn them to stop. In all travelling by these vehicles, I counsel patience, good-humour, and politeness—the best manners of the first-class railway carriage. The lower the neighbourhood you are passing through, the more will this conduct be appreciated; and there is often more necessity for you to ride outside to oblige a working-woman in Shoreditch or Whitechapel, than a lady in Kensington or Bayswater. The latter may have a choice of vehicles; the first has none. So well is this understood by the conductors of omnibuses on the common routes, that you will probably hear a conversation like the following going on over the roof, if you have not acted with the usual politeness:

Conductor to Driver. "Bill, when's a man not a man?"
Driver to Conductor. "Give it up."
Conductor to Driver. "When he won't get out to 'blige a female."

In concluding my remarks upon land travelling, I may observe that night-trains for long distances—except for the post-office, luggage traffic, and passengers journeying under the spur of some sharp necessity—are a delusion and a snare. The time supposed to be saved by such travelling is never really saved; the traveller is exhausted for one or more days; and discovers, too late, that neither warm baths, strong tea, nor soda-water, at repeated intervals, will make up for a lost night's rest. Excursion-trains of the wild order, such as go to Paris and back in three days, are another travelling mistake; for no men see so little of the world as those who hurry through it like steeplechasers.

33

MISS. MULOCH (DINAH MARIA MULOCK CRAIK), *A LIFE FOR A LIFE: A NOVEL* (NEW YORK: CARLETON, 1864), PP. 196–197

His story

Dec. 31st, 1856.

THE merry-making of my neighbors in the flat above—probably Scotch or Irish, both of which greatly abound in this town—is a sad counteraction of work to-night. But why grumble, when I am one of the few people who pretend to work at all on so merry a night, which used to be such a treat to us boys? The sounds overhead put me in mind of that old festival of Hogmanay, which, for a good many things, would be "more honored in the breach than the observance."

This Liverpool is an awful town for drinking. Other towns may be as bad; statistics prove it; but I know no place where intoxication is so open and shameless. Not only in by-streets and foul courts, where one expects to see it, but every where. I never take a short railway journey in the after part of the day but I am liable to meet at least one drunken "gentleman" snoozing in his first-class carriage; or, in the second class, two or three drunken "men" singing, swearing, or pushed stupidly about by pale-faced wives. The sadness of the thing is, that the wives do not seem to mind it—that every body takes it as a matter of course. The "gentleman," often gray-haired, is but "merry," as he is accustomed to be every night of his life; the poor man has only "had a drop or two," as all his comrades are in the habit of taking whenever they get the chance; they see no disgrace in it, so they laugh at him a bit, and humor him, and are quite ready to stand up for him against all in-comers who may object to an intoxicated fellow-passenger. *They* don't, nor do the women belonging to them, who are well used to tolerate drunken sweethearts, and lead about and pacify drunken husbands. It makes me sick at heart sometimes to see a decent, pretty girl sit tittering at a foul-mouthed beast opposite; or a tidy young mother, with two or three bonny children, trying to coax home, without harm to himself or them, some brutish husband, who does not know his right hand from his left, so utterly stupid is he with drink. To-night, but for my chance-hand at a railway station, such a family-party as this might have reached home fatherless—and no great misfortune, one might suppose. Yet the wife had not even looked sad—had only scolded and laughed at him.

34

FRANCES ELEANOR TROLLOPE, *VERONICA*, 'THE RAILWAY WAITING ROOM', IN *ALL THE YEAR ROUND*, NEW SERIES V.2 (SEPTEMBER 25, 1869), P. 386

They were in London. The railway station looked inexpressibly dreary, with its long vistas ending in black shadow, its sickly lamps blinking like eyes that have watched all night and are weary, and its vast glazed roof, through which the grey dawn was beginning to glimmer.

It was yet too early to attempt to go to Mrs. Lockwood's house. They must wait at least a couple of hours. The vicar looked so worn, aged, and ill, that Maud tried to persuade him to seek some rest at the hotel close to the station, promising that he should be roused in due time. But he refused to do so.

"Sit here," he said, leading Maud into a waiting-room, where there was a dull coke fire smouldering slowly, and where a solitary gas-light shed a yellow glare over a huge, bare, shining centre table, leaving the rest of the apartment in almost darkness. "You will be safe and unmolested here. I must go and make some inquiries—try to find some trace—. Remain here till I return."

Maud thought she had never seen a room so utterly soul-depressing. No place would have appeared cheerful to her at that moment; but this railway waiting-room was truly a dreary and forlorn apartment. She sat there cowering over the dull red fire, sick, and chilly, and sad; listening nervously to every echoing footfall on the long platform without; to the whistle of some distant engine, screaming as though it had lost its way in the labyrinthine network of lines that converged just outside the great terminus, and were wildly crying for help and guidance; listening to the frequent clang of a heavy swing-door, the occasional sound of voices (once a man laughed aloud, and she involuntarily put her hands up to her startled ears to shut out the sound that jarred on every quivering nerve with agonising discord), and to the loud, deliberate ticking of a clock above the waiting-room door.

35

G. K. CHESTERTON, 'THE PREHISTORIC RAILWAY STATION', IN *TREMENDOUS TRUFFLES* (NEW YORK: DODD, MEAD, 1909), PP. 260–267

A RAILWAY station is an admirable place, although Ruskin did not think so; he did not think so because he himself was even more modern than the railway station. He did not think so because he was himself feverish, irritable, and snorting like an engine. He could not value the ancient silence of the railway station.

"In a railway station," he said, "you are in a hurry, and therefore, miserable"; but you need not be either unless you are as modern as Ruskin. The true philosopher does not think of coming just in time for his train except as a bet or a joke.

The only way of catching a train I have ever discovered is to be late for the one before. Do this, and you will find in a railway station much of the quietude and consolation of a cathedral. It has many of the characteristics of a great ecclesiastical building; it has vast arches, void spaces, coloured lights, and, above all, it has recurrence or ritual. It is dedicated to the celebration of water and fire the two prime elements of all human ceremonial. Lastly, a station resembles the old religions rather than the new religions in this point, that people go there. In connection with this it should also be remembered that all popular places, all sites, actually used by the people, tend to retain the best routine of antiquity very much more than any localities or machines used by any privileged class. Things are not altered so quickly or completely by common people as they are by fashionable people. Ruskin could have found more memories of the Middle Ages in the Underground Railway than in the grand hotels outside the stations. The great palaces of pleasure which the rich build in London all have brazen and vulgar names. Their names are either snobbish, like the Hotel Cecil, or (worse still) cosmopolitan like the Hotel Metropole. But when I go in a third-class carriage from the nearest circle station to Battersea to the nearest circle station to the *Daily News*, the names of the stations are one long litany of solemn and saintly memories. Leaving Victoria I come to a park belonging especially to St. James the Apostle; thence I go to Westminster Bridge, whose very name alludes to the awful Abbey; Charing

Cross holds up the symbol of Christendom; the next station is called a Temple; and Blackfriars remembers the mediæval dream of a Brotherhood.

If you wish to find the past preserved, follow the million feet of the crowd. At the worst the educated only wear down old things by sheer walking. But the educated kick them down out of sheer culture.

I feel all this profoundly as I wander about the empty railway station, where I have no business of any kind. I have extracted a vast number of chocolates from automatic machines; I have obtained cigarettes, toffee, scent, and other things that I dislike by the same machinery; I have weighed myself, with sublime results; and this sense, not only of the healthiness of popular things, but of their essential antiquity and permanence, is still in possession of my mind. I wander up to the bookstall, and my faith survives even the wild spectacle of modern literature and journalism. Even in the crudest and most clamorous aspects of the newspaper world I still prefer the popular to the proud and fastidious. If I had to choose between taking in the *Daily Mail* and taking in the *Times* (the dilemma reminds one of a nightmare), I should certainly cry out with the whole of my being for the *Daily Mail*. Even mere bigness preached in a frivolous way is not so irritating as mere meanness preached in a big and solemn way. People buy the *Daily Mail*, but they do not believe in it. They do believe in the *Times*, and (apparently) they do not buy it. But the more the output of paper upon the modern world is actually studied, the more it will be found to be in all its essentials ancient and human, like the name of Charing Cross. Linger for two or three hours at a station bookstall (as I am doing), and you will find that it gradually takes on the grandeur and historic allusiveness of the Vatican or Bodleian Library. The novelty is all superficial; the tradition is all interior and profound. The *Daily Mail* has new editions, but never a new idea. Everything in a newspaper that is not the old human love of altar or fatherland is the old human love of gossip. Modern writers have often made game of the old chronicles because they chiefly record accidents and prodigies; a church struck by lightning, or a calf with six legs. They do not seem to realise that this old barbaric history is the same as new democratic journalism. It is not that the savage chronicle has disappeared. It is merely that the savage chronicle now appears every morning.

As I moved thus mildly and vaguely in front of the bookstall, my eye caught a sudden and scarlet title that for the moment staggered me. On the outside of a book I saw written in large letters, "Get On or Get Out." The title of the book recalled to me with a sudden revolt and reaction all that does seem unquestionably new and nasty; it reminded me that there was in the world of to-day that utterly idiotic thing, a worship of success; a thing that only means surpassing anybody in anything; a thing that may mean being the most successful person in running away from a battle; a thing that may mean being the most successfully sleepy of a whole row of sleeping men. When I saw those words the silence and sanctity of the railway station were for a moment shadowed. Here, I thought, there is at any rate something anarchic and violent and vile. This title, at any rate, means the most disgusting individualism of this individualistic world. In the fury of my bitterness and passion I actually bought the book, thereby ensuring that my enemy would get some of my money. I opened it prepared to find some brutality, some blasphemy, which would really be an exception to the general silence and sanctity of the railway station. I was prepared to find something in the book that was as infamous as its title.

I was disappointed. There was nothing at all corresponding to the furious decisiveness of the remarks on the cover. After reading it carefully I could not discover whether I was really to get on or to get out; but I had a vague feeling that I should prefer to get out. A considerable part of the book, particularly towards the end, was concerned with a detailed description of the life of Napoleon Bonaparte. Undoubtedly Napoleon got on. He also got out. But I could not discover in any way how the details of his life given here were supposed to help a person aiming at success. One anecdote described how Napoleon always wiped his pen on his knee-breeches. I suppose the moral is: always wipe your pen on your knee-breeches, and you will win the battle of Wagram. Another story told that he let loose a gazelle among the ladies of his Court. Clearly the brutal practical inference is—loose a gazelle among the ladies of your acquaintance, and you will be Emperor of the French. Get on with a gazelle or get out. This book entirely reconciled me to the soft twilight of the station. Then I suddenly saw that there was a symbolic division which might be paralleled from biology. Brave men are all vertebrates; they have their softness on the surface and their toughness in the middle. But these modern cowards are all crustaceans; their hardness is all on the cover and their softness is inside. But the softness is there; everything in this twilight temple is soft.

Part 6

SUBTERRANEAN RAILWAYS AND THE UNDERGROUND
High Victorian railway cultures

36

'THE METROPOLITAN SUBTERRANEAN RAILWAY', *THE TIMES* (LONDON), NOVEMBER 30, 1861, P. 5

A quick and safe means of communication beneath the overcrowded streets of London has always been the great ideal of modern engineers. The public, however, have, perhaps not unnaturally, regarded the scheme as little less than Utopian, and one which, even if it could be accomplished, would certainly never pay. A subterranean railway under London was awfully suggestive of dark, noisome tunnels, buried many fathoms deep beyond the reach of light or life; passages inhabited by rats, soaked with sewer drippings, and poisoned by the escape of gas mains. It seemed an insult to common sense to suppose that people who could travel as cheaply to the city on the outside of a Paddington 'bus would ever prefer, as a merely quicker medium, to be driven amid palpable darkness through the foul subsoil of London. The pertinacity, too, with which the scheme at first hung fire strengthened not a little the incredulity of those who from the beginning had disbelieved it altogether. The Subterranean Railway has been talked about for years, and nothing done, till the whole idea has been gradually associated with the plans for flying machines, warfare by balloons, tunnels under the Channel, and other bold but somewhat hazardous propositions of the same kind. Yet many enterprising men have always adhered to the Subterranean Railway, have advocated its feasibility, and supported its use, till they at last brought about a result even more difficult to accomplish, if possible, than that of constructing the line itself—they got the capital for it. With the money for the undertaking, and with Mr. John Fowler as engineer, the rest has been comparatively easy. Working quietly under ground, only stopping up a thoroughfare now and then, or making an awful crack here and there in the walls of some houses under which it passed, the line has been slowly but very surely progressing from west to east, till the greater part of it is now far advanced towards completion, and the first length will actually be opened for public traffic, from the Victoria-street Station to Paddington, before the 1st of next May—the date by which it is, of course, sought to complete all our improvements in the means of metropolitan communication. When it is opened, we venture to think the public will be agreeably surprised to find that this underground railway is for nearly half its length not underground at all, and that where it does pass for various lengths beneath the streets, the tunnels, instead of being close, dark, damp, and ill-smelling passages, are wide, spacious, clean, and excellently well lit, reminding one, in fact, more of a well-kept street by night than a subterranean passage through the very heart of this dense metropolis. Whether the railway is one which will or will not remunerate the shareholders we venture no opinion, but both as one of the most novel and important works of the kind that have yet entered the city, and as one which, we think, must prove of the greatest convenience to the public, it deserves full notice in our columns. The present powers of the company only allow them to carry their line from Paddington to Finsbury-circus, a distance of four and a half miles, and of this length, as we have said, more than three miles, from Paddington to the Victoria-street Station, are in many parts quite complete, and in others nearly so, with perfect working junctions with the Great Western and Northern Railways. It commences at the Paddington Station, and is continued thence, in an almost direct line, towards the New-road, passing beneath the Edgware-road at right angles, and intersecting in the same manner Lisson-grove-road and Upper Baker-street, skirting along, beneath, and just outside the southern extremity of Regent's Park. Thence it passes under the houses at the eastern extremity of Park-crescent (some three or four houses in which have been by no means improved by its passage), continues beneath Tottenham-court-road into the New-road, and, passing close by Euston-square, turns at King's-cross to effect a junction with the up and down lines of the Great Northern Railway. From King's-cross a great part of the line is an open cutting, except for a length of about 600 yards beneath Bagnigge-wells-road and Coppice-row, where again, for the length we have said, a tunnel intervenes. From this to the Victoria-street Station it is nearly all a fair open cutting, and up to this point the line is nearly ready. From the Victoria-street Station, to be erected on the dirty waste ground, beyond Holborn, which is now dignified with the name of Victoria-street, the line is soon to have two branches, one intersecting Holborn-hill, or rather Skinner-street, and, continuing its course due south under the site of the old Fleet Prison, effecting a junction with the Chatham and Dover line, which is to cross the Thames at Blackfriars. The other and more important branch—in fact, the main line—is to be continued under the ground north of Smithfield and south of Charterhouse-square, and will pass beneath Barbican into Finsbury-circus. At this terminus it is intended, for the present at least, to stop; though there is not the least doubt but, as the advantages which this quick mode of communication will afford and the relief which it must give to the enormously overcrowded traffic of our streets become more generally known and appreciated, the shareholders themselves will find their own account in extending their branches to all the chief suburban districts of the metropolis. As it is, even completed to the Victoria-street Station, and communicating with the Chatham and Dover-bridge when finished, the facilities which it will offer to rapid travelling will be immense. A person starting from Brighton or Dover will be put down almost at his own door at Bayswater, instead of, as now, taking almost as much time to travel from London-bridge to

Bayswater as to perform a long journey by rail. In like manner, those coming from the North—from Edinburgh, Liverpool, or Manchester—will be able to book direct through to Dover or Southampton without the loss of a minute on their journey. It is not too much to say that for passengers pressed for time the two or three miles interval between the northern and southern stations of the metropolis are equal in actual delay to 200 or 300 miles distance on an unbroken journey. But though most of our readers know the fact of the delay, many of them may ask, why was it necessary to take the line underground? To this we can only reply, in the words of the company, that it was not necessary at all, but that as by so doing they could effect a very great saving in the cost of the undertaking, it was thought to be most desirable. Sewers were not to be interfered with, gas-pipes were to be regarded as sacred, water-pipes not to be touched, churches to be avoided, and houses to be left secure. With these trifling drawbacks, Mr. Fowler was at liberty to take his tunnel through a labyrinth of sewers and gas and water mains if he could. At every step vestries, gas and water companies, and the Board of Works had to be consulted, and but for the kind and liberal spirit in which the company was met, and the fair efforts which were everywhere made by these bodies to help them over their great difficulties, the railway could never have been made at all. Perhaps, however, a short rough outline of the portion of the line now nearly completed will give our readers the best idea of what these difficulties were. To the Victoria-street Station the line is nearly 3½ miles long, having stations at Paddington, Edgware-road, Baker-street, Portland-road, Euston-square, King's-cross, and Victoria-street. From west to east the average slope downwards of the whole line is about 1 in 300 feet, though after entering the city it again rises, but there is no steeper gradient throughout than 1 in 100. Its greatest curve is of 200 yards radius, and its greatest depth from the ground above to the rails not less than 54 feet, and there are not more than 1,200 yards of straight line throughout. The span of the arch of the tunnel is 28½ feet, its form is elliptical, and its height 17 feet, except in the parts where there is great superincumbent pressure, when the form of the arch is altered to give it greater strength and to take the crown to a height of 19 feet. The foundations of the tunnel go from four to five feet into the solid ground on each side below the rails, except in some few places, where the close vicinity of very heavy buildings rendered extra strength necessary, and here the tunnel has been driven like a shaft, and is a solid ring of massive brickwork above and below; in fact, in all parts of the tunnel itself the most zealous care has been taken to insure the structure being everywhere greatly in excess of the strength it actually requires. Thus, even the lightest parts of the tunnel have six rings of brickwork, though railway arches of seven feet greater span are never built with more than five. The outer sides of the arches also are filled in with solid beds of concrete, and the whole covered over with a layer of asphalte to keep it watertight. In fact, the tunnel has been formed on what engineers call the "cut and cover" principle; that is, the ground has been opened to the base of the intended tunnel, the tunnel built, covered with concrete, and asphalte and filled in again with earth and the roadway paved over as before. On this plan and working in

12ft. lengths the tunnel has actually been constructed at the rate of 72ft. a week, quicker than any work of the kind has ever yet been accomplished. It has not all, however, been knocked off at this rapid rate. Passing near churches and heavy buildings the tunnel has been regularly driven in four-feet lengths by skilled miners; and such portions, being conducted with the most zealous care, have advanced but slowly. At the western extremity, where the soil was a fine gravel, the works were at one time greatly impeded by the water, which in that district is abundant everywhere at about 14ft. from the surface. This it was useless to try pumping out, as the pumps brought up sand and gravel as well as water, and would, had the attempt been persevered in, have brought up the very foundation of the surrounding houses also. It was necessary at last to make regular drains into the low-level sewers in order to keep the works free. Through the gravel and through the London clay the labour has been very easy, but in parts where there was light, loose, sandy soil a great deal of difficulty was experienced. All the really difficult parts have now, however, been surmounted, and the tunnel built in the most solid manner. The lines of rails are laid through many lengths, each line being double gauge, intended for both the broad and narrow traffic. Where the junctions have been effected at Paddington and King's-cross it was necessary at the point where the switch rails joined to widen the tunnel, and at these parts make it, in fact, like the mouth of a trumpet. This was the most difficult operation ever attempted in either tunnelling or brickwork, but Mr. Fowler has surmounted all the obstacles in a masterly manner. What made the work at King's-cross more difficult than all was that at precisely the most difficult part of all the junctions the great Fleet Ditch sewer crossed it right through the crown of the tunnel arch. As the sewer, of course, could not be disturbed, the obstacle was met by carrying it across, slung, as it were, in a powerful cast-iron trough, and there it now hangs, peering through the brickwork like a colossal main, and with all beneath it as dry and sweet-smelling as if Fleet Ditch—that fullest and foulest of all London's sewers—were 100 miles away. It is but justice to Mr. Jay, the contractor, for all this end of the works from Euston-square to say that he has accomplished all the designs in the most massive and careful manner, and that, in fact, the works here are regarded among engineers as positive models of what contract labour should be. The stations along the line which we have already enumerated will, all but two, be open-air stations, and even those that are to be underground will be amply lit by daylight coming through apertures in the roof of the arch. But one of the greatest difficulties of all the many that had to be overcome consisted in constructing an engine that should be at once of great power and speed, capable of consuming its own smoke, and, above all, to give off no steam. Ordinary engines passing through tunnels so completely enclosed would in a very short time fill them with such a mixture of steam and smoke as would be very nearly suffocating, would make signals almost useless, and, in short, render the traffic not only disagreeable but dangerous. To avoid all these complicated evils Mr. Fowler has invented an engine which, while in the open air, works like a common locomotive, but, when in the tunnel, consumes its own smoke, or rather makes none, and by condensing its own steam gives off not a particle of vapour.

On Thursday last Mr. Wilkinson, the chairman of the company, with Mr. Alderman Rose, Mr. Pearson, and a number of gentlemen connected with the company, the City Corporation, and the Board of Works, were invited to Paddington to witness a trial of this engine. They were received by Mr. T. M. Johnson, the resident engineer, under whose personal superintendence all the works of the line have been effected. The engine (which was of the broad gauge) was duly examined and admired, though, truth to say, there is nothing particularly attractive in its external appearance. The whole party then mounted trucks provided for the occasion, and the engine took the train along the first tunnel to the open station in course of building in the Edgware-road. As long as the engine had building in the Edgware-road. As long as the engine had remained in the open air at Paddington it had fizzed and simmered like any other locomotive; but the instant it entered the tunnel it condensed its steam, and scarcely a mark of vapour was perceptible, while, from the flues into the smoke-box being damped, not the least smell of smoke was given off. As upon the success of this engine the successful working of the line depends, the result of the experiment was watched with a good deal of anxiety. It, however, was perfectly satisfactory, and not even the most distant lamps in the long vista down the sides of the tunnel were dimmed in the slightest degree—in short, nothing could have been more entirely complete and satisfactory. Having gone through the tunnel, the engine returned down the same track, and when in the centre of the tunnel, to show the difference, the engine was allowed to work upon the usual plan, and in a few instants the whole place was full of vapour, which was so thick that even when the visitors returned through for the third time the lamps were still scarcely visible.

The party were then invited to leave the train and to walk along the line as far as the Great Northern station, at King's-cross. In some parts of this route, where the tunnelling was still going on, the way was dark, sometimes difficult, and always dirty. Where the works were complete and the rails laid, the whole aspect of the tunnel lit with gas was light, warm, and cheerful. In at most three or four months more our readers will have an opportunity of judging of this wonderful work for themselves, and we think a single trip will suffice, even with the most fastidious, to upset all preconceived ideas as to the discomforts of subterranean railways in London. The through trains from east to west, and *vice versâ*, will, we believe, be arranged to start every 10 minutes, to accomplish the distance from end to end in 13 minutes, at a rate of fares which it is said will compete with those of the cheapest omnibuses. If this is so the line ought to prove remunerative to the shareholders, though whether it is so or not it must be an immense convenience to the public.

37

MORTIMER COLLINS, *THE VIVIAN ROMANCE* (NEW YORK: HARPER, 1870), PP. 31–32

Four-in-hand

"But put your best foot forward, or I fear
That we shall miss the mail."

ALACK, Mr. Tennyson, I have missed the mail for more years than I wish to reckon—missed the wholesome travel with the wind on your face, and the passage swift, but not too swift, through ever-varying scenery, and the gay interchange of welcome and humor, and the stoppages at roadside inns, and the cheery tankard, and all the possibility of adventures. Railways are excellent things, and I wonder how the world got on without them; but twenty or thirty miles on the best line in England thrills every nerve in my body, and makes my brain throb, and causes me to feel so grimy that I abhor myself. Then the hideous smell of the engine, the dust and ashes that attack your eyes and nostrils, the fustiness of the carriages, the maniacal scream of the steam-whistle, the grinding and groaning noises of the whole machine—are not these abominations?

The Poet Laureate has ventured to versify the visions of those who expect that the air will be the highway of the future. I hope it may.

Those who have never sailed in a balloon can not conceive how perfect a mode of motion it is. In calm weather the car seems stationary; the earth seems to be descending from it or approaching it, as the case may be. And then the exquisite silence of the mid-ether—sound of the world below reaching you with increasing faintness as you rise into the serene realm of air. And consider what a blessing the balloon system would be to those who don't travel and don't want to. What can be more irritating to a quiet man, leaning over his garden gate than to see restless people whirling by in all kinds of vehicles, raising clouds of dust and making an objectionable noise?

A landscape photograper once told me that he had never taken a picture in any part of England without discovering a clothes-line in it. Is there any spot between the four seas where you may not sometimes hear the scream of the locomotive? And, to make matters worse, the highways and by-ways are now infested by the agricultural engines.

38

M. E. BRADDON, 'ON THE TRACK', FROM *HENRY DUNBAR: THE STORY OF AN OUTCAST*, THREE VOLS. (LONDON: J. MAXWELL, 1866), III, PP. 187–201

The railway journey between Shorncliffe and Derby was by no means the most pleasant expedition for a cold spring night, with the darkness lying like a black shroud on the flat fields, and a melancholy wind howling over those desolate regions, across which all night-trains seem to wend their way. I think that flat and darksome land which we look upon out of the window of a railway carriage in the dead of the night must be a weird district, conjured into existence by the potent magic of an enchanter's wand,—a dreary desert transported out of Central Africa, to make the night-season hideous, and to vanish at cock-crow.

Mr. Carter never travelled without a railway rug and a pocket brandy-flask; and sustained by these inward and outward fortifications against the chilling airs of the long night, he established himself in a corner of the second-class carriage, and made the best of his situation.

Fortunately there was no position of hardship to which the detective was unaccustomed; indeed, to be rolled up in a railway rug in the corner of a second class carriage, was to be on a bed of down, as compared with some of his experiences. He was used to take his night's rest in brief instalments, and was snoring comfortably three minutes after the guard had banged-to the door of his carriage.

But he was not permitted to enjoy any prolonged rest. The door was banged open, and a stentorian voice bawled into his ear that hideous announcement which is so fatal to the repose of travellers, "Change here!" &c. &c. The journey from Shorncliffe to Derby seemed almost entirely to consist of "changing here;" and poor Mr. Carter felt as if he had passed a long night in being hustled out of one carriage into another, and off one line of railway on to another, with all those pauses on draughty platforms which are so refreshing to the worn-out traveller who works his weary way across country in the dead of the night.

309

At last, however, after a journey that seemed interminable by reason of those short naps, which always confuse the sleeper's estimate of time, the detective found himself at Derby, still in the dead of the night; for to the railway traveller it is all dead of night after dark. Here he applied immediately to the station-master, from whom he got another little note directed to him by Mr. Tibbles, and very much resembling that which he had received at Shorncliffe.

> *"All right up to Derby,"* wrote Sawney Tom. *"Gent in furred coat took a ticket through to Hull. Have took the same, and go on with him direct.— Yours to command,*
>
> *T. T."*

Mr. Carter lost no time after perusing this communication. He set to work at once to find out all about the means of following his assistant and the lame traveller.

Here he was told that he had a couple of hours to wait for the train that was to take him on to Normanton, and at Normanton he would have another hour to wait for the train that was to carry him to Hull.

"Ah, go it, do, while you're about it!" he exclaimed bitterly, when the railway official had given him this pleasing intelligence. "Couldn't you make it a little longer? When your end and aim lies in driving a man mad, the quicker you drive the better, *I* should think!"

All this was muttered in an undertone, not intended for the ear of the railway official. It was only a kind of safety-valve by which the detective let off his superfluous steam.

"Sawney's got the chance," he thought, as he paced up and down the platform; "Sawney's got the trump cards this time; and if he's knave enough to play them against me— But I don't think he'll do that; our profession's a conservative one, and a traitor would have an uncommon good chance of being kicked out of it. We should drop him a hint that, considering the state of his health, we should take it kindly of him if he would hook it; or send him some polite message of that kind; as the military swells do, when they want to get rid of a pal."

There were plenty of refreshments to be had at Derby, and Mr. Carter took a steaming cup of coffee and a formidable-looking pile of sandwiches before retiring to the waiting-room to take what he called "a stretch." He then engaged the services of a porter, who was to call him five minutes before the starting of the Normanton train, and was to receive an illegal douceur for that civility.

In the waiting-room there was a coke fire, very red and hollow, and a dim lamp. A lady, half buried in shawls, and surrounded by a little colony of small packages, was sitting close to the fire, and started out of her sleep to make nervous clutches at her parcels as the detective entered, being in that semi-conscious state in which the unprotected female is apt to mistake every traveller for a thief.

Mr. Carter made himself very comfortable on one of the sofas, and snored on peacefully until the porter came to rouse him, when he sprang up refreshed to continue his journey.

"Hull, Hull!" he muttered to himself. "His game will be to get off to Rotterdam, or Hamburg, or St. Petersburg, perhaps; any place that there's a vessel ready to take him. He'll get on board the first that sails. It's a good dodge, a very neat dodge; and if Sawney hadn't been at the station, Mr. Joseph Wilmot would have given us the slip as neatly as ever a man did yet. But if Mr. Thomas Tibbles is true, we shall nab him, and bring him home as quiet as ever any little boy was took to school by his mar and par. If Mr. Tibbles is true,—and as he don't know too much about the business, and don't know any thing about the extra reward, or the evidence that's turned up at Winchester,—I daresay Thomas Tibbles will be true. Human nature is a very noble thing," mused the detective; "but I've always remarked that the tighter you tie human nature down, the brighter it comes out."

It was morning, and the sun was shining, when the train that carried Mr. Carter steamed slowly into the great station at Hull—it was morning, and the sun was shining, and the birds singing, and in the fields about the smoky town there were herds of sweet-breathing cattle sniffing the fresh spring air, and labourers plodding to their work, and loaded wains of odorous hay and dewy garden-stuff were lumbering along the quiet country roads, and the new-born day had altogether the innocent look appropriate to its tender youth,—when the detective stepped out on the platform, calm, self-contained, and resolute, as brisk and business-like in his manner as any traveller in that train, and with no distinctive stamp upon him, however slight, that marked him as the hunter of a murderer.

He looked sharply up and down the platform. No, Mr. Tibbles had not betrayed him. That gentleman was standing on the platform, watching the passengers step out of the carriages, and looking more turnip-faced than usual in the early sunlight. He was chewing nothing with more than ordinary energy; and Mr. Carter, who was very familiar with the idiosyncrasies of his assistant, knew from that sign that things had gone amiss.

"Well," he said, tapping Sawney Tom on the shoulder, "he's given you the slip? Out with it; I can see by your face that he has."

"Well, he have then," answered Mr. Tibbles, in an injured tone; "but if he have, you needn't glare at me like that, for it ain't no fault of mine. If you ever follered a lame eel—and a lame eel as makes no more of it's lameness than if lameness was a advantage—you'd know what it is to foller that chap in the furred coat."

The detective hooked his arm through that of his assistant, and led Mr. Tibbles out of the station by a door which opened on a desolate region at the back of that building.

"Now then," said Mr. Carter, "tell me all about it, and look sharp."

"Well, I was waitin' in the Shorncliffe ticket-offis, and about five minutes after two in comes the gent as large as life, and I sees him take his ticket, and I hears him say Derby, on which I waits till he's out of the offis, and I takes my own ticket, same place. Down we comes here with more changes and botheration than ever was; and every time we changes carriages, which we don't seem to do much else the whole time, I spots my gentleman, limpin' awful, and lookin' about him suspicious-like, to see if he was watched. And, of course, he weren't watched—oh, no; nothin' like it. Of all the innercent young men as ever was exposed to the temptations of this wicked world, there never was sech a young innercent as that lawyer's clerk, a carryin' a blue bag, and a tellin' a promiskruous acquaintance, loud enough for the gent in the fur coat to hear, that he'd been telegraphed for by his master, which was down beyond Hull, on electioneerin' business; and a cussin' of his master promiskruous to the same acquaintance for telegraphin' for him to go by sech a train. Well, we come to Derby, and the furry gent, he takes a ticket on to Hull; and we come to Normanton, and the furry gent limps about Normanton station, and I sees him comfortable in his carriage; and we comes to Hull, and I sees him get out on the platform, and I sees him into a fly, and I hears him give the order, 'Victorier Hotel,' which by this time it's nigh upon ten o'clock, and dark and windy. Well, I gets up behind the fly, and rides a bit, and walks a bit, keepin' the fly in sight until we comes to the Victorier; and there stoops down behind, and watches my gent hobble into the hotel, in awful pain with that lame leg of his, judgin' the faces he makes; and he walks into the coffee-room, and I makes bold to foller him; but there never was sech a young innercent as me, and I sees my party sittin' warmin' his poor lame leg, and with a carpet-bag, and railway rug, and sechlike on the table beside him; and presently he gets up, hobblin' worse than ever, and goes outside, and I hears him makin' inquiries about the best way of gettin' on to Edinborough by train; and I sat quiet, not more than three minutes at most, becos', you see, I didn't want to *look like* follerin' him; and in three minutes' time, out I goes, makin' as sure to find him in the bar as I make sure of your bein' close beside me at this moment; but when I went outside into the hall, and bar, and sechlike, there wasn't a mortal vestige of that man to be seen; but the waiter, he tells me, as dignified and cool as yer please, that the lame gentleman has gone out by the door lookin' towards the water, and has only gone to have a look at the place and get a few cigars, and will be back in ten minutes to a chop which is bein' cooked for him. Well, I cuts out by the same door, thinkin' my lame friend can't be very far; but when I gets out on to the quay-side, there ain't a vestige of him; and though I cut about here, there, and every where, lookin' for him, until I'd nearly walked my legs off in less than half an hour's time, I didn't see a sign of him, and all I could do was to go back to the Victorier, and see if he'd gone back before me.

"Well, there was his carpet-bag and his railway rug just as he'd left 'em, and there was a little table near the fire all laid out snug and comfortable ready for him; but there was no more vestige of hisself than there was in the streets where I'd been lookin' for him; and so I went out again, with the prespiration streamin' down my face, and I walked that blessed town till over one o'clock this mornin', lookin' right and left, and inquirin' at every place where such a gent was likely to try and hide hisself, and playin' up Mag's divarsions, which, if it was divarsions to Mag, was oncommon hard work to me; and then I went back to the Victorier, and got a night's lodgin'; and the first thing this mornin' I was on my blessed legs again, and down at the quay inquirin' about vessels, and there's nothin' likely to sail afore to-night, and the vessel as is expected to sail to-night is bound for Copenhagen, and don't carry passengers; but from the looks of her captain,

I should say she'd carry any think, even to a churchyard full of corpuses, if she was paid to do it."

"Humph! a sailing vessel bound for Copenhagen; and the captain's a villanous-looking fellow, you say?" said the detective, in a thoughtful tone.

"He's about the villanousest I ever set eyes on," answered Mr. Tibbles.

"Well, Sawney, it's a bad job, certainly; but I've no doubt you've done your best."

"Yes, I have done my best," the assistant answered, rather indignantly; "and considerin' the deal of confidence you honoured me with about this here cove, I don't see as I could have done hany think more."

"Then the best thing you can do is to keep watch here for the starting of the up-trains, while I go and keep my eye upon the station at the other side of the water," said Mr. Carter. "This journey to Hull may have been just a dodge to throw us off the scent, and our man may try and double upon us by going back to London. You'll keep all safe here, Sawney, while I go to the other side of the compass."

Mr. Carter engaged a fly, and made his way to a pier at the end of the town, whence a boat took him across the Humber to a station on the Lincolnshire side of the river.

Here he ascertained all particulars about the starting of the trains for London, and here he kept watch while two or three trains started. Then, as there was an interval of some hours before the starting of another, he recrossed the water, and set to work to look for his man.

First he loitered about the quays a little, taking stock of the idle vessels, the big steamers that went to London, Antwerp, Rotterdam, and Hamburg—the little steamers that went short voyages up or down the river, and carried troops of Sunday idlers to breezy little villages beside the sea. He found out all about these boats, their destination, and the hours and days on which they were to start, and made himself more familiar with the water-traffic of the place in half an hour than another man could have done in a day. He also made acquaintance with the vessel that was to sail for Copenhagen—a black sulky-looking boat, christened very appropriately the Crow, with a black sulky-looking captain, who was lying on a heap of tarpauling on the deck, smoking a pipe in his sleep. Mr. Carter stood looking over the quay and contemplating this man for some moments with a thoughtful stare.

"He looks a bad 'un," the detective muttered as he walked away; "Sawney was right enough there."

39

M. E. BRADDON, *THE LOVELS OF ARDEN* (LEIPZIG: B. TAUCHNITZ, 1871), PP. 92–97

She had been alone like this about half an hour, when the crackling of the brambles near her warned her of an approaching footstep. She looked up, and saw a stranger approaching her through the sunlight and shadows of the wood—a tall man, in a loose gray overcoat.

A stranger? No. As he came nearer to her, the face seemed very familiar; and yet in that first moment she could not imagine where she had seen him. A little nearer, and she remembered all at once. This was her companion of the long railway journey from London to Holborough. She blushed at the recollection, not altogether displeased to see him again, and yet remembering bitterly that cruel mistake she had made about Arden Court. She might be able to explain her error now, if he should recognise her and stop to speak; but that was scarcely likely. He had forgotten her utterly, no doubt, by this time.

She went on with her sketching—a trailing spray of Irish ivy, winding away and losing itself in a confusion of bramble and fern, every leaf sharply defined by the light pencil-touches, with loving pre-Raphaelite care—she went on, trying to think that it was not the slightest consequence to her whether this man remembered their brief acquaintance of the railway-carriage. And yet she would have been wounded, ever so little, if he had forgotten her. She knew so few people, that this accidental acquaintance seemed almost a friend. He had known her brother, too; and there had been something in his manner that implied an interest in her fate.

She bent a little lower over the sketch-book, doing her uttermost not to be seen, perhaps all the more because she really did wish for the opportunity of explaining that mistake about Arden Court. Her face was almost hidden under the coquettish gray hat, as she bent over her drawing; but the gentleman came on towards her with evident purpose. It was only to make an inquiry, however.

"I am looking for a picnic party," he said. "I discovered the *débris* of a luncheon yonder, but no human creature visible. Perhaps you can kindly tell me where the strayed revellers are to be found; you are one of them, perhaps?"

Clarissa looked up at him, blushing furiously, and very much ashamed of herself for the weakness, and then went on with her drawing in a nervous way, as she answered him,

"Yes, I am with Lady Laura Armstrong's party; but I really cannot tell you where to look for them all. They are roaming about in every direction, I believe."

"Good gracious me!" cried the gentleman, coming a good deal nearer—stepping hastily across the streamlet, in fact, which had divided him from Clarissa hitherto. "Have I really the pleasure of speaking to Miss Lovel? This is indeed a surprise. I scarcely expected ever to see you again."

"Nor I to see you," Clarissa answered, recovering herself a little by this time, and speaking with her accustomed frankness. "And I have been very anxious to see you again."

"Indeed!" cried the gentleman eagerly.

"In order to explain a mistake I made that night in the railway-carriage, in speaking of Arden Court. I talked of the place as if it had still belonged to papa; I did not know that he had sold it, and fancied I was going home there. It was only when I saw my uncle that I learnt the truth. You must have thought it very strange."

"I was just a little mystified, I confess, for I had dined at the Court with Mr. Granger."

"Papa had sold the dear old place, and, disliking the idea of writing such unpleasant news, had told me nothing about the sale. It was not wise, of course; but he felt the loss of Arden so keenly, I can scarcely wonder that he could not bring himself to write about it."

"It would have been better to have spared you, though," the unknown answered gravely. "I daresay you were as fond of the old home as ever your father could have been?"

"I don't think it would be possible for any one to love Arden better than I. But then, of course, a man is always prouder than a woman—"

"I am not so sure of that," the stranger muttered parenthetically.

"—And papa felt the degradation involved in the loss."

"I won't admit of any degradation in the case. A gentleman is none the less a gentleman for having spent his fortune rather recklessly, and the old blood is no less pure without the old acres. If your father were a wise man, he might be happier now than he has ever been. The loss of a great estate is the loss of a bundle of cares."

"I daresay that is very good philosophy," Clarissa answered, smiling, beguiled from painful thoughts by the lightness of his tone; "but I doubt if it applies to all cases—not to papa's, certainly."

"You were sketching, I see, when I interrupted you. I remember you told me that night of your fondness for art. May I see what you were doing?"

"It is hardly worth showing you. I was only amusing myself, sketching at random—that ivy straggling along there, or anything that caught my eye."

"But that sort of thing indicates so much. I see you have a masterly touch for so young an artist. I won't say anything hackneyed about so fair a one; for women are showing us nowadays that there are no regions of art closed against them. Well, it is a divine amusement, and a glorious profession."

There was a little pause after this, during which Clarissa looked at her watch, and finding it nearly five o'clock, began to put up her pencils and drawing-book.

"I did not think that you knew Lady Laura Armstrong," she said; and then blushed for the speech, remembering that, as she knew absolutely nothing about himself or his belongings, the circumstance of her ignorance on this one point was by no means surprising.

"No; nor did I expect to meet you here," replied the gentleman. "And yet I might almost have done so, knowing that you lived at Arden. But, you see, it is so long since we met, and I—"

"Had naturally forgotten me."

"No, I had not forgotten you, Miss Lovel, nor would it have been natural for me to forget you. I am very glad to meet you again under such agreeable auspices. You are going to stay at the Castle a long time, I hope. I am booked for an indefinite visit."

"O no, I don't suppose I shall stay very long. Lady Laura is extremely kind; but this is my first visit, and she must have many friends who have a greater claim upon her hospitality."

"Hale Castle is a large place, and I am sure Lady Laura has always room for agreeable guests."

"She is very, very kind. You have known her a long time, perhaps?"

"Yes, I have been intimate with the Challoners ever since I was a boy. Lady Laura was always charming; but I think her marriage with Fred Armstrong—who worships the ground she walks on—and the possession of Hale Castle have made her absolutely perfect."

"And you know her sister Lady Geraldine, of course?"

"O yes, I know Geraldine."

"Do you know Mr. Fairfax, the gentleman to whom she is engaged?"

"Well, yes; I am supposed to have some knowledge of that individual."

Something in his smile, and a certain significance in his tone, let in a sudden light upon Clarissa's mind.

"I am afraid I am asking very foolish questions," she said. "You are Mr. Fairfax?"

"Yes, I am George Fairfax. I forgot that I had omitted to tell you my name that night."

"And I had no idea that I was speaking to Mr. Fairfax. You were not expected till quite late this evening."

"No; but I found my business in London easier to manage than I had supposed it would be; so, as in duty bound, I came down here directly I found myself free. When I arrived at the Castle, I was told of this picnic, and rode off at once to join the party."

"And I am keeping you here, when you ought to be looking for your friends."

"There is no hurry. I have done my duty, and am here; that is the grand point. Shall we go and look for them together?"

"If you like. I daresay we shall be returning to the Castle very soon."

They sauntered slowly away, in and out among the trees, towards a grassy glade, where there was more open space for walking, and where the afternoon sun shone warmly on the smooth turf.

40

GUSTAVE DORÉ, THE WORKMEN'S TRAIN, LUDGATE HILL, AND OVER THE CITY BY RAILWAY. ILLUSTRATIONS ORIGINALLY PRINTED IN DORÉ AND BLANCHARD JERROLD, *LONDON: A PILGRIMAGE*. (LONDON: GRANT, 1872)

Figure 40.1 Gustave Doré

41

LADY MARGARET MAJENDIE, 'A RAILWAY JOURNEY', *BLACKWOOD'S MAGAZINE* 121 (APRIL 1877), PP. 497–503

A CLOSE cab laden with luggage drove up to Euston Station in time for the 7.30 A.M. train for the north. While the porters surrounded the boxes, the occupants of the cab passed straight through on to the platform, looking rather nervously about them. They were two—a very pretty girl in a most fascinating travelling costume of blue serge and fur, and an elderly woman, who, from her appearance, might have been her nurse.

"Sit here, and don't move, Miss Edith, while I take your ticket: now, mind you don't stir;" and she deposited her on a bench.

"Are you the young lady as has ordered a through carriage reserved?" asked a guard, with official abruptness.

"Yes."

"Then come along of me, miss."

"No, no; I must wait," and Edith, who was quite unused to travelling, grasped her bag and did not move. The guard looked astonished, but only shrugged his shoulders and walked off. Presently he came back.

"You'll be late, miss," he said, not encouragingly. "Train 'ill be off in another minute." Edith looked at him in despair. Should she leave her post? Would Jenkins never come back? A loud aggressive bell began to ring. Edith started up; she seized all the things Jenkins had put under her charge—rugs, carpet-bag, umbrella-case, loose shawl, and provision-basket—and was trying to stagger away under the load, when Jenkins came back very hot and flurried, seized half the packages, and hurried her to the train. The guard unlocked the special carriage, and put her in.

"No hurry, ma'am," he said; "four minutes still."

"I don't at all like it, now it has come to the point, Jenkins," said Edith, leaning out of the window.

"Nor I, miss; and how your mamma could let you go all alone like this, passes me; but I have spoken to the guard and written to the station-master, and you've a good bit to eat, and not a blessed soul to get into the carriage from end to end; so don't be afraid, my dear, and I make no doubt that your dear uncle will meet you at the other end."

"I have no doubt that one of my uncles will—I hope Uncle John, as I have never seen Uncle George."

"Everything you want, miss?" said an extra porter. "I have put in all the rugs and a hot-water-tin, and the luggage is all right in the van just behind."

"All right, all right!" said Mrs Jenkins.

"Thank you, ma'am," said the porter, pocketing a shining half-crown.

A gentleman suddenly came running on to the platform; the train was just about to start. "Here, porter, take my portmanteau; quick—smoking carriage!"

"All full, sir! quick, sir, please!"

"It's Mr George!" cried Jenkins, suddenly. Edith started forward. "Oh!"

The gentleman caught sight of Jenkins. "Here, guard, guard! put me in here!"

"Can't, sir—special."

"Quick; let me in! it's—it's my niece!"

The train began to move.

"Confound you, be quick!"

The door was opened just in time, and Edith, as excited as Mr George, seized him with both hands by the coat-sleeve, and pulled him in with all her might into the carriage. They were off.

Mr George sat down opposite to Edith with a sigh of relief.

"I am so glad to see you, Uncle George," said Edith, timidly; "for though I am generally bold enough, I was rather afraid of this long journey."

"I will take care of you," said the uncle. "I am very glad to make your acquaintance, my dear." The "my dear" sounded a little strained, as though it were not a common expression on Uncle George's lips, and Edith looked up at him. She had not expected her uncle to be so young in appearance; but she had often heard her mother say that he was the youngest-looking man of his age she had ever known; and now she quite agreed,—for though she knew him to be really about fifty-eight years of age, he might from his appearance be taken for five-and-twenty, or even less. He was remarkably good-looking—more so than she had expected—and his eyes looked very young, and frank, and blue. There was a twinkle in them also; she was sure that he was fond of fun. Edith felt quite fond of her uncle; she was not one bit afraid of him—his face was so open, and good, and kindly.

"Now we must make ourselves comfortable," said Uncle George, and he proceeded to set to work. He put the rugs and baskets into the nets, he pushed the carpet-bag and portmanteau under the seat, took off his hat, put on a very becoming Turkish fez, extracted newspapers from his pocket, spread a shawl over Edith's knees, and then wriggled himself comfortably into a corner seat.

"How well old Jenkins wears!" he said. "She looks like a young dairy-maid."

"Oh!" said Edith, a little shocked at his irreverence.

"I remember how she used to feed me with dried fruit and macaroons out of the store-room."

"Really! surely she is not old enough for that?"

"Oh, ah! I forget her age; but the fact was, I wasn't of course a boy."

"Of course not. Why, I think mamma said that you and Jenkins were born the same day—or was she the eldest?"

"Oh, I was the eldest."

"No, you were not; I remember she was three weeks older than you, and it was because she was your foster-sister that she always was so fond of you. Indeed, mamma said that she wanted to leave her to go to you and Aunt Maria when your eldest children were born, even out to India."

"My eldest children! what do you mean? Oh! by the by, yes; they are dead."

"Dead! my cousin George dead?"

"Yes, yes, my dear."

"Poor little Addie? was it true that George never got over her loss?"

"Don't!" said Uncle George, abruptly; and he held up a newspaper upside down.

Edith touched his arm very gently.

"I am so sorry, Uncle George," she said, sweetly. "If I had known that you had lost them both, I would not have said anything; please forgive me. And poor Aunt Maria, too! Oh, I beg your pardon."

Uncle George threw down his paper and looked smilingly at her.

"Does your mamma ever speak of me?"

"Constantly, perpetually;" said Edith, her voice still a little choked.

"And what does she say of me?"

"She says that you are the dearest, kindest, warmest-hearted, most sweet-dispositioned old gentleman existing; she says you have been a gallant officer, and a loyal, true-hearted soldier." Edith's eyes kindled. "And I have heard how you distinguished yourself in India, and I—I am very glad to see you, Uncle George."

"Yes, yes, he is all that," said he, with enthusiasm.

"What? who?" asked Edith, confused.

"My father—I—I—I mean my son."

"Poor George! he was a most distinguished soldier also. I wish I had known him. No, Uncle George, I won't speak so—I do not want to pain you."

"I like to hear all you tell me about him, my dear."

"I have only heard how good a soldier he was, and that he was so handsome and so good."

"And had he faults and defects?"

Edith looked surprised.

"I used to hear that he was conceited."

"No, no," said Uncle George, hastily; "he never was that. He was proud, I grant—perhaps too proud—but never conceited."

"Poor George!" sighed Edith; "I had so looked forward to knowing him."

"Had you really?"

"Yes; I never had a companion of my own age. Do tell me, shall I like my cousins at Hatton?"

"I think so, some of them: do you mean Uncle John's daughters, or his step-children?"

"Both."

"I think you will like Mary, tolerate Susan, abhor Agatha, admire Jane, and adore Alice."

"Alice is the adorable one, is she?" said Edith, laughing; "and is she the one they say is so pretty?"

"Oh no; poor Alice is deformed, and can never leave the sofa; but she has the sweetness of an angel and the courage of a martyr: she is not in the least pretty."

"Oh, what a trial! always on the sofa!"

"What a sweet little thing this is!" thought Uncle George, but he said nothing.

"How comes it that you know none of your cousins?" said he, suddenly.

"Why do you want me to tell you what you know so much better than I do, Uncle George?"

"Yes, yes, of course; but naturally I want to know your side of the story. Have you never been at Hatton?"

"Never; and I thought it so very kind of you to induce Uncle John to persuade mamma to let me go."

"Yes; I thought, you know, that a few companions of your own age would do you good. How old are you?"

"Did you not get mamma's letter, in which she told you that I was to be eighteen to-morrow?"

"No; it must have been late. I never heard of it."

"How very unfortunate! Then no one will know I am coming. She asked you to tell Uncle John about the trains and things."

"Oh, ah! *that* letter! oh, of course, that is all right. I don't—I—I sometimes don't read letters through."

Edith laughed.

"I will tell you one version of my story. Mamma being papa's widow, and papa having been the eldest son, had to leave Hatton when I was born and turned out to be a stupid little girl; and she went abroad because she was so delicate, and became a Roman Catholic."

"Holloa!"

"What is it, Uncle George?"

"You are not one, I hope?"

Edith looked rather indignant. "It is *very* odd of you to say that," she said, "when you know as well as I do all that you did about it; indeed I shall never forget your kindness. I was very unhappy when mamma wanted me to change; and Uncle John's letters and all Aunt Maria wrote made it worse than ever, only your letters made all smooth; and mamma was so much touched by the one you wrote to her about papa's trust in her, and my not being hers only, and all that, that, indeed, I have always loved you—you have seemed to me like my own dear father."

"I am very glad, my dear child, and I hope that in future you will be guided by my advice."

"I hope I shall see a great deal of you, Uncle George, for I know how fond I shall be of you, for my mother loves you dearly."

"It is very kind of her."

"And do you know, since we came to live in England, I have never paid a single visit, or been for one week away from home. Oh, it is such fun going to Hatton! Do my cousins ride?"

"Yes, a great deal; are you fond of it?"

"I love it; there is nothing in the world to me like a good gallop. Ah, it was the greatest trial of all my life when Queen Mab was sold!"

"When was that?"

"Mamma made me give up riding, or rather I gave it up of myself, because it made her so nervous."

"What else do you care for?—dancing?"

"Oh, I love it; but I have never been to a ball in my life."

"There are to be two at Hatton next week, and you must promise me the first valse at each."

"Do *you* valse?"

"Oh yes. You see I am not such an old fogy as you expected."

"No; nobody would believe you to be fifty-eight, except for one thing."

"What is that?"

But Edith blushed and would not answer.

"You need not mind, child—I never was at all sensitive; and alas! now my memory is not what it was."

"That's it," said Edith, eagerly; "only I did not like to say it. Here we are at a station."

It was now ten o'clock; Uncle George bought the 'Times' and 'Daily News,' and they both began to read. About twelve o'clock the pangs of hunger began to assail Edith, and she exclaimed –

"Uncle George, it is only twelve o'clock, and I must eat to live."

"I have been existing merely for the last hour with the greatest difficulty, but I have got nothing wherewith to refresh exhausted nature; I calculated on a bun at Carlisle."

"Hours hence! No, I am amply provided. Will you have beef or chicken sandwiches, or cold partridge, or what?"

They made a very good lunch, and uncle and niece grew hourly better acquainted.

"I believe we ought to look out of the window," said he, presently. "My father said that the country about here was quite beautiful."

"That must have been before the days of railways," said Edith, gravely. "Those coaching days must have been quite delightful."

"They were."

"Mamma has told me about that extraordinary adventure you and papa had on the Aberdeen coach."

"It was extraordinary."

"Papa caught the branch of a tree, did he not?"

"Yes; and do you remember what I did?"

"You jumped out just as the coach upset, and sat on all the horses' heads."

"And a most uneasy seat it must have been; and did Uncle Arthur—I mean your papa—remain suspended in mid-air?"

"No, he swung into the tree. I have often heard of your climbing exploits, and that when you were young you could climb any tree."

"I have not lost the power," said Uncle George, stretching himself. "Holloa!"

"What is the matter?" said Edith, startled.

"Nothing—nothing—sit still!"

But she followed the direction of his eyes. The train (a very long one), was going round a sharp curve, they were in one of the last carriages, and to her horror and terror, she saw, about a hundred yards in front of the train, a whole herd of cows on and off the line—two or three frantically galloping.

All heads were stretched out of the windows, clamouring tongues and even cries resounded from the other carriages, but neither Edith nor George uttered a sound, only she put back her hand and caught his; he seized it very tightly in the suspense, knowing well that a terrible accident might be impending. It was hardly a second, but it seemed a lifetime. The frantic cattle rushed off the line in a body, all but one unfortunate beast. The guards put on the very heaviest brakes, but the impetus was so great that the slackening was hardly perceptible. It may have been fortunate that it was so, for instead of upsetting the train, the cow was tossed off the line utterly destroyed, and the engine rushed on in safety.

George and Edith sat down opposite to each other; both were very pale.

"Thank God!" said Edith, and she covered her face with one hand. George did not speak, but he took off his cap and looked out of the window for one minute.

"Now I shall give you some sherry," he said, suddenly. "You are the pluckiest little brick I ever came across. Any other girl would have screamed."

"I never scream," said Edith, indignantly; "and I don't want any sherry."

"I am your uncle, and I say you are to have some—drink it up."

"I hate wine," she said, giving back the flask.

"There, good child, to do as you are told."

At the next station a perfect crowd of passengers was waiting for the up-train. A great *fête* was going on in the next town for the visit of some royal personage, and the train was filled to overflowing. Presently the civil guard came up to the special carriage and said most deprecatingly that there was one gentleman, who couldn't find a place anywhere; and as he was only going to the next station, would they admit him just for that twenty minutes? Uncle George consented very discontentedly, and very grudgingly moved his long legs to admit of the entry of a very stout old gentleman, who sat heavily down, and received into his ample lap a perfect pile of packages and baskets, and a brace of hares, and a rabbit tied by the legs which he had dexterously suspended by a string round his neck.

"Not worth while, indeed, my dear madam," he said, as Edith began to make room for his things. "Only twenty minutes—no inconvenience, I assure you."

The heavily-weighted train moved off. The old gentleman now began a series of playful bows which made the hares and rabbits dance up and down.

"It really was too good of you to admit an old fogy like me," he said, blandly; "for of course with half an eye I can see the tender situation."

A deep growl from Uncle George. He gave a little start and went on to himself—"Sweet young couple! just wedded, eh?"

Edith felt half choked with laughter, but she managed to say convulsively—"Will you give me my book, Uncle George?"

The old gentleman started, cocked his head as a blackbird does when he perceives a very fat worm, and muttered—

"Impossible!"

Edith and George were wrapped in their respective novels. The old gentleman fidgeted, sighed, and arranged his features into a most sanctimonious expression. There was dead silence till he reached his station, where he descended. The departure bell was ringing, when his head suddenly reappeared at the window, the hares and rabbit streaming wildly from the back of his neck.

"My children," he said, "take my advice—go back to your friends. This—" A little shriek ended his discourse; the train was going on; and he, being borne along on the step involuntarily, two stout porters rushed to the rescue and lifted him off. Edith and George laughed till the tears ran down their cheeks.

"I could eat again, with a little persuasion," said George, presently.

"Why, what o'clock is it?"

"Just five, and we shall not get in till eight-thirty. Remember that we had our luncheon at twelve."

"Very well." And they proceeded to eat.

The sun had gone down, and the whole sky was gorgeous with gold and crimson light, on which great black clouds floated prophetically.

"What a grand sky!" said Edith.

"Magnificent! Nowhere does one see such clouds as in England."

"Were you very fond of India?"

"Of course I am; my work lies there, my hopes, my future."

Edith looked astonished. "I should have thought," she said, "that *now* you would have been content to rest at home; but I admire you for loving work. Shall you go out again?"

"That depends very much upon circumstances. It would be a great grief to me to give up my profession."

"It is very odd, but I certainly thought that mamma told me you had given up your profession."

"She was mistaken," said Uncle George, shortly.

"I have often longed to go to India," cried Edith.

"Have you?" said George, very eagerly.

"Oh yes, beyond anything; life there gives everybody a chance. I mean, heroic men and great characters are formed in India, and men have great responsibilities and development for quite a different class of most desirable qualities there."

"That is quite true; and you are just the sort of woman to help a man to do anything."

"I am so glad you think so, Uncle George," she said, laughing and blushing.

At seven o'clock they reached a very large station, where the train had half an hour to wait. They got a cup of tea, and then, both being rather cold, they began to walk vigorously up and down to the very end of the terminus. It was quite dark at the far end, and they stood side by side, looking up into the mouth of the great station with its mighty arch. Trains rushed past, or heavily moved away with a harsh, discordant whistle. Great red lamps loomed out of the darkness like dragon's eyes. George drew Edith hastily on one side that she might not be struck by the chain of a huge cart-horse which passed close by them, on its way to bring up a coal-truck. It was very cold, and they stamped up and down, and George enjoyed a fragrant cigar.

"Take your seats!" shouted the porter. "Take your seats!" And they resumed their places.

"Them's a bride and bridegroom," said a stout country-woman to a friend; and the loud guttural "Lor!" with which the news was received reached the ears of the travellers.

A blazing lamp was in the carriage, and under its yellow light Edith tried to read.

"Don't read, Edith," said the young uncle, suddenly. "Talk instead."

She shut up her book.

"To tell you the truth, Uncle George," she said, "we are getting so near that I am beginning to feel ridiculously nervous."

He looked at his watch, and suddenly started.

"So late," he said. "We shall be there in ten minutes."

"Oh!"

"And the fact is," he began, restlessly fidgeting; "the fact is—a—a—I have got a confession to make to you."

"To me! oh, Uncle George!"

"D—n Uncle George!"

Edith looked startled beyond measure.

"The fact is, Edith, I am not my father."

"What do you mean?"

"I mean I am my son."

"But he is dead."

"No, no; only, what was a fellow to say when you pressed me so hard? I am your cousin George!"

"Oh!"

"And we have been such friends, you won't be angry? Are you vexed, Edith?" and he took both her hands.

"No; only astonished. I think—on the whole, I am rather—glad."

"That's all right; for, do you know, Edith, I seem to have known you for years! You have shown to-day every good quality a woman can possibly possess."

"Don't spoil me by such sayings."

"And Edith, dear Edith, do you know—confound it! here we are!—only this, I should like to go on travelling with you, like this, for ever and ever—and—"

Hatton! Hatton! tickets, please. Hatton!

"Here, Jones! take Miss Edith's bag. Is the carriage up?"

"Yes, sir."

"And a cart? there is a heap of luggage."

"All right, sir."

"Come along, Edith! here we are, and my father is in the carriage."

42

COVER ILLUSTRATION OF H. L. WILLIAMS'S ADAPTATION OF DION BOUCICAULT'S PLAY *AFTER DARK* (1880s), DEPICTING RAILWAY RESCUE SCENE IN THE LONDON UNDERGROUND/SUBTERRANEAN RAILWAY

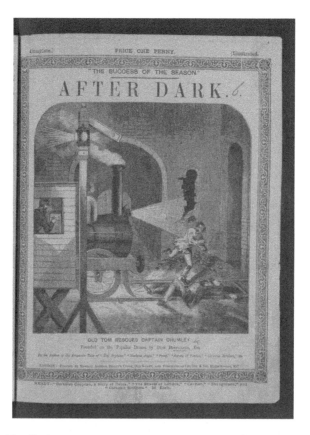

Figure 42.1 After Dark

43

DION BOUCICAULT, SCENE II FROM *AFTER DARK: A DRAMA OF LONDON LIFE IN 1868, IN FOUR ACTS.* (NEW YORK: DEWITT, N.D.) PP. 36–37

Scene II.—*Cellar in 1st grooves. Gas down.*

Enter, L., TOM

TOM. Caged, trapped by the villains! Oh, Gordon Chumley, what have they done with him, since they dragged me here. Where am I? Oh, that fiend Knatchbull. After I had dogged him to this place, and then to lose him at the hour of triumph. Is there no means of escape from this place? (*whistle, sound of train approaching,* R.) What's that? (*run train* R. *to* L. *and off over platform; sees air-hole in flat*) I may be able to climb up and look out. (*looks out of hole*) It looks like a long dark street, with green and red lights in the distance. Oh, I know it, I know it now. It is the underground railway. (*comes down from steps. Light shown* L. 2 E.) What's that? a light in the adjoining cellar. A door! some one is in the next cellar. Surely that is Dicey's voice. I may hear what he says. Ah! a keyhole! Morris and Knatchbull. What are they carrying between them? The body of a man! Oh, it is Gordon—Gordon Chumley. They have murdered him and have brought him here to bury him. What is it they are saying? "Is the hole large enough?" And Morris says: "Yes." Knatchbull speaks: "Is the line clear?" I hear footsteps returning. Ah, what do they say? "Brick up the hole again!" Ah! they have thrown the insensible man into some hole or blind well! (*light removed*) I must escape from this. What's this under my hand? a bar! a fastening to the door. (*seizes bar*) Come on, come on! (*through his set teeth—breaks bar away*) Ah! With this I can make the hole larger and escape. To work, Frank Dalton, to work! I must first find a barrel, or something to stand on to work. Here, here!

[*Exit* L., *groping with bar before him.*

Scene changes to

Scene III.—*Discover* TOM *at hole* L. *in flat, working with bar to widen it;* CHUMLEY *on track* L. C.

TOM. I have got the bricks out—nearly room enough to squeeze through. (*suddenly*) What's that lying on the line! it does not move, yet it looks like a man. Ah, it is Gordon Chumley! (*bell rings faintly, then loudly, whistle, same;*

the sound of train approaching begins and is continued till end. Get train ready, R. U. E. *Music to correspond*) I must be free now. Gordon, I am here, I am here! Oh, God, they have placed him there to die. Gordon, Gordon! I will save you. Oh, the train! the coming train! Good heart, courage, Gordon! (*jumps down, falls upon* CHUMLEY *and rolls with him upon stage, front, clear*) You are saved. (*run train on.*)

QUICK CURTAIN.

Part 7

NETHERWORLDS AND NOSTALGIA

Late Victorian and Edwardian railway cultures

44

GEORGE GISSING, '10 SATURNALIA!', IN *THE NETHER WORLD* (LONDON: SMITH, ELDER, & CO., 1890), PP. 105–113

At Holborn Viaduct there was a perpetual rush of people for the trains to the 'Paliss.' As soon as a train was full, off it went, and another long string of empty carriages drew up in its place. No distinction between 'classes' to-day; get in where you like, where you can. Positively, Pennyloaf found herself seated in a first-class carriage; she would have been awe-struck, but that Bob flung himself back on the cushions with such an easy air, and nodded laughingly at her. Among their companions was a youth with a concertina; as soon as the train moved he burst into melody. It was the natural invitation to song, and all joined in the latest ditties learnt at the music-hall. Away they sped, over the roofs of South London, about them the universal glare of sunlight, the carriage dense with tobacco-smoke. Ho for the bottle of muddy ale, passed round in genial fellowship from mouth to mouth! Pennyloaf would not drink of it; she had a dread of all such bottles. In her heart she rejoiced that Bob knew no craving for strong liquor. Towards the end of the journey the young man with the concertina passed round his hat.

Clem Peckover had come by the same train; she was one of a large party which had followed close behind Bob and Pennyloaf to the railway station. Now they followed along the long corridors into the 'Paliss,' with many a loud expression of mockery, with hee-hawing laughter, with coarse jokes. Depend upon it, Clem was gorgeously arrayed; amid her satellites she swept on 'like a stately ship of Tarsus, bound for the isles of Javan or Gadire;' her face was aflame, her eyes flashed in enjoyment of the uproar. Jack Bartley wore a high hat—Bob never had owned one in his life—and about his neck was a tie of crimson; yellow was his waistcoat, even such a waistcoat as you may see in Pall Mall, and his walking-stick had a nigger's head for handle. He was the oracle of the maidens around him; every moment the appeal was to 'Jeck! Jeck!' Suke Jollop, who would in reality have preferred to accompany Bob and his allies, whispered it about that Jack had two-pound-ten in his pocket, and was going to spend every penny of it before he left the 'Paliss'—yes, 'every bloomin' penny!'

Thus early in the day, the grounds were of course preferred to the interior of the glass house. Bob and Pennyloaf bent their steps to the fair. Here already was gathered much goodly company; above their heads hung a thick white wavering cloud of dust. Swing-boats and merry-go-rounds are from of old the chief features of these rural festivities; they soared and dipped and circled to the joyous music of organs which played the same tune automatically for any number of hours, whilst raucous voices invited all and sundry to take their turn. Should this delight pall, behold on every hand such sports as are dearest to the Briton, those which call for strength of sinew and exactitude of aim. The philosophic mind would have noted with interest how ingeniously these games were made to appeal to the patriotism of the throng. Did you choose to 'shy' sticks in the contest for cocoa-nuts, behold your object was a wooden model of the treacherous Afghan or the base African. If you took up the mallet to smite upon a spring and make proof of how far you could send a ball flying upwards, your blow descended upon the head of some other recent foeman. Try your fist at the indicator of muscularity, and with zeal you smote full in the stomach of a guy made to represent a Russian. If you essayed the pop-gun, the mark set you was on the flank of a wooden donkey, so contrived that it would kick when hit in the true spot. What a joy to observe the tendency of all these diversions! How characteristic of a high-spirited people that nowhere could be found any amusement appealing to the mere mind, or calculated to effeminate by encouraging a love of beauty.

Bob had a sovereign to get rid of. He shied for cocoanuts, he swung in the boat with Pennyloaf, he rode with her on the whirligigs. When they were choked, and whitened from head to foot, with dust, it was natural to seek the nearest refreshment-booth. Bob had some half-dozen male and female acquaintances clustered about him by now; of course he must celebrate the occasion by entertaining all of them. Consumed with thirst, he began to drink without counting the glasses. Pennyloaf plucked at his eldow, but Bob was beginning to feel that he must display spirit. Because he was married, that was no reason for his relinquishing the claims to leadership in gallantry which had always been recognised. Hollo! Here was Suke Jollop! She had just quarrelled with Clem, and had been searching for the hostile camp. 'Have a drink, Suke!' cried Bob, when he heard her acrimonious charges against Clem and Jack. A pretty girl, Suke, and with a hat which made itself proudly manifest a quarter of a mile away. Drink! of course she would drink; that thirsty she could almost drop! Bob enjoyed this secession from the enemy. He knew Suke's old fondness for him, and began to play upon it. Elated with beer and vanity, he no longer paid the least attention to Pennyloaf's remonstrances; nay, he at length bade her 'hold her bloomin' row!' Pennyloaf had a tear in her eye; she looked fiercely at Miss Jollop.

The day wore on. For utter weariness Pennyloaf was constrained to beg that they might go into the 'Paliss' and find a shadowed seat. Her tone revived tenderness in Bob; again he became gracious, devoted; he promised that not another glass of beer should pass his lips, and Suke Jollop, with all her like, might go to perdition. But heavens! how sweltering it was under this glass canopy! How the dust rose from the trampled boards! Come, let's have tea. The programme says there'll be a military band playing presently, and we shall return refreshed to hear it.

So they made their way to the 'Shilling Tea-room.' Having paid at the entrance, they were admitted to feed freely on all that lay before them. With difficulty could a seat be found in the huge room; the uproar of voices was deafening. On the tables lay bread, butter, cake in hunches, tea-pots, milk-jugs, sugar-basins—all things to whomso could secure them in the conflict. Along the gangways coursed perspiring waiters, heaping up giant structures of used plates and cups, distributing clean utensils, and miraculously sharp in securing the gratuity expected from each guest as he rose satiate. Muscular men in aprons wheeled hither the supplies of steaming fluid in immense cans on heavy trucks. Here practical joking found the most graceful of opportunities, whether it were the deft direction of a piece of cake at the nose of a person sitting opposite, or the emptying of a saucer down your neighbour's back, or the ingenious jogging of an arm which was in the act of raising a full tea-cup. Now and then an ill-conditioned fellow, whose beer disagreed with him, would resent some piece of elegant trifling, and the waiters would find it needful to request gentlemen not to fight until they had left the room. These cases, however, were exceptional. On the whole there reigned a spirit of imbecile joviality. Shrieks of female laughter testified to the success of the entertainment.

As Bob and his companion quitted this sphere of delight, ill-luck brought it to pass that Mr. Jack Bartley and his train were on the point of entering. Jack uttered a phrase of stinging sarcasm with reference to Pennyloaf's red feather; whereupon Bob smote him exactly between the eyes. Yells arose; there was a scuffle, a rush, a tumult. The two were separated before further harm came of the little misunderstanding, but Jack went to the tea-tables vowing vengeance.

Poor Pennyloaf shed tears as Bob led her to the place where the band had begun playing. Only her husband's anger prevented her from yielding to utter misery. But now they had come to the centre of the building, and by dint of much struggle in the crowd they obtained a standing whence they could see the vast amphitheatre, filled with thousands of faces. Here at length was quietness, intermission of folly and brutality. Bob became another man as he stood and listened. He looked with kindness into Pennyloaf's pale, weary face, and his arm stole about her waist to support her. Ha! Pennyloaf was happy! The last trace of tears vanished. She too was sensible of the influences of music; her heart throbbed as she let herself lean against her husband.

Well, as every one must needs have his panacea for the ills of society, let me inform you of mine. To humanise the multitude two things are necessary—two things of the simplest kind conceivable. In the first place, you must effect an entire change of economic conditions: a preliminary step of which every tyro will recognise the easiness; then you must bring to bear on the new order of things the constant influence of music. Does not the prescription recommend itself? It is jesting in earnest. For, work as you will, there is no chance of a new and better world until the old be utterly destroyed. Destroy, sweep away, prepare the ground; then shall music the holy, music the civiliser, breathe over the renewed earth, and with Orphean magic raise in perfected beauty the towers of the City of Man.

Hours yet before the fireworks begin. Never mind; here by good luck we find seats where we can watch the throng passing and repassing. It is a great review of the People. On the whole how respectable they are, how sober, how deadly dull! See how worn-out the poor girls are becoming, how they gape, what listless eyes most of them have! The stoop in the shoulders so universal among them merely means over-toil in the workroom. Not one in a thousand shows the elements of taste in dress; vulgarity and worse glares in all but every costume. Observe the middle-aged women; it would be small surprise that their good looks had vanished, but whence comes it they are animal, repulsive, absolutely vicious in ugliness? Mark the men in their turn: four in every six have visages so deformed by ill-health that they excite disgust; their hair is cut down to within half an inch of the scalp; their legs are twisted out of shape by evil conditions of life from birth upwards. Whenever a youth and a girl come along arm-in-arm, how flagrantly shows the man's coarseness! They are pretty, so many of these girls, delicate of feature, graceful did but their slavery allow them natural development; and the heart sinks as one sees them side by side with the men who are to be their husbands.

One of the livelier groups is surging hitherwards; here we have frolic, here we have humour. The young man who leads them has been going about all day with the lining of his hat turned down over his forehead; for the thousandth time those girls are screaming with laughter at the sight of him. Ha, ha! He has slipped and fallen upon the floor, and makes an obstruction; his companions treat him like a horse that is 'down' in the street. 'Look out for his 'eels!' cries one; and another, 'Sit on his 'ed!' If this doesn't come to an end we shall die of laughter. Lo! one of the funniest of the party is wearing a gigantic cardboard nose and flame-coloured whiskers. There, the stumbler is on his feet again. ''Ere he comes up smilin'!' cries his friend of the cardboard nose, and we shake our diaphragms with mirth. One of the party is an unusually tall man. 'When are you comin' down to have a look at us?' cries a pert lass as she skips by him.

A great review of the People. Since man came into being did the world ever exhibit a sadder spectacle?

Evening advances; the great ugly building will presently be lighted with innumerable lamps. Away to the west yonder the heavens are afire with sunset, but at that we do not care to look; never in our lives did we regard it. We know not what is meant by beauty or grandeur. Here under the glass roof stand white forms of undraped men and women—casts of antique statues—but we care as little for the glory of art as for that of nature; we have a vague feeling that, for some reason or other, antiquity excuses the indecent, but further than that we do not get.

As the dusk descends there is a general setting of the throng towards the open air; all the pathways swarm with groups which have a tendency to disintegrate into couples; universal is the protecting arm. Relief from the sweltering atmosphere of the hours of sunshine causes a revival of hilarity; those who have hitherto only bemused themselves with liquor now pass into the stage of jovial recklessness, and others, determined to prolong a flagging merriment, begin to depend upon their companions for guidance. On the terraces dancing has commenced; the players of violins, concertinas, and penny-whistles do a brisk trade among the groups eager for a rough-and-tumble valse; so do the pickpockets. Vigorous and varied is the jollity that occupies the external galleries, filling now in expectation of the fireworks; indescribable the mingled tumult that roars heavenwards. Girls linked by the half-dozen arm-in-arm leap along with shrieks like grotesque mænads; a rougher horseplay finds favour among the youths, occasionally leading to fisticuffs. Thick voices bellow in fragmentary chorus; from every side comes the yell, the cat-call, the ear-rending whistle; and as the bass, the never-ceasing accompaniment, sounds myriad-footed tramp, tramp along the wooden flooring. A fight, a scene of bestial drunkenness, a tender whispering between two lovers, proceed concurrently in a space of five square yards.—Above them glimmers the dawn of starlight.

For perhaps the first time in his life Bob Hewett has drunk more than he can well carry. To Pennyloaf's remonstrances he answers more and more impatiently: 'Why does she talk like a bloomin' fool?—one doesn't get married every day.' He is on the look-out for Jack Bartley now; only let him meet Jack, and it shall be seen who is the better man. Pennyloaf rejoices that the hostile party are nowhere discoverable. She is persuaded to join in a dance, though every moment it seems to her that she must sink to the ground in uttermost exhaustion. Naturally she does not dance with sufficient liveliness to please Bob; he seizes another girl, a stranger, and whirls round the six-foot circle with a laugh of triumph. Pennyloaf's misery is relieved by the beginning of the fireworks. Up shoot the rockets, and all the reeking multitude utters a huge 'Oh' of idiot admiration.

Now at length must we think of tearing ourselves away from these delights. Already the more prudent people are hurrying to the railway, knowing by dire experience what it means to linger until the last cargoes. Pennyloaf has hard work to get her husband as far as the station; Bob is not quite steady upon his feet, and the hustling of the crowd perpetually excites him to bellicose challenges. They reach the platform somehow; they stand wedged amid a throng which roars persistently as a substitute for the activity of limb now become impossible. A train is drawing up slowly; the danger is lest people in the front row should be pushed over the edge of the platform, but porters exert themselves with success. A rush, a tumble, curses, blows, laughter, screams of pain—and we are in a carriage. Pennyloaf has to be dragged up from under the seat, and all her indignation cannot free her from the jovial embrace of a man who insists that there is plenty of room on his knee. Off we go! It is a long third-class coach, and already five or six musical instruments have struck up. We smoke and sing at the same time; we quarrel and make love—the latter in somewhat primitive fashion; we roll about with the rolling of the train; we nod into hoggish sleep.

The platform at Holborn Viaduct; and there, to Pennyloaf's terror, it is seen that Clem Peckover and her satellites have come by the same train. She does her best to get Bob quickly away, but Clem keeps close in their neighbourhood. Just as they issue from the station Pennyloaf feels herself bespattered from head to foot with some kind of fluid; turning, she is aware that all her enemies have squirts in their hands, and are preparing for a second discharge of filthy water. Anguish for the ruin of her dress overcomes all other fear; she calls upon Bob to defend her.

But an immediate conflict was not Jack Bartley's intention. He and those with him made off at a run, Bob pursuing as closely as his unsteadiness would permit. In this way they all traversed the short distance to Clerkenwell Green, either party echoing the other's objurgations along the thinly-peopled streets. At length arrived the suitable moment. Near St. James's Church Jack Bartley made a stand, and defied his enemy to come on. Bob responded with furious eagerness; amid a press of delighted spectators, swelled by people just turned out of the public-houses, the two lads fought like wild animals. Nor were they the only combatants. Exasperated by the certainty that her hat and dolman were ruined, Pennyloaf flew with erected nails at Clem Peckover. It was just what the latter desired. In an instant she had rent half Pennyloaf's garments off her back, and was tearing her face till the blood streamed. Inconsolable was the grief of the crowd when a couple of stalwart policemen came hustling forward, thrusting to left and right, irresistibly clearing the corner. There was no question of making arrests; it was the night of Bank-holiday, and the capacity of police-cells is limited. Enough that the fight perforce came to an end. Amid frenzied blasphemy Bob and Jack went their several ways; so did Clem and Pennyloaf.

Poor Pennyloaf! Arrived at Shooter's Gardens, and having groped her way blindly up to the black hole which was her wedding-chamber, she just managed to light a candle, then sank down upon the bare floor and wept. You could not have recognised her; her pretty face was all blood and dirt. She held in her hand the fragment of a hat, and her dolman had disappeared. Her husband was not in much better plight; his waistcoat and shirt were rent open, his coat was filth-smeared, and it seemed likely that he had lost the sight of one eye. Sitting there in drunken lassitude, he breathed nothing but threats of future vengeance.

An hour later noises of a familiar kind sounded beneath the window. A woman's voice was raised in the fury of mad drunkenness, and a man answered her with threats and blows.

'That's mother,' sobbed Pennyloaf. 'I knew she wouldn't get over to-day. She never did get over a Bank-holiday.'

Mrs. Candy had taken the pledge when her husband consented to return and live with her. Unfortunately she did not at the same time transfer herself to a country where there are no beer-shops and no Bank-holidays. Short of such decisive change, what hope for her?

Bob was already asleep, breathing stertorously. As for Pennyloaf, she was so overwearied that hours passed before oblivion fell upon her aching eyelids. She was thinking all the time that on the morrow it would be necessary to pawn her wedding-ring.

45

JAMES JOHN HISSEY, *THROUGH TEN ENGLISH COUNTIES* (LONDON: RICHARD BENTLEY & SON, 1894), PP. 392–393

As we had a long day's drive before us, we left Berkhampstead early next morning. I am afraid, however, we were not in our usual buoyant spirits, for it was the last day of our tour; and though all good things must come to an end in this imperfect world, still the end was unwelcome.

Just beyond our inn, close to an old milestone inscribed "To London. 26 Miles"—that has been curiously preserved in the heart of the town—we noticed a charming time-mellowed old house of three gables, with stone-mullioned windows of leaden lattice lights; and this was really the last noticeable picturesque house on the journey. It seemed to us to give a grace and a dignity to the rather commonplace street. These modest old English homes that are so comfortable to live in, as well as pleasant to look at, are to the modern villa as a diamond is to paste.

Our way lay now along a wooded valley; some of the hedges we observed were of clipped beech, and chestnut trees began to make their welcome appearance in the landscape, and for a time road, railway, and canal ran close together—the railway too close indeed for the comfort of our horses. The scenery was very pretty in places, and there was plenty of life in the prospect, with the rapid rush of trains on one hand, and the slow progress of canal boats on the other. Great was the contrast between the two modes of transit; the one a sudden roar, a rush of steam, a cloud of dust, a shrill metallic shriek, and before you had hardly time to think about the matter an express train had come and gone; the other an almost noiseless and tediously slow movement of towed barges. England is a country of sharp contrasts, for in it the old and the new are so frequently thrown into close proximity, as where the railway goes beneath the feudal castle walls, or in some ancient churches the electric light glows in the medieval gloom, and lights up tombs of olden knights in their armoured effigies.

46

THOMAS HARDY, *JUDE THE OBSCURE* (NEW YORK: HARPER AND BROTHERS, 1896), PP. 341–343

THE purpose of a chronicler of moods and deeds does not require him to express his personal views upon the grave controversy above given. That the twain were happy—between their times of sadness—was indubitable. And when the unexpected apparition of Jude's child in the house had shown itself to be no such disturbing event as it had looked, but one that brought into their lives a new and tender interest of an ennobling and unselfish kind, it rather helped than injured their happiness.

To be sure, with such pleasing anxious beings as they were, the boy's coming also brought with it much thought for the future, particularly as he seemed at present to be singularly deficient in all the usual hopes of childhood. But the pair tried to dismiss, for a while at least, a too strenuously forward view.

There is in Upper Wessex an old town of nine or ten thousand souls; the town may be called Stoke-Barehills. It stands with its gaunt, unattractive, ancient church, and its new red brick suburb, amid the open, chalk-soiled cornlands, near the middle of an imaginary triangle which has for its three corners the towns of Aldbrickham and Wintoncester, and the important military station of Quartershot. The great western highway from London passes through it, near a point where the road branches into two, merely to unite again some twenty miles farther westward. Out of this bifurcation and reunion there used to arise among wheeled travellers, before railway days, endless questions of choice between the respective ways. But the question is now as dead as the scot-and-lot freeholder, the road wagoner, and the mail coachman who disputed it; and probably not a single inhabitant of Stoke-Barehills is now even aware that the two roads which part in his town ever meet again, for nobody now drives up and down the great western highway daily.

The most familiar object in Stoke-Barehills nowadays is its cemetery, standing among some picturesque mediæval ruins beside the railway; the modern chapels, modern tombs, and modern shrubs having a look of intrusiveness amid the crumbling and ivy-covered decay of the ancient walls.

On a certain day, however, in the particular year, which has now been reached by this narrative—the month being early June—the features of the town excite little interest, though many visitors arrive by the trains; some down trains, in especial, nearly emptying themselves here. It is the week of the Great Wessex Agricultural Show, whose vast encampment spreads over the open outskirts of the town like the tents of an investing army. Rows of marquees, huts, booths, pavilions, arcades, porticoes—every kind of structure short of a permanent one—cover the green field for the space of a square half-mile, and the crowds of arrivals walk through the town in a mass, and make straight for the exhibition ground. The way thereto is lined with shows, stalls, and hawkers on foot, who make a market-place of the whole roadway to the show proper, and lead some of the improvident to lighten their pockets appreciably before they reach the gates of the exhibition they came expressly to see.

It is the popular day, the shilling day, and of the fast-arriving excursion trains two from different directions enter the two contiguous railway-stations at almost the same minute. One, like several which have preceded it, comes from London, the other by a cross-line from Aldbrickham; and from the London train alights a couple: a short, rather bloated man, with a globular stomach and small legs, resembling a top on two pegs, accompanied by a woman of rather fine figure and rather red face, dressed in black material, and covered with beads from bonnet to skirt, that made her glisten as if clad in chain-mail.

They cast their eyes around. The man was about to hire a fly, as some others had done, when the woman said, "Don't be in such a hurry, Cartlett. It isn't so very far to the show-yard. Let us walk down the street into the place. Perhaps I can pick up a cheap bit of furniture or old china. It is years since I was here—never since I lived as a girl at Aldbrickham, and used to come across for a trip sometimes with my young man."

"You can't carry home furniture by excursion train," said, in a thick voice, her husband, the landlord of The Three Horns, Lambeth; for they had both come down from the tavern in that "excellent, densely populated, gin-drinking neighborhood," which they had occupied ever since the advertisement in those words had attracted them thither. The configuration of the landlord showed that he, too, like his customers, was becoming affected by the liquors he retailed.

"Then I'll get it sent, if I can see any worth having," said his wife.

They sauntered on, but had barely entered the town when her attention was attracted by a young couple leading a child who had come out from the second platform, into which the train from Aldbrickham had steamed. They were walking just in front of the innkeepers.

"Sakes alive!" said Arabella.

"What's that?" said Cartlett.

"Who do you think that couple is? Don't you recognize the man?"

"No."

"Not from the photos I have shown you?"

"Is it Fawley?"

"Yes—of course."

47

ARTHUR QUILLER-COUCH, 'THE CUCKOO VALLEY RAILWAY' AND 'PUNCH'S UNDERSTUDY', IN *THE DELECTABLE DUCHY: STORIES, STUDIES, AND SKETCHES* (NEW YORK: C. SCRIBNERS' SONS, 1898), PP. 61–69, 107–115

Cuckoo Valley Railway

THIS century was still young and ardent when ruin fell upon Cuckoo Valley. Its head rested on the slope of a high and sombre moorland, scattered with granite and china-clay; and by the small town of Ponteglos, where it widened out into arable and grey pasture-land, the Cuckoo river grew deep enough to float up vessels of small tonnage from the coast at the spring tides. I have seen there the boom of a trading schooner brush the grasses on the river-bank as she came before a southerly wind, and the haymakers stop and almost crick their necks staring up at her top-sails. But between the moors and Ponteglos the valley wound for fourteen miles or so between secular woods, so steeply converging that for the most part no more room was left at the bottom of the V than the river itself filled. The fisherman beside it trampled on pimpernels, sundew, watermint, and asphodels, or pushed between clumps of *Osmunda regalis* that overtopped him by a couple of feet. If he took to wading, there was much ado to stand against the current. Only here and there it spread into a still black pool, greased with eddies; and beside such a pool, it was odds that he found a diminutive meadow, green and flat as a billiard-table, and edged with clumps of fern. To think of Cuckoo Valley is to call up the smell of that fern as it wrapped at the bottom of the creel the day's catch of salmon-peal and trout.

The town of Tregarrick (which possessed a gaol, a workhouse, and a lunatic asylum, and called itself the centre of the Duchy) stood three miles back from the lip of this happy valley, whither on summer evenings its burghers rambled to eat cream and junket at the Dairy Farm by the river bank, and afterwards sit to watch the fish rise, while the youngsters and maidens played hide-and-seek in the woods. But there came a day when the names of Watt and Stephenson waxed great in the land, and these slow citizens caught the railway frenzy. They took it, however, in their own fashion. They never dreamed of connecting themselves with other towns and a larger world, but of aggrandisement by means of a railway that should run from Tregarrick to nowhere in particular, and bring the intervening wealth to their doors. They planned a railway that should join Tregarrick with Cuckoo Valley, and there divide into two branches, the one bringing ore and clay from the moors, the other fetching up sand and coal from the sea. Surveyors and engineers descended upon the woods; then a cloud of navvies. The days were filled with the crash of falling timber and the rush of emptied trucks. The stream was polluted, the fish died, the fairies were evicted from their rings beneath the oak, the morals of the junketing houses underwent change. The vale knew itself no longer; its smoke went up week by week with the noise of pick-axes and oaths.

On August 13th, 1834, the Mayor of Tregarrick declared the new line open, and a locomotive was run along its rails to Dunford Bridge, at the foot of the moors. The engine was christened *The Wonder of the Age;* and I have before me a handbill of the festivities of that proud day, which tells me that the mayor himself rode in an open truck, "embellished with Union Jacks, lions and unicorns, and other loyal devices." And then Nature settled down to heal her wounds, and the Cuckoo Valley Railway to pay no dividend to its promoters.

It is now two years and more since, on an August day, I wound up my line by Dunford Bridge, and sauntered towards the Light Horseman Inn, two gunshots up the road. The time was four o'clock, or thereabouts, and a young couple sat on a bench by the inn-door, drinking cocoa out of one cup. Above their heads and along the house-front a vine-tree straggled, but its foliage was too thin to afford a speck of shade as they sat there in the eye of the westering sun. The man (aged about one-and-twenty) wore the uncomfortable Sunday-best of a mechanic, with a shrivelled, but still enormous, bunch of Sweet-William in his buttonhole. The girl was dressed in a bright green gown and a white bonnet. Both were flushed and perspiring, and I still think they must have ordered hot cocoa in haste, and were repenting it at leisure. They lifted their eyes and blushed with a yet warmer red as I passed into the porch.

Two men were seated in the cool tap-room, each with a pasty and a mug of beer. A composition of sweat and coal-dust had caked their faces, and so deftly smoothed all distinction out of their features that it seemed at the moment natural and proper to take them for twins. Perhaps this was an error: perhaps, too, their appearance of extreme age was produced by the dark grey dust that overlaid so much of them as showed above the table. As twins, however, I remember them, and cannot shake off the impression that they had remained twins for an unusual number of years.

One addressed me. "Parties outside pretty comfortable?" he asked.

"They were drinking out of the same cup," I answered.

He nodded. "Made man and wife this mornin'. I don't fairly know what's best to do. Lord knows I wouldn' hurry their soft looks and dilly-dallyin'; but did 'ee notice how much beverage was left in the cup?"

"They was mated at Tregarrick, half-after-nine this mornin'," observed the other twin, pulling out a great watch, "and we brought 'em down here in a truck for their honeymoon. The agreement was for an afternoon in the woods; but by crum! sir, they've sat there and held one another's hand for up'ards of an hour after the stated time to start. And we ha'nt the heart to tell 'em so."

He walked across to the window and peered over the blind.

"There's a mort of grounds in the cocoa that's sold here," he went on, after a look, "and 'tisn't the sort that does the stomach good, neither. For their own sakes, I'll give the word to start, and chance their thankin' me some day later when they learn what things be made of."

The other twin arose, shook the crumbs off his trousers, and stretched himself. I guessed now that this newly-married pair had delayed traffic at the Dunford terminus of the Cuckoo Valley Railway for almost an hour and a half; and I determined to travel into Tregarrick by the same train.

So we strolled out of the inn towards the line, the lovers following, arm-in-arm, some fifty paces behind.

"How far is it to the station?" I inquired.

The twins stared at me.

Presently we turned down a lane scored with dry ruts, passed an oak plantation, and came on a clearing where the train stood ready. The line did not finish: it ended in a heap of sand. There were eight trucks, seven of them laden with granite, and an engine, with a prodigiously long funnel, bearing the name *The Wonder of the Age* in brass letters along its boiler.

"Now," said one of the twins, while the other raked up the furnace, "you can ride in the empty truck with the lovers, or on the engine along with us—which you like."

I chose the engine. We climbed on board, gave a loud whistle, and jolted off. Far down, on our right, the river shone between the trees, and these trees, encroaching on the track, almost joined their branches above us. Ahead, the moss that grew upon the sleepers gave the line the appearance of a green glade, and the grasses, starred with golden-rod and mallow, grew tall to the very edge of the rails. It seemed that in a few more years Nature would cover this scar of 1834, and score the return match against man. Rails, engine, officials, were already no better than ghosts: youth and progress lay in the pushing trees, the salmon leaping against the dam below, the young man and maid sitting with clasped hands and amatory looks in the hindmost truck.

At the end of three miles or so we gave an alarming whistle, and slowed down a bit. The trees were thinner here, and I saw that a highroad came down the hill, and cut across our track some fifty yards ahead. We prepared to cross it cautiously.

"Ho—o—oy! Stop!"

The brake was applied, and as we came to a standstill a party of men and women descended the hill towards us.

"'Tis Susan Warne's seventh goin' to be christen'd, by the look of it," said the engine-driver beside me; "an', by crum! we've got the Kimbly."

The procession advanced. In the midst walked a stout woman, carrying a baby in long clothes, and in front a man bearing in both hands a plate covered with a white cloth. He stepped up beside the train, and, almost before I had time to be astonished, a large yellow cake was thrust into my hands. Engine-driver and stoker were also presented with a cake a-piece, and then the newly-married pair, who took and ate with some shyness and giggling.

"Is it a boy or a girl?" asked the stoker, with his mouth full.

"A boy," the man answered; "and I count it good luck that you men of modern ways should be the first we meet on our way to church. The child 'll be a go-ahead if there's truth in omens."

"You're right, naybour. We're the speediest men in this part of the universe, I d' believe. Here's luck to 'ee, Susan Warne!" he piped out, addressing one of the women; "an' if you want a name for your seventh, you may christen 'en after the engine here, the *Wonder of the Age*."

We waved our hats and jolted off again towards Tregarrick. At the end of the journey the railway officials declined to charge for the pleasure of my company. But after some dispute, they agreed to compromise by adjourning to the Railway Inn, and drinking prosperity to Susan Warne's seventh.

Punch's understudy

THE first-class smoking compartment was the emptiest in the whole train, and even this was hot to suffocation, because my only companion denied me more than an inch of open window. His chest, he explained curtly, was "susceptible." As we crawled westward through the glaring country, the sun's rays reverberated on the carriage roof till I seemed to be crushed under an anvil, counting the strokes. I had dropped my book, and was staring listlessly out of the window. At the other end of the compartment my fellow-passenger had pulled down the blinds, and hidden his face behind the *Western Morning News*. He was a red and choleric little man of about sixty, with a protuberant stomach, a prodigious nose, to which he carried snuff about once in two minutes, and a marked deformity of the shoulders. For comfort—and also, perhaps, to hide this hump—he rested his back in the angle by the window. He wore a black alpaca coat, a high stock, white waistcoat, and trousers of shepherd's plaid. On these and a few other trivial details I built a lazy hypothesis that he was a lawyer, and unmarried.

Just before entering the station at Lostwithiel, our train passed between the white gates of a level crossing. A moment before I had caught sight of the George drooping from the church spire, and at the crossing I saw it was regatta-day in the small town. The road was thick with people and lined with sweet-standings; and by the near end of the bridge a Punch-and-Judy show had just closed a performance. The orchestra had unloosed his drum, and fallen to mopping the back of his neck with the red handkerchief that had previously bound the panpipes to his chin. A crowd still loitered around, and among it I noted several men and women in black—ugly stains upon the pervading sunshine.

The station platform was cram-full as we drew up, and it was clear at once that all the carriages in the train would be besieged, without regard to class. By some chance, however, ours was neglected, and until the very last moment we seemed likely to escape. The guard's whistle was between his lips when I heard a shout, then one or two feminine screams, and a company of seven or eight persons came charging out of the booking-office. Every one of them was apparelled in black: they were, in fact, the people I had seen gaping at the Punch-and-Judy show.

In a moment one of the men tore open the door of our compartment, and we were invaded. One—two—four—six—seven—in they poured, tumbling over my legs, panting, giggling inanely, exhorting each other to hurry—an old man, two youths, three middle-aged women, and a little girl about four years old. I heard a fierce guttural sound, and saw my fellow-passenger on his feet, choking with wrath and gesticulating. But the guard slammed the door on his resentment, and the train moved on. As it gathered speed he fell back, all purple above his stock, snatched his malacca walking-cane from under the coat-tails of a subsiding youth, stuck it upright between his knees, and glared round upon the intruders. They were still possessed with excitement over their narrow escape, and unconscious of offence. One of the women dropped into the corner seat, and took the little girl on her lap. The child's dusty boots rubbed against the old gentleman's trousers. He shifted his position, grunted, and took snuff furiously.

"That was nibby-jibby," observed the old man of the party, while his eyes wandered round for a seat.

"I declare I thought I should ha' died," panted a robust-looking woman with a wart on her cheek, and a yard of crape hanging from her bonnet. "Can't 'een find nowhere to sit, uncle?"

"Reckon I must make shift 'pon your lap, Susannah."

This was said with a chuckle, and the woman tittered.

"What new-fang'd game be this o' the Great Western's? Arms to the seats, I vow. We'll have to sit intimate, my dears."

"'Tis First Class," one of the young men announced in a chastened whisper: "I saw it written on the door."

There was a short silence of awe.

"Well!" ejaculated Susannah: "I thought, when first I sat down, that the cushions felt extraordinary plum. You don't think they'll fine us?"

"It all comes of our stoppin' to gaze at that Punch-an'-Judy," the old fellow went on, after I had shown them how to turn back the arm-seats, and they were settled in something like comfort. "But I never *could* refrain from that antic, though I feels condemned too, in a way, an' poor Thomas laid in earth no longer ago than twelve noon. But in the midst of life we are in death."

"I don't remember a more successful buryin'," said the woman who held the little girl.

"That was partly luck, as you may say, it bein' regatta-day an' the fun o' the fair not properly begun. I counted a lot at the cemetery I didn' know by face, an' I set 'em down for excursionists, that caught sight of a funeral, an' followed it to fill up the time."

"It all added."

"Oh, aye; Thomas was beautifully interred."

By this time the heat in the carriage was hardly more overpowering than the smell of crape, broadcloth, and camphor. The youth who had wedged himself next to me carried a large packet of "fairing," which he had bought at one of the sweet-stalls. He began to insert it into his side pocket, and in his struggles drove an elbow sharply into my ribs. I shifted my position a little.

"Tom's wife would ha' felt it a source o' pride, had she lived."

But I ceased to listen; for in moving I had happened to glance at the further end of the carriage, and there my attention was arrested by a curious little piece of pantomime. The little girl—a dark-eyed, intelligent child, whose pallor was emphasised by the crape which smothered her—was looking very closely at the old gentleman with the hump—staring at him hard, in fact. He, on the other hand, was leaning forward, with both hands on the knob of his malacca, his eyes bent on the floor and his mouth squared to the surliest expression. He seemed quite unconscious of her scrutiny, and was tapping one foot impatiently on the floor.

After a minute I was surprised to see her lean forward and touch him gently on the knee.

He took no notice beyond shuffling about a little and uttering a slight growl. The woman who held her put out an arm and drew back the child's hand reprovingly. The child paid no heed to this, but continued to stare. Then in another minute she again bent forward, and tapped the old gentleman's knee.

This time she fetched a louder growl from him, and an irascible glare. Not in the least daunted, she took hold of his malacca, and shook it to and fro in her small hand.

"I wish to heavens, madam, you'd keep your child to yourself!"

"For shame, Annie!" whispered the poor woman, cowed by his look.

But again Annie paid no heed. Instead, she pushed the malacca towards the old gentleman, saying—

"Please, sir, will 'ee warm Mister Barrabel wi' this?"

He moved uneasily, and looked harshly at her without answering. "For shame, Annie!" the woman murmured a second time; but I saw her lean back, and a tear started and rolled down her cheek.

"If you please, sir," repeated Annie, "will 'ee warm Mister Barrabel wi' this?"

The old gentleman stared round the carriage. In his eyes you could read the question, "What in the devil's name does the child mean?" The robust woman read it there, and answered him huskily—

"Poor mite! she's buried her father this mornin'; an' Mister Barrabel is the coffin-maker, an' nailed 'en down."

"Now," said Annie, this time eagerly, "will 'ee warm him same as the big doll did just now?"

Luckily, the old gentleman did not understand this last allusion. He had not seen the group around the Punch-and-Judy show; nor, if he had, is it likely he would have guessed the train of thought in the child's mind. But to me, as I looked at my fellow-passenger's nose and the deformity of his shoulders, and remembered how Punch treats the undertaker in the immortal drama, it was all plain enough. I glanced at the child's companions. Nothing in their faces showed that they took the allusion; and the next moment I was glad to think that I alone knew what had prompted Annie's speech.

For the next moment, with a beautiful change on his face, the old gentleman had taken the child on his knee, and was talking to her as I dare say he had never talked before.

"Are you her mother?" he asked, looking up suddenly, and addressing the woman opposite.

"Her mother's been dead these two year. I'm her aunt, an' I'm takin' her home to rear 'long wi' my own childer."

He was bending over Annie, and had resumed his chat. It was all nonsense—something about the silver knob of his malacca—but it took hold of the child's fancy and comforted her. At the next station I had to alight, for it was the end of my journey. But looking back into the carriage as I shut the door, I saw Annie bending forward over the walking-stick, and following the pattern of its silver-work with her small finger. Her face was turned from the old gentleman's, and behind her little black hat his eyes were glistening.

48

GEORGE JOHN WHYTE-MELVILLE, *THE BROOKES OF BRIDLEMERE* (LONDON: WARD, LOCK, 1899), PP. 156–161, 200–205

Perhaps it is the pace at which we speed, suggestive in itself of abnormal energy and power, and comparative ubiquity, that makes things appear feasible when we travel by railway, though we considered them perfectly impossible before we took our tickets, and shall find them extremely difficult to accomplish when we have arrived. It has never been my good fortune to cleave the skies like Dædalus, or Mr. Glaisher, in a balloon; nor am I likely to do so, unless the "*Deus qui vult perdere, prius dementat;*" but I have no doubt that every man begins to feel a hero at an elevation of a thousand feet, and I fancy that for consciousness of capability, and a general conviction of superiority to his kind, as the horseman is to the pedestrian, so is the railway traveller to the horseman, and the aëronaut to the railway traveller, though the last fly through space at the rate of sixty miles an hour, on the wings of the Liverpool express.

Multiple's brain was seldom idle, but it did not usually work so fast as now, while he traversed the wide green pastures grown lately so familiar, that told him he was approaching Middlesworth station. He felt none of the diffidence, none of the misgivings, none of the conflict of hopes and fears, half-cherished, half-repressed, that chequer the anticipations of a true lover in his meeting with her whom he has taught himself to esteem fairer, and wiser, and better, and harder to win than all the other daughters of Eve. He neither trembled when he thought of his princess, nor did his heart thrill, and his cheek burn to feel that every minute and every mile brought him closer to her presence; that nothing but the near horizon now divided him from the palace in which she lived; that yonder line of wooded hills was within the range of her vision as of his; that the very breeze which stirred the clump of leafless poplars at the station where he gave up his ticket would but dally with that half dozen of elms, a mile off on the height, ere it passed on to whisper amongst the evergreens in Helen's garden, under her windows at Bridlemere. These are lovers' fancies, fond, foolish, yet engrossing for the time. Multiple was no fond, foolish lover, but a wooer—fierce, resolute, and not to be denied.

While the train slackened speed to glide into Middlesworth station, he clenched both his hands tight, till the costly rings he wore printed marks in his soft white fingers, smiling with the smile of one who has taken a prey for which he feels no pity, and got an enemy at a disadvantage to whom he will extend no grace.

Miss Brooke's walk was over just about the time Mr. Multiple's train stopped at its last station but one. Helen had paid her usual visit to Dame Batters, whose remarks were more inconsequent, as her rheumatism seemed more troublesome, than common. The girl entered her own garden with drooping head and slow, listless step. Somebody had compared her to a lily once, in Philip Stoney's hearing. It was long ago. She knew exactly how long, and could have named the very day of the month on which this exceedingly trite simile was proclaimed. She also remembered how a young man in company had clandestinely gathered one of those spotless flowers soon after, and, too shy to wear it in his button-hole, had twirled it about between his fingers till the stalk broke. She had not forgotten how he picked up the head and put it away somewhere—probably in his pocket—with great care and secresy, believing himself unobserved. And so he was by all but her. She was like a lily still; but a poor, faded lily now—drooping, forlorn, dejected; no longer the priestess of the garden and the pride of the summer's day.

She felt oppressed by one of those strange, dim forewarnings of evil to which we are subject all our lives, but especially in the sensitive season of youth. Forewarnings, that overshadow us with no kind of reason, and that arise from no phantom revelations of the future, but from the certain influence of the past. Medically speaking—not romantically—they are apt to originate in affections of the heart. Derangement of the liver, I suspect, and disorder of the stomach will also create these depressing sensations; but though often the effect of bodily ailment, a long course of mental anxiety is sure to produce them in their most distressing form. If any particular misfortune happens to us, after one of these morbid attacks, we hold up our hands, and talk vaguely about mysterious affinities, and the wonderful presentiments of the soul. If, as is usually the case, nothing out of the common way takes place, we forget all about them directly; change of scene, or diet, or society, has drawn them from our minds.

Helen felt low and nervous when she went to dress. Sitting down before her glass, and looking on the lovely image it reflected, her thoughts flowed back in the contemplation of her own face, to him for whose sake alone she prized the beauty, which she could not but be aware she possessed. It was sad, it was humiliating, yet it was not entirely displeasing, to feel how everything now reminded her of *him;* and when she considered that soon it would be a crime to think of him at all, she felt justified in indemnifying herself by present rebellion, for the loyalty that must never again be shaken after the fatal day on which she had passed her word.

The maid, who had been with her young mistress in the nursery, and who was an execrable hairdresser, pulled, and parted, and brushed out Helen's long locks, chattering volubly the while, with that happy insensibility to the low spirits of others, enjoyed by so many of her class. She was especially fluent to-night on Mr. John's abrupt departure, an occurrence sufficiently unprecedented to have occasioned many surmises below stairs, and condoled with Helen on the probability of her sitting down alone, in the event of his not returning to dinner.

No lady's-maid—even if she lived in a booking-office—would be likely to have the remotest idea of the time at which any train in the twenty-four hours was due at a station; and though people were continually arriving at Bridlemere by this method of transit, Helen's attendant entertained no more distinct notions of when, or how, or why they got to Middlesworth, than if she had resided in another kingdom, instead of the adjoining parish.

When, therefore, the grinding of wheels was heard outside, followed by an alarming peal at the door-bell, it never occurred to her that this was the most probable hour at which the young Squire would return by the quick afternoon train in time for dinner, having been up to London for the day.

He was soon back at the railway station, and in direct infringement of the company's by-laws, tendering half-a-crown to the guard of the train on the understanding that this incorruptible functionary should reserve a carriage expressly for himself and his friends.

I think I have observed of late years that young men travel with more impediments in the way of luggage, than was the practice long ago in the days of my youth. I have seen, in that primeval age, a rampant dandy of his time making the transit from London to Doncaster outside the mail, which, by the way, he drove, or *worked*, as we used to call it, fully half the distance, with no more superfluities than a shawl-handkerchief; no more necessaries than a sherry-flask, and a cigar-case the size of a portmanteau. But to-day they seem to have advanced a whole century in matters of comfort and convenience. The modern traveller who takes a first-class ticket requires as many luxuries as an Eastern potentate. In addition to railway rugs and wrappers of every description, he must be further encumbered by a faggot of sticks and umbrellas, securely strapped together like the bundle in the fable, by an embroidered cap, a travelling lamp, an uncut novel, a paper-knife, *The Times* (with supplement), the *Globe*, a sporting paper, and the *Saturday Review*, nor can any of these extras apparently be crammed into a large leathern reticule, with a pocket in its stomach like a female kangaroo, already stuffed with writing materials, cigar cases, eau de Cologne, hair-brushes, and, as I am informed, all the materials for an elaborate toilet.

Each of Walter's three friends possessed the paraphernalia pertaining to his station. There was but little room in their "engaged" compartment for the half-dozen new packs of cards, without which it was impossible to travel over a score of miles. These lively young gentlemen were going down to join the hunting-party at St. Barbs, and had arranged to dine with Walter at the barracks; and then catch a late train on a branch line, which would bring them to the Duke's about midnight. The day would be thus passed in change of scene and excitement. There remained but the period occupied by their journey from London to Middlesworth. This blank, it had been decided, could be agreeably filled up with whist.

The party consisted of Viscount Mexico, an exceedingly rich and uninteresting Peer, supposed to be somewhat deficient in brains, but well known at Eton, Oxford, and subsequently in London, as sufficiently careful of his own interests, and not too stupid to play a remarkably good rubber: or to square accounts with his agent scrupulously once a month, whereby the family property, little damaged by a shamefully inadequate settlement on his Lordship's mother, did by no means deteriorate under his administration. This young nobleman was very properly the great gun of the party.

The other two, of smaller bore, so to speak, and inferior calibre, were as well known in London as Northumberland House or the Duke of York's Column. Captain Belt of the Life Guards, christened Augustus, but known in the regiment as Tom, was a fair specimen of a class that delights to throw away its advantages, and waste its energies on frivolous pursuits, for which it cares nothing at heart. Tom Belt, with courage, good humour, good health, and good abilities, was satisfied, or I should say, resigned, to pass his days in the narrowest possible circle, even of those amusements for which he seemed to live. To shoot pigeons at Hornsey, to lose glove-bets at Ascot, to be well dressed, and ride a neat hack in the Park— these were the aims and endeavours of his existence. He had talents of which he was scarcely conscious, for he had never cultivated them. He had affections, frittered away on a hundred different objects, of which he preferred the most unworthy. He had a large estate which he neglected; but, fortunately for him, an agent, who allowed no "pickings" but his own. He had all the accessories that go to form a man of influence in his generation, and what was the result? Tom Belt, with his cheery manner, his pleasant smile, his good set of teeth, had the reputation of being not quite an idiot, only because he could play a fair rubber at whist!

How many men there are about London completely thrown away from sheer want of a plunge into cold water; who, when braced up by danger, difficulty, or affliction, prove themselves capable of great things; and who, even in the natural and tranquil course of events, do sometimes get tired of frivolity at middle-age, and turn to the real working purposes of life. Perhaps, if they *will* do nothing but waste their time till they are ruined, the best thing for them is to get rid of their money as fast as they can. Yet it does seem a pity to lose all the golden years of youth, all the resources and advantages of wealth, because people persist in making a business of pleasure, thereby losing the exquisite flavour afforded by the one, as well as the substantial-food comprised in the other.

Tom Belt might well be called one of the drones in the hive. Not so little Champignon, sitting on the opposite seat, and presenting Lord Mexico with a paper cigarette of undeniable quality, imported direct from Madrid, as he assures his Lordship, who, possibly in complete ignorance of that capital, seems but little impressed with the fact.

Champignon has worked hard all his life. Nobody knows who he is—nobody thinks of asking. From some men society requires that they should bring their credentials in their hand; others it accepts, as we accept the swallows in the spring, without troubling ourselves where they came from.

Champignon's name is French; his low stature, olive complexion, and dark, piercing eyes, argue a Spanish origin; but when he opens his lips, you are satisfied that English is his mother-tongue. There is a tradition that he speaks many continental languages like a native. Possibly he may; but there is no mistake about his English; and no foreigner, I think, however great his proficiency, ever yet succeeded in deceiving our national ear. There is also a superstition that he is connected in some mysterious manner with the Government, and this indefinite link seems unaffected by a change of Ministry. Also he disappears suddenly on occasion, even in the middle of the season, for weeks at a time. Vague rumours then arise that he is engaged in important political missions at foreign capitals. On his return, invitations to dinner pour in without number, and his admirers become more infatuated than ever to observe, as he takes care they shall, that he is hand-and-glove with every *attaché* in London, and that ambassadors themselves clap him on the shoulder, and call him *Mon cher* in the Park.

The little man loses nothing, depend upon it, by being a secret from the crown of his French hat to the tips of his nice boots. Nobody knows what he does with himself all the morning, or why he is regularly seen by his acquaintance, which means everyone in London, yet never twice by the same person in the afternoon. Nobody knows whether he lives at the address on his cards, or where he dines when not engaged to one of his noble friends, or why people so often miss him at those great parties in the lists of which his name invariably appears next day. Nobody knows if he is, or is not, connected with several daily, and one weekly paper; or why he is half-an-hour in advance of the world regarding telegrams, official news, horrible accidents, and domestic scandal. He himself knows everything—where you can get unadulterated sherry; who was the first person to throw himself off the Monument, and where he fell; why Lady Macallummore's hair all came down at the Caledonian ball; how she sent her maid away, and where the maid is gone. Ere he has been twelve hours at St. Barbs he will tell the Duchess of Merthyr-Tydvil of a shop for cleaning old lace in the Barbican, and what to give her love-birds for the gapes. He will warn the Duke of a certain favourite likely to be "made safe" for the Two Thousand; and he will show the land-agent a diagram of a new subsoil plough. Lady Julia calls him "The Pocket Companion and Universal Referee." Perhaps, if obliged to go out, he will enjoy his day's hunting less than any other country amusement; but he will ask his host honestly to put him on a quiet horse, and will get through even this ordeal quietly and creditably enough.

In appearance he is not prepossessing, but he looks what he is—a hard and wiry man, though small. He speaks little, notwithstanding his amount of information, and drinks less; but he smokes cigarettes from morning till night, and makes a fair annual income by his skill in the noble game of whist.

The train has panted out of the station; cleared off a few short white puffs of smoke, as though to bring its lungs into play; indulged in a strange, shrill shriek, like a wild cry of freedom from some living monster, and is fairly settled to its work, thirty miles an hour, over the beautiful pastoral country that lies to the north of London. There is a forty-shilling penalty for smoking, wisely advertised in each carriage, to enhance the forbidden pleasure of a cigar. It is needless to say that three of these, and a cigarette, are already in full process of consumption. The fellow-travellers talk a little, read a little, find the latter an unpleasant process, and somebody says something about "whist."

"The very thing!" observes Tom Belt, turning from the window, out of which he has been scanning the country, searching, I imagine, for the easy places in the fences, and thinking how tempting they look to ride over—"the very thing. Play all the way down; make the time pass. Not too high, I vote. What say you, Brooke? Quiet rubber in the old form; pound points?"

"Pounds and fives," answered Walter, carelessly, strong in the possession of ready money; "or ponies, if you like it better. I don't care. Bet what you please."

The hussar was a proficient in the game—perhaps one of the best in London, for his years. Its intricacies suited his turn of mind, and he had made many a welcome hundred by the self-taught habit of remembering every card as it came out. He felt now that he was a turn better than any of his company: for of the other three, though sound average players, Champignon could alone be considered even second-rate. The higher the stakes, therefore, the more profitably, he thought, could he employ his time. Why, he might win enough in a couple of hours to take him well over the next three months; and something seemed to tell him he was in a run of luck just now. So he shuffled the cards, and cut Champignon for a partner, with very decided anticipations of success.

They won the first game triumphantly. Honours divided. Cards pretty equal; but Tom Belt, possibly unused to whist at the rate of thirty miles an hour, committed an egregious blunder, and Mexico might have made more of his diamonds. "Play must tell," thought Walter, as he prepared to deal; and he laid the life guardsman thirty pounds to twenty, with considerable *sang froid*.

The next was not so prosperous. The adversaries' cards were of a nature to override any amount of play, and the inferior performers, as Mexico pleasantly observed, "had it all their own way from first to last, and won in a canter."

49

H. G. WELLS, *WHEN THE SLEEPER WAKES* (NEW YORK: HARPER & BROS., 1899), PP. 201–211

Some hundred feet or more sheer below him was one of the big wind-vanes of south-west London, and beyond it the southernmost flying stage crowded with little black dots. These things seemed to be falling away from him. For a second he had an impulse to pursue the earth. He set his teeth, he lifted his eyes by a muscular effort, and the moment of panic passed.

He remained for a space with his teeth set hard, his eyes staring into the sky. Throb, throb, throb—beat, went the engine; throb, throb, throb,—beat. He gripped his bars tightly, glanced at the aëronaut, and saw a smile upon his sun-tanned face. He smiled in return—perhaps a little artificially. "A little strange at first," he shouted before he recalled his dignity. But he dared not look down again for some time. He stared over the aëronaut's head to where a rim of vague blue horizon crept up the sky. For a little while he could not banish the thought of possible accidents from his mind. Throb, throb, throb—beat; suppose some trivial screw went wrong in that supporting engine! Suppose—! He made a grim effort to dismiss all such suppositions. After a while they did at least abandon the foreground of his thoughts. And up he went steadily, higher and higher into the clear air.

Once the mental shock of moving unsupported through the air was over, his sensations ceased to be unpleasant, became very speedily pleasurable. He had been warned of air sickness. But he found the pulsating movement of the aëropile as it drove up the faint south-west breeze was very little in excess of the pitching of a boat head on to broad rollers in a moderate gale, and he was constitutionally a good sailor. And the keenness of the more rarefied air into which they ascended produced a sense of lightness and exhilaration. He looked up and saw the blue sky above fretted with cirrus clouds. His eye came cautiously down through the ribs and bars to a shining flight of white birds that hung in the lower sky. For a space he watched these. Then going lower and less apprehensively, he saw the slender figure of the Wind-Vane keeper's crow's nest shining golden in the sunlight and growing smaller every moment. As his eye fell with more confidence now, there came a blue line of hills, and then London, already to leeward, an intricate space of roofing. Its near edge came sharp and clear, and banished his last apprehensions in a shock of surprise. For the boundary of London was like a wall, like a cliff, a steep fall of three or four hundred feet, a frontage broken only by terraces here and there, a complex decorative façade.

That gradual passage of town into country through an extensive sponge of suburbs, which was so characteristic a feature of the great cities of the nineteenth century, existed no longer. Nothing remained of it but a waste of ruins here, variegated and dense with thickets of the heterogeneous growths that had once adorned the gardens of the belt, interspersed among levelled brown patches of sown ground, and verdant stretches of winter greens. The latter even spread among the vestiges of houses. But for the most part the reefs and skerries of ruins, the wreckage of suburban villas, stood among their streets and roads, queer islands amidst the levelled expanses of green and brown, abandoned indeed by the inhabitants years since, but too substantial, it seemed, to be cleared out of the way of the wholesale horticultural mechanisms of the time.

The vegetation of this waste undulated and frothed amidst the countless cells of crumbling house walls, and broke along the foot of the city wall in a surf of bramble and holly and ivy and teazle and tall grasses. Here and there gaudy pleasure palaces towered amidst the puny remains of Victorian times, and cable ways slanted to them from the city. That winter day they seemed deserted. Deserted, too, were the artificial gardens among the ruins. The city limits were indeed as sharply defined as in the ancient days when the gates were shut at nightfall and the robber foeman prowled to the very walls. A huge semi-circular throat poured out a vigorous traffic upon the Eadhamite Bath Road. So the first prospect of the world beyond the city flashed on Graham, and dwindled. And when at last he could look vertically downward again, he saw below him the vegetable fields of the Thames valley—innumerable minute oblongs of ruddy brown, intersected by shining threads, the sewage ditches.

His exhilaration increased rapidly, became a sort of intoxication. He found himself drawing deep breaths of air, laughing aloud, desiring to shout. After a time that desire became too strong for him, and he shouted.

The machine had now risen as high as was customary with aëropiles, and they began to curve about towards the south. Steering, Graham perceived, was effected by the opening or closing of one or two thin strips of membrane in one or other of the otherwise rigid wings, and by the movement of the whole engine backward or forward along its supports. The aëronaut set the engine gliding slowly forward along its rail and opened the valve of the leeward wing until the stem of the aëropile was horizontal and pointing southward. And in that direction they drove with a slight list to leeward, and with a slow alternation of movement, first a short, sharp ascent and then a long downward glide that was very swift and pleasing. During these downward glides the propellor was inactive altogether. These ascents gave Graham a glorious sense of successful effort; the descents through the rarefied air were beyond all experience. He wanted never to leave the upper air again.

For a time he was intent upon the minute details of the landscape that ran swiftly northward beneath him. Its minute, clear detail pleased him exceedingly.

He was impressed by the ruin of the houses that had once dotted the country, by the vast treeless expanse of country from which all farms and villages had gone, save for crumbling ruins. He had known the thing was so, but seeing it so was an altogether different matter. He tried to make out places he had known within the hollow basin of the world below, but at first he could distinguish no data now that the Thames valley was left behind. Soon, however, they were driving over a sharp chalk hill that he recognised as the Guildford Hog's Back, because of the familiar outline of the gorge at its eastward end, and because of the ruins of the town that rose steeply on either lip of this gorge. And from that he made out other points, Leith Hill, the sandy wastes of Aldershot, and so forth. The Downs escarpment was set with gigantic slow-moving wind-wheels. Save where the broad Eadhamite Portsmouth Road, thickly dotted with rushing shapes, followed the course of the old railway, the gorge of the Wey was choked with thickets.

The whole expanse of the Downs escarpment, so far as the grey haze permitted him to see, was set with wind-wheels to which the largest of the city was but a younger brother. They stirred with a stately motion before the south-west wind. And here and there were patches dotted with the sheep of the British Food Trust, and here and there a mounted shepherd made a spot of black. Then rushing under the stern of the aëropile came the Wealden Heights, the line of Hindhead, Pitch Hill, and Leith Hill, with a second row of wind-wheels that seemed striving to rob the downland whirlers of their share of breeze. The purple heather was speckled with yellow gorse, and on the further side a drove of black oxen stampeded before a couple of mounted men. Swiftly these swept behind, and dwindled and lost colour, and became scarce moving specks that were swallowed up in haze.

And when these had vanished in the distance Graham heard a peewit wailing close at hand. He perceived he was now above the South Downs, and staring over his shoulder saw the battlements of Portsmouth Landing Stage towering over the ridge of Portsdown Hill. In another moment there came into sight a spread of shipping like floating cities, the little white cliffs of the Needles dwarfed and sunlit, and the grey and glittering waters of the narrow sea. They seemed to leap the Solent in a moment, and in a few seconds the Isle of Wight was running past, and then beneath him spread a wider and wider extent of sea, here purple with the shadow of a cloud, here grey, here a burnished mirror, and here a spread of cloudy greenish blue. The Isle of Wight grew smaller and smaller. In a few more minutes a strip of grey haze detached itself from other strips that were clouds, descended out of the sky and became a coastline—sunlit and pleasant—the coast of northern France. It rose, it took colour, became definite and detailed, and the counterpart of the Downland of England was speeding by below.

In a little time, as it seemed, Paris came above the horizon, and hung there for a space, and sank out of sight again as the aëropile circled about to the north again. But he perceived the Eiffel Tower still standing, and beside it a huge dome surmounted by a pinpoint Colossus. And he perceived, too, though he did not understand it at the time, a slanting drift of smoke. The aeronaut said something about "trouble in the underways," that Graham did not heed at the time. But he marked the minarets and towers and slender masses that streamed skyward above the city windvanes, and knew that in the mattter of grace at least Paris still kept in front of her larger rival. And even as he looked a pale blue shape ascended very swiftly from the city like a dead leaf driving up before a gale. It curved round and soared towards them growing rapidly larger and larger. The aëronaut was saying something. "What?" said Graham, loth to take his eyes from this. "Aëroplane, Sire," bawled the aëronaut pointing.

They rose and curved about northward as it drew nearer. Nearer it came and nearer, larger and larger. The throb, throb, throb—beat, of the aëropile's flight, that had seemed so potent and so swift, suddenly appeared slow by comparison with this tremendous rush. How great the monster seemed, how swift and steady! It passed quite closely beneath them, driving along silently, a vast spread of wire-netted translucent wings, a thing alive. Graham had a momentary glimpse of the rows and rows of wrapped-up passengers, slung in their little cradles behind wind-screens, of a white-clothed engineer crawling against the gale along a ladder way, of spouting engines beating together, of the whirling wind screw, and of a wide waste of wing. He exulted in the sight. And in an instant the thing had passed.

It rose slightly and their own little wings swayed in the rush of its flight. It fell and grew smaller. Scarcely had they moved, as it seemed, before it was again only a flat blue thing that dwindled in the sky. This was the aëroplane that went to and fro between London and Paris. In fair weather and in peaceful times it came and went four times a day.

They beat across the Channel, slowly as it seemed now, to Graham's enlarged ideas, and Beachy Head rose greyly to the left of them.

"Land," called the aëronaut, his voice small against the whistling of the air over the wind-screen.

"Not yet," bawled Graham, laughing. "Not land yet. I want to learn more of this machine."

"I meant—" said the aëronaut.

"I want to learn more of this machine," repeated Graham.

"I'm coming to you," he said, and had flung himself free of his chair and taken a step along the guarded rail between them. He stopped for a moment, and his colour changed and his hands tightened. Another step and he was clinging close to the aëronaut. He felt a weight on his shoulder, the pressure of the air. His hat was a whirling speck behind. The wind came in gusts over his wind-screen and blew his hair in streamers past his cheek. The aëronaut made some hasty adjustments for the shifting of the centres of gravity and pressure.

"I want to have these things explained," said Graham. "What do you do when you move that engine forward?"

The aëronaut hesitated. Then he answered, "They are complex, Sire."

"I don't mind," shouted Graham. "I don't mind."

There was a moment's pause. "Aëronautics is the secret—the privilege—"

"I know. But I'm the Master, and I mean to know." He laughed, full of this novel realisation of power that was his gift from the upper air.

The aëropile curved about, and the keen fresh wind cut across Graham's face and his garment lugged at his body as the stem pointed round to the west. The two men looked into each other's eyes.

"Sire, there are rules—"

"Not where I am concerned," said Graham. "You seem to forget."

The aëronaut scrutinised his face. "No," he said. "I do not forget, Sire. But in all the earth—no man who is not a sworn aëronaut—has ever a chance. They come as passengers—"

"I have heard something of the sort. But I'm not going to argue these points. Do you know why I have slept two hundred years? To fly!"

"Sire," said the aëronaut, "the rules—if I break the rules—"

Graham waved the penalties aside.

"Then if you will watch me—"

"No," said Graham, swaying and gripping tight as the machine lifted its nose again for an ascent. "That's not my game. I want to do it myself. Do it myself if I smash for it! No! I will. See. I am going to clamber by this—to come and share your seat. Steady! I mean to fly of my own accord if I smash at the end of it. I will have something to pay for my sleep. Of all other things—. In my past it was my dream to fly. Now—keep your balance."

"A dozen spies are watching me, Sire!"

Graham's temper was at end. Perhaps he chose it should be. He swore. He swung himself round the intervening mass of levers and the aëropile swayed.

"Am I Master of the earth?" he said. "Or is your Society? Now. Take your hands off those levers, and hold my wrists. Yes—so. And now, how do we turn her nose down to the glide?"

"Sire," said the aëronaut.

"What is it?"

"You will protect me?"

"Lord! Yes! If I have to burn London. Now!"

And with that promise Graham bought his first lesson in aërial navigation. "It's clearly to your advantage, this journey," he said with a loud laugh—for the air was like strong wine—"to teach me quickly and well. Do I pull this? Ah! So! Hullo!"

"Back, Sire! Back!"

"Back—right. One—two—three—good God! Ah! Up she goes! But this is living!"

And now the machine began to dance the strangest figures in the air. Now it would sweep round a spiral of scarcely a hundred yards diameter, now it would rush up into the air and swoop down again, steeply, swiftly, falling like a hawk, to recover in a rushing loop that swept it high again. In one of these descents it seemed driving straight at the drifting park of balloons in the southeast, and only curved about and cleared them by a sudden recovery of dexterity. The extraordinary swiftness and smoothness of the motion, the extraordinary effect of the rarefied air upon his constitution, threw Graham into a careless fury.

But at last a queer incident came to sober him, to send him flying down once more to the crowded life below with all its dark insoluble riddles. As he swooped, came a tap and something flying past, and a drop like a drop of rain. Then as he went on down he saw something like a white rag whirling down in his wake. "What was that?" he asked. "I did not see."

The aëronaut glanced, and then clutched at the lever to recover, for they were sweeping down. When the aëropile was rising again he drew a deep breath and replied. "That," and he indicated the white thing still fluttering down, "was a swan."

"I never saw it," said Graham.

The aëronaut made no answer, and Graham saw little drops upon his forehead.

They drove horizontally while Graham clambered back to the passenger's place out of the lash of the wind. And then came a swift rush down, with the wind-screw whirling to check their fall, and the flying stage growing broad and dark before them. The sun, sinking over the chalk hills in the west, fell with them, and left the sky a blaze of gold.

Soon men could be seen as little specks. He heard a noise coming up to meet him, a noise like the sound of waves upon a pebbly beach, and saw that the roofs about the flying stage were dark with his people rejoicing over his safe return. A dark mass was crushed together under the stage, a darkness stippled with innumerable faces, and quivering with the minute oscillation of waved white handkerchiefs and waving hands.

50

HENRY JAMES, 'LONDON', *ENGLISH HOURS* (BOSTON: HOUGHTON, MIFFLIN AND CO., 1905), PP. 36–39

Of course it is too much to say that all the satisfaction of life in London comes from literally living there, for it is not a paradox that a great deal of it consists in getting away. It is almost easier to leave it than not to, and much of its richness and interest proceeds from its ramifications, the fact that all England is in a suburban relation to it. Such an affair it is in comparison to get away from Paris or to get into it. London melts by wide, ugly zones into the green country, and becomes pretty insidiously, inadvertently—without stopping to change. It is the spoiling perhaps of the country, but it is the making of the insatiable town, and if one is a helpless and shameless cockney that is all one is obliged to look at. Anything is excusable which enlarges one's civic consciousness. It ministers immensely to that of the London-lover that, thanks to the tremendous system of coming and going, to the active, hospitable habits of the people, to the elaboration of the railway-service, the frequency and rapidity of trains, and last, though not least, to the fact that much of the loveliest scenery in England lies within a radius of fifty miles—thanks to all this he has the rural picturesque at his door and may cultivate unlimited vagueness as to the line of division between centre and circumference. It is perfectly open to him to consider the remainder of the United Kingdom, or the British empire in general, or even, if he be an American, the total of the English-speaking territories of the globe, as the mere margin, the fitted girdle.

Is it for this reason—because I like to think how great we all are together in the light of heaven and the face of the rest of the world, with the bond of our glorious tongue, in which we labour to write articles and books for each other's candid perusal, how great we all are and how great is the great city which we may unite fraternally to regard as the capital of our race—is it for this that I have a singular kindness for the London railway-stations, that I like them æsthetically, that they interest and fascinate me, and that I view them with complacency even when I wish neither to depart nor to arrive? They remind me of all our reciprocities and activities, our energies and curiosities, and our being all distinguished together from other people by our great common stamp of perpetual motion, our passion for seas and deserts and the other side of the globe, the secret of the impression of strength—I don't say of social roundness and finish—that we produce in any collection of Anglo-Saxon types. If in the beloved foggy season I delight in the spectacle of Paddington, Euston, or Waterloo,—I confess I prefer the grave northern stations,—I am prepared to defend myself against the charge of puerility; for what I seek and what I find in these vulgar scenes is at bottom simply so much evidence of our larger way of looking at life. The exhibition of variety of type is in general one of the bribes by which London induces you to condone her abominations, and the railway-platform is a kind of compendium of that variety. I think that nowhere so much as in London do people wear—to the eye of observation—definite signs of the sort of people they may be. If you like above all things to know the sort, you hail this fact with joy; you recognise that if the English are immensely distinct from other people, they are also socially—and that brings with it, in England, a train of moral and intellectual consequences—extremely distinct from each other. You may see them all together, with the rich colouring of their differences, in the fine flare of one of Mr. W. H. Smith's bookstalls—a feature not to be omitted in any enumeration of the charms of Paddington and Euston. It is a focus of warmth and light in the vast smoky cavern; it gives the idea that literature is a thing of splendour, of a dazzling essence, of infinite gas-lit red and gold. A glamour hangs over the glittering booth, and a tantalising air of clever new things. How brilliant must the books all be, how veracious and courteous the fresh, pure journals! Of a Saturday afternoon, as you wait in your corner of the compartment for the starting of the train, the window makes a frame for the glowing picture. I say of a Saturday afternoon, because that is the most characteristic time—it speaks most of the constant circulation and in particular of the quick jump, by express, just before dinner, for the Sunday, into the hall of the country-house and the forms of closer friendliness, the prolonged talks, the familiarising walks which London excludes.

51

HENRY JAMES, 'ISLE OF WIGHT', *PORTRAITS OF PLACES* (BOSTON: HOUGHTON, MIFFLIN AND CO., 1911), PP. 292–294

The Isle of Wight is disappointing at first. I wondered why it should be, and then I found the reason in the influence of the detestable little railway. There can be no doubt that a railway in the Isle of Wight is a gross impertinence; it is in evident contravention to the natural style of the place. The place is minutely, delicately picturesque, or it is nothing at all. It is purely ornamental; it exists for the entertainment of tourists. It is separated by nature from the dense railway-system of the less diminutive island, and it is the corner of the world where a good carriage-road is most in keeping. Never was there a better place for sacrificing to prettiness; never was there a better chance for not making a railway. But now there are twenty trains a day, and the prettiness is twenty times less. The island is so small that the hideous embankments and tunnels are obtrusive; the sight of them is as painful as it would be to see a pedlar's pack on the shoulders of a pretty woman. This is your first impression as you travel (naturally by the objectionable conveyance) from Ryde to Ventnor; and the fact that the train rumbles along very smoothly, and stops at half a dozen little stations, where the groups on the platform enable you to perceive that the population consists almost exclusively of gentlemen in costumes suggestive of unlimited leisure for attention to cravats and trousers (an immensely large class in England), of old ladies of the species denominated in France *rentières*, of young ladies of the highly-educated and sketching variety, this circumstance fails to reconcile you to the chartered cicatrix which forms your course. At Ventnor, however, face to face with the sea, and with the blooming shoulder of the Undercliff close behind you, you lose sight to a certain extent of the superfluities of civilisation. Not, indeed, that Ventnor has not been diligently civilised. It is a well-regulated little watering-place, and it has been subjected to a due measure of cockneyfication. But the glittering ocean remains, shimmering at moments with blue and silver, and the large gorse-covered downs rise superbly above it. Ventnor hangs upon the side of a steep hill, and here and there it clings and scrambles, it is propped and terraced, like one of the bright-faced little towns that look down upon the Mediterranean. To add to the Italian effect, the houses are all denominated villas, though it must be added that nothing is less like an

Italian villa than an English one. Those which ornament the successive ledges at Ventnor are for the most part small semi-detached boxes, predestined, even before they had fairly come into the world, to the entertainment of lodgers. They stand in serried rows all over the place, with the finest names in the British *Peerage* painted upon their gate-posts. Their severe similarity of aspect, however, is such that even the difference between Plantagenet and Percival, between Montgomery and Montmorency, is hardly sufficient to enlighten the puzzled visitor. An English watering-place is much more comfortable than an American; in a Plantagenet villa the art of receiving "summer guests" has usually been brought to a higher perfection than in an American rural hotel. But what strikes an American, with regard to even so charmingly-nestled a little town as Ventnor, is that it is far less natural, less pastoral and bosky, than his own fond image of a summer-retreat. There is too much brick and mortar; there are too many smoking chimneys and shops and public-houses; there are no woods nor brooks, nor lonely headlands; there is none of the virginal stillness of Nature. Instead of these things, there is an esplanade, mostly paved with asphalt, bordered with benches and little shops, and provided with a German band. To be just to Ventnor, however, I must hasten to add that once you get away from the asphalt there is a great deal of vegetation. The little village of Bonchurch, which closely adjoins it, is buried in the most elaborate verdure, muffled in the smoothest lawns and the densest shrubbery. Bonchurch is simply delicious, and indeed in a manner quite absurd. It is like a model village in imitative substances, kept in a big glass case; the turf might be of green velvet and the foliage of cut paper.

52

E. NESBIT, 'SAVIOURS OF THE TRAIN', *THE RAILWAY CHILDREN* (LONDON AND NEW YORK: MACMILLAN, 1906), PP. 127–137

"Hush. Stop! What's that?"

"That" was a very odd noise indeed,—a soft noise, but quite plainly to be heard through the sound of the wind in the tree branches, and the hum and whirr of the telegraph wires. It was a sort of rustling, whispering sound. As they listened it stopped, and then it began again.

And this time it did not stop, but it grew louder and more rustling and rumbling.

"Look—" cried Peter, suddenly—"the tree over there!"

The tree he pointed at was one of those that have rough gray leaves and white flowers. The berries, when they come, are bright scarlet, but if you pick them, they disappoint you by turning black before you get them home. And, as Peter pointed, the tree was moving,—not just the way trees ought to move when the wind blows through them, but all in one piece, as though it were a live creature and were walking down the side of the cutting.

"It's moving!" cried Bobbie. "Oh, look! and so are the others. It's like the woods in Macbeth."

"It's magic," said Phyllis, breathlessly. "I always knew this railway was enchanted."

It really did seem a little like magic. For all the trees for about twenty yards of the opposite bank seemed to be slowly walking down towards the railway line, the tree with the gray leaves bringing up the rear like some old shepherd driving a flock of green sheep.

"What is it? Oh, what is it?" said Phyllis; "it's much too magic for me. I don't like it. Let's go home."

But Bobby and Peter clung fast to the rail, and watched breathlessly. And Phyllis made no movement towards going home by herself.

The trees moved on and on. Some stones and loose earth fell down and rattled on the railway metals far below.

"It's *all* coming down," Peter tried to say, but he found there was hardly any voice to say it with. And, indeed, just as he spoke, the great rock, on the top of which the walking trees were, leaned slowly forward. The trees, ceasing to walk, stood still and shivered and shivered. Leaning with the rock, they seemed to hesitate a moment, and then rock and trees and grass and bushes, with a rushing sound, slipped right away from the face of the cutting and fell on the line with a blundering crash that could have been heard half a mile off. A cloud of dust rose up.

"Oh," said Peter, in awestruck tones, "isn't it exactly like when coals come in—if there wasn't any roof to the cellar and you could see down."

"Look what a great mound it's made!" said Bobbie.

"Yes, it's right across the down line," said Phyllis.

"That'll take some sweeping up," said Bobbie.

"Yes," said Peter, slowly. He was still leaning on the fence. "Yes," he said again, still more slowly.

Then he stood upright.

"The 11.2 down hasn't gone by yet. We must let them know at the station, or there'll be a most frightful accident."

"Let's run," said Bobbie, and began.

But Peter cried, "Come back!" and looked at Mother's watch. He was very prompt and businesslike, and his face looked whiter than they had ever seen it.

"No time," he said; "it's two miles away, and it's past eleven."

"Couldn't we," suggested Phyllis, breathlessly, "couldn't we climb up a telegraph post and do something to the wires?"

"We don't know how," said Peter.

"They do it in war," said Phyllis; "I know I've heard of it."

"They only *cut* them, silly," said Peter, "and that doesn't do any good. And we couldn't cut them even if we got up, and we couldn't get up. If we had anything red, we could get down on the line and wave it."

"But the train wouldn't see us till it got round the corner, and then it could see the mound just as well as us," said Phyllis; "better, because it's much bigger than us."

"If we only had something red," Peter repeated; "we could go round the corner and wave to the train."

"We might wave, anyway."

"They'd only think it was just *us*, as usual. We've waved so often before. Anyway, let's get down."

They got down the steep stairs. Bobbie was pale and shivering. Peter's face looked thinner than usual. Phyllis was red-faced and damp with anxiety.

"Oh, how hot I am!" she said; "and I thought it was going to be cold; I wish we hadn't put on our—" she stopped short, and then ended in quite a different tone—"our flannel petticoats."

Bobbie turned at the bottom of the stairs.

"Oh, yes," she cried; "*they're* red! Let's take them off."

They did, and with the petticoats rolled up under their arms, ran along the railway, skirting the newly fallen mound of stones and rock and earth, and bent, crushed, twisted trees. They ran at their best pace. Peter led, but the girls were not far behind. They reached the corner that hid the mound from the straight line of railway that ran half a mile without curve or corner.

"Now," said Peter, taking hold of the largest flannel petticoat.

"You're not—" Phyllis faltered—"you're not going to *tear* them?"

"Shut up," said Peter, with brief sternness.

"Oh, yes," said Bobbie, "tear them into little bits if you like. Don't you see, Phil, if we can't stop the train, there'll be a real live accident, with people *killed*. Oh, horrible! Here, Peter, you'll never tear it through the band!"

She took the red flannel petticoat from him and tore it off an inch from the band. Then she tore the other in the same way.

"There!" said Peter, tearing in his turn. He divided each petticoat into three pieces. "Now, we've got six flags." He looked at the watch again. "And we've got seven minutes. We must have flag-staffs."

The knives given to boys are, for some odd reason, seldom of the kind of steel that keeps sharp. The young saplings had to be broken off. Two came up by the roots. The leaves were stripped from them.

"We must cut holes in the flags, and run the sticks through the holes," said Peter. And the holes were cut. The knife was sharp enough to cut flannel with. Two of the flags were set up in heaps of loose stones between the sleepers of the down line. Then Phyllis and Roberta took each a flag, and stood ready to wave it as soon as the train came in sight.

"I shall have the other two myself," said Peter, "because it was my idea if we waved something red."

"They're our petticoats, though," Phyllis was beginning, but Bobbie interrupted—

"Oh, what does it matter who waves what, if we can only save the train?"

Perhaps Peter had not rightly calculated the number of minutes it would take the 11.29 to get from the station to the place where they were, or perhaps the train was late. Anyway, it seemed a very long time that they waited.

Phyllis grew impatient. "I expect the watch is wrong, and the train's gone by," said she.

Peter relaxed the heroic attitude he had chosen to shew off his two flags with. And Bobbie began to feel sick with suspense.

It seemed to her that they had been standing there for hours and hours, holding those silly little red flannel flags that no one would ever notice. The train wouldn't care. It would go rushing by them and tear round the corner and go crashing into that awful mound. And every one would be killed. Her hands grew very cold and trembled so that she could hardly hold the flag. And then came the distant rumble and hum of the metals, and a puff of white steam showed far away along the stretch of line.

"Stand firm," said Peter, "and wave like mad! When it gets to that big furze bush step back, but go on waving! Don't stand *on* the line, Bobbie!"

The train came rattling along very very fast.

"They don't see us! They won't see us! It's all no good!" cried Bobbie.

The two little flags on the line swayed as the nearing train shook and loosened the heaps of loose stones that held them up. One of them slowly leaned over and fell on the line. Bobbie jumped forward and caught it up, and waved it; her hands did not tremble now.

"Keep off the line, you silly cuckoo!" said Peter, fiercely.

It seemed that the train came on as fast as ever. It was very near now

"It's no good," Bobbie said again.

"Stand back!" cried Peter, suddenly, and he dragged Phyllis back by the arm.

But Bobbie cried, "Not yet, not yet!" and waved her two flags right over the line. The front of the engine looked black and enormous. It's voice was loud and harsh.

"Oh, stop, stop, stop!" cried Bobbie. No one heard her. At least Peter and Phyllis didn't, for the oncoming rush of the train covered the sound of her voice with a mountain of sound. But afterwards she used to wonder whether the engine itself had not heard her. It seemed almost as though it had—for it slackened swiftly, slackened and stopped, not twenty yards from the place where Bobbie's two flags waved over the line. She saw the great black engine stop dead, but somehow she could not stop waving the flags. And when the driver and the fireman had got off the engine and Peter and Phyllis had gone to meet them and pour out their excited tale of the awful mound just round the corner, Bobbie still waved the flags but more and more feebly and jerkily.

When the others turned towards her she was lying across the line with her hands flung forward and still gripping the sticks of the little red flannel flags.

The engine-driver picked her up, carried her to the train, and laid her on the cushions of a first-class carriage.

"Gone right off in a faint," he said, "poor little woman. And no wonder. I'll just 'ave a look at this 'ere mound of yours, and then we'll run you back to the station and get her seen to."

It was horrible to see Bobbie lying so white and quiet, with her lips blue, and parted.

"I believe that's what people look like when they're dead," whispered Phyllis.

"*Don't!*" said Peter, sharply.

They sat by Bobbie on the blue cushions, and the train ran back. Before it reached their station Bobbie had sighed and opened her eyes, and rolled herself over and begun to cry. This cheered the others wonderfully. They had seen her cry before, but they had never seen her faint, nor any one else, for the matter of that. They had not known what to do when she was fainting, but now she was only crying they could thump her on the back and tell her not to, just as they always did. And presently, when she stopped crying, they were able to laugh at her for being such a coward as to faint.

When the station was reached, the three were the heroes of an agitated meeting on the platform.

The praises they got for their "prompt action," their "common sense," their "ingenuity," were enough to have turned anybody's head. Phyllis enjoyed herself thoroughly. She had never been a real heroine, and the feeling was delicious. Peter's ears got very red. Yet he, too, enjoyed himself. Only Bobbie wished they all wouldn't. She wanted to get away.

"You'll hear from the Company about this, I expect," said the Station Master.

Bobbie wished she might never hear of it again. She pulled at Peter's jacket.

"Oh, come away, come away! I want to go home," she said.

So they went. And as they went Station Master and Porter and guards and driver and firemen and passengers sent up a cheer.

"Oh, listen," cried Phyllis; "that's for *us*!"

"Yes," said Peter, "I say, I am glad I thought about something red, and waving it."

"How lucky we *did* put on our red flannel petticoats!" said Phyllis.

Bobbie said nothing. She was thinking of the horrible mound, and the trustful train rushing towards it.

"And it was *us* that saved them," said Peter.

"How dreadful if they'd all been killed!" said Phyllis, with enjoyment; "wouldn't it, Bobbie?"

"We never got any cherries, after all," said Bobbie.

The others thought her rather heartless.

53

E. M. FORSTER, *HOWARDS END* (NEW YORK: G. P. PUTNAM SONS, 1911), PP. 12–19

Might it really be best to accept Aunt Juley's kind offer, and to send her down to Howards End with a note?

Certainly Margaret was impulsive. She did swing rapidly from one decision to another. Running downstairs into the library, she cried: "Yes, I have changed my mind; I do wish that you would go."

There was a train from King's Cross at eleven. At half-past ten Tibby, with rare self-effacement, fell asleep, and Margaret was able to drive her aunt to the station.

"You will remember, Aunt Juley, not to be drawn into discussing the engagement. Give my letter to Helen, and say whatever you feel yourself, but do keep clear of the relatives. We have scarcely got their names straight yet, and, besides, that sort of thing is so uncivilised and wrong."

"So uncivilised?" queried Mrs. Munt, fearing that she was losing the point of some brilliant remark.

"Oh, I used an affected word. I only meant would you please talk the thing over only with Helen."

"Only with Helen."

"Because—" But it was no moment to expound the personal nature of love. Even Margaret shrank from it, and contented herself with stroking her good aunt's hand, and with meditating, half sensibly and half poetically, on the journey that was about to begin from King's Cross.

Like many others who have lived long in a great capital, she had strong feelings about the various railway termini. They are our gates to the glorious and the unknown. Through them we pass out into adventure and sunshine, to them, alas! we return. In Paddington all Cornwall is latent and the remoter west; down the inclines of Liverpool Street lie fenlands and the illimitable Broads; Scotland is through the pylons of Euston; Wessex behind the poised chaos of Waterloo. Italians realise this, as is natural; those of them who are so unfortunate as to serve as waiters in Berlin call the Anhalt Bahnhof the Stazione d'Italia, because by it they must return to their homes. And he is a chilly Londoner who does not endow his stations with some personality, and extend to them, however shyly, the emotions of fear and love.

To Margaret—I hope that it will not set the reader against her—the station of King's Cross had always suggested Infinity. Its very situation—withdrawn a little behind the facile splendours of St. Pancras—implied a comment on the materialism of life. Those two great arches, colourless, indifferent, shouldering between them an unlovely clock, were fit portals for some eternal adventure, whose issue might be prosperous, but would certainly not be expressed in the ordinary language of prosperity. If you think this ridiculous, remember that it is not Margaret who is telling you about it; and let me hasten to add that they were in plenty of time for the train; that Mrs. Munt, though she took a second-class ticket, was put by the guard into a first (only two "seconds" on the train, one smoking and the other babies—one cannot be expected to travel with babies); and that Margaret, on her return to Wickham Place, was confronted with the following telegram:

"All over. Wish I had never written. Tell no one.—HELEN."

But Aunt Juley was gone—gone irrevocably, and no power on earth could stop her.

MOST complacently did Mrs. Munt rehearse her mission. Her nieces were independent young women, and it was not often that she was able to help them. Emily's daughters had never been quite like other girls. They had been left motherless when Tibby was born, when Helen was five and Margaret herself but thirteen. It was before the passing of the Deceased Wife's Sister Bill, so Mrs. Munt could without impropriety offer to go and keep house at Wickham Place. But her brother-in-law, who was peculiar and a German, had referred the question to Margaret, who with the crudity of youth had answered, "No, they could manage much better alone." Five years later Mr. Schlegel had died too, and Mrs. Munt had repeated her offer. Margaret, crude no longer, had been grateful and extremely nice, but the substance of her answer had been the same. "I must not interfere a third time," thought Mrs. Munt. However, of course she did. She learnt, to her horror, that Margaret, now of age, was taking her money out of the old safe investments and putting it into Foreign Things, which always smash. Silence would have been criminal. Her own fortune was invested in Home Rails, and most ardently did she beg her niece to imitate her. "Then we should be together, dear." Margaret, out of politeness, invested a few hundreds in the Nottingham and Derby Railway, and though the Foreign Things did admirably and the Nottingham and Derby declined with the steady dignity of which only Home Rails are capable, Mrs. Munt never ceased to rejoice, and to say, "I did manage that, at all events. When the smash comes poor Margaret will have a nest-egg to fall back upon." This year Helen came of age, and exactly the same thing happened in Helen's case; she also would shift her money out of Consols, but she, too, almost without being pressed, consecrated a fraction of it to the Nottingham and Derby Railway. So far so good, but in social matters their aunt had accomplished nothing. Sooner or later the girls would enter on the process known as throwing themselves away, and if they had delayed hitherto, it was only that they might throw themselves more vehemently in the future. They saw too many people at Wickham Place—unshaven musicians, an actress even, German cousins (one knows what foreigners are), acquaintances picked up at Continental hotels (one knows what they are too). It was interesting, and down at Swanage no one appreciated culture more than Mrs. Munt; but it was dangerous, and disaster was bound to come. How right she was, and how lucky to be on the spot when the disaster came!

The train sped northward, under innumerable tunnels. It was only an hour's journey, but Mrs. Munt had to raise and lower the window again and again. She passed through the South Welwyn Tunnel, saw light for a moment, and entered the North Welwyn Tunnel, of tragic fame. She traversed the immense viaduct, whose arches span untroubled meadows and the dreamy flow of Tewin Water. She skirted the parks of politicians. At times the Great North Road accompanied her, more suggestive of infinity than any railway, awakening, after a nap of a hundred years, to such life as is conferred by the stench of motor-cars, and to such culture as is implied by the advertisements of antibilious pills. To history, to tragedy, to the past, to the future, Mrs. Munt remained equally indifferent; hers but to concentrate on the end of her journey, and to rescue poor Helen from this dreadful mess.

The station for Howards End was at Hilton, one of the large villages that are strung so frequently along the North Road, and that owe their size to the traffic of coaching and pre-coaching days. Being near London, it had not shared in the rural decay, and its long High Street had budded out right and left into residential estates. For about a mile a series of tiled and slated houses passed before Mrs. Munt's inattentive eyes, a series broken at one point by six Danish tumuli that stood shoulder to shoulder along the highroad, tombs of soldiers. Beyond these tumuli, habitations thickened, and the train came to a standstill in a tangle that was almost a town.

The station, like the scenery, like Helen's letters, struck an indeterminate note. Into which country will it lead, England or Suburbia? It was new, it had island platforms and a subway, and the superficial comfort exacted by business men. But it held hints of local life, personal intercourse, as even Mrs. Munt was to discover.

"I want a house," she confided to the ticket boy. "Its name is Howards Lodge. Do you know where it is?"

"Mr. Wilcox!" the boy called.

A young man in front of them turned round.

"She's wanting Howards End."

There was nothing for it but to go forward, though Mrs. Munt was too much agitated even to stare at the stranger. But remembering that there were two brothers, she had the sense to say to him, "Excuse me asking, but are you the younger Mr. Wilcox or the elder?"

"The younger. Can I do anything for you?"

"Oh, well"—she controlled herself with difficulty. "Really. Are you? I—" She moved away from the ticket boy and lowered her voice. "I am Miss Schlegel's aunt. I ought to introduce myself, ought n't I? My name is Mrs. Munt."

She was conscious that he raised his cap and said quite coolly, "Oh, rather; Miss Schlegel is stopping with us. Did you want to see her?"

"Possibly—"

"I'll call you a cab. No; wait a mo—" He thought. "Our motor's here. I'll run you up in it."

"That is very kind—"

"Not at all, if you'll just wait till they bring out a parcel from the office. This way."

"My niece is not with you by any chance?"

"No; I came over with my father. He has gone on north in your train. You'll see Miss Schlegel at lunch. You're coming up to lunch, I hope?"

"I should like to come *up*," said Mrs. Munt, not committing herself to nourishment until she had studied Helen's lover a little more. He seemed a gentleman, but had so rattled her round that her powers of observation were numbed. She glanced at him stealthily. To a feminine eye there was nothing amiss in the sharp depressions at the corners of his mouth, or in the rather box-like construction of his forehead. He was dark, clean-shaven, and seemed accustomed to command.

"In front or behind? Which do you prefer? It may be windy in front."

"In front if I may; then we can talk."

"But excuse me one moment—I can't think what they're doing with that parcel." He strode into the booking-office, and called with a new voice: "Hi! hi, you there! Are you going to keep me waiting all day? Parcel for Wilcox, Howards End. Just look sharp!" Emerging, he said in quieter tones: "This station's abominably organised; if I had my way, the whole lot of 'em should get the sack. May I help you in?"

"This is very good of you," said Mrs. Munt, as she settled herself into a luxurious cavern of red leather, and suffered her person to be padded with rugs and shawls. She was more civil than she had intended, but really this young man was very kind. Moreover, she was a little afraid of him; his self-possession was extraordinary. "Very good indeed," she repeated, adding: "It is just what I should have wished."

"Very good of you to say so," he replied, with a slight look of surprise, which, like most slight looks, escaped Mrs. Munt's attention. "I was just tooling my father over to catch the down train."

"You see, we heard from Helen this morning."

Young Wilcox was pouring in petrol, starting his engine, and performing other actions with which this story has no concern. The great car began to rock, and the form of Mrs. Munt, trying to explain things, sprang agreeably up and down among the red cushions. "The mater will be very glad to see you," he mumbled. "Hi! I say. Parcel. Parcel for Howards End. Bring it out. Hi!"

A bearded porter emerged with the parcel in one hand and an entry book in the other. With the gathering whir of the motor these ejaculations mingled: "Sign, must I? Why the—should I sign after all this bother? Not even got a pencil on you? Remember next time I report you to the station-master. My time's of value, though yours may n't be. Here"—here being a tip.

"Extremely sorry, Mrs. Munt."

"Not at all, Mr. Wilcox."

"And do you object to going through the village? It is rather a longer spin, but I have one or two commissions."

"I should love going through the village. Naturally I am very anxious to talk things over with you."

As she said this she felt ashamed, for she was disobeying Margaret's instructions. Only disobeying them in the letter, surely. Margaret had only warned her against discussing the incident with outsiders. Surely it was not "uncivilised or wrong" to discuss it with the young man himself, since chance had thrown them together.

A reticent fellow, he made no reply. Mounting by her side, he put on gloves and spectacles, and off they drove, the bearded porter—life is a mysterious business—looking after them with admiration.

The wind was in their faces down the station road, blowing the dust into Mrs. Munt's eyes. But as soon as they turned into the Great North Road she opened fire. "You can well imagine," she said, "that the news was a great shock to us."

Part 8

THE RAILWAY ACCIDENT, PUBLIC HEALTH, AND MILITARY DEPLOYMENT

54

'WOLVERHAMPTON', *THE SPECTATOR*, FEBRUARY 24, 1838, PP. 176–177

On the night of Tuesday week, a serious accident occured on the Liverpool and Birmingham Railway. As the mixed train was proceeding down the inclined plane between Wolverhampton and Birmingham, it came in contact with a horse, which had strayed upon the railway from the adjoining fields. The consequences are detailed as follows—

"The affrighted animal fell across the rails; and the engine, tender, and many of the carriages, passed over his body; and such was the violence of the shock occasioned by its resistance to the moving vehicles, that the engine shot off the lines with prodigious force, dragging with it, down the embankment of five or six feet high, the ponderous vehicle, the tender, and several of the carriages, smashing some into splinters, prostrating others, and displacing all more or less. The tender fell upon the body of one of the conductors of the engine, who was instantly crushed to death; the other (his brother) retained his hold upon the machine, and escaped without injury. The three first carriages contained horses; which, of course, were dreadfully mangled and bruised. The next and first carriage in the train containing passengers was upset, and thrown upon its side upon the railway; but, marvellous to relate, neither the passengers inside nor the guard upon the top, who was hurled headlong into the ditch below, sustained any injury. The numerous passengers in the other vehicles retained their seats; and, beyond the shock and alarm, and delay, sustained no inconvenience."

The next train from Liverpool was warned in time to prevent its running against the first train—

"In order to get into the other line of railway, it had to retrace the ground to Wolverhampton; and there, whilst in the act of passing from one line to the other, owing to some derangement of the moveable points of intersection of the rails, the engine and tender ran off the rails with a violence which separated them from the train, which, with its numerous cargo of passengers, was thus left without any means of reaching its destination at midnight, fourteen miles from Birmingham."

55

'IN THE TEMPLE GARDENS', *TEMPLE BAR* 2 (JULY, 1861), PP. 286–287

I beckoned to her. She quickly understood my meaning, rose, and, with a noiseless tread, followed me from the room. I determined to take advantage of the mother's drugged sleep, and give the poor child a change from the depressing monotony of the sick-room.

"We set out for a walk then, Lily gradually resuming her old sunny manner. Not far from the house were then open fields. I speak of some years back, remember. In a cutting through these ran the Birmingham Railway, and it was a great delight to the child to sit on the well-turfed slope of the cutting and watch the trains as they dashed past to and fro. To this spot, then, we once more directed our steps, took our seats, and commenced counting the lines of carriages which the shrieking engine whirled away from us. Lily was busy, too, making daisy-chains, and tying up bouquets of clover, and decking me with wild flowers.

"For a few minutes my thoughts wandered back into the past, to my counting-house life—to my deep love—to my dead wife—to my lost son. Then I thought of that angry sick woman, racked by her fierce jealous passions; and lastly of the poor child Lily, whom I was forbidden to love, who was forbidden to love me, and whose company I could only enjoy by stealth. I started from my reverie. I looked round for Lily. To my horror, I found that she had descended the incline, and, in her anxiety for daisies, had wandered on to the line of the railway, and was plucking them close to the very rails. I called to her in an agony. She looked up with a crow of delight, holding overhead a little bunch of daisies. Then—then—O God! came the hideous shriek—the whirling train grinding on its grim iron way! She saw her danger, gave a little scream of terror, and hurried back towards the slope. Too late! too late! The monstrous engine struck her cruelly. She was flung forward several yards on to the side of the cutting; a terrible wound was shining on her forehead, and the red blood clogging and soiling her golden hair.

"Half swooning with fright, I hurried towards her; a look of suffering and alarm was upon her face—with mouth half open, showing the tiny pearly teeth within, and eyes staring under raised and rigid brows. I felt for her heart's beating, but could detect no pulsation. Not a soul was near to proffer aid or counsel. The train had hurried by this time a mile away; my heart was throbbing with a violence that was exquisitely painful, my head burned, and strange shapes seemed to dance before my eyes. I *knew that she was dead*, yet I would not know it.

"I took her in my arms—heavy and motionless, with swinging limbs—God, how it sickened me to see her so!—and ran back all the way to my house. A superhuman strength seemed given me to accomplish this, or perhaps I should say rather the force of insanity assisted me, for at that moment I felt I was mad.

"She stood at the door-step—up and dressed, and leaning on her stick—wan and pale, with dark circles round her great staring eyes, and the red light burning fiercely in them. She thrust forth her thin trembling hand as she saw me.

" 'Where is the child?' she said, her fingers clutching out claw-wise.

" 'Be calm; pray compose yourself,' I murmured, as well as I was able.

" 'Where is she?' she shrieked. 'What has happened? Lily! Lily! Give her me.'

"Her glance fell upon the dead child in my arms. I covered over with my hand the poor head, lest she should see the red stains among the silky curls. She was too quick for me.

" 'Take away your hands. Lilian, my own—my own, own darling. Monster, you have murdered her! O God! see the blood upon his hands—he has killed her.'

"With the scream of one insane, she flung herself upon me and tore away the child. She hugged the body tight to her heart, and kissed the wounded head till her white face was blotched and stained with blood. Suddenly she swooned back and fell heavily on the floor, still clasping the dead child to her heart. She never spoke sensibly again. She lived through that night and the following day; but she died the next evening, with the child still in her arms. One grave contained them both, and I was left alone—how sad, God only knows."

56

'ARMAGH', *THE SPECTATOR*, JUNE 15, 1889, 813

The worst railway accident ever reported from Ireland occurred on the 12th inst., on the Great Northern line. An excursion had been arranged on that day for the Sunday-school children of Armagh, and at 9.30 a train of fifteen carriages left the station, laden with a thousand boys and girls, and their teachers and friends. It was soon perceived that the engine was not strong enough for its work, and about two miles from the town, near the top of a steep incline, the train came to a standstill. According to the officials, the couplings broke; according to all independent witnesses, the driver and guard uncoupled the last seven carriages, "propping" that section with a stone or two under the wheels. The section with the engine then moved on, and the section left behind, jarred by the jerk, knocked aside the stones and rolled back towards Armagh down the incline. Gathering speed from its own weight, it dashed on at forty miles an hour, and crashed into a slowly moving train just come out of Armagh. Two of the carriages were telescoped, and eighty children and grown-up persons were killed, sixty more being seriously injured. The scene was so indescribably shocking, that a carman named Hughes, who came up to assist, died of horror at the sight. Assistance of every kind was immediately procured, the neighbourhood turning out for miles; but nothing could be done except for the wounded, and the whole town is plunged in grief and mourning. The officials appear to be gravely to blame: first, for allowing the train to be overpacked—an average of twenty-two to a compartment—secondly, for supplying insufficient draught-power; and thirdly, for carelessness, if that part of the story is correct, in leaving the last section of the train to run back. Their culpable failure has cost perhaps a hundred innocent lives and an untold amount of domestic misery, and may cost a fine on the shareholders which will spoil the dividend for a year.

57

'THE INFLUENCE OF RAILWAY TRAVELLING ON PUBLIC HEALTH', *THE LANCET*, 1862, PP. 15–17

Report of the Commission

IN the year 1825 there was, in the whole world, only one railway carriage, built to convey passengers. It ran on the first railway between Stockton and Darlington, and bore on its panels the motto—

"Periculum privatum, publica utilitas."

The generation, which then was young, and now is old, has seen mighty changes such as it was never before given to one generation to witness. But none of these changes have been more remarkable than those which trace their origin in clear line to the ugly yellow carriage that passed almost unnoticed in the opening procession slowly dragged by the first engine along the first railway line.

From the time of this trial trip there was no longer any question as to the public utility of the new system of travelling; and the lapse of a third of a century has proved to demonstration how aptly chosen were the words "publica utilitas," selected by George Stephenson as best describing the purpose his grand project was destined to subserve. He foresaw "the day when railways would come to supersede almost all other modes of conveyance in this country, and railroads become the great highway for the King and all his subjects." These were his own words, and the hearer of them lives to witness their exact fulfilment.

But if there was no question as to public utility, yet the first words of the motto—that this new method of travelling was void of danger—met no such ready assent; for the most alarming conjectures were put forth as to injurious influences on public health which railway travelling must produce, and awful dangers were described as impending over rash adventurers who should thus risk their safety.

A century and a half previous to the earliest times of railway travelling, similar warnings had been uttered about a new-fangled mode of conveyance just then introduced; and stage coaches were described as "one of the greatest evils that had happened to the kingdom." The injury to health from their use was only one of many disastrous results. Those who travelled by these coaches, it was urged, became weary and listless, and contracted an idle habit of body. "What advantage is it to men's health," asks one author, "to be called out of their beds into their coaches an hour before day in the morning, to be hurried in them from place to place till one hour, two, or three within night, after sitting all day, in the summer time stifled with heat and choked with dust, or in the winter starving and freezing with cold? What addition is it to men's health or business to ride all day with strangers, oftentimes sick, ancient, diseased persons, or young children crying; many times poisoned with their nasty scents? Is it for a man's health to be laid fast in foul ways, and forced to wade up to the knees in mire,—to travel in rotten coaches, necessitated to bait or lodge at the worst inn on the road?"—and so on until the writer had made a case sufficient to demand the immediate suppression of stage coaches. With custom and after experience the influence of coach travelling on health and comfort came to be very differently estimated. Pennant says the coaches of his time (1739) were fitted for the conveyance of "the soft inhabitants of Sybaris;" and a scientific dictionary (1763) says, "at present they seem to want nothing either with regard to ease or magnificence." Yet some thirty years after this, when the late Lord Campbell first travelled by coach from the north to London, he was gravely advised to stay a day at York, as the rapidity of motion (eight miles per hour) had caused several through-going passengers to die of apoplexy.

The dangers from railway travelling with which the public were at first threatened were innumerable. The immense velocity (for some rash speculators had hinted at a pace of twenty miles an hour) was fraught with danger to the respiration, and the carbonic acid generated by the fuel when passing through long tunnels would inevitably produce suffocation by "the destruction of the atmosphere." Tunnels would expose healthy people to colds, catarrhs, and consumptions. Boiling and maiming were to be every-day occurrences. And numbers of less demonstrative people looked on the suggested innovation either as a wicked tempting of Providence, or a wild scheme too visionary to be worthy of serious consideration.

We have outlived the time of these prejudices. We have reached a period when loose inferences and vague surmises should no longer be permitted to usurp the place of exact knowledge. For the immense collection of facts and data already made in reference to railways, and the experience accumulated by the rapid development of railway travelling, supply materials abundantly sufficient to justify a systematic inquiry into the influence on health of railway travelling, with reasonable prospect of attaining reliable results and determining many harassing doubts.

Medical men are often asked whether they consider railway travelling prejudicial to health. Usually some case is cited on which the question is made to turn; precision as to history and symptoms being more or less disregarded. But the very frequency of the interrogation points to the same conclusion which careful inquiry has led us to form—that there has been gradually growing up in the public mind a suspicion of dangers from railway travelling widely different from that apprehension with which the thoughts of travellers were at first uneasily possessed. It is no longer the fear of accidents so much as a vague dread of certain undefined consequences to health resulting from influences peculiarly produced by this mode of travelling; and we find that those little likely to form decided opinions without careful inquiry share this feeling, and do not hesitate to express it. In his evidence before a Committee of the House of Commons in 1859, Lord Shaftesbury said, "The very power of locomotion keeps persons in a state of great nervous excitement, and it is worthy of attention to what an extent this effect prevails. I have ascertained that many persons who have been in the habit of travelling by railway have been obliged to give it up in consequence of the effect on the nervous system. I think that all these things indicate a tendency to nervous excitement, and in what it may issue I do not know." In the course of this inquiry, it is proposed to consider the evidence on which rests the prevailing public opinion very fairly represented by the remarks of this careful observer.

It is due, however, that we first mention the actual amount of railway travelling according to the latest estimates, and then consider the extent of those immediate dangers to life and limb usually grouped under the common term of railway accidents; in order that these may not interfere with subsequent considerations as to other influences of railway travelling, apart from the immediate risk of personal injury.

There are now about 11,000 miles of railway, mostly double lines, in operation in Great Britain; equivalent to the total length of all the railways in the rest of Europe, according to the last returns. The number of individual journeys undertaken in the United Kingdom have increased, during the last ten years, at the rate of nearly ten millions per annum. The distance now daily travelled by passenger-trains would circle the whole world six times. The separate journeys made during the year 1860 amounted to 164,633,028, the average length of each journey being rather more than fourteen miles.

The saving of time by railway as compared with the best of other modes of conveyance is about one hour in each twelve miles. And so, in the course of a twelvemonth there is added to the available time of the community a period of upwards of 20,000 years; or, in other words, there is a number three times as great as this added to the effective working population of the country, reckoning eight hours as the work-time in each day. Certain reservations must, however, be borne in mind so far as these figures are concerned, since journeys now rendered easy by rail would never have been undertaken but for its facilities. Allowing the widest margin for this and other exceptions, there still remains a clear annual saving, which may be reckoned by hundreds of years; and this has an indirect bearing on the subject of public health which may be here alluded to.

For people in the present day do more work, with less recreation, or provision of rest for the mind and exercise for the body, than at any previous time. In the middle ages, the number of feasts and holidays ordered by the Church or established by custom ensured many days in the year when no business was thought of. In large towns, it was the duty of citizens to encourage and join in athletic games and exercises, for which certain hours were set apart, and which inured men to resist the influences of cold, of discomfort, and even of disease. In London, occupations of this salutary kind were solemnly enjoined, and, from the account of Stowe, must have absorbed a considerable amount of time. In the eighteenth century, general holidays and festivals decreased in number, and public exercises were gradually discontinued. But, even then, a journey by horse or coach, tedious and uncomfortable as it now seems, had yet the advantage of affording a period of rest from anxieties whilst on the road, and of physical exercise or motion in the open air; the mind being necessarily diverted by the personal incidents of the journey. With the increase of railway travelling, and the greater facilities for transaction of business which rapid communication affords, there has been a corresponding change in the habits of the people, a devotion of more time to the work of life, and a neglect of means adapted to ensure vigorous and resistent physical health.

For that important social change during late years, a progressive increase in the number of the middle classes, which is in great measure attributable to railways, affords the means of avoiding many of those unhealthy influences with which a worse clothed, worse housed, and worse fed population had formerly to contend. There is strength and stamina sufficient to get comfortably through life, but very little of that surplus physical health which we have named resistent. There are the means to fly, but not the power to fight. And so, when a warning comes that the energies of the mind or the endurance of the body have been overtaxed and broken down, it not unfrequently happens that the real source of the mischief is disregarded, the *post* and *propter* are confused, and the disastrous result is attributed to some cause of really secondary importance. This consideration should especially be borne in mind in all cases where impairment of health is attributed exclusively to the influence of railway travelling.

RAILWAY ACCIDENTS.—The information possessed as to the extent and character of accidents occurring on railways is very precise, while other means are available for comparing them with accidents from other modes of travelling. The passenger-trains of the United Kingdom travelled over nearly 50,000,000 of miles in 1859. In 1860, the distance had increased to 52,816,579 miles. The number of railway accidents in four years was as follows:—

Year.	Accidents.	Killed.	Injured.
1857	62	26	657
1858	56	35	467
1859	56	13	386
1860	68	37	515

In the Metropolis alone there were 70 persons killed and 910 injured by coach and carriage accidents in 1859. In Paris, the numbers in 1860 were 30 killed and 579 injured. The average number of deaths in coal-mines in this country is 1000 per annum; and it is calculated that a British vessel is wrecked in each tide throughout the year. Here is proof sufficient of the comparative safety of railways compared with other modes of travelling and with other conditions of life in which the individual does not rely on himself for security.

Furthermore, it is readily seen what is the average risk to each individual traveller. Of persons killed by railway accidents in the United Kingdom, the proportion to the whole number of travellers was, in 1854, 1 in 7,195,342. In 1860, it was 1 in 5,677,000. In France, it was 1 in 7,000,000. In Belgium, 1 in 8,860,000. In Prussia, 1 in 17,500,000 of all travellers. The proportion of persons killed whilst travelling by diligences in France was 1 in 335,000—about equal to the proportions of both *killed and injured* on English and French railways. On the railways of the United States these amount, however, to 1 in 188,000; but there the cost incurred in constructing the lines is two-thirds less than on European railways.

Railway travelling, then, as at present conducted, is more free from actual danger to life and limb than any other mode of conveyance. But the returns which show this, also help to prove something more. It would be beyond our province to discuss all the causes which endanger the safety of travellers by rail, for this would involve entering into all the details of railway management. But after long and careful investigation, we deem it right to direct attention here to one source of danger so little known to the public that not even the continual recurrence of accidents clearly traceable to this source has as yet aroused attention to this increasing cause of risk.

COLLISIONS.—Of the whole number of railway accidents (242) occurring during four years, 149 were due to collisions. Of 2136 deaths and injuries in the same time, 1643 were attributable to collisions. In the last six months of the year (during the time when irregular or excursion trains run) the number of collisions was 93, as compared with 56 in the first half of the year.

At any given time, and in the most perfectly appointed train travelling on the most exactly laid line, the lives and safety of the passengers are in the keeping of three men, on whose clearness of head, knowledge of their business, and command of all their faculties, everything depends. These are the signal-man, the engine-driver, and the guard. It is therefore a matter of vital importance that every possible precaution should be adopted to insure that each of these men, when on duty, is at all times in fullest possession of those qualifications essential to the safe conduct of the train. Were this always the case, it is difficult to understand how a collision could possibly occur. If he did not know his business, he should not have been appointed; if he would not attend to it, he was guilty of manslaughter if death ensued. But if he could not do his work, and that through no fault of his own—how then?

Suppose that men wearied out by long journeys and exhausted by fatigue and want of sleep are ordered, on pain of dismissal, to undertake immediately fresh duties for which they are rendered incapable by previous exhaustion of body and mind. Would it not then appear little short of miraculous if some accident did not result? The worn-out engine-driver nods, and a hundred lives are in jeopardy; the signal-man, dazed by want of sleep, becomes confused, and in a moment the engines are pounding up human beings between them. The acute faculties of the guard are blunted by long unrest, the danger-signal passes unnoticed, the break does not second the efforts of the alarmed engine-driver, and next morning there is recorded in the papers another railway accident.

The supposition suggested and these illustrations of accruing results may appear exaggerations to those who for the first time consider this subject; but careful inquiries have afforded us convincing evidence that the system of railway management, so far as concerns the duties of guards, engine-drivers, and signal-men, evinces very little regard to those particular conditions which we have mentioned as essential to render trains ordinarily safe from risk of collision. It is only necessary to cite a few cases by way of illustration, preferring those which have appeared in public print; since the majority of direct personal communications made to us were in confidence—for obvious reasons.

When the collision occurred in a tunnel on the Brighton line last August, the signal-man stated in evidence, "I went on duty at eight in the morning, and should have remained on for twenty-four hours. Twenty-four hours I consider as a hard day's work. I am always glad when it's over—I know that." A letter in the *Times*, *à propos* of this, mentions that a signal-man at Brighton had been thirty consecutive hours on duty.

In the collision which occurred shortly after on the North London line, the signal-man stated that he was on duty when the accident occurred from seven in the morning till ten at night.

On another line, a most intelligent guard informed us that on one occasion he was for forty-six hours without taking his clothes off and in charge of passenger-trains, during this time having only an hour and a half's rest. He believed that he was not equal to his work during the last hours, being dead beat.

An engine-driver on a fourth line said that he had been thirty-six hours on his engine without any interval, taking his meals on the way; acknowledged that few men could stand this; he did not regularly sleep at all during the time, but had a "sort of dog-sleeps;" often had from sixteen to eighteen hours a day on duty for four and sometimes six days a week.

A guard on another line said he had been three days and two nights constantly in charge; and a responsible official on the same line, having peculiar opportunities of obtaining information, testified that this system of imposing extra and unexpected work on the men very generally prevails.

It might be supposed that these are exceptional instances during unusual traffic pressure. But this is not so; and even were it the case, would afford no excuse. For it were far better not to start a train than to send it forth under the charge of wearied men unequal to their duty, and at such risks as we have described.

Fairly worked, there are few operatives so intelligent and trustworthy as railway officials. But they are men, not machines. They have no alternative but dismissal if they demur to orders from superiors, and it is a rule on railways that the last order given is to be obeyed. If dismissed, they have no appeal. There are plenty to take their places, for the pay is high—porters anxious to become guards, firemen ambitious to become drivers. They have appealed to the directors on several occasions without results, and even now a protest is being prepared on the subject. As it is, they have no alternative but to do as they are bid, and we all know that sooner or later discontented men cease to be trustworthy servants.

And not only is the endurance of the men occasionally overstrained to a dangerous extent, but on some lines a regular system of overwork of a most injurious kind has been introduced. The guards are paid by time when on duty; they are thus induced to work for sixteen or eighteen hours a day for four or five days a week, resting on the other days, and receiving no pay; or work the same number of hours during three weeks, and have shorter time on the fourth. The engine-drivers are paid by the trip, with the same result, practically ensuring a temptation to earn extra pay by over-work. Again, it is a rule that men sleeping from their homes have a small allowance as bed-money. To save this, one of the railways has recently directed that the guards of one route, after travelling nearly two hundred miles, shall return the same day, and without any interval of rest, in charge of another train.

We select these particulars from a large number of similar cases, to indicate where blame must lie for proceedings so unjust to the men, dangerous to the public, and injurious to the interests of the companies. For exemption from danger under circumstances such as we have described must tend to make men over-confident or careless, and this must lead to accidents. The impolicy of the present system seems sufficiently evident; but the reports made from time to time by the official Government inspectors do not indicate much likelihood of reform by railway executives, who "seem to prefer the risk of paying enormous sums of money-compensation for accidents and damage, to attempting any improvement."

The remedy is the simple one of fixing a maximum time of work. It has already been found necessary to adopt this system for Post-office officials travelling on railroads, who are not permitted to exceed a certain number of hours on duty. If such a regulation be found necessary for the work of sorting letters, it is tenfold more needful where the lives of passengers are at stake. It is a duty devolving on Government to provide the remedy and compel attention to it.

58

JOHN CHARLES HALL, 'RAILWAY ACCIDENTS', IN *MEDICAL EVIDENCE IN RAILWAY ACCIDENTS* (LONDON: LONGMANS & CO. 1868), PP. 27–42

Case IV

An elderly gentleman, travelling in a second-class railway carriage, suddenly found himself at the bottom of the carriage, his train having run into some coal trucks. When I saw him, three hours after the collision, he was confused, and could give me no very clear account beyond what I have already stated; that he found himself with his hat off at the bottom of the carriage; and that he was helped out. How long he had been insensible he knew not, but said that he sat on the bank of the railway and felt cold, and that a gentleman had lent him a rug. He had come on by train for some miles after the accident. He felt sick, and attempted to vomit; but did not bring anything from his stomach. Pulse 58, feeble; skin cold. He was put to bed; a cup of hot tea given to him; a good fire lighted in his bed-room; and a hot-water tin placed at his feet.

Next morning he appeared confused; and, when seen by myself and an old personal friend who had known him many years, he said his head ached, and that the light from the window caused him annoyance. His pulse was 60; temperature normal; tongue furred. He had perfect command over his sphincters. He complained of pain in the head, and great tenderness along the whole of his cervical region, over which he thought he had been struck. There was no mark on the skin, nor was the part swollen. He could not read, and asked me to read a letter for him; when he attempted to read, the words ran into each other. His sleep was disturbed and broken; he awoke with a start, and was remarkably irritable, and predicted the most fearful results from the injury he had sustained.

His friend informed me that some years previously he had been injured in a railway collision; that he was then for a long time unable to attend to business; and hence, probably, the disposition to look gloomily on the future. He continued in this state for several days; the exalted sensibility of the whole nervous system was most marked. When he attempted to walk he said "his legs failed him." There was slight ptosis of the right eye-lid; and the vessels of the conjunctiva on that side were injected. He almost shuddered when the eye was examined by the ophthalmoscope; and a hot sponge applied to the upper part of the spine caused him to cry out with pain. The temperature in every part of the body was normal. Dr. Fletcher, Dr. Bartolomé, and Mr. W. F. Favell, saw this gentleman with me. The conclusion at which we arrived was, that no permanent injury had been received; and that with perfect rest, and abstaining from business and all mental exertion, in three months he would be quite well.

The case was settled out of court by the payment of £500 and the costs. I have seen this gentleman several times since. There is no ptosis, nor any single trace of the accident. He is able to carry on his business, and is in every respect quite well.

Case V

The Rev. J. B., aged 61, April, 1867, travelling on the Great Northern Railway in a third class carriage, was looking out of the window, when the passenger train ran into a luggage train. He was violently shaken at the time, and received a severe blow on the right side of his head; his hat had been broken by the force of the blow. He was senseless for a short time, then felt sick, and reeled at first like a drunken man, but soon recovered, and proceeded up to London; and went, after taking tea with a friend, to buy a new hat. He preached on the following day (Sunday), to a large congregation, but felt often at a loss for a word; he was a good deal exhausted after service, and at once went to bed. On the following evening, he commenced the first of a course of lectures, but broke down from exhaustion. He returned home to Sheffield the next day by railway, having been about five hours on the road, and immediately sent for me to attend him. He was very feeble, and spoke with difficulty; his face on the right side was partially paralysed. He could not read; the light gave him pain; and when a candle was held to his eyes, he frowned and asked that it might be taken away. On putting out his tongue, it was seen to be drawn to the left side of the mouth, and this continued for nearly a month. He walked with great difficulty, and complained that his legs were cold; there was a constant desire to pass urine. His urine was acid; specific gravity 1019; pulse 66.

With perfect rest, and abstaining from all mental exertion, and a few weeks spent at the seaside, in three months from the receipt of the injury, this minister resumed his usual duties and perfectly recovered.

The case was settled out of court, the patient and the company having mutually agreed that the sum to be paid should be fixed by myself.

Case VI

Mr.—, a gentleman in middle life, had the misfortune to be riding in a second class carriage at the time of a collision on a railway. After the accident, he proceeded some distance, and at the end of his journey he was seen by the surgeon of the company. He complained of pain over the dorsal and lumbar regions, on which, he said, he had been bruised; and, in addition, of an inability to walk without pain.

He returned to his home from London in a first class carriage, was immediately attended by his family surgeon, and was seen by myself for the first time, seven days after the accident.

I found him in bed laid on his back. He told me "he was suffering very great pain along the whole course of the spine, and that he had not power to move his legs or even to turn in bed." The temperature of the whole body was normal. He had perfect command over the bladder and rectum. He said that at first he had "difficulty with his water, but that was improved." His pulse was 76; but as he spoke of the severe injuries he had sustained by the negligence of the company, and the heavy damages (two or three thousand pounds) he would make the directors pay, he became very excited, and his pulse rose to 98.

On getting him out of bed, he was unable, he said, to walk or to bear any of the weight of the body on his feet; he supported himself by the table, and insisted on being again carried immediately to his bed. There was no mark on any part of the back. During the whole of my attendance these symptoms remained. He complained of a sensation of pins and needles in both legs; there was no reflex action; no drawing up, or starting of the legs; no wasting.

As we saw him in bed, he appeared a stout healthy man, but he told us, again and again, "that he had no power over his limbs, and that he was unable to walk." In the absence of all objective symptoms, I ventured to express a very strong opinion, that no permanent injury to the spine or spinal chord had been sustained; and in this opinion three other medical gentlemen concurred.

Having satisfied myself that he not only could walk without assistance, but that he had actually done so, and that, too, at the time when he assured me that he was altogether incapable of moving his limbs, I discontinued my attendance.

A gentleman of great skill and long experience was now called in, and through trusting to subjective symptoms only, was led to conclude that the injury to the spine and spinal chord was severe, and probably permanent.

About three months after the accident the case was compromised, on the payment by the company of several hundred pounds. It is, doubtless, a consolation to this gentleman and his friends now to know, that my prognosis was correct; and that his and their fears proved altogether groundless. Shortly after the case was settled, he was observed walking about in the street. He has almost ever since attended to his business; and no trace of the injury remains.

Case VII

C. W., aged 23, whose income was about £70 a year, was injured in an accident on a railway, June, 1866. He was shaken and bruised, and sustained a simple fracture of the fibula. At the end of July, he complained for the first time of having "nervous fits" and of a "peculiar sensation in his head." This state of things continued until the end of August, when he told his medical attendant that "his eye-sight was impaired." In September, the sense of taste was said to be lost; there was loss of sensation also, and he swallowed his food with apparent difficulty.

The case came before a jury, at the Assizes, the end of the same year. He was brought into court on crutches. He could bear strong ammonia (N H^3) to the nose, which only produced a little watering of the eyes. The loss of taste was shewn by the impunity with which he could take a spoonful of mustard; and the loss of sensation, by his indifference to the application of a pin to all parts of the face and neck.

The medical men called on his behalf told the jury that "*as four of the special senses were impaired or lost, there must be disease of the base of the brain, resulting from the accident; that he could never be in so good a condition of health as before the accident; and that he might die in less than two years.*"

The Company, under the advice of counsel, called no witnesses—relying on a speech in mitigation of damages. The jury returned a verdict for the plaintiff—damages £1,500.

Very soon after the trial, he was seen walking in the town with the help of a stick. Next, he was observed running after a railway train when in motion, for the starting of which he was too late, and which he was prevented from entering by the officials. The last report I had of him was, that "he was in good health, going about as usual, and no worse for the injuries he had sustained."

Case VIII

W. B., aged 30. This gentleman was in the same train as the last patient, whose case has been narrated. After the accident, he had symptoms of cerebral and spinal concussion, and also many of the nervous subjective symptoms so often present in patients who have been in a collision on a railway. These symptoms will be found fully described in the next case.

The medical attendants of this gentleman expressed the opinion that "it was altogether impossible that he could resume his occupation as a commercial traveller in less than two years." On the company proposing a compromise, £1,500 was demanded. The sum paid in the end was £1,000.

I am informed that "three weeks after the settlement of his claim, this person resumed his usual occupation, and that he has been perfectly well and able to do his work ever since."

Case IX

Mr. H., aged 46, a stout and well formed man (who although of a nervous temperament, had always enjoyed good health), was waiting in one of the third-class carriages of an excursion train, at a station, expecting every minute that it would start on the return journey, when owing to a mistake in the signals, his train was run into by another. The door of his carriage being open, he was thrown by the force of the collision upon the platform. He remained for some time insensible. Mr. Benson, his medical attendant, informed me that at the time of the accident

Mr. H. had symptoms of concussion of the brain, and that the right arm and shoulder were bruised, much discoloured, and very painful.

The accident happened on the 12th of June, but he was not seen by me until the 6th of the following August. At first he appeared to have had the usual symptoms of slight concussion of the brain. Then he slept but little, and when he did so awoke with a start, and fancied that he was falling. He tells me now "that his sleep is broken and uncomfortable," that he does not know what it is to enjoy a good night's rest; that he has fearful dreams; and he added "I have not had a good night's rest since it happened."

The power of attending to his business in a great measure is lost, for he cannot direct his attention to any one subject long together. He is one of the Board of Directors of a large company, and it had been his duty to reckon the wages, and to cast up the books of the workmen. He can no longer do so. His family tell me "he is a changed man, and now irritable and discontented." His tongue is furred. He has no appetite; no inclination to do anything; "feels best when sitting in his chair." He can walk well, though he feels very weak, and as though his legs would give way under him. The utterance is not affected; still, he appears, now and then, at a loss for the right word to complete a sentence; his taste and smell are not impaired; there is slight intolerance of light. He stated that "loud noises distressed him very much." The sense of touch is not impaired. He can read, but it makes him "mazey." There appeared some difference of power on the two sides; he did not grasp with the right hand so firmly as he did with the left. He had perfect command over the sphincters; the bowels were inclined to be constipated; pulse 76.

He was advised to go immediately to the sea-side; to keep his mind altogether at rest; and to leave his warehouse in charge of others for a month or two.

The case was settled out of court by the payment of £500. When I saw this gentleman some months afterwards, all traces of the accident had passed away.

Two other persons, both young, were in the same carriage with this gentleman, and were also injured. One, a young gentleman, that I saw, had ptosis, the result of a cut over the eye-brow, but who perfectly recovered in a few months. The other was a young lady, who had slight concussion of the brain. There was nothing in either of these cases calling for comment, and they are only mentioned as illustrative of the different degrees in which persons travelling in one carriage may be injured by the same collision on a railway.

Case X

Mrs.—, aged 32, married to a respectable artisan, and the mother of several children, three days before I saw her in consultation with Mr. Morton, had been in a collision on a railway. She was at the time of the accident for a short period insensible, and on recovering consciousness felt very sick and faint. I found her in bed, with inability to move, from "feeling sore and bruised all over." There was considerable pain in the left shoulder, also over the collarbone, and in the axilla on that side. There was a somewhat severe contusion just above the collar-bone, and extending backwards. She said, "she was thrown forward against some part of the carriage," and the shoulder had evidently been severely struck, probably in the recoil. The pulse was 86; the pupils acted well; there was no intolerance of light. She had some pain in the head, and slight tenderness on pressure at the cervical portion of the spine.

There was a marked difference of temperature between the two sides. This was tested very carefully by a thermometer, which showed the difference to be no less than four degrees. The difference of temperature, however, was also quite evident to the touch. The pulse on the left side was weaker than on the right. She described the left hand as being "dead." A silver spoon dipped into hot water could be felt along the spine and over the right arm; no sensation was produced on passing it over the left arm and fore arm.

Mr. Morton and myself came to the conclusion that the present condition of the left arm was the result of pressure from effused blood; and that as this became absorbed the symptoms would disappear. I was the more decided in this prognosis, because it was clear to me that the cause was local, and that the brain and spinal chord had sustained no injury.

The treatment consisted in keeping the patient in bed; rubbing the arm, neck, and shoulder with the belladonna liniment, and wrapping the arm in a flannel bandage. Day by day the difference in the temperature became less and less; in a week, there was no difference between the two sides as regards temperature; neither was there any difference in the pulse. When I saw her last, about a month after the accident, beyond looking a little thin and pale—and her surgeon said "she always did so"—I could detect nothing to lead to the conclusion that her recovery would not be perfect; and she was left with the assurance that she would very soon be quite well. The case was settled by a payment of £100; and I am happy to add when I last heard of her she was in every respect as well as usual.

In this case of somewhat severe railway accident, there are many points of very great interest. 1. More especially the marked difference in pulse and temperature, between the right and left side. 2. That this only came on two days after the injury had been received. 3. That as the effused blood became absorbed, the parts resumed their normal condition. 4. The perfect recovery.

Case XI

Mr. R. M., aged 62, a very temperate, respectable, and industrious hard-working smith, using a very heavy hammer in his trade, was in a carriage next to the one which was thrown off the line in a railway collision.

I saw him a few days after the accident, in consultation with my friend, the late Mr. Sykes. When I called he had gone out to the back of his house; and he came into the room where we were seated, walking with difficulty, and leaning on a stick. He told us "that at the time of the accident he was looking out of the window of a second-class carriage; that his head was knocked backwards and forwards; that he fell with his back on to the top of one of the seats; that his eye was bruised; and that two of his teeth were knocked out;" that "he was bruised all over, more particularly on the back, and on the right arm; that he could not walk without great pain and difficulty; and that he had lost the power of grasping with the right hand." There was pain on pressure over the lower portion of the spine; this was red from the application of hot fomentations and embrocations when I saw him; but the principal injury appeared to me to be over the right gluteal region, the skin over that part being tender, swollen, and discoloured. There was also a somewhat large bruise over the right elbow, extending up the arm for some inches on that side. The pulse was 76. He complained of pain in the head, and there was a slight cut on the right side of the head, near the eye. The eyes were carefully examined with the ophthalmoscope. No intolerance of light or impaired vision was at this time complained of.

He was under my care for about five weeks, during which time he gradually improved, although he still told me that "he had lost all power over the right hand and arm, and that he had no power to grasp anything."

The opinion I formed was that the injury was not permanent; that the brain and spinal chord had not, in any degree, been injured; and that it was in the highest degree ridiculous, to suppose for a moment that such a blow as had been received at the elbow and on the front of the arm, could possibly lead to a permanent loss of power.

An action was tried at the assizes, and very heavy damages were claimed. The plaintiff appeared with his arm in a sling, said he had still little or no power in his right hand and right arm, that he had lost flesh, and he complained also of such an affection of vision as set at naught all our previous notions of optics.

Three medical gentlemen, two of them having had a large hospital and private practice, swore that "in all probability the injuries received would lead to a permanent loss of power in the right hand and arm." How such an injury could possibly lead to such a result, I freely confess my inability to discover.

I was not examined, but three medical practitioners of the highest attainments, and very large experience, confirmed my opinion on oath in the witness box. They testified that it was only a matter of time; and that the man would soon be able to work again at his trade. No one denied that the man had been injured, the only question was the *degree and probable duration of the effects of the accident.*

The Company had paid, I think, £75 into court. The jury doubled that sum, giving £150. Mark the result. On the 13th of November—exactly five months after the accident—R. M. called at my consulting room. He shewed me his arm. He had the most perfect use of it (he doubled his fist, flexed his fore-arm, and firmly grasped my hand); for a man of his age, he was well nourished and muscular. He said "he was going to commence his work in a day or two." The last time I saw him was in the street; not a trace of the accident remained! He had the perfect use of his arm.

Case XII

Mrs. M., aged 37, married, and in the seventh month of pregnancy, was in the third carriage from the engine in a railway collision. I attended her, in consultation with my friend Mr. Morton. She was removed from the carriage by her husband in a state of insensibility, and so she continued for many hours. When in this state, she was seen by Dr. Younge and Mr. Browning.

At the time of the accident, she had been thrown forward on her stomach; the abdominal muscles, and the muscles over one hip were swollen, and the skin discoloured. From the time of recovering her senses she had been constantly sick; temperature of the body increased; pulse slow and feeble.

Her medical attendant was fearful that premature labour would come on; but I am correct in stating that such is not a very usual result of railway accidents. The continued increased temperature, and slow pulse, were to me by far the most serious causes of anxiety; for, *in all cases of severe concussion that I have seen, nothing has pointed so clearly to the probability of an unfavourable termination as a feeble slow pulse, and an increased heat of skin.*

After a long and tedious illness, this lady improved, went to her full time, and ultimately recovered. The case was settled out of court for far less than is usual where injuries so severe have been sustained.

The symptoms present in this patient supply an opportunity for speaking of the use of

The thermometer in diseases

What has already been said of the ophthalmoscope, applies with equal force to the thermometer; and those physicians and surgeons who place "no reliance" either on the one or on the other, possibly do so from not having taken the trouble to ascertain how valuable may be the assistance rendered by them in the investigation of certain affections following railway accidents. The use of the thermometer, in diseases, will always be regarded as valuable, by all who have made themselves masters of the indications which its readings convey.

A high temperature, and a slow and feeble pulse, after a concussion of the brain or spinal chord in a railway accident, are most unfavourable, although not always fatal, symptoms.

In erysipelas, in some few cases of pneumonia, and fever, temperatures above 105° may be met with without being necessarily of evil prognostic omen, but, in most other diseases, a mid-day temperature above 105° is a decidedly grave symptom.

If the pulse and general symptoms of a patient are favourable, the thermometer, in spite of this, marking a high temperature, the former symptoms are to be chiefly relied on in forming a prognosis, though the latter should make us still more careful in searching for any intercurrent disease, especially inflammation of the lungs.

Where the general symptoms are perplexing, one counterbalancing the other, a very high temperature registered by the thermometer, throws one more weight into the scale for forming an unfavourable prognosis, and *vice versâ*.

Where the pulse and general symptoms, on the one hand, indicate danger, the temperature, on the other hand, not raising alarm from being either very high or very low, the pulse and general symptoms are by far the more trustworthy in forming a correct prognosis.

Case XIII

November 9th. Mr. G. R., aged 35, on the second of the previous October, was in a second-class carriage of a railway train, which came into collision with another train in a tunnel. He stated that he was struck between the shoulders, and that even now the skin was "tender, and smarted when touched." He complained of a feeling of numbness in the left arm, fore-arm, and fingers; but, there was no prickling sensation. He went out of his house and walked about the day after the accident. Was at church a week ago—walked more than a mile to his place of worship, "but not in his usual way." Pulse 76; tongue clean. The pupils act equally and perfectly. Can read, but thinks the left eye is not so good as the right. He has perfect command over the bladder and rectum, and can grasp firmly with both hands. I saw this gentleman with Mr. Favill and Dr. Younge.

February 10th. I did not see him again until today—three months from my last visit. He has not worked yet; walks out every day a little, but cannot walk well; vision appeared perfect, for we found him seated in his chair, and reading a newspaper without spectacles; states that he has lost flesh, but he appeared to Mr. Favill and myself well nourished and muscular; the muscles of his legs and arms felt firm; his chest measured 39, and expanded to 41 inches; the abdomen measured 38 inches. There was no difference of circumference between the right and left arms, or the right and left thighs or legs. He still complained of being unable to attend to his business—why this was so did not appear evident. Gently passing the finger along the spine was said to cause much pain, but his attention being directed from this part, considerable pressure was borne without remark.

From the first, we could detect no evidence of injury to the spinal chord. The muscles of the back had doubtless been bruised, but of the many severe bruises of those parts that I have seen resulting from blows, the inflammation has not extended to the spinal chord; and it has been found, both in hospital and private practice, that such contusions, as a rule, do not lead to inflammation of the chord. In severe sprains, sometimes, pain is felt for a longer or shorter period, but even severe sprains seldom lead to permanent spinal impairment.

The case was settled out of court, on the payment of £150, and I am happy to add the last report I had of this gentleman fully justified the prognosis of Mr. Favill and myself.

From the time when I was first consulted, the symptoms of Mr. G. R. were subjective only. The most careful examination of Dr. Fletcher, Dr. Younge, Mr. Favill, and myself, failed to discover a single objective symptom of injury to the brain or spinal chord; nor could we detect, on using the ophthalmoscope, any difference between the right eye and the left—his vision not having in the slightest degree suffered.

Case XIV

Mr.—, an agent, aged 42, December, 1857, was in a railway collision. Severe blow on back of head; side bruised; bleeding from ears and nose; insensible for half an hour. When he recovered, noticed dimness of vision in left eye, with severe pain in the head. After two or three weeks, the dimness of vision improved in the left eye, then returned with a prismatic halo around objects. Two months from this time right eye affected also; in four months he was quite blind; suffered severe pain in the head, with tremor, wasting, and some loss of power over the limbs.

1863. Six years after the accident; blind of both eyes; general health good; can walk well; no paralysis; memory and mental faculties healthy.

This case, taken from the work of Dr. Fletcher, is instructive, as showing that from the receipt of the blow on the head there were symptoms indicative of injury to the brain—immediate insensibility after the accident, and continuing for some time; bleeding from the nose and ears; impaired vision—a progressive change from bad to worse, and ending in permanent loss of sight.

Cases 1, 2, 3, 4, 5, 9, and 14 clearly prove what pathology had previously taught us to expect, namely, that injury to the brain and spinal chord is immediately followed by objective symptoms pathognomonic of such injury.

59

'NAVVIES FOR THE CRIMEA' AND 'THE BALACLAVA RAILWAY CORPS', *ILLUSTRATED LONDON NEWS*, 13 JANUARY 1855, 28–29, 304

THE departure of the second detachment of the men engaged by Messrs. Peto and Betts to construct the railway from Balaclava to the trenches before the heights round Sebastopol, which we briefly noticed last week, was witnessed by a large party of noblemen and gentlemen. The "navvies," who are nearly all young men in the prime of vigorous manhood, presented all those evidences of stalwart strength and endurance for which their class is proverbial.

Every navvy, besides his pay and rations, has given to him gratuitously complete suits of clothing adapted for every variety of weather and work in which he may be engaged. They consist of a striped cotton shirt, over which a large red flannel shirt of stout quality. The trousers are of moleskin, lined throughout with flannel; strong worsted stockings, with laced boots, technically known as "ankle-jacks." The waistcoat is also of moleskin; and the coat a sort of "pea-jacket," which is also padded and lined with flannel. Some of the gangs were supplied with large roomy white flannel shirts or smocks. When working in boggy soil or in water, high boots are to be worn, as shown in our Illustration. We also give the costume to be adopted in wet weather, consisting of a complete suit of waterproof, with a "south-wester," instead of the woollen cap to be ordinarily worn. It is needless to add that the whole of the clothes are of excellent quality, and well adapted for the wear and tear they will have to undergo. The men themselves, who may be said to be the best judges, were highly pleased, and expressed themselves well contented with their "rig."

A large crowd assembled on the Brunswick Pier to witness their departure. Shortly after two o'clock the men were mustered on the foredeck in their new clothing, to hear addresses from Capt. W. S. Andrews, managing director of the North of Europe Steam Navigation Company, and Lord Henry Clinton, who, with a party of gentlemen connected with the enterprise, were on the platform amidships.

Capt. Andrews addressed the navvies in brief but homely and energetic terms which elicited hearty plandits from his hearers. He told them that though the accommodation to be found on board ship necessarily differed considerably from what they had been accustomed to, yet nothing had been neglected that could contribute during the voyage to their comfort and the preservation of that health and strength on which so much reliance was placed, not only by their employers, but by the whole country. Everything that could be done had been done as far as human foresight could effect it for them; and if they would only be united and cordial among themselves—exhibiting good temper, cheerfulness, docility, and confidence and respect towards those placed over them on board—they would be as happy as the circumstances of the case would permit in a lengthened voyage at this period of the year. For his own part, he could unhesitatingly say, that he never knew an emigrant vessel—and he had known many—that had furnished quarters in any respect preferable to those on board the *Hesperus*. He then explained the more immediate objects of the expedition, and dwelt upon its importance as an auxiliary to the operations of our gallant countrymen in the Crimea. They were going to the aid of our heroic defenders, who had not only to fight—and how they fought the whole world would for ever admiringly testify—but had also to work and perform many duties for which it could not be expected that soldiers were so well adapted as the skilled and trained men who were now going out to relieve them, and leave them at full liberty to deal with the enemy as they had done in the dashing rush at Alma and the immortal conflict at Inkerman. The future success of the siege operations, and of other operations, too, in the Crimea, would depend in a great measure on the present expedition; and it might be said, accordingly, with far more truth of Peto's navvies than of more aspiring experimentalists, that "the eyes of Europe were upon them." They must expect, and would not be cast down by, hardships and privations; some of these, perhaps, would not appear so very terrible in the Crimea as at home. There would be no public-house to go to; but there would be plenty of good substantial refreshments always available when needed; and while that was the case he had no fear that there would be much grumbling at whatever work might be expected at their hands. They were not like Russian serfs, who dare not call their souls their own, but who must slay and be slain without asking why or wherefore. They were free Englishmen, volunteers at perfect liberty to go or stay just as they pleased, according to their own unbiassed judgment, without the least undue influence, concealment, artifice, or exaggeration used to warp their opinion one way or the other. All that was said or done was to guarantee them good clothing, good food, good pay, a good ship, and a good Captain. They had a good cause—the cause of the country, the cause of justice, and fair play. They would bring good hearts to the cause—English hearts that never recoiled from the obligations of duty, come in what shape they might, whether at the point of the pick or the bayonet; and he doubted not that the British navvy would prove himself as great a benefactor in repelling the evils of barbarism abroad as he had been in extending the blessings of civilisation at home. At the invitation of Captain Andrews, who was loudly applauded, three cheers were given for the Queen, and three for Messrs. Peto and Betts.

    Lord Henry Clinton then addressed them, and said that it had been the intention of his brother, the Duke of Newcastle, to have been present, as his Grace would have been proud to make the acquaintance of the men who were going with so much alacrity to the aid of an object he had so much at heart as the Balaclava and Sebastopol Railway, but was unable to attend, owing to a Cabinet Council being held that day, and at that hour. His Lordship also dwelt on the importance of the undertaking, and enforced Captain Andrews's admonition as to the desirability of maintaining sobriety, union, and good humour in the face of every annoyance to which they might unavoidably be exposed; for then he was sure that the energy for which they were so deservedly famous would carry them triumphant over every impediment. The disinterested, self-sacrificing promptitude with which Mr. Peto had acted upon the suggestion which led to the present magnificent enterprise was beyond all praise, even the praise it had everywhere been met with. As it was raining, and time pressed, he would not detain them with a long speech, but would conclude by earnestly wishing them a safe and pleasant voyage, and a speedy return to their families and to their country, which they might be sure would welcome them as they deserved.

Three cheers were given for his Lordship, and three for the Duke of Newcastle, by whom, on the part of the Government, this undertaking has been entered upon. Captain Raymond, the Marine Superintendent of the intended works, and Mr. Kellock, Superintendent in the Crimea, each spoke a few words of encouragement, which were received with great cordiality; the cheering being renewed as the visitors and officials put off for shore in a waterman's boat. The *Hesperus* then steamed down the river.

By way of summary, it may be stated, that, from the original conception of the plan to the completion of the final details thus far, everything connected with the expedition has been conducted not only with the greatest celerity, quite unprecedented in an undertaking or this magnitude, but with uninterrupted success. The great secret of this has been a judicious division of labour, and the entrusting of each department to a competent official; the whole being supervised by the experienced eye, and stimulated by the energetic example, of Captain Andrews— whose varied knowledge of administrative requirements in controlling large bodies of men proved of the utmost value in an enterprise of such very miscellaneous characteristics as the present. All the vessels of the "navvy" fleet have now sailed, with the exception of the *Levant*, which sails this day One of the firm of Peto and Co. has had an interview during the present week with Sir De Lacy Evans, by whom the plans of operation in connection with the Railroad have been thoroughly approved of; but the nature of these plans is, for obvious reasons, not permitted to be made public. Enough to say, however, that there is substantial ground for calculating with confidence that the expectations formed of the efficacy of the navvy corps will be completely realised in the Crimea; and that, if even peace should supervene, and there be no absolute necessity for employing them in actual belligerent purposes against Sebastopol, enough will remain to be done to demonstrate the sagacity of intrusting its execution to such hands, and to render it certain that the precedent now adopted will be followed on all occasions of a like nature for the future, if such occasions should unfortunately arise. We may, perhaps, take this opportunity of saying that the suggestion offered in a leading journal by Sir F. B. Head, as to the preferability of plank-roads, on the Canadian plan, over the proposed railway, would be quite inapplicable to the circumstances of the case in the Crimes. The delay in obtaining huts for the men all this winter is conclusive as to the impracticability of procuring wood of a kind suitable to roads—to say nothing of the difficulty of having it sawn and dressed in a proper manner, and in the enormous quantity that would be needed for the distance from Balaclava to the heights around Sebastopol; while a scarcely less serious objection arises from the wide-spread injury to the road itself, and to all in the neighbourhood, from the splinters that would be caused by the Russian shot and shell falling upon so exposed and fragile a surface. The engineers entrusted with the construction of the Balaclava Railway are perfectly conversant with the merits of all modes of traction in all parts of the world, and not less so in Canada than elsewhere; and we may be quite sure they will adopt that which is best suited to the present undertaking, in every respect.

Previous to the departure of the ships from Blackwall, all the men were assembled in the premises occupied as storehouses by the Crimean Expedition, and, under the able superintendence of Captain Raymond, the Commodore of the fleet of those transports, each man was furnished with his kit. The beds were first carried on board, and then the individual parties returned for the remainder of their outfits, the last article delivered to them being a stout leather strap capable of embracing all the articles delivered to them. On getting on board, most of the men immediately equipped themselves in their new outer clothing, and in it exhibited themselves to the people on shore. One navigator distinguished himself by ascending to the foretop of the *Hesperus*, in full costume, and cheering his friends from his elevated position, to the great amusement of the assembled crowd.

The *Prince of Wales*, with fifty more men on board, left Blackwall on Friday afternoon, the 5th instant, and proceeded to sea on Sunday last.

The Balaclava Railway

One of the recent accounts received from Balaclava opens thus:—"The navvy, his barrow, and pick-axe, are in possession, and he is 'master of the situation.' The noise of 'blasts' in the rock, the ring of hammers, the roll of the train, the varying din of labour, sound all around the harbour. The railway has crept up the hill, about three miles outside the down, and two engines have been dragged up to the top of the greatest elevation which the engineers will have to surmount, and will speedily be at work moving the drum to drag up the heavy trains laden with shot, and shell, and provisions."

Another account states:—"The progress which this tramway is making as perfectly marvellous. It is now progressing at the rate of a quarter of a mile per day, including all the delays which arise from bridging small streams, levelling and filling up inequalities, &c. Half the men are employed in laying down the rails and sleepers during the day, and the remainder work all night in boxing up with earth and stones the spaces left between each sleeper. As an instance of the rapidity with which the work proceeds, a pile-driving machine was landed one evening, and carried piecemeal up to where it was necessary to sink piles for a stout wooden bridge across a small, but very muddy stream, which runs into the harbour. The machine was erected early the following morning, and before that evening the piles were all driven, the machine removed, the bridge finished, and the rails laid down for the space of 100 yards beyond."

A Correspondent in the Royal Artillery, who writes from the "Balaclava Lines," has enabled us to present the accompanying Scene of the Railway operations by night.

60

'THE INVASION OF THE FREE STATE', *THE SPECTATOR*, MARCH 17, 1900, 229

WE write before we can obtain knowledge of the results of Lord Roberts's advance into the Free State, but taken altogether the prospects seem most promising. At any rate, the moment is an opportune one for reviewing the military situation as a whole. In Natal everything depends upon how long Ladysmith can hold out, and this again depends upon the amount of food still in the place. That the enemy will not now take Ladysmith by storm seems certain. Again, we do not think that Ladysmith will succumb owing to the garrison being prostrated by disease. No doubt the place is not healthy, but there is nothing like a plague, and garrisons do not yield from ill-health. As we have said, then, it is a case of food. But unless we are mistaken the food will certainly last another fortnight, and most probably another three or even four weeks. Therefore there is still time for the effects of General Roberts's advance to be felt and for Ladysmith to be relieved indirectly, before the grim necessity for cutting their way out is presented to the garrison. That they will lay down their arms and allow themselves to be made prisoners we absolutely refuse to believe. In addition there is still the chance that General Buller may be able to force his way through, or, at any rate, to seize a position which will enable him to hold out a helping hand to Sir George White. We need not, therefore, assume with the pessimists that Ladysmith must be counted as already lost. No doubt its fate hangs in the balance, but not till another two weeks have passed will it be reasonable to give up hope.

On the southern frontier the position is most curious. We hear of little or no activity being displayed by General Gatacre, but round Rensburg what was formerly General French's command is being very closely pressed upon by the Colesberg Boers, who have been very heavily reinforced. So hard pressed, indeed, has been the attack that our soldiers have been obliged to fall back at all points. As long, however, as our troops do not let themselves be surrounded, this advance by the Boers is by no means a matter for alarm or depression. In fact, the further we can lure them into the Colony in this direction the better. Every mile they move forward makes greater the risk they are running of being cut off by a flank movement from Orange River Station to Fauresmith and Trompsburg. This flank movement seems, in fact, to have already begun, and we shall not be surprised to hear very shortly of large developments. Still more important is the great movement undertaken by Lord Roberts. This movement is, of course, a great deal more than an effort to relieve Kimberley. That would only be an incidental result of its success. Its main object is evidently the seizure of Jacobsdal and, if possible, the capture there of the Boer stores from which the force round Kimberley has been supplied. If our readers will look at a map they will realise the strategic conditions of the movement. Jacobsdal lies in the triangle formed by the junction of the Riet River and the Modder River, which junction takes place at our camp at Modder. What Lord Roberts appears to have done was to send a body of his troops, under General French, some twenty miles down the Riet River to Dekil's Drift. There they crossed, and hurried at once across country about twenty-five miles till they reached the Modder River, where they seized and occupied several drifts. Thus French's force is now stretched across the land between the rivers, and bars the direct retreat of the Boers from Jacobsdal. The Boers, therefore, have two courses open to them. They must either attempt to defend Jacobsdal—a very difficult task, considering their situation between the rivers—or else they must evacuate Jacobsdal, and evacuate by a movement away from Bloemfontein and the Free State. But the evacuation of Jacobsdal, it would seem probable, must also mean the evacuation of the position at Magersfontein. It may be, however, that there will be a severe struggle on the part of the Boers to regain the positions they have lost, and as we are learning, nothing is so uncertain as the fate of battle. Still, as far as one can see, it looks as if in a very few days the road would be open into the Free State, and with no very serious obstacle between General Roberts and Bloemfontein.

The actual invasion of the Free State suggests many very interesting problems. It was generally supposed in the autumn that our troops would follow the railway line, and therefore advance *viâ* Colesberg. It seems possible, however, now that the advance will be along the main road from Jacobsdal to Bloemfontein,—a distance of not much more than one hundred miles. It is possible that a field railway may be laid as the troops advance. There are not any rivers or mountains to cross, and if the railway could be laid at two miles a day it might not be far from Bloemfontein at the end of six weeks. Possibly, however, this would not be considered worth while, and all the railway enterprise available will be devoted to repairing and reopening the line between Kimberley and Mafeking. The distance is very great, but if some seven thousand men could be added to the force now in Mafeking, and to the troops under Colonel Plumer, which will soon, we hope, join them, Mafeking might be made the base for a direct advance upon Pretoria. Nothing would more quickly end the war than an advance from that side, and we shall be very much surprised if Lord Roberts has not all along kept this possibility in view. Even if no attempt is made to lay a railway from Jacobsdal to Bloemfontein we may be sure that railway communication will not be neglected, and that every effort will be made to seize Springfontein, the very important junction within the Free State, where the lines *viâ* Colesberg and *viâ* Albert Junction meet. When once we have got Springfontein, and the country behind us has been cleared of the enemy, the regular railway route to Bloemfontein is clear.

We may end by a word as to the political aspects of the invasion of the Free State. We trust that every effort will be made to reassure the inhabitants, to explain to them that we have no sort of intention of depriving them of their liberties, and to make them realise that as soon as the military period is concluded the rights of self-government and of individual liberty will be as securely and as liberally enjoyed as they ever were in the Free State and far more securely and far more liberally than they have been in the Transvaal. We know this so well that we hardly think it worth reiterating, but let us remember that the Free Staters do not know it. They have had the poison of anti-British prejudice so persistently instilled into their minds for the last five or six years, that they really believe we are coming to enslave them, or at any rate to treat them as they have seen the Outlanders treated at Johannesburg,—*i.e.*, made into white Kaffirs. The sooner we begin the attempt to disabuse them of these notions the better it will be for them, for us, and for the peace of South Africa.

61

BOER WAR: DIARY OF EYRE LLOYD, 2ND COLDSTREAM GUARDS, ASSISTANT STAFF OFFICER, COLONEL BENSON'S COLUMN, KILLED AT BRAKENLAAGTE, 30TH OCTOBER 1901 (LONDON: ARMY AND NAVY COOPERATIVE SOCIETY, 1905), PP. 3–6, 17–19, 27–28, 43, 45, 56–58, 63, 66–67, 71–78, 105–118, 124, 131, 137–141, 153, 169–171, 187, 242, 249–250, 260, 288–289

> *November* 12*th, Sunday.*—Reach Cape Town about 2.30 p.m. Wanted at once at the front, and so unload ship as soon as possible and go up in two trains; 1st train 9.30 p.m., 2nd train 2.30 a.m. on Monday. Officers only to take 35 lbs. of luggage. This will probably not be strictly enforced so long as the bulk is not too great, so we all put a few extras in our valises at the last minute. All other luggage to be left at Cape Town.

Men's valises left behind and everything put in their great coats and haversacks. Colonel Pole-Carew came to see us and was cheered. He came with Lady Ned Cecil (Ned is in Mafeking) and Lady Charlie Bentinck (he is at Kimberley, wounded) and Davies' Grenadiers. Could not get all luggage out in time.

> *November* 13*th, Monday.*—Sutton (in command), Baring, Acheson, Gell, Burton, Campbell, and self, start from Cape Town at 2.30 a.m., amid cheers. Breakfast, Wellington. Lunch, Worcester. Dinner, Matjesfontein. Most of the journey lovely scenery. Great cheering whereever we meet anyone. All very happy and cheery, men very keen. Write home. Train

very comfortable, 4 officers in each carriage and there is room for us all to lie down. Men's carriages also are well fitted up and make into 6 beds and one sleeps on the floor. Food at the stations very good. We are travelling without any baggage. I think our 35 lbs. is in one of the trucks, but am not sure. I had a great bother with the horses, I had to fill up spaces with tents.

November 15*th, Wednesday.*—Entrained at 4.30 a.m. Arrived Orange River about 9 a.m., where we had breakfast. We encamp across the river where our other half battalion is already bivouacked. Little, 9th Lancers, asked me to lunch, try to go over there on Julian Steel's horse, but horse jibs badly and was evidently ill, was caught in a storm and had to get back by 2 p.m., just managed it minus lunch. Eat tongue, bully beef, bread, cold gravy, whisky and dirty water—enjoyed myself thoroughly. Acheson, Burton and I, in a tent together. Fred comes over from 9th Lancer camp. No. 3 company mounts inlying picquet at 5 p.m. I am captain of the day.

December 4*th, Monday.*—Highland Brigade filling up. We shall soon have 2 Horse batteries, 3 Field batteries, and the naval gun. At the Modder battle we only had 1 battery F. A. and 4 guns and sailors. 15,000 Boers said to be at Spytfontein. Scouts fired on 3 miles from here. A squadron of the 12th Lancers have arrived, the rest of the 12th and the Carabineers are coming. On fatigue, building railway bridge. We are probably going to fortify this place. Had a slight go of diarrhœa.

December 5*th, Tuesday.*—12th Lancers arrive. Naval big gun has arrived; this will counteract the Boer "Long Tom," but it is too heavy to move from railway. Rumour that Carabineers not allowed to come up, because they looted at Southampton. Went on out-post parade at 3.30 p.m., in reserve this time. Quite well again. Shute, Steele, Hardy, Towny, G. Baring and several others are seedy with the same complaint.

December 6*th, Wednesday.*—Nothing happened on outpost, except that Wilty saw a line of wagons moving northwards. Keswick, 12th Lancers, passed through the out-posts awfully pleased because he had been nearly shot. Geoffrey Stewart returned to-day, cured, but still looking pale.

December 7*th, Thursday.*—Boers cut railway at Enselin siding last night. Brigade attack parade. Frank Farquhar arrived, and is posted to my company, and Gell returned to No. 5. All the Highland Brigade have now arrived. Fearful dust. Frank says Acheson and Claude are getting on well.

Joe Laycock dines with me.

Boers were driven off at Enselin siding, but not before they had blown up three culverts and cut several miles of wire. A few Boers have taken up their old position at Gras Pans.

December 8*th, Friday.*—Left half battalion paraded for fatigue at 4 a.m.; right half paraded at 2.15 p.m. We built part of a redoubt on the island, good position. Temporary railway bridge finished. G. battery R.H.A. have arrived.

December 26th, Tuesday.—Paraded 4.45 a.m. Railway fatigue. A little shelling done on both sides. Muller's house blown up. Desultory shelling goes on nearly every day. Our guns were ordered not to fire on Christmas Day. Cavalry draw Boer fire and find they have 4 new guns. Heavy firing all along the Boer position at about 8 p.m. Don't know what at. Boers have strengthened their right on the railway.

February 12th, Monday.—Start for Lemonfontein to-day at 2 p.m., train delayed all down the line. Get some dinner in hospital train.

February 19th, Monday.—Arrive Modder River about midnight. Hear that Magersfontein is evacuated. Sleep on in train. Battalion said to be at Magersfontein.

February 20th, Tuesday.—Hear that battalion is probably at Klip Drift, having started at 2 hours' notice on Sunday night. Julian and I hire a cart and drive to Jacobsdal, where we catch up our transport.

March 15th, Thursday.—Baring mounts guard at Field Marshal's quarters (Steyn's house). Grenadier and Scots Guards go down the line by train to Glen up the railway. I escort 64 prisoners to the Provost Marshal from the Fort; all except 21 are released on taking the oath not to take up arms again or give information to the enemy.

April 7th, Saturday.—Get orders to entrain for Kaffir River, 6 p.m. train, entrain at about 10 p.m. Get to Kaffir River at about midnight. No. 5 company remains in Bloemfontein.

April 8th, Sunday.—Our 2 battalions and 5 companies Cameron Highlanders and a battery of artillery here. Boers said to be threatening railway bridge. Go on out-post at 4.30 p.m.

April 18th, Wednesday.—Beresford and Cruikshank go to Cape in hospital train. Still raining. 2 more patients arrive. Fine night. Tents went to Kaffir River early this morning.

April 19th, Thursday.—Polly-Carew says the brigade can't come back till Chermside's division can advance. The latter can't move on account of the going being too heavy from rain for transport to move. He also says the Brigade have had a very bad time in this rain.

April 21st, Saturday.—Come out of hospital at 2 p.m. Orders to march, sent Kaffir River; C.O. and self will ride out to-morrow. Division's destination is Springfield, with orders to take Waterworks.

April 22nd, Sunday.—Direction altered, Brigade at Fereira Siding. C.O., Romilly, (joining 1st battalion reserve of officers), and self go down by train.

May 4th, Friday.—Remain at Brandfort. Engineer construction train comes up to repair bridge. Basuto workmen.

May 6th, Sunday.—March to Small Deel, the junction for Winburg. Vet River bridge badly destroyed. Baggage takes a long time crossing bridge and does not arrive till late. 98th joins the Guard's Brigade till they can rejoin their own.

May 9th, Wednesday.—March to Welgelegen—do flank guard to baggage.

May 10th, Thursday.—Paraded 6.15. March to Reit Spruit on the Zand River. Fight expected on the Zand River. Fighting all the morning on our right, probably Tucker's division. We march about 20 miles. Tucker does well. Hear that 30 Inniskilling Dragoons shot under white flag. Baggage very late. Cross the Zand River without opposition.

May 11th, Friday.—March to within 1 mile of Geneva Siding.

May 12th, Saturday.—Paraded 5.45 a.m. Advance guard expect a fight to get into Kroonstad, but all the Boers have bolted. Long tiring march. March past Lord Roberts in the market square of Kroonstad. Bivouac 2 miles the other side of town. Boers evidently on the run. War will soon be over. Baggage very late. Average time for dinner during this march has been about 7.30 p.m.

May 15th, Tuesday.—A patrol was fired on to-day out of a house flying white flag. A squadron sent out and farm burnt at once. Parade railway fatigue 8 p.m.

May 17th, Thursday.—More wild rumours, the best lie being that all is settled for peace except the indemnity. Kitchener has stopped all our mails at Zand River and they say we shall not get a mail before we get to Pretoria. Rather a nuisance as I am anxious to hear about the horses at home. No answer ever comes to questions about horses, and the winter seems to have been wasted. Paraded 7.30 for railway fatigue, 8 to 12 p.m.

May 22nd, Tuesday.—Left Kroonstad, marched to Honnings Spruit station, about 20 miles.

May 23rd, Wednesday.—Parade 8 a.m. March about 17 miles to the Rhenoster River. The Boers had prepared this for defence, but did not wait for us. They have blown up all the bridges.

May 24th, Thursday.—French's cavalry cross the Vaal. Orange Free State annexed and declared British territory. Marched to Vredefort station, about 15 miles.

May 25th, Friday.—Paraded 6.45 a.m. Very cold. Marched to 3 miles beyond Grootvlei station, about 13 miles. The map we have been given is all wrong. Hamilton's mounted infantry a few miles ahead.

May 27th, Sunday.—*Crossed the Vaal.* Paraded 6.45 a.m. Marched to Vereeniging *across the Vaal*, at Viljoen's drift, without opposition. Cavalry are checked at a drift 10 miles east. There are a few coal mines here, but hardly any town. It is a horrid dusty place. The cavalry were here in time yesterday to save the mines from being blown up and we have captured 4 days' supplies, which will enable us to go on to-morrow. Only one span of bridge blown up.

May 28th, Monday.—Paraded about 7 a.m. Marched about 22 miles to Klip River station. On out-post. Boers came down to defend the place, but went away again by train at once on our arrival. Very cold night, 10 degrees of frost. Had to keep two nigger prisoners all night without blankets.

May 29th, Tuesday.—Marched about 20 miles to Germaston. We were told we were only going 12 miles. Bridge over Klip River broke and all the transport got stopped. We did not get our transport till midnight. Mounted infantry were fired on in Germaston, 1 killed. We took 3 engines and 40 trucks. A train went down at once to the Vaal for supplies. We extended for attack, but found no one. Got into camp after dark.

August 30th, Thursday.—Paraded with the Grenadiers at 7 a.m., and marched to Helvetia, where we found the rest of the Brigade. We all then went on to Watervaal Onder. At the end of this valley we again come on a change of scenery, quite precipitous valleys and wilder and higher mountains. Watervaal Onder just like a Swiss village. There is a tunnel on the railway west of this with a cog wheel in the middle owing to the steepness of the fall of the line. The Boers all bolted except a few snipers. 1800 prisoners were released by Boers at Nooitgedacht.

September 5th, Wednesday.—Buller's guns heard to-day. Four trains are said to be captured by the Boers. War seems less likely than ever to finish yet. Buller has gone towards Lydenburg and they say he is held up on the road and wants help.

September 9th, Sunday.—Captain of the day; rumours that Steyn and Kruger have bolted out of the country. Jenkins arrives out of hospital from Pretoria, his train was nearly blown up near Brugspruit. John Campbell returns from hospital here.

September 10th, Monday.—Four companies Grenadiers go up the line to guard construction train. Rumour that we all go on to-morrow.

September 13th, Thursday.—Paraded 6.30 a.m. Marched to Godwaan River, very long tiring march. Had to march along the railway in file all the way; passed enclosure where the prisoners were, an oblong surrounded by 2 barbed wire fences and electric light all round. Had a delightful bathe in Elands River when we arrived. Scots Guards ordered on here late in afternoon.

September 14th, Friday.—Scots Guards arrive here 3.30 a.m. Paraded 6 a.m., bad luck on kiddies; all by bad management of Divisional Staff. March to De Kaap Hoof, wonderful scenery. French supposed to have got 67 engines, 3 weeks' food and 2 weeks' forage in Barberton. We had a very stiff and tiring climb.

September 17th, Monday.—Paraded 5.45 a.m. Marched to North Kaap station on the Barberton Kaapmûnden Railway. Ever since we have left Watervaal Onder, it has been dangerous marching, but nothing has happened, the road is through hills all the way.

September 18*th, Tuesday*.—Paraded 11.30 a.m., rear-guard. Marched to about 3 miles beyond Avoca. We got a lot of engines at Avoca, about 50. This is all gold country. Got in about 6 p.m.

September 19*th, Wednesday*.—Paraded 7 a.m. Marched to about 2 miles beyond Louws Creek Station. Only got on very slowly as the wood had to be cleared of undergrowth all the way.

September 20*th, Thursday*.—Paraded 6 a.m. Marched to Kraapmûnden. All the transport are dead beat, they have had no forage for two days.

September 21*st, Friday*.—Paraded 4.50 a.m. Marched 20 miles. Very hot and trying march, long waits in early morning for transport. Marched all through the heat of the day. Only 1st line of transport came on. Blankets were to have gone on by train, but they could not work the engine. Reached break in the line and bivouacked at about 5.30 p.m. about a mile from Crocodile River. Cook's wagon arrived 11 p.m. Mess carts did well and arrived 10 minutes after us. 30 men fell out. Clive fainted. 102 in the shade. No forage for mules or horses. Ox wagon broke down. Coming on tomorrow, very bad road. No blankets, but luckily warm night. Men ate emergency ration.

September 22*nd, Saturday*.—Had nice bathe in Crocodile River. Brooks not in yet. Paraded 2.30 p.m. Marched to Hector's Spruit, where I found Brooks. Weather very hot now. Only about 1000 feet above the sea. Warned that we shall be without water at the next halt. Nice in this heat! About 5 miles. Twenty guns found destroyed here by the Boers.

September 24*th, Monday*.—Paraded 5 a.m. Marched to Komati Poort, where we arrived about 11 a.m. and had a good drink in the river. Very hot, Boers all gone. Mercenaries gone to Delagoa Bay. 7 miles of rolling stock found here on the Selati railway. All the rolling stock is now accounted for. Had a lovely bathe in the Crocodile River. Komati Bridge all right. Portuguese frontier about 1½ miles beyond bridge lined with Portuguese flags.

September 26*th, Wednesday*.—Mail goes out. Hamilton's brigade arrives. Mail arrives in the evening. Rumour that we start very soon for home. Lord Kitchener has arrived and worked wonders among the rolling stock. We are to have a ceremonial parade on 28th in honour of the King of Portugal's birthday. I don't know who cares about the King of Portugal or who was the ass who discovered his birthday.

September 27*th, Thursday*.—1st Battalion Coldstream ordered to entrain 9 a.m., presumably for home; but don't entrain till about 2 p.m.

September 28*th, Friday*.—3rd Grenadiers start early by train, they don't get further than Hector's Spruit. 1st Battalion Coldstream only as far as Nels Spruit. Paraded for King of Portugal's birthday. Portuguese Governor of Resand Garcia attended. Lunch with Johnny White. See Madocks, Hamilton's A.D.C.

September 29*th, Saturday*.—Paraded for train at 10 a.m. We go in 3 trains, Nos. 3, 5, 6 and 8 in 3rd train, starting at 1.45 p.m. Amateur engine drivers!

We get as far as Hector's Spruit at about 8 p.m., where we stop for the night. Grenadiers at Kaapmunden. 1st battalion at Nels Spruit.

September 30th, Sunday.—Started from Kaapmunden at 3.45 a.m. Nearly ran into the train in front and were nearly run into ourselves. Beautiful scenery between Kaapmunden and Krokodil Poort. Arrived Waterval Onder about 9 p.m. Stayed the night there.

October 1st, Monday.—Great delay about starting, got to Waterval Boven about 11 a.m. Gradient over cog line, 1 in 20, went on very slowly, engine often breaking down. At 9.30 p.m., about 1½ miles from Pan, Boers had taken up a rail. Engine ran off the line and Boers began shooting within 100 yards, dark night, most of us asleep. Tumbled out of wagons as fast as possible. Four wagons of Boer prisoners had been attached to us at Belfast. One Boer seriously wounded. Fortunately Boers did not come on. Our 4 companies lost, 5 killed and 14 wounded. Private Fortune killed, Private Lilly wounded. Heywood slightly wounded, graze in head. Very stupid allowing train to run at night.

October 2nd, Tuesday.—An American doctor arrived on a truck early from Pan. About 1 a.m. a Mounted Infantry man arrived to ask what had happened. A construction train arrived about 7 a.m. to put the engine on the line again. Our store wagon had 46 bullet holes and the last one 25. We were lucky to get off so cheap. Wounded went back in construction trains, also Boer prisoners. Both at Wonderfontein and at Pan warning had come that the Boers were up to mischief, so it was disgraceful letting us go at night. We buried 5 of our dead, Shute read the Service. If the Boers had gone on shooting, in about 20 minutes, we must have been done. We were completely surprised. It is wonderfully lucky they bolted. I expect they thought we were a provision train and bolted when they saw half battalion turning out.

October 3rd, Wednesday.—Left Middelburg 4 a.m. The bumping of these amateur engine drivers is very unpleasant! If asleep it makes one think one is held up again. Reached Pretoria at 1 p.m. Polly-Carew came out on the 2nd during the day and was very annoyed about the attack. He has given orders that no more trains of his division are to run at night. It is lucky we did not go over the embankment when we were derailed. Healey (Doctor) was with us by the merest chance. His first orders had been to go by the 2nd train. Wire broken from Middelburg.

November 4th, Sunday.—Paraded 12.15. Entrain 3.45 p.m., no one knew we were moving till we arrived at the station. Met Dr. Ker, Aunt Maria's stepson, very nice man. Dine at Elansfontein. Sleep at Johannesburg.

November 5th, Monday.—Went to Pretoria. General Hart did not know we were coming. General Barton had a very mismanaged fight apparently, here, a short time ago.

Decmeber 18th, Tuesday.—Train held up between here and Potchefstroom by Boers with one gun!

January 13*th, Sunday.*—Parcel mail arrives. News that Boers attacked and were beaten at several places along Komati railway.

January 17*th, Thursday.*—Mail goes out 5 p.m. Get an answer from Baillie, who asked me to go and stay with him. Concert in railway station.

January 21*st, Monday.*—Went by 6.50 train to Potchefstroom to see Baillie at Vyv Hoek Farm. He is an old man of about 65, was in 7th Hussars and has farmed here for 25 years, his nephew has been with him for 8 years, helping him. Saw all his farm. The chief objections to farming here are locusts and hail; labour and manure are scarce and expensive, but possibilities are very great. Slept at Vyv Hoek.

January 23*rd, Wednesday.*—News arrived that the Queen died last night at 6.30 p.m. I only heard she was ill last night. It must have been very sudden.

January 24*th, Thursday.*—Geoffrey Stewart went by 6.50 train to Johannesburg. 21 guns fired at noon to-day in honour of His Majesty King Edward VII.'s Accession. There was no black powder, and blank charge of cordite only fizzled out of the muzzle, so salute could not be fired. Out-post. Flags raised to mast head at noon.

January 25*th, Friday.*—81 guns ordered and flags half mast at noon for the Queen till

March 9*th, Saturday.*—Leave Klerksdorp, 6.30 train, with servant and two horses. Find Colonel Benson's Column at Potchefstroom. I take over duties of Staff-officer to Mounted troops under command of Wormald. Very grateful to Skeff over this job. Wormald has about 530 mounted troops, consisting of 12th Lancers, 1 L. H., Imp. Y. 1 B., and Kitchener's Horse. Benson's Column consists of 6 companies of Infantry, Cheshire, R.W.F., Derby, and Northampton, 4 R.H.A. guns, 2 R.F.A., 1 howitzer, 2

April 7*th, Sunday.*—Scottish Horse scheme off, but go on with Colonel Benson all the same. Our train due to start 8 a.m., but didn't leave till 12 o'clock. Destination Middelburg, only got as far as Balmoral. Dined with the Buffs.

April 14*th, Sunday.*—148 M.I. remounts and 40 Scottish Horse remounts arrived last night. Scottish Horse remounts very good, M.I. remounts very bad. The M.I. remounts have been in the train since last Tuesday without anyone to look after them, and consigned to no one; they were only watered by the kindness of various railway staff officers, and I expect were hardly fed at all; it is disgusting. Railway seems to be very badly run.

May 9*th, Thursday.*—With great difficulty we loaded a truck with foals and then we were told no train would go, so we had to let all the foals out again. Got a very fine cake from aunt Alice Nevile, also a Ross telescope from home. A few days ago, Macan and 2 companies 18th M. I. went out to fetch in a Boer family, one company went off "on its own" after some cattle, and got 3 men wounded, 1 died.

May 10*th, Friday.*—Mares and foals (90) and 12 donkeys were sent off to Elandsfontein. Played polo.

September 5th, Thursday.—Paraded 7 a.m. Marched to—mine. Colonel Benson, Jackson, and I, rode into Brugspruit and went on by train to Middelburg. We heard to-day of poor Vandeleur's death, shot in a train on the Petersburg line. He seems to have been shot in cold blood. An Hospital nurse was also shot in the same train. Hinton, the Boer Commander, held a thanksgiving service. Remounts very scarce, General Walter Kitchener seems to have taken everything.

September 20th, Friday.—Paraded 6.30 a.m. and marched to Tovreden. Col. Benson and 19th M. I. went to dig up a reported Boer gun near Lake Chrissie, but it was not found, we always seem to get very little ammunition with the Boers we capture. Information reports that they never carry much but whenever they want ammunition they can get it. I suppose the Commandants must have ammunition hidden all over the country. We captured a German ambulance and 2 doctors with the Boers. They say the war will go on for another 6 years! They told me that the Boers believe that the French have bought Delagoa Bay Railway and have landed 50,000 men to help the Boers! They will go to Wonderfontein and thence return to the Boers. The Boers see all the English Pro-Boer papers and speeches.

October 17th, Thursday.—Went to see Marker. He is A.D.C. to Kitchener. He mounted me on Maxwell's ponies. They were excellent ponies. We played Brigade of Guards *v.* Rest. Won by 1 goal to nil. Marker, Stanley, self and Bonham (Hon. member because he has a cousin in the Grenadiers!) played for the Brigade. We had quite a good game. We slept in the train.

My Dear Kennedy,

I feel I ought to have written to you ages ago as I daresay you would be interested to hear how things are getting on out here. I have often intended writing but somehow time has slipped by and I have not done so. I have been out here 20 months now and have seen every phase of the war. I was with my regiment till last March and have since then been on Colonel Benson's Staff. His Column consists mostly of mounted troops, and certainly mounted work is much more interesting than foot-soldiering in a country like this.

My regiment went up the Western Side in 1899 with Lord Methuen and we were all through Belmont, Graspan, Modder River and Magersfontein, a pretty hard three weeks. We fought Belmont, Graspan and Modder River in the first 6 days and Magersfontein 10 days after. I am very glad to have been through these as nothing but personal experience can teach one the effect of modern rifle fire in an Infantry attack. Modder River was the severest as far as I was concerned. I lost 18 men and an officer killed and wounded in my Company alone.

We then had a long monotonous time at Modder River till Lord Roberts's advance and the relief of Kimberley. After Cronje's surrender at Paardeberg, we marched straight to Bloemfontein with little fighting. Our last march was 40 miles, which we did in 22 hours. This is heavy marching when you consider the amount of weight the men have to carry and the short rations.

We started again from Bloemfontein on May 1st and our Infantry only came into action twice, at Johannesburg and Pretoria. We entered Pretoria on 5th June, my battalion being the first to enter, which made it rather exciting. We then thought the war was over! However we soon found out we were wrong and had to march to Koomatie Poort and fought two big battles on the way, Diamond Hill and Belfast. When we got to Koomatie Poort we were entrained and Kitchener told us we were going straight home! On the way back to Pretoria our train with half a battalion in it was derailed in the night, and the Boers shot at us from 70 yards off, killing 5 and wounding 19. The whole thing was over in about five minutes and the Boers bolted. Once more we were due for home when Lord Roberts left, but we were unexpectedly entrained and sent to Potchefstroom, which the Boers attacked the night we arrived! Fortunately we had no casualties that time.

Last December I was sent on detachment to Klerksdorp, where we had an anxious time as our garrison was very weak, but we were never attacked seriously. Last March I went as Staff Officer to Wormald, who was commanding Benson's Mounted Troops. I have had an excellent time since then. That Column was broken up last April and then Colonel Benson took me on his own Staff. He is a most charming man and the best soldier I have served under out here. He is very fond of galloping at the Boers and there is nothing the Boers hate so much! This war is dragging on fearfully. We made a great mistake in dealing so leniently at first and allowing oaths of surrender, etc. The Boers have no sense of honour or of the obligation of an oath, and simply surrendered to tide over an inconvenient stage of the war and took up arms again as soon as they could with safety. But I think the worst offenders are the pro-Boers at home. Nothing is bad enough for them.

Part 9

THE GREAT WAR AND INTERWAR RAILWAY CULTURES

62

'RAILWAYS AND THE WAR', IN *THE TIMES HISTORY OF THE WAR* 6 (1915), PP. 161, 167, 169–174

On the outbreak of the Great War it was not easy for the average person to grasp the essential fact that the railways over which in normal times he travelled for purposes of business or pleasure were not only an indispensable part of the war machine, but perhaps the most powerful weapon in the armoury of the nations. There were wars before railways were built, and mankind will probably retain force as the final international court of appeal when railways shall have been superseded by other methods of land transport. The European War was, however, more than any conflict between the armed forces of mankind which preceded it, a war of railways.

In the Great War the railways exercised a constant influence on the course of the fighting. The campaigns in Belgium, France, Russia, in Northern Italy, and the great thrust into the Balkans, by which the enemy sought to gain possession of the through railway route to Constantinople, furnished many illustrations of the tendency in modern warfare to wage battles for the possession of transport facilities, and to utilize to the fullest extent the mobility which railways confer. Germany made free use of her railway system to transfer large forces from one battle front to the other and to hold up each in turn during the early stages of the war; the excellent employment made of French railways enabled our Ally to be at least partially prepared to deal with the invader, and it was largely by means of her railways that Russia mobilized in a period of time which surprised the enemy and occupied territory in East Prussia at a moment when Germany was concentrating on the march to Paris. The fine use which was made of the railways by the combatant armies was often overlooked for the simple reason that they were common features of every-day life.

In Great Britain there was, of course, with one possible exception, no such thing as a strategic railway. The main lines of communication and practically every branch railway were constructed to serve ordinary commercial needs. The building of strategic railways had always been the business of the State, and in Great Britain there were no State railways, although the Government in virtue of the powers vested in it took possession of the railway system when war was declared.

The position on the Continent was very different. The policy of building railways by which military forces could be rapidly placed on artificially created frontiers had been pursued for many years. In this respect Germany had taken the lead, and had constructed a large mileage of railway lines for which there was military but certainly no commercial justification. It was a simple task indeed for any railway expert to destroy the whole edifice of German sophistry regarding the responsibility for the war by a reference to the policy pursued by Germany in strategic railway construction. It was plain that the invasion of France through Belgium was an essential part of the plan of invasion. There could be no other reason for the remarkable network of lines which had been constructed on the frontiers of Belgium, and which when the time came were employed for the invasion of that unhappy country. The only excuse that the Germans could offer for their railway policy was that the best defensive consists in preparedness for an offensive. The work of constructing these railways was simplified by the fact that the German railway system was owned and worked by the Government.

In a war which in its character was so often a struggle for lines of communication, every mile of the railway was an asset. The following table, compiled for the *Great Eastern Railway Magazine*, from which some of the maps in this chapter have been reproduced, may, therefore, be regarded as possessing historical interest, as it represents the railway conditions as they existed at the outbreak of war:

–		Miles of Railway.	Area Sq. Miles per Railway Mile.	Population per Railway Mile.
Great Britain	about	23,450	5 1/7	1,930
Belgium	,,	5,000	4	2,400
France	,,	30,000	8	1,650
Russia	,,	39,000	234	3,500
Germany	,,	38,000	6	1,700
Austria-Hungary	,,	27,000	10	2,000
Italy	,,	10,800	10 1/4	3,211

The table reveals the disadvantage at which Russia was placed in relation to Germany, and why the latter country was confident of holding up the slow-moving Russian armies while France was being beaten to her knees. That, with a railway system so inferior to that of the enemy, Russia was able to mobilize her forces for the invasion of East Prussia at so early a stage in the conflict was one of the marvels of a war which was full of surprises.

Germany, with that genius for organization which proved to be one of her great assets in the long struggle, had, during the forty years of peace which followed the war with France in 1870, created a railway system which, however well it may have served the needs of the travelling and commercial community, had, as indicated above, been largely built with a view to military needs. It is obvious to anyone who studies the accompanying maps that the possession of railways which covered the frontiers of France, Belgium, and Poland, which provided duplicate routes between East and West, which linked all the railway centres by direct lines with the frontiers, was a great military asset. The trunk lines were all important, but it was some of the smaller railways on the frontier that held the main interest for the military chiefs. These were, indeed, of supreme importance to Germany. The line between Emden and Munster afforded connexion across the marshy country of Ems; its branch lines were also of military value. In the triangle formed by Cologne, Aix la Chapelle, Emmerich, Limburg and the Rhine, Germany had multiplied strategic lines to the point of apparent confusion. These, in addition to controlling the frontiers, served Essen and other industrial towns.

A glance at a map shows how important, apart from its influence on the Belgian campaign, was the seizure of Luxemburg. It gave a straight road from Verviers to Metz, with connexions on the Rhine. Into this line and the territory behind it between Cologne and Saarburg many branch lines and connexions had been constructed. So military in purpose were some of the railways on which Germany relied for the rapid invasion of Belgium that they had never been used for ordinary traffic before the war. One of these secret lines was that connecting Malmedy and Stavelot. Yet its existence was almost essential to the success of German military plans. The line linking Malmedy with Weymertz was another important strategic route. Major Stuart Stephens had reminded us that without the aid of these short lines the troops entrained at Coblenz, Cologne, Bonn and Gladbach could not be secretly projected on the Belgian frontier. As a blind to the real intentions in constructing these particular railway links, Germany had provided an alternative route between Aix and St. Vitti, but this was not built as a military railway, and had, before Germany was ready for war, to be superseded by a high-level line. As a corollary to the little Stavelot—Malmedy line four million pounds were expended in building this high level line between Weymertz and Malmedy. It was designed to be finished in June, 1914, and as is now known war broke out at the beginning of August in that year. Such was the gigantic "bluff" put up by Germany in regard to the reasons for building these two lines—the Stavelot-Malmedy and the Weymertz-Malmedy—that a considerable portion of the capital was provided by Belgium, and that country actually at its own cost linked these lines, designed to facilitate the rapid invasion of its territory, with the Belgian railway system. The annexation of Luxemburg was, of course, a very simple affair. The railways were already in German hands, and it was an easy task to transport an army into the capital of the Duchy and announce its annexation for the purposes of the war.

There were other points in the German railway policy before the war to which attention should be directed to show the determination to be ready for war, although it was known, in the phrase used by Sir James Yoxall, that in the months preceding the outbreak of hostilities "grass grew hay-high between the rails of the few French strategic railways." The same writer furnished some striking information as to what the Germans had been doing in constructing railways through the volcanic province of the Eifel, just inside the German frontier. Ten years ago the railway was a simple single line, but by the time war was declared it had been straightened, doubled, and throughout its steeper gradients flattened; in certain sections it had been tripled and quadrupled, and sidings, absurdly large for the trading or social needs of the population, were laid out near any railway station which was in flat open country and itself situated on level ground with plenty of space in the vicinity of the station. At Gerolstein, a village with 1,200 inhabitants, sidings suitable for the traffic of a large town had been laid out.

A marked feature of German railways was that there were very few heavy gradients, and that on many of the main lines there was not a single tunnel. That routes had been selected for the railways which presented so few natural obstacles was a great advantage as long as the railways remained in German possession, but in the event of invasion, which a military Power such as Germany probably never contemplated when laying out the railway system, it would clearly be very difficult for German armies in retreat to damage the railways to an extent which would prevent their use by an invading army for anything more than a short period.

It may be pointed out that even during peace time German railways were administered by military methods. On the mobilization of the army they were immediately taken over by the military authorities, under the guidance of the Railways Section of the Great General Staff. The German railway administration was of a somewhat complicated character, but the Imperial Government had always possessed arbitrary powers in connexion with railway construction, and it had been no unusual circumstance for military lines to be constructed through territory in opposition to the will of the inhabitants. To such a degree of completeness had the German railway organization been brought that rules had been framed before the war governing the administration of railways in foreign countries which were occupied by the German army.

No doubt many fine feats in transport were achieved by German railways during the war, but some of the stories concerning the rapid movement of troops from east to west or the converse which were published in the Press were obvious exaggerations. There is a limit in transportation of which every practical railway man is fully aware, and some of the performances with which rumour credited the German railway organization were of an impossible character. One fine achievement, however, stands to the credit of Von Hindenburg who, in spite of the handicap of air reconnaissance, succeeded by the transfer of a large force from the Cracow and Czenstochau districts in effecting a surprise upon the Russian forces in the neighbourhood of Kalisch. In a period of four days Von Hindenburg transported a force of nearly 400,000 men over a distance of 200 miles. The fact that it took four days to move this army over a comparatively short distance, although in itself a good performance, gave an index to the time which would be occupied in transferring any large body of troops from the eastern to the western front, a journey which in peace times occupied about twenty hours by express train and which, even when the necessary rolling stock had been assembled at the point of departure, a long and wearisome business in itself, would under military traffic conditions take many times as long. Even when credit is given for all the advantage which followed the fact that Germany was fighting on interior lines, a majority of the stories which gained currency at various times during the war may be relegated to the same category as that of the transport of a Russian army through England.

The French railway system, although it was not constructed for strategic purposes, was admirably adapted for the rapid transport of troops and material of war. The lines along the eastern frontier from Boulogne, through Amiens, Tergnier, Laon, Reims and Verdun commanded the German frontier and that through Cambrai and Mons to Brussels enabled troops to be transported to the Belgian frontier. These, however, were commercial railways, not strategic in the ordinary meaning of the word, nor was the frontier, as was the case with Germany, a maze of railways whose only functions were that of army transport. Under normal peace conditions the French railways were under the control of the Minister of Public Works, but as was the case in Great Britain, they were automatically taken over by the Government on the outbreak of war.

It will be interesting to show in some detail how the French railways were managed during the war. The whole of the railways were operated under the condition even in times of peace that if the Government required to transport troops and supplies to any point on any railway system the Company must immediately place all its facilities at the service of the State. As this obligation had existed for a period of forty years a permanent military organization was in existence whose duties were to prepare the railways for service in time of war. According to an account of the system in force which appeared in the *Journal des Transports*, each of the large railways had attached to it a Committee of two, known as the Commission de Réseau, composed of a technical member, usually the general manager of the railway, and a military member, who was a high officer of the general staff nominated by the Minister of War. The duties of this Committee were to investigate in all its bearings in the light of strategic requirements the manner in which the railway could be utilized for the purposes of war. In addition to the Commissions de Réseau a Military Railways Committee had been created in the year 1898. This Committee, which was presided over by the Chief of the General Staff, consisted of six military officers of high rank, three representatives of the Ministry of Public Works, and the members of the Commissions of the different railways. The functions of this Committee were mainly advisory, but it sat in judgment on all questions relating to military transport, and assented or dissented from measures proposed by the Commissions de Réseau.

Special regulations affecting railway employees came into force on the declaration of war. These provided that when a railwayman was called to the colours he was mobilized as a railwayman, and the working of this system was successfully tested during the railway strike of 1910, the railway men being then called out under martial law. On the first day of mobilization the railways were required to place at the disposal of the military authorities the whole of their transport facilities either over the whole of the systems or on certain specified routes. The railway system of France was on mobilization divided into two zones which, although administered by different authorities, were both under military control. The army zone was placed under the control of the Commander-in-Chief of the armies in the field, to whose staff was attached an officer whose status was that of Manager of the army railways. This zone was subdivided into the sections of line which were within and without the actual sphere of military operations. Within the zone of actual field operations the service was conducted by military units, while the sections of line outside that area were manned by the employees of the company who were mobilized under a territorial system for that purpose. The other railway zone, known as the interior zone, was under the direction of the Minister of War, who gave authority to the Commission de Réseau of each railway to carry out executive functions, each of the two members of the Committee retaining individual responsibility, the military member being entrusted with military measures, and the technical member being charged with the provision of rolling stock and other technical requirements.

While precedence was given to the transport of troops and materials of war, provision was also made for the carriage of food-stuffs and general commercial merchandise. Within the army zone ordinary traffic was entirely suspended except on the order of the Commander-in-Chief. In the interior zone ordinary passenger and goods traffic was carried according to the conditions prescribed by the Minister of War, who had the power after mobilization and concentration were completed to authorize the partial or complete resumption of ordinary passenger and freight traffic.

The French Army at the outset of the war was undoubtedly under the handicap of having a much smaller mileage of strategic railways than Germany. The deficiency was to a certain extent remedied during the progress of the war. The French had a valuable asset in a fine corps of railway engineers, and in connection with the repair of railways damaged during the march on Paris and the subsequent advance the services of British railwaymen were requisitioned both for this repair work and for the building of new lines.

An account of the fine work done on the French railways during the early days of the war was furnished by the French authorities, and the report indicated with what remarkable precision the transport system worked. Its first great task was the transport of the "troupes de couverture," the army sent to the frontier to meet the first shock of the enemy, a proceeding which enabled the mobilization of the main armies to be carried out undisturbed.

This was the work of the first department of the three heads into which the French transport service was divided. The second department was charged with the regular supply of men, horses, provisions, ammunition and material to the armies in the field. The third department was responsible for the transport of troops from one part of the theatre of war to another where their presence would contribute to the success of an operation. The transport of the "troupes de couverture" commenced on the evening of July 31, 1914, and was completed on August 3 at noon without any delay either in the departure or arrival of trains, and before any of the ordinary services had been suspended. Nearly 600 trains were required on the Eastern system alone, and the merit of this fine feat in transportation was enhanced by the fact that the transport of troops in connection with the general mobilization commenced on August 2 and was, therefore, partially concurrent with the movement of the first armies to the frontier. The transports needed for the concentration of the armies generally commenced on August 5, the most urgent period ending on August 12. During these eight days no fewer than 2,500 trains were dispatched, of which only 20 were subjected to slight delays, and during a period of fourteen days nearly 4,500 trains were dispatched, and in addition 250 trains loaded with siege supplies for the fortresses. These excellent results of French railway organization were rendered the more noteworthy from the fact that the original destination of four army corps was changed after mobilization had commenced.

63

EDWIN A. PRATT, 'EMPLOYMENT OF WOMEN AND GIRLS', IN *BRITISH RAILWAYS AND THE GREAT WAR: ORGANISATION, EFFORTS, DIFFICULTIES AND ACHIEVEMENTS*, 2 VOLS. (LONDON: SELWYN AND BLOUNT, 1921), PP. 475–482

RAILWAY companies were among the first, even if they were not actually the first, of the great employers of labour to resort to the expedient of engaging women and girls as substitutes for men in order that a larger number of the latter might be released for service with the Colours. Not only, also, were they pioneers in this direction but the number they eventually took on assumed exceptionally large proportions, while the experiences they thus had occasion to gain in comparing the respective merits of masculine and feminine labour in a wide range of railway activities offer many points of public interest.

It was as early in the war as February, 1915, that the British railway companies began to realise the possibilities open to them in the directions stated. There had been conferences between Lord Kitchener and representatives of the Railway Executive Committee as to what could be done to permit of the enlistment of railwaymen in still greater numbers, and the suggestion was made that one means towards the achievement of this purpose would be found in the taking of a greater number of women into the railway service than were then already employed. In certain grades, as, for instance, those of engine-drivers, firemen and shunters, a substitution of women for men would, admittedly, be impracticable; but there were many others in regard to which it was felt that women might readily take the place of men for the duration of the war.

How, following upon this, the Railway Executive Committee appointed a sub-committee to deal with the question of releasing men for enlistment in the Army, and how this sub-committee, meeting first on March 24th, 1915, proposed, among other things, that the employment of women should be extended, Here it may be added that the late Mr. Potter, General Manager of the Great Western Railway, and Chairman of the sub-committee in question, took a special interest in this question of employing women substitutes, and that the results of the recommendations made by the sub-committee were soon manifested. The greatest increase at first was naturally found in the employment of women and girls for clerical duties; and more and still more were soon being taken on as booking-clerks, parcel clerks, ticket-collectors, ticket-examiners, dining-car attendants, porters, carriage-cleaners, telegraphists, etc.

These developments gave rise to some degree of concern on the part of the National Union of Railwaymen, and that organisation asked for an assurance from the railway companies that the taking on of women in capacities in which they were not formerly employed was an emergency provision arising out of the circumstances created by the war, and one that would not prejudice any undertaking given by the companies as to the re-employment, on the conclusion of the war, of men who had joined the Colours. An assurance to this effect was given, and it was further placed on record that the employment of women during the war in capacities in which they had not previously been employed was without prejudice to the general question of the employment of women.

One almost inevitable result of the taking over of men's work by women was the adoption by the latter of men's attire when the conditions rendered the resort to this expedient especially advantageous. The precedent was, it is believed, first set by the women carriage-cleaners employed at the London and South Western Railway Company's Wimbledon Park sidings. They made for themselves some masculine garments which they found so well adapted to the duties of carriage-cleaning that other women workers followed their example alike in this and in various other occupations. Thereupon the company undertook to supply the garments in question, regarding them as in the nature of "uniform" for their women employees. Before long the wearing of men's clothes by women workers in various grades of railway employment was generally adopted, and it led to a great advance in the employment of women as substitutes for men, thus allowing of the latter being released in still greater number for service with the forces.

As the war progressed and the demand for men became more urgent than ever, women were employed by the railway companies on a variety of other non-feminine occupations, some of which might well be regarded as involving so great a strain on the physical powers of the worker as not to be suitable for women at all. There came a time, in fact, when women, in addition to their range of light employments in the railway service, engaged in so much manual labour formerly undertaken exclusively by men that they were to be found in almost every grade on which it was practicable to employ them and for which previous training was not an essential qualification.

In August, 1916, returns were obtained from sixty-eight railway companies, comprising a large number of small companies and a few large ones, as to the extent to which the substitution of female for male employees had been adopted by them. Considerable difference was found in the action taken by the companies concerned. Some were still employing no women at all. Others had not increased their number during the war. These conditions related mainly to the smaller companies. The returns from larger ones were much more satisfactory. The London, Brighton and South Coast Company, for example, had increased the number of their women workers from ninety-nine to 683, and the Glasgow and South Western from 442 to 1,095. The largest increase shown by the companies included in the return was in respect to women clerks, the aggregate having risen from a pre-war total of 2,104 to 13,930. Twenty-three companies were then employing women as porters; twenty-nine had women ticket-collectors; eight had women engine-cleaners and twelve employed women in workshops.

At the end of October, 1916, the Railway Executive Committee obtained a fresh set of returns, furnished by twelve leading companies; and here, again, much interesting information was presented.

The total number of women and girls then in the service of these twelve companies was over 33,000. This figure compared with 13,046, the total for the whole of the British railway companies on the outbreak of the war, namely, 4,564 engaged on railway work proper and 8,482 in "other categories," such as waitresses in refreshment rooms, waiting-room attendants, hotel staffs, washerwomen, charwomen, etc. The 33,000 of the later date included 1,068 waitresses and 2,825 office-cleaners, so that to this extent, at least, essentially feminine occupations were being followed; but the special interest in the list now drawn up, apart from the sum total of the figures, lay in the fact that no fewer than 135 separate and distinct occupations then being followed by girls and women on British railways were specified. Nor did the list profess to be anything like complete in this respect, 2,189 out of the 33,000 being grouped under the heading of "miscellaneous."

How varied the occupations then being followed on the railway by women and girls had become, and the numbers engaged in various grades or departments (apart from those in the non-specified miscellaneous group), may be shown by the following typical examples: Clerks, 13,904; carriage-cleaners, 2,173; workshop women (various), 1,278; platform porters, 1,098; munition workers, 1,046; goods porters, 901; ticket-collectors or ticket-examiners, 706; gatekeepers, 705; engine-cleaners, 587; labourers, 239; machinists, 178; messengers, 150; parcel porters, 147; horse-cloth and sack repairers, 121; painters, 99; dining-car attendants, 93; number-takers, 79; cellar and page girls, 40; weighing-machine attendants, 23; brass lacquerers, 23; letter-sorters, 15; horse-keepers, 14; carters, 12; train attendants, 11; cloak-room attendants, 10; luggage-room porters, 10; wagon repairers, 8; hotel porters, 6; harness-cleaners, 6; warehousewomen, 5; train-information attendants, 4; crockery collectors, 4; ferry attendants, bridge-keepers, blind-pullers, wharfingers and flag makers, two each, and gardener, carver, printer, billiard-marker and signal cleaner and lighter, one each.

Taking individual companies, it was shown that at this date one company (the Great Central) had increased the number of its women clerks from seventy to 1,526, and employed eighteen women ticket-collectors, 186 women carriage-cleaners, fifty-five signal-cleaners, and 454 porters. Another (the Midland) had

480 women carriage-cleaners, 475 engine-cleaners, 226 labourers in workshops and thirty-seven other women labourers. Still another, while employing women neither as engine-cleaners nor labourers, had 142 as ticket-collectors.

A subsequent list of grades in which women were being employed by various companies included the following, in addition to those already mentioned: Call girl, check-office assistant, stores assistant, lamp-room attendant, tube-cleaner, cabin attendant, luggage-weigher, searcher, gate-keeper, lock-keeper, lamplighter, weighing-machine attendant, canal-traffic enterer, time-keeper, polisher, coil-winder, concrete-block maker, cellar and page girl, baker, halt attendant, stationery packer, coal storer, signal-cleaner and lighter, crane-driver, stable-washer, van-washer and yard woman.

By the end of 1916 the number of women employed on the making of munitions of war in railway workshops was 2,251. This figure steadily increased until the end of October, 1917, when it attained a maximum of 4,698. From that time it decreased month by month until, by the end of October, 1918 (the latest date of the periodical returns collected in respect to all companies), it had fallen to 2,045. The number of women and girls employed on "railway work," as distinct from munition work and "other categories," rose from 4,564 on August 4th, 1914, to 34,272 on December 31st, 1916, and to 50,828 on December 31st, 1917. A maximum of 55,942 was reached on September 30th, 1918. The greatest number of women engaged on railways in "other categories" was attained on October 31st, 1918. The figure then stood at 10,718. Taking the sum total of women and girls employed by British railway companies in all capacities, one finds that this was as follows at the dates mentioned:—August 4th, 1914: 13,046; December 31st, 1916: 46,316; December 31st, 1917: 65,389; September 30th, 1918: 68,801 (the maximum; October 31st, 1918: 68,637.

The maximum of 68,800 relates, of course, to the number of women and girls still in the railway service on the date mentioned. If allowance is made for those who had taken up railway work but kept to it for short or comparatively short periods only, the aggregate would be far in excess of the figure stated.

According to later returns obtained by the Ministry of Transport, and quoted in the House of Commons on November 10th, 1919, by the Parliamentary Secretary of that department, the number of women employed by fourteen principal British railway companies on November 11th, 1918, was 55,796, while the number on July 30th, 1919, was 34,545. Sir Rhys Williams added: –

Most of the women still employed are only retained temporarily pending the return of the men who left the companies' service to join the Army and have not yet been demobilised but who have been promised that the positions which they left shall be kept open for them.

The value of the services rendered by so considerable a body of women in enabling many more railwaymen to join the Colours than could otherwise have been spared if the railways were to carry on is beyond all question, and the women who undertook the duties thus assigned to them are deserving of the gratitude of the country, and are entitled to consider that they, also, helped to win the war, just as though they had themselves been qualified to take part in the fighting.

If, however, it should be asked what conclusions as to the suitability of women to undertake railway work under normal conditions can be based on the experience of their labour under the abnormal conditions of war, the reply to be given must vary according to (1) the position filled, (2) the local circumstances thereof, and (3) certain general considerations.

The greatest success of war-time women workers on railways was attained in respect to clerical duties. Some of them, holders of University degrees, and employed in the offices of General Managers or other high officers who may not have had lady clerks before, were found to be most capable women, and the work they did was done very well indeed. In head offices and large goods offices women in general were regarded as eminently suited to minor clerical work so long as this was mainly of a routine kind. In such matters as typing and simple accounts, the work of women and girls compared, according to one authority, with that of younger men and boys. In any case they were so far successful, especially when working under male supervision, that in January, 1918, fifty per cent. of the clerical staff employed on the principal railways were women. Generally speaking, however, women clerks were found to be more lacking in initiative than men; they were less useful to the companies than men because they could not be so readily transferred from one sphere of duties to another, while, as a rule, three women were required to do the work of two men, although it is possible that the position would be improved in proportion as the women gained more experience.

As booking-clerks, women who took up the work did so with less training than, in pre-war days, would have been undergone by the average male booking-clerk; but they did very well at large stations where the conditions allowed of their being allotted day-turns of duty. On some of the suburban lines, however, there is practically an all-night service; on others the ordinary trains which run till midnight or up to 1 a.m., are succeeded by workmen's trains which start between 4 a.m. and 5 a.m. Here it was, of course, necessary that the booking-offices should be kept open to suit these trains; but there was an obvious inexpediency in the taking on of either the very late or the very early turns of duty by women and girls, who, from this point of view, at least, could not be considered equal to men.

Similar conditions in respect to large stations and hours applied to women as ticket-collectors, with the further consideration that at smaller stations women did not take over the full range of duties previously performed by men who not only collected tickets but helped with parcels or luggage and made themselves generally useful. Neither, again, as ticket-collectors or ticket-examiners on the trains were women found to be so expeditious as men.

As porters, again, the employment of women was mainly limited to the larger stations; and even there they were not always equal to the handling of the heavier luggage—a consideration which led to the weight allowed to travellers being restricted. At smaller stations where the male porter had not only looked after the passengers and dealt with luggage of whatever bulk but could fill up his time with shunting, lighting signal-lamps, etc., a woman was clearly not an adequate substitute. Nor could women porters be called upon, in the same way as men porters, to act when necessary as railway guards. In any case, also, the rule of three women being wanted in place of two men prevailed throughout all the porterage grades.

Women carriage-cleaners had proved their usefulness prior to the outbreak of hostilities. The number now taken on for an occupation well suited to those belonging to the working classes assumed considerable proportions, and the results were eminently satisfactory. It was said of them that they took more time over what they did, and that their output was only about fifty per cent. of that done by men; but they cleaned the insides of the carriages more thoroughly, and in this respect the sympathies of railway travellers would certainly favour the women.

In all manual work involving any degree of strain upon the physical system of the worker, women, as might well be expected, were not nearly as efficient as men. This was especially shown in such grades as that of goods porter. Not only had the weight of the consignments to be taken into account, but, while the pushing of a loaded trolley on the level might be within the capacity of the woman worker, a much greater effort was required to get the same trolley up the incline leading to the goods wagon into which the commodities might have to be loaded. It was then that the strain really began to tell. Much of the work, in fact, in connection with the handling of goods was of so laborious a type that women should not, it was considered, be allowed to undertake it at all except under conditions of grave emergency. Taking all the grades here concerned, it was once more found that in almost every instance three women were wanted to do the work of two men.

There was at one time a tendency on the part of certain railway companies to put women into signal boxes on branch and subsidiary lines, but although the companies themselves considered that the women were equal to the work, the men in signal boxes alongside were apt to raise objections and declare that "they could not accept the responsibility."

Coming now to general considerations, the view taken by probably the majority of railway officials was that, whilst women could carry out the less important duties connected with railway work, they were not, as a body, equal to men in the more important posts; they were not physically fitted for the heavier duties; they were not so well qualified to deal with the emergencies always liable to arise on railways, while, through a lack of railway training, they could not, however proficient in one grade, be called upon readily to take up the work of absentees in another grade.

To this last-mentioned statement it might be replied that women could acquire the said training, and thus qualify for other grades than those in which they actually worked. Here, however, one must bear in mind that the outlook of the average boy, youth or man who enters the railway service differs essentially from that of the average girl or woman. In the former case the new railway worker expects to spend his life at railway work, as his father and grandfather may have done before him; and he knows, whether he begins as clerk or as porter, that there are open to him possibilities of promotion which may lead to his eventually attaining to what he would regard as a very desirable post indeed. Hence the junior, or the subordinate, generally welcomes any opportunity that may be offered to him of showing his fitness for promotion. As against all this, the average girl or woman is more apt to regard her post on the railway as a temporary one and one that in the event of her marriage she would not want to occupy any longer. Whatever her prospects in this direction, she is generally more ready to settle down to the routine work to which she may find herself allocated, and not only does not seek for the opportunities to fill temporarily the more important posts which are so welcome to an aspiring youth, but rather shrinks from assuming responsibilities she may regard as beyond her powers. For these reasons, apart from the conscientious performance of her ordinary duties, she probably does not take the same direct interest in railway work as a man, and, consequently, is of less value to a company.

One must, however, remember that the women and girls who took on this wartime railway work were expressly warned that their engagement was a temporary one only, and that they must not look forward to a permanency. In these circumstances there was still less encouragement even for the more intelligent of those in the clerical grades to qualify for higher positions which they would have to give up as soon as the men for whom they were acting as substitutes came back from the war.

The lack of desire for training in higher branches of railway work was especially characteristic of women employed in the manual grades. These women were almost invariably content to follow instructions in regard to the work to which they were put and did not aspire to anything better. Their periods of service, too, were in many cases very short, as though they either soon wearied of the work or else realised their physical unfitness for it. Out of a total of 1,483 women employed at the London stations of one of the principal companies during the course of the war, 633 resigned after one month's service, 126 after two months, 124 after three months and the remainder after varying periods up to about eighteen months. In the Goods Department of the same company, out of a total of 1,022 resignations, 548 were within one month, and 104 after more than one month and less than two months. The number who had been in the company's service in December, 1918, for periods of eighteen months and over was only 108. Then the women employed in manual work at the company's principal goods station were especially bad time-keepers. Forty-two of them lost sixty days through being absent without leave. Out of a staff of 152 women, 116 lost 165 hours in a single week by arriving late on duty. Men workers were found to stay away less and to keep much better time than the women. Among the clerical staff punctuality was much better observed, though the percentage of absence through illness was higher among the women than among the men.

In regard to the claims which have been advanced that women in the railway service should have rates of pay equal to those of men in corresponding grades and positions, it is held that, inasmuch as the value of female labour to a railway company is not equal to that of men, any attempt to enforce the principle of equality in remuneration would lead to a discontinuance of the employment of women save, perhaps, under exceptional conditions.

64

THOMAS HARDY, 'MIDNIGHT ON THE GREAT WESTERN', IN *THE POETICAL WORKS OF THOMAS HARDY*, 2 VOLS. (LONDON: MACMILLAN, 1919), I, P. 483

In the third-class seat sat the journeying boy,
    And the roof-lamp's oily flame
Played down on his listless form and face,
Bewrapt past knowing to what he was going,
    Or whence he came.

In the band of his hat the journeying boy
    Had a ticket stuck; and a string
Around his neck bore the key of his box,
That twinkled gleams of the lamp's sad beams
    Like a living thing.

What past can be yours, O journeying boy
    Towards a world unknown,
Who calmly, as if incurious quite
On all at stake, can undertake
    This plunge alone?

Knows your soul a sphere, O journeying boy,
    Our rude realms far above,
Whence with spacious vision you mark and mete
This region of sin that you find you in,
    But are not of?

65

LORD MONKSWELL, 'MAKING UP LOST TIME', *THE RAILWAY MAGAZINE* 50 (JAN.–JUNE 1922), PP. 157–160

PERFECT punctuality, which renders unnecessary the making up of lost time, is no doubt the ideal at which railways should aim. But in this imperfect world that ideal, though it may be more or less nearly approached, can never be completely attained. Even on the best managed railways there will always be a certain number of cases in which time is lost, and when this happens what ought to be done?

The particular drawback attaching to unpunctuality on a railway is that the loss of time by one train inevitably involves the delay of others. If one train is behind time all trains connecting with it, those timed to follow it closely and, very likely too, some which have to cross its path are affected. Indeed, it may safely be said that as a rule the unpunctuality of one important train affects detrimentally the whole of the traffic of all the districts through which it passes.

Unpunctuality is wasteful in two ways. First and foremost it wastes time, which is life. The life of each one of us consists of so much time. This time once wasted is gone for ever. It can never be replaced. Time unnecessarily lost through railway unpunctuality is a dead loss of national efficiency, in that it deprives those railway passengers whose time is of any value of a certain part of this valuable time. The sum of the amount of human efficiency lost through the unpunctuality of some important train containing several hundred passengers and involving the further unpunctuality of many other trains, all with their own complements of passengers, may be very great and represent the loss of a large sum of money.

Secondly, there is the direct financial loss due to disorganisation caused by unpunctuality. Every extra stop costs something in increased wear and tear, and all the work in connection with the delayed trains has to be done at some time other than that foreseen and can hardly help causing unnecessary expense both to the railway itself and to its customers.

Causes of late running

Unpunctuality is therefore, an expensive thing in itself, and from mere motives of economy should be reduced to the lowest point. When time has once been lost the only way of setting things right again, or at any rate of minimising the trouble, is to make up the time lost as quickly as possible.

What are the objections to doing this? I can think of three:—

(1) *Restricted Engine Power.*—The engine may not be sufficiently powerful to put forth the extra effort required. If this is so there is obviously nothing to be done and the case calls for no further consideration.

(2) *Danger.*—A great deal of vague nonsense is talked about the danger from excessive speed due to the making up of lost time. Actually, of course, the possible dangers arising from excessive speed are accurately known and perfectly easily guarded against. For the most part they arise on secondary lines where the permanent way is not sufficiently solid to bear the strain of a train running beyond a certain speed. There are also certain types of vehicle, particularly engines, that cannot with safety be allowed to exceed certain prescribed speeds. With first-class rolling-stock running over the solidly constructed and carefully maintained permanent way of main lines of railway there is clearly no danger from excessive speed, except at particular places, such as sharp curves, where it is always necessary to reduce speed whether a train is making up time or not. Very high speeds have so often been authentically recorded on suitable parts of almost all the principal main lines of the world that there can no longer be any serious question of danger about them. And if it is thought inadvisable to give the drivers permission to go "all out" down hill, nothing is easier than to prescribe the limits that must not be exceeded, as is habitually done on the Continent of Europe. It really makes very little difference to timekeeping what are the maximum speeds downhill. Where time is to be gained is by increased speed uphill and on the level. By running at 90 m.p.h. instead of 80 m.p.h. downhill 5 sec. are gained each mile, but by running uphill at 60 m.p.h. instead of 50 m.p.h. 12 sec. are gained each mile.

At the sharp curves and other places where speed must be limited it is no doubt important to take precautions by means of automatic recorders to ensure that the safe limit of speed should not be exceeded. But this is equally the case whether time is being made up or not, and to suggest that a driver who has received suitable instructions and who knows that any failure to comply with his instructions will be detected, cannot be trusted to carry them out when making up time, appears to me fantastic.

(3) *Expense.*—To make up time the engine will no doubt have to work harder and will consume more coal, and the strain on the boiler and possibly on the machinery will be increased. It is, of course, difficult to give exact estimates as to what the extra expense is likely to amount to. It would be very interesting if anyone who has access to any information that may exist on the subject would deal adequately with that point. My own belief is that it would amount

to a very small fraction of the sum lost by refraining from making up lost time. Even, for instance, with coal at the present abnormal price, circumstances could hardly be found in which the making up of all the lost time possible would work out at more than 6*d*. a mile.

Practice in other countries

On general principles, therefore, it appears that the making up of lost time has everything to recommend it. I suggest that the matter ought to be carefully thought out by the railway companies and precise, printed instructions issued to the engine drivers setting out exactly what is expected of them. This has for long been done in France, where many years ago it was specifically recognised by the Ministry of Public Works that the making up of lost time was conducive to safety.

In the year 1895, some question having arisen whether premiums paid to the engine drivers for the making up of lost time should be discontinued, the French Ministry of Public Works addressed a circular to the various companies containing a passage of which the following is a literal translation:—

> "But if it is important to avoid excessive speed it is not less indispensable to prevent delays as far as possible or to attenuate those which occur on the way. Independently of the disturbance which these irregularities import into the service and of the complaints on the part of the public to which they give rise, they often become the cause of serious accidents."

So far as I know it is, and always has been, the practice in France to pay the drivers so much for every minute of lost time which they regain.

The following is a translation of the printed instructions issued to engine drivers by the Paris-Orleans Railway regarding the making up of lost time:—

> "When a delay has taken place enginemen must make every effort to regain on the remainder of the run the time lost on the first part of it; they must, however, always have their train under control and be able to stop, if necessary within a distance of 800 metres (½ mile).
>
> "The additional speed must never exceed half the regulation speed of the train on gradients which rise or fall less steeply than 1 in 100, and a third of the regulation speed on gradients of 1 in 100 or steeper."

All this is subject to the rule that the maximum speed on French railways must never exceed 120 km. (74½ miles) an hour.

As to the regulation speed of a train it should be explained that in the working time-tables of French lines each train is given a "regulation speed." This regulation speed is about equal to the average full speed of the train, say 3 m.p.h. faster than the average start to stop speed of its fastest run.

As regards Germany very similar instructions are issued to the engine drivers, at any rate, on the Prussian State Railways, which comprised at least two-thirds of the German railways before the war. (Since the war all the German lines have, I believe, been amalgamated into one Imperial system.)

These instructions are, moreover, really acted upon both in France and Germany.

Experience in France

The first time I ever travelled on a French locomotive, more than twenty years ago, we made up 20 min. in a run of slightly over 80 miles. It was the afternoon boat train from Calais to Paris. This train at that time was given 103 min. for the run of 81¼ miles from Amiens to Paris. Leaving Amiens about 20 min. late we were stopped outside the Gare du Nord in just over 82 min. from Amiens. On this occasion we ran for something over 20 miles up gradients averaging about 1 in 350 at 60 m.p.h.—an experience entirely new to me in the year 1898, and one which I imagine would then have been new to most other people. Downhill only 16 km. (10 miles) all told, were run at 70 m.p.h. or over.

The late Mr. Charles Rous-Marten has recorded an instance of a Paris-Lyons-Mediterranée train, which, leaving Dijon 55 min. late, had regained 35 min. by the time it reached Laroche (99 miles).

While this important question is thus carefully considered and arranged for on the principal railways of the Continent, the matter seems to have been, and to be, almost entirely neglected in Great Britain. I write subject to correction, as in spite of many endeavours on my part I have never yet been able to ascertain how the matter really stands on most of the principal British lines.

British drivers not encouraged

But so far as my investigations go I have been unable to discover that British drivers receive any printed instructions beyond the rule in the rule-book which directs them to work their train as nearly as possible in accordance with the booked times and in such a manner as to avoid excessive speed or loss of time. It is hardly possible to imagine anything more unsatisfactory than this rule. The language, which ought to be of the most precise possible kind, so as to leave no loophole for misunderstanding is, when examined, found to be vague to such a point as to have practically no meaning whatever. In particular there is no definition of "excessive speed," and as regards the expression "loss of time," there is nothing to show whether "loss of time" includes casual delays which should, therefore, be made up, or whether when casual delays have taken place the driver is not expected to trouble about them but just to go on keeping up the original booked speed. I suppose that some general understanding exists on these points and that the drivers probably receive verbal instructions about the making up of lost time. What a man in the position of an engine driver should have are definite printed instructions setting forth in detail exactly what he is expected to do in each case, and he should be able to appeal to the actual text of his instructions if he wishes to do so. In a matter of high policy such as the making up of lost time all responsibility in principle should clearly rest with the officers of the line, and a subordinate like a driver should only have the responsibility for carrying out the clearly expressed orders of his superior officers.

Whatever may be the real state of the case as regards the instructions given to the locomotive men, I have no hesitation in saying that the way in which the making up of lost time is taken in hand in Great Britain has, in my experience, been extremely bad. Some railways are better than others, and an energetic driver will sometimes, apparently on his own initiative, make up time where a less energetic driver on the same railway will not. But in the whole of my experience on British railways the making up of lost time has been the exception, and I should say that when a train has been late in at least four cases out of five no attempt whatever has been made to regain time. In the case of some important railways, indeed, I have been informed definitely on the highest authority that the making up of lost time is not encouraged.

Each train in its place

All this is very odd and illogical. The smooth working of a railway depends so obviously on each train being in the proper place at the proper time that I do not think that the paramount importance of working with the least possible departure from the pre-arranged plan can be challenged seriously. And it is particularly from the point of view of the utmost attainable measure of safety that I wish to direct attention to this matter. Clearly the possibility of mistakes taking place is much reduced if each train is, as far as possible, in the place assigned to it in the time-table. The supreme object lesson as to the danger of failing to make up lost time is furnished by the Gretna accident in 1915 on the Caledonian Railway, in which it is estimated that 227 persons were killed and 246 persons were injured. In this case it will be remembered that owing to the lateness of the express a slow train, timed to leave Carlisle after the express, was allowed to leave Carlisle in front of the express. At Quintinshill, near Gretna, this slow train was shunted on to the up line to allow the express to pass, and while standing on the up line was run into by a troop train. This accident could not have taken place if the London and North Western Railway had brought the Glasgow express punctually into Carlisle on the morning on which it occurred. In making this remark I impute blame to nobody. I am not aware whether this particular train on this particular night could have made up time or whether circumstances existed which rendered the making up of time an impossibility, and on this point no light is thrown by the Board of Trade report. I am aware also that in the matter of making up time the practice of the London and North Western Railway seems in general to be less unsatisfactory than that of most British lines. I merely point out that for some reason or other time was lost and had not been regained, so that the train was late at Carlisle, and that if the lost time had been regained so as to make the train punctual at Carlisle the accident could not have taken place.

A further remark which suggests itself is that it is extremely odd that the Board of Trade inspector did not consider it his duty to investigate in any way the reasons for the failure of the London and North Western Railway to bring the express punctually into Carlisle. It can only be supposed that the matter lay outside the scope of his instructions. As this unpunctuality was the predisposing cause of the accident to which all the other irregularities which took place were merely accessory, it may be suggested that the sooner the Board of Trade (or the Ministry of Transport, whichever department may happen at the moment to be responsible) widen the scope of their inspectors' instructions the better. It is indeed most strange that that department did not long ago realise the extreme importance, from the point of view of the safety of the travelling public, which attaches to the making up of lost time, so as to reduce unpunctuality to a minimum, and that it does not insist that every effort should always be made by the railways to make up as much lost time as possible, subject, of course, to any speed restrictions that, in their turn, may be essential to safety.

If the matter of the making up of lost time is not taken in hand seriously (and at the present time there are absolutely no signs whatever to indicate that this will be done) it may be predicted with the utmost assurance that in the future avoidable accidents will take place, which, looked at from the lowest point of view, will cost the railway companies in the repair of damaged road and rolling-stock and in compensation for deaths and personal injuries, many times as much as the economies which will be effected by abstaining from making up all the lost time possible.

66

'RAILWAY ART AND LITERATURE IN 1922', *THE RAILWAY MAGAZINE* 51 (JULY–DEC. 1922), PP. 59–66

When the Railway Magazine made its first appearance on the bookstalls in 1897, British and Irish railways did not number among their excellences a true appreciation of the aid that art and literature contributes in expanding the volume of holiday travel with consequent benefit to railway receipts. So long as the patient public were plentifully provided with timetable information, surely that was sufficient! The picture poster and the artistically illustrated booklet were not unknown, but the output was diminutive compared with the avalanche of literature and the plentitude of posters that heralded each summer season in the early days and during the adolescence of the twentieth century. Then came the war and a gradual stoppage of all enticement, much more inducement, to travel, until in fact the fares were raised for the avowed purpose of compelling the would-be traveller to stay at home and thus avoid congesting the lines needed for military traffic. Fares thus raised were afterwards maintained and further increased to meet growing railway expenditure, but since then—and particularly pronounced it is in this year of grace 1922—there has been a tendency to give the holiday maker such advantages, he will seek recreation by travel, and that in comfort by railway, rather than by racing the roads in motor coaches where he will, as the poet puts it, "breathe clouds of dust and call it country air." As a result we are witnessing some return to the pre-war standard of railway art and literature and not a few Railway Magazine readers are watching the developments with keen interest.

Caledonian

It is as easy to write with enthusiasm as it is difficult to express in terms that could justly be called exaggerated, the appreciation one feels of the pictorial excellence of the posters now exhibited by the Caledonian Railway. True, the scenic grandeur of Bonnie Scotland lends itself with equal facility to portrayal by the artist's brush as it does to the descriptive powers of the poet's pen. Gleneagles, of course, holds pride of place among the subjects chosen by the Caledonian authorities for the mural decoration of railway stations and other points of vantage. The proud boast "There is no better golf course in Great Britain than Gleneagles" in white letters on a green ground, with a lady golfer in a red jersey watching the flight of her ball makes an exceedingly effective poster, while other "Gleneagles" pictures, entitled "The 'Howe o' Hope,' " "The 'Lover's Gait,' " "The Witches' Bowster," are equally meritorious. Another magnificent combination of the poster painters' art and of the colour printers' skill is a picture portraying that lovely lake—Loch Tay overshadowed by the bold summit of Craig Chailliach and the cairn-crowned Ben Lawers, the monarch of the scene. This picture should be particularly potent in luring the tired-eyed city man from the dusty recesses of his business environment for a healthy holiday in the Highlands of the north. One other notable Caledonian publicity product illustrates in effective colouring, Moffat the holiday resort of the Scottish lowlands, and yet another, Loch Awe hotel, which is reached by the Callander and Oban line.

In the production of holiday books the Caledonian Railway has, for a long course of years, been well to the fore, and this season is no exception to the rule. There are new editions of all the popular publications that have earned so much approbation in the past. These include an illustrated guide containing particulars of hotels, boarding-houses and furnished apartments and also an angler's guide. Very useful to intending visitors to Scotland are the booklets issued in conjunction with the Glasgow and South Western and North British Railways providing particulars of the steamboat services to and from the Clyde coast.

Furness

No fewer than eleven golf courses in the Lake District are served by the Furness Railway and these form the subject of a new poster. Printed in blue, black and green on a white ground and including a map of the railway with the golf courses distinctly marked, it answers its purpose admirably. For the holiday maker and tourist a revised edition of the company's illustrated guide has been published, together with various leaflets and a folder concerning circular and other tours through Lakeland.

Glasgow and South Western

>   It was the poet Thompson who inquired
>   Who can paint like nature?
>   Can imagination boast amid its gay creation,
>   Hues like hers?

The pictorial posters of the Glasgow and South Western Railway for the current year are doing their best to supply the answer, and *inter alia* induce the Southron to say with Shakespeare, "I will resolve for Scotland." A cynic has said that the best scenery in the world is improved by the presence of a good hotel in the foreground. Perhaps the Glasgow and South Western "Turnberry" poster will convince him that the sea in the foreground, a good golf course in the centre and a thoroughly modern and convenient hotel slightly to the rear, have in them the making of a perfect holiday haunt. Attractive to many who find a pleasure in going down to the sea in ships—but not too far—is the big colour picture showing the paddle-steamer "Glen Sannox," making a trip to the Clyde watering places. In these days—or nights—of the ubiquitous whist-drive there is a topical touch in the "All Trump" poster proclaiming that eliminating chance by selecting an Ayrshire coast resort as a holiday centre is "Not a gamble" Topical too, is the "clock-face" poster recalling the co-incidence of holiday time with "summer time" and naming a dozen centres on the Glasgow and South Western system where the seeker after rest and recreation may find health-giving ozone, golfing, bathing and boating.

In addition to a new edition of the company's well-known pocket guide to the golfing resorts it serves, the Glasgow and South Western Railway is gratuitously circulating an excellent 32-page booklet illustrated by colour pictures and a map and entitled, "Scotland's Playground." It describes the south-west of Scotland, the country of Caledonia's national poet, Burns, where focussed and epitomized the traveller from afar will find Scottish history, Scottish scenery, Scottish comedy and tragedy, all of which combined to inspire "Robbie" so that he wrote:—

> O Scotia! my dear, my native soil!
> For whom my warmest wish to Heaven is sent!

Great Central

For the summer of 1922, a new edition of this company's guide to holiday resorts, hotels, boarding houses and apartments contains a useful map of the Great Central Railway and its connections. As in former years, the book is profusely illustrated. Particulars of South of England resorts are included for the guidance of the large number of holiday makers resident in northern and midland counties who desire to travel by the Great Central line to London, where they may either break their journey, or at once cross to another railway's terminus *en route* to a southern seaside resort. Cleethorpes is the maritime holiday attraction of the Great Central itself, and in conjunction with the Cleethorpes' Council a new and attractive poster, printed in colours is being exhibited. It is entitled "A Gigantic Wave of Happiness"—aptly named it depicts juvenile joy *par excellence*.

Great Eastern

This railway was one of the first British lines to realise the power of the printing press in promoting passenger traffic, and to-day, so far from being a lost art at Liverpool Street, the well-tried policy of publicity is vigorously pursued. The new posters for 1922 are letterpress in well-matched colours, and in addition to those advertising happy, healthy holidays at East Coast resorts, prospective holiday-makers are reminded by others of the inexpensiveness of Belgium and the advantages of the Harwich-Antwerp route. Another announces week-end tickets to Zeebrugge via Harwich, June to September, and gives details of fares, availability of tickets, trains, &c., and last, but not least, mentions the fact that these holders of week-end tickets require no passports, provided they are British subjects, or Belgian subjects, or French citizens resident in the United Kingdom.

In the way of guide books the Great Eastern has a prime assortment. "Evenings by the Sea," a 24-page pamphlet, contains eleven choicely coloured pictures portraying the after dark delights of Yarmouth, Lowestoft and other east coast holiday haunts. "Seaside and Countryside by the Great Eastern Railway" (price 6d.), edited by Percy Lindley, is replete with pictures in colour and in halftone. A pamphlet by the same author, entitled "An Ideal Holiday," describes and illustrates the district of the Broads and eloquently appeals to lovers of things aquatic. For intending travellers to the Continent several profusely illustrated booklets are provided, while for the American visitor to England, "Cambridge University"—a guide to the Colleges, issued by the Great Eastern Railway—may be strongly recommended, and to other visitors too, if unacquainted with the architectural glories and romantic history of the ancient University town, the Camboritum of Roman days and Cantebrigge of Chaucer's pilgrim. Then again, there has just been published the first of a series of four booklets descriptive of the historic and literary features of East Anglia. These books are being written by Mr. F. V. Morley, a Rhodes Scholar now at Oxford University, and are personal impressions of a series of pleasant journeys through East Anglia. Entitled "The English Orient," the books are sold at One Shilling each, and may be obtained at 71, Regent Street, W.1, at the Enquiry Office, Liverpool Street, or by post from the Publicity Office, General Manager's Department, Liverpool Street Station, E.C.2.

Great Northern

Posters produced at King's Cross are always noteworthy. RAILWAY MAGAZINE readers require no reminder of the bracing Skegness picture that achieved astonishing fame. This year's output is worth more than passing notice and it may be safely said the pictures will attract considerable attention wherever exhibited. It is not to the holiday maker alone that the Great Northern makes its appeal. Speed, combined with comfort and convenience, is a business proposition and one of the most striking posters intimates the advantages of travel by the Great Northern line for men engaged in commercial pursuits. Others tell of the bracing character of the east coast—Southend, Sutton-on-Sea and Mablethorpe are each the subject of animated pictures—Southend "for bounding spirits" will appeal to all who have an eye for life and movement, as well as gay colouring.

The Great Northern Railway tourist programme from June 1 to October 31, contains a wealth of information concerning fares, break of journey, reserved seats, ticket offices, and so forth, but to help the prospective holiday maker to make his decision a capital selection of holiday literature is provided, together with the inevitable down-to-date and carefully corrected edition of the 1922 hotel and apartments guide.

Great North of Scotland

For those who desire a dry bracing climate the Aberdeenshire and Banffshire Highlands in summer may be recommended, and for the service of travellers from afar a useful book giving particulars of furnished lodgings in the districts served by the Great North of Scotland Railway is published year by year. The edition for 1922 includes a map in colours, showing railway lines, coach and steamer routes and the roads traversed by the almost ubiquitous motor omnibus. The premier holiday attraction of this railway is its "Three Rivers Tours" by rail, motor and coach via the Dee, Don and Spey. Full facts may be gleaned from the book which is issued gratuitously from the General Manager's office at Aberdeen.

Great Western

Serving as it does, that painter's paradise, the Cornish Coast, it is quite in accordance with the fitness of things that the Great Western's latest contribution to holiday art should be a realistic poster portraying a gorgeous marine sunset. The picture is called "The Golden West" and the artist is Arthur Sowyer. Critics unacquainted with the charms of Cornwall, or the delights of Devon, may vainly imagine the glowing hues of the picture to be far-flung artistic fancy, or at least exaggerated in the warmth of its tones, but those who know and love the natural wiles of the west will admit its general faithfulness. Another artistic production, is a double-crown poster illustrating in exquisite colouring St. Ives Bay, Cornwall and the Tregenna Castle Hotel, St. Ives. This fine hotel is railway owned and stands in grounds of one hundred acres. It commands magnificent marine views and is within a few minutes' walk, through the gardens, of the railway station.

For holiday booklets, the Great Western has a long established name and fame. A novelty this year is a dozen four-paged booklets, each telling a different story under the general heading of "The Line to Legend Land." Those who find pleasure in the pranks of "piskies" and stories of giants, pious mediæval monks, mermaids and other small deer of bygone days will delight in these. Each one is illustrated on the front page by a quaint and appropriate picture, while the fourth page bears a map showing the Great Western lines and connections.

Highland

Among the posters this year decorating the notice boards there is a particularly distinctive one that advertises "The Highlands of Scotland" and the various hotels owned and managed by the Highland Railway. It illustrates in fine and profuse colouring the glories of the highlands, while prominently in the foreground a young lady in a red jersey is holding a deer-hound by a leash. Another quite new Strathpeffer Spa poster used this year by the Highland Railway is an admirable example of colour printing. RAILWAY MAGAZINE readers should look out for it. Strathpeffer Spa is a great asset to Scotland. It obviates the need for travel to some foreign spa for hydrotherapeutic treatment, and for the information of health seekers and holiday-makers the Traffic Manager of the Highland Railway, Inverness, is distributing a well-illustrated booklet. From Inverness, likewise, comes a new edition of the "Official A.B.C. Tourist Guide to the Highlands of Scotland via the Highland Railway." This latter guide gives evidence of the realisation of the interest there is to the general public in railway features as well as in scenery, for the illustrations include a full-page photographic view of the Highland Railway 4–6–0 locomotive, *Clan Campbell*.

London and North Western

Second to none was the pre-war reputation of the London and North Western Railway in regard to its holiday literature which had, for its leading characteristics, both quality and quantity. Vast numbers of booklets were distributed, not in the British Isles only, but on the Continent and in the United States of America, while the hoardings and the railway station notice boards of the homeland were resplendent with the pictorial posters published at Euston. This great reputation is one that requires an effort to maintain, but it is being done in spite of all the disadvantages of the post-war period. This year the publicity department in addition to issuing the usual guides to the various holiday districts served by the London and North Western system, such as "Washington and Franklyn's Country" and the "Spas of Central Wales" has produced for circulation, principally in the North and the Midlands, a charming guide entitled "Southern England—the Land of Flowers and Sunshine," written by Basil M. Bazley, the author of that pleasing guide first issued last year, "The Charm of England," specially intended for distribution in America. Mr. Bazley is an admirable cicerone—always entertaining, never wearisome, apt in quotation, and a friendly philosopher from whom the reader parts with regret. The country described in Mr. Bazley's pages is not, of course, "North-Western" territory, but comprises the four seaboard counties of Kent, Sussex, Hampshire and Dorset together with the inland county of Surrey and some corners of Devon, Somerset and Wiltshire. To reach the places described by Mr. Bazley's facile pen, the denizen of industrial England usually has at his service the London and North Western route with its splendid permanent-way and magnificent rolling-stock.

Recently a new North Wales poster has appeared. It depicts Conway Castle in the background, while the front portion of the picture shows a smart yacht riding at anchor, what time on her deck a leisurely yachtsman smokes the pipe of peace and contentment. A scene refreshing, indeed, these hot afternoons.

London and South Western

For health and pleasure this line serves some of the finest districts in England, and the publicity department at Waterloo makes good use of the splendid material at its disposal in the 1922 edition of "Hints for Holidays." An admirable guide is this to the south and west of England and the Channel Islands. It contains lists of hotels, boarding houses and apartments, and likewise caters for the commercial man by including particulars of business houses. Altogether the book contains much that is attractive and well worthy of close perusal. The illustrations are fine and include no fewer than sixteen colour pictures. The numerous maps are clear and reliable. It is an ideal guide and reflects great credit upon those responsible for its production.

In March last a dainty booklet was issued entitled "Early Holiday Delights in the South West." Quite up to the usual Waterloo standard of excellence, this well-illustrated brochure of 32 pages is calculated to set the townsman's heart yearning for the sylvan scenes and sunny shores it so exquisitely epitomizes.

Quiet holidays in Normandy and Brittany appeal to many, and the company has published a new edition of its guide to those two fascinating provinces of France. The book is full of useful information for every type of tourist, in spite of its modest disclaimer that it is not intended to replace Baedeker. All the same, ecclesiologists, golfers, sea-bathers, cyclists, students of language and of history, also those ordinary persons who form the principal portion of the population, will find in it just the helpful holiday hints that they require.

One cannot over-praise the 1922 poster output of the London and South Western Publicity Department. It is a superb collection. Several beautifully printed in colours are called "district posters." The object of the district poster is two-fold, first to attract visitors to the district, and then to encourage such travellers from afar, to take short railway trips when they are there, a copy of the poster being exhibited at each railway station in the district, as well as elsewhere, so that holiday makers may see how easily other resorts may be reached by railway. The district posters illustrate North Devon, East Devon, Dorset, North Cornwall, New Forest, and the Channel Islands. They are designed on the "Old Style Map" principle. This system has been adopted for book illustration, but not hitherto, so far as we can remember, has it been employed in poster production. Pride of place, however, must be given the Chertsey poster. This is a remarkably fine specimen of the latest rotogravure work. It is the first of this character to be printed by Messrs. Waterlow and Sons, Limited, but we understand others, in similar style, are to follow. Posters of Guildford, Exeter, Godalming, Jersey, &c., have been produced in conjunction with the various local advertising committees, and the company have also published a number of letterpress posters in connection with the Continental and excursion arrangements. In combination with other railways, the London and South Western Railway, has been advertising on the street hoardings the advantages of early holidays.

Just another poster calls for special mention. Its official title "The Holiday Problem Solved" conveys no suggestion of the artist's subject, a seashore scene in which animated nature claims first attention in the form of a cheerful, chubby, and altogether lovable specimen of human babyhood—naked and unashamed—who with an equally cheerful canine companion, is watching the very unmilitary march of a mammoth crab from the shingle to the sad sea waves. The title of the picture is taken from the fact that across the bottom is the inscription:—To solve the holiday problem, get a copy of—"Hints for Holidays" at London and South Western Railway stations and offices, or send three penny stamps to Publicity Department, Waterloo Station, S.E: 1.

London, Brighton and South Coast

Publicity on the "Brighton" is always conducted on high-grade lines. Good taste in art and literature are its prevailing characteristics and at the same time it never lacks freshness or variety. To attract visitors to the sunshine and sea breezes of the sunny south, well-chosen posters adorn the hoardings of the industrial north and midlands, and other suitable spots. But in merely magnetising the traveller from afar the department does not deem its duty done; it still has to make easy the path of the pleasure-seeking pilgrim. In connection with the "Sunny South Special" a through train every week-day, consisting of corridor carriages and a tea car to (and from) Birmingham, Manchester, Liverpool, &c., and Brighton and Eastbourne, &c., *via* Willesden, Kensington and East Croydon, a useful pamphlet is issued describing the resorts served and including a map of the route. For those who desire accommodation there is a well illustrated book containing an official list of hotels and apartments. Then there is a 16-paged booklet for wanderers by field-path, wayside and woodland, over turf-clad downs and heathery commons, bearing the title of "The Surrey Hills"; and for invalids and jaded workers who require a rest in healthy surroundings, the company distributes an informing pamphlet entitled "Nature's Finest Tonic."

Of the nine "Brighton" posters the present writer has before him, the two of greatest distinction—all nine are good—are those proclaiming "The Sunny South" They are an admirable pair, and the one is the necessary complement of the other, for one of them illustrates no fewer than fourteen finely-frocked young ladies seated (in deck chairs) on the sands facing west, while the other depicts the same number of holiday-garbed gentlemen of more or less youthful appearance similarly occupied, but delightedly gazing east!

London Underground Electric

One versed in phrenology would probably affirm that the head of the publicity department of the London Electric Underground lines and associated train and omnibus companies is blessed with an uncommonly big botanical bump. Anyway the floral posters issued from Electric House are as charming as they are numerous and that they are genuinely effective is beyond all question. Crocus time, daffodil time, bluebell time and chestnut time each in its order has its appropriate picture poster and they are eagerly looked for by thousands of Londoners who speculate upon what will be the next. But the Underground does not depend upon floral schemes alone to induce city and suburban people to seek fresh fields and pastures new. Quaintness has its uses and so has the historic building properly pictured. The Underground is catholic in its tastes and consequently appeals to an enormous public.

The booklets produced under the same auspices are equally creditable and are calculated to suit the mentality of all sorts and conditions of people both old and the young.

Metropolitan

On this railway publicity work is in the hands of the Commercial Manager and is always well done. Its holiday books and its souvenirs are, without exception, the last words in artistic production. Lately some very fine posters have been issued, and one of them is reproduced on this page. The originals are printed by colour-type process in brown, sepia and green. The one illustrated is attracting much attention among the visitors to London. It advertises a day at the Zoological Gardens, and is a fine piece of work. The massive head of the King of Beasts shows up with remarkable detail in the original. The Metropolitan Railway serves some of the most suitable spots in or around London, for school treats, annual outings, pleasure parties and the like. This fact is made the subject of a particularly pleasing pictorial poster.

Midland

We have been privileged to inspect the proofs of a new Midland Railway guide-book, "The Peak of Derbyshire," and in its preface we are reminded that it was that accepted judge of the beautiful in nature, Lord Byron who wrote:

> "There are prospects in Derbyshire as noble as any in Greece or Switzerland."

Travellers whose only knowledge of the district is derived from the views obtained from the trains on the Midland line will readily accept Lord Byron's dictum, even had he not the support of many other famous writers such as Sir Walter Scott and John Ruskin. The book, which is well-illustrated and of convenient size for the pocket, begins with Derby, the centre of the English midlands, which, in addition to being famous as a pre-eminent railway town is one of the most ancient boroughs in the land and possesses many features of antiquarian interest. The most valuable relic of old Derby stands on one end of Derwent Bridge. It dates from the fourteenth century and is the "Chapel of Our Lady of ye brigg." The present porcelain works, wherein is made the famous Derby china, are within a few minutes' walk of the Midland Railway station. These facts and hundreds of others referring to the villages and towns of the "Peak District" may be gleaned from the well-written guide book under notice.

For those seeking country and seaside holidays, the Midland Railway has issued the 1922 edition of its official directory of apartments, hotels, boarding houses, &c. The book likewise provides a list, of what to many youthful holiday makers, are the black clouds that loom through the latter days of golden summer, viz:—schools. The northern counties of Ireland too, have their Midland Railway connection via Heysham and are included in the book, the compilers of which must have taken "thorough" as their motto, so well and so exhaustively have they performed their task.

North Eastern

A very fine series of holiday-resort posters has been issued for 1922, and we are reproducing a striking example on this page. Arresting and notable are the designs of other posters depicting the scenic glories of such places as Bridlington, Scarborough, Whitby, Harrogate, Whitley Bay, Northumberland, &c.

North Staffordshire

Although in the opinion of Dean Inge the Staffordshire characters in Mr. Arnold Bennett's novels are people not worth writing about, there are others who think differently. Impressions as to Staffordshire as a holiday haunt likewise may vary. Known principally to the public beyond its borders, by reason of its famous pottery, the county has other claims to distinction, and to make these better known, the North Staffordshire Railway has provided two particularly informing posters. One of these, centred by a useful map, sets out the attractions for tourists, excursionists, pleasure and picnic parties to the following places celebrated for scenery of rock, water, wood and dale:—Ashbourne, Dovedale, Trentham, Sandon, Weston (Ingestre), Great Haywood and Colwich for Cannock Chase and Thugborough. Other points mentioned are Alton, Rudyard Lake, Rushton for Dane Valley, Biddulph, Keele, Norton-in-Hales, Mow Crop and the Manifold Valley. This long list is augmented by the information that Stoke-on-Trent and the federated pottery towns are situated upon this line of railway and are distinguished for their productions in china, earthenware and tesselated tiles for walls and pavements. In addition to views of scenery and churches, this poster includes the reproduction of a photographic print showing a train on the Manifold (Toy) Railway near Waterhouses station. The other North Staffordshire Railway poster—attractively printed in green and sepia—advertises the attractions of Rudyard Lake. This is a fine stretch of water of about 200 acres. The lake provides fishing and boating, and there is golfing amid charming scenery close at hand, the golf course in fact being at the north end of the lake, close to Rudyard Lake station.

South Eastern and Chatham

This railway has a fine selection of holiday literature and an excellent poster display. In our August issue we shall deal fully with the uncommon characteristics of both.

67

'FLYING SCOTSMAN'S FIRST RUN', *TIMES* (LONDON), 2 MAY 1928, P. 13

The longest non-stop service

The longest regular non-stop railway service in the world, between King's Cross and Edinburgh, a distance of 392½ miles, was started yesterday by the London and North Eastern Railway. Yesterday also the London Midland and Scottish Railway, which last week ran a non-stop train from Euston to Edinburgh, a distance of 399 miles, began a regular service having no stop at a station, though a halt is made outside Carlisle to change engines. It is expected that this will become a non-stop service later, but the company are not at present prepared to make any statement as to their plans. It is officially denied, however, that they are building new engines for the service.

The departure platform at King's Cross Station was crowded at 10 a.m. yesterday, when the "Flying Scotsman" started its initial non-stop run. Curious spectators had made a careful examination of the new train, which contains several new features, including a hairdressing saloon with a waiting room, a ladies' retiring room, and an electric kitchen. The greatest interest was taken in the engine with its corridor connexion enabling the relief driver and fireman to pass from the train behind to the footplate when half the journey has been accomplished.

The LORD MAYOR (Sir Charles Batho), who attended at King's Cross to see the "Flying Scotsman" start, congratulated the railway company on a wonderful achievement. He shook hands with the drivers and firemen, congratulated them, and wished them the best of luck. Loud cheers were given as the "Flying Scotsman" left the station.

Simultaneously with the departure of the "Flying Scotsman" from King's Cross the service to King's Cross from Waverley Station, Edinburgh, was started. On the platform was a large crowd of spectators. BAILIE HAY, the senior magistrate of Edinburgh, in the absence of the Lord Provost, said a few words to the drivers and firemen, and his daughter pinned on their breasts sprigs of white heather. A large beribboned horseshoe was placed on the engine.

Ahead of time

The train from London arrived at Edinburgh at 6.3 p.m., 12 minutes ahead of scheduled time. On the journey the passengers collected subscriptions for the drivers and firemen, and they were presented with pocket-books at Edinburgh as a memento of the occasion.

The train from Edinburgh to London arrived at King's Cross Station at 6.12 p.m., two-and-a-half minutes in front of scheduled time. Mr. William Whitelaw, the chairman of the company, Sir Ralph Wedgwood, the chief general manager, and Lady Wedgwood congratulated the two drivers and the two stokers on their work on the journey and presented them with pocket-books with silver inscriptions as a souvenir of the successful run. The timing of the train to London was as follows:—

> Berwick, one minute early: Newcastle, three minutes late: York, one minute early: Doncaster, three minutes early: Grantham, two minutes early: Peterborough, one minute early: Hatfield, one minute late: King's Cross, two-and-a-half minutes early.

68

FRANK PARKER STOCKBRIDGE, 'CARGOES THROUGH THE CLOUDS', *HARPER'S* 140, 1919–1920, PP. 189–191

We have seen "the nations' airy navies, grappling in the central blue," and we are about to see fulfilled the rest of Tennyson's prophecy, the "pilots of the purple twilight, dropping down with costly bales."

For the purposes of this article, let prophecy stop there. The chance of any particular prophet predicting with accuracy either the course which the development of air-borne commerce will follow or what it will be like when it has been fully developed is too remote to be worth taking. It can, of course, be forecast of commercial aviation that it must pass through certain stages common to the development of all new inventions and enterprises. Radio-telegraphy, motion pictures, the automobile, each is a familiar recent example of the progress of an art from its inception in the brain of an inventor, or a group of inventors, through the period of endless experimentation, adaptation and change, to its final establishment as a popular and commercial success on the securities of which one may borrow money from his banker. That aerial navigation will, in its turn, pass through these stages of development and, before the children of to-day have reached maturity, become so merged in the routine of our everyday life as no longer to be the subject of wonder or comment, is hardly to be doubted.

Commercial aerial navigation, the thing itself, is here. There is no important section of the known world in (and above) which airplanes or dirigibles, or both, are not being used for some form of transportation which can be distinctly termed commercial, or where, at least, there are no well-matured, adequately financed plans for the establishment of commercial aviation actually in process of development. The newspapers have already announced the opening of booking-offices in London for air passengers to Brazil. This is merely one of the commercial aviation enterprises inaugurated since the war. A quick glance around the world discloses scores of other commercial uses of aircraft.

While the frequent flights between London and Paris made by Mr. Andrew Bonar Law in the course of his attendance as one of the British plenipotentiaries to the Peace Conference, in an airplane "equipped with all the luxuries of a Pullman," as one enthusiastic correspondent put it, received considerable notice in the newspapers, little has been said about the regular express airplane service that has been in operation between the French and British capitals for many months. Grand pianos are not the type of freight one thinks of first in connection with aerial commerce, but for advertising purposes an instrument of this sort was carried by airplane from the London store of which we hear most in America to a customer in France. And this across the English Channel, the flight over which by Bleriot less than ten years ago was an achievement so spectacular that the details were cabled around the world! Merchandise of every sort is transported by airplane daily on regular schedule between these two European cities.

The British Postmaster-General announced in the House of Commons, on July 18th, that aerial mail service to foreign countries was being seriously considered; it might not be long, he said, before mails would be carried to China and Australia in a few hours. Regular mail service by air post between Paris and Geneva was established on May 26th, when the Swiss airman, Durafour, made the trip of two hundred and fifty miles in five and one-half hours, including half an hour's forced landing on French soil because of fog.

A British airplane company announces that it has been offered a carriage rate of five dollars an ounce for transporting from Shanghai to London certain essences used in the manufacture of perfumes.

Airplane lines for the regular transportation of merchandise between Brussels and Paris have been established. Five hundred pounds of lobsters constituted the cargo of the first plane to make the flight from Paris.

Regular daily newspaper delivery by airplane was inaugurated last May by the London Daily Mail, which sent packages of its Manchester edition to Carlisle, Dundee, Aberdeen, and Montrose by the air route. The papers are dropped from the 'planes in bundles attached to parachutes. The regular railroad time between Manchester and Aberdeen is thirteen hours, ten minutes; the newspaper 'plane makes it in three hours and a half.

At Johannesburg, South Africa, a commercial aviation company has been formed for the purpose of establishing passenger and express service between that city and Pretoria, Maritzburg, Durban, and Cape Town.

Australia has already established a transcontinental airway, from Sydney 2,330 miles across country to Port Darwin on the north coast. Landing-stations and relay and fuel depots have been established at distances of 390 miles apart. The survey by airplane of an alternative interior route has been begun.

It is 1,135 miles from Calcutta to Simla (a distance that strikes the American who knows India only from the maps in his school-books with a distinct shock of surprise). The railway fare, first class, is a little more than £8. And, as every reader of Kipling and Flora Annie Steele knows, it is a long, hot, tiresome journey. But now, or very shortly, one may literally fly from the stifling heat of the Hoogli flats to the cool hills of the "Plain Tales" in a third of the time and for less than twice the money. The newly organized commercial aviation company of India, with three million pounds sterling of capital, projects a Calcutta-Simla passenger-line that will cut the distance to 950 miles and make the trip in twelve to fifteen hours as against the forty-two hours which the train takes, for a fare of £15 17s. This route will be flown *via* Delhi; another line will run from Calcutta to Bombay, another from Calcutta to Darjeeling, and a fourth from Calcutta to Puri, the average fare being sixpence per mile.

The St. Maurice Valley Forest Protective Association, with the co-operation of the Canadian government, has established an airplane forest-fire patrol.

Even as the proof of this article is being revised comes the cabled report of the airplane "timber cruisers," twenty men with three machines, back from a month's exploration of two million square miles of Labrador timber and pulp-wood lands, with sketches and photographic maps revealing millions of dollars worth of accessible wealth as yet untapped.

One of the largest American aircraft manufacturers recently received a request for prices from the Congo Mission of the Disciples of Christ, which proposes to replace its fleet of steam-launches with flying-boats, the better to spread the gospel among the natives of the Belgian Congo. Half a dozen other foreign mission stations have also made similiar inquiries. "Sky-pilot" may soon be more than a mere figure of speech to the natives of many lands.

Lord Northcliffe, whose offer of a $50,000 prize was one of the stimuli of the men who undertook to fly across the Atlantic last spring, was quick to see the possibilities of closer Anglo-American relations which the flight in sixteen hours of Alcock and Brown from Newfoundland to Ireland opened up. "A warning to cable monopolists," he termed the feat, adding that the voyage was quicker than the average time of press messages in 1919. "I look forward with certainty," he said, "to the time when the London morning newspapers will be selling in New York in the evening, allowing for the difference between British and American time, and *vice versa* in regard to the New York evening newspapers reaching London the next day. Then we shall no longer suffer from the danger of garbled quotations due to telegraphic compression. Then, too, the American and British peoples will understand each other better, as they are brought into closer daily touch."

So far we have been talking about airplanes. The successful transatlantic round trip of the R-34 is the most convincing evidence that in the discussion of aerial transportation the dirigible balloon must not be forgotten. In fact, the only important commercial use of aircraft prior to the European war was the system of passenger-carrying Zeppelins. Immediately upon the signing of the armistice the Germans resumed the operation of passenger service by Zeppelins. Regular voyages on a fixed schedule between Berlin and Constantinople, *via* Munich and Vienna, have been made for several months.

Announcement was made in June of the formation of a combination of British airship interests, with several million pounds sterling available capital, for the establishment of airship lines literally encircling the earth. Moderate-sized dirigibles (there ought to be a better word for this craft) are being built for carrying express and mail matter, together with passengers; for long-distance flights carrying no cargo but passengers, ships of large size and high speed will be used; equally large craft, with lower engine power and slower speed, but large carrying capacity, will be constructed for general freight purposes. The largest of these airships yet planned is to have a cubic capacity of 3,500,000 feet, or nearly twice that of the R-34; it is expected to carry fifteen tons of passengers and mail for a distance of 4,500 miles at a speed of sixty miles an hour. The first of these new ships will be of 1,250,000 cubic feet capacity.

These are hard-headed British business men, who are preparing to stake their millions on the feasibility of operating airship routes from London to the four corners of the earth. Two main lines across the western ocean are planned; a London-New York route either direct or *via* Lisbon and the Azores, and a London-Rio Janeiro route, *via* Lisbon and Sierra Leone. Tickets (at £1,000) from London to Rio and return are already on sale for the first voyage. Schedules of two days and a half to New York, seven days to Perth, Australia, five days and a half to Cape Town, four days to Rio, a day and a half to Cairo—these are the space-ignoring, time-destroying details of this gigantic project.

To travel by airship over a shrunken world will not be as expensive as traveling about New York in a taxicab; ten cents a mile, against thirty; £50 from London to New York; threepence-halfpenny to send a letter. These are the tariffs already announced; that they will eventually be reduced is not to be doubted.

I have tried to indicate with the utmost brevity some of the things the rest of the world is doing in commercial aviation. These involve big plans and big figures. So far in America, the land of the airplane's nativity, nothing approaching these foreign achievements and projects in any important way has been undertaken or even seriously planned, with the sole exception of the United States aerial mail service.

Part 10

RAILWAY CULTURES OF SCOTLAND AND IRELAND

69

ANON. (DAVID CROAL), *EARLY RECOLLECTIONS OF A JOURNALIST, 1832–1859* (EDINBURGH: ANDREW ELIOT, 1898), PP. 8–10

There will be many yet alive among the citizens of Edinburgh who remember the means adopted by the Post Office authorities of the day to accelerate the speed of the mails, and get letters and newspapers a little earlier from the south. The railway system had not penetrated further than Morpeth at the time referred to, from which point the old mail coach, doing its eight or nine miles an hour, was employed to convey the bags to Edinburgh. The saving of even a few hours was regarded as a matter of importance when events of national interest were engaging the attention of the people of Scotland. To secure this result horseflesh was the only available agency. A light two-horse curricle, with a red-coated guard in charge, was daily despatched from the Post Office in Edinburgh as far as Morpeth in time for the arrival of the train from the south with the mails. These were transferred to the curricle, which at once set out on its 120 miles journey northwards. Frequent relays of horses, and the lightness of the vehicle, enabled the latter to anticipate the regular coach by several hours. It was an animating sight to follow with the eye the sweating team, as they dashed along Nicholson Street and the Bridges on their way to the Post Office, laden with their budget, and one that never failed to awaken the interest of the passer-by, for who could tell, in those stirring days, what might be the tenor of the despatches? No telegraphic wires were then in existence to anticipate them.

70

CHARLES RICHARD WELD, *TWO MONTHS IN THE HIGHLANDS, ORCADIA, AND SKYE* (LONDON: LONGMANS, GREEN, LONGMAN, AND ROBERTS, 1860), PP. 4–6

The heavy baggage is packed, and on its sea way to the North, and light-hearted we are about speeding after it by rail to the granite city, when, enter our servant with a telegraphic despatch.

Now, as we are not, thank the Fates, in the habit of receiving these documents—fancy what the lives of those business men must be who, not satisfied by the twenty or so daily delivery of letters in our huge metropolis are perpetually receiving telegrams!—a telegraphic despatch is by no means calculated to have a soothing influence, and now, just as we were singing in the outburst of our joy:

"Dear, damn'd, distracting town, farewell."

—the words are Pope's—here is a message flashed upon us with electric speed, which for all that we know may wither up holiday plans and pleasures, nay, crush the very soul and manhood out of us. But courage, courage, break the seal, better to know the worst than linger in agonising uncertainty. So we tear the envelope open—and, oh! joy, with what relief we read—"*Stop at Symington Station where my carriage will meet you.*" This being interpreted meant that the chief of our party, a great Scotch Laird, and as good as he is great; not being able to proceed to the shooting quarters in the North as soon as he expected, dexterously managed to hit me with a telegram inviting me to join him at his seat in Peeblesshire, and thus diverted my proposed direct route from London to Aberdeen.

So transferring my patronage from the Great Northern Railway to the North Western, I found myself shortly after 9 P.M. whizzing to the North. Fortune favoured me. I had but one fellow-passenger to whom I was indebted for a much more comfortable night than I expected to pass in the semi-cushioned second-class carriage. The said passenger, judging by the amazing number and variety of flat, square, round, and oval packages which were stowed under the seats, was a commercial traveller. When we dashed into the dark night he proceeded to arrange these packages very methodically, adjusting them on the seats in such a manner that they enabled us to recline comfortably and obtain some hours' sleep. Commercial gentlemen dislike having inquisitive questions put to them respecting their profession, so I bridled my curiosity to know what the packages contained. Certainly, not hardware, more probably silk or woollen goods, for they were extremely soft and really did good mattress service. At all events, the hours sped swiftly, as they generally do during night travel; and when I rubbed my eyes after a wild unearthly dream of rushing down slopes on fiery dragons, I found that we were in border-land, and ere the sun had kissed the Cumberland hills, the train stopped at Symington. There was my friend's carriage, and there his servant looking out for the gentleman from London.

Heavens! what a change. We get out of the close railway carriage, the heat of London in us still, and a sharp bracing frosty air blows on our face.

71

W. EDMONDSTOUNE AYTOUN, *NORMAN SINCLAIR* 3 VOLS. (EDINBURGH: WILLIAM BLACKWOOD AND SONS, 1861), I, PP. 250–251, 271–274, II, PP. 102–114

Early on the day appointed, Carlton and I ascended as outside passengers the glorious "Defiance," which in those times, when the railway system was yet in its infancy, was the pride and wonder of the road. Much as our comfort has been enhanced by the traction of what a modern poet has called "the resonant steam-eagles," I am not sure that the new mode of locomotion is so hilarious as the old. In a railway train you profit little by the scenery—you dash so rapidly past town and grange that you hardly have a glimpse of their outline—and you are utterly precluded from the grand old amusement of studying character on the road. The stage-coach, on the contrary, carried you into the very heart of the country; gave you time to enjoy the scenery; brought under your notice many a curious specimen of life and manners; and enabled you, if the coachman or guard were disposed to be communicative, as was usually the case, to form a tolerably accurate estimate of the peculiarities and history of the neighbourhood. But it is of no use instituting comparisons between the living and the dead. Stage-coaches, except in a few very remote districts, are as defunct as the hand-loom or spinning-wheel, and will ere long become mere matters of tradition. I sometimes wonder what was the fate of all those gorgeous "Defiances," "Eclipses," "Lightnings," "Rattlers," and "Sohos?" Did the indignant proprietors when they found that they were fairly beaten off the road, and totally unable to compete with the screaming metallic competitors, bring together their defeated chariots, and sacrifice them as a magnificent holocaust? Or have they been consigned to the infamy and disgrace of a back-shed, therein to remain until they rot to pieces, being tenanted in the mean time by cocks and hens, for lack of better company?

No sooner had we passed the London suburbs, than the atmosphere became clear as by magic; and on either hand was opened up an expanse of landscape, winter-clad indeed, but enlivened by the rays of the sun.

Important towns, great seats of manufacture and marts of trade, had been brought into more intimate connection by the locomotive engine; and trunk lines to convey passengers and expedite traffic from one end of the kingdom to the other were now in the course of construction. The necessity for, at least the great advantage of such communication being admitted, the movement so far was considered a good and wholesome one. It was calculated to benefit the labourer, the mechanics, and the iron-master—it opened a new field, and apparently a favourable one, for the investment at home of capital which otherwise might have been squandered or lost in foreign speculation or loan—and to the tourist and traveller it promised advantages, which a few years before would have been regarded as equally fabulous with the mode of transport by means of magical carpets so frequently referred to in the *Arabian Nights' Entertainments.* Here and there, indeed, some great landed proprietor, the sanctity of whose parks or the privacy of whose domain was to be violated by the screaming engine, made fierce opposition to the lines; but the directors, justly conceiving that human squires would not prove more inexorable than the Colchian dragon, took occasion to administer such copious draughts of the *aurum potabile* as disarmed the hostility of their opponents.

But, as at the Californian or Australian diggings, the discovery in a new locality of a single nugget of gold instantly creates the rush of a thousand desperadoes towards the spot, so did the success of those early railways, and the high price which their shares commanded in the market, stimulate the cupidity of the British public, and transport them utterly beyond the boundaries of reason and of prudence. Trunk communication, it was confidently asserted, was not sufficient, even with the aid of branches which might subsequently be made, for the pressing wants of the country. The system so developed must go on, and that immediately, until Britain should be covered by a vast network of railways. To lag behind when others were pushing forward was a palpable folly and a positive crime—to let capital remain idle when it could be so usefully employed, was next thing to insanity. The true Dorado which Raleigh had crossed the ocean to seek for and explore, was at last discovered to be our native English soil.

The lawyers scented the prey from afar, and chuckled gloatingly at the prospect of unlimited fees. Engineers by the hundred sprang up into life and being, like the stones which Deucaleon hurled over his shoulder. Projectors mapped out the country, and compiled outrageous advertisements. Traffic-takers betook themselves to the practical study of the whole art of lying. Men, whose entire worldly property did not exceed fifty pounds, or who were positively worth less than nothing, contracted engagements for thousands, in the full confidence that, long before payment was required, they could dispose of their scrip at a profit. Talk of *roulette* or *rouge-et-noir!* Continental gambling shrunk into insignificance when compared with the magnitude of English Railway hazard!

Railways, however, cannot be constructed without ground on which to lay them down; and many proprietors, taking alarm at the extent of the mania, and perhaps not feeling quite satisfied as to the sufficiency of the security tendered, were unwilling that their lands should be bisected and cut up, and would not even allow the projectors to make a preliminary survey. But the crafty engineering staff was not to be so baffled. What they could not take by force they were resolute to compass by guile; and accordingly they made their way over the country in all manner of disguises, attracting as little attention as possible when noting down their observations; or, when challenged as trespassers, abandoning their design by day to renew it by night with aid of moon or lantern. Many strange stories were told of encounters that had taken place under such circumstances; but on the whole it was generally allowed that the surveyors had the best of it, their superior astuteness enabling them to throw dust in the eyes of the stolid watchmen.

"So it is actually proposed to make a railway from Goatshead to Ditchington," said Sir John Hawkins, a burly representative of the order of baronets. "That is really too bad! There is no call whatever for such a line, and it will cut up both our properties, Stanhope. I don't know what you may be inclined to do, but I am determined to oppose it, even though I should be compelled to go to the House of Peers."

"Well, I suppose there can be no doubt of their intentions," said Mr Stanhope. "They made application to me—quite civilly, I must say—for permission to take a survey; but as I am as much against the line as you are, I thought it my duty to refuse."

"Quite right! There is no standing the impudence of those fellows. What title have they to ask Parliament to compel me to surrender the land which my family have possessed since the reign of Henry the Fifth, for the purpose of trundling along their bales of cotton and calico? Have they not a canal already, and is that not sufficient for their wants? I tell you what, Stanhope; I don't like the posture of things at all. It appears to me that Peel is systematically playing into the hands of the manufacturers, and using our support in the mean time to throw us ultimately overboard."

"Nay, nay!" said Sir George Smoothly; "You must not judge Sir Robert too harshly. It cannot be denied that he is a very sagacious man. That was a wonderful idea of his advising us to attend to the registers."

"I can see nothing wonderful in it," said Sir John Hawkins. "It was sound common sense, to be sure; but Peel had not the credit of originality. The advice was first given to the party by Alison, and Peel adopted it verbatim."

"That shows his great talent for appropriation," said Sir George. "Of what use is a good idea unless it be practically enforced?"

Railway morals

MY duty as observer and chronicler of the progress of the railway movement led me often to Westminster, where the committee-rooms exhibited a most extraordinary spectacle. It has been doubted by many persons, whose practical experience was such as to give great weight to their opinion, whether committees of either House of Parliament were the best tribunals which could have been devised for adjudicating upon what were, in reality, gigantic public works, albeit promoted by private enterprise and capital. I confess, after mature deliberation on what I have seen, that I more than participate in such doubts, and that I have arrived at the conclusion that Parliament, in order to retain the confidence and command the respect of the nation, must sooner or later delegate no inconsiderable portion of its powers to be exercised by a judicial body, as remote from influence and as little liable to suspicion as are the judges of the land. We have arrived now—indeed, we arrived long since—at this discreditable position, that only a fractional part of the public business, which Ministers have declared to be urgent, can be carried through in the course of a protracted session. Some measures, specially recommended in the Speech from the Throne to the consideration of Parliament, are abandoned from sheer lack of time to pass them through the formal stages; whilst others, equally important, and affecting large interests, are hurried forward with precipitate and indecent haste, which precludes the possibility of objection, or of a fair and impartial discussion. In fact, more work is thrust before Parliament than it can, under any circumstances, overtake. Even if the whole body of members was composed of men of first-rate business talent, resolute for despatch, never wandering from the point immediately before them, and eschewing talking for mere talking's sake, they could not accomplish the feat of satisfactorily disposing of the whole enormous programme. But we know very well that, for one man possessed of such qualifications, there are at least three quidnuncs who are absolute obstacles to business; being either inveterate chatterers, whose sole object it is to have their speeches reported in the papers, or stolid monomaniacs, who advocate some monstrous impracticability, or cankered objectors-general, who consider it their duty to challenge every proposition. Night after night is the time of the great council of the nation abused and frittered away by those merciless and intolerable pests; and the consideration of public business is continually postponed to an hour, long before the arrival of which honest men, who are not connected with Parliament, have sought the solace of their pillows.

In the days of the railway mania, so numerous were the applications to Parliament that the majority of the House of Commons were drafted out into committees to hear, yawn, and determine. Unless the prevalent idea that judicial talent is comparatively rare be altogether erroneous, it would seem difficult to defend an arrangement which left interests representing millions of capital and realised property to the tender mercies of gentlemen who were for the most part utterly ignorant of the rules of evidence, unused to be addressed by lawyers, apt to be confounded and puzzled by details, sometimes actuated by prejudice, and always liable to be swayed by external influences. No man, who had a personal cause of his own impending, would have selected such a tribunal; but it was deemed quite good enough for companies who were claiming a monopoly, and for proprietors who were defending their possessions. And as if to make the thing more glaringly absurd, the ordinary judicial safeguards were dispensed with. No oath was administered to witnesses, who, being thus relieved from the moral guilt and final consequences of perjury, did certainly oftentimes hazard the most astounding assertions. I shall not go the length of saying that false evidence was given as to what was strictly matter of fact; but as to matters of opinion, there was amazing discrepancy. Engineer testified against engineer as to the merits and practicability of competing lines; valuators reported thousands or hundreds, according as they were engaged for the landlords or for the companies; fertile regions became sterile, or sterile regions fertile, as occasion suited or interest required. Vast mineral beds yet unopened, and the extent of which it was utterly impossible to compute, would be made available to the country if one line was granted; whereas another, leading through a district already glowing with furnaces, could be of very little use, because, in the opinion of men of skill, the seams were well-nigh exhausted.

I had the pleasure one day of hearing my friend Davie Osett examined as a witness; and certainly a richer scene it was hardly possible to conceive. Davie had gone through his examination as a surveyor of the Goatshead and Ditchington Junction in a highly creditable manner, for he was thoroughly master of his craft, and had only to speak to the gradients; but he had been impressed as a witness by some company that had started a line on the Border, and was required to speak, from local knowledge, of the advantages which the scheme held forth. In answer to the friendly questions put by the counsel for the promoters, Davie testified valiantly; but I could perceive that the opposing barrister, whose powers of badgering a witness were reputed to be extraordinary, intended, if possible, to break him down. It must be premised that, before these railway committee tribunals, learned gentlemen did not think it necessary to be very courteous in their demeanour or fastidious in the style of their examinations, but assumed a licence which certainly would have been checked in a regular court of justice. This particular barrister was a beetle-browed, flat-nosed man, with something of the look of a bull-dog; evidently a dangerous customer, and one from whom mischief was to be expected.

This gentleman, after taking a long and deliberate survey of Davie through his glasses, rose up; and, giving to his forensic gown a peculiar jerk, which was meant as an intimation to the committee that he intended thoroughly to demolish the witness, began his cross-examination.

"I think you have told us, Mr Osett, that you are a surveyor?"

"That is just what I said," replied Davie.

"Then, may I ask if you have been professionally consulted, or in any way engaged, in connection with this line, the advantages of which you have detailed with such wonderful precision?"

"Not I," said Davie. "I have not been in Scotland since the line was projected."

"That was not what I asked you, sir!" said the counsel, whose name was Churnley. "No prevarication, if you please! Answer me—yes or no—have you seen any plan or section of the line?"

"I have seen no sections, but I have seen a plan."

"Aha! I thought we should get at the truth at last. And what sort of plan was it?"

"That's easily answered," said Davie, "for that's it hanging on the wall."

"And you mean to say you have seen no other?"

"Ye have said it, sir," replied Davie, lapsing into the vernacular.

"Then, sir, will you inform the committee how it is that you are able to speak with such confidence as to the resources of the district?"

"Just because I was born there, have lived there a' my days, and ken the country as weel as ye ken the streets of London."

"You described yourself as the son of a Mr Osett of the Birkenshaws, if I recollect aright?"

Davie assented.

"Now, sir, I ask you, is your father proprietor of that place?"

"Dear me! No, sir; he's only the tenant, as his father was before him."

"Then how came you, sir, to be so audacious as to attempt to impose upon this honourable committee by giving your father, whom you now admit to be a mere tenant, a territorial designation?"

"It's easy to see you never crossed the Border," replied Davie. "Ilka tenant amang us gets the name of his steading."

"Do you absolutely, sir, mean to persist in such a statement, in order to cover your imposture?"

"Troth, if I'm an impostor, there's another I am speaking to," said Davie.

"Is that insolence, sir?" blustered the lawyer. "I call upon the chairman of the committee for protection."

"O man, can ye no protect yoursel'? Wha's going to meddle wi' ye? But I'll tell you what I mean, and make gude my words. Are na ye Mr Churnley of Lincoln's Inn?"

"Well, sir, what of that?"

"Just this—that Lincoln's Inn nae mair belongs to you—that is, in the way of absolute property—than the Birkenshaws does to my father. Sae ye see, Mr Churnley, you should think twice afore ye begin to misca' folk."

This sally provoked a roar of laughter from the audience, with whom Mr Churnley was no favourite, albeit he was patronised by some solicitors on account of his pre-eminence in browbeating.

"I think," said the chairman of the committee, a mild-looking gentleman, who was evidently amused by the encounter—"I think that the learned counsel need not press that point any farther. Indeed, I happen to know that what the witness has said regarding the prevalent custom on the Scottish Border is correct."

"Very well, sir!" said Mr Churnley, with a suppressed snort. "If the members of committee are satisfied—which I am not—that this young man intended to make no misrepresentation, I shall proceed to more important matters. Now, sir, attend to me if you please. You have said that this line of railway passes for the greater portion of its length through a pastoral country. Now, I ask you what may be your estimate of the number of sheep annually reared in the district?"

"I could not answer that question with anything like precision."

"I don't expect you to inform me as to the exact number," said Churnley; "I only ask for an approximation. Speaking so confidently as you have done of the large traffic to be derived from that source, you must of course have formed an estimate."

"Indeed, sir, I have formed naething of the kind," said Davie. "I am a surveyor by trade, and not a traffic-taker."

"Then, sir, will you state for the satisfaction of the committee, the grounds upon which you rest so very confident an opinion?"

"I'll do that, sir," replied Davie, with the best goodwill in the world. "Ye see, sirs," said he, addressing himself to the committee, "that if it were a question whether London would afford sufficient traffic to maintain a line, it would be a clean waste of time to inquire how many souls dwelt within the city. Ae glance at the streets wad satisfy ony reasonable man without condescending on particulars. Now, if you were in that district about which I was speaking, in the springtime, you could hardly hear yourselves speak for the crying of the ewes and the bleating of the lambs, that are as thick on the hill-sides amaist as are the gowans. Nae man can count them. Ye might as weel try to count the bees that are humming by, or the butterflies that are flaunting past, or the trouts in the water, or the crows that are clavering in the wood. And what ye see for twenty lang miles on either side of the road is but a sma' portion of the stock that is bred up in the glens and high farms. This gentleman is very good at speering, but I'se wager he canna tell me how many cab-horses there are in London, ony mair than he can specify how many hairs there are in his wig!"

"Then, sir, you admit you have been speaking at random?" said Mr Churnley.

"I admit naething of the kind. I never made even a rough guess at the numbers, which indeed would be a kittle job; for what wi' hoggs and gimmers—"

"Aha, my friend! have I caught you tripping? Confine yourself to the question of sheep, and not of other animals."

"Weel—that's just what I'm doing."

"Not at all, sir! Take care what you are about. You were beginning to estimate the number of pigs in the district."

"Troth, sir, ye maun be dull o' hearing. Feint a word have I said about pigs this day."

"Will you have the audacity to deny, sir, that you particularly mentioned hogs?"

"Lord save us!" cried Davie, "here's a man that disna ken a hogg frae a sow!"

This caused another shout of laughter, which was not allayed by a malicious suggestion made by the counsel for the promoters of the bill, who expressed his regret that before handling so technical a subject, his learned brother had not taken the pains to consult the well-known tractate of the Ettrick Shepherd, *Hogg upon Sheep*. It cost the chairman of the committee, who evidently was conversant with agricultural affairs, no little pains to persuade the discomfited and fuming Churnley that, in Scotland, a sheep of a year old was technically termed a hogg. That legal luminary seemed inclined to maintain an argument upon the interpretation given in Johnson's Dictionary, and rather imprudently indulged in some derogatory remarks on the barbarous customs and jargon of the north, whereupon the junior counsel on the opposite side, a fiery young advocate from the Scottish bar, started to his feet, and made a stinging rejoinder, noways complimentary to the called of Lincoln's Inn.

This fracas being over, Mr Churnley, who now appeared to suspect that he had caught a Tartar in the person of the redoubted Davie, continued his examination more cautiously and less offensively than before. He now shifted to another topic.

"On referring to my notes, Mr Osett," he said, "I find you state that you expect a considerable traffic in wood and timber. That, I think, was the purport of your evidence in chief?"

"That is what I said, undoubtedly."

"Sheep you consider to be one of the staples of the district?"

"That I stand by."

"And wood also is a commodity which, in your opinion, will be conveyed along the line!"

"That also is my opinion."

"Then, Mr Osett, will you inform the committee whether, in that district, there is any tract of planted land which can with propriety be called a forest?"

"As to propriety I cannot weel say; but the whole district is known, and has been known for hundreds of years, by the name of The Forest."

"Then am I to understand you to say that there is much valuable timber growing in the neighbourhood?"

"That ye never heard me say. There might be natural wood enough, if the sheep didna eat it down; but beyond auld thorn-trees, and a wheen elms, and birks, and rowans, that are gey and plenty in the cleughs, and some young larch plantations, I can hardly say that you will find muckle standing timber."

"Enough to make sleepers for the railway—eh, Mr Osett?"

"Indeed no, sir. There's barely enough to shelter the gowks and cushie-doos."

"And I presume there is not much extent of the other kinds of wood you have specified. An American, no doubt, would consider that the country was very well cleared?"

"I'm thinking that would be his view," replied Davie.

"Then, sir, answer me distinctly—how do you reconcile those admissions with the statement that you expect a traffic in timber?" And Mr Churnley rested his hands on his hips, and glared on his victim.

"How do I reconcile it?" said Davie, "Why, of course, on the principles of political economy."

"Oho! I have brought you to that, have I? Well, Mr Scot, expound your theory. I am curious to learn how you will contrive to conjure a trade out of nothing."

"It's not to be supposed," said Davie, "that a gentleman like you can be ignorant of the leading doctrine propounded by Adam Smith, and supported by other able writers, of demand and supply."

"Come, come, Mr Osett! you are following the disreputable practice of your countrymen, who, whenever they find it inconvenient to answer a plain question, skulk into a thicket of metaphysics. You admit that there is no timber, or next to none, in the district—how then can you expect a traffic in that commodity?"

"Just because, as we grow no timber ourselves, we must get it from elsewhere. Can ye no see that a railway must thrive by the wants as weel as the produce of a district? Is there ony cotton grown in Manchester? and yet what keeps that wealthy city afloat, and gives good dividends to the railway company, but the transmission of American bales? In the Forest, though it may be a contradiction of terms, we want timber, and must have it for many purposes, building and agricultural, and this railway will bring it to our doors far cheaper than by ony other conveyance. If you want to examine me further, Mr Churnley, since that's your name, ye may go on as long as ye like, but I warn you it's no in your power, clever as ye may be, to catch me in ony contradiction."

The ringing of the bell, as an intimation that the Speaker had gone to prayers, broke up the sitting of the committee; and on the following day Mr Churnley declined to proceed further with the examination of the acute surveyor.

Such fencing-matches as that which I have just described were very common; but beyond relieving the monotony of details as to gradients and sections, and affording some amusement to the audience, they were of little use. The fact is, that members of committees, being for the most part strangers to the districts through which it was proposed to carry the lines, were very much influenced by the opinions, of course cautiously expressed, of other members of Parliament who were intimately connected with the localities. As it frequently was the case that the latter had a direct pecuniary interest in the success of those enterprises, they were not scrupulous as to the means they employed for advancing them; and a good deal of delicate negotiation and private earwigging was practised, which hardly would have stood the test of a rigid investigation before a court of honour.

72

C. F. GORDON CUMMING, *IN THE HEBRIDES* (LONDON: CHATTO & WINDUS, 1883), PP. 201–204, 420–422

The Sunday war

The beginning of June 1883 furnishes a very remarkable study of sundry characteristics of the Isles. Towards the close of May the Hebridean shores were visited by vast shoals of herring. The fishers from the east coast, ever on the alert, captured such enormous quantities that the market was glutted, and the fish-curers were positively unable to take them off their hands. On Saturday, June 2nd, two steamers were loaded at Stornoway (Isle of Lewis) with fresh and kippered herring, and despatched to the railway terminus at Strome Ferry (Isle of Skye), whence a special Sunday train was to convey these "perishable goods" to Inverness to catch the south trains.

This, however, was not to be. The men of Lewis, now effectually stirred up by sundry agitators to the consideration of their "grievances," could not spare time to secure their share of the bountiful Heaven-sent supply. They were busy preparing for a great "demonstration" at Stornoway, at which all their wrongs—real and imaginary—were set forth at full length, and thus two precious days were wasted, while the east-coast boats were reaping an abundant harvest. The next day was Saturday, which comes so near Sunday that they could not think of launching their boats till Monday (by which time the herring would probably be gone). So they stayed on land bewailing their poverty, and letting the remedy slip away from their grasp.

Equally remarkable was the scene enacted at Strome Ferry on the arrival of the fish-laden steamers at about 1 a.m. on Sunday morning. The railway servants, numbering about a dozen men, at once commenced to transfer the fish to the railway waggons, but soon learnt that the fishers had resolved to put a stop to such "Sabbath desecration." Whether this determination was a spontaneous outburst of genuine Puritanism, or whether it was inspired by jealousy of the more energetic men who had reaped their neglected harvest, is hard to say, but it is certain that they acted in obedience to some general summons, for the Company's servants had scarcely begun their work, when a body of about fifty fishers from the immediate neighbourhood assembled, and announced their resolution to prevent this unlawful Sabbath work.

As their words were ignored, they seized the man in charge of the steam crane, dragging him violently away, and effectually stopping its work. Later, the railway porters endeavoured to discharge the cargo by hand, whereupon the fishers pushed the waggons away, and, their numbers being now augmented to about 150 men, mostly armed with stout sticks, they fairly drove the railway men off the pier,—not without a very serious scrimmage. All the morning fresh boat-loads of these rigid Sabbatarians continued to arrive from all parts of the coast, evidently deeming their own action a display of most righteous zeal. Entreaties, remonstrances, arguments were all in vain. A small body of police arrived from Dingwall in the forenoon, but found themselves quite unable to cope with the Puritanic mob, who could see no Sabbath-breaking in their own act of rowing across Loch Carron to molest peaceful railway servants in the discharge of their duty! It is said that two hundred men crossed the hill from Lochalsh district, and spent the night signalling by fires to the men in boats on the loch. So the fishers held their ground and guarded the pier till midnight, when, the Sabbath being ended, they allowed work to proceed, and the fish finally reached the London market, considerably deteriorated in value.

Were this principle to be faithfully carried out, it is obvious that the men of the Outer Isles must give up all thought of fishing for the market on Friday and Saturday, as their cargoes would be left to decay at Strome Ferry!

After all this excitement we may safely assume that the Sabbatarian party did not obey the injunction to labour on the first of the "six days," and that Monday's shoals did not suffer at their hands! Indeed the greater part of the week was devoted to arranging a plan of action for the following Saturday night, when the rioters were resolved to muster in much larger numbers, and so put an effectual stop to this "Sabbath breaking" by the railway authorities.

These, however, took active measures for the repression of such interference. A body of about two hundred police was brought together from various districts, so far south as Lanark, and assembled at Strome Ferry. A detachment of troops was also despatched from Edinburgh to Fort George, where a special train was in readiness to convey them to the scene of action, should their presence be required.

Late on Saturday night the Sabbatarian party mustered in force, and great excitement prevailed. Happily the clergy of the district, who had hitherto been absent at the General Assembly in Edinburgh, arrived in time to counsel the people to disperse without creating any further disturbance; and their words, combined with the awe-inspiring presence of so large a police force, induced the crowd to return to their boats about midnight.

About ten of the ringleaders were arrested, and were treated as martyrs to the good cause.

A few days later a large meeting was held on the sea-shore at Strome Ferry, presided over by a considerable number of the clergy and elders of the Free Church from neighbouring districts, to demonstrate that Sunday work is contrary to the established law of Scotland, which orders that the Sabbath shall be kept free from work. Parallels were drawn between the demonstration at Strome Ferry and the action of Nehemiah (chap. xiii. 15), and resolutions were passed to resist to the uttermost all attempts to authorize any such evil-doing in their midst. It was resolved that funds should be collected for the defence of the young men who had been apprehended. One of the reverend speakers declared "that he could authoritatively say, on behalf of many in Inverness and the north generally, that they approved of the stand the men had made against the work carried on at Strome on Sunday. He knew that it would not be allowed to go on in any other place except there, and the company was taking advantage of the people of the district."

Perhaps the quaintest illustration of a hospitable board literally groaning under the weight of good things heaped upon it, was a great dinner given to Argyle by M'Eachin, in Cantyre, whereat every creature he could possibly lay hands on, was roasted whole and set on the table "standing on its stumps!" There was an ox, a goat, a sheep, a stag, a roe, hares, rabbits, and all manner of poultry, and many another good thing, cooked in such fashion as might well have given Soyer a dream of Bedlam!

At length the sad day came, when we were compelled to bid adieu to beautiful Skye—its mountains, and its kindly people. We took the coach to dreary Broadford, where visitors are now landed by steamers from Strome Ferry, the new railway terminus. Just imagine the snorting iron horses having found their way even to these wilds (solitudes no longer), and making those grand misty summits echo back their hideous shriek and whistle. The poet's nightmare of seeing a railway "bridge the Hebrides" has well-nigh been rendered a vulgar fact, and his wail over the great Saxon invasion keeps ringing in our ears—

> "Land of Bens and Glens and Corries,
>   Headlong rivers, ocean floods!
> Have we lived to see this outrage
>   On your haughty solitudes?
>
>   .   .   .   .   .   .
>
> Strange to them the train—but stranger
>   The mixed throng it bubbles forth,
> Strand and Piccadilly emptied
>   On the much-enduring North!"

All of which is very fine theoretically; but practically it must be confessed that a luxurious railway *coupé* has *some* advantages over a crowded coach; and as to our brethren of the city, I only hope they may all carry away as sunny memories of Skye as have clung to me. To them above all others, the four-and-twenty hours which transport them from the heart of London to the farthest limits of these wild hills should be a concentrated essence of delight—and no British railway could possibly lie through scenes more beautiful than does the new Skye line.

The old folk will tell you that the railway is no new idea to them, for, just as the making of the Caledonian Canal had long been foretold by seers, who beheld ships with great white sails passing to and fro, where other men could see only broom and heather,—so, more than two hundred years ago, Coignoch Oig, the prophet of Brahan in Ross-shire (many of whose prophecies have already been strangely verified), foretold that a day was coming when every stream in this wild region would be bridged, when a white house should stand on every hill, and balls of fire would pass rapidly up and down Strathpeffer!

More especially, for the last thirty years have they expected the railway, for it was about that time, "just thirty years syne," that the folk travelling by the coach, between Loch Carron and Strome Ferry (by the old road, which ran very near where the railway now goes), were startled one dark winter night by seeing a great light coming towards them, and as it drew nearer they saw that it was a huge dark coach with fiery lamps—they could see no horses; only a great glare of flames and sparks, and it rushed past them at a place where there was no road, and vanished among the mountains. After this, the mysterious coach was seen at frequent intervals for two or three years—till at last the coachman could no longer stand the constant strain on his nerves, and gave up running at night.

This is the story that you may hear from any old "*cailliach*" as she sits in the gloaming, crooning her old songs by the light of the red peat fire, or spinning her endless yarns to the group of barelegged and bare-armed lassies, whose bright eyes glitter in the ruddy light as they press around her, or cling closer one to another, as the interest of the story becomes more thrilling. Presently the lads will join them, for the day's work is done, and "e'en brings a' hame" to the pleasant fireside.

And already we look back to "the old coaching days" as to a dream of the past! Yet there are people still living who remember when the coaches first began to run regularly north of Aberdeen, and what a grand thing *that* was thought! Nay, more; there are many gentlemen who can vividly recollect going from here to London in a sailing smack, as the simplest and least troublesome route. How often I have heard my father describe such voyages, and the annoyance of being becalmed for days together! Then came the coasting steamers; a grand improvement, and many a merry run we have had in them between London and Moray. Now all these are things of the past. You breakfast one morning in sight of the great Skye hills, and the next finds you at Euston Square—a process so simple, that life becomes one incessant railway journey, for ever whirling to and fro!

73

C. F. GORDON CUMMING, *MEMORIES* (EDINBURGH: W. BLACKWOOD, 1904), PP. 440–441

In those days few people ever left their homes. In the whole parish of Elgin there were not more than four gigs in use, and it was a very rare thing for any one to go so far as Edinburgh; few indeed had ever visited London. There was no public conveyance north of Aberdeen. A mail-coach was started about 1812 to run between Aberdeen and Inverness. This it did very slowly, being run by only a pair, and those between Elgin and Forres are said to have been very decrepit old horses.

About the year 1819 a four-horse coach was started, which, leaving Inverness at 6 A.M., reached Aberdeen at 10 P.M. The original mail-coach followed suit, and the competition improved matters. About 1826 "The Star" was started, to leave Aberdeen at 8 A.M. and reach Elgin at 5 P.M. Other local coaches were started, but were frequently half empty. In 1835 "The Defiance" was started. Well do I remember it with its first-class team, and the scarlet coats of the cheery driver and guard, whose brass horn was the signal that news from the south was arriving.

In those days postage was so costly that letters were few and far between. So small was the correspondence even in the beginning of the nineteenth century, that the mail-bags containing a very few letters were carried by a post-rider on horseback three times a week. And now our half-a-dozen heavy posts each day are too few for the present generation, who must needs telegraph about every trifle, often to the exceeding disgust of the country recipients of totally unnecessary messages, for which they have to pay large sums as porterage.

"The Defiance" continued to keep up its credit, till it was driven aside by the arrival of the railway, which was somewhat late in the day, as the idea that so gigantic an undertaking could ever pay, was considered preposterous, more especially the Highland line between Forres and Perth, crossing barren mountains. However, energetic men pushed the matter, and bit by bit from the year 1846 onwards, local railways were made, and finally in 1865 all were amalgamated under the name of The Highland Railway Company, with branches in every direction, and crowds of busy folk and tourists from every corner of the world—a change indeed since 1800! with the solitary post-runner and an occasional gig or post-chaise.

One very important reason against travelling on wheels was that till quite recent times there were no bridges: small streams were crossed on stepping-stones, and large ones by ferry-boats, and when rivers were in flood, passengers had to wait till the waters subsided, sometimes being detained for days in most uncomfortable quarters, while each year had a record of persons drowned in rashly attempting to ford the rivers.

With the exception of an old wooden bridge which crossed the Spey at Boat of Bridge, and which was ruined at the time of the Reformation, and a few other slight wooden bridges, there were none north of Aberdeen till the early part of the sixteenth century, when the first stone bridge over the Lossie was erected—a single arch founded on each side on the rock, and consequently so secure that it remains in use to this day. Unmindful of the wisdom of the earlier builders, a two-arch stone bridge across the Lossie was built in 1814, but being founded on gravel, it was swept away in the flood of 1829. Now we have stone or metal bridges for road or rail in every direction.

74

'THE DUBLIN AND KINGSTOWN RAILWAY', *DUBLIN PENNY JOURNAL* 3, 113, 30 AUGUST 1834, PP. 65–68

In the last number but one of our second volume, with two or three engravings suited to the subject, we took the opportunity of pointing out the great importance of establishing railroads in various directions throughout this country—we described the construction, and stated the expense of several of those at present used in England; and now proceed, according to our promise in that number, to lay before our readers some particulars relative to the new line which is nearly completed between our city and Kingstown; a work, which we have no hesitation in saying, reflects the highest credit on all the parties engaged in its construction—on those with whom the idea originated—on those who had the public spirit to embark their capital in such a concern—on the engineer who planned the work and carried the design into execution—as well on the various individuals who in subordinate situations, have lent their varied talents and their energies to its completion. Were it not that under present circumstances it might appear a work of supererogation, we should have felt disposed to notice some of the many calumnies which we have from time to time heard poured forth on the promoters and designers of this important national undertaking. We forbear, however, under the impression that the authors of such calumnies have seen their errors, and that they will hereafter judge of the railway by its own merits. At the same time, it would be unjust if the deserved meed of praise were not given to the spirited and liberal minded body of Directors, who have weathered the storm, and who have thus successfully introduced into Ireland the best promoter of internal peace—rapidity, facility, and economy of communication. But we now proceed to the railway itself.

The Entrance Station is on the east side of Westland Row. The design is sufficiently characteristic of a public building without any attempt at embellishment. The chief points worthy of attention are the beautiful granite door-cases, and cornices, from the rocks near Seapoint cliffs, and the light elegant iron roof over the passengers' station. The details of the internal arrangements for the reception and distribution of passengers can only be explained by inspection, or by an examination of the plans and drawings; but it appears evident that the public accommodation has been studied in every respect. Indeed nothing but system and simplicity could effect the arrival and departure of trains of carriages every quarter of an hour without danger or confusion.

To preserve the ordinary traffic of the public thoroughfares, the railway starts at an elevation of about twenty feet from the surface, and spans in succession over each street by flat elliptical arches. For the more important streets, smaller arches for the foot-ways have been made on each side of the principal openings.

The intervals between the streets consist of high retaining walls of limestone, obtained from the Donnybrook quarries, the space between which has been filled with sand, gravel, dry rubbish, and similar materials; the cartage gave employment during the whole of the last autumn, winter, and spring, to hundreds of the humble proprietors of carts and cars.

The breadth of the railway from Westland Row to Barrow-street, beyond the Grand Canal docks, is nearly sixty feet between the parapets, and is calculated to receive four lines of rails: the two central roads for the going and returning passenger trains, and the two exterior ones for the coal, granite, timber, and general merchandize-waggons, which will load and unload with great facility at the sides, and without the slightest interruption to the continual stream of the passenger traffic.

The railway is carried across the quays, and a part of the Grand Canal docks, by a granite bridge of three oblique arches of peculiar workmanship, which, though well known in England, is now introduced for the first time in Ireland, and has drawn the attention and admiration of all the operative mechanics. One arch is intended for a future street, marked out, to pass parallel to the docks: a second is for the business of the quays—the third is to pass the boats of the trade, and is provided with a towing-path, ranging with the general line of the dock wall. This bridge will form one of the most remarkable features of the works.

Some difficulties appear to have occurred in getting the railway past the distillery near the docks, at which it ought to be mentioned that a large station or depot is provided for the accommodation of trade. Over Barrow-street the arch is built with what is technically called *knee'd or elbow quoins*; the stones being cut so as to form an oblique or skew bed on the face of the ring, and to return to a square bed within: these quoins are of granite—the rest of the arch stones are of the usual limestone. At this place also the rail-road contracts to a breadth of thirty feet, being adapted for two lines only for the remainder of the distance, the breadth between each of the lines of railway track, being as much, however, as eight feet.—The bridge over the Circular road is square, but across the Irishtown road the angle of intersection is only fifty-three degrees; and a granite elliptical arch, built on the oblique principal, has been introduced with good effect. The intervals between the bridges are still sustained by certaining walls, which, however, diminish in height, and the crossing at Haig's distillery is the first accessible point to the railway from Dublin. This being but little frequented, the roadway has been raised by gentle approaches, and passes on the level of the rail-road. A neat lodge is built, and, according to the act of parliament, gates will be placed across the railway, and a vigilant watch kept. We next come to a handsome bridge of three arches, across the river Dodder, with a side opening for foot passengers. The railroad here approaches the surface of the country, A little further forward, and on the north side, are erecting the buildings for the repairs and construction of the locomotive engines, coaches, waggons, &c.; and the other necessary shops and conveniences for the company.

At Serpentine avenue the railroad crosses on the present level of the road, with gates, lodge, &c., as before.—All appearance of masonry now ceases; a green sod bank marks the boundary on each side, with a double row of quick-set plants on the top, which, in a few years, will form a fine hedge. Externally, the mound is formed like a slight field fortification, with a berm or set off, on which another hedge-row is planted. A very wide and deep trench forms an effectual fence against cattle and trespassers; and thus the line runs on through Simmonscourt-fields, crossing Sandymount-lane and Sydney Parade, which will be protected, like the other roads, with gates, lodges and watchmen. At Merrion the Strand road is crossed close to the old baths, with similar protection, but on account of the liability of intrusion, the railway from Merrion-hall on to the strand is guarded by high stone fence-walls. From Old Merrion to the place where stood the bathing places at Black Rock, the railroad is elevated across the strand, and at high water appears like a long mole stretching into the sea. A smile will be raised at the recollection of the many good-natured predictions of the direful and destructive effect the winter-storms were to produce upon this attempt to force nature; and observing the facility and rapidity with which this embankment was completed, as well as that the effect of the storms has been to accumulate a protecting bank at the footings of the outer slope: not the slightest apprehension can be entertained of any future danger from the severest eastwardly gales, when the stone facing next the sea is finished all along, as it has been completed in parts. To afford additional stability and protection, an increased breadth is given to the banks seaward, which will form a delightful promenade on fine summer evenings. A cross embankment is made from opposite Booterstown-lane to the railway, to give an access to passengers; and it is the intention of the noble lord of the manor to cultivate the land thus redeemed by the railway operations, which will, therefore, in the course of a few months, present the appearance of a luxuriant garden, where lately was only a barren sandy beach. The quantity of land to be brought into useful occupation is about fifty English acres. At Williamstown, the railway nearly touches the shore by Seafort Parade, and another access is afforded: while ample culverts allow the water to flow in as usual to the bathing places all along the coast, which now, that the construction of the sea embankment is nearly finished, will be as pure as ever, with the additional advantage of being always smooth and still.

At Black Rock, the company are constructing bathing accommodation for both sexes, on the outer sides of the railway enbankment, to which approach will be had by a handsome foot-bridge from the high ground. These baths, will be, as nearly as practicable, on their former sites.—Access will also be had by a second cross embankment from the railway to Merrion avenue, and handsome lodges with waiting-rooms for passengers, will be constructed at this station, as also at the cross bank from Booterstown.

From Black Rock to Kingstown, the character of the work changes continually—high walling on the land side, and open to the sea; then passing under Lord Cloncurry's demesne, among the beautiful granite pavilions erecting for his lordship; next, below the noble archway or tunnel; and beyond, through a deep, rocky excavation, upwards of forty feet in depth; and below, the bridge connecting the severed portions of the elegant lawn of Sir Harcourt Lees; emerging from whence, the eye catches the noble sea-view, with the distant harbour. The road will now pass close under Seapoint boarding-house, which has been accommodated with a bridge over the railroad, descending to neat baths, and to a boat pier, and other conveniences. Again occurs a portion of deep cutting, through granite rocks, with a handsome bridge of granite, to the Martello tower at Seapoint, from whence to Salthill the railroad runs at the bottom of Monkstown cliffs, with an ample promenade on the sea side, and divided from the new foot-path by a neat iron railing. All the rugged cliffs have been levelled down, and formed into pleasing slopes, which the taste of the owner of the adjacent cottages will soon cover with flowers and shrubs.—The house at Salthill is now converting, with vast additions, into a splendid tavern, which will rival its celebrated namesake in the vicinity of Eton college in all, it is to be hoped, except its extravagant charges; and the hill itself will be cut into beautiful terraces and slants, and planted in an ornamental manner. To this extent, terminating on the western pier of the old harbour of Dunleary, the works of the company are completed, and nearly ready for opening; but the last portion, on which a commencement is now making, yet remains to be described. Four acts or scenes have been passed over, viz: –

1 The city, or mural portion, from Westland-row to Serpentine avenue.
2 The country or rural district, from that station to Old Merrion.
3 The isolated sea embankments, as far as Black rock, and,
4 The coast road portion under the cliffs, and among the rocks, with the boating and bathing accommodations seaward, as far as Salthill. What follows, though less beautiful, is not less useful, and may be styled the 5th or commercial district.

It commences by striking a chord line across a segment of the old harbour of Dunleary, which segment will be filled up, and, ere long, probably covered with bonded warehouses and yards. With the accommodation of an ample wharf, sufficient cranage and other conveniences—the cargoes of colliers, steamers, and all trading vessels may be quickly and economically transported to the railway waggons, and by these brought into Dublin at a very low rate.

The old harbour traversed, the railway will pass between the Martello tower and the battery opposite Crofton terrace. It will here be in deep cutting, and a granite bridge will preserve the communication with the old pier and landing place, with a considerable improvement in the approaches. Between the battery and the admiralty stores, the railroad will closely border on the harbour, and a convenient bonding-yard for timber may be formed with ready communication with the railway, whereby a great convenience would be afforded to the Canada and Baltic merchants. The road then goes at the back of the admiralty stores, and close to the boat harbour and landing place of the Royal harbour, and thence runs to a termination on the large open space opposite the Commissioners'-yard and what is termed the Forty-foot road, being immediately connected with the magnificent quay and landing-place, now in course of construction by government, for the accommodation of the Post Office and other steamers, and when the works are completed, passengers may step from the railway coaches to the steamers, and again, on arriving will, with the mail bags, be conveyed in a quarter of an hour from the Royal Harbour of George the Fourth to the centre of the Irish metropolis.

Stations will be erected at this end of the railway; and for the protection of the public, an iron railing will be placed between the railway and the common road, for the whole length of the harbour, from Dunleary to the Forty-foot road, and such communications will be made across as the harbour commissioners may direct.

In addition to the tavern at Salthill, a new hotel near Seapoint Martello Tower, is spoken of. It is understood also that the company are about to erect splendid baths on a scale of accommodation hitherto unknown in this country; and in every point of view, the taste, the wants, and the wishes of the public will be studied and provided for; an excellent policy, which will be well compensated by the additional intercourse of passengers upon the railway.

The preceding outline will convey to the distant reader, who may be familiar with the country between Dublin and Kingstown, some idea of the works, and of their general character; but to those who have not seen the beauties of Dublin bay and its vicinity, it will be difficult to convey an accurate impression of the effect the railway will present. Hurried by the invisible, but stupendous agency of steam, the astonished passenger will now glide, like Asmodeus, over the summits of the houses and streets of a great city—presently be transported through green-fields and tufts of trees—then skim across the surface of the sea, and taking shelter under the cliffs, coast among the marine villas, and through rocky excavations, until he finds himself in the centre of a vast port, which unites in pleasing confusion the bustle of a commercial town with the amusements of a fashionable watering place. Of the manner in which the work has been executed, it is sufficient to observe that the utmost solidity and severest simplicity mark the entire. The formation of the railway bed consists of layers of gravel and concrete, with longitudinal and numerous cross drains. Immense blocks of granite, at intervals of three feet, support the iron rails, by means of supports called chairs; at every fifteen feet a larger block extends across and unites the two rails together, and the appearance of firmness and solidity is very remarkable in the course of construction, though at the parts which are quite finished off, nothing is to be seen except four parallel lines of iron bars, laid with almost geometrical precision. To those who may interest themselves in the details which combine, it is believed, all the most recent improvements, it may be satisfactory to know, that at the offices of the company every facility is afforded for the inspection of the working, as well as the embellished drawings, and that a morning will be satisfactorily employed in examining these as well as the various models.

Six locomotive engines have been built for the Dublin and Kingstown railway: three of these are from the manufactory of Messrs. George Forrester, and Co., of Liverpool; and three from the house of Messrs. Sharp, Roberts, and Co., of Manchester. The greatest mechanical perfection has been attained in these machines; and the useful and honorable rivalry between two such eminent houses, cannot but result in advantage to the present company as well as to the public, by combining superiority of workmanship with the most improved adaptation of principles. A great and interesting experiment is also conducting at the same time, inasmuch as the working parts of the engines is totally different by each house. Messrs. Forrester have horizontal cylinders, fore and hind wheels of unequal diameter, elastic pistons working with improved valves, a small number of tubes in the boiler, &c. Messrs. Sharp Roberts and Co. have introduced vertical cylinders, the whole of the wheels alike; bell-crank motion, solid pistons, patent valves without friction; numerous tubes, &c. Both have put unequalled workmanship—both have adopted wrought iron frames, and straight axles, and it is believed have avoided all the errors and weaknesses observed in the locomotive engines hitherto produced.

The carriages for the accommodation of passengers are of three classes: most of these have been made in Dublin by Mr. Dawson, of Capel-street; and by Messrs. Courteney and Stephens, of Blackhall-place. A few only were made in Manchester. The wheels, axles, &c. were necessarily constructed in England. Trucks are also provided for conveying gentlemen's carriages, &c.

The railway coaches of the first and second class may be almost called elegant; the third class carriages are superior to those in use on the English railways, and all are covered. The fares will be on a very low scale.

It is impossible to describe all the details connected with the railway establishment, and indeed they would scarcely be interesting to the general reader. To form an accurate judgment, the work itself should be seen; and as it is now opened, public curiosity and individual enquiry will be fully gratified.

The character of the works, the variety of the different constructions, and the costly expenditure upon the Dublin and Kingstown railway, form a remarkable contrast to the appearance of flatness which the country presents to the eye of a casual observer, which glancing over the level ground, between the south side of Dublin and the shores of the bay, prompts the not unnatural remark, of the cheapness and facility with which a railway might have been constructed. But many causes have concurred in requiring a continual change in the transverse section of the railway, which have, certainly, greatly added to the novelty and interest of the work, though, at the same time, difficulties have been increased, and expenses augmented far beyond what has ever yet been required to force a level passage through the most difficult districts where railways have been introduced.

Among those causes may be enumerated the expediency of penetrating deeply into the centre of the metropolis; the attention requisite to be paid to public safety, and to vested and incorporated rights; the great value of the property, whether as building or suburban grounds; the interposition of secluded demesnes; the preservation of the bathing, boating, and other accommodations of individuals, and of the public along the coast; the necessity of making the course of the road as direct as possible, and of connecting the several changes of direction by easy curves, and the caution to be exercised in tracing a complete and isolated route, for the peculiar machines to be employed, through the rich and populous district in the vicinity of a large commercial city, to a termination on the quays of the finest artificial harbour in the world; where the smallest nautical conveniences had to be preserved from interference, or to be amply compensated for and replaced; and close to the streets of a rising and populous borough, the conveniences and even the apprehensions of whose inhabitants had to be consulted.

The original intention was to have commenced the railway at the rere of the college buildings, and to have skirted the college park, parallel to Great Brunswick-street. This would have made the starting point about the Clarendon stables, and within a very short distance of the very centre of Dublin business. Vague fears, misrepresentations, and other causes created an outcry against such a proposition, which it is hoped at a future and not distant period may still be realized.

Indeed it is fondly anticipated that this measure may be the means of introducing the railway system generally into Ireland, and, independent of all other considerations, this is the light in which it becomes most interesting to every well-wisher for the happiness and prosperity of our country. Capital, intelligence, and enterprize exist abundantly in Ireland; and nothing is wanting to render it the most flourishing part of the empire but confidence, and the diffusion of information.—What can more readily bring these than railroads, whereby the English landlord and the traveller may visit the remotest parts of Ireland with the same rapidity and safety with which he now posts down from London to Brighton. When the landed proprietor can have the means of visiting his estates frequently and expeditiously, he will perceive that to the want of employment and education are to be attributed the whole of the evils of Ireland.

There is nothing exhibits so much the overgrown amount of the population in Ireland, when brought into comparison with its capital and property, as the lowness of wages. In many parts of Ireland, labour is not higher than it was when Arthur Young wrote his travels; fifty years ago his report of the wages of the labouring poor, shows the rate to have been nearly, if not altogether, as high as it is now; and while all kinds of agricultural produce have nearly doubled in price, the labourer must still put up with six-pence or eight-pence per day; and moreover, happy is that poor peasant, who is sure of constant employment even at that rate. Let railways be introduced in various directions throughout the country, and this will not long be the case. Give the landlord an opportunity of adding to his rent-roll, or even of improving his estate, by transporting the produce of his grounds from the interior of the country, at nearly the same rate of charge as those now living on the coast, and even were there no higher motive than self-interest, he will soon give employment to numbers of those who are now dragging out a miserable existence in poverty and wretchedness. But we must also remark, that to enable the people to benefit by the advantages which railways will offer, they must be educated. The great deficiency of the Irish is in the quantum of educated labour that is amongst them; and therefore it is, that though the market is overstocked with gross, untrained, shall we say, brute labour, yet there is a lamentable deficiency in those minds and hands that are requisite to carry into effect the nicer operations of art, or agriculture, or manufacture. It is, therefore, essential that our people should be educated: educated up to trustworthiness—educated so as to be capable of productive labour—educated so as to have a respect for themselves—educated so as to acquire a religious restraint over their hitherto uncurbed passions—educated so as to acquire a dislike for secret association, and a respect for the law—educated as becomes Christian freemen, and Ireland will yet be the finest and fairest portion of the British empire.

The evils that counteract the great natural blessings which Providence has showered down on this country, are of long standing—they have existed before history had a record—they have exercised their baneful influence on the character of the people for centuries; and it cannot be the work of a day to remove what is wrong and replace it with what is right: still let us hope that the introduction of steam navigation, and the construction of railroads throughout the land, will prove one great step towards abating the evil.

75

J. JAY SMITH, *A SUMMER'S JAUNT ACROSS THE WATER* (PHILADELPHIA: J. W. MOORE, 1846), PP. 46–47

Dublin, May, 1845.

ONE of the first places to which my friends took me on arriving at Dublin, was the Atmospheric Railway, connecting with the Kingston; its commencement is seven miles from our Imperial Hotel in the great thoroughfare of Sackville Street. Its terminus is at Dalkey, a distance of one mile and three-quarters, which we ran in the unusually slow time of four minutes: the route has been frequently traversed in one minute and three-quarters, or sixty miles an hour, on an ascending grade, and with a weight attached of seventy tons. You know the mode of exhausting the pipe by a steam-engine of one hundred horse power, and inserting a piston in a cylinder in the centre of the track; the opening in the fifteen-inch tube is immediately closed by a wheel running over plates of iron, about five inches long, and replacing them in a slight bed of luting, such as is employed to grease cartwheels or of that consistence, but by no means in such quantity or so fluid as I had imagined from the descriptions. We ascended a grade, recollect, of seventy-six feet, in less than two miles. It is considered here a successful invention and likely to be generally introduced. A committee of Parliament reported favourably on it last week. The Americans must take up and improve this plan. No railroad should be now commenced in the United States without ascertaining fully the benefits and economy of this important invention. Various charters for this improved mode have been granted in England, and many routes are now in progress, with prospects of complete success.

76

FREDERICK RICHARD CHICHESTER, *MASTERS AND WORKMEN: A TALE ILLUSTRATIVE OF THE SOCIAL AND MORAL CONDITION OF THE PEOPLE*, 3 VOLS. (LONDON: NEWBY, 1851), I, PP. 7–17

It was near the end of July, but though the vegetation of summer was in its richest luxuriance, there seemed no gladness on the face of the earth. The dull, heavy, sunless air was hot and oppressive as in the chamber of death, and quick lightning flashed at intervals from masses of murky clouds, long gathering in the horizon. The cattle panting for want of water, stood in little groups together on the parched fields; not a bird flitted across the sky; only man—restless man was actively struggling forwards—forwards in pursuit of his daily bread, or of the thousand other objects, which civilization has taught him to covet, whether for good or for evil, who shall decide! The clang of enormous hammers rang on the still air, from a line of long black buildings near the margin of a once romantic river, where a hundred coal fires, white with intensity of heat, glowed doubly bright, as the gloomy day waned dark and dim, and clouds of smoke burst from many of those giant chimneys, which are the true obelisks of modern times.

The whole scene gave the strongest evidence that a servile imitation of the remains of the old races has ceased, their work is done. The busy multitudes of living men, are creating monuments to themselves, as their fathers did of yore; monuments of knowledge, and industry, more vast, and more noble in their simple utility, than all the vain erections of the slaves of Egypt, or of Rome.

The long tyranny of exalted individuals and exclusive classes over the multitude, if not yet extinct in Europe, has taken a milder form in England, and energy and talent are there chiefly directed, not to make slaves of human beings, but of matter; not to enchain the free born soul, but to govern the elements, that they may work under the controul of mind, for the general benefit of the human race. Industry and science are daily breaking down the old barriers of exclusive privileges, and enabling the poor and the humble, to participate in many of the advantages of civilization, which wealth was once inadequate to procure.

A great change is quietly going on in social existence, for the benefit of the lower classes, and the rich, whilst seeking to obtain interest for their capital, though they may increase luxury, are, at the same time, advancing intellectual activity, which can alone counteract its evils, and affording to the poor many advantages and conveniences which, by ameliorating their physical condition, tend to elevate their moral character. Some men who see nothing but demoralization in the progress of the people, make futile efforts to arrest the inevitable movement of society, whilst others, anxious for the welfare of all mankind, exert themselves, not to check, but to direct to worthy objects, the restless activity of the age. To them, even the blackness and dense atmosphere of a great manufacturing town, and the clang of the hammer, and the rush of the steam carriage, have their charms and their inspiration, though well aware that evil can never be banished from the face of the earth, nor the heart of man entirely changed.

Yonder flying vehicles, smoking and groaning along the railroad to the magnificent station of one of England's dark cities of industry, though a minister of good, yet bears within itself the evidence, that joy and sorrow, vice and virtue, wealth and poverty must continue to travel on together to the grave, as long as society exists. In those carriages, as in life, there is a first, a second, and a third class, all profitting, in a certain degree, by the inventions of the age, yet all retaining unchanged their early destination.

The young countess, who leans back against the luxurious cushions of a first class carriage, and weeps because her only child has recently been laid in the grave, sheds not less bitter tears because she is borne along, thirty miles an hour instead of ten. The wealthy banker in the next carriage, who hopes to secure a profit of twenty thousand pounds, by the rapidity of his journey, and his gorgeous wife, who is more engaged with her lap-dog than her husband, are not less proud and insolent, because they do not travel post. The old workman, with his pretty little grandchild on his knee, in the second class, is not less industrious, or honest, because he has been able, for a trifling sum, to travel fifty miles and return in one day, to visit his sick son. No! he is telling his neighbour, a railway is a grand invention for the poor, to whom time and labour are the only capital, and the same thought occupies the minds of many of the motley crowd, who with baskets and small bundles fill the third class carriages. Even that tall, sorrowful-looking man, in a thread-bare suit, who is counting so anxiously the few shillings that remain in his purse, smiles as he looks on the delicate, slender girl of seventeen at his side, and remembers how many hours of fatigue she has been spared, by that railroad. But though he has this one cause for rejoicing, other sorrows rankle unchanged in his heart, and when the train rolled rapidly along a terrace commanding an extensive view of the smoking city it approached, tears rose to the poor man's eyes. No one marked his emotion, save his companion, who watched him ever anxiously, and understanding his feelings, she gently pressed his hand in hers, as the fiery course of the carriages finished, under the lofty arch of the station. In another moment, the imprisoned crowd rushed from the vehicles on to the platform. All was bustle and confusion. Some of the passengers were crying out for carpet-bags, others were eagerly claiming trunks, as they were pulled forth from their hiding-places, into the light of the gas; one old gentleman was in despair, that another had walked off with his portmanteau; the banker's wife vainly offered a sovereign to a policeman to catch her lap-dog, which had disappeared amidst the crowd, till her rage was directed against her maid, who had forgotten a variety of travelling baskets, books, and umbrellas, at the last station, where they had changed carriages.

The melancholy traveller by the third class, was exempt from such troubles; his whole luggage was contained in a small bundle he carried under his arm. As he observed the confusion and anxiety of those around him, he felt that poverty has some advantages, after all, and with his young companion at his side, he quietly endeavoured to make his way amidst the crowd.

He stopped as he approached the gateway leading to the town, and taking a letter from his pocket, held it up to the gas-light, to look once more at the direction. He had scarcely read it, when some one behind him desired him, in a haughty voice, to stand aside, and not to stop up the public passage. He looked up, and his eyes met the imperious glance of the banker, who had travelled by the first class.

"Wealth, and success, and good living, had greatly altered this man, since they had last met, for many years had passed since then; but he knew him instantly, to be James Graves, the son of a smuggling ship captain, who had once been the lowest clerk in the bank, of which he was now the leading partner.

A cold shudder passed over the poor man, from head to foot, as the haughty gentleman, in passing, slightly touched his shoulder, but he gave no sign of recognition. The banker evidently knew him not. He paused, with some curiosity under the gateway, to watch the rich man enter the handsome carriage that was waiting for him, and take his place at the side of his murmuring and discontented wife. The rain was falling in torrents, and a short sigh burst from the poor traveller's lips, when, after the carriage had rolled away, he drew his young companion's arm within his, and putting up a torn cotton umbrella, stepped out in the muddy road. There was no envy in his heart; he was incapable of envying any man's wealth; but the remembrance of injustice, forced that sigh from his heart.

In silence he led his young companion by the shortest foot-way, towards the centre of the busy, populous town, through squalid gloomy streets, from whence the houses nearly excluded the light of day. There is nothing more loathsome and revolting to a benevolent heart, than these secret and long hidden recesses of great cities, which, in many instances, have been suddenly broken open by the social earthquake of modern railways and laid bare, with all their filth and their poverty, and their dense population, to the public eye. These plague spots of our great commercial towns are no longer hidden by plaster palaces and flaunting gin shops, from the fastidious eyes of luxury, but rent asunder by a railway, it seems if the very worst parts of these wretched dwellings were displayed, to arouse the passers by to a sense of the duty and necessity of endeavouring to improve the moral and physical condition of those whom destiny has condemned to inhabit such abodes.

77

ANDREW DICKINSON, *MY FIRST VISIT TO EUROPE* (NEW YORK: G. P. PUTNAM, 1851), PP. 48–50

Poor Ireland has been doctored almost to death, and then turned out to die like an old worn-out-horse, whose labour has fattened his master. Poor Pat has committed many grievous sins; but one can hardly believe they will all be visited on him alone. Naturally honest, confiding, and easily led, he has too often been the dupe of mere demagogues, who had their ends to serve by fleecing him for his special good; and repudiating the culture of the soil by their advice, what must follow but beggary and starvation? Who is to be scape-goat is not for me to say. Somewhere will fall a heavy vengeance.

But as sure as I live, here we are in Drogheda in an hour and a quarter! We must get out here and pass the Boyne waters by coach, from the windows of which I view the field where the famous battle of the Boyne was fought in 1690 between James II. and William III. This battle, with a loss on both sides of 2000 men, decided the fate of James. The field has undergone some changes. It looks like any other field, covered with the grass of summer; yet I could imagine the "confused noise and garments rolled in blood," and the awful clangour of battle. But look at that group of half-starved, hatless tatterdemalions, with no covering but a few ancient rags dangling from the knees and elbows! Was ever such a picture of wretchedness seen in my native land? They shout incessantly, " 'ape'ny! 'ape'ny!" A few half-pence are thrown from the coach-top and windows; "but what are they among so many?" Besides, it aggravates the misery of the wretched sufferers who get none in the desperate scramble. Ah! why was I born in a land that floweth with milk and honey, while these fellow-beings almost "perish with hunger?" Our coach rolls over the bridge that crosses the Boyne: they follow imploringly; but their voices are drowned by the rattling of wheels. In the brief interval of taking seats in the railway, their deafening shouts are renewed with despairing energy. They run after the train, but alas! the modern railroad improvements have not improved their condition—they are distanced! Poor fellows! Their voices are annihilated; we hear and see them no more! Look at those princely castles on the hills! All around are luxury and refinement; and amid all this overgrown wealth, gross ignorance and gaunt beggary in mud huts! Overcome by this heart-rending scene, I was for some time unable to enjoy some of the richest scenery in this lower world—the very prototype of green Eden. It seems as if some parts of this country had escaped the primeval curse; but the poverty of the working classes tells a true tale of the first and last curse. Dunleer, Dundalk, and many smaller towns, sweep by us with American railroad velocity. At Inneskeen, I saw them cutting bogs with a slane or spade, about four inches broad, with a steel blade the same width, at right angles with the edge of the spade. The turf is cut in the shape of bricks, and stacked in pyramids so as to admit the air through the interstices. Turf is a capital substitute for coal. Large tracts of bog land have been reclaimed and made the best of arable land.

From Castle Blaney to Armagh it is fourteen miles by coach. During the half hour in getting ready for a start, another scene in the Beggars' Opera came off with some variations—a heart-sickening, tragical sight. A number of poor squalid creatures followed the coach full two miles, with yelling cries for a pitiful brass farthing or two, over which they luxuriated with mad joy, like some California gold-seeker, when he finds a whole mountain of the precious yellow dust. Their cries were very annoying; but they had the worst of it. Our way to Belfast was through the counties of Dublin, Westmeath, Louth, and Down; and in beauty often surpassed the vivid pictures imagination had drawn. Never was fitter name than the Green Isle; although this country, like England, is rather bare of trees. My eye rested on the hills and valleys of lively green with unceasing delight; and as the landscape glided from my view, the thought that I should never see those beautiful scenes again was painful.

Armagh lies on gracefully swelling hills. At a distance of ten miles, I could see its celebrated cathedral on a commanding height covered with luxuriant green, forming a beautifully picturesque landscape. On a neighbouring hill another splendid cathedral was erecting. From Armagh to Belfast is an excellent railway, equal to any in England. Along this part of the route the scenery is charming, the prospect being very extensive. Leftward, twenty-five miles off, is a splendid sheet of water, twenty-five miles long and half that width, and from its azure tint, might be mistaken for a strip of sky. On the right are the highest mountains in Ireland, stretching from Dundrum Bay to Belfast. At Lisburn and other places millions of yards of linen spread over the green lawns for miles, gave the country the appearance of winter. At six in the evening I reached Belfast, surprised at its beauty, extensive trade, increasing prosperity, and the comparative cheapness of many commodities, lower than I found them in England or Ireland.

78

SIR FRANCIS BOND HEAD, *A FORTNIGHT IN IRELAND*, 2ND ED. (LONDON: JOHN MURRAY, 1852), PP. 70, 108–114

DURING the few days I was in Dublin, I perceived that it was not only agreed upon by everybody I had the happiness to converse with that I ought to make a tour in Ireland, but everybody was obliging enough to tell me exactly where I ought to proceed. "You must go to *Cork*," said one; "*Belfast* is the place that YOU should visit," said another. All said "*Of course* you'll go to KILLARNEY!" After gratefully thanking everybody for their kind endeavours to steer a compassless and rudderless bark into its proper harbour, I asked—as it were quite incidentally—in what part of Ireland was to be seen the greatest amount of poverty and misery; and as almost everybody, in reply, named the counties of Mayo and Galway, in the secret chamber of my mind I quietly determined that, without saying a word to any one, I would make my tour in that direction. Everybody was so obliging, that I believe I could have obtained a sackfull of letters of introduction; and like a postman, could have spent the whole of my time in delivering them. On reflection, however, I considered that, instead of going to strange people who would often encumber me with help, the best mode of summarily obtaining the simple information I desired would be to get an order to the constabulary, who, throughout Ireland, are ubiquitous. I conceived that this highly intelligent body of men would of course be intimately acquainted, not only with their respective localities, but with the persons within them best competent to instruct me. Lastly, it was evident that an order addressed to the constabulary would also, on production, be a pass into any jails or workhouses I might desire to visit.

Accordingly, the evening before my departure, without mentioning my route, I obtained what proved to be of inestimable assistance to me—namely, a general firman, from the chief constabulary office in Dublin, directing the force to afford me "all possible information and assistance."

With this in my pocket, and with a small carpetbag by my side, I drove early next morning to the railway station, and, after paying for my ticket, took possession of a first-class coupé, which I knew I should have entirely to myself.

For nearly an hour, in beautiful sunshine, I flew across a verdant country, nearly as flat as Hounslow, intersected by low hedges into small fields, in which were standing large cocks of hay, corn in sheaves, and here and there poppies, thistles, with yellow, white, and red weeds, which, as true children of Nature, appeared to be enjoying themselves wherever they could steal an opportunity. In the picture, which now became more undulating, I observed a few small woods, some stone walls, and, scantily dotted about, a few low stone cottages thatched—some dilapidated, others milk white.

The country seemed to be troubled neither with towns nor cities. The railway fence was often nothing but a slight ditch bounded by a couple of stout wires running through slight posts, about two feet high.

The coupé was so large and so high, that with the greatest ease I could pace from one side to another with my hat on; and then, resuming my seat, it was really quite delightful to find oneself in a quiet study with large plate-glass windows, contemplating, not little bits of painted canvas, but Ireland itself, passing in review, with growing crops, living cows, sheep, goats, and horses grazing, swine rooting, an Irish lamb gambolling, and in its immediate neighbourhood, lying on the green bank, an Irish child, the loveliest ornament of the soil on which it slept. Suddenly, from the most beautiful verdure, we passed through a large dark level, looking as if it had been convulsed by an earthquake that had just rudely thrown up a substratum to the surface. Among it, here and there, were to be seen women and a few men, stacking peat into tumuli of various picturesque shapes. The barren bog, however, suddenly changed into heather in bloom, in which occasionally appeared heaps of peat; and thus for some time flowers and fuel were to be seen in juxtaposition, in a beautiful variety of different proportions.

In about forty miles the fences of the country changed into banks protected by single or double ditches. The railway on which I travelled appeared to have been admirably executed. On one of its sides, indolently hanging in the air, were two wires, ready for electrical communication on any subject.

On stopping for a few minutes to allow our hot engine to drink, I observed, ranged along and resting upon the coping of a railway bridge, scarcely twenty yards from us, a series of Irish faces, of various ages and of both sexes, which would have formed an amusing as well as interesting study for any artist.

At fifty miles from Dublin we came to Mullingar, the centre and the principal town of the county of Westmeath. It appeared to contain a substantial gaol surrounded by high walls, a court-house, extensive barracks, a handsome Roman Catholic chapel on an elevated site, a nunnery, a union workhouse, and a variety of other civilized comforts and luxuries. About two miles to the south lives Lough Ennell, a shining patch of water between four and five miles long, and about one and a half broad.

The station was exceedingly clean; and when we left it, and an erect, intelligent, well-dressed station-man, who at about half a mile from it, in a well-appointed uniform, appeared standing on the green bank, motionless as a statue, I could not help feeling that his outstretched arm not only showed us the way we were to go, but, morally speaking, demonstrated most indisputably the facility with which a railway, wherever it runs, establishes habits of order, discipline, and cleanliness, which have been declared to be impossible to inculcate.

After flying across a capital stone-wall-hunting country, in which I observed at work a number of very well-dressed men in clean shirts (it was Monday), healthy children, and women whose bare red legs appeared for some reason or other to have a propensity to whiten in proportion to their distance from the earth, and a quantity of black cattle, I began to examine the little chamber in which I was receiving so much placid enjoyment.

My attention to it was first attracted by an unusual-looking object immediately before me, which proved to be a blue cloth covered table, suspended at a convenient level by a pair of small hinges, which enabled me, with the assistance of a small contrivance beneath, to raise and fix it.

I next discovered a sliding door, by which the coupé could be divided into two chambers; and on continuing my search, I observed several trifling indications of another hidden luxury, which, on unbuttoning a hasp, proved, to my great astonishment, to be two comfortable double beds and hair mattresses, in which two couples, closing the intermediate door, might separately sleep as comfortably and as innocently as if they were at home.

At seventy-eight miles from Dublin the train stopped at a large grey town, divided apparently into about equal halves by the Shannon, which was rushing through it with considerable violence. It was Athlone, the most important town between Dublin and Galway; indeed, not only is it about half way between the Irish Channel and the Atlantic, but as nearly as possible in the very centre of Ireland, the river forming the boundaries of the counties of Westmeath and Roscommon, and, of course, of Leinster and Connaught; moreover, by the subdivision of the water, one-half of the town is in the one county, and the opposite one in the other.

At this central point I had determined to leave the train; and accordingly, descending from my coupé, I found myself in one moment in the centre of a great crowd of clean, well dressed people, some, like myself, just arrived, others just departing. There were also a considerable number of spectators; among whom, worming their way with trunks, bags, boxes, and bandboxes, on their shoulders, in their arms, and pendent in their hands, were to be seen several men, dressed in blue, with yellow worsted lace—railway porters—employed in transporting luggage either to or from the train. Calmly observing this grand scene of only apparent confusion stood the station-master, distinguished by a blue embroidered collar.

I would fain have stopped a moment to have admired the beautiful bridge and castle of Athlone, but I was in a stream of human beings, and had only to follow it; no sooner, however, was I outside the station-gate than my carpet-bag was a signal for boys to assail me in all directions. Philosophically speaking, I could only give it to one; and having done so, I expected I should have been deserted by the rest, but three or four honest-looking lads kept following me, as if they considered I was about to produce another carpet-bag. "Will you pick the marn's pockut?" exclaimed one of them, by way of reproof to his comrade, who appeared from his propinquity to be the successful candidate.

At a short distance I found a public car with three horses, that had been waiting for the train, and was about to start for Tuam; accordingly depositing my bag on it, I told the driver I would walk on. After proceeding about one hundred yards, on coming to a turning I said to an old woman as I passed her, "Is this the road to Tuam?" "Oh yus!" she replied; adding, with an arch smile, "it wull be, when you're *there*."

When the car overtook me, there were seated on each side of it two or three well-dressed people, one of whom with his right hand made a slight beckoning sign to me. I, however, scrambled up to the driver, and although there was scarcely room for us both, and although the iron rail pressed very hard against my left thigh, I consoled myself with the reflection that I was probably the only person travelling through Ireland who was not taking a one-sided view of the country, and of the manners, social, moral, religious, and political, of its inhabitants. Whoever could have invented the art not only of journeying and of thinking elbow foremost, but of sitting for hours together back to back with fellow-creatures with whom it may be desirable to converse, I am totally unable to conceive. The fellow, whoever it was, grievously annoyed me the whole of the short time I was in Ireland. His invention was to my eyes what the sound of setting a saw is to my ears.

My Siamese companion—for we were literally one flesh—was a strong, healthy, bony (of *that* I am quite sure) man of about fifty-five years of age, with an intelligent, pleasing, and yet very serious countenance. We had scarcely proceeded two hundred yards when a fine rosy-faced boy with naked feet came running towards us to beg of me. My friend—for such he had dubbed himself the instant I sat beside him—made a furious pretended attempt to strike the suppliant across the face with his whip, but the little fellow, without raising a hand, and with a confidence that would have disarmed anybody, beautifully smiled at him, although he was quite within reach of the lash.

Dublin, in the direction in which we were travelling, has no suburbs, and so in a few minutes we were all flying through flat, rural scenery, strongly resembling England, excepting that the colour of the grass as it flitted by was certainly, if possible, rather more beautiful. In the fields, which were small, and bounded by hedges, we continually passed close to groups of sturdy reapers, and their living attitudes, and open, sunburnt breasts, contrasted with the motionless yellow sheaves that stood around them, formed a pleasing picture of "harvest home." Alongside of us, as we glided on, was—as is usually the case in railway travelling—a canal, the horses and boats of which appeared by comparison to be moving backwards.

By the time we had gone fifteen miles, the speed of the train evidently began to diminish, and, continuing to slacken, it had scarcely stopped, when I heard loudly ejaculated by a monotonous, psalm-singing voice, which on two legs was evidently rapidly approaching me, the word "MAY-nooth!" and on looking out of the window, a neat white station, bounded on each side by a high bright pea-green paling, a pea-green lamp-post, a pea-green ladder, and a pea-green bell-post, all newly painted, was standing close before me.

79

GEORGE FOXCROFT HASKINS, *TRAVELS IN ENGLAND, FRANCE, ITALY AND IRELAND* (BOSTON: P. DONAHOE, 1856), PP. 265–266, 269

Cork

From Dublin we travelled to Cork by railroad. The journey is not by any means so agreeable as one I formerly made by the mail coach and Bianchoni's cars. In that journey I passed through a country diversified with hills and valleys, of surpassing beauty; through parks, and fields of wheat, and every kind of luxuriant vegetation, rivalling the most attractive plains of Italy and Switzerland. Palaces and mansions, denoting wealth and social comfort, appeared on every side; packs of hounds, the winding horns of hunters, and herds of deer, agreeably diversified the scene and added to its interest. The cabins of the peasantry lined the roads, revealing a population of vast extent, each cabin swarming with beautiful and rugged children. Fifty years ago, the celebrated Dr. Milner, speaking of the Catholic population of Ireland, after two centuries and a half of depression, poverty, and persecution, wrote as follows: "The history of the human race furnishes but one parallel to it—the increase of the Israelites in Egypt; and this, notwithstanding the vast and incessant drains upon the young men to supply the army and navy, and the constant and prodigious efflux of the poor from their own country." In this journey by railroad, on the contrary, we passed through a country of bogs and pastures, without inhabitants. Now and then we saw the remains of a burned or decayed cottage, or hamlet; and when, at times, we passed through a fine and florid country, we exclaimed, "Beautiful! but where are the inhabitants?" Alas! vast changes have taken place in Ireland within ten years. Villages are depopulated—whole counties are comparatively deserted. Fever, famine and persecution, enlistments and emigration, have created a terrible void in the population.

We found excellent lodgings and sumptuous fare at the Imperial Hotel, one of the most comfortable public houses in the United Kingdom. We engaged a carriage, and rode about the city and its environs. Cork holds rank as the second city in Ireland, in extent, population, and commercial importance. It is delightfully situated on the banks of the River Lee, which flows through its heart. The Lee is a river of singular beauty; it winds gracefully among verdant hills, and through the most luxurious plains that mortal eye hath ever seen; and the wild and the cultivated are so happily mingled, that it would seem as if the hand of taste had been every where employed skilfully to improve nature. The hills are clad from the summit to the water's edge with every variety of foliage; graceful villas and ornamental cottages are scattered among them in profusion, and here and there some ancient ruin recalls a story of the past. The principal streets in Cork are wide, straight, and neatly paved; in the suburbs and outskirts, they are narrow and dirty. From the number of carts, carriages, and loaded wagons, and the noise and bustle along the quays, I should suppose that business was very active, and the inhabitants industrious and prosperous. Even in the poorer quarters, I did not find so much poverty and wretchedness as I had expected. Beggars were few in number, and by no means importunate or annoying. There were people in rags, but they looked cheerful and healthy.

My stay in Cork was by far too brief. With a sigh of deep regret, I parted from my faithful, warm-hearted friends, to see them perhaps no more, and proceeded swiftly by railroad towards Killarney. All the way the scenery was most beautiful; but who can attempt to describe scenery seen from a railway carriage? You might as well try to count the spokes in a swiftly revolving wheel. Immediately on our arrival at Killarney, we engaged a jaunting car to take us to Milltown. It was Saturday afternoon, and we wished to pass the Sunday with my old and venerable friend, the Rev. Bartholomew O'Connor, P. P., familiarly known among his devoted parishioners as "Father Bat." It was a lovely day, and the road over which we rolled was more like the avenue to the mansion of a prince than like a public highway. On our right we passed the venerable ruins of Aghadoe, consisting of the walls of a cathedral, of which the main doorway is in a good state of preservation; the remains of a round tower, some twelve or fourteen feet high; and the base of a castle, called by the inhabitants the Bishop's Chair, or See, perhaps because it was the place of his residence.

80

MICHAEL CAVANAGH (ED.), *MEMOIRS OF GENERAL THOMAS FRANCIS MEAGHER COMPRISING THE LEADING EVENTS OF HIS CAREER* (WORCESTER, MASS.: THE MESSENGER PRESS, 1892), PP. 245–253

"Taking the field"

(From "Meagher's Memoirs of Forty-Eight.")

"When we reached the Council-Rooms we found —— and McGee there, and, after a short conversation with them, it was arranged that the former should leave in the evening for Paris, put himself immediately into communication with the most influential Irishmen residing in that city, and leave nothing undone to procure a military intervention, in the event of the insurrection we contemplated taking place.

"In a few hours he sailed from Kingstown; and I have lately heard, from a trusted source, that the duties he undertook were performed by him with great ardor, intelligence and success; that, in fact, owing to his earnest representations, the armed intervention of the French government would have taken place, had we made a good beginning, and shown ourselves worthy of so honorable an assistance.

"As for McGee, he volunteered to start the same evening for Belfast, cross over to Glasgow, and lie concealed there until he heard from Dillon. Should he receive any favorable information, he was to summon the Irish population of that city to rise and attack whatever troops were intrusted with its defence. In case of these troops being overpowered, he should seize two or three of the largest merchant steamers lying in the Clyde; with pistols to their heads, compel the engineers and sailors to work them out; steer round the north coast of Ireland; and at the head of two thousand men, or more, if he could get them, make a descent on Sligo; fight his way across the Shannon and join us in Tipperary.

"This project may now appear a monstrously absurd one. At the time, however, many circumstances concurred to give it a rational, sober, practicable character.

Adventurous, bold, and dangerous in the highest degree, it certainly was, to the individual who proposed and ventured to conduct it. But, once taken in hand by our countrymen in Glasgow, no doubt could have been entertained of its accomplishment. Not alone, that the Irish there numbered several thousands; not alone that Chartism was on the watch there, and panting for an outbreak; but the city was almost wholly defenceless; the troops of the line had been drafted off to other places; and, as a substitute an awkward militia force had been hastily patched up, and strapped together.

"The project, however,—whether it was good or bad—did not originate exclusively with McGee. In proposing it to us, he was acting in obedience to the wishes of three Delegates who had arrived in Dublin the previous evening, and had been instructed by a large body of Irishmen, resident in Glasgow, to lay the project in question before the chief men of the Clubs, and urge them to sanction, encourage, and direct it.

"That evening, McGee started for Belfast; and, next day, crossed over to Scotland; where, I have since learned, from a Catholic clergyman of high integrity and intellect, he went through the difficult and perilous business he had undertaken, with singular energy, tact and firmness; and for several days stood fully prepared to carry out the views just stated had Dillon or I sent him word to do so.

"Why we failed to communicate with him will be easily learned from the sequel of this letter.

"Yet, upon a moment's reflection, I think it may be more satisfactory for me to state at once, that in consequence of no decisive blow having been struck in Tipperary, we felt we could not be justified in bringing our friend, and the men under him, into collision with the Government. He was to take the field in the event of our establishing a good footing in the South; and this not having been accomplished, it would have been treacherous on our part to have written a line directing him to explode the conspiracy he had organized.

"Having parted with —— and McGee, Dillon and I went up stairs to the room used for private committees, took down the large map of Ireland which hung there, and folding it up with the intention of bringing it with us to the country, returned to the room in which Halpin and his assistants were at work.

"We desired the former to let Duffy, Martin, and the other Confederates in Newgate, know of our going to the country, and our resolution of commencing the insurrection, if possible, in Kilkenny.

> *"We further desired him to communicate, in the course of the evening, with the officers of Clubs; inform them of our intentions; and desire them to be in readiness to rise, and barricade the streets, when the news of our being in the field should reach them; and when, as an inevitable result, three or four regiments from the Dublin garrison had been drawn off to reinforce the troops of the southern districts."*

[I have italicized the foregoing paragraph in Mr. Meagher's narrative, for the purpose of directing my readers' particular attention to the important statement made therein—and, because I intend to show, in the next chapter of this work, that not only were the Clubs *not* notified on the evening in question of the instructions left by the members of the Executive Council for their guidance, but that,—*two days afterwards*—in answer to a direct question—Mr. Halpin denied positively having received any instructions whatsoever for the guidance of the Clubs, from the gentlemen in question before their departure from Dublin.]

"We had wished good-bye to Halpin, and were going out, when young R— H— and Smyth came up. We told them the arrangements we had made; intreated them to go round to the different clubs that evening—state openly to the members what we proposed doing—communicate to them our wishes; and exhort them to observe a calm, patient attitude, until the moment we designated for their coming into action had arrived.

"They promised faithfully to do so.

"We arrived at the Kingstown railway station just in time to catch the 5 o'clock train.

"The carriages were crowded, and the conversation very noisy about the Suspension Act. I retain a vivid picture of one gentleman in particular; a very stiff, cold, sober gentleman, with red whiskers and a gambouge complexion; who took occasion to remark, in quite a startling and fragmentary style, that 'the Government had done the thing—the desirable thing—at last—time for them—should have been done long ago—country had gone halfway to the devil already—Whigs always infernally slow—had given those scoundrels too much rope—but they'd hang themselves—he'd swear it—that he would.'

"I nudged Dillon at the conclusion of these consoling observations. He threw a quiet, humorsome look at the loyal subject with the red whiskers and gambouge complexion, and burst out laughing. He was joined by some gentlemen, and two or three ladies, who recognized us, but little suspected, I should say, the errand we were on.

"At Kingstown we got upon the Atmosphere Railway, and rattled off to Dalkey. Half an hour after, we were at dinner in Druid Lodge, Killiney, where Mrs. Dillon was staying at the time.

"I should have mentioned, before this, that whilst Dillon and I were at the Council Rooms in D'Olier street, Lawless went to the office of the Wexford coach, and engaged for us two inside seats, as far as Enniscorthy, in that night's mail, leaving word with the clerk that the gentlemen for whom he had engaged the seats were to be taken up at Loghlinstown; a little village seven miles from Dublin, and little more than two from Druid Lodge.

"The places were taken in the name of Charles Hart, with a view to conceal our departure from the police, who were on the alert; picking out, in every nook and corner, information relative to our movements.

"At half-past eight we left Druid Lodge for Loghlinstown. We did not enter the village, however; but drew up at the tree, opposite, I believe, to Sir George Cockburn's demesne.

"There, underneath that fine old tree, we remained for about twenty minutes, until the coach came up, and, whilst we were standing in silence under it, surrounded by the darkness, which the deepening twilight, mingling with the shadow of the leaves, threw round us, I could not but reflect, with something of a heavy heart, upon the troubled Future, within the confines of which I had set my foot, never to withdraw it.

"The evening, which was cold and wet, the gloom and stillness of the spot, naturally gave rise to sentiments of a melancholy nature. But, above all, a feeling, which, for many days, had more or less painfully pressed upon my mind, and which, in some of the most exciting scenes I had lately passed through, failed not to exercise a saddening influence upon my thoughts and language—the feeling that we were aiming far beyond our strength, and launching our young resources upon a sea of troubles, through which the Divine hand alone could guide and save them; this feeling, more than all, depressed me at the moment of which I speak, and I felt far from being happy.

"At that moment, I entertained no hope of success. I knew well the people were unprepared for a struggle; but, at the same time I felt convinced that the leading men of the Confederation were bound to go out, and offer to the country the sword and banner of Revolt, whatever consequences might result to themselves for doing so.

"The position we stood in; the language we had used; the promises we had made; the defiances we had uttered; our entire career, short as it was, seemed to require from us a step no less daring and defiant than that which the Government had taken.

"Besides, here was an audacious inroad upon the liberty of the subject! The utter abrogation of the sacred personal inviolability, guaranteed by sound old law, to all people linked by rags or golden cords to the Brunswick Crown! Was it not the choicest ground of quarrel, upon which a people, provoked and wronged like the Irish people had been for years and years, could fling down the gauge of battle.

"Was it not said, too, by the most peaceable of our Repealers, that, the moment the Constitution was invaded, they would sound the trumpet, and pitch their tents? Was it not said over and over again, by these sensitive, scrupulous, pious, poor men—by these meek, forbearing, mendicant Crusaders—that they would stand within the Constitution? On both feet within it? But that the very instant the soldier or the lawyer crossed it, they would unsheathe the sword of Gideon, and with a mighty voice, call upon the Lord of Hosts, and the Angel of Sennacherib!

"I hold that the leaders of the Confederation were bound to give these men an opportunity to redeem their pledges; bound to give the people, who honestly and earnestly desired to change their condition, an opportunity to attempt such a change, if it so happened that all they required was the opportunity to make the attempt; bound, at all events, and whatever might be the result to themselves, to mark, in the strongest and most conclusive manner, their detestation of an act which left a great community to be dealt with, just as the suspicions of a Police Magistrate, a Detective, or a Viceroy might suggest.

"And what is the befitting answer of a people to the Parliaments, the Cabinets, or Privy Councils, that deem it 'expedient' to brand the arms, and gag the utterance of a nation? There is but one way to reply to them, and that is, by the signal-fires of insurrection.

"Then again had we not gone out upon the Suspension Act, and written our protest against that measure upon the standard of Rebellion, the English officials would have been led to believe that the privileges of Irish citizens might be abused, not only with perfect impunity, but without one manly symptom of resentment. We preferred risking our lives, rather than suffer this contemptuous impression to go abroad.

"Thoughts such as these crossed my mind—as hastily and irregularly as I have now written them—whilst we were waiting for the coach. In giving them to you, I have made no effort to mould them into anything like an accurate and graceful form. Yet, misshapen as they are, you may, perhaps, glean from them the motives that prompted me to an enterprise which I felt convinced would fail, and learn the views I took, at the last moment, of our position and its duties, the difficulties by which it was surrounded, and the sacrifices which it exacted.

"At nine o'clock the coach came up; and having wished Charles Hart, who had accompanied us from Druid Lodge, an affectionate farewell, Dillon and I took our places; the guard sung out 'All right!' and in a second or two, we were dashing away, in gallant style, along the road to Bray.

"We were the only inside passengers, and we had the good fortune not to be interrupted until we came to Enniscorthy.

"At Rudd's hotel we dismounted and ordered a car for Ballinkeele. It was little more than five o'clock, and the morning was bitterly cold. A clear, bright sun, however, was melting the thin frost which had fallen in the night, and changing into golden vapor the grey mist which arched the gentle current of the Slaney. Not a soul was stirring in the streets; the hotel itself was dismally quiet; the fowls in the stable-yard, and the gruff old dog, beside the soft warm ashes of the kitchen-fire, were all at rest.

"Whilst the car was getting ready, I sat down before the fire, and taking out the last number of the *Felon*, read for Dillon, the beautiful, noble appeal—written, as I have understood since, by James Finton Lalor—which ended with this question:—

"*Who will draw the first blood for Ireland? Who will win a wreath that shall be green forever?*"

"Passing out of the town, the first object which struck us was Vinegar Hill, with the old dismantled wind-mil, on the summit of it, sparkling in the morning light. You can easily imagine the topic upon which our conversation turned, as we passed by it.

"Alas! it is a bitter thought with me whilst I write these lines—more bitter, far, a thousand times, than the worst privations of prison-life—that, unlike those gallant Wexford men of '98, we have left behind us no famous field, within the length and breadth of our old country, which *men* could point to with proud sensation, and fair hands strew with garlands.

"After an hour's drive we arrived at Ballinkeele, and, having asked for Smith O'Brien, were shown by the servant to his room.

"We found him in bed. He did not seem much surprised at the news we told him, and asked us what we proposed to do? Dillon replied, there were three courses open to us. The first to permit ourselves to be arrested. The second, to escape. The third, to throw ourselves upon the country, and give the signal of insurrection.

"O'Brien's answer was just what we had expected. As to effecting an escape, he was decidedly opposed to it; whatever might occur, he would not leave the country; and as to permitting ourselves to be arrested, without first appealing to the people, and testing their disposition, he was of opinion we would seriously compromise our position before the public, were we to do so. The suspension of the Habeas Corpus Act was an event, he conceived, which should excite, as it would assuredly justify, every Irishman in taking up arms against the government—at all events he felt it to be our duty to make the experiment.

"I told him we had come to the same conclusion previous to our leaving Dublin, and were prepared to take the field with him that day.

"He then got up, and having sent for Mr. Maher, informed him of the news we had brought. It was arranged we should breakfast immediately, and leave Ballinkeele with as little delay as possible.

"At ten o'clock we were seated in Mr. Maher's carriage, and on our way to Enniscorthy. Whilst we drove along, different plans of operation were discussed of which the one I now state to you was, in the end, considered the best.

"From all we had heard, we were of opinion it would not be advisable to make our first stand in Wexford; very few Confederates having been enrolled from that county, and our political connection with it, consequently, being extremely slight. Indeed, there was scarcely a single man of influence in the county, with whom we could put ourselves in communication; and, without taking other circumstances of an unfavorable nature into consideration, it appeared to us, that, this being our first visit amongst them, it was too much to expect that the Wexford men would rally round us with the enthusiasm which the people, in other parts of the country, where we were better known, would be sure to exhibit. It was absolutely necessary to commence the insurrection with heart and vigor, and, at a glance, we saw, that, in Waterford, in Kilkenny, in Tipperary, we might calculate upon the manifestation of the warmest and boldest spirit.

"At first O'Brien was strongly in favor of going to New Ross. I was opposed to this, and argued against it, with no little anxiety; urging upon him the serious disadvantage it would be to us—in case the people of New Ross responded to our appeal—to commence the fight in a town so helplessly exposed to the fire of the war-steamers then lying in the Barrow, and the number of which, in little more than two hours, would certainly be increased by a contingent from the larger ones which were anchored in the Suir, abreast of Waterford.

"The like objection prevailed against our selection of the latter place; and we finally determined upon making for Kilkenny. The same plan, in fact, which Dillon and I thought of, the day before, was agreed to by O'Brien.

"It seemed to him, as it had seemed to us, that Kilkenny was the very best place in which the insurrection could break out. Perfectly safe from all war-steamers, gun-boats, floating-batteries, standing on the frontiers of the three best fighting counties in Ireland, Waterford, Wexford and Tipperary—the peasantry of which could find no difficulty in pouring in to its relief; possessing from three to five thousand Confederates, the greater number of whom we understood to be armed; most of the streets being extremely narrow, and presenting, on this account, the greatest facility for the erection of barricades; the barracks lying outside the town, and the line of communication between the principal portions of the latter and the former, being intercepted by the old bridge over the Nore, which might be easily defended, or, at the worst, very speedily demolished; no place, it appeared to us, could be better adapted for the first scene of the revolution, than this, the ancient 'City of the Confederates.'

"In making this selection, there were one or two considerations, of temporary interest, which influenced us to some extent.

"The railway from Dublin was completed to Bagnalstown only, leaving fourteen miles of the ordinary coach road still open between the latter place and Kilkenny. The thick shrubberies and plantations; the high bramble fences, and at different intervals, the strong limestone walls which flank this road; the sharp twists and turns at certain points along it; the alternations of hill and hollow, which render a journey by it so broken and diversified; its uniform narrowness, and the steep embankments, which, in one or two places, spring up where its width measures scarcely sixteen feet; everything was in favor of its being converted, by an insurgent population, with almost certain security and ease, to the most successful enterprises.

"Along this road, as they left the station-house at Bagnalstown, and marched upon Kilkenny, whole regiments, draughted off from the Dublin and Newbridge garrisons, might have been surprised and cut to pieces had the country once been up.

"Then the Royal Agricultural Society was on the eve of holding its annual cattle show in Kilkenny; specimens of the choicest beef and mutton had already arrived, and, in full clover, were awaiting the inspection of the highest nobles, and the wealthiest commoners of the land. Many, too, of these proud gentlemen had themselvss arrived; and carriages might have been met, each hour, along the different avenues to the town, freighted with the rank, the gaiety and fashion of the surrounding country. In case of a sustained resistance, here was a creditable supply of hostages and provisions for the insurgents!

"With some hundred head of the primest cattle in the island, we could have managed admirably behind the barricades for three or four days; whilst with a couple of Earls, from half a dozen to a dozen Baronets, an odd Marquis, or. "the only Duke" himself, in custody, we might have found ourselves in an exellent position to dictate terms to the Government.

C. O. BURGE, *THE ADVENTURES OF A CIVIL ENGINEER: FIFTY YEARS ON FIVE CONTINENTS* (LONDON: ALSTON RIVERS, 1909), PP. 8–13, 47–53

An old woman was travelling on the same line with her son, and the guard, collecting tickets at the end of the journey, objected to his half-ticket, alleging that he was over the age-limit and should pay full fare. "But," said the mother, "he was all right when we started, but your train was so long a comin' that the lad has grow'd since."

Much passenger travelling was done in pre-railway days, and for some time after, by canal as well as mail coach. I remember what were called "fly-boats," which carried a great number of passengers, with handsomely fitted up cabins and towed by a team of horses. A great speed was attained, and the wash on to the canal banks following the boat was very great. Dublin and the river Shannon and many other inland places were thus connected. People, especially in the country parts of Ireland, were so ignorant that I remember, long before *through* tickets were thought of, hearing an old woman asking, at a country booking office, for a ticket to America. Possibly she thought that the train would land her there.

The first railway station ever built—Westland Row, on the Dublin and Kingstown Railway—was within a mile of our house. This was not the first railway, however, but the one or two lines constructed in England before it had no stations, in the present sense of the word, the passengers getting up from and down to the road side, as in the case of the mail coach. It was a considerable time after the introduction of railways before travelling by road in private carriages by the wealthier classes was abolished. They hesitated for a long time to travel in vehicles in which they might be brought into contact with their tradespeople, commercial travellers, etc., and for some time only made use of them to send their servants and luggage. When they did use them personally they had their private carriages loaded up on railway trucks and sat in them. But in 1847, a countess travelling with her maid in this way was nearly killed by her carriage being set on fire by an engine spark while going at full speed. The maid jumped off and was severely injured, and, the train drawing up at a station, the mistress was rescued. The incident put an end to the practice. The late Queen did not travel by train until seventeen years after the first railway was opened, and the Duke of Wellington, who was present at the first railway accident when Mr. Huskisson, the prominent politician, was killed, never entered a railway train after that until a few years before his death, some twenty years later, when he was obliged to do so in travelling from London to Windsor in attendance on the Queen. I remember one of our boyish excitements in connection with the new method of travelling was to slip through the railway fence and put on the rails fourpenny pieces, which have since been superseded by threepenny bits. After the train had passed over these they were expected to be flattened into sixpences, with the object of getting more tops or toffee for them. This practice could not be, in principle, distinguished from coining or passing bad coin, but I do not think that we thought of that. The commercial speculation by which 50 per cent profit was hoped for was not, however, on the whole, a success, many of the coins being struck away and lost in the ballast.

One of the early railways was worked by air, and was located close to Dublin. A tube was fixed between the rails, and the leading carriage (for there was no engine) was attached to a piston within the tube, the air in front being exhausted by a stationary steam engine at one end of the line. The train was, in this way, sucked along the rails. The railway was on a steep grade, so that the return journey was effected by gravity. I frequently travelled by these trains, which went at great speed, but the working was found not to be so economical as by the locomotive, so that the system was abandoned in favour of the latter.

The entry of the young Queen Victoria with Prince Albert into Dublin took place in 1849—a great excitement, for no sovereign had visited Ireland for nearly thirty years. We had seats in a friend's window from which to see the royal procession. The Queen, then about thirty years of age, had a slight figure, and the Prince of Wales, now King Edward VII, was a small boy dressed in Highland costume. At night the city was illuminated, but not as such displays are exhibited now with brilliant devices in gas, for this illuminant was chiefly limited to street lamps, private houses generally using oil lamps and candles. There was no plate-glass, and to the centre of each small pane, twelve to eighteen to each window, an ordinary tallow candle was fixed. No pane was without its light, for otherwise the glaziers were considered to have an unwritten right to throw stones and break the offending pane. Self-interest rather than excess of loyalty was, no doubt, the actuating motive. Candles and oil lamps, chiefly the former, were, as a rule, the only indoor illumination, and a pair of silver snuffers on a tray was indispensable in every living-room. The former was like a large pair of scissors with a sort of box on one blade which was the receptacle for the wick cut off. One of the youngsters' practical jokes of that time was to fill the box surreptitiously with gunpowder, and watch the result when some timid person would use it.

Dublin was a great place for military displays, there being a large garrison in view of possible rebellion, for revolution was not only in the air in those days, but in some foreign countries had come down very much to the ground. The Queen's birthday, but much more notably the anniversary of Waterloo, then well within the memory of most people, was always celebrated by a review and sham fight on a large scale in Phœnix Park, and the military uniforms being much more gorgeous than in these days, it was a magnificent sight. All the pride, pomp, and circumstance of glorious war with none of its miseries were there. We used to go in my uncle's open carriage, from which, like all others, the horses were detached during the fight. My father only kept a single-horse closed brougham. The great feature was the cavalry charges delivered with swords flashing, and at such speed and ever increasing roar right up against the line of carriages, that it was almost impossible to conceive that the troops could draw up in time to avoid overwhelming us. The pedestrians around us could not stand it, but fled. Nevertheless, we longed for repetition. This is a curious tendency of the human mind, and no doubt accounts for many a desperate deed, such is the fascination of danger. I know of a small boy who quite recently longed to be taken on to an open foot-bridge under which enormous express trains, at perhaps seventy miles an hour, would pass. These would so greatly frighten him temporarily, with noise and smoke, that he would cling to his nurse, crying frantically, and yet next day he would beg to be taken again.

The south of Ireland was then full of the freaks of a Marquis of Waterford who had been killed hunting a few years before. It was said of him that, being anxious to see the effects of a railway collision—at that early period not as well known as now—he tried to induce the directors of the Great Southern and Western Railway of Ireland to cause two empty trains to meet at full speed, he paying all expenses, but the directors, not having the same sporting proclivities, declined. Subsequently, having some grievance against the company with regard to what he believed to be exorbitant first-class fares, he is said to have hired a large number of chimney-sweeps and paid their first-class fares for several months, to occupy each one a separate compartment. They were to be in working costume, brushes and soot and all. This led, as might be supposed, to the second-class becoming more fashionable, which was a considerable loss to the company.

The engineering works with which I was connected in Ireland were of an unimportant nature, more especially in comparison with the large works abroad with which I had subsequently to deal. In Kilkenny, however, where for the first time I was put in responsible charge, I built a viaduct which was rather remarkable from its being constructed entirely of black marble, not for ornamental reasons, but because that material was the most accessible and cheapest.

My first railway accident happened about this time. For some time previous, the development of railway travelling had so far progressed in the first quarter-century of its existence that the excursion trip had been invented, and an advertisement induced me and some companions to take advantage of one to see Paris, which, though I had been to the Continent as a boy, I had not seen. Going by South Wales, and approaching Swansea Station, we ran bump, smash into a goods train. Sitting opposite to me with his back to the engine was a portly old gentleman particularly well upholstered, and the sudden check to our progress sent me bodily into this soft cushion. At that period I was a slender youth, as full of angles as a proposition in Euclid, so that the old man got considerably the worst of it. "Beg pardon," said I. "Don't mention it," said he; and as our carriage was uninjured, we resumed our positions as if nothing had happened. There were others, however, in the train who were severely injured, though nobody was killed.

I was inexperienced in those days, or should have claimed compensation for shock to system, or something of that kind, which reminds me of a fellow-countryman who was hurt in a collision. He claimed and got compensation for not only himself but his wife, who had not been injured by the accident. "An' how did ye manage it?" said a friend. "Shure an' hadn't I the prisince of mind to fetch her one in the head before they dragged us out," was the reply.

Poster advertisements, such as we see everywhere now, even defiling the most beautiful landscapes, were then unknown, but large printed ones were beginning to crowd the railway station platforms, though even these had not been introduced abroad. On our return, coming from Dover to London, after passing several intermediate stations, a French fellow-passenger, who was in England for the first time, exclaimed, "*Mon Dieu! quel drôle de chose, que toutes les stations se nomment Colman's Mustard!*" I shall not mention my impressions of Paris, for no doubt they were the same as those of hundreds of others visiting in youth that brilliant city for the first time; but I must say, having been there so often since, there seems to have been a great sobering down of the national character in the fifty years. The modern Parisian is much more staid and business-like than of old. The Palais Royal was then full of brilliant shops devoted to luxurious ware of all kinds, which, with the bands in the middle of the square and other attractions, have all disappeared, and apparently have not migrated to any other quarter.

THE preparation of plans, etc. for Parliament called for much more of the engineer's energies at the time I am now dealing with than latterly. Railways were being pushed forward in every conceivable direction, to the great comfort of the traveller of to-day, and the plans and estimates of proposed railway bills had to be lodged in London at the proper office before midnight on the 30th November each year, in order to entitle them to be dealt with in the following session. If the lodgment were attempted to be made at 12.1 a.m. on December 1st it would be refused, and a year would be lost. Not properly realizing the amount of time necessary for engineers to survey lines and furnish estimates of the cost, promoters often left their schemes till there was very little time for them, the question of raising money also causing delay. As nearly every engineer in the country, competent or otherwise, was in fierce demand at the same time, large fees, unheard of since, were flying about, and though the work, day and night, was strenuous and exciting, it had its due reward to follow. London seemed to us on these occasions a land flowing with turtle soup and green Chartreuse, and we began to understand the great cost of the initial proceedings of getting, or often failing to get, a railway bill through Parliament.

I remember coming over to London with a large party, under a temporary employer, for a work of this kind, for we were to finish our office work in Westminster, which, by the way, is the head-quarters of engineering, owing to its nearness to Parliament House. The express trains in the sixties were nearly as fast as those of to-day, though much lighter and less frequent, and of course there were no such things as sleeping-cars, or refreshments except at large stations. We were timed by our train to stop two minutes at Rugby, but this was insufficient for our chief to refill his brandy flask at the refreshment bar. Like Odysseus, a man of many devices, on drawing up at the platform, he shouted to the passing porters a terminological inexactitude, as we should now call it, to the effect that a frightful noise had been going on under the carriage for several miles past, and that he feared something was wrong. The station-master was summoned, and directly a crowd of mechanics were under the vehicle seeking in vain the cause of the trouble, while our resourceful chief was quietly restoring his flask to a temporary state of repletion, not destined, however, to last long.

My original chief was by this time increasing his English work, and one of his parliamentary schemes in conjunction with another leading engineer, was that of the Mid-London Railway, which was to follow practically the same route as the tube with the almost similar name "Central London," since constructed. It was, however, on the same principle as the present Metropolitan Railway, close to the surface. The shopkeepers, however, objected to the temporary interruption to their business by the opening up of the street, and also thought that owing to the public being partly diverted from the footway to the underground line, they would lose patronage. They forgot, however, as has since been shown by the construction of the Central London Tube, that by giving better access to the street from greater distances, much more custom would be gained than would be lost through the local diversion of the traffic. The scheme was therefore rejected at their instance, and the shops lost for many years this advantage, while the public now has the otherwise unnecessary trouble and delay of going up and down lifts to reach the trains, instead of having them at the foot of a short flight of stairs. It seemed hard to us that a work which would have provided us with fairly lucrative employment for some years, and, as the subsequent adoption and success of the Twopenny Tube, on a similar route, shows, would have been a public benefit, was thrown out, under a misapprehension, after a lively debate.

Very few of these railway bills, however, were honoured by a debate, they were mostly left to parliamentary committees, in business attendance on which I heard many eminent men. Sir William Vernon Harcourt, subsequently a prominent politician; Sir Edmund Beckett, afterwards Lord Grimthorpe, of church bell fame; and Hope Scott, a son-in-law of Sir Walter, whose surname he assumed. For his able advocacy of, or opposition to, railway and other schemes, the latter was said to be fee'd at the rate of a guinea for every word uttered. Carlyle, who was then living, wrote, "Speech is silvern but silence is golden." In Hope Scott's case it was speech that was golden.

82

J. M. SYNGE, *IN WICKLOW, WEST KERRY AND CONNEMARA* (DUBLIN: MAUNSEL, 1911), PP. 65–67, 157–165

In West Kerry

At Tralee station—I was on my way to a village many miles beyond Dingle—I found a boy who carried my bag some way along the road to an open yard where the light railway starts for the west. There was a confused mass of peasants struggling on the platform, with all sort of baggage, which the people lifted into the train for themselves as well as they were able. The seats ran up either side of the cars, and the space between them was soon filled with sacks of flour, cases of porter, chairs rolled in straw, and other household goods. A drunken young man got in just before we started, and sang songs for a few coppers, telling us that he had spent all his money, and had nothing left to pay for his ticket. Then, when the carriage was closely packed, we moved slowly out of the station. At my side there was an old man who explained the Irish names of the places that we came to, and pointed out the Seven Pigs, a group of islands in the bay; Kerry Head, further off; and many distant mountains. Beyond him a dozen big women in shawls were crowded together; and just opposite me there was a young woman wearing a wedding ring, who was one of the peculiarly refined women of Kerry, with supreme charm in every movement and expression. The big woman talked to her about some elderly man who had been sick—her husband, it was likely—and some young man who had gone away to England, and was breaking his heart with loneliness.

'Ah, poor fellow!' she said; 'I suppose he will get used to it like another; and wouldn't he be worse off if he was beyond the seas in Saint Louis, or the towns of America?'

This woman seemed to unite the healthiness of the country people with the greatest sensitiveness, and whenever there was any little stir or joke in the carriage, her face and neck flushed with pleasure and amusement. As we went on there were superb sights—first on the north, towards Loop Head, and then when we reached the top of the ridge, to the south also, to Drung Hill, Macgillicuddy's Reeks, and other mountains of South Kerry. A little further on, nearly all the people got out at a small station; and the young woman I had admired gathered up most of the household goods and got down also, lifting heavy boxes with the power of a man. Then two returned American girls got in, fine, stout-looking women, with distress in their expression, and we started again. Dingle Bay could now be seen through narrow valleys on our left, and had extraordinary beauty in the evening light. In the carriage next to ours a number of herds and jobbers were travelling, and for the last hour they kept up a furious altercation that seemed always on the verge of breaking out into a dangerous quarrel, but no blows were given.

At the end of the line an old blue side-car was waiting to take me to the village where I was going. I was some time fastening on my goods, with the raggedy boy who was to drive me; and then we set off, passing through the usual streets of a Kerry town, with public-houses at the corners, till we left the town by a narrow quay with a few sailing boats and a small steamer with coal. Then we went over a bridge near a large water-mill, where a number of girls were standing about, with black shawls over their

From Galway to Gorumna

SOME of the worst portions of the Irish congested districts—of which so much that is contradictory has been spoken and written—lie along the further north coast of Galway Bay, and about the whole seaboard from Spiddal to Clifden. Some distance inland there is a line of railway, and in the bay itself a steamer passes in and out to the Aran Islands; but this particular district can only be visited thoroughly by driving or riding over some thirty or forty miles of desolate roadway. If one takes this route from Galway one has to go a little way only to reach places and people that are fully typical of Connemara. On each side of the road one sees small square fields of oats, or potatoes, or pasture, divided by loose stone walls that are built up without mortar. Wherever there are a few cottages near the road one sees bare-footed women hurrying backwards and forwards, with hampers of turf or grass slung over their backs, and generally a few children running after them, and if it is a market-day, as was the case on the day of which I am going to write, one overtakes long strings of country people driving home from Galway in low carts drawn by an ass or pony. As a rule one or two men sit in front of the cart driving and smoking, with a couple of women behind them stretched out at their ease among sacks of flour or young pigs, and nearly always talking continuously in Gaelic. These men are all dressed in homespuns of the grey natural wool, and the women in deep madder-dyed petticoats and bodices, with brown shawls over their heads. One's first feeling as one comes back among these people and takes a place, so to speak, in this noisy procession of fishermen, farmers, and women, where nearly everyone is interesting and attractive, is a dread of any reform that would tend to lessen their individuality rather than any very real hope of improving their well-being. One feels then, perhaps a little later, that it is part of the misfortune of Ireland that nearly all the characteristics which give colour and attractiveness to Irish life are bound up with a social condition that is near to penury, while in countries like Brittany the best external features of the local life—the rich embroidered dresses, for instance, or the carved furniture—are connected with a decent and comfortable social condition.

About twelve miles from Galway one reaches Spiddal, a village which lies on the borderland between the fairly prosperous districts near Galway and the barren country further to the west. Like most places of its kind, it has a double row of houses—some of them with two storeys—several public-houses with a large police barrack among them, and a little to one side a coastguard station, ending up at either side of the village with a chapel and a church. It was evening when we drove into Spiddal, and a little after sunset we walked on to a rather exposed quay, where a few weather-beaten hookers were moored with many ropes. As we came down none of the crews were to be seen, but threads of turf-smoke rising from the open manhole of the forecastle showed that the men were probably on board. While we were looking down on them from the pier—the tide was far out—an old grey-haired man, with the inflamed eyes that are so common here from the continual itching of the turf-smoke, peered up through the manhole and watched us with vague curiosity. A few moments later a young man came down from a field of black earth, where he had been digging a drain, and asked the old man, in Gaelic, to throw him a spark for his pipe. The latter disappeared for a moment, then came up again with a smouldering end of a turf sod in his hand, and threw it up on the pier, where the young man caught it with a quick downward grab without burning himself, blew it into a blaze, lit his pipe with it, and went back to his work. These people are so poor that many of them do not spend any money on matches. The spark of lighting turf is kept alive day and night on the hearth, and when a man goes out fishing or to work in the fields he usually carries a lighted sod with him, and keeps it all day buried in ashes or any dry rubbish, so that he can use it when he needs it. On our way back to the village an old woman begged from us, speaking in English, as most of the people do to anyone who is not a native. We gave her a few halfpence, and as she was moving away with an ordinary 'God save you!' I said a blessing to her in Irish to show her I knew her own language if she chose to use it. Immediately she turned back towards me and began her thanks again, this time with extraordinary profusion. 'That the blessing of God may be on you,' she said, 'on road and on ridge-way, on sea and on land, on flood and on mountain, in all the kingdoms of the world'—and so on, till I was too far off to hear what she was saying.

In a district like Spiddal one sees curious gradations of type, especially on Sundays and holidays, when everyone is dressed as their fancy leads them and as well as they can manage. As I watched the people coming from Mass the morning after we arrived this was curiously noticeable. The police and coastguards came first in their smartest uniforms; then the shopkeepers, dressed like the people of Dublin, but a little more grotesquely; then the more well-to-do country folk, dressed only in the local clothes I have spoken of, but the best and newest kind, while the wearers themselves looked well-fed and healthy, and a few of them, especially the girls, magnificently built; then, last of all, one saw the destitute in still the same clothes, but this time patched and threadbare and ragged, the women mostly barefooted, and both sexes pinched with hunger and the fear of it. The class that one would be most interested to see increase is that of the typical well-to-do people, but except in a few districts it is not numerous, and it is always aspiring after the dress of the shop-people or tending to sink down again among the paupers.

Later in the day we drove on another long stage to the west. As before, the country we passed through was not depressing, though stony and barren as a quarry. At every crossroads we passed groups of young, healthy-looking boys and men amusing themselves with hurley or pitching, and further back on little heights, a small field's breadth from the road, there were many groups of girls sitting out by the hour, near enough to the road to see everything that was passing, yet far enough away to keep their shyness undisturbed. Their red dresses looked peculiarly beautiful among the fresh green of the grass and opening bracken, with a strip of sea behind them, and, far away, the grey cliffs of Clare. A little further on, some ten miles from Spiddal, inlets of the sea begin to run in towards the mountains, and the road turns north to avoid them across an expanse of desolate bog far more dreary than the rocks of the coast. Here one sees a few wretched sheep nibbling in places among the turf, and occasionally a few ragged people walking rapidly by the roadside. Before we stopped for the night we had reached another bay coast-line, and were among stones again. Later in the evening we walked out round another small quay, with the usual little band of shabby hookers, and then along a road that rose in some places a few hundred feet above the sea; and as one looked down into the little fields that lay below it, they looked so small and rocky that the very thought of tillage in them seemed like the freak of an eccentric. Yet in this particular place tiny cottages, some of them without windows, swarmed by the roadside and in the 'boreens,' or laneways, at either side, many of them built on a single sweep of stone with the naked living rock for their floor. A number of people were to be seen everywhere about them, the men loitering by the roadside and the women hurrying among the fields, feeding an odd calf or lamb, or driving in a few ducks before the night. In one place a few boys were playing pitch with trousers buttons, and a little further on half-a-score of young men were making donkeys jump backwards and forwards over a low wall. As we came back we met two men, who came and talked to us, one of them, by his hat and dress, plainly a man who had been away from Connemara. In a little while he told us that he had been in Gloucester and Bristol working on public works, but had wearied of it and come back to his country.

'Bristol,' he said, 'is the greatest town, I think, in all England, but the work in it is hard.'

I asked him about the fishing in the neighbourhood we were in. 'Ah,' he said, 'there's little fishing in it at all, for we have no good boats. There is no one asking for boats for this place, for the shopkeepers would rather have the people idle, so that they can get them for a shilling a day to go out in their old hookers and sell turf in Aran and on the coast of Clare.' Then we talked of Aran, and he told me of people I knew there who had died or got married since I had been on the islands, and then they went on their way.

83

J. M. SYNGE, *THE ARAN ISLANDS*, 4 VOLS. (DUBLIN: MAUNSEL, 1912). I, PP. 115–120

I have left Aran. The steamer had a more than usually heavy cargo, and it was after four o'clock when we sailed from Kilronan.

Again I saw the three low rocks sink down into the sea with a moment of inconceivable distress. It was a clear evening, and as we came out into the bay the sun stood like an aureole behind the cliffs of Inishmaan. A little later a brilliant glow came over the sky, throwing out the blue of the sea and of the hills of Connemara.

When it was quite dark, the cold became intense, and I wandered about the lonely vessel that seemed to be making her own way across the sea. I was the only passenger, and all the crew, except one boy who was steering, were huddled together in the warmth of the engine-room.

Three hours passed, and no one stirred. The slowness of the vessel and the lamentation of the cold sea about her sides became almost unendurable. Then the lights of Galway came in sight, and the crew appeared as we beat up slowly to the quay.

Once on shore I had some difficulty in finding anyone to carry my baggage to the railway. When I found a man in the darkness and got my bag on his shoulders, he turned out to be drunk, and I had trouble to keep him from rolling from the wharf with all my possessions. He professed to be taking me by a short cut into the town, but when we were in the middle of a waste of broken buildings and skeletons of ships he threw my bag on the ground and sat down on it.

'It's real heavy she is, your honour,' he said; 'I'm thinking it's gold there will be in it.'

'Divil a ha'p'orth is there in it at all but books,' I answered him in Gaelic.

'Bedad, is mor an truaghé' ('It's a big pity'), he said; 'if it was gold was in it it's the thundering spree we'd have together this night in Galway.'

In about half an hour I got my luggage once more on his back, and we made our way into the city.

Later in the evening I went down towards the quay to look for Michael. As I turned into the narrow street where he lodges, someone seemed to be following me in the shadow, and when I stopped to find the number of his house I heard the 'Fáilte' (Welcome) of Inishmaan pronounced close to me.

It was Michael.

'I saw you in the street,' he said, 'but I was ashamed to speak to you in the middle of the people, so I followed you the way I'd see if you'd remember me.'

We turned back together and walked about the town till he had to go to his lodgings. He was still just the same, with all his old simplicity and shrewdness; but the work he has here does not agree with him, and he is not contented.

It was the eve of the Parnell celebration in Dublin, and the town was full of excursionists waiting for a train which was to start at midnight. When Michael left me I spent some time in an hotel, and then wandered down to the railway.

A wild crowd was on the platform, surging round the train in every stage of intoxication. It gave me a better instance than I had yet seen of the half-savage temperament of Connaught. The tension of human excitement seemed greater in this insignificant crowd than anything I have felt among enormous mobs in Rome or Paris.

There were a few people from the islands on the platform, and I got in along with them to a third-class carriage. One of the women of the party had her niece with her, a young girl from Connaught, who was put beside me; at the other end of the carriage there were some old men who were talking in Irish, and a young man who had been a sailor.

When the train started there were wild cheers and cries on the platform, and in the train itself the noise was intense; men and women shrieking and singing and beating their sticks on the partitions. At several stations there was a rush to the bar, so the excitement increased as we proceeded.

At Ballinasloe there were some soldiers on the platform looking for places. The sailor in our compartment had a dispute with one of them, and in an instant the door was flung open and the compartment was filled with reeling uniforms and sticks. Peace was made after a moment of uproar and the soldiers got out, but as they did so a pack of their women followers thrust their bare heads and arms into the doorway, cursing and blaspheming with extraordinary rage.

As the train moved away a moment later, these women set up a frantic lamentation. I looked out and caught a glimpse of the wildest heads and figures I have ever seen, shrieking and screaming and waving their naked arms in the light of the lanterns.

As the night went on girls began crying out in the carriage next us, and I could hear the words of obscene songs when the train stopped at a station.

In our own compartment the sailor would allow no one to sleep, and talked all night with sometimes a touch of wit or brutality, and always with a wonderful fluency with wild temperament behind it.

The old men in the corner, dressed in black coats that had something of the antiquity of heirlooms, talked all night among themselves in Gaelic. The young girl beside me lost her shyness after a while, and let me point out the features of the country that were beginning to appear through the dawn as we drew nearer Dublin. She was delighted with the shadows of the trees—trees are rare in Connaught—and with the canal, which was beginning to reflect the morning light. Every time I showed her some new shadow she cried out with naïve excitement:

'Oh, it's lovely, but I can't see it.'

This presence at my side contrasted curiously with the brutality that shook the barrier behind us. The whole spirit of the west of Ireland, with its strange wildness and reserve, seemed moving in this single train to pay a last homage to the dead statesman of the east.

84

JOSEPH TATLOW, *FIFTY YEARS OF RAILWAY LIFE IN ENGLAND, SCOTLAND AND IRELAND* (LONDON: THE RAILWAY GAZETTE, 1920), PP. 110–111

Golf, the diamond king, and a steam-boat service

Thought not a golfer myself, never having taken to the game in earnest, or played on more than, perhaps, twenty occasions in my life, I may yet, I think, in a humble way, venture to claim inclusion amongst the pioneers of golf in Ireland, where until the year 1881 it was unknown. In the autumn of that year the Right Honourable Thomas Sinclair, Dr. Collier, of "British History" fame, and Mr. G. L. Baillie, a born golfer from Scotland, all three keen on the game, set themselves in Belfast to the task of establishing a golf club there. They succeeded well, and soon the Belfast Golf Club, to which is now added the prefix *Royal*, was opened. The ground selected for the links was the *Kinnegar* at Holywood, and on it the first match was played on St. Stephen's Day in 1881. That was the beginning of golf in Ireland. Mr. Baillie was the Secretary of the Club till the end of 1887, when a strong desire to extend the boundaries of the Royal game in the land of his adoption led him to resign the position and cast around for pastures new. Portrush attracted him, engaged his energies, and on the 12th May, 1888, a course, which has since grown famous, was opened there. About this time I made his acquaintance and suggested Newcastle, the beautiful terminus of the County Down railway, as another likely place. On a well remembered day in December, 1888, he accompanied me there, and together we explored the ground, and finished up with one of those excellent dinners for which the lessee of our refreshment rooms and his capable wife (Mr. and Mrs. Lawrence) were famous, as many a golfer I am sure, recollects. Mr. Baillie's practised eye saw at once the splendid possibilities of Newcastle. Like myself, he was of an enthusiastic temperament, and we both rejoiced. I remembered the shekels that flowed to the coffers of the Glasgow and South-Western from the Prestwick and Troon Golf Courses on their line, and visions of enrichment for my little railway rose before me. Very soon I induced my directors to adopt the view that the railway company must encourage and help the project. This done the course was clear. They were not so sanguine as

I, but they had not lived in Scotland nor seen how the Royal game flourished there and how it had brought prosperity to many a backward place. Mr. Baillie's energy, with the company's cooperation to back it, were bound to succeed, and on the 23rd March, 1889, with all the pomp and ceremony suitable to the occasion (including special trains, and a fine luncheon given by the Directors of the Company) the Golf links at Newcastle, Co. Down, were formally opened by the late Lord Annesley. From that time onward golf in Ireland advanced by leaps and bounds. Including Newcastle, there were then in the whole country, only six clubs and now they number one hundred and sixty-eight! The County Down Railway Company's splendid hotel on the links at Newcastle, with its 140 rooms, and built at a cost of £100,000, I look upon as the crowning glory of our golfing exploration on that winter day in 1888. To construct such a hotel, at such a cost, was a plucky venture for a railway possessing only 80 miles of line, but the County Down was always a plucky company, and the Right Honourable Thomas Andrews, its Chairman, to whom its inception and completion is chiefly due, was a bold, adventurous and successful man.

85

PADRAIC COLUM, 'INTO MUNSTER: ON THE TRAIN', *THE ROAD ROUND IRELAND* (NEW YORK: MACMILLAN, 1926), PP. 416–419

I BEGIN to hear the sound that belongs to Cork more than do the Bells of Shandon even—the chime of the Cork sentence. "D'ye see thon wee cuttie wi' the weans?" a man in Derry had said to me when I had asked him the way, pointing out a girl with children. It stayed in my memory as the typical Northern sentence, spoken as if the man wanted to keep his lips tightly shut. "I wonder in the world would you give me a little kiss?" A girl speaking to a child she is minding says it; it stays with me as the typical Cork sentence, spoken on a rising stress, the last word coming like a bursting bud. In the railway-carriage I am in all are speaking with this rising inflection.

"I must say that you seem to be ignorant of the rudiments of logic," a young man says to someone in the group that he belongs to. He puts the argument into a mathematical form, and goes on to prove his point in terms of A, B, and X. They all have the accent; they all have the intellectual qualities of their county—intelligence, assertiveness, and humorous scepticism. One dominates the group; he has power of language and energy of gesture. He tells of getting off the train at Mallow and going into the refreshment-room. A sandwich with the bread dry and the ham like an autumn leaf! And then the price asked for a bottle of stout—that in the middle of a Christian country! While the train delayed he had run down the platform to get a box of matches. "In the excitement of the moment I put a half-a-crown into the slot-machine." He couldn't retrieve the coin; the way he spoke of the place made me think of Mallow as a calamitous spot.

The same man tells of a prize-fight that he had gone up to Dublin to see. He was in the crowd that rushed into the seats in the theatre. Having secured his seat he went into the bar to get some refreshment before the long engagement in the ring began. He came back to his seat; before him there was a man standing up and putting on his coat. "'Sit down,'" said I, "'I paid to see this fight.'" "'Fight,' said the lad, 'the fight is over.' And it was over just like that." "Now, wasn't that the worst that ever happened to a man!" said one of his auditors, "you having paid for your seat and all!" "It was nearly the worst. But I had the presence of mind to go down the stairs and sell my ticket to a lad in the crowd."

At the other side of the carriage there is a large woman, clothed in black, with round and frightened eyes. A depressed man is with her. She had identified him on the platform as the train came into the last station. They were friends, but they had not met for years. The woman looks as if she kept a shop in some rather prosperous town; the man may be an auctioneer or a clerk in a solicitor's office.

"And so you buried your Grannie?" she says.

"Three months ago. We had an announcement in all the papers."

"And what about Sara?"

"Sara's in England. She got burnt—an oil-stove. It's not known whether she's marked for life. Michael can't travel on account of his heart. When I was in Glasgow he came to the train to see me. He's white on the head now. He'll be handing in his gun soon."

"Do you hear anything from Dunn's now?"

"I wrote to them when they got the legacy, and I had one letter."

"I hear they aren't a bit better off than they used to be."

"Worse. A mare kicked and broke two of her hind legs. The bog used to be some good to them, but it has been all let to the other tenants."

"And Gracie—any sign?"

"Divil a sign. And she's not young any more."

"I hear James is sick."

"He's always sick. The poor man is only just there."

"What else was I going to ask you? Did Daniel get much of a fortune with Kate?"

"No. Not nearly as much as they said he'd get."

"And how is your own people? . . ."

"There will be no more salmon between Castleconnel and Athlone." The man dominating the other group makes this melancholy announcement. The electrical works on the Shannon will prevent the salmon going up, and the great fish will never again be in the greatest of Irish rivers. "I know a man who is paying fifty pounds for a mile of the Blackwater, and be it known to you it's not worth my pipe." "I could tell you of a river that has more salmon in it than all the other rivers of Ireland put together," another man says. This is something worth hearing about. But then the train stops, the group get off, and I missed hearing the name of that salmon-abounding river.